Thomas Walter Perry, Charles H Terrot

Some Historical Considerations Relating to the Declaration on

Kneeling

Thomas Walter Perry, Charles H Terrot

Some Historical Considerations Relating to the Declaration on Kneeling

ISBN/EAN: 9783744718103

Printed in Europe, USA, Canada, Australia, Japan

Cover: Foto ©Lupo / pixelio.de

More available books at **www.hansebooks.com**

SOME

HISTORICAL CONSIDERATIONS

RELATING TO THE

DECLARATION ON KNEELING,

APPENDED TO THE

Communion Office of the English Book of Common Prayer:

A LETTER,

ADDRESSED PRIVATELY IN 1858, TO

THE RIGHT REV. CHARLES H. TERROT, D.D.,

BISHOP OF EDINBURGH AND THEN PRIMUS.

TO WHICH IS ADDED,

A Postscript of further Authorities and Arguments;

INCLUDING AN

EXAMINATION OF STATEMENTS IN A WORK & SUPPLEMENT ON THE EUCHARIST,

BY THE VERY REV. W. GOODE, D.D., DEAN OF RIPON.

BY THE

REV. THOMAS WALTER PERRY,

ASSISTANT CURATE OF S. MICHAEL AND ALL ANGELS, BRIGHTON.

LONDON:

JOSEPH MASTERS, ALDERSGATE STREET,

AND NEW BOND STREET.

OXFORD: J. H. & J. PARKER; CAMBRIDGE: DEIGHTON, BELL, & Co.;

EDINBURGH: GRANT & SON.

MDCCCLXIII.

ADVERTISEMENT.

THE origin of the following LETTER and of the Postscript whereby it has expanded into this VOLUME is sufficiently stated, at pp. 1, 2, and 76, to render needless any further explanation here, as to the reason for preparing and now publishing these "Historical Considerations," beyond saying—that the writer was encouraged, in pursuing the investigation and in deciding to make public its results, by the reliable opinions of some who were cognizant of the Pamphlet when, five years ago, it was only privately circulated.

But it may be desirable to mention, with reference to the main line of argument therein adopted,—touching the belief of the leading English Reformers, on the Eucharistic Presence, having been *unchanged* subsequent to 1549—That, though perhaps somewhat novel, it is very important to be established, provided an appeal to Evidence strictly warrants such a conclusion. That there is *prima facie* ground for contending the point, may be most reasonably inferred from the consideration of a Doctrinal identity *really* subsisting, and here shewn, between the *First* and the *Second* Liturgies of K. Edward VI., notwithstanding that the case is commonly believed to be, and apparently is, otherwise: it strengthened the writer's convictions on this point to find that Mr. Freeman's independent examination of these two Eucharistic Services, (*Principles of Divine Service*. Vol. i.) led him to a similar opinion concerning them.

Further, it is of very material consequence to point out, that—in order to determine accurately the precise opinions, regarding Eucharistic Presence, held by those who are cited as witnesses in these pages—it is essential to bear in mind constantly *the exact sense* in which the words are used which are printed throughout in a prominent **Egyptian** type.

A few additions have been made to the original Letter, these are distinguished by being inserted within square brackets.

Some inconvenience may probably attend the, unavoidable, absence of a systematic arrangement of the Postscript which forms the bulk of the Volume; but this is, perhaps, in part remedied by a copious Table of Contents.

It is only respectful to the Dean of Ripon, some of whose statements and arguments are herein contested, to explain that—a portion of the remarks having been printed before he was elevated to his present Dignity, it was thought he would be best identified by continuing to call him " Mr. Goode."

The Reader will see that the Letter when first issued was signed " Presbyter Anglicanus "; this anonymous subscription was adopted no less from the writer's own wish, than in deference to the counsel of others. In subsequently determining to own its Authorship he was influenced, chiefly, by the knowledge that the Letter had been attributed to one whom it would be a serious injustice to hold responsible for any errors of fact or argument it may contain.

The Author's thanks are especially due, and are hereby tendered, to the Hon. G. F. Boyle, of Cumbrae, for much pains most kindly bestowed in attentively perusing and obligingly criticizing, at different stages of its progress, the Volume which is now presented to the candid judgment of those who may be induced to give it a patient perusal.

T. W. P.

Feast of the Ascension, 1863.

ADDENDA AND CORRIGENDA.

Page 2, line 7, *for* "from those usually held" *read* "from those opinions usually held."

,, 35, Note, line 10, *for* "consecrated" *read* "unconsecrated."

,, 67, line 3 from bottom, *for* "organicas" *read* "organical."

,, 71, line 20, *for* "vol" *read* "fol."

,, 120, line 11, *for* "if by is meant" *read* "if by this is meant."

,, 128, Note, line 4, *for* "prace" *read* "peace"; and, line 6, *for* "Corp" *read* "Conf."

,, 142, line 4, *for* "given" *read* "give."

,, 145, line 6, *for* "kind" *read* "principle."

,, 201, line 8 from bottom, *insert* "to" *after* "papist."

,, 218, Note, *after* "Lambeth Library" *add* "nor yet at C. C. College, Cambridge."

,, 262, Note, line 3, *for* "Edw. had" *read* "Edw. vi. had"; and *for* "235" *read* "211."

,, 272, Note, line 10 from bottom, *for* "Line" *read* "Linc."

,, 289, lines 3 and 7 from bottom, *for* "Bishop" *read* "Doctor."

,, 309, Note, line 6 *for* "without the Declaration" *read* "without Adoration."

,, 358, line 16, *for* "Declara" *read* "Declaration."

,, 391, Note, line 2, *for* "a sunguinis" *read* "ac sanguinis."

CONTENTS.

b

HISTORICAL CONSIDERATIONS,

.ETC.

———

My Lord,

Scarcely a fortnight ago I heard, with much concern, that a Synod of the Scottish Bishops had been specially summoned for the 27th of this month, to consider whether any and what steps should be taken by their Lordships in consequence of grave complaints which have been made imputing heterodoxy to certain statements in the Bishop of Brechin's Primary Charge.

In common with others I was aware that these charges (which, as is publicly known, were brought before the Synod of Bishops by the Bishop of Glasgow some months ago) threatened to occupy their Lordships' attention in the coming September : though, indeed, we indulged a hope—that the excitement and agitation, so strangely caused, becoming allayed and the Bishop of Brechin's own explanations and proofs of his statements in his recently published 2nd Edition being attentively considered, either the promoter or pro-moters of the Charges might be led to withdraw them, or that the Synod would deem it best not to entertain them.

In this hope we have been unhappily disappointed ; and we cannot but be doubly anxious as to any statement which may be put forth by the Synod now summoned, so unex-pectedly and suddenly, to debate certain Propositions, which it is understood the Bishops are to be asked to affirm, condem-natory of points in that Charge.

B

There seems reason to think that the questions to be discussed may be materially affected by the meaning which the Synod might attach to the well known Declaration on Kneeling which is appended to the English Communion Office.

Some little time since I happened to mention to a friend that I had reason to think there were grounds for forming an opinion of this Declaration different from those usually held; my observation having been quoted by him at a meeting of gentlemen assembled in consequence of the announcement of the coming Synod, I was asked by them to put together at once any statements or facts which had led to that opinion.

This, my Lord, I now proceed to do in the form of a Letter to yourself: only premising that the very limited time allotted to me will I fear prevent so ample an examination of the subject as its great importance demands.

The Declaration in question, as it originally appeared in the 2nd Prayer Book of Edw. VI., A. D. 1552, commences thus:—

" Althoughe no ordre can be so perfectlye deuysed, but it may be of some, eyther for theyr ignorance and infirmite, or els of malice and obstinacie, mysconstrued, depraued, and interpreted in a wrong parte. And yet because brotherly charitie willeth, that so muche as conueniently may be offences should be taken away : therefore we willing to dooe the same."

Then follows the form which (with such verbal changes as will be seen by a comparison of the two texts) also appeared in the revised Book of Charles II., A. D. 1662. The words printed here, and throughout the following pages, in Egyptian type, indicate the expressions on which the present controversy turns.

1552.	1662.
" Whereas it is ordeyned in the Booke of Common Prayer, in the administracion of the Lordes Supper, that the Communicantes kneelynge should receiue the Holye Communion : whiche thynge beynge well mente for a sygnificacyon of the hum-	" Whereas it is ordained in this Office for the administration of the Lord's Supper, that the Communicants should receive the same kneeling; (which Order is well meant, for a signification of our humble and grateful acknowledgement of the benefits

ble and gratefull acknowledgeyne of the benefites of Christe, given unto the woorthye receyuer, and to auoyde the prophanacion and dysordre whiche about the Holye Communion myghte elles ensue. Lest yet the same kneelynge might be thought or taken otherwyse, we dooe declare that it is not mente thereby, that any adoracion is doone, or oughte to bee doone, eyther unto the Sacramentall bread or wyne there bodelye receyued, or unto any **reall** and **essenciall** presence there beeyng of Chrystes **naturall** fleshe and bloude. For as concernynge the Sacramentall bread and wyne, they remayne styll in theyr verye naturall substaunces and therefore may not bee adored, for that were Idolatrye to be abhored of all faythfull Christians. And as concernynge the **naturall** bodye and bloud of our Sauiour Christ, they are in heauen and not here : for it is agaynst the trueth of Christes **true naturall** bodye, to be in moe places then in one at one tyme."

of Christ therein given to all worthy Receivers, and for the avoiding of such profanation, and disorder in the Holy Communion, as might otherwise ensue ;) Yet, lest the same kneeling should by any persons, either out of ignorance and infirmity, or out of malice and obstinacy, be misconstrued and depraved ; it is here declared, that thereby no Adoration is intended, or ought to be done, either, unto the Sacramental bread or wine, there bodily received, or unto any **corporal** presence of Christ's **natural** Flesh and Bloud. For the Sacramental bread and wine remain still in their very natural substances, and therefore may not be adored : (for that were idolatrie to be abhorred of all faithful Christians ;) and the **natural** Body and Bloud of our Saviour Christ are in heaven, and not here ; it being against the truth of Christ's **natural** Body to be at one time in more places than one."

Two opinions have, more or less, prevailed with regard to this Declaration ; the one—that, in *both* its forms, it was designed to exclude *any* doctrine of a Real Presence : the other—that the earlier form had this object, but that the later, by the substitution of the word "*corporal*," for the words "*real* and *essential*," was meant to maintain the Catholic doctrine of the Real Presence, as opposed to that doctrine of the Real Presence which is held to be involved in the dogma of Transubstantiation.

I venture to think that neither of these views is the true one: but (1) That *both* forms of the Declaration were intended to express the same thing ; and (2) That the precise object of both was, neither more nor less than—*To disclaim for the Church of England a belief in any* VISIBLE *or* INVISIBLE *Presence of Christ's* NATURAL *Body and Blood* LOCALLY *in the Eucharist.*

Any tone of faith, however strong ; any terms conveying it, however exalted; these, I humbly believe, were designed to be allowed; provided they did not involve that Doctrine which, I allege, was disavowed in the Declaration; while a definite Corporal Act was *prescribed*, adequate to express the highest belief, and that THE ACT OF KNEELING.

Now, the real question to be considered is not,—What can this Declaration be fairly made to mean by strict, much less by ingenious, criticism ? but—To what conclusion shall we be led by an induction of Historical facts and opinions connected with its promulgation at both periods ?

It is my present conviction that the interpretation I have alleged is *that* interpretation which Documentary evidence goes to prove ; and this is what I purpose now to endeavour to establish in the following Historical enquiry.

I have suggested that the *earlier*, equally with the later, form of the Declaration was designed *only* to exclude any doctrine of a LOCAL NATURAL (*i.e.* a carnal, physical, organical) Presence in the Sacrament of the Lord's Supper. The question then obviously arises, and must first be answered, Was such a Presence maintained by any in the Church of England in 1552, when this Declaration was put forth ? History proves that it was; and moreover it also proves that the Declaration under consideration (though issued, as will be seen hereafter, by way of explanation to the Puritan, rather than as a protest against the Roman party) was only one in a series of endeavours to extirpate a doctrine which had taken root, and had propagated itself widely among both clergy and people.

The period which this enquiry must embrace commences naturally with the reign of Edward VI.; but it may be useful to notice the doctrine which was authoritatively insisted upon just prior to his Accession ; perhaps this may be conveniently done by referring to the test then applied to *Shaxton*, Bishop of Salisbury. This Prelate, as his Injunctions of 1538 prove, was in the matter of Ceremonies, a Reforming Bishop ; and Burnet, writing of 1546, says :—

"*Nicholas Shaxton*, that was bishop of Salisbury, had been long prisoner ; but this year, he had said in his imprisonment, in the Counter in Bread-street, *that Christ's* natural *Body was not in the Sacrament, but that it was a Sign and Memorial of His Body that was crucified for us.* Upon this he was indicted and condemned to be burnt. But the King [Hen. viii.] sent the Bishops of London and Worcester to deal with him to recant ; which on the 9th of July he did, acknowledging," That, (to quote his letter to the King as given by Foxe) " within this yere I have fallen into that mooste detestable and mooste abhomynable heresye of them that bee callid Sacramentaries denyeing wretchedlie the presence of Chryst's bleassed body in tholye Sacrament of the aultare."

Among the recantation Articles, which he says, " I with my harte doo believe, and with my mouthe doo confesse," are the following :

" The fyrste. Allmightie God by the power of His woorde pronounced by the Priest at Masse in the consecration, turneth the breade and wyne into the very naturall body and blood of oure Saviour Jhesu Chryste. Soo that after the consecration there remayneth noo substaunce of breadde and wyne, but onely the substaunce of Cryste, God and man.

" The thyrd. The same bleassed Sacrament being consecrate ys and ought to be worshipped and adored with godly honour where-soever yt ys : forasmoche as yt ys the bodie of Cryste inseperably unyted to the Deitie.

" The fyfte. The same body and bloude whiche ys offered in the Masse ys the very propitiation and satisfaction for the synnes of the woorlde forasmoche as yt ys the selfsame in substuance whiche was offered upon the crosse for oure redemption.

" The nynth. The Masse used in this Realme of Englande ys agreeable to thinstitution of Chryste. And wee have in this Churche of Englande the verie true Sacrament whiche ys the very body and bloudde of oure Savyour Chryste under the forme of bredde and wyne."—*Burnet, Hist. Ref.* vol. 1, bk. 3, p. 325, fol. 1715 ; and *Foxe, Acts and Mon.* vol. v., app. 17. Ed. 1846.

Now whether *Shaxton* held (as is probable) the more refined view which is implied in what was then known as the *invisible* Corporal Presence, these Articles do not enable us to determine : but that a grosser view of the Presence of Christ's NATURAL Body was extensively held, is plain from one of the earliest acts of Edward's Council after his Accession.

On Nov. 4th, 1547, was passed the statute 1 Edw. VI. c.i. intitled " An Act against such as shall unreverently speak against the Sacrament of the Altar, and of the receiving thereof in both kinds." The Act recites that, owing to " certain abuses heretofore committed of some," others had

" contemptuously depraved, despised, or reviled the same " most holy and blessed Sacrament." (*Stephens' Eccl. Stat.*, vol. 1., p. 292). What had in part produced this re-actionary irreverence may be gathered from the Royal Proclamation, founded upon this Statute, which was issued on the 27th December following. It relates that :

" Some of " the King's " subjects, not contented with such words and terms as scripture doth declare thereof......and that the Body and Bloud of Jesu Christ is there......search and strive unreverently whether the Body and Bloud aforesaid is there **really** or **figurately**, locally or circumscriptly, and having quantity and greatness, or but substantially and by substance only, or els but in a figure and manner of speaking ; whether His blessed Body be there, head, leggs, armes, toes, and nails, or any other ways, shape and manner, naked or clothed ; whether He is broken and chewed, or He is always whole ; whether the bread there remaineth as we see, or how it departeth ; whether the flesh be there alone, and the blood, or part, or ech in other, or in th'one both, in th'other but only bloud ; and what bloud ; that only which did flow out of the side, or that which remained........"

Consequently all persons were prohibited from *open* controversy and strife on the subject, and from

" affirming any more termes of the said blessed Sacrament, than be expressly taught in the Holy Scripture, and mentioned in the foresaid act,"

until authority should

" define, declare and set furthe an open doctrine thereof, and what termes and words may justly be spoken thereby, other than be expressly in the Scripture contained in the Act before rehearsed." —*Cardwell*, Doc. Ann. vol. I, pp. 35-7.

In proof of the existence of this very *carnal* opinion, two years later, I may cite a Conversation between *Cranmer* and *Bonner*, Bishop of London, on Sept. 10, 1549 : the Archbishop, in consequence of some remarks which Bonner made,

" ....said unto him, ' My Lord of London ! ye speak much of a presence in the Sacrament ; what presence is there, and of what presence do you mean ?' Wherewith the Bishop......spake again to the Archbishop very earnestly, and said, ' *What presence*, my Lord ? I say and believe that there is the **very true** presence of the Body and Blood of Christ. What believe *you*, and how do *you* believe, my Lord ?' Upon which words the Archbishop .....asked him further, whether He were there, face, nose, mouth, eyes, arms, and lips, with other lineaments of His Body ?"

Bonner, indeed, apparently disavowed such a physical notion, for, besides a previous complaint that Hooper misunderstood him, he, shaking his head observed, as Foxe says, "Oh! I am right sorry to hear your Grace speak these words." (*Acts & Mon.* vol. v. p. 752). Yet the very fact of the Archbishop mooting the point argues his knowledge that it was still held even by some in authority, if not by Bonner.

Against, then, this prevalent doctrine of a carnal Presence in the Eucharist, *Cranmer*, *Ridley*, and others who were, more or less directly, concerned in preparing the First Book of Common Prayer, watchfully and determinedly set themselves. *Ridley* since 1545 when he began to study Ratramn's book "on the Body and Blood of the Lord," and *Cranmer* since 1546, when *Ridley* told him of his changed views on the Eucharist, had been carefully investigating the subject of Transubstantiation, and the errors of doctrine or practice which it theoretically or practically involved.

It was under such circumstances that the task of revising the Public Service Books was completed; and this fact on the one side, coupled with the fact on the other side—that Edward's first Prayer-book was thought to be, and was, of such a character that even the unreforming party and the adherents of the Pope could and did use it—may serve to shew that its language was accounted both an adequate exponent of ancient doctrine and a security against popular corruptions of it.

That it was so accounted may be gathered, I think, (1) from a Document (Domestic Edw. VI. vol vii.) in the State Paper Office, (hitherto unpublished I believe) viz.: A letter from the "Duke of Somerset to Cardinal Pole, dated 4th June, 1549, replying to his letters "of the Sixth of Maie." In this Epistle, which mainly relates to questions arising out of the then relative claims and positions of England and the See of Rome, reference is made to the new Service Book in the following passage:—

"The conclusion and that yt ye make thextreme peryll and daungier maie peradventure be knowen to you at Rome, of a dissencion amonges our Busshops uppon the chiefeest poyntes of Religion, We here do knowe no such thinge, but on the contrary, by a common agreement of all the chief learned men in the realme, the thing of longe time and maturely debated emonges them which had most opinyon of learninge in the scriptures of God, and were likeliest to give lest to affeccon as well Busshops as other equaly and indifferently chosen of judgment not coacted with superior authoritie, nor otherwise invited but of a common agreament emonges them ther was first agreament on pointes, and then same cominge to the judgement of the hole parliament, not severaly devided, but all men admitted to the hearinge and debatinge at large, before all states and persones hearinge what could be said against it by one hole consent of thupper and nether house of the parliament finally concluded and aproved, and so a forme and rite of service, a trade and doctryne of relligion by that authoritie and after that sort allowed, set forthe and establisshed by act and statute, and so publisshed and divulged to so great a quiet as ever was in Englond, and as gladly received of all partes, whereof ye your self if ye had bene here and did bere that affeccon ye pretend to your contrey shuld have had great cause to rejoise. Yf yet in a schole poynt or two som one or two peradventure will be singuler in opinion and not be satisfied in thinges which be not in that boke, Whither he be Busshop or other, as ever hitherto it hathe bene sene in all metinges of learned men, What doth that derogate the quyet of the Realme when thei receyve the lawe and be obedient unto it.

. . . .

" And to thiutent ye may the better know of our doeings We have delivered to those which brought you letters the Boke of Common service, the same whereof heir before we have spoken, agreed on in the Parliament. In the which yf ye can fyend eny faulte we shall gladly receyve yor lettres and here yor judgment given therupon, and shall as gently cawse the reasons to be rendred unto you, wherewith we do not fere ye shalbe satisfied."

The Duke concludes by inviting the Cardinal to return to England—

" Not dowbting but sufficient reason grounded uppon Godes word shalbe given unto you for every poynt betwixt us and you in variance. And we are not in muche feare but that it may welbe if ye did se thinges here with your eyes and conferred with learned men the reasones and causes of our doinges the which now ye do not learn, but by report, which in tyme and distaunce encreaseth, and made of them which favoreth not the thing ys exaggerated to the worse, ye wold peradventure condiscend your self and be in all poyntes satisfied as at this present many bothe of Busshops and other learned men be, which at the first did miche repyne, fare you well. From Greenwiche, the 4th of June, 1549.

Yor lovyng freende if you
acknowledge yor dutie to
the Ks. Mat^e.

E. S."

Such a letter and invitation could not, surely, have been sent to Pole if the first reformed Liturgy had not bespoken itself with sufficient plainness to be Catholic in its character and language.

(2) Next, Gardiner, Bishop of Winchester, who may be taken as a fair type of a large party not favourable to the Reformation, did nevertheless, as we shall see hereafter, testify to the fitness of most of what was done and, in particular, frequently quoted the new Prayer Book (whether always effectively or not is another question) in support of his own Doctrinal opinions which yet were vigorously combated by Cranmer and others.

Now it is important to notice that in the very month in which Somerset's letter to Pole was written, Public Disputations were held in the two Universities, before the King's Visitors and Commissioners, on the Eucharistic controversy; and moreover that in those Disputations language was occasionally employed by the Reforming party which (if it stood alone and were criticized apart from the Prayer Book, which they professed to accept, and upon which some of them had been engaged) would certainly favour the notion that they held a most lax and indefinite view of the Real Presence: yet I think it will appear from a careful examination of their arguments and a generous interpretation of their words, that their great anxiety was—not to lend themselves in any degree to an apparent support of that doctrine of a CARNAL Presence which was then sought to be eradicated; and that this accounts for much of their seemingly contradictory language. In saying this I am neither defending it nor attempting to reconcile it.

First of all, considering his public position and his relations to the English Reformers at this time, it will be well to notice Peter Martyr's Disputation at Oxford, June 11th to 15th 1549.

Foxe's opinion of the *object* and *purport* of P. Martyr's discussion is shortly stated in these words: it was, he says :—

" ...... that the substance of bread and wine was not changed in the Sacrament, and that the Body and Blood of Christ were not carnally and bodily in the bread and wine, but united to the same sacramentally."—Vol. v., p. 800.

c

The following is an analysis of it.

" Peter Martyr being called by the king to the public reading of the Divinity Lecture in Oxford, amongst his other learned exercises did set up in the public schools three conclusions of Divinity, to be disputed and tried by argument ; at which disputations were present the King's Visitors, to wit, Henry, Bishop of Lincoln ; Dr. Coxe, Chancellor of that university ; Dr. Hains, Dean of Exeter ; Master Richard Morison, Esquire ; and Christopher Nevinson, Doctor of Civil Law.

" The conclusions propounded were these :—

" First. ' In the Sacrament of Thanksgiving there is no **transubstantiation** of Bread and Wine into the Body and Blood of Christ.

" Secondly. ' The Body and Blood of Christ be not **carnally,** or **corporally in** the Bread and Wine, nor, as others use to say, **under** the kinds of bread and wine.

" Thirdly. ' The Body and Blood of Christ be united to bread and wine **sacramentally.**

" They that were the chief Disputers against him on the contrary side were, Dr. Tresham, Dr. Chedsey, and Morgan."

From " The Reasons and principal Arguments of Peter Martyr," I extract the following :—

" *The argument of Peter Martyr upon the first conclusion.*

After quoting Holy Scripture, he says—

" Ergo. We also, with the Scriptures,' ought not to **exclude bread** from the nature of the Sacrament."

Quoting St. Cyprian, he says—

" Ergo. As in the person of Christ, so in the Sacrament, both the natures ought still to remain."

Quoting Gelasius, St. Augustine, and Theodoret, he says

" Ergo. Like as the Body of Christ remained in Him, and was not changed into His Divinity ; so **in** the Sacrament, the bread is not changed into the Body, but **both the substances** remain whole."—*Foxe*, Acts and Mon. Vol. vi. p. 299.

In the following " Argument" he *appears* to contradict these last two conclusions :—

" The words of the Evangelist, speaking of that which Christ took, blessed, brake, and gave, do import it to be bread, and nothing else but bread."

Yet his conclusion agrees with them : for he only says "Ergo, the substance of bread is not to be *excluded* out of the Sacrament :" (p. 300). He does not say that the Body and Blood of Christ is *not in* the Sacrament.

" Arguments of Peter Martyr. disputing with Martin Chedsey upon the first question.

" Every Sacrament consisteth in two things, that is, in the thing signifying, and the thing signified."

. . . .

He contends that Transubstantiation " is false."

" I. First, by these words of the Scripture, when He saith, ' Do this in remembrance of Me,' forasmuch as remembrance properly serveth not for things corporally present, but for things rather being absent. [*i.e.* corporally absent.]

" II. Secondly, where He saith, ' Until I come ;' which words were vain if He were already come [*i e.* corporally] by consecration.

" IV. Furthermore, whereas the Lord biddeth them to take and eat, it is evident that the same cannot be understood, without a trope, forasmuch as He cannot be eaten and chewed with teeth, as we use properly, in eating other meats, to do.

. . . .

" The second cause why the words of Christ, ' This is My Body,' cannot be literally expounded without a trope, is the nature of a sacrament ; whose nature and property is to bear a sign or signification of a thing to be remembered, which thing, after the substantial and real presence is absent........

" The third cause why the words of consecration are figuratively to be taken, is the testimony of the ancient doctors.

" Tertullian saith, ' This is My Body ;' that is to say, This is a figure of My Body.

" Augustine saith, ' Christ gave a figure of His Body.' Also he saith, ' He did not doubt to say, *This is My Body*, when He gave a sign of His Body.'

" Jerome saith, ' Christ represented unto us His Body.'

" Augustine, in his book, ' De Doctrina Christiana,' declareth expressly that this speech of eating the Body of Christ, is a figurative speech.'

" Ambrose saith, ' As thou hast received the similitude of His Death ; so thou drinkest the similitude of His precious Blood.' "

" Argument.

" The Death of Christ is not present really in the Sacrament, but by similitude.

" The precious Blood of Christ is present in the Sacrament, as His death is present.

" Ergo. The precious Blood of Christ is not present really in the Sacrament.

" The minor of this argument is proved before by the words of Ambrose."

" The argument of Peter Martyr, upon the Second Conclusion.

" The **true natural** body of Christ is placed in Heaven.

" The **true natural** body of man can be but in one place at once, where he is.

" Ergo, The **true natural** Body of Christ can be in no place at once, but in heaven where He is.

" The major is plain by the Scriptures."—St. Mark xvi. 19 ; St. John xii. 8. and xvi. 28 ; St. Matt. xxiv. 23 ; Acts iii. 21 ; Coloss. iii. 1.

" The minor, likewise, is evident by St. Austin, who speaking of the glorified Body of Christ, affirmeth the same to be in one certain place, ' Propter veri corporis modum,' that is, for the manner of a true body."

" Argument.

" Every **true natural** body requireth one certain place.

" Augustine saith, Christ's Body, is a **true natural** Body.

" Ergo, Christ'sBody requireth one certain place."—p. 302.

. . . .

" Argument.

" We must not so defend the Divinity of Christ, that we destroy His humanity.

" If we assign to the Body of Christ plurality of places, we destroy His humanity.

" Ergo, we must not assign to the body of Christ plurality of places."

. . . .

" Argument.

" If Christ had given His Body **substantially** and **carnally** in the supper, then was that Body either passible or impassible.

" But neither can you say that body to be passible or impassible, which He gave at supper.

" Ergo, He did not give His Body **substantially** and **carnally** at supper."

" Argument.

" Bodies **organical**, without quantity, be no bodies.

" The Pope's Doctrine, maketh the Body of Christ in the Sacrament to be without quantity.

" Ergo, The Pope's Doctrine maketh the Body of Christ in the Sacrament to be no body."—p. 303.

Strype, in relating this Disputation, quotes P. Martyr as reporting of it to the Archbishop, thus :—

" ' That his doctrines he then maintained might not altogether square with Bucer's judgment. But he said in his own justification, that he granted the Body of Christ was present to us by faith, and that we are incorporated into Him by communication.........
that we do partake of the matter of the Sacrament, namely, the Body and Blood of Christ ; but he meant it in **mind** and **faith** ......

13

that the Holy Ghost is efficacious in the Sacrament, by virtue of the Lord's institution. But that which he **especially endeavoured** to assert was, that they mixed not the Body and Blood of Christ **carnally** with the bread and wine by **any corporeal** Presence. Nor yet would he have the Sacrament to be symbols without honour and reverence. Another thing he asserted, which he thought might offend Bucer, was, that it was not agreeable to the Body of Christ, however glorified, to be in many places at once.—*Strype's Cranmer*, Bk. ii., c. 14.

Next, in order of time, we come to the Disputations at Cambridge on the Eucharist: of these there were three, conducted by the persons named in Ridley's " Determination."*

" *The first disputation holden at Cambridge, the 20th day of June, A.D.* 1549, *before the King's Majesty's Commissioners, by Dr. Madew respondent, ...*"

In his Declaration against transubstantiation he says:—". . . some papists dream and fancy, such a **corporal, real,** and **gross** presence of Christ's Body in the Sacrament, as they affirm it to be there, even **as verily** as it was upon the Cross. Indeed the bread is changed after a certain manner into Christ's body; for Christ gave not His own **natural** Body to His Disciples at His last supper, but only a sign, or figure thereof. Christ's Body **is there with** the Bread; our senses cannot be deceived about the substance of bread, but they do judge there to be but one body, that is of bread : *ergo,* so it is. Also the very definition of a Sacrament doth plainly repugn unto transubstantiation.................. Now, indeed, there be two manner of signs ; one that signifieth only, the other that doth **exhibit** the thing itself. The first is applied to the old law chiefly, the other to the law of grace. ......

" ......Even as we are changed into Christ by receiving the Sacrament, so the bread is changed into the Body of Christ. But our **substance** is not changed into Christ's **substance.** Ergo, the **substance** of the bread is not changed into Christ's Body. ...."— p. 307.

One of the Disputants, Dr. Glyn, pressed upon Dr. Madew that—

" St. Austin saith thus, ' Lo no man eateth of that bread, except he first adore and worship it.'

" *Madew.* ' By your patience, St. Austin, in that place, speaking of the honouring of Christ's Body now sitting in heaven.'

" *Glyn.* ' Yea, master doctor, think you so ? And why not also of His blessed Body in the Sacrament, seeing that He saith It is there ?........And why then ought we not to honour It **in** the Sacrament ? or how many bodies hath Christ, seeing you do grant His Body in Heaven to be honoured, but not his Body here **in** the Sacrament ?'

* See p. 18.

" *Madew.* ' Forsooth He hath but one very Body and no more ; but the same is sacramentally in the Sacrament, and substantially in Heaven : here by faith and there in deed.' "—p. 310.

Glyn next repeated his argument, upon which *Ridley*, then Bishop of Rochester, said—

" ......I do grant unto you, master opponent, that the old ancient fathers do record and witness a certain honour and adoration to be due unto Christ's Body, but they speak not of It in the Sacrament, but of It in Heaven at the right hand of the Father, as holy Crysostom saith, ' Honour thou It and then eat It :' but that honour may not be given to the outward sign, but to the Body of Christ itself in Heaven.. For that Body is there only in a sign virtually, by grace, in the exhibition of It in spirit, effect, and faith, to the worthy receiver of It. For we receive virtually only Christ's Body in the Sacrament."

" *Glyn.* ' How then if it please your good Lordship, doth Baptism differ from this Sacrament ? for in that, we receive Christ also by grace and virtually.'

"*Rochester.* 'Christ is present after another sort in Baptism than in this Sacrament ; for in that, He purgeth and washeth the infant from all kind of sin, but here, He doth feed spiritually the receiver in faith with all the merits of His blessed death and passion. And yet He is in Heaven still really and substantially, as for example : the King's Majesty, our Lord and Master, is but in one place, wheresoever that his royal person is abiding for the time; and yet his mighty power and authority is everywhere in his realms and dominions : so Christ's real Person is only in Heaven substantially placed, but His might is in all things created effectually ; for Christ's Flesh may be understood for the power or inward might of His Flesh.' "*—p. 311.

" *Glyn.* 'Holy St. Ambrose saith, *the Body there made by the mighty power of God's word, is the Body* [*taken*] *of the Virgin Mary.*'

" *Rochester.* ' That is to say, that by the word of God the thing hath a being that it had not before, and we do consecrate the body, that we may receive the grace and power of the Body of Christ in Heaven by this sacramental body.'—p. 312.

" *Glyn.* ' So, I perceive you would have me to grant that the Sacrament is but a figure, which Theoplylact doth deny.'

" *Rochester.* ' You say truth, he denieth it indeed to be a figure, but he meaneth that it is not only a figure."—p. 313.

After some further discussion between *Glyn* and *Ridley*,

* Compare with this argument of Ridley, the following argument on the Roman side :—
" *Weston.* Now then take this argument : wheresover God's authority is, there is Christ's Body : but God's authority is in everyplace : Ergo. What letteth the Body of Christ to be in everyplace ? "—*Disputation with Cranmer at Oxford*, April 14, 1553.

the argument was taken up by "*Master Langdale,*" who quoted *Erasmus* as saying—

" The Church of Christ hath determined, very lately, transubstantiation. It was of a long season enough to believe Christ's Body to be either under the bread consecrated, or else to be present after any other manner."

Madew (accepting, of course, Erasmus as an authority, seeing that his Paraphrase on the Gospels was then in public use in the Churches by the King's Injunctions of 1547) said in reply :—

" . . . . . . it is most constant and sure, that Erasmus was of that mind and opinion, that it was enough for a Christian to believe Christ's Body and Blood to be in the Sacrament, in what manner or condition soever it were."—p. 314.

Then *Langdale* asked—

" . . . . . . whether that this sentence ' This is my Body,' be spoken of Christ figuratively or not?

" *Madew.* ' After the mind of the common gloss of Cyprian and Origen, it is so taken in very deed.'

" *Langdale.* ' That cannot be, by your patience ; for it is taken there substantially: ergo, not figuratively.

" *Madew.* ' I deny your argument.'

" *Langdale.* I prove my argument good, thus : This word *substance* doth plainly repugn, and is contrary to, this word *figure*: ergo, substantially and figuratively do also repugn. Moreover, I ask of you, whether that this be a true proposition or not: *Bread is Christ's Body.*'

" *Madew.* ' Yea, forsooth it is a true proposition.'

"*Langdale.* 'Then thus to you: Christ's Body was given for us, but you say that bread is Christ's Body : ergo, bread was given for us.'

"*Rochester.* 'Not so, sir, for your former proposition is of double understanding.'

" *Langdale.* ' Well, yet you, master doctor, do grant that Christ is substantially in the Sacrament.'

" *Madew.* ' No : I deny that I said so ever.

" *Langdale.* 'Yea, do you so ? Well, I pass not thereupon greatly; for I will prove it by another means.—Christ did suffer His most glorious passion for us really and substantially : Ergo, He is also in the Sacrament substantially. The argument is good, because that it is the same here, that was there crucified for us : howbeit here invisibly, indeed spiritually and sacramentally; but there visibly, and after a mortal and most bloody manner.'

" *Rochester.* ' Master Langdale, your argument doth well conclude in case that His Body were here, in the Sacrament, after such a sort as it was when He was betrayed. But that is not so; for He was betrayed and crucified in His natural Body, substantially and really, in very deed; but in the Sacrament he is not so, but spiritually and figuratively only.'

"*Langdale.* ' By your good Lordship's favour that is not so ; for He is there not figuratively, but verily and indeed, by the power of His mighty word : yea, even His very own natural Body, under the Sacrament duly performed by the lawful minister.' "—p. 315.

To this statement *Madew* and *Ridley* gravely objected.

In reply to an argument of "*Master Segewick,*" another opponent, *Ridley* said :—

" I do grant it [the Bread of the Sacrament] to be Christ's true Body and Flesh, by a property of the nature assumpted to the God-head ; yea, and we do really eat and drink his Flesh and Blood after a certain real property."—p. 316.

Then they proceeded to another point, which was thus stated by *Segewick* :—

" Now, as touching our second conclusion, this I say : wheresoever, Christ is ; there is a sacrifice propitiatory; but, in the Lord's Supper is Christ : ergo, in the Lord's Supper is a sacrifice propitiatory."

Madew. " Christ is not offered in the Lord's Supper, but is received spiritually."

Segewick. "The Priesthood and the Sacrifice be correspondent together ; but Christ's Priesthood, after the order of Melchizedeck, is perpetual ; ergo, also so is His Sacrifice.

Rochester " Christ is a Priest for ever ; that is to say, His Priest-hood and Sacrifice, offered once for all, is available for ever ; so that no other shall succeed Him."

Segewick. "Where there is no Oblation, there is no Sacrifice : ergo, if Christ be not perpetually offered, there is no perpetual Sacri-fice. Item, the same bloody Sacrifice of Christ upon the Cross was the very fine and end of all the bloody Sacrifices figured in the Law after the order of Aaron's Priesthood. Wherefore, you must needs grant that He offered Himself also, at His last Supper, after the order of Melchizedeck, under the forms of Bread and Wine, or else you must show the Scripture where He did so, which I can-not perceive to be done but at His last Supper only, after an un-bloody manner. Item, He is offered for the remission of sins daily : ergo, He is a Sacrifice propitiatory still, in the new Law, as St. Augustine saith, expounding these words of the Psalm, ' Thou hast not willed to have Sacrifice and Oblation, but,' &c.

"*Rochester.* "St. Cyprian speaketh much like that sort, where he saith thus, ' It is the Lord's Passion, which we do offer,' &c."—p. 317.

In " *The second Disputation holden at Cambridge the 24th day of June,* 1549," *Dr. Glyn* commenced with a Declaration upon each of his two Conclusions argued at the former meeting; upon which "*Master Perne*" said to him:—

" . . . . You left transubstantiation, and endeavour yourself to prove **the real Presence in the Sacrament**: whereas we deny nothing less than His **Corporal** Presence, or the absence of His **substance in** the Bread."—p. 320.

Grindal then followed, and argued against the change of the **substance** of the Bread, that—

" If it be the **real** and **substantial** Body of Christ, because Christ said ' This is my Body ;' ergo, because the Lord said ' I will not drink of the fruit of this vine,' and Paul calleth it Bread after the consecration, it is therefore Bread and Wine."—p. 322.

A little after, *Grindal* remarked—

" Augustine upon the thirty-third psalm saith, ' Christ bare Himself in His own Hands, after a sort ; not **indeed** or **truly**,' &c." —p. 324.

Then *Gest* followed, and contended against a change of substance, saying—

" If the bread be changed, it is made the [**natural**] Body of Christ: but that is not so ; ergo, it is not changed."

" *Glyn*. ' I deny your minor.'

" *Gest*. ' It is not generate or begot:

" Ergo, it is not the Body.'

" *Glyn*. ' That followeth not ; as though to be made, and to be generate or begot, were all one thing ; or as though there were no other mutation than a generation : and so you impugn a thing that you know not. But what call you the generation ? '

" *Gest*. ' The generation is the production of the accidents.'

" *Glyn*. ' A new definition of a new philosopher.'

" *Gest*. ' That which he took He blessed ; that which He blessed He brake, and gave it unto them : ergo,' &c.

" *Glyn*. ' Christ took bread, brake bread, and gave His Body, that is the **substance** of His Body: saying, *This is my Body*.'

" *Gest*. 'The Bread is not changed into the Blood of Christ : ergo, not into His Body either.'

" *Glyn*. ' I deny your antecedent.'

" *Gest*. ' The Master of the sentences saith it.'

" *Glyn*. You understand him not ; for the bread is changed into the **Body** of Christ by the power of God's word."

" *Rochester*. Ye dream of a **real presence** of Christ's Body in the Sacrament, by the force of the words spoken ; which the Holy Scripture doth impugn."

" *Gest*. If there were any transubstantiation, the accidents should not remain still ; for they have no matter whereto they may lean or cleave. But the accidents remain not themselves alone : ergo,' &c.''—p. 325.

In "the third Disputation, holden at Cambridge, as before," *Master Perne*, having made his Declaration upon the two Conclusions, said in his argument against Parker (not *Matthew*, afterwards Archbishop)—

"I grant unto you that Christ is in the Sacrament truly, wholly, and verily, after a certain property and manner : I deny not His presence, but His real and corporal presence I utterly deny ; for doubtless His true and natural Body is in Heaven, and not in the Sacrament : notwithstanding He dwelleth with us, and in us, after a certain unity. And also in the sixth chapter of John, He speaketh not of the Flesh of Christ crucified,' &c.

"*Parker.* The flesh of Christ as it is in the Sacrament, is quick and giveth life : ergo, His real and substantial flesh is in the Sacrament."

. . . .
. . . . . .

"*Rochester.* ....these words 'This is My Body.' are meant thus : by grace it is My true Body, but not My fleshly Body, as some of you suppose."—p. 329.

In reply to *Master Vavasor*, who had drawn an argument from *St. Augustine*, in Ps. xcviii.—

"Christ of the earth received earth, and of the flesh of Mary He received flesh."

Ridley said :—

"I acknowledge not His real substance to be there ; but the property of His substance."—p. 331.

Supplementary to these arguments we have Ridley's "Determination concerning the Sacrament, made at Cambridge, after three Disputations held there, June 20, 1549."

The King's Commissioners.—Bishops of Rochester [Ridley] and Ely [Goodrich], Mr. (afterwards Sir John) Cheke, Dr. May, and Thomas Wendy, Physician to the King.

> 1st Disputation, Dr. Madew v. Dr. Glyn, Segewick, Langdale, and Young.
> 2nd Disputation, Dr. Glyn v. Grindal, Perne, Gest, and Pilkington.
> 3rd Disputation, Perne v. Parker, Pollard, Vavasor and Young.

He decides that TRANSUBSTANTIATION is disproved, as being

> 1. "Clean against the words of the Scripture."—viz. St. Matt.

xxvi. 29; St. Mark xiv. 25; Exod. xii. 46; 1 Cor. xi. 24; St. John vi. 27, 28, 29, 50, 54, 55, 62, 63.

2. Against " The Ancient Fathers a thousand years past,"— viz.;—Dionysius Pseudo Areopagita : St. Ignat. Ep. ad Philad.: St. Iren. cont. Heres. lib. iv. c. 18 : Tert. adv. Marc. iii : St. Cyp. ad. Cæcil. i. 6 : Theodoret: Gelasius: St. Cyril : St. August. The places either not named or the same as those in his Treatise on Transubstantiation.

3. Against " the nature of the Sacrament, which consisteth in three things, that is, Unity, Nutrition, and Conversion."

4. Because " They which say that Christ is carnally present in the Eucharist, do take from Him the verity of man's nature....

5. Contrary to the Article of the Creed, " He ascended into heaven," &c.

And from these premises, together with Heb. ix. 11, 26, 28; x. 14, and St. Aug. ad Bonif. Ep. 23 : and Faust. xx. c. 18, he holds it proved—

" That there is no other [real or carnal] oblation of Christ.... but that which was once made upon the Cross."— *Works.* Parker Society.—pp. 171-9.

In the next year, 1550, Cranmer published his " Defence of the True and Catholic Doctrine of the Sacrament:" to which Bishop Gardiner having made a reply, the Archbishop printed his " Answer" in the latter part of 1551 : as his original work and Bishop Gardiner's criticims are sub-stantially comprised in Cranmer's " Answer " it is desirable to extract a few passages from it, both as serving to shew (1) The nature of the controversy with Gardiner ; (2) The continuous identity of the Archbishop's statements touching the PHYSICAL Presence in the Sacrament; and (3) The occa-sional convergence of the two Prelates' views on points which are involved in the terms of the Declaration on Kneeling at the Sacrament.

It is true, indeed, that, in both cases, it is often most difficult to gain a clear notion of what the respective writers maintain; and to determine how far they are consistent with themselves : yet if this is more especially the case with Cranmer, from whatever cause, he has furnished certain keys to this controversial work of his. For in his "Preface to the reader," he thinks "it good..to admonish [him] of certain words and kinds of speeches which," as he says, " I do use sometimes in this mine answer....lest in mistaking thou do as it were stumble at them."

Thus he says :—

" This word ' Sacrament' I do sometimes use (as it is many times taken among writers and holy doctors) for the sacramental bread, water, or wine ; as when they say that, *sacramentum est sacræ rei signum*, ' a Sacrament is the sign of an holy thing.' But where I use to speak sometimes (as the old authors do) that Christ is in the Sacraments, I mean the same as they did understand the matter ; that is to say, not of Christ's carnal Presence in the outward Sacrament, but sometimes of His sacramental presence. And sometime by this word ' Sacrament :' I mean the whole ministration and receiving the Sacraments......"— *Works, Parker Society*, vol. i. p. 3.

It may be a fit introduction to any extracts from this "Answer" and also a legitimate comment upon them where of doubtful meaning, to notice Cranmer's estimate of Bertram whose Book I have already alluded to in connection with the Archbishop : thus in reply to Gardiner he observes :—

" And as for Bertram, he did nothing else but, at the request of King Charles, set out the true doctrine of the Holy Catholic Church, from Christ unto his time, concerning the Sacrament. And I never heard nor read any man that condemned Bertram before this time : and therefore I can take no hindrance, but a great advantage at his hands : for all men that hitherto have written of Bertram, have much commended him. And seeing that he wrote of this Sacrament at King Charles's request, it is not like that he would write against the received Doctrine of the Church in those days. And if he had, it is without all doubt that some learned man, either in his time or sithence, would have written against him, or at the least not have commended him so much as they have done."*— p. 14, see also p. 77.

The following are some extracts from Cranmer's "Answer," they are but a few out of many passages to the like purport.

(I) "....as He giveth the bread to be eaten with our mouths, so giveth He His very Body to be eaten with our faith. And therefore I say, that Christ giveth Himself truly to be eaten, chewed and digested ; but all is spiritually with faith, not with mouth. And yet you would bear me in hand, that I say that thing which I say not : that is to say that Christ did not give His Body, but the figure of His Body."—p. 15.

" And therefore to answer you plainly, the same flesh that was given in Christ's last supper, was given also upon the Cross, and is given daily in the ministration of the Sacrament. But although

* Compare the Bp. of St. Davids' remarks on Mr. Freeman's opinion of Bertram's views, in his charge of 1857, Appendix B. p. 118.

it be one thing, yet it was diversely given. For upon the Cross Christ was carnally given to suffer and to die ; at His last supper he was spiritually given in a promise of His death; and in the Sacrament He is daily given in remembrance of His death. And yet it is all but one Christ that was promised to die, that died indeed, and whose death is remembered ; that is to say, the very same Christ, the eternal Word that was made flesh. And the same flesh was also given to be spiritually eaten, and was eaten in deed, before His supper, yea, and before His incarnation also. Of which eating, and not of sacramental eating, He spake in the sixth of John : " My flesh is very meat, and My blood is very drink. He that eateth My flesh, and drinketh My blood, dwelleth in me, and I in him."—p. 24.

" And, although Christ in His human nature, substantially, really, corporally, naturally, and sensibly, be present with His Father in heaven, yet sacramentally and spiritually He is here present. For in water, bread, and wine, he is present, as in signs and sacraments ; but He is indeed spiritually in those faithful, Christian people, which according to Christ's ordinance be baptized, or receive the Holy Communion, or unfeignedly believe in him.."

" The papists' say, that evil and ungodly men receive in this Sacrament the very body and blood of Christ, and eat and drink the selfsame thing that the good and godly men do. But the truth of God's word is contrary, that all those that be godly members of Christ, as they corporally eat the bread and drink the wine, so spiritually they eat and drink Christ's very flesh and blood. And as for the wicked members of the devil, they eat the sacramental bread, and drink the sacramental wine, but they do not spiritually eat Christ's flesh, nor drink His blood, but they eat and drink their own damnation."—p. 47.

Gardiner had said, in reply to Cranmer's "Defence," that it was not true to charge his side with holding.—

" . . . . . . that Christ is in the bread and wine, but they agree in form of teaching with that the Church of England teacheth at this day, in the distribution of the Holy Communion, in that it is there said, the Body and Blood of Christ to be under the form of bread and wine.—p. 51.

To this Cranmer rejoins truly enough thus, for the phrase occurred only as a notice, at the end of the First Book of Homilies, of an intended Homily; though indeed it was the alleged *physical* statement which he was denying :—

" And as concerning the form of doctrine used in this Church of England in the Holy Communion, that the body and blood of Christ be [i.e. carnally] under the form of bread and wine, when you shall shew the place where this form of words is expressed, then shall you purge yourself of that, which in the meantime I take to be a plain untruth."—p. 53.

" And how sure be you that Christ is in **substance** present because He is **truly** present ? Are you assured that this your doctrine agreeth with God's word ? Doth not God's word teach a **true** presence of Christ in spirit, where He is not present in His **corporal** substance ? As when He saith : " Where two or three be gathered together in My name, there am I in the midst of them." And also when He saith : " I shall be with you till the end of the world." Was it not a **true** presence that Christ in these places promised ? And yet can you not of this **true** presence gather such a **corporal** presence of the **substance** of Christ's **manhood**, as you unlearnedly, contrary to the scriptures, go about to prove in the Sacrament ? For when Christ said, ' This is My body,' it was bread which is called His body in a figurative speech, as all old authors teach, and as I have proved in my third book, the eighth and eleventh chapters. And the manner how Christ carried Himself in His own hands, St. Augustine declareth it to be figuratively."—p. 61.

" They say that Christ is **really** and **corporally** in the sacramental bread being reserved, so long as the form of bread remaineth, although it be an whole year and more; but after the receiving thereof, He flieth up from the receiver into heaven, as soon as the bread is chewed in the mouth or digested in the stomach. But we say, that after what manner Christ is received of us, in the same wise He remaineth in us, so long as we remain the members of Christ."—p. 61.

" And as for the Book of Common Prayer, although it say, that in each part of the bread broken is received the whole body of Christ yet it saith not so of the parts unbroken, nor yet of the parts or whole reserved, as the papists teach. But, as in Baptism we receive the Holy Ghost, and put Christ upon us, as well if we be christened in one dish full of water taken out of the font, as if we were christened in the whole font or river ; so we be as truly fed, refreshed, and comforted by Christ, receiving a piece of bread at the Lord's holy table, as if we did eat an whole loaf. For, as in every part of the water in baptism is whole Christ and the Holy Spirit, sacramentally, so be they in every part of the bread broken, but not **corporally** and **naturally**, as the papists teach."—p. 64.

" Who is so ignorant that hath read anything at all, but he knoweth that distinction of three eatings? But no man that is of learning and judgment, understandeth the three diverse eatings in such sort as you do, but after this manner ; that some eat only the Sacrament of Christ's Body, but not the very Body itself : some eat His Body, and not the Sacrament : and some eat the Sacrament and Body both together. The **Sacrament** (that is to say, the Bread) is **corporally** eaten and chewed with the teeth in the mouth : the very Body is eaten and chewed with **faith** in the Spirit. Ungodly men, when they receive the Sacrament, they chew in their mouths, like unto Judas, the **sacramental bread**, but they eat not the **celestial** Bread, which is Christ. Faithful Christian' people, such as be Christ's true disciples, continually from time to time record in their minds the beneficial death of our Saviour Christ, chewing it by faith in the cud of their spirit, and digesting it in their hearts, feeding and comforting themselves with that heavenly meat, although they daily receive not the Sacrament thereof; and so they eat Christ's Body spiritually, although not the Sacrament thereof. But when such men, for their more comfort and confirmation of eternal life, given unto them by Christ's death, come unto the Lord's holy table, then, as before they fed spiritually upon Christ, so now they feed corporally also upon the sacramental bread: by which sacramental feeding in Christ's promises, their former spiritual feeding is increased, and they grow and wax continually more strong in Christ, until, at the last, they shall come to the full measure and perfection in Christ. This is the teaching of the true catholic church, as it is taught by God's word. And, therefore St. Paul, speaking of them that unworthily eat, saith, that they eat the bread, but not that they eat the body of Christ, but their own damnation......."—p. 71.

" The papists say, that the body of Christ that is in the Sacrament, hath His own proper form and quantity. We say, that the body of Christ hath not His proper form and quantity, neither in the Sacrament, nor in them that receive the Sacrament; but is in the Sacrament sacramentally, and in the worthy receivers spiritually, without the proper form and quantity of His body......."—p. 72

" I never said that Christ is utterly absent, but I ever affirmed that He is truly and spiritually present, and truly and spiritually exhibited unto the godly receivers; but corporally He is neither in the receivers, nor in or under the forms of bread or wine, as you do teach clearly without the consent of master Bucer [whom Gardiner had quoted] who writeth no such thing."—p. 127.

" As for the real presence of Christ in the Sacrament, I grant that He is really present after such sort as you expound really in this place, that is to say, in deed, and yet but spiritually. For you say yourself, that He is but after a spiritual manner there, and so is He spiritually honoured, as St. Augustine saith."—p. 127.

" For my doctrine is, that the very body of Christ, which was born of the Virgin Mary, and suffered for our sins, giving us life by His death, the same Jesus, as concerning His corporal presence, is taken from us, and sitteth at the right hand of His Father; and yet is He by faith spiritually present with us, and is our spiritual food and nourishment, and sitteth in the midst of all them that be gathered together in His name. And this feeding is a spiritual feeding, and an heavenly feeding, far passing all corporal and carnal feeding; and therefore there is a true presence and a true feeding in deed, and not 'in a figure only, or not at all,' as you most untruly report my saying to be. This is the true understanding of the true presence, receiving and feeding upon the Body of our Saviour Christ; and not, as you deprave the meaning and true sense thereof, that the receiving of Christ truly and verily is the receiving corporally with the mouth corporal, or that the spiritual receiving is to receive Christ only by His Divine Nature, which thing I never said nor meant."......p. 185.

" .... what made the people to run from their seats to the

altar, and from altar to altar, and from sacring (as they called it) to sacring, peeping, tooting, and gazing at that thing which the Priest held up in his hands, if they thought not to honour that thing which they saw ? What moved the priests to lift up the Sacrament so high over their heads; or the people to cry to the priest, 'Hold up! hold up!' and one man to say to another, 'Stoop down before;' or to say, 'This day have I seen my Maker;' and, 'I cannot be quiet, except I see my Maker once a day?' What was the cause of all these, and that as well the priest as the people so devoutly did knock and kneel at every sight of the Sacrament, but that they worshipped that **visible thing** which they saw with their eyes, and took it for very God? For if they worshipped in spirit only Christ sitting in heaven with His Father, what needed they to remove out of their seats to toot and gaze, as the Apostles did after Christ, when He was gone up into heaven ? If they worshipped nothing that they saw ; why did they rise up to see ? Doubtless, many of the simple people worshipped that thing which they saw with their eyes.

"And although the subtle papists do colour and cloke the matter never so finely, saying that they worship not the **sacraments** which they see with their eyes, but **that thing** which they believe with their faith to be **really** and **corporally** in the sacraments ; yet why do they run from place to place, to gaze at the things which they see, if they worship them not, giving thereby occasion to them that be ignorant to worship that which they see ? Why do they not rather quietly sit still in their seats, and move the people to do the like, worshipping God in heart, and in spirit, than to gad about from place to place to see that thing, which they confess themselves is not to be worshipped ?

" And yet, to eschew one inconvenience, (that is to say the worshipping of the **sacrament**,) they fall into another as evil, and worship nothing there at all. For they worship that thing, (as they say) which is **really** and **corporally**, and yet **invisibly** present **under** the kinds of bread and wine, which (as before is expressed and proved) is utterly nothing. And so they give unto the ignorant occasion to worship bread and wine, and they themselves worship nothing there at all.—p. 229.

" And where you say that 'it were not well' to worship Christ in the Sacrament, if nothing be there (as you say I teach,) if you mean that Christ cannot be worshipped but where He is **corporally** present, (as you must needs mean if your reason should be to purpose,) then it followeth of your saying, that we may not worship Christ in baptism, in the fields, in private houses, nor in no place else where Christ is not **corporally** and **naturally** present, But the true teaching of the holy Catholic Church is, that although Christ, as concerning His **corporal** presence, be continually resident in heaven, yet He is to be worshipped not only there, but here in earth also, of all faithful people, at all times, in all places, and in all their works.

" Hear now what followeth further in my book :

" But the papists, for their own commodity to keep the people still in idolatry, do often allege a certain place of St. Augustine upon the Psalms, where he saith, that 'no man doth eat the flesh of Christ, except he first worship it,' and that 'we do not offend in worshipping thereof, but we should offend if we should not worship it.'

" That is true which St. Augustine saith in this place. For who is he that professeth Christ, and is spiritually fed and nourished with His flesh and blood, but he will honour and worship Him, sitting at the right hand of His Father, and render unto Him from the bottom of his heart, all laud, praise, and thanks for His merciful redemption ?"—p. 230.

. . . .

" These words of St. Augustine, with the other before recited, do express his mind plainly, that Christ is not otherwise to be eaten than **spiritually,** (which **spiritual** eating requireth no **corporal** presence) and that he intended not to teach here **any adoration,** either of the **visible** sacraments or of any thing that is **corporally in** them. For indeed there is nothing **really** and **corporally in** the bread to be worshipped, although the papists say that Christ is [**corporally**] in every consecrated bread."—p. 231.

" But this doctrine, which the holy doctors do teach, is agreeable to holy scripture, necessary for all Christian persons to believe for their everlasting salvation, and profitable for their spiritual comfort in this present life ; that is to say, that the sacrament of Christ's body and blood in the natures and substances of bread and wine is distributed unto all men, both good and evil which receive it, and yet that only faithful persons do receive **spiritually** by faith the **very** body and blood of our Saviour Christ. So that Christ's **natural** body is not in the sacrament **really, substantially,** and **corporally,** but only by representation and signification, and in His lively members by spiritual and effectual operation."—p. 283.

" And howsoever the body and blood of our Saviour Christ be there present, they may as well be present there with the substance of bread and wine, as with the accidents of the same, as the school authors do confess themselves, and it shall be well proved, if the adversaries will deny it. Thus you see the strongest arguments of the papists answered unto, and the chief foundation whereupon they build their error of **transubstantiation** utterly subverted and overthrown."—p. 304.

" And where you allege, that in the book of Common Prayer it is set forth, how in each part of what is broken of the consecrated bread is the whole body of our Saviour Christ, what could you have alleged more against yourself? For if the consecrated bread be broken in parts, how can you 'answer truly by faith, as a believing man,' which answer you make straightways after, that,' ' that which is broken is no bread ?' And if you would answer, as you be wont to do, that the accidents of bread be called bread, yet that collusion will not serve you in this place. For seeing that this place speaketh of consecrated bread, answer me to this, whether the substance or accidents be consecrated ? And if you say the accidents, then for as much as consecration, by your doctrine, is conversion, it must follow that the accidents of bread be converted, and not the substance ; and so should you call it transaccidentation, and not transubstantiation ; and if you say, that the substance of bread is consecrated, then forasmuch as that which is consecrated is divided into parts, and in every part is the whole body of Christ, you must confess that the substance of bread remaineth with the parts thereof, wherein is received the body of Christ."—p. 327.

Other passages of a kindred character will be found at pp. 22, 47, 73, 79, 112, 188, 190, 227, 228, 366, and elsewhere throughout the volume.

Gardiner (according to the custom of those times, pursued by both sides alike, towards their opponents, when they had the power,) was now in prison, on charges such as were not uncommon in that age, and which may, perhaps, be best described as *politico-ecclesiastical nonconformity* : his several Examinations show what I have already remarked—that he was of a numerous party in those days who (while they had been more or less averse, on various grounds, from helping on the changes which had taken place) yet acquiesced in the ecclesiastical arrangements, with a good or a bad grace, content to think or believe that they were comprehensive enough to include their faith and practice.

This Prelate had already in his sermon before the King on the Feast of St. Peter, June 29, 1548, expressed his approval of the Act and Proclamation already mentioned, enforcing Communion in both kinds, and condemning the irreverent talkers of the Sacrament: morover, he added " That if Chantries were abused by applying the Mass for the satisfaction of sin, or to bring men to Heaven, or to take away sin, or to make men, of wicked—just, I like the Act [that suppressed them] well." And again, " I like well the rest of the King's Majesty's proceedings concerning the Sacrament." —*Foxe*, vol. vi. pp. 89 and 92.

In " The 4th Session against him, Jan. 8, 1550-1, in his ' Long Matter Justificatory,' Art. lxiv. we read :—

".... The said Bishop then told them why he liked the said book, and noted unto them how, notwithstanding the alteration, yet touching the truth of the very presence of Christ's most precious Body and Blood in the Sacrament, there was as much spoken in that book as might be desired ; and that although the elevation was taken away, yet the alteration in one special place, was indeed reserved : and showed it them, adding, it must needs be so ; affirming also, that there was never more spoken for the sacrament than in that book, wherewith might be confuted all that spoke against it, if they would take it for authority."—p. 114, see also pp. 169, 200, 201, 203, 204, and 322, for the confirmatory testimony of the various witnesses as given in the several sessions.

In the 9th Session, Jan. 21, 1550-1, among the " Articles, additional exhibited by Gardiner," he declares :—

" First, that the Bishop of London that now is [Ridley], then being Bishop of Rochester, did openly in his sermon made at Paul's Cross, in the month of November or December, or thereabouts, in the first year of the King's Majesty's reign* that now is, very earnestly and vehemently preach and teach the true presence of Christ's most Precious Body to be in the Sacrament of the Altar.

" Item, That Dr. Redman, in a sermon which he preached before the King's Majesty in Lent, the second year of his Majesty's reign, did preach and teach to be believed for the true Catholic Faith, that the true presence of Christ's Body and Blood was in the Sacrament of the Altar.

" Item, That my Lord Archbishop of Canterbury, about the time that the Bishop of Winchester aforesaid [viz. himself] preached a sermon on St. Peter's Day, at Westminster, before the King's Majesty, in a booke by him translated, called Catechism,† did affirm, publish, and set forth, the true presence of Christ's most Precious Body and Blood to be in the Sacrament of the Altar....."—p. 125.

The Articles also contain similar statements as to others.

Again, in the 20th Session, Feb. 3, 1550-1, "John White" Warden of Winchester, being "sworn and examined" before the King's Commissioners, deposed concerning the 37th Article, in which Gardiner had pleaded that he had not infringed any authorized prohibitions by preaching of " the very Presence of Christ's Body in the Sacrament."

" .... that ever since his time, that doctrine of the Presence of Christ in the Sacrament hath been received, acknowledged, and agreed upon, by the whole Clergy and temporalty learned of this Realm, and by Acts of Parliament and synods established, and by the Prelates and other learned men set forth in books and open sermons, until within two years since [i. e. after Edward's First Book came into use], or thereabout, one Peter Martyr, in Oxford, in his Lectures (as this deponent hath heard say), called the thing again in question ; whereupon ensued contention, and afterwards disputation....p. 24.   See also other testimonies in pp. 222, 225, 226, 231, and 239.

* i. e. Almost two years after he had begun to study Bertram's book.
† i. e. Justus Jonas's Catechism.

On the other hand it should be observed that, in this same Session, "The Lord Paget," another witness, said that, in the Sermon in question, the Bishop's advocacy of the Mass went to prove "a CARNAL Presence."—p. 162.

"But," as Foxe says, "against this Dr. Gardiner, we will sit and watch, on the contrary side, Dr. Redman." In a Document called

" A Note of the Communication that I, Richard Wilkes, had with Master Doctor Redman, being sick at Westminster on his death bed, but of good memory, the 2nd day of November, 1551, in the presence of Master Young, and another whom I did not know, and two of Master Doctor Redman's servants, the one called Ellis, and the other unknown," occur the following passages :—

"Then I asked him of the presence of Christ.—He said, Christ was present with His Sacrament, and in those that received it as they ought. And there was 'mira unitio,' a wonderful union (for that word was named), betwixt Christ and us, as St. Paul saith : . . . . ' Ye be bone of His bone, and flesh of His flesh :' the which union was ineffable.

"Then I asked him what he thought of the opinion that Christ was there [*i. e.* in the Sacrament] **corporally, naturally,** and **really.** He answered, 'If you mean by **corporally, naturally,** and **really,** that He is there present (**vere,**) I grant.

"Then I asked, how he thought of that which was wont commonly to be spoken, that Christ was there **flesh, blood,** and **bone;** as I have heard the stewards in their Leets give charge when the Six Articles stood in effect, and charge the inquest to inquire, that if there were any that would deny that Christ was present in the Sacrament of the Altar, in **flesh, blood,** and **bone,** they should apprehend them. He said that it was too gross, and could not well be excused from the opinion of the Capernaites.

"Then I asked him, ' Inasmuch as Christ is there (**vere,**) how do we receive Him ? in our minds and spiritual parts, or with our mouths, and into our bodies; or both ?' He said, ' We receive Him in our minds and souls by faith.'

"Then, inasmuch as he was much on this point, that there was 'mira unitio,' 'a marvellous union' betwixt us and Christ, in that we were 'caro ex carne ejus, et os ex ossibus ejus,' 'bone of His bone and flesh of His flesh ;' I desired to know his opinion, whether we received the **very** body of Christ with our mouths and into our bodies, or no ?—Here he paused and held his peace a little space ; and shortly after he spake, saying, ' I will not say so ; I cannot tell; it is a hard question : but surely,' saith he, ' we receive Christ in our souls by faith. When you do speak of it otherways, it soundeth grossly, and savoureth of the Capernaites.' "—*Foxe, Acts and Monuments,* vol. vi., p. 267. ed. 1846.

So again in

"*Another Communication between Dr. Redman, lying in his death-bed, and Master Nowel, then schoolmaster in Westminster, and certain others, with Notes of his Censure and Judgment touching certain points of Christ's religion,*" we read :—

" V. Item—That the wicked are not partakers of the body of Christ, but receive the outward Sacrament only.

" VI. Item—That the Sacrament ought not to be carried about in procession ; for it is taught what is the use of it in these words, ' Accipite, manducate, et bibite,' and ' Hoc facite in mei memoriam ;' ' Take, eat, and drink,' and ' Do this in remembrance of Me.'

" VII. Item—That nothing which is seen in the Sacrament, or perceived with any outward sense, is to be worshipped.*

" VIII. Item—That we receive not Christ's body, ' corporaliter, id est crasse,' corporally, that is to say, grossly, like other meats, and like as the Capernaites did understand it.

IX. Item—That we receive Christ's body, ' sic spiritualiter, ut tamen vere ;' so spiritually that nevertheless truly."

The following *Declaration* of John Young, (one of the witnesses who attested these items,) as to No. V., is given by Foxe :—

" Imprimis —That Dr. Redman said more, whereas St. Augustine said ' Quod Judas idem accepit quod Petrus,' ' that Judas received the same that Peter did,' he said, that he understood that of the Sacrament, and that after the same phrase a man might say ' Quod Simon Magus idem baptisma recepit quod apostoli,' ' That Simon Magus received the same baptism that the Apostles did,' when he did receive only the outward Sacrament to his condemnation ; for he said that he thought Christ would not vouchsafe to give His holy flesh to an ungodly man : and this, he said, was always his mind, though he knew well that other men did otherwise think."—*Ibid* pp. 269-70.

Redman's views are more fully set out in " *The Letter of Master Young to Master Cheke concerning Dr. Redman, translated out of Latin into English.*" Nowell, afterwards Dean of St. Paul's, came to Dr. Redman during his illness, to ask his opinion on several points :—

" When he was asked whether wicked and ungodly people, in the Holy Communion, did eat the body of Christ and drink His blood, he answered, that such kind of men did not eat Christ's most blessed flesh, but only took the Sacrament, to their own damnation ; saying that Christ would not give His most pure and holy flesh to be eaten of such naughty and impious persons, but would withdraw Himself from them . . . . . ' [they] do receive the Sacrament

* The opposite then is implied.

and the selfsame which good and godly men receive; but the Body of Christ they do not receive, for Christ doth not vouchsafe to deliver it to them.' And thus, he said, was his opinion and belief, although he knew others to be of a contrary judgment.

"Being then after this demanded, whether he thought Christ's presence to be in the Sacrament, or no; he answered that Christ did give and offer to faithful Christian men His **very real** Body and Blood **verily** and **really, under** Sacraments of Bread and Wine; insomuch that they which devoutly come to be partakers of that Holy Food, are, by the **benefit** thereof, united and made one with Christ in His Flesh and Body. And therefore, he said, that Christ did **distribute** His Body **spiritually**; that He **gave** it **truly**; yet not so, nevertheless, that by these and the like words, we should conceive any **gross, carnal** intelligence, such as the Capernaites once dreamed of; but that (quoth he) we might labour and endeavour to express by some kind of words, the ineffable majesty of this mystery. For the manner whereby Christ is there present, and ministereth to the faithful His Flesh, is altogether inexplicable; but we must believe (quoth he) and think, that by God's mighty power, and the holy operation of His Spirit, this so notable a mystery was made; and that heaven and earth were joined together in that moment, as the blessed man, St. Gregory saith, ' the lowest parts are joined with the highest,' by which is understood that holy food whereby they which be regenerate by the Holy Ghost in baptism are nourished to immortality. And further he said, that Christ's Body was received in the said Sacrament by faith, which being received, both body and soul were quickened to everlasting life."—*Ibid* pp.272—3.

HOOPER, Bishop of Gloucester, may be regarded as another important witness to the language of this period on the Real Presence: in his "Visitation Book" of 1551-2, among his "Articles concerning the Christian Religion," we read thus:—

" X. Item, that in the Sacrament of the Body and Blood of the Lord there is no **transubstantiation** of the bread and wine, into the Body and Blood of Christ, or **any manner** of **corporal** or **local** presence of Christ **in, under,** or **with** the bread and wine.. ......"—-*Later Writings of Bishop Hooper*, Parker Society, p. 122.

" Again, in the " Articles whereunto William Phelps, pastor and curate of Cirencester....consented....ministered unto him by John Hooper, Bishop of Gloucester, the 29th day of April, in the 5th year of the reign of King Edward the Sixth, 1551," we find:—

"Item, that the same Holy Word of God doth confess, hold, defend, acknowledge and maintain, that the **very natural, substantial, real,** and **corporal** Body of Christ, concerning His humanity, is only and solely in Heaven and not in the Sacrament and Communion of His precious Body and Blood......"

"As for the eating of His Flesh and drinking of His Blood **really, corporally, materially,** or **substantially,** it is but a carnal and gross opinion of men......"—p. 153.

So, too, in "An Assertion and defence of the true knowledge and use of the Sacrament of Christ's Precious Body and Blood, made by John Wynter, Master of Arts, Parson of Stawnton, and professed by him in the Cathedral Church of Gloucester, 8 November, Anno Domini, 1551." He says:—

"......That in the same Sacrament by no manner of means, reasons, or ways, the Body and Blood of Christ is **carnally, bodily, really,** or **substantially** present, but only **spiritually** to the soul and eye of faith;........And as in the breaking of the bread in the Sacrament, after the words of Christ which be these 'That is given for you,' there is no **sensible** feeling or painful passion, nor **killing again** of Christ's precious Body, no more is there **in** the bread, or **under** the bread of the Sacrament, after the words, which be these, 'This is My Body,' any **natural, corporal,** or **substantial** presence of the Body that died, or of the Blood that was shed; but that the bread and wine remaining in their substance be Sacraments of Christ's Body and Blood, which be present unto the eyes spiritually of faith, ·which is in the receiver, and not **substantially** nor **corporally** in the elements of bread and wine. And whosoever be of the contrary opinion and would defend **transubstantiation** or **corporal** presence, I do condemn his faith as an error and opinion contrary to the express Word of God...... .."—p. 155.

Having thus considered the opinions on the Real Presence prevalent at this time among the leading persons who conducted Ecclesiastical Affairs, we are brought in historical order to the Articles and the Prayer Book of 1552. For the purpose of this enquiry, it is not material to ascertain whether the XXIXth of these 42 Articles had been finally settled at the time when the Prayer Book was published: there seems indeed no reason to think the contrary: for although the Book came into use on the 1st November, and the Articles did not receive the Archbishop's last corrections until the 24th of the same month, and were only published in the May of the following year (1553), there is nothing in the language of the Article which (judging from what we have already seen) could well be a subject of dispute among the authors and revisers of it. The Article runs thus:

(1.) "XXIX. *Of the Lord's Supper*. The Supper of the Lorde is not onely a sign of the loue that Christiens ought to haue among theimselues one to another, but rather it is a Sacrament of our redemption by Christ's death, insomoche that to soche as right-lie, woorthelie, and with faieth receiue the same, the breade whiche we breake is a communion of the bodie of Christe. Likewise the Cuppe of blessing is a Communion of the bloude of Christe.

(2.) "Transubstanciation, or the chaunge of the substaunce of breade and wine into the substaunce of Christes bodie and bloude cannot be proued by holie writte, but is repugnant to the plaine woordes of Scripture, and hath giuen occasion to many supersticions.

(3.) "Forasmoche as the trueth of mannes nature requireth, that the bodie of one, and theself same manne cannot be at one time in diuerse places, but must nedes be in some one certeine place: Therefore the bodie of Christe cannot bee presente at one time in many and diuerse places. And because (as holie Scripture doeth teache) Christe was taken up into heauen, and there shall continue unto thende of the worlde, a faithful man ought not, either to beleue, or openlie to confess the **reall** and **bodelie** [*Realem et Corporalem*] presence (as thei terme it) of Christes **flesh** and **bloude, in** the Lordes Supper.

(4.) "The Sacramente of the Lordes Supper was not commaunded by Christes ordinaunce to be kepte, carried about, lifted up, nor worshipped."

Now, it must be plain, I think, that the 3rd paragraph of this Article is the deliberate judgment of the Convocation* of 1552 on a point which, as we have seen, had been long debated in connection with the docrine of Transubstantiation; and the Church of England, thus speaking Synodically, cautiously limits herself to a *negative* statement; that statement is simply and solely a denial and a condemnation of the, then still prevalent, opinion or belief that Christ's NATURAL FLESH AND BLOOD was present in the Sacrament of the Altar in some "REALL and BODILIE" *i. e.*, in some CARNAL, PHYSICAL ORGANICAL, and withal LOCAL manner. The expression "as thei terme it," interpreted, as it must be, by the language which has been already quoted from controversial and other Documents of the six preceding years, seems to me to demonstrate this. *Such* a belief, and moreover the open profession of it, was, in the judgment of the Synod, what "a faithful

* The title proves this:—"*Articles agreed on by the Bishops and o'her learned men in the synod at London, in the year of our Lord God* 1552, *for the avoiding of controversy in opinions, and the establishment of a godlie concord in certain matters of Religion.* Published by the King's Majesty's commandment, in the month of May, 1553. Rich. Graftonus, typographus regius excudebat. Lond. mense Junii, 1553."

man ought not " to hold or promulge: *how much* he might or must hold, or *what language* he should use to express his belief in the Eucharistic Presence, the Synod did not attempt to determine: indeed we may fairly presume that the various opinions of its members must have been an effectual bar to any such definition, if it had been even thought of: *all* that the Convocation decreed was—that a specific belief, and its recognized verbal expression, which were avowedly one logical result of the theory of Transubstantiation, "ought not" to be persisted in—*all* that it seems to have meant was, to discountenance, discourage, and prevent the continuance of this belief and form of words.

Coeval with this Synodical decision appeared the 2nd Prayer Book of Edward VIth : certain complaints which, as is well known, had been made by the more eager of the reforming party in England, and in particular the censures of Bucer, are stated to have led to the revision of the former Book. Whether the concessions which this revision implied were wise or not, it is unnecessary and might look immodest for me here to discuss. But it is of consequence to ask—was the new Book, with its altered language and arrangement, designed to teach *another* and a *lower* doctrine than that embodied in the earlier Book ? To this question I feel no hesitation in replying, as my firm conviction, that it was not. Such indeed is but the recorded opinion of many who have critically compared the two ; though some of them have thought that the Doctrine of the first Book, on the Eucharist especially, was but barely saved in the Second. Without attempting here, however, any proof, from internal evidence, of the conviction just expressed, it must suffice (and is more to the purpose probably) to look for some Historical attestations of it; and the three following seem enough for the purpose :—

" First: we have the witness of the Act of Uniformity, which authorized the Book. In that Statute, the 5 and 6 Edw. VI. c. i. A.D. 1552, which (considering the co-operation of the Ecclesiastical and Civil Legislatures in those days) must be held to embody the opinion of both the Bishops and the Parliament, the First Prayer Book is spoken of as—

" ....a very godly order.... agreeable to the Word of God and the Primitive Church, very comfortable to all good people desiring to live in Christian conversation, and most profitable to the estate of this realm....."

And then the Act proceeds to state in the 5th Section that—

" Because there hath arisen in the use and exercise of the aforesaid Common Service in the Church heretofore set forth, divers doubts,"

not, be it observed, as to its Doctrinal teaching but—

(1) " for the fashion and manner of the ministration of the same,"

while even this was not really owing to anything in the Book itself, but grew

"rather by the curiosity of the Minister and Mistakers, than of any other worthy cause ; therefore, as well for the more plain and manifest explanation hereof, as for the more perfection of the said Order of Common Service, in some places where it is necessary to make the same prayers and fashion of service more earnest and fit to stir Christian people to the true honouring of Almighty God :"

(a practice in which, as the Preamble states, " a great number" of people proved themselves very deficient, by their choosing to

(2) " Abstain and refuse to come to their Parish Churches and other places where Common Prayer, administration of the Sacraments, and preaching of the word of God, is used upon Sundays and other days ordained to be holy days")

on *these two* accounts (1 and 2) it was that

" The aforesaid Order of Common service " had been " faithfully and godly perused, explained, and made fully perfect."

Next: we have the testimony of LATIMER, a most competent witness, who (in the "Disputation at Oxford " of 1554, to be noticed hereafter, when in the course of the argument, *Weston* was led to ask him " Which Communion [Book] ?— the first, or the last"—*i. e.* the Liturgy of 1549 or 1552—he referred to?) said :—

" I find no great diversity in them ; they are one supper of the Lord : but I like the last very well."

" *Weston*. Then the first was naught, belike."

"*Latimer*. I do not well remember wherein they differ."

" *Weston*. Then cake-bread and loaf-bread are all one with you."—p. 504.

Thirdly : there are the two considerations ; (1) First that the

Book was not, so far as I am aware, held at the time to teach a doctrine contrary* to that of the former Book: (2) Secondly, that it was the same Book, with no *material* alterations, which satisfied the Roman party in England for the first ten years of Elizabeth's reign, and which, as we have strong ground for believing, would have received the Pope's confirmation, had the Queen chosen to acknowledge his Supremacy.

I say—with no *material* alterations; because it cannot be seriously contended, I imagine, that the terms used in delivering the Sacrament destroyed its orthodoxy in 1552, and revived it in 1559; or were so designed by the revisers at those periods.

Now, it was in this 2nd Book of Edward VI. that the Declaration on Kneeling first appeared. The history of its introduction plainly shews that the revisers did not contemplate its being there. The book, as settled by Convocation and authorized by Statute, did not contain it: many of the copies apparently were printed† without it; nor was it until " the 27th of October, 1552," four days before the Feast of All Saints, the day on which its use was to begin, that, as Burnet states—

" The Council Book mentions also a letter written to the Lord Chancellor to add in the Edition of the new Common Prayer Book, a Declaration touching Kneeling at the receiving of the Communion." —*Hist. Refor.* Part 3, Bk. 4, fol. p. 210.

It is not difficult, I think, to account for this step: the

---

* The Rubric in Edward's 2nd Book declaring what Bread "shall *suffice*" to be used in the Celebration, has often in our own times been appealed to as demonstrating that those who inserted it made altogether light of Consecration, because of the concluding words "And if any of the bread or wine remain, the Curate shall have it to his own use," which they assume to refer to the Consecrated elements. But this is wholly a mistake. The new practice *permitted* [apparently in 1550 (see passage from p. 64 of Cranmer's " Defence"—*sup.* p. 22) and now recognized as a permission,] by the earlier part of the Rubric, no doubt created the need for this latter part: [since it would naturally become a question—how to dispose of such consecrated *Bread* as had been offered, seeing that it, unlike Wafers, could not be kept for future Celebrations.] The Clergy of that day could be at no loss what to do with the remaining Consecrated elements when not reserved for sick Communions, as I apprehend, from the Office for Communion of the sick, they still were when needed.

Be it observed, too, that the same Rubric was continued in Elizabeth's Book.

† " Sept. 27th an order came to Grafton the printer in any wise to stay from uttering any of the books of the new service. And if he had distributed any of them among his company (of stationers) that then he give strait commandment not to put any of them abroad until certain faults therein were corrected."— *Strype*, Memorials, Ed. vi.

tide, which in the reign of Elizabeth it was found so almost impossible to stem, had already set in against Ceremonies, and in particular against external reverence in the ministration of the Holy Communion : Cranmer and others could not but perceive this, and may easily have foreseen the evils which might arise in the use of a Book which, to allay prejudices, had been shorn of all which it could safely part with consistently with preserving at least a decent ministration of its Offices, and especially that of the Holy Communion. Remembering, too, the objections which had been made to "knocking and kneeling," at the celebration of the Eucharist, it was a likely supposition that the accustomed gesture would be sought to be abandoned by many of the people who, perhaps, would be encouraged in not a few cases by their Clergy. To place a direction for "kneeling" before words of delivery which certainly *sounded* less reverential than the old form, would be a probable security for the continuation of an external reverence which we must believe the Bishops had every intention to preserve.

But then, the very fact that this direction was an *addition*, and had no counterpart in the Office which had been censured as too Ceremonial, would easily excite suspicion, and promote criticism. What more probable, then, than that objections were urged upon the Council against the direction, and that its omission was pressed for? This may have been the occasion of the order to the Printer to stay the issue, on the plea of correcting "certain faultes." Yet the considerations which I have surmised to have prompted the direction were doubtless equally weighty in inducing the Bishops and the Privy Council to determine on retaining it in the Book. To explain however to the objectors that it was not to be construed *as in any way countenancing* TRANSUBSTANTIATION, was a natural resort ; and what terms so likely to suggest themselves as those of the xxixth. Article which had then been prepared. Accordingly, as I think a comparison of the Article and the Declaration must show, the latter was framed upon that model and added to the Book upon the Council's authority to meet the case of the objectors.

We know that one of Bucer's Censures was that the Consecration Prayer in the 1st Book "favoured Transubstantiation too much:" I can conceive nothing so probable as that the objectors to the Rubric for "kneeling" thought the same. The Bishops were most desirous to eliminate that Doctrine: this, as I have already urged, seemed to be their ONE aim with regard to the Eucharistic controversy. Did they mean anything more when they sanctioned this new Declaration? I most entirely believe that they did not.

This persuasion derives some strength from such an occurrence as the following, which happened only three months afterwards.

During the reign of Edward VI. (viz. about January, 1553-4) there were, as *Foxe* relates, certain "Articles and Informations to the King's Honourable Council, put up and exhibited by Hugh Rawlins and Thomas Lee, against the blessed man of God, *Master Ferrar*, Bishop of St. David's." Among these were some which charged him with "*Maintenance of Superstition* contrary to the King's Ordinances and Injunctions." The Charges were preferred by some members of his Cathedral. To the XXIst Article, which charged that "He, being often in Cærmarthen, and other places in the Chancel, at the time of Holy Communion, not only tarried there himself, neither communicating nor ministering, bareheaded and uncoiffed, reverently kneeling; but also permitteth the people there to continue, the chancel and choir full, kneeling and knocking their breasts: which manner is yet used in all the Diocese, without any reformation or gainsay of him or any of his officers:—"

" ....he saith, that he hath been divers times in the Choir of Caermarthen, and hath tarried there in the communion-time, not communicating himself; and that in every church where he cometh on the holy-day to preach, or to pray, he kneeleth in the choir, bareheaded, as well at Matins before the communion, as at Evensong after, without any superstition: he thinketh it not necessary for the Communion's sake to leave kneeling to Christ, But he hath diligently taught the people not to kneel nor knock to the visible show, or external show of the Sacrament. And the choirs of Caermarthen and other places there, are not close at the sides, so that the people may come in and forth at their pleasure.

Moreover the King's ordinances do not authorize him to rebuke the people for knocking on their breasts, in token of repentance of their sins; nor for kneeling in token of submission to God for mercy in Christ."—Foxe, vol. vii., pp. 6 and 13.

It is just worth while to remark that *Foxe* speaks of Ferrar as "the virtuous and godly Bishop," and calls the charges "the quarrelling and frivolous articles of his present adversaries:" also that through various delays upon these charges, he "was detained in prison till the death of King Edward, and the coming in of Queen Mary and popish religion, whereby a new trouble rose upon him, being now accused and examined for his faith and doctrine," (pp. 16 and 21,) for which he was ultimately put to death.

Still more to the purpose, as showing the continuous identity of language on the Eucharistic Presence with that used alike in 1549 and 1552, are the Writings and Examinations of such of the Prelates and other Clergy as were put on their trial during the reign of Mary. It will be found that then, as before, it was the doctrine of *Transubstantiation* which was the key to all their statements against what continued to be known as the REAL Presence.

Upon the Accession of Mary, a Disputation was held in the Convocation House at London, commencing Oct. 18, 1553. On the fourth day, Oct. 25, *John Philpot*, Archdeacon of Winchester, being the Disputant, prefaced his argument with an oration, in which he said thus:—

" 'But before I bring forth any argument, I will, in one word, declare what manner of presence I disallow in the Sacrament, to the intent the hearers may the better understand to what end and effect mine arguments shall tend : not to deny utterly the presence of Christ in his Sacraments, truly ministered according to His institution ; but only to deny that gross and carnal presence, which you of this house have already subscribed unto, to be in the Sacrament of the Altar, contrary to the truth and manifest meaning of the Scriptures : That by transubstantiation of the sacramental bread and wine, Christ's natural Body should, by the virtue of the words pronounced by the priest, be contained and included under the forms or accidents of bread and wine. This kind of Presence, imagined by men, I do deny,' quoth Philpot, 'and against this I will reason.' "—p. 401.

Dr. Chedsey, in reply, contended for an "*invisible presence*" of Christ's *natural* Body in the Sacrament; and that Christ's *Flesh* is *visibly* ascended into Heaven, and *invisibly* abideth still in the Sacrament of the Altar"—p. 403.

In the argument on the 30th of October, *Philpot* said thus :—

" But **bodily** to be present, and **bodily** to be absent ; to be on earth and to be in heaven, and all at one present time ; be things contrary to the nature of a **human** body : ergo, it cannot be said of the **human** Body of Christ, that the **selfsame** Body is both in heaven, and also in earth at one instant, either visibly or invisibly." —p. 408.

Again, take the following extract from—

" A Conference between NICHOLAS RIDLEY, sometime Bishop of London, and SECRETARY BOURN, with others, at the Lieutenant's table at the Tower." A.D. 1553.

" Mr. Fecknam perceiving whereunto my talk went, ' Why,' quoth he, ' what circumstances can ye shew me that should move you to think of any other sense, than as the words plainly say, *Hoc est corpus meum, quod pro vobis tradetur?* This is My Body which shall be betrayed for you.'

"' Sir,' said I, ' even the next sentence that followeth : *Hoc facite in meam commemorationem.* Do this in My remembrance. And also by what reason ye say the bread is turned into Christ's **carnal** Body; by the same I may say, that it turned into His mystical Body. For as that saith of it, ' *Hoc est corpus meum quod pro vobis tradetur :*' so Paul which spake by Christ's spirit saith, ' *Unus panis et unum corpus multi sumus omnes, qui de uno pane participamus.* We being many are all but one bread, and one body, in as much as we are partakers of one bread.' "—p. 157.

Afterwards Ridley refers them to *Bertram's* Book, professing his agreement with it.

So, too, the same expressions are to be gathered from

" *The Disputation had at Oxford the 18th day of April, 1554, between Master Hugh Latimer, Answerer, and Master Smith and others, Opposers.*" I extract the following. To the first Conclusion, viz :—

" That in the Sacrament of the Altar, by the virtue of God's word pronounced by the Priest, there is **really** present the **natural** Body of Christ, conceived of the Virgin Mary, **under** the kinds of the appearances of bread and wine : in like manner His Blood."

Latimer replied .—

" ......I say, that to the right celebration of the Lord's supper there is no other presence of Christ required, than a **spiritual** presence : and this presence is sufficient foe a Christian man, as a presence by which we abide in Christ, and Christ abideth in us, to the obtaining of eternal life, if we persevere. And this same presence may be called most fitly a **real** presence ; that is a presence not figured, but a **true** and a **faithful** presence : which thing I here rehearse, lest some sycophant or scorner should suppose me, with the Anabaptists, to make nothing else of the Sacrament, but a naked and a bare sign. As for that which is feigned of many concerning their **corporal** presence, I, for my part, take it but for a papistical invention ; therefore think it utterly to be rejected."—p. 501.

It was asked by *Tresham*—

" Of what Flesh meant Christ ? His **true** Flesh or no ?"

" *Latimer*. Of His **true** Flesh, **spiritually** to be eaten in the supper by faith, and not **corporally**."—p. 506.

Again *Seton*, quoting St. Cyprian *De coena Domini*, enquired, " ....where doth it [the New Testament] command the drinking of Blood ?"

" *Latimer*. In these words, ' Bibite ex hoc omnes ;' *i.e.* ' Drink ye all of this ?' "

" *Seton*. Then we taste **true** Blood."

" *Latimer*. We do taste **true** Blood, but **spiritually** ; and this is enough."

" *Weston*. Augustine upon the XLVth. Psalm, saith : ' Drink boldly the Blood which ye have poured out.'—Ergo, It is Blood."

" *Latimer*. I never denied it nor ever will I go from it, but that we drink the **very** Blood of Christ **indeed**, but **spiritually** : for the same St. Augustine saith, ' Believe and thou hast eaten.' "—p. 507.

" *Latimer*. The **substance** of Blood is drunk, but not in one manner.

" *Pie*. It doth not require the same manner of drinking."

" *Latimer*. It is the **same thing**, not the **same manner**. I have no more to say.

" Here *Weston* cited the place of Crysostome, of Judas's treason : ' O the madness of Judas ! He made bargain with the Jews for thirty pence to sell Christ, and Christ offered him His Blood, which he sold.' "

" *Latimer*. I grant He offered to Judas His Blood, which he sold, but in a Sacrament."

" *Cartwright.* Linus and all the rest do confess the body of Christ to be in the Sacrament; and St. Augustine also, upon Psalm xcviii. upon this place, 'Adorate scabellum pedum,' &c., granteth that It is to be worshipped."

" *Latimer.* We do worship Christ in the Heavens, and we do worship Him in the Sacrament : but the massing is not to be used."

" *Smith.* Do you think that Cyril was of the ancient Church ?"

" *Latimer.* I do think so."

" *Smith.* He saith (in Johan I. x. c. xiii.) ' that Christ dwelleth in us **corporally.**' These be Cyril's words of the mystical benediction."

" *Latimer.* That ' **corporally** ' hath another understanding than you **grossly** take it."—*Foxe* vi. pp. 508-9

Or take the two following instances :

(1) First, the case of " *John Bradford*, Martyr," who, in his second examination before the Lord Chancellor, Jan. 29th, 1554-5, in reply to his Lordship's question, " Well, then, how say you to the blessed Sacrament ? Do you not believe there Christ to be present concerning his *natural* Body ?" Answered—

" My Lord, I do not believe that Christ is **corporally** present at and in the due administration of the Sacrament. By this word '**corporally**' I mean that Christ is there present **corporally unto faith.**"—Foxe, vol. vii., p. 157.

So, too, in his " *Last Examination*," referring to the former, the Chancellor said—

" Why ! didst not thou deny Christ's presence in the Sacrament ?"

" *Bradford.* No ! I never denied nor taught, but that to faith, whole Christ, Body and Blood, was **as** present **as** bread and wine to the due receiver."

" *L. Chancellor.* Yea, but dost thou not believe that Christ's Body **naturally** and **really** is there, **under the forms of bread and wine ?**"

" *Bradford.* My Lord, I believe Christ is present there to the faith of the due receiver : as for **transubstantiation,** I plainly and flatly tell you, I believe it not."

" Here was Bradford called diabolus, a slanderer ; ' for we ask no question,' quoth my Lord Chancellor, ' of transubstantiation, but of Christ's Presence.' "

" *Bradford.* I deny not His Presence to the faith of the receiver ; but deny that He is **included** in the bread, or that the bread is **transubstantiate.**"

" *Worcester.* If He be not included, how is He then present?"

" *Bradford.* Forsooth, though my faith can tell how, yet my tongue cannot express it ; nor you otherwise than by faith, hear it, or understand it."—p. 163.

(2) Next; in the second Examination of *John Rogers,* Vicar of St. Sepulchre's, Jan. 29, 1554-5, he saith—

" ......I cannot understand ' **really** and **substantially** ' to signify otherwise than **corporally**: but **corporally** Christ is only in Heaven, and so cannot Christ be **corporally** also in your Sacrament."—p. 598.

The like language we find in the

" Conferences between *Ridley* and *Latimer* during their imprisonment, A.D. 1555."

" *Ridley.* v. They do servilely serve the holy sign, as St. Augustine speaketh, (de doct. Christ. lib. iii. c. 9.) instead of the thing signified, whilst the **Sacramental Bread** (by a solemn or common error) is adored and worshipped for the flesh taken of the Son of God.

" *Latimer.* If ye deny unto them their **corporeal** presence, and **transubstantiation,** their fantastical adoration will (by and by) vanish away. Therefore be strong in denying **such** a presence, and then ye have won the field.

" Furthermore, in the first Supper, celebrated of Christ Himself, there is no mention made of adoration of the **elements.** Who said, ' Eat ye, and drink ye,' not worship ye. Therefore, against adoration may be spoken that saying of Christ concerning divorce, ' From the beginning it was not so '........—"p. 106.

" *Ridley.* vi. They pluck away the honour from the only sacrifice of Christ, whilst this sacramental and mass-sacrifice is believed to be propitiatory, and **such** a one as purgeth the souls, both of the quick and the dead. Contrary to that is written to the Hebrews, ' With one offering hath He made perfect for ever them that are sanctified.' And again, ' Where remission of these things (that is, of sins) is, there is no more offering for sin."—p. 107.

" *Latimer.* ' By His own Person He hath purged our sins." These words ' by His own Person,' have an emphasis or vehemence, which driveth away all sacrificing priests from **such** office of sacrificing ; seeing that, which He hath done by Himself, He hath not left to be **perfected** by others ; so that the **purging** of our sins may more truly be thought past and done, than a thing to come and to be done......"—p. 107.

" *Ridley.* ' Upon the which vouchsafe to look with Thy merciful and cheerful countenance.' What meaneth this prayer for the Sacrament itself, if it be, as they say, the Body of Christ, if it be **God** and **man**? How should the Father not look with a cheerful countenance upon His only well-beloved Son ?......' —p. 109.

" *Latimer.* To this let them answer, that so pray ; except peradventure, this prayer was used long before it was esteemed to be the Body of Christ **really** and **corporally.** And then this prayer maketh well to destroy the popish opinion, that it is not the opinion of the Church, nor so ancient as they babble...."—p. 109.

To turn now to a published Treatise of *Ridley*, in " A brief Declaration of the Lord's Supper," &c. A.D. 1555. Written " during his imprisonment."

Having quoted St. Matthew xxvi. 26—30; St. Luke xxii 19 & 20; 1 Cor. x. 16 & 17; xi. 23—28; and argued from these passages—

" That with the receipt of the Holy Sacrament of the Blessed Body and Blood of Christ is received of every one, good or bad, either life or death ; .... ;" he declares (p. 9.) " so far as I know, there is no controversy among them that be learned among the Church of England, concerning the matter of this Sacrament, but all do agree, whether they be new or old ; and to speak plain, and as some of them do.odiously call each other, whether they be Protestants, Pharisees, Papists, or Gospellers."—*Works.* Parker Society, p. 9.

Then he proceeds (p. 11) to show

" Wherein the dissension doth stand ; " and says, " It is neither to be denied nor dissembled, that in the matter of this Sacrament there be divers points, wherein men counted to be learned cannot agree as,

" [*a*] Whether there be any **transubstantiation** of the bread or no ?

" [*b*] Any **corporal** and **carnal** presence of Christ's **substance,** or no ?

" [*c*] Whether **adoration,** only due unto God, is to be done unto the **Sacrament,** or no ?

" [*d*] And whether Christ's Body be there offered in **deed** unto the Heavenly Father by the priest, or no ?

" [*c*] Or whether the evil man receiveth the **natural** Body of Christ, or no ?"

But he states that

" .... All five aforesaid points do chiefly hang upon this one question, which is, what is the **matter** of the Sacrament, whether it is the **natural** substance of bread, or the **natural** substance or Christ's own Body ?"

" For," he argues " if it be Christ's own **natural** Body, born of the Virgin ; then assuredly (seeing that all learned men in England, so far as I know, both new and old, grant there to be but one substance) then, I say, they must needs grant

" [*a*] transubstantiation, that is, a change of the **substance** of bread into the **substance** of Christ's Body :

" [*b*] .... the **carnal** and **corporal** presence of Christ's Body :

" [c.] then must the **Sacrament** be adored with the honour, due unto Christ Himself, for the unity of the two natures in one Person :

" [d] then, if the Priest do offer the Sacrament, he doth offer **in deed** Christ Himself:

" [e] and finally, the murderer, the adulterer, or wicked man, receiving the Sacrament must needs then receive also the **natural** substance of Christ's own Blessed Body, both Flesh and Blood.

But (p. 12.) " if,....it be found that the [**natural**] substance of bread is the material substance of the Sacrament [confessed of all that be named to learned, so far as I do know in England] ; although, for the change of the use, office, and dignity of the bread, the bread indeed sacramentally is changed into the Body of Christ, as the water in baptism is sacramentally changed into the fountain of regeneration, and yet the material substance remaineth all one, as was before ;....then

" [a] there is no such thing indeed and in truth as they call transubstantiation, for the substance of bread remaineth still in the Sacrament of the Body :

" [b] ..the **natural** substance of Christ's human nature, which He took of the Virgin Mary, is in heaven, where it reigneth now in glory, and not here inclosed under the form of bread :

" [c] that godly honour, which is only due unto God the Creator, *may* not be done unto the creature without idolatry and sacrilege, *is* not to be done unto the **Holy Sacrament** :

" [d] ....Christ's Blessed Body and Blood, which was once only offered and shed upon the Cross, being available for the sins of all. the whole world, is offered up no more in the **natural** substance thereof, neither by the priest, nor any other thing."

" [e] the wicked, I mean the impenitent, murderer, adulterer, or such like, do not receive the **natural** substance of the Blessed Body and Blood of Christ :

Before going on to prove from Holy Scripture " the truth" of this, he anticipates the enquiry—

" Whether they, that thus make answer and solution unto the former principal question, **do take away simply and absolutely the presence of Christ's Body and Blood from the Sacrament,** ordained by Christ, and duly ministered according to His holy ordinance and institution of the same ?" and replies " Undoubtedly, they do deny that utterly, either so to say or so to mean."—p. 12.

And refers to their Books for proof.

Moreover, he adds (p. 13)—

" Now then you will say, what kind of presence do they grant, and what do they deny ? Briefly, they deny the presence of Christ's Body in the **natural** substance of His human and assumed nature, and grant the presence of the same by grace......Even as, for example, we say the same sun, which, in substance, never removeth his place out of the heavens, is yet present here by its beams, light and natural influence, where it shineth upon the earth. For God's Word and His Sacraments be, as it were, the beams of Christ, which is sol justitiæ (Mal. iv.) the Sun of righteousness."

From the account of the Institution given by the Evangelists and St. Paul, he argues thus (p. 15)

" So it appeareth plainly that Christ called very bread His Body. But very bread cannot be His Body, in **very substance** thereof:" yet it "retaining still its own very **natural substance**, may be thus by grace, and in a sacramental signification, His Body : whereas else the very bread, which He took, brake, and gave them, could not be in any wise His **natural** Body, for that were confusion of substances. And therefore the very words of Christ, joined with the next sentence following, both enforce us to confess the very bread to remain still, and also open unto us how that ,bread may be and is thus, by His Divine Power, His Body which was given for us."—p. 15.

Then he proceeds to argue similarly " of the Lord's Cup," from the words of Institution.

And ends by supporting his arguments with the following Patristic authorities.—*Origen*, in Matt. xxv. Hom 11 ; Hom. super Levit. vii. ; *S. Chrysostom*, in Matt. Hom. xi. (Op. imp.) Ep. ad Cæs. Mon.; *Theodoret*, Dial. 1 and 2, cont. Eut. ; *Tertullian*, Adv. Marc. iv. c. 40, and i. c. 14.; *St. Augustine*, cont. Faust. xx. c. 21 ; Ps. xcviii ; de Fide ad Petrum, c. 19; Ps. iii. Ep. xxiii. Quæst. lib. iii. Ep. cii. Cont. Max. lib. ii. c. 22. Tract. in Johan. c. 12.*

We come now to an important occurrence, considering who was the chief person in it, namely Cranmer's " Disputation at Oxford," April 16th, 1555.

The Articles to be disputed were these :—

" I. In the Sacrament of the Altar is the **natural** Body of Christ conceived of the Virgin Mary, and also His Blood, present **really** under the forms of bread and wine, by virtue of God's word pronounced by the Priest.

" II. There remaineth no **substance** of bread and wine after the consecration, nor any other **substance** but the **substance** of (Christ) God and Man.

" III. The lively sacrifice of the Church is in the Mass, propitiatory as well for the quick as the dead."— *Works*. Parker Society, vol. ii. p. 394.

In answer to Chedsey, who said " His **true** Body is in the Sacrament," it was replied by *Cranmer :*—

* The passages are most of them in Dr. Pusey's Catena. The Parker Society's Editor has collated them, distinguishing the doubtful, as in fact Ridley had partly done.

" His **true** Body is **truly** present to them that truly receive Him : but **spiritually.** And so is It **taken** after a **spiritual** sort. For when He said, ' This is My Body,' it is all one as if He had said— This is the breaking of My Body ; this is the shedding of My Blood : as oft as you shall do this, it shall put you in remembrance of the breaking of My Body, and the shedding of My Blood ; that as truly as you receive this Sacrament, so truly shall you receive the benefit promised by receiving the same worthily.

" *Chedsey.* Your opinion differeth from the Church, which saith, that the **true** Body is in the Sacrament : Ergo—your opinion therein is false.

" *Cranmer.* I say and agree with the Church, that the Body of Christ is **in** the Sacrament **effectually,** because the passion of Christ is **effectual.**

" *Chedsey.* Christ, when He spake these words, ' This is My Body,' spake of the **substance,** but not of the **effect.**

" *Cranmer.* I grant He spake of the **substance,** and not of the **effect,** after a sort : and yet it is most true, that the Body of Christ is **effectually in** the Sacrament. But I deny that He is there **truly** present **in** bread, or that **under** the Bread in [? is] His **organical** Body . . . ,"—*Writings and Disputations of Cranmer,* Parker Society 1844, p. 394.

Then *Cranmer* handed up a written reply, in which he said :—

" In the first conclusion, if ye understand by this word ' really,' *re ipsa, i.e.* ' in **very deed** and **effectually,'** so Christ, by the grace and efficacy of His Passion, is **in deed** and **truly** present to all His true and holy members.

" But if ye understand by this word ' really,' *corporaliter, i.e.* **'corporally,'** so that by the Body of Christ is understanded a **natural** Body and **organical,"**

this he declared to be opposed to the Scriptures and the Catholic Church, which affirm—

" Christ to have left the world, and to sit at the Right Hand of the Father till He come to judgment."

The 2nd and 3rd Propositions he said also differed from the " accustomed manner and speech of Scripture."

Chedsey held this to mean—

" the Body of Christ to be **in** the Sacrament only by the way of participation, insomuch as we communicating thereof, do participate the **grace** of Christ ; so that you mean hereby only the **effect** thereof. But our conclusion standeth upon the **substance,** and not the **efficacy** only. . . . . .

" *Cranmer.* Thus you gather upon mine answer as though I did mean of the **efficacy** and not of the **substance** of the Body ; but I mean of them **both,** as well of the **efficacy** as of the **substance.**

And forsomuch as all things come not readily to memory, to a man that shall speak extempore, therefore for the more ample and fuller answer in this matter, this writing here do I exhibit."—pp. 395-6.

In this writing *Cranmer* states—

I. That " Christ at the time of His Maunday....did institute a perpetual memory of this His death, to be celebrated among Christians in bread and wine;......The Sacrament and Mystical Bread being broken and distributed after the institution of Christ, and the mystical wine likewise being taken and received, be not only Sacraments of the flesh of Christ wounded for us, and of His blood-shedding, but also be most certain Sacraments to us, and, as a man would say, seals of God's promises and gifts, and also of that holy fellowship which we have with Christ and all His members. Moreover they be to us memorials of that heavenly food and nourishment wherewith we are nourished unto eternal life, and the thirst of our boiling conscience quenched, and, finally, whereby the hearts of the faithful be replenished with unspeakable joy, and be corroborated and strengthened unto all works of godliness. ' We are many,' saith St. Paul, ' one Bread and one Body, all we which do participate of one bread and cup.' And Christ saith ' Eat ye ; this is My Body :' and, 'Drink ye ; this is My Blood :' and, ' I am the Living Bread which came down from Heaven. He that eateth me shall also live for me. Not as your fathers did eat manna in the desert, and are dead. He that eateth Me shall also live for Me.' Thus therefore true bread and true wine remain still in the Eucharist, until they be consumed of the faithful, to be signs, and as seals unto us, annexed unto God's promises, making us certain of God's gifts towards us. Also Christ remaineth in them, and they in Christ, which eat His flesh and drink His blood, as Christ Himself hath promised : ' they that eat My flesh and drink My blood, abide in Me, and I in them.' Moreover, He abideth also in them which worthily receiveth the outward Sacrament ; neither doth He depart so soon as the Sacrament is consumed, but continually abideth, feeding and nourishing us so long as we remain bodies of that Head, and' members of the same. I acknowledge not here the **natural** Body of Christ, which is only spiritual, intelligible, and unsensible, having no distinction of members and parts in it; but that Body only I acknowledge and worship, which was born of the Virgin, which suffered for us, which is visible, palpable, and hath all the form and shape and parts of the true natural body of man."

" 2......the old doctors do·call this speaking of Christ [*i.e.* ' Take, eat,' &c.] tropical, figurative, anagogical, allegorical ; which they do interpret after this sort, that although the substance of bread and wine do remain, and be received of the faithful, yet notwithstanding, Christ changed the appellation thereof, and called the bread by the name of His Flesh, and the wine by the name of His Blood, *non rei veritate, sed significante mysterio ; i.e.* ' not that it is so **in very deed**, but signified in a mystery;' so that we should consider, not what they be in their own nature, but what they do import to us and signify ; and should understand the Sacrament, not **carnally**, but spiritually ; and should attend, not to the **visible** nature of the Sacraments, neither have respect only to the outward bread and cup, thinking to see there with our eyes no other things but only bread and wine ; but that, lifting up our minds, we should look up to the Blood of Christ with our faith, should touch Him with our mind, and receive Him with our inward man ; and that, being like eagles in this life, we should fly up into Heaven in our hearts, where that Lamb is resident at the Right Hand of His Father, which taketh away the sins of the world . . . .

" 3. The only oblation of Christ (. . . . upon the Altar of the Cross . . . .) was of such efficacy, that there is no more need of any sacrifice for the Redemption of the whole world . . . . Whosoever shall seek any other Sacrifice propitiatory for sin, maketh the Sacrifice of Christ of no validity, force, or efficacy . . . ." —pp. 396-9.

After this they proceeded again to argue, *Chedsey* declaring—

"That the **natural** Body is **in** the Sacrament."
Cranmer replied. "To your argument I answer : If you understand by the Body **natural**, *organicum*, that is, having such proportion and members as He had living here, then I answer negatively.

Chedsey then argued from the words of Institution :—

" That thing is here contained that is given for us :
" But the substance of bread is not given for us :
" *Ergo*. The substance of bread is not here contained.
" *Cranmer*. I understand not yet what you mean by this word ' contained:' if ye mean **really**, then I deny your major.

. . . .

" *Chedsey*. If you ask what is the thing therein contained ; because His Apostles should not doubt what Body it was that should be given, He saith : ' This is My Body which shall be given for you,' and ' My Blood which shall be shed for many.' *Ergo*, here is **the same substance** of the Body, which the day after was given, and **the same Blood** which was shed. And here I urge the Scripture, which teacheth that it was no phantastical, no feigned, no **spiritual** Body, nor Body in faith, but **the substance** of the Body.
" *Cranmer*. You must prove that it is contained ; but Christ said not, ' which is contained.' He gave bread, and called that His Body. I stick not in the words of the Scripture, but in your word, which is feigned and imagined of yourself."—p. 400.

Weston then quoted S. Chrys., Hom. lxi. ad Pop. Antioch "*Necessarium est*" &c., and argued from it thus:—

" The same flesh, whereby Christ is made our brother and kinsman, is given of Christ to us to be eaten :"

" Christ is made our brother and kinsman by His **true, natural,** and **organical flesh :**

" *Ergo.* His **true, natural,** and **organical** flesh is given to us to be eaten.

" *Cranmer.* I grant the consequence and the consequent.

" *Weston.* Therefore we eat it with our mouth.

" *Cranmer.* I deny it. We eat it through faith.

Weston repeated his argument; to which it was replied by

" *Cranmer.* I grant He took and gave **the same true, natural, and organical flesh wherein He suffered ;** and yet He feedeth **spiritually,** and that flesh is received **spiritually.**

" *Weston.* He gave us **the same flesh** which He took of the Virgin :

" But He took not His **true flesh** of the Virgin **spiritually,** or in a figure :

" *Ergo.* He gave His **true, natural** flesh, not **spiritually.**

" *Cranmer.* Christ gave to us His own **natural** flesh, **the same** wherein He suffered, but feedeth us **spiritually.**"—pp. 402 & 3.

. . . .

" *Weston.* When Christ said ' Eat ye,' whether meant He, by the mouth or by faith ?

" *Cranmer.* He meant that we should **receive** the Body by faith, the bread by the mouth."

" *Weston.* Nay, the Body by the mouth."

" *Cranmer.* That I deny."

In proof, *Weston* quoted St. Chrys. on Ps. 50 " *Erubescit fieri nutrix,* &c., and Hom. 83 on St. Matt. 26, " *Non enim sufficit,*" &c. *Cranmer* replied—

" I grant we make one nature with Christ: but that to be done with the mouth we deny."

" *Weston.* Chrysostom, 2 Cor., cap. xiii. Hom. 29 hath these words : .... ' No little honour is given to our mouth, receiving the Body of the Lord.'

" *Cranmer.* This I say, that Christ entereth into us both by our ears and by our eyes. With our mouth we receive the Body of Christ, and tear it with our teeth ; that is to say, the Sacrament of the Body of Christ. Wherefore I say and affirm, that the virtue of the Sacrament is much : and therefore Chrysostom many times speaketh of Sacraments no otherwise than of Christ Himself, as I could prove, if I might have liberty to speak, by many places of Chrysostom, where he speaketh of the Sacrament of the Body of Christ."

" *Cole*....denied it to be the Sacrament of the Body of Christ, save only of the mystical Body, which is the Church."

Cranmer defended his position by S. Chrys. de Sacerd. lib. 3, c. iii.—

" O miracle ! O the good-will of God towards us! which sitteth above at the right hand of the Father, and is holden in men's hands at the sacrifice time, and is given to feed upon, to them that are desirous of Him.   And that is brought to pass by no subtlety or craft, but with the open and beholding eyes of all the standers-by."

Upon which *Cranmer* remarked—

" Thus you hear Christ is here in earth every day, is touched, is torn with the teeth, that our tongue is red with His blood ; which no man having any judgment will say or think to be spoken without trope or figure."—pp. 404 & 5.

Weston then quoted S. Chrys., Hom. 24—

" I shew forth that thing on the earth unto thee, which is worthy the greatest honour," &c., and argued (together with *Cole* and *Chedsey*) "that the Body of Christ is shewed us upon the earth," in "**sub-stance,**" not in "**figure,**" "not **sacramentally** only, but **in very deed** also ;" is touched "as Thomas touched Christ," touching whom he touched "the Lord God.' "

Cranmer contended that, though

" in the Sacrament only" was That to be seen which is " worthy greatest honour," yet Christ is not seen "upon the earth" save "with the eyes of our mind, with faith and spirit ;" that Christ is touched in the Sacrament in the same sense as Thomas touched God, of whom it is not "sound doctrine to affirm, that God is touched."—pp. 405-7

Cranmer uses the expression " He touched not God, but Him which was God :" yet, looking at the nature of his argument, and considering the unreserved way in which he had just before adopted St. Chrysostom's strong expressions as to the Eucharist, he would seem sufficiently shielded from any accusation of *Nestorianism*: not to say that elsewhere his writings are an adequate defence.

His opponents then pressed him with *Tertullian*, De Resurrectione, Carnis, c. viii. "*Videamus de propria Christiani hominis forma,*" &c. and *Photius* on 1 Cor. xi, 27, arguing from them thus :—

" The flesh eateth Christ's Body, that the soul may be fed therewith :
" The soul is not fed with the Sacrament, but with Christ's Body.
" *Ergo.*   The **flesh** eateth the body of Christ."

To which *Cranmer* answered :—

" The Sacrament is one thing; the matter of the Sacrament is another. Outwardly we receive the Sacrament ; inwardly we eat the body of Christ." And again "the flesh, I say, eateth the Sacrament; it eateth not Christ's body. For Tertullian speaketh of the Sacrament; and the place hath not *inde* ' thereof,' but *de Deo* ' of God.' "—pp. 407-9.

After some dispute on a passage of *St. Hilary*, de Trin. lib. viii. *Young* said—

" Against him that denieth principles we must not dispute. Therefore that we may agree of the principles, I demand whether there be any other Body of Christ than His instrumental Body ?

Cranmer. " There is no natural Body of Christ but His organical Body."—p. 414.

An argument then arose touching what Christ did in the Institution of the Eucharist, in the course of which *Young* asked—

" The thing signified in the Sacrament, is it not in that Sacrament?" *Cranmer.* " It is. For the thing is ministered in a sign. He followeth the letter that taketh the thing for the sign. Augustine separateth the Sacrament from the thing. 'The Sacrament,' saith he, ' is one, and the thing of the Sacrament another.' "—p. 415.

Again, *Pie* said—

" The words of Christ, as Ambrose saith, are of strength to work. What do they work? Ambrose saith, they make the Blood which redeemed the people :

" *Ergo.* The natural Blood is made.

" *Cranmer.* The Sacrament of His Blood is made. The words make the Blood to them that receive it : not that the Blood is in the cup, but in the receiver."

This expression being demurred to, *Cranmer* referred to *S. Ambrose* de Sacramentis l. iv., c. iv. (which *Weston* quoted) and remarked—

" .... But what is that He saith : Thou receivest for a similitude ?' I think he understandeth the Sacrament to be the similitude of His Blood."—p. 418.

Again, *Chedsey* argued—

" As Christ is truly and really incarnate, so is He truly and really in the Sacrament :

" But Christ is really and truly incarnate :

" *Ergo.* The Body of Christ is truly and really in the Sacrament."

" *Cranmer.* I deny the major."

" *Chedsey.* I prove the major out of Justine, in his Second Apology......' As by the word of God Jesus Christ our Saviour being made flesh had both Flesh and Blood for our salvation; so we are taught, that the meat consecrated by the word of prayer instituted of Him, whereby our blood and flesh are nourished by communion, is the Flesh and Blood of the same Jesus which was made flesh.'"

"*Cranmer.* You have translated it well; but I deny your major. This is the sense of Justin; that that bread is called the Body of Christ, and yet of that sanctified meat our bodies are nourished."

"*Chedsey.* Nay, he saith, of that sanctified meat both our bodies and souls are nourished."

"*Cranmer.* He saith not so; but he saith that it nourisheth our flesh and blood: and how can that nourish the soul, that nourisheth the flesh and blood?"

"*Cole.* It feedeth the body by the soul."

"*Cranmer.* Speak uprightly. Can that which is received by the soul and the spirit, be called the meat of the body?"—p. 420.

.   .   .   .

"*Cranmer.* We ought not to consider the bare bread; but whosoever cometh to the Sacrament, eateth the **true** Body of Christ." —p. 421.

Lastly, we shall do well to consider attentively the

"Disputation at Oxford between Dr. Smith, with his other colleagues and Doctors, and Bishop Ridley." A.D. 1555.

"*Weston, the Prolocutor.* Good Christian people and brethren, we......are entering into a controversy,......concerning the **verity** of the Body of our Lord Jesu Christ in the Eucharist....

"*Dr. Smith.* This day, right learned Master Doctor, three questions are propounded......to wit:

"First. Whether the **natural** Body of Christ our Saviour, conceived of the Virgin Mary, and offered for man's redemption on the Cross, is **verily** and **really** in the Sacrament by virtue of God's word spoken by the priests, &c.

"Secondly. Whether in the Sacrament, after the words of consecration, be any other **substance**, &c.

"Thirdly. Whether in the mass be a sacrifice propitiatory, &c.

"Touching the which questions.... I will essay again to demand your sentence in the first question—whether the **true** Body of Christ, after the words pronounced, be **really** in the Eucharist, or else only the **figure**......—pp. 191-2.

Ridley then protests his submission to the Church, his lack of time and books, and his right to correct his statements afterwards.

"The First Proposition.

"In the Sacrament of the Altar, by the virtue of God's word spoken of the priest, the **natural** Body of Christ, born of the Virgin Mary, and His **natural** Blood, are **really** present under the forms of bread and wine.

Ridley complains (1) that this statement

" is very obscure and dark, by means of sundry words of doubtful signification. And being taken in the sense which the schoolmen teach, and at this time the Church of Rome doth defend, it is false and erroneous . . . ."—p. 195.

(ii.) Of the

" ambiguity in this word 'really,' whether it be to be taken as the logicians term it 'transcendenter ;' that is, most generally : and so it may signify **any manner of thing** which belongeth to the Body of Christ, **by any means**: after **which sort** we also grant Christ's Body to be **really** in the Sacrament of the Lord's Supper . . . . or whether it be taken to signify the **very same thing, having body, life, and soul, which was assumed and taken of the word of God unto the unity of person. In which sense,** since the Body of Christ is **really** in Heaven, because of the **true** manner of His Body, it may not be said to be here in the earth."—p. 196.

(iii.) Of the

" further doubtfulness in these words, 'under the forms of bread and wine,' whether the **forms** be there taken to signify the only **accidental** and outward shews of bread and wine ; or therewithal the **substantial** natures thereof, which are to be seen by their qualities, and perceived by exterior senses. Now the error and falseness of the proposition, **after the sense of the Roman Church and Schoolmen,** may hereby appear, in that they affirm the bread to be **transubstantiated** and changed into **the flesh** assumed of the Word of God . . . . . . and so they gather that Christ's Body is **really** contained in the Sacrament of the Altar . . . . . ."—p. 196.

In " *Confirmation of the aforesaid Answer,*" he puts a syllogism, one proposition of which is that

" This doctrine," which he opposes, "maintaineth a **real, corporal** and **carnal** presence of Christ's Flesh, assumed and taken of the word, to be in the Sacrament of the Lord's Supper, and that not by **virtue** and **grace** only, but also by the whole **essence** and **substance** of the Body and Flesh of Christ."—p. 197.

He goes on to argue that—

" This **carnal** presence is contrary 'to' St. John xvi. 7 ; Acts iii. 21 ; St. Matt. ix. 15 ; St. John xvi. 22 ; xiv. iii. ; St. Matt. xxiv. 23, 28.

(ii.) Varies from the Creed " He ascended," &c.

(iii.) " It destroyeth and taketh away the Institution . . . . which was . . . . to be used and continued until the Lord himself shall come . . . . for a remembrance is not of a thing present, but of a thing past and absent . . . . as one of the Fathers saith ' A figure is in vain when the thing figured is present.'

(iv.) " . . . . . . it affirmeth that . . . . . . the wicked and faithless, mice, cats, and dogs also may receive the very **real** and **corporal** Body of the Lord . . . . .

(v.)   " It confirmeth........that.... cruelty of the ' Anthro-
pophagi ' ......for it is a more cruel thing to devour a quick man
than to slay him.

(vi.)   " It forceth men to maintain many monstrous miracles," *e.g.*
"that the accidents remain without any subject," also " Christ's Body
without His qualities, and the true manner of a body," &c.

(vii.)   It gives occasion to such heresies as those of Marcion and
Eutyches.

(viii.)   " It falsifieth the sayings of the godly Fathers .... Justin,
Irenæus, Tertullian, Origen, Eusebius, Emissenus, Athanasius, Cyril,
Epiphanius, Jerome, Chrysostom, Augustine, Vigilius, Fulgentius,
Bertram, and other most ancient Fathers."—pp. 198-201.

Next he proceeds to deny that he intends

" To take away the true presence of Christ's Body in His Supper
rightly and duly ministered, which is grounded upon the word of
God, and made more plain by the commentaries of the faithful
fathers....."

" I say and confess with the Evangelist Luke, and with the
Apostle Paul, that the bread on the which thanks are given, is the
Body of Christ in the remembrance of Him and His death, to be set
forth perpetually of the faithful until His coming.

" I say and confess, the bread which we break to be the communion and partaking of Christ's Body, with the ancient and
faithful fathers.

" I say and believe, that there is not only a signification of Christ's
Body set forth by the Sacrament, but also that therewith is given
to the godly and faithful the grace of Christ's Body, that is, the
food of life and immortality.   And this I hold with Cyprian.

" I say also with St. Augustine, that we eat life and we drink
life ; with Emissene, that we feel the Lord to be present in grace ;
with Athanasius, that we receive celestial food, which cometh from
above ; the property of natural communion, with Hilary ; the
nature of flesh, and benediction which giveth life, in bread and
wine, with Cyril ; and with the same Cyril, the virtue of the very
flesh of Christ, life and grace of His Body, the property of the
Only Begotten, that is to say, life ; as He Himself in plain words
expoundeth it.

" I confess also with Basil, that we receive the mystical advent
and coming of Christ, grace and the virtue of His very nature ; the
sacrament of His very Flesh, with Ambrose ; the Body by grace,
with Epiphanius : spiritual flesh, but not that which was crucified,
with Jerome ; grace flowing into a sacrifice, and the grace of the
Spirit, with Chrysostom ; grace and invisible verity, grace and
society of the members of Christ's Body, with Augustine.

" Finally, with Bertram......I confess that Christ's Body is in
the Sacrament in this respect ; namely, as he writeth, because there
is in it the Spirit of Christ, that is, the power of the word of God,
which not only feedeth the soul, but also cleanseth it.   Out of these
I suppose it may clearly appear unto all men, how far we are from

that opinion, whereof some go about falsely to slander us to the world, saying, we teach that the godly and faithful should receive nothing else at the Lord's table, but a figure of the Body of Christ." —pp. 201 & 2.

" *The Second Proposition.*

" After the consecration there remaineth no substance of bread and wine, neither any other substance, than the substance of God and man."

For the answer to this he refers to his arguments against Prop. 1, and strongly insists upon the authority of *Bertram* as supporting him.

" *The Third Proposition.*

. " In the Mass is the lively sacrifice of the Church, propitiable and available for the sins as well of quick as of the dead."

Ridley objects (1) that in the

" Words 'the lively sacrifice of the Church,' there is a doubt whether they are to be understood figuratively and sacramentally, for the sacrament of the lively sacrifice (after which sort we deny it not to be in the Lord's Supper), or **properly** and without any figure : after the which manner there was but one only sacrifice, and that once offered, namely, upon the Altar of the Cross.

(ii.) " There is also a doubt in the word ' propitiable,' whether it signify here, that which taketh away sin, or that which may be made available [orig. *an quod potest reddi propitium.* Ed.] for the taking away of sin ; that is to say, whether it is to be taken in the active or in the passive signification.

(iii.) That " the words seem to import ......the quick and lively body of Christ, **flesh,** united and knit to the Divinity, to lie hid under the accidents and outward shews of bread and wine. . ."—p. 207

Among his *Arguments* against the proposition are these :—

(*a*) " All remission of sins cometh only by shedding of blood.
" In the Mass there is no shedding of blood :
" Ergo, in the Mass there is no remission of sins ; and so it followeth also, that there is no propitiatory sacrifice.

(*b*) " In the Mass the passion of Christ is not in **verity,** but in a mystery representing the same.
" But where Christ **suffereth** not, there He is not offered in **verity.**
" Ergo, in the Mass there is no propitiatory sacrifice......"
—p. 209.

Dr. Smith, in reply, objected to Ridley's argument—that Christ's *Ascension* and *Session* "hinder not his REAL presence in the Sacrament."

Ridley. " ...... If you take the **real** presence of Christ according to the **real** and **corporal** substance which He took of the Virgin, THAT Presence being in Heaven, cannot be on the earth also. But, if you mean a real presence 'secundum rem aliquam quæ ad corpus

Christi pertinet,' *i. e.* according to something that appertaineth to Christ's Body, certes the ascension and abiding in Heaven are no let at all to that presence. Wherefore Christ's Body, after that sort, is here present to us in the Lord's Supper; by grace, I say, as Epiphanius speaketh of it.

"*Weston.* I will cut off from henceforth all equivocation and doubt: for whensoever we speak of Christ's Body, we mean that which He took of the Virgin.

"*Ridley.* Christ's ascension and abiding in Heaven cannot stand with His Presence."—p. 213.

Then *Smith* and *Weston*, in a long argument, contended that Christ *could* now be present "corporally and really" and had thus appeared since his Ascension, viz., to St. Stephen, St. Paul, and St. Peter. *Ridley* does not deny that Christ *can* thus be present, *if He will*, but says they must prove that will; he disputes that the vision to SS. Stephen and Paul revealed Christ *on earth*, and will not deny that the account mentioned by some Fathers of the appearance to St. Peter may be true; yet he contends (1) that these are too *doubtful* to argue from; and (2) that if true, they do not invalidate his position; and (3) requires them to prove that Christ was corporally in Heaven "at the same time when He was corporally on earth.'

Weston quoted St. Chrysostom, Hom. xvii. in Heb. c. 10, and St. Bernard: *Ridley*, while denying that the latter makes for his opponents, rejects him as *too late* an authority: of the former he says:—

"I remember the place well," but remarks—" And whereas you allege out of Chrysostom, that Christ is offered in many places at once (both here full Christ and there full Christ), I grant it to be true; that is, that Christ is offered in many places at once, in a **mystery** and **sacramentally**, and that He is **full** Christ in all those places; but not after the **corporal** substance of our **flesh** which He took, but after the benediction which giveth life; and He **is given** to the godly receivers **in** bread and wine, as Cyril speaketh. Concerning the oblation of Christ, whereof Chrysostom here speaketh he himself doth clearly shew what he meaneth thereby, in saying by the way of correction, ' We always do the selfsame, howbeit by the recordation or remembrance of His sacrifice."—p. 217.

Again, *Smith* quotes St. Chrysostom *de Sacerdotio*, lib. iii. c. 4. *Ridley* accepts the passage, and says—

"He that sitteth there, is *here* present in **mystery** and by **grace;**

and is holden of the godly, such as communicate Him; not only sacramentally with the hand of the body, but much more wholesomely with the hand of the heart, and by inward drinking is received : but by the sacramental signification He is holden of all men."—p. 223.

Further on, *Ward*, quoting the words

"Take eat, this is My Body," asks " Gave He bread made of wheat and material bread?"

"*Ridley.* I know not whether He gave bread of wheat; but He gave true and material bread.

" *Ward.* I will prove the contrary by Scriptures.

" He delivered to them that which He bade them take.

" But He bade them not take material bread, but His own Body.

" Ergo, He gave not material bread, but His own Body.

" *Ridley.* I deny the minor. For He bade them take His Body sacramentally in material bread ; and after that sort it was both bread which He bade them take; because the substance was bread, and that it was also His Body, because it was the Sacrament of His Body, for the sanctifying and the coming of the Holy Ghost, which is always assistant to those mysteries which were instituted of Christ, and lawfully administered."—p. 228

This argument Ridley says he derived from Theophylact, on St. Matt. xxvi. and he adds—

" I grant the bread to be converted and turned into the flesh of Christ; but not by transubstantiation, but by sacramental converting or turning. ' It is transformed,' saith Theophylact in the same place, ' by a mystical benediction, and by the accession or coming of the Holy Ghost, unto the flesh of Christ.' He saith not, by expulsion or driving away the substance of bread, and by substituting or putting in its place the corporal substance of Christ's flesh. And whereas he saith, ' It is not a figure of the Body,' we should understand that saying, as he himself doth elsewhere add ' only,' that is, it is no naked or bare figure *only*. For Christ is present in His mysteries; neither at any time, as Cyprian saith, doth the Divine Majesty absent Himself from the Divine Mysteries." —pp. 229, 30.

Again, *Ward* quoted St. Aug. on Ps. xcvi. "Worship His Footstool," &c. After some dispute about it, in which *Ridley* asserted that he

" never yet spake contumeliously" of " the Sacraments;" adding " I grant that Christ hath here His Church in earth ; but that Church did ever receive and acknowledge the Eucharist to be a Sacrament of the Body of Christ, yet not the Body of Christ really, but the Body of Christ by grace.

" *Glyn.* Then I ask this question: Whether the Catholic Church hath ever or at any time been idolatrous ?

" *Ridley.* The Church is the pillar and stay of the truth, that

I

never yet hath been idolatrous in respect of the whole ; but, per-adventure, in respect of some part thereof, which sometimes may be seduced by evil pastors, and through ignorance.

" *Glyn.* That Church ever hath **worshipped the flesh** of Christ in the Eucharist.

" But the Church hath never been idolatrous.

" Ergo, it hath alway judged **the flesh** of Christ to be in the Eucharist.

" *Ridley.* And **I also worship Christ in the Sacrament,** but not because He is **included in** the Sacrament : like as I worship Christ also in the Scriptures, not because He is really included in them. Notwithstanding I say, that the Body of Christ **is present in the Sacrament;** but yet **sacramentally** and **spiritually** (according to His grace) giving life, and in that respect **really,** that is, according to His benediction, giving life. Furthermore, I acknowledge gladly the **true** Body of Christ to be **in** the Lord's Supper, in such sort as the Church of Christ......doth acknowledge the same. But the true Church of Christ doth acknowledge **a presence** of Christ's Body in the Lord's Supper to be communicated to the godly by **grace,** and **spiritually,** as I have often shewed, and by a **sacramental** signification ; but not by the **corporal** presence of the Body of His **flesh.**

" *Glyn.* Augustine against Faustus [saith] ' Some there were which thought us, instead of Bread and of the Cup, to worship Ceres and Bacchus.' (lib. xx. c. 13.) Upon this place I gather, that there was an adoration of the Sacrament among the Fathers ; and Erasmus, in an Epistle to the brethren of Lower Germany, saith, that the **worshipping of the sacrament** was before Augustine and Cyprian.

" *Ridley.* We do handle the signs reverently : but we worship the Sacrament as a Sacrament, not as a thing signified by the Sacrament.

" *Glyn.* What is the symbol of the Sacrament ?

" *Ridley.* Bread.

" *Glyn.* Ergo, We worship bread.

" *Ridley.* There is a deceit in this word ' adoramus.' We **worship the symbols, when reverently we handle them.** We **worship Christ wheresoever we perceive His benefits;** but we understand His benefits to be **greatest in the Sacrament.**

" *Glyn.* So I may fall down before the bench here, and worship Christ ; and if any man ask me what I do, I may answer, I worship Christ.

" *Ridley.* **We adore and worship Christ in the Eucharist.** And if you mean the external Sacrament ; I say, **that also is to be worshipped as a Sacrament.**

" *Glyn.* So was the faith of the primitive Church.

" *Ridley.* Would to God we would all follow the faith of that Church !

" *Glyn.* Think you that Christ hath now His Church ?

" *Ridley.* I do so.

" *Glyn.* But all the Church **adoreth** Christ **verily** and **really** in the Sacrament.

" *Ridley.* You know yourself, that the Eastern Church would not acknowledge **transubstantiation**; as appeareth in the Council of Florence."—pp. 235-37.

Then *Weston* and *Curtop* argued, after each other, that

" That which is in the cup, is the **same** that flowed from the side of Christ."

Ridley admitted that it was,

" but not **after the same manner**, after **which** manner it sprang from His side : " he said it " is **in** the Chalice indeed, but not in the **real** presence, but by grace and in a Sacrament.

" *Weston*. That is very well. Then we have Blood in the Chalice.

" *Ridley*. It is true; but by grace, and in a Sacrament." —pp. 237, 238.

Watson then asked this question—

" When Christ said in John vi., ' He that eateth My flesh,' &c., doth He signify in those words the eating of His **true** and **natural Flesh**, or else of the bread and symbol ?

" *Ridley*. I understand that place of the **very Flesh** of Christ to be eaten, but **spiritually**; and further I say, that the Sacrament also pertaineth to the **spiritual manducation**: for without the Spirit to eat the Sacrament is to eat it unprofitably; for whoso eateth not **spiritually**, he eateth his own condemnation."—p. 238.

Further, *Watson* argued—

" This promise [i. e. of ' Society betwixt Christ and us '] is made to the Flesh and Blood of Christ, and not to the bread and wine."

" Ergo, The Sacrament is not bread and wine, but the Body and Blood of Christ.

" *Ridley*. There is no promise made to him that taketh common bread and common wine ; but to him that receiveth the sanctified bread, and bread of the Communion, there is a large promise of grace made : neither is the promise made to the symbols, but to the **thing** of the Sacrament. But the **thing** of the Sacrament is the **Flesh** and **Blood**."—p. 240.

Next *Tresham* said—

" Evil men do eat the **natural** Body of Christ : Ergo, the **true** and **natural** Body of Christ is on the altar.

" *Ridley*. Evil men do eat the **very true** and **natural** Body of Christ **sacramentally**, and no further; as St. Augustine saith. But good men do eat the **very true** Body, both **sacramentally**, and **spiritually** by grace."—p. 246.

Again, in reply to *Tresham*, who quoted St. Aug. cont Donat. v. c. 8, *Ridley* said

" It is the Body to them [the wicked,] that is, the Sacrament of the Body : and Judas took the Sacrament of the Lord to his con-demnation. Augustine hath distinguished these things well in another place, where he saith, ' The bread of the Lord, [and] the bread the Lord. Evil men eat the bread of the Lord, but not the bread the Lord : but good men eat both the bread of the Lord, and Bread the Lord.' "

Then *Weston* quoted Theophylact—

"....Judas....tasted the Lord's Flesh," &c.: to which *Ridley* replied "This phrase to Divines is well known, and used of the doctors: He tasted the Flesh of the Lord 'insensibiliter' 'insensibly;' that is, the Sacrament of the Lord's Flesh."—p. 247.

Watson, again, quoted the Council of Nice, c. xxx.; of which *Ridley* said it "is to me a great authority;" when *Watson* pressed the sentence "The Lamb of God lieth on the Table:" *Ridley* said:

"....that Heavenly Lamb, is (as I confess) **on** the table; but by a **spiritual** presence, by grace, and not after any **corporal** substance of His Flesh taken of the Virgin Mary......"—p. 249.

Afterwards *Pie* asked

"What say you to that Council, where it is said, that the Priest doth offer an unbloody sacrifice of the Body of Christ?

"*Ridley.* I say, it is well said, if it be rightly understood.

"*Pie.* But he offereth an unbloody sacrifice.

"*Ridley.* It is called unbloody, and is offered after a certain manner, and in a mystery, and as a representation of that bloody sacrifice: and he doth lie, who saith Christ to be offered."—p. 250.

Weston next referred to St. Chrys. Hom. xxxiv., on 1 Cor. x., and urged from it by another syllogism that "the **real** [*i. e.* **natural**] Body of Christ is in the Eucharist;" on which *Ridley* observed—"We worship, I confess, the same true Lord and Saviour of the world, which the wise men worshipped in the manger; howbeit we do it in a mystery, and in the Sacrament of the Lord's Supper, and that in spiritual liberty, as saith St. Augustine, not in carnal servitude: that is, we do not worship servilely the signs for the things: for that should be, as he also saith, a part of a servile infirmity. But we behold with the eyes of faith Him present after grace, and spiritually set upon the table; and we worship Him which sitteth above, and is worshipped of the angels. For Christ is always assistant to His mysteries, as the said Augustine saith. And the Divine Majesty, as saith Cyprian, doth never absent Itself from the Divine Mysteries: but this assistance and presence of Christ, as in Baptism it is wholly **spiritual,** and by **grace,** and not by any **corporal** substance of the **Flesh,** even so it is here in the Lord's Supper, being rightly and according to the Word of God duly ministered.

"*Weston.* That which the woman did hold in her womb, the same thing holdeth the Priest.

"*Ridley.* I grant the Priest holdeth the **same thing,** but after another manner. She did hold the **natural** Body; the Priest holdeth the **mystery** of the Body."—p. 251.

Weston then dissolved the Disputation, exclaiming, and calling upon those present to join with him, "Verity hath the victory."

Other, and equally strong, statements of Ridley, occur in

his last examination before the Commissioners at Oxford, Sept. 30, 1555. To take but one passage :

" .... both you and I agree herein, that in the Sacrament is the very true and natural Body and Blood of Christ, even that which was born of the Virgin Mary, which ascended into Heaven, which sitteth at the Right Hand of God the Father, which shall come from thence to judge the quick and dead ; only we differ *in modo*, in the way and manner of being : we confess all one thing to be in the Sacrament, and dissent in the manner of being there......to the question thus I answer, that in the Sacrament of the Altar is the natural Body and Blood of Christ *vere et realiter*, indeed and really, for spiritually by grace and efficacy ; for so every worthy receiver receiveth the very true Body of Christ. But if you mean really and indeed, so that thereby you would include a lively and a moveable Body under the forms of Bread and Wine, then, in that sense, is not Christ's Body in the Sacrament, really and indeed."—p. 274.

We have now seen what was the, apparently, all-absorbing topic in the writings, disputations, and conversations of Cranmer, Ridley, and others (who are known to have been responsible for the Revisions of the Public Offices of the Church of England both in 1549 and 1552) *prior* to the publication of the contested Declaration on Kneeling: we have learned that that topic was the Doctrine of Transubstantiation and its real or alleged theoretical and practical results : we have further ascertained that the first Book of Common Prayer embodied such Eucharistical Doctrine as satisfied the defenders and (apparently) the opposers of that view of the Real Presence which was based upon Transubstantiation: we have noticed that the second Book of Common Prayer was held to teach substantially the doctrine of the former Book, and as such was accepted : we have found that *at* and *subsequent to* the publication of this *later* Book (which moreover contained the famed Declaration), the synodical, official, and personal statements of those concerned in it were precisely of the same kind, in reference to the chiefly debated questions on the Eucharist, as those which they had made *at* and *before* the appearance of the *earlier* Book: and further we have observed that the statements of others (either but little or not at all responsible for the authorized changes, yet representing no doubt the views and opinions of a large number of the Clergy and probably of many educated laity of that period) are of a like stamp and character.

Further, it can hardly have escaped observation that certain phrases and words (which, in order to draw attention to them, I have printed in a distinct type) continually recur throughout the several Documents already quoted; and moreover that they are constantly interchanged and used as equivalents. On the one hand we have the following :—

(1) *Flesh, blood, bone, essence, substance, very substance, natural substance, corporal substance, same substance, self-same in substance, form, quantity, corporal presence of the substance of Christ's manhood, essence and substance of the body and flesh of Christ, true and natural flesh, true natural organical flesh not spiritually, real and bodily presence of Christ's flesh and blood, transubstantiation or corporal presence, real presence, God and man, contained and included under the forms or accidents, there with the bread, mixed: gross, corporal, corporeal, carnal, real, natural, organical, true, corporaliter* id est *crasse, sensible, essential, true natural, very natural, very, substantial, indeed, self-same, human, local: naturally, corporally, grossly, bodily, materially, truly and really, substantially, locally, circumscriptly, properly, carnally, invisibly, verily, fleshly, organically, sensibly, not sacramentally only, verily and indeed, killing again, not in figure.*

While on the other hand we find these :—

(2) *Substance, virtue, efficacy, mystery, very flesh, full Christ, presence of Christ in spirit, very true and natural body sacramentally, natural body and blood of Christ vere et realiter, present in mystery and by grace, same thing, true natural organical flesh but spiritually: very, real, indeed, converted, true, mixed not, sacramental, faithful, spiritual, very real, remembrance, property, certain real property: very deed and effectually, in deed and truly, really, spiritually, verily, substantially, figuratively, properly, sacramentally, virtually, verily and really, wholly, corporally unto faith, after a certain property or manner, turned not by transubstantiation but sacramentally, vere=corporally naturally really, so spiritually that nevertheless truly.*

Now it must be conceded, I think, that these terms so used all mean the same thing and all point to one conclusion. The former (1) are simply *negations* of a certain kind of

Presence in the Holy Eucharist which was, or was alleged to be, held by (what I may conveniently call) the Papal party ; and which was declared by the Reforming party, whether English or Foreign, to be a Presence alike opposed to Scripture, to the consent of the Ancient writers, to the continuous teaching of the Church, to philosophy, to reason, and to faith. The latter (2) are definitions of the sort of Presence which the *English* Reformers, as a whole, allowed to be consistent with the tests just named; but they must not, I venture to suggest, be accounted as *exclusive* definitions, but only as a terminology which to their minds was adequate to teach the *Catholic* doctrine and (what it seems likely was even of more importance to their minds *then*, in their estimate of what was essential to be done) would effectually supersede the popular belief in Transubstantiation, and with it would break down the evils which they pointed to as having flowed from it.

These considerations, I cannot but think, must be the safest guides to the interpretation of the Declaration on Kneeling (or *Black Rubric* as it is commonly but inaccurately called) appended to the Communion Office in the Prayer Book of 1552: if so, it is of the utmost importance that we should not affix to it a meaning exceeding in the slightest degree what its framers designed it to convey: we may not I conceive, narrow its terms or assume them to be positive definitions of *what*, and *what only*, the English Churchmen of that day were free to hold and to teach: our true course, it seems to me, is to affix to it only that character which it will be found *Historically* to bear: what that character is I described at the commencement of these remarks, and I am emboldened to think that the evidences since examined are adequate to prove that it was not untruly drawn.

It is well known that the DECLARATION disappeared from the 2nd Prayer Book when revised for use at the commencement of Elizabeth's reign, and was not restored until the last revision in 1662. The cause of its non-appearance in the Book of 1559 may be easily, and probably accurately, surmised, though I am not aware of any more precise evidence on the subject than the statement of Bp. Burnet (for which, however, he gives no proofs) that it "........was by Queen Elizabeth ordered to be left out of the Common Prayer Book ! since it might have given offence to some, otherwise the belief of the Corporal Presence."—*Hist. Ref.* Pt. ii. Bk. i. p. 162, fol. 1715.

Now, looking at the general history of the period, no doubt this remark of Burnet furnishes a most probable reason for the omission of the Declaration: indeed, we learn from *Collier*, who may be regarded as Burnet's Historic rival, that Elizabeth's Cabinet, on her Accession, impressed upon her that—" To prevent discontent, the reformed Liturgy ought to be reviewed, and made as inoffensive to all parties as may be." (*Eccles. Hist.*, vol. ii. p. 410, fol. 1714): and this, so far as the Papal party were concerned, well agrees with another remark made by Burnet, namely, that " The Queen . . . . . . inclined . . . . . . to have the manner of Christ's Presence in the Sacrament left in some general words; that those who believed the CORPORAL Presence might not be driven away from the Church by too nice an explanation of it." (*Hist. Ref.* vol. ii. bk. 3, p. 376.) Certainly, on the face of it, the Declaration does look like a denial of the Real Presence, and therefore must have been an annoyance, if not an obstacle, to the Roman party, who would naturally construe its terms as a reproach to views which they held, and against which, as we have seen, it was directed.

But, it is worth considering whether this alleged wish of the Queen stood alone, in inducing Abp. Parker and his Episcopal brethren to omit the Declaration: it seems to me that their knowledge of the tendencies of the extremer Reforming party in Edward's later years, their fears of a re-actionary irreverence consequent upon the contemplated alteration in the Religious Offices, *Mary* being dead, and their commencing experience of those whose course after-wards proved so fertile a source of trouble to both Parker and Grindal (though the latter somewhat sympathized with them)—were points which, in all likelihood, assisted to determine their judgment in favour of the omission.

It was, indeed, made a subject of enquiry, whether kneeling at the Sacrament should be insisted on in the Book then to be prepared: for, among the questions proposed by *Cecil* to *Guest* (afterwards Bishop of Rochester) the 10th was " Whether the Sacrament were to be received standing or kneeling? (*Strype's Ann.* vol. i. p. 83.) *Guest* thought it should be *indifferent*: this opinion, however, was not acted upon: though, if it had been, that would have furnished no satisfactory proof of a *denial* of the Real Presence, seeing it was the external form of devotion in the Greek Church. Indeed, the language of Guest, in a controversy already quoted (p. 17) quite agreed with that of his contemporaries, who yet insisted upon *kneeling* being the rule ; and unless we are to suppose that his views had become higher when, in 1566, he wrote his lately-discovered remarkable letter to Cecil—a supposition which certainly lacks proof—we must believe that he advocated what he considered to be an act of reverence equally demonstrative with kneeling, *if* made the rule of the Church.

True it is that later in Elizabeth's reign the Puritans, as they had then begun to be called, pressed upon the Bishops to allow them to receive the Eucharist *standing :* but this was only when they found that their demands to be allowed *to sit* were again and again rejected : indeed I remember to have seen it stated somewhere (by Strype, I think, though the passage was not noted down at the time and cannot now be searched for) that some of them even proposed to *prostrate* themselves : their object in this, as in their other proposals apparently being simply to avoid a Rule authoritatively laid down, and the more so as that Rule was the one also observed in the rest of the Western Church.

That Parker and Grindal were both concerned to secure reverence in the celebration of the Eucharist (though the latter proved himself throughout Elizabeth's reign considerably anti-ceremonial) is plain from the fact that not long after the publication of the Prayer Book of 1559—indeed almost contemporaneous with it — the Queen upon their recommendation (*Parker Corresp.* p. 378) issued an Injunction, in virtue of the power vested in her by Sec. xxvi of her Act of Uniformity, directing *Wafer Bread* to be used " for the more reverence to be given to these Holy Mysteries "— an Injunction which provoked controversy and opposition during the whole of her reign.   These considerations, apart from others which could be produced did my present limits permit, seem sufficient to establish the view suggested—that a fear of its abuse by the Puritan party, as well as an un-

K

willingness to offend the Roman party, concurred to keep out from Elizabeth's Prayer Book a Declaration which, as it was verbally obnoxious to the latter so, was not incapable of perverse and mis-directed criticism by the former.

It is wholly out of my power now, from the want of time, to attempt any examination of controversial Documents in this Reign, touching the question of the Real Presence, similar to that pursued in Edward's reign: it would be much to the purpose, for example, to analyze Jewel's famous controversy with Harding; it may be observed, however, that it would probably yield the like results and, too, would exhibit more consistent and definite language than some of that which has been quoted.

But the prominent part taken by Grindal in this Reign, first as Bishop of London, then Archbishop respectively of York and Canterbury, renders it desirable not to pass over a tract of his upon this subject which seems to have been written just after his return to England upon the accession of Elizabeth. We have already seen something of his views in the discussion given at (p. 17): it is most unlikely that his opinions on this point became more Catholic during his residence among the continental Protestants: if this be so, we are entitled to regard the tract just mentioned as explanatory of his former statement.

Strype (Life of Grindal, p. 464) having stated that *Grindal* was the author, speaks of it as—

".....written in a clear method, and with much rational evidence, against the **real**, that is, the **gross** and **corporal** presence in the Sacrament.

In this imaginary Dialogue *Custom* asks at the outset—

" What! are you so great a stranger in these quarters? Hear you not how that men do daily speak against the Sacrament of the Altar, denying it to be the **real** Body of Christ ?

Verity pleads in excuse for his ignorance that he has " returned but of late into this country."

Custom having cited the text " This is my Body," as expressing the REAL Presence, *Verity* proposes to " Declare the meaning of the words .... and next in what sense the Church and the old Fathers have evermore taken them."

We are bound, therefore, to assume that *Verity* means to speak in a Catholic sense.

In the course of this argument, *Custom* having alleged "Christ hath not so gross and fleshly, (as you think) but a spiritual and ghostly body; and therefore, without repugnance, it may be in many places at once," *Verity* puts this Syllogism.

"No body, being **real, natural**, and **organical**, and not **spiritual** can be in many places at once:

"Christ's Body in the Sacrament was in the Apostles' hands and mouths at one time: which were many places:

"Ergo, Christ's Body in the Sacrament was not a **real, natural,** and **organical** Body, but **spiritual**."—pp. 50 and 51.

Further on, he argues against the *real,* that is the *carnal* presence, from the case of unworthy receivers, summing up his position in these words:—

"Thus, by the Word of God, by reason, and by the old Fathers, it is plain that sinful men eat not the Body of Christ, receive they the Sacrament never so oft: which thing could not be, if in the Sacrament there remained nothing but the Body of Christ."—p. 59.

It is unnecessary to quote more from this Dialogue : but it is of consequence to notice the expression in the last extract, "If in the Sacrament there remained *nothing but* the Body of Christ."

Grindal's words, "nothing but," taken by themselves, would naturally convey the belief that he held a Real Objective Presence; denying at the same time the truth of the alleged Roman theory which asserted the absence of the *substance* of the Bread and Wine as distinguished from their *accidents* which were held to remain. He tells "Custom," (p. 42) "I conclude by your own argument, that we ought not only to say, but also to believe, that in the Sacrament there remaineth bread": and then he quotes St. Augustine's definition "(in Joan. tract. 26) *Aliud est sacramentum, aliud res sacramenti. Sacramentum est quod in corpus vadit: res autem sacramenti est corpus Domini nostri Jesu Christi.*" His argument seems to be—that as the *res sacramenti* is "spiritual" not "organicas" IT can only be matter for *spiritual manducation;* but this being an act of *lively* "faith," which the wicked have not, therefore "Christ's Body cannot be eaten of the wicked : which thing must necessarily ensue, if the bread were turned into the body of Christ," for then IT must be " eaten with the teeth....of the body :" which is impossible. Grindal like the other writers of that period, especially those whom I have been quoting, was combating the *carnal* Presence then, as we have seen, popularly held ; and then too, as now, *imputed* to Transubstantiation. If Roman Catholics now *repudiate* this view, and try to reconcile diffi- culties by attributing to *accidents* the properties which Grindal assigned to *substance ;* then, however inconsistent or illogical their argument may be thought, CHARITY at least should forbid us from endeavouring to fasten upon them what they *now* disown ; though, as will have been observed in the course of these quotations, some of their leading con- troversialists formerly *insisted* upon the popular belief.

There are no Writings of Abp. Parker to which we can turn to ascertain with precision what were his views on this Doctrinal question ; but so far as we can gather from his general statements and conduct during his Primacy, it is certain that they were *not lower* than Grindal's : his con- tinued residence in England during the reign of Mary no doubt preserved him from much of that deteriorated Doctrine which the contact with Genevan Divines produced in some of his contemporaries : indeed the accusations made against him by (the Roman) *Dorman* on the one hand and by many of the Puritans on the other hand, of being a *Lutheran,* plainly shew that his tendencies were in what we should term the *Catholic* direction.

But it is much to the purpose to observe that the Arch- bishop put forth, in 1556, jointly with *Grindal* and *fourteen* other Bishops, Ælfric's Anglo-Saxon Homily of " the Paschall Lamb," in the Preface to which they state that—

" .... almost of the whole sermon is about the understanding of the Sacramentall bread and wine howe it is the bodye and bloude of Christ our Saviour, by which is reuealed and made knowen, what hath been the common taught doctrine of the Church of England on this behalfe many hundreth years agoe, contrarye unto the unadvised writing of some nowe a days."

The Preface specifies, too, certain points in the Sermon

which the Episcopal publishers accounted "not consonant
to sounde doctrine," and, throughout the Sermon, notes
indicate their views upon various statements in it: it is just
worth while to notice, however, that the expression "once
suffred Christe by hym selfe, but yet neuertherless his suf-
frynge is daylye renued at the masse through mysterye of
the holye housell "—is not marked as objectionable by the
Bishops, though they do in the Preface take exception to the
sentence which immediately follows—"Therefore the holye
Masse is profitable both to the lyuing and to the dead."
Is it improbable that—having regard to the whole tenor of
the Sermon, based too as it is said to have been upon Bertram's Book—they considered the language sound? Indeed
a comparison of it with many passages in the Writings
already quoted would perhaps answer this enquiry affir-
matively. Plainly the great value of Ælfric's Homily in
the minds of the Elizabethan Bishops was its witness
against *Transubstantiation:* if the above expression did not
involve that tenet, and it would be hard to prove that it
does—they would in all likelihood, I think, be unwilling to
condemn it even if they thought it *undesirable;* though,
indeed, that they did so regard it must first be shewn.

I can only now simply notice one other important fact
in connection with this omission of the Declaration in
Elizabeth's Book, namely, that the third paragraph (p. 32) of
the xxixth of Edward's Articles was omitted in the xxxix
Articles of 1571. Now considering that that paragraph was,
as I have already shown, the probable basis of the Declaration
in the Prayer Book of 1552, this omission seems to strengthen
the notion that not only did the Elizabethan Bishops, of whom
be it remembered *Gest* the framer of the present xxviiith
Article was one—desire not needlessly to alienate the
Roman party, but that they wished to afford as much
latitude of language as could possibly consist with a denial
of Transubstantiation. What kind of language they approved may be seen from the Saxon Homily already mentioned: but we have no warrant, I think, for supposing that
they wished to *limit* others to that if only they repudiated
the Roman Doctrine.

It was not until the Revision of 1662 that the Declaration again found its way into the Prayer Book. The Nonconformist party at that time desired these two things, among others, with reference to the Administration of the Holy Communion; first:—(1) " ....that the kneeling at the Sacrament (it being not that gesture which the Apostles used, though Christ was personally present amongst them, nor that which was used in the purest and primitive times of the Church) may be left free, as it was 1 and 2 Edw., ' As touching kneeling, &c., they may be used or left as every man's devotion serveth without blame.'" (2) Next the restoration of the Declaration on Kneeling.

The *Bishops* in their " Answer " to these " Exceptions " of the *Ministers* defended the " position of Kneeling," assigning their reasons in §§ 10 and 15: to the other demand they replied :—

§ 12. This Rub. is not in the liturgy of Queen Elizabeth, nor confirmed by law; nor is there any great need of restoring it, the world being now in more danger of profanation than of idolatry. Besides the sense of it is declared sufficiently in the 28th Article of the Church of England."—*Card. Hist. Conf.* p. 354.

After this refusal on the part of the Bishops how came it then to be inserted? Burnet, who as a near contemporary must be accounted a competent witness, thus answers the question: he is replying to *Collier's* criticism on his History:—

" The next, and indeed the last particular that out of many more I will mention, is the setting down the explanation that was made upon the order for kneeling at the Sacrament in King Edward's time, wrong in a very material word: For in that, the words were : *That there was not in the Sacrament any Real or Essential Presence of Christ's Natural Flesh and Blood :* but he instead of that puts *Corporal Presence.* It seems in this he only looked at the Rubrick, as it is now at the end of the Communion Service, upon a conceit that it stands now as it was in King Edward's Book ; though it was at that time changed ; and we know who was the author of that change, and who pretended that a *Corporal Presence* signified such a presence as a body naturally has, which the assertors of Transubstantiation itself do not, and cannot pretend is in this case, where they say the body is not present corporally, but spiritually, or as a spirit is present. And he who had the chief hand in procuring this alteration, had a very extraordinary subtilty, by which he reconciled the opinion of a Real Presence in the Sacrament with the last words of the Rubrick, *That the Natural Body and Blood of Christ were in Heaven, and not here; it being against the truth of Christ's Natural Body, to be at one Time in more Places than one.* It was thus : a Body is in a Place, if there is no intermediate Body, but a Vacuum between it and the place. And he thought that by the Vertue of the Words of Consecration, there was a *Cilinder* of a *Vacuum* made between the elements and Christ's Body in Heaven ; So that no body being between, it was both in Heaven and in the elements. Such a solemn Piece of Folly as this, can hardly be read without Indignation. But if our Author favors this conceit, yet when he sets down that which was done in King Edward's reign, he ought not to have changed the word, especially such an important one. I shall say no more of that work, but that there appeared to me quite through the second volume, such a constant inclination to favour the Popish doctrine, and to censuré the Reformers, that I should have had a better opinion of the author's integrity, if he had professed himself not to be of our communion, nor of the communion of any other Protestant Church.—*Burnet*, Hist. Ref. Part iii. preface p. 5. vol. 1715.

The words "real and essential " of the original Declaration were, however, changed into " corporal," and it will be seen that Burnet says "we know who was the author of that change:" in the margin he puts the letters " D. P. G," meaning I suppose *Dominus*, or *Doctor Peter Gunning*, and then he tells us why the change was made—a statement which beyond all question leads to a persuasion amounting almost to certainty, (1) first, that the term now substituted was meant to remove any *doubt* which might hang upon the original words ; (2) next, that the Declaration not only was not designed to *exclude* a very high doctrine of the Real Presence, but was purposely intended to *include* those who held it, if only they disallowed Transubstantiation.

But there is another piece of evidence furnished by Burnet in this matter in the following passage :—

" [Some other lesser additions were made. But care was taken, that nothing should be altered, so as it had been moved by the Presbyterians ; for it was resolved to gratify them in nothing.] One important addition was made, chiefly by *Gawden's* means ; he pressed that a declaration, explaining the reasons of their kneeling at the Sacrament, which had been in King Edward's Liturgy, but was left out in Queen Elizabeth's time, should again be set where it had once been. The Papists were highly offended, when they saw such an express declaration made against the Real Presence,

and the Duke told me that when he asked *Sheldon* how they
came to declare against a doctrine, which he had been instructed
was the doctrine of the Church, *Sheldon* answered, ask *Gawden*
about it, who is a Bishop of your own making; for the King had
ordered his promotion for the service he had done.—*Hist. of his
own time.* Vol. 1, p. 183, fol. ed. 1724.

" Now who was "the Duke" thus speaking to Burnet? I
suppose the Duke of York, afterwards James II : * if so, did
his views of the Real Presence incline to the *Roman* or to
the *Anglican* phase of that doctrine? His subsequent
history will probably answer that it was to the *Roman* aspect:
in that case it is easy to understand that he should suppose
the Declaration to be directed "against a doctrine, which he
had been instructed was the doctrine of the Church [of
England] :" but this would tend to shew that it was aimed
at Transubstantiation and nothing more, and this was quite
enough to account for the fact that " the Papists were highly
offended." Is there any evidence to shew that *Gawden* did
not hold high views of the Real Presence though denying
Transubstantiation? I am unable at present to answer this
question. If he did, then we must suppose that he and
Gunning (if it was Gunning, as I believe, to whom Burnet
referred in the other passage) co-operated in clearing the old
Declaration of what probably they thought a misleading
term, and substituting a definition not liable to the same
objection and withal only denying Transubstantiation. If he
did not, then we may imagine that though Gawden pressed
for the re-insertion of the Declaration, he only gained his
point by conceding the use of an expression which Gunning

* [For Burnet, writing of the authorship of Εἰκὼν Βασιλικὴ, says " I
was not a little surprised, when in the year 1673, in which I had a great share of
favour and free conversation with the then Duke of York, afterwards King
James the Second, as he suffered me to talk very freely to him about matters of
religion, and as I was arguing with him somewhat out of his father's book, he
told me that book was not of his father's writing, and that the letter to the
Prince of Wales was never brought to him. He said, Dr. Gawden writ it: after
the restoration he brought the Duke of Somerset and the Earl of Southampton
both to the King and to himself, who affirmed that they knew it was his
writing; and that it was carried down by the Earl of Southampton, and shewed
the King during the treaty of Newport, who read it and approved of it as containing his sense of things. Upon this he told me, that though Sheldon and
the other Bishops opposed Gawden because he had taken the Covenant, yet the
merits of that service carried it for him, notwithstanding the opposition made to
it."—(*Hist. of Own Time*, Vol. I. p. 51, fol.; *or* Vol. I. p. 81, 8vo. Oxford,
1823.)]

" the [supposed] author " of it intended to admit his view of
the Presence.

But we cannot fairly presume that either of these courses
was adopted without the sanction of the rest, or at least the
major part, of the Bishops: which of the two views represented their own, makes no material difference to the conclusion which seems to follow from it, and which has been
already stated, namely, That the Declaration is *nothing more*
than a *negation* of Transubstantiation.

If, indeed, I have at all succeeded in shewing that this was
all that was designed by the *original* Declaration, the circumstances attending its revision and re-introduction, so far as
we seem to know them, cannot possibly make it to mean
more. Then comes the very natural question—What license
is to be allowed, what limits are to be imposed, in enuncia-
ting the Doctrine of the Real Presence? Again, I venture
to repeat, that the one cardinal point of TRANSUBSTANTIATION
seems to have been meant to decide it.

The expressions used by Cranmer, Ridley, and others
whom I have quoted: the way in which they professed to
accept the high language of Antiquity: these alike appear
to say that they had no wish to pare down any statement
which should invest the Sacrament of the Altar with the
greatest possible dignity and should secure for it the deepest
reverence, if only it did not run up into an admission of
that particular belief against which they were contending.
Indeed considering some of their staments, especially those
of Ridley, it is hard to say why they were burned for their
alleged recusancy. Can it be shewn that the statements of
the Bp. of Brechin and others, now complained of, exceed
them? How near *Cranmer* and *Gardiner* approached in
1550 may be seen from the following passage :

In his reply to the " Defence " Gardiner quoted a passage
from Bucer, which he thus translated:—

" ' As the sun is truly placed determinately in one place of the
visible heaven, and yet is truly and substantially present by means of
his beams elsewhere in the world abroad; so our Lord, although
He be comprehended in one place of the secret and divine heaven,
that is to say, the glory of His father, yet, nevertheless by His

L

word and holy tokens He is exhibit present truly whole God and man, and therefore in substance in His holy supper; which presence man's mind, giving credit to His words and tokens, with no less certainty acknowledgeth, than our eyes see, and have the sun present, exhibited, and shewed with his corporal light. This is a deep secret matter, and of the New Testament, and a matter of faith; and therefore herein thoughts be not to be received of such a presentation of the body as consisteth in the manner of this life transitory, and subject to suffer. We must simply cleave to the word of Christ, and faith must relieve the default of our senses.'" —*Answer* p. 90.

To this appeal on Gardiner's part, Cranmer thus answers:—

" In this comparison, I am glad that, at the last, we be come so near together; for you be almost right heartily welcome home, and I pray you let us shake hands together. For we be agreed, as me seemeth, that Christ's Body is present, and the same Body that suffered; and we be agreed also of the manner of His presence. For you say that the Body of Christ is not present but after a spiritual manner, and so say I also. And if there be any difference between us two, it is but a little, and in this point only; that I say that Christ is but spiritually in the ministration of the Sacrament, and you say that he is but after a spiritual manner in the Sacrament. And yet you say that he is corporally in the Sacrament, as who should say that there were a difference between spiritually, and a spiritual manner; and that it were not all one to say that Christ is there only after a spiritual manner, and not only spiritually.

" But if the substance of the Sun be here corporally present with us upon earth, then I grant that Christ's Body is so likewise: so that he of us two that erreth in the one, let him be taken for a vain man, and to err also in the other. Therefore I am content that the reader judge indifferently between you and me, in the corporal Presence of the Sun, and he that is found to err, and to be a fool therein, let him be judged to err also in the corporal Presence of Christ's Body.

" But now, Master Bucer, help this man at need: for he that hath ever hitherto cried out against you, now being at a pinch, driven to his shifts, crieth for help upon you: and, although he was never your friend, yet extend your charity to help him in his necessity. But Master Bucer saith not so much as you do; and yet if you both said that the beams of the Sun be of the same substance with the Sun, who would believe either of you both? Is the light of the candle the substance of the candle? or the light of the fire the substance of the fire? Or is the beams of the Sun anything but the clear light of the Sun? Now, as you said even now of me, if you err so far from the true judgment of natural things, that all men may perceive your error, what marvel is it if you err in heavenly things?

" And why should you be offended with this my saying, that Christ is spiritually present in the assembly of such as be gathered together in His name? And how can you conclude hereof, that this is a plain abolition of the mystery of the Sacrament, because that in the celebration of the Sacrament I say that Christ is spiritually present? Have not you confessed yourself that Christ is in the Sacrament but after a spiritual manner? And after that manner He is also among them that be assembled togethether in His name. And if they that say so do abolish the mystery of the Sacrament, then do you abolish it yourself, by saying that Christ is but after a spiritual manner in the Sacrament, after which manner you say also that He is in them that be gathered together in His name, as well as I do, that say He is spiritually in both. But he that is disposed to pick quarrels, and to calumniate all things, what can be spoken so plainly, or meant so sincerely, but he will wrest it unto a wrong sense? I say that Christ is spiritually and by grace in His supper as He is when two or three be gathered together in His name, meaning that with both He is spiritually, and with neither corporally; and yet I say not that there is no difference. For this difference there is, that with the one He is sacramentally, and with the other not sacramentally, except they be gathered together in His name to receive the Sacrament. Nevertheless, the selfsame Christ is present in both, nourisheth and feedeth both, if the Sacrament be rightly received. But that is only spiritually, as I say, and only after a spiritual manner, as you say.

"And you say further, that before we receive the Sacrament, we must come endued with Christ, and seemly clothed with Him. But whosoever is endued and clothed with Christ hath Christ present with him after a spiritual manner, and hath received Christ whole both God and man, or else he could not have everlasting life. And therefore is Christ present as well in Baptism as in the Lord's Supper. For in Baptism be we endued with Christ, and seemly clothed with Him, as well as in his Holy Supper we eat and drink Him.—*Ibid* pp. 91-2.

The illustration here used is Ridley's also: I am not competent to decide the nice *philosophical* question which alone seemed to divide the belief of *Cranmer* and *Gardiner* at that time: but it appears to deserve a careful consideration. Absolute lack of time hinders any pursuit now of the thoughts which it involves and of the enquiries which I have only just been able to indicate in these latter pages: they have been thrown hastily together, as possibly furnishing some few suggestions which may shew the importance of further examination and serious deliberation before arriving at any conclusions, supposed to be deducible from the Declaration on Kneeling, adverse to recently promulged and now contested statements on the doctrine of the Real Presence in the Holy Eucharist.

In this crude shape and with all their imperfections I have ventured, my Lord, to address these remarks to your Lordship, *in an unpublished and very incomplete form :* thinking that if they do perchance contain any new fact or argument they may not be unacceptable to your Lordship at this seemingly critical time; and beliving also that in so doing I am not wanting in due respect to your high and responsible Office in the Church of Christ.

> I have the honour to be, my Lord,
>> Your Lordship's faithful Servant in Christ,
>>> PRESBYTER ANGLICANUS.

₊*₊ P.S. Wholly too late to examine it, and much less to have it copied and printed in time to accompany this letter, I noticed in looking through Mr. Lemon's recently published Calendar of State Papers, an apparently important Document in " Vol. xv. Domestic. Edward VI. No. 15, Oct. 7, 1552," intitled " Archbp. Cranmer to the Council. Has received their directions that the Book of Common Prayer should be diligently pursued, and the printer's errors therein amended. Arguments defending the practice of Kneeling at the Sacrament ? "

It will be seen that the date of this letter coincides with the dates from which I have argued at p. 37 that resistance was probably made by the Bishops to the demand for withdrawing the order for Kneeling at Communion. I need scarcely say that Cranmer's Arguments for Kneeling, contained in this State Paper, may throw light upon the purpose of the original Declaration : and this is a strong ground for suspending judgment upon it. I hope to produce this State Paper with as little delay as may be : and at the same time to complete this letter.

May 25th, 1858.

POSTSCRIPT, No. 2.

Since the above Letter was printed I have been endeavouring to collect any other materials which might confirm or
further elucidate the views and position therein taken: the
result of such searches as time and opportunity afforded,
together with some observations unavoidably omitted in the
Letter, I now submit for consideration in this Postcript;
only making this further preliminary remark,—that it would
probably be an error to suppose that a longer investigation
would not furnish new or additional facts and arguments of
the like character and tendency.

I. And, first of all, it will be best to produce and notice
the State Paper mentioned in my former P.S. The following
is an accurate transcript of the original Document remaining
in the STATE PAPER OFFICE, and marked :—

" Domestic. Edward VI. Vol. 15, No. 15."

" After my right humble commendations unto yor good Lord-
shipps—Where I understaunde by your L. ltres that the Kings Matie his
pleasure is that the boke of commen service shoulde bee diligentlye
perused and therin the prynters errourse to bee amendid : I shall
travaile therin to the uttermost of my power albeit I had neade first
to have had the boke written wch was passed by acte of Parliament
and sealed w^t the greate seale wch remaynith in the handes of
Mr Spilman clerke of the Parlament, who is not in London nor I
cannot learne where he is. Nevertheles I have gotten the copie
wch Mr Spilman delivered to the printers to printe by, wch I thinke
shall serve well enough. And where I understaunde further by
yor L. ltres, that some bee offended w^t kneeling at the tyme of the
receavinge of the Sacrament, and woulde that I callinge to me the
bushop of London and some other learned men as Mr Peter Martyr
or suche like should w^t theim expend and waye the said prescription
of kneelinge whether it bee fitt to remayn as a commaundement or to
bee left out of the boke. I shall accomplish the Kings Matie his
commaundement albeeit I trust that wee w^t just ballaunce waied
this at the makinge of the boke, and not onlie wee but a greate
menny bushops and other of the best learned w^{t}in this realme and
appoincted for that purpose. And nowe the boke beinge read and
approved by thole state of the Realme in the high courte of Parlament w^t the Kings Matie his roiall assent, y^t this shoulde bee nowe
altered againe w^{t}out Parlament, of what importaunce this matter is,

I referr to your L. wisdome to considre. I knowe yor L. wisdome
to bee suche, that I trust ye will not bee moved w^t thes gloriouse
and unquiet spirites wch can like nothing but that is after their own
fansye and cease not to make troble and disquietnes when thinges
bee most quiet and in goode ordre. If suche men should bee
hearde although the boke were made everye yere anewe, yet should
it not lacke faultes in their opinion. But (saie thei) it is not commaunded in the scripture to kneele, and whatsoever is not commaunded in the scripture is against the scripture and utterly unlaufull
and ungodlie. But this saing is the chief foundation of therro^r of
thanabaptists and of divers other sectes. This sainge is a subvertion
of all ordre aswell in religion as in common pollicye. If this sainge
bee true, take awaie the hole boke of service. For what should men
travell to sett an ordre in the forme of service, if no ordre can bee
sett, but that is alreadye prescribed by the scripture. And because
I will not troble yor L. w^t recitinge of manny scriptures or proves in
this matier, whosoever teacheth anny suche doctrine (if yor L. will
geave me leave) I will sett my fote by his to bee tried by fier, that
his doctrine is untrue, and not onlie untrue but also seditiouse and
p[er]illouse to bee hearde of anny subjectes, as a thinge breakinge
the bridle of obedience and losinge theim from the bonde of all
princes lawes. My good L. I praye youe to considre that there bee
two praiers wch go before the receavinge of the Sacrament and two
ymmediatlie followe all wch tyme the people praying and geavinge
thanckes, do kneele ; and what inconvenience there is that it may
not bee thus ordered I knowe not. If the kneelinge of the people
shoulde bee discontynued for the tyme of the receavinge of the
Sacrament, so y^t at the recept therof thei shoulde rise up and staunde
or sitt, and then ymmediatlie kneele downe againe, it should rather
importe a contemptuouse then a reverent receavinge of the Sacrament. But it is not expreslye conteigned in the scripture (saie thei)
that Christ ministred the sacrament to his apostles kneelinge. Nor
thei finde it not expresly in scriptur that he ministered it staundinge
or sittinge ; but if wee will followe the plaine wourdes of scripture,
wee shall rather receave it lyinge downe on the grounde, as the
custome of the wourlde at that tyme almost every where, and as the
Tartars and Turkes use yet at this daie to eate their meate lying
upon the grounde. And the wourdes of the Evangelist importe the
same, wch bee ἀνάκειμαι and ἀναπίπτω whiche signifie properlie to
lie downe upon the floure or grounde and not to sitt apon a forme or
stole. A [nd] the same speache use thevangelists where thei sh [ew]
that Christ fead five thowsaunde w^t v loves, wh [ere] it is plainlie
expressede that thei satt down upon the grounde and not upon stoles.
I beseche yor L. to take in good parte this my longe babelinge wch I
write as of my self onlie, because the bushop of London is not yet
come, and yor L. required aunswer w^t speede, and therfore ame I
constrayned to make some aunswer to yor L. afore his coming. And
thus I praye god longe to preserve yor L. and to increase the same

in all prosperitie and godlines. At Lambieth This vijth of Octobr
1552.

" Yo^r Lordeshipps to commaunde

" T. Cantr

(Indorsed) "To my veray goode Lordes of the Kings most
honorable councell.

"7, octob. 1552 Bish. of Cant'b. to ye Cll. de gennaflect in communio. ευχαριστ."

Now it will be seen that this Letter of Archbishop Cranmer
most entirely confirms the suggestions I have offered in p. 36:
for although it makes no allusion to any intended Declaration
on Kneeling to be added to the Book, it proves distinctly, as
I surmized, that "objections were urged upon the Council
against the direction" to kneel at receiving the Sacrament,
" and that its omission was pressed for." It further attests the
conviction there expressed, that "the considerations which"
had "prompted the Direction" to kneel at receiving "were
doubtless equally weighty in inducing the Bishops and the
Privy Council to determine on retaining it in the Book."
Nothing can be plainer than that Cranmer was deeply impressed with the necessity of not yielding this point, as well
as other points, to the "gloriouse and unquiet spirites" of
that day ; and his language in this Letter ought to have considerable weight with those in our own time who, while professing their great reverence for the Archbishop, are treading
in the very steps of that extreme Reforming party in 1552
whose conduct the Primate thus severely censures. That
Ridley and the other leading Bishops concurred with Cranmer
in this determination as to kneeling at Communion might be
inferred from the consideration that the Archbishop was probably disposed to go beyond them in consulting the prejudices
of those whom they were all desirous to comprehend if they
could in the Church of England : but here is Cranmer's testimony that "at the makinge of the boke " this "prescription of
kneelinge" was determined upon by "a great menny bushops
and other of the best learned ": we may be sure, therefore,
that they, like him, refused to alter it. That the King and
Council *deferred* to the Bishops even if they *differed* from

them (of which, however, there is no proof), is clear from the fact that the Order was not withdrawn.

Probably, however, it will be objected—that the Reasons which Cranmer assigns in this Letter for " Kneeling at the tyme of the receavinge of the Sacrament" are no proof that he held the Doctrine of the Real Presence. But surely it would be fairer to ask—Do they contain any indication that he did not hold it? In answering this question, it is of consequence to bear in mind the character of the complainants and the ground of their complaint: both are described by the Archbishop in his Letter: he saw clearly enough that they were not to be satisfied with such a concession as they required, even if he had been disposed to make it; and we may well believe him to have felt that, whatever their faith or misbelief as to the Real Presence, any argument upon it would be out of place with those who demanded license to do as they list because "it is not expressly conteigned in the scripture (saie thei) that Christ ministered the sacrament to his apostles kneelinge." It was, then, only prudent and politic in one who was evidently bent upon carrying his point, not to risk the loss of it by furnishing the Council with arguments which perhaps some of them might refuse to endorse, and which, even if all concurred in them, would be no answer to the opponents of the Rubric, whatever their opinion on the then debated question of Christ's presence in the Sacrament: for, no doubt, they would have retorted— That the Apostles did not kneel even when Christ was *visibly* present.

It would be most unjust therefore to Cranmer, to accuse him, on such a ground as this, of not holding the Catholic Doctrine: rather it would be due to him to think that he was unwilling to peril its acceptance by employing it to defeat an opposition which, however *truly*, was not then *ostensibly* based upon the non-recognition of it.

Moreover, it would appear that the Archbishop quite understood the weakness of those who professed to " bee offended," and well knew how to turn their own inconsistency into an argument for the rule and practice which he was defending. For it seems that they limited their objection to kneeling, to " the tyme of the *receavinge* of the Sacrament":

this, no doubt, was highly important in the estimation of the Zwinglian and stricter Sacramentarian party, who wished to disconnect from the reception of the Eucharistic elements every idea of their being the *media* of *conveying* to any the Body and Blood of Christ. To kneel at receiving them would be the recognition of a belief which even Calvin and the more moderate Sacramentarians held—that *simultaneously* with the participation of the bread and wine the Body and Blood of Christ were *communicated* to the elect, or those in a state of grace. It is obvious, therefore, that if the protestation thus involved in *not kneeling* at the *time of receiving*, were allowed, kneeling at other parts of the Service would not be an *obstacle* with them, though they might *prefer* some other attitude. It is easy, then, to conceive, that under these circumstances Cranmer felt it necessary to meet the objectors on their own ground, and to furnish the Council with an answer which (while perhaps it was necessary for some of the Councillors themselves) should enable it to appease the complainants without adverting to any Doctrinal dispute.

The consideration, then, that the objectors acquiesced in the rule of kneeling at other parts of the Communion Office (and thus maintained some external reverence in what they regarded as no more than a commemorative rite) coupled with their non-belief of any Objective Presence resulting from Consecration, appears to have provided the Archbishop with his answer to their cavil: he simply contents himself with calling the Council's attention to the fact " that there bee two praiers which go before the receavinge of the Sacrament and two ymmediatlie followe all which tyme the people praying and geavinge thanckes, do kneele". These four prayers were, (1) The Prayer of access, " We do not presume," &c.; (2) The Consecration Prayer, " Almighty God our heavenly Father," &c.; (3) The Lord's Prayer; (4) The Prayer of Thanksgiving, " O Lord and heavenly Father," &c., or, " Almighty and everlasting God," &c., as in our present Office. On what principle, asks the Archbishop, in effect, can they kneel during these prayers, and refuse to kneel

M

during that act which they would acknowledge as designed to quicken their intellectual apprehension of Christ—which perhaps some of them would even regard as the obsignation of the benefits of Christ's death? They cannot merely wish, he virtually says, to exhibit less devotion at the moment when they would intensify their mental union with Christ, or realize the sealing of His grace, than when they ask Him to bestow these blessings or thank Him for having vouchsafed them! Even on their own view of the nature and use of the Lord's Supper, if " at the recept " of the Sacrament the people " shoulde rise up and staunde or sitt, and then ymmediately kneele down againe, it should rather import a contemptuouse then a reverent receavinge of the Sacrament."

This, I think, is the very lowest construction which can be put upon the Archbishop's Letter: his argument was one which the necessity of the case appears to have required, and which, were it needful, might be justified by the example of an Apostle who said, " being crafty I caught you with guile." Yet it must not be taken as the measure of Cranmer's own belief: *that*, to be rightly estimated, must be sought either in his own positive teaching or in controversies with the Papal party: in these we should expect to find how much he deliberately held; and some tolerable notion of what he did believe on the Real Presence will have been gathered from the passages already cited.

I can readily imagine, however, some one appealing to this Letter from Cranmer to the Council as a proof of what has been sometimes asserted—that the Archbishop, when he prepared Edward's Second Book, did not believe in Consecration. It will be asked, I have no doubt, does not the fact that Cranmer here speaks of the Prayer of Consecration in precisely the same language which he applies to the Prayer of Access and to the two Post-communion Prayers, prove that he could not have attributed any peculiar value to the act of Consecrating the Eucharist?

For the reasons already given it would be enough to answer—that Cranmer's view of Consecration must not be gathered from language used on an occasion when to have urged the importance of Consecration would probably have only had the mischievous effect of provoking a clamorous demand to expunge the Prayer itself from the Book which had just received the sanction of the Crown and of Parliament; and that Cranmer had some reason to fear the Council would not refuse to employ its extensive powers in altering the Book, if it so pleased them, is plain from his referring it to their "wisdome to considre" of " what importaunce" it was, even for the Rubric on Kneeling to "bee nowe altered againe without Parliament." Yet, perhaps, in that very silence which was only politic, we may trace a latent defence of Consecration. It can scarcely have been absent from the Archbishop's mind—that the objectors to the Rubric must have been fully conscious of the importance attached to this Prayer of Consecration by, at least, the greater proportion of a Clergy who had only four years before been constantly using the old Mass Office, and who at that very time were accustomed to so definite a form of Consecration as that in Edward's 1st. Book. His own sagacity moreover, must surely have suggested to him that (though the Prayer as altered in the 2nd Book, and especially the omission of the Rubrics requiring the manual acts, might satisfy the Clerical as well as the Lay malcontents) the complainants could not disguise from themselves the distinctive character of a Prayer which " the Priest " was still ordered to offer " standing up" and which they would certainly believe him, in the majority of cases, to use with the same intention which he had always had : not to say that they would expect to find the Priests, generally, continuing to use those same Manual Acts to which up to that time they had been accustomed and which, be it observed, they were not *forbidden* to employ : for to suppose that the Clergy of 1552 in any numbers, and, much more, suddenly, made so great a change in their habitual practice; is a notion as wholly improbable as the supposition—that if the present Prayer Book were now revised and the Rubrics in the Consecration Prayer *omitted*, any considerable number of the Clergy of the present day would cease to Consecrate the Eucharist with the Manual Acts *now* prescribed.

Now mark how the Archbishop turns to account this impression, which we cannot deny he was *likely* to have had, of the objectors' mental consciousness as to the prevailing belief touching this Prayer: he makes no *special* allusion to the Prayer itself; that would, in all likelihood, have been a signal for reclamation on their part and would have added force to their objection to kneeling at the reception, as recognizing a Real Presence due to Consecration: but, ignoring for the time their own disbelief and their conviction of others' belief in Consecration, he contents himself with noticing the fact that at that Prayer and three other Prayers intimately related to it " the people praying and geaving thanckes, do kneele ;" leaving it to them to reconcile it to their own consciences how (while objecting to kneel at receiving) they could unite in an *external act* which *implied* acquiesence in a theory they themselves disavowed. It was no part of his duty *then* to sound in unwilling ears the Doctrine of the Church: enough if he could compel uncandid minds to yield assent to a Rule which he was not prepared to abandon, though that assent was secured by an argument which condemned their own palpable inconsistency.

But we are not without distinct evidence as to Cranmer's views at this time touching *Consecration*: his " Defence of the True and Catholic Doctrine of the Sacrament " (already quoted at pp. 19—26) will tell us what they were: the " Defence " was written in 1550 *i.e.* the year after the publication of Edward's 1st Book; its *object* and the Archbishop's *status* at that time on the Eucharistical question are thus described by Foxe, A.D. 1563, in his " LIFE, STATE, AND STORY OF THOMAS CRANMER :" the *Italics* are mine :—

" During all this mean time of King Henry aforesaid, *until* the entering of King Edward, it seemeth that Cranmer was scarcely yet thoroughly persuaded in the *right knowledge* of the Sacrament, or at least, was not yet *fully ripened* in the same : wherein shortly after he being more groundly confirmed by conference with Bishop Ridley, in process of time did so profit in more riper knowledge, that at last he took upon him the defence of that whole doctrine, that is, to refute and throw down first, the *corporal* presence ; secondly, the *phantastical transubstantiation ;* thirdly, the *idolatrous* adoration ; fourthly, the false error of the papists, that wicked men do eat the *natural* body of Christ ; and lastly, the *blasphemous* sacrifice of the mass. Whereupon in conclusion he wrote five books for the public instruction of the Church of England, which instruction yet to this day standeth and is received in this Church of England."—*Cranmer on the Lord's Supper.* Works, Parker Society p. xix, or *Foxe, Acts and Mon.* Vol. 8, p. 34, ed. 1849.

The following is Cranmer's statement upon Consecration, as quoted by him from *The Defence* in his *Answer* to Bishop Gardiner's strictures upon that Book :—

" And now I will come to the saying of St. Ambrose, which is always in their mouths. ' Before the consecration,' saith he, as they allege, ' it is bread, but after the words of the consecration it is the body of Christ.'

" For answer hereunto, it must be first known what consecration is.

" Consecration is the separation of anything from a profane and worldly use unto a spiritual and godly use.

" And therefore when usual and common water is taken from other uses, and put to the use of baptism in the name of the Father, and of the Son, and of the Holy Ghost, then it may rightly be called consecrated water, that is to say, water put to an holy use.

" Even so, when common bread and wine be taken and severed from other bread and wine to the use of the holy communion, that portion of bread and wine, although it be of the same substance that the other is from the which it is severed, yet it is now called consecrated, or holy bread and holy wine.

" Not that the bread and wine have or can have any holiness in them, but that they be used to an holy work, and represent holy and godly things. And therefore St. Dionyse (*De Eccl. Hierar.* cap. 3,) called the bread· holy bread, and the cup an holy cup, as soon as they be set upon the altar to the use of the holy communion.*

" But specially they may be called holy and consecrated, when they be separated to that holy use by Christ's own words, which He spake for that purpose, saying of the bread, ' This is my body,' and of the wine, ' This is my blood.'

" So that commonly the authors, before those words be spoken, do take the bread and wine but as other common bread and wine ; but after those words be pronounced over them, then they take them for consecrated and holy bread and wine.

" Not that the bread and wine can be partakers of any holiness or godliness, or can be the body and blood of Christ, but that they represent the very body and blood of Christ, and the holy food and

* This statement of Cranmer's at once suggests that, though in Edward's 2nd Book the Rubric for the oblation of the Elements was omitted, the Abp. could not have contemplated the modern (but now pronounced illegal) practice of neglecting this act : for, as will be seen presently, his views were the same in 1552.

nourishment which we have by him. And so they be called by the names of the body and blood of Christ, as the sign, token, and figure is called by the name of the very thing which it sheweth and signifieth.

"And therefore as St. Ambrose, in the words before cited by the adversaries, saith, that 'before the consecration it is bread, and after the consecration it is Christ's body,' so in other places he doth more plainly set forth his meaning, saying these words : ' Before the benediction of the heavenly words, it is called another kind of thing ; but after the consecration, is signified the body of Christ. Likewise before the consecration it is called another thing; but after the consecration it is named the blood of Christ *(De his qui mysteris initiantur,* cap. ult.) And again he saith : 'When I treated of the Sacraments, I told you that that thing which is offered before the words of Christ, is called bread: but when the words of Christ be pronounced, then it is not called bread, but it is called by the name of Christ's body.' *(De sacramentis, Lib.* v. cap. 4.)

"By which words of St. Ambrose it appeareth plainly, that the bread is called by the name of Christ's body after the consecration ; and although it be still bread, yet after consecration it is dignified by the name of the thing which it representeth :* as at length is de-

---

* It is of importance not to mistake Cranmer's use of this expression which, in other forms also, he often employs: we may be tolerably certain that his meaning is best represented by the terms *"no bare sign, no untrue figure of a thing absent"* which occur in the first part of "An Homily of the worthy receiving and reverent esteeming of the Sacrament of the Body and Blood of Christ," even if we knew that this Homily of the 2nd Book was not written by him or at his instance, whereas the probability is that he was its author.

In confirmation of this it may be remarked—that *Cranmer* could not have held *lower* views on this point than *Calvin* whose doctrine the Archbishop must have well known : it may elucidate this, and other statements in this Letter, to quote the following account of *Calvin's* belief as given by Bishop Cosin; bearing in mind, however, how it was affected by his theory of Grace already referred to.

"Now because great is the fame of Calvin, (who subscribed the Augustan Confession and that of the Switzers,) let us hear what he writ and believed concerning this sacred mystery. His words in his Institutions and elsewhere are such, so conformable to the style and mind of the ancient fathers, that no Catholic protestant would wish to use any other. 'I understand,' saith he, ' what is to be understood by the words of Christ, that He doth not only offer us the benefits of His death and resurrection, but His very Body wherein He died and rose again. I assert that the Body of Christ is really, (as the usual expression is,) that is, truly, given to us in the sacrament, to be the saving food of our souls.' (Comm. on 1 Cor.) Also, in another place: 'Item, that word cannot lie, neither can it mock us; and, except one presumes to call God a deceiver, he will never dare to say that the symbols are empty, and that Christ is not in them. Therefore, if by the breaking of the bread our Saviour doth represent the participation of His Body, it is not to be doubted but that He truly gives and confers it. If it be true that the visible sign is given us to seal the gift of an invisible thing, we must firmly believe that, receiving the signs of the Body, we also certainly receive the Body itself. Setting aside all absurdities, I do willingly admit all those terms that can most strongly express the true and substantial communication of the Body and Blood of Christ granted to the faithful with the symbols of the Lord's Supper; and that, not as if they received only by the force of their imagination, or an act of their minds, but really so as to be fed

clared before in the process of transubstantiation, and specially in the words of Theodoretus.

" And as the bread is a corporal meat, and corporally eaten, so, saith St. Ambrose (*De sacramentis*, Lib. vi. cap. 1,) ' is the body of Christ a spiritual meat, and spiritually eaten,' and that requireth no corporal presence. ' "—*Works*, Parker Society pp. 177-8.

Such was Abp. Cranmer's deliberately recorded opinion on this subject in 1550: Bishop Gardiner in his reply controverted the Primate's views: as however, we are not now seeking *Gardiner's* but *Cranmer's* belief, it is not necessary to quote the argument of the former, especially as it is substantially incorporated with Cranmer's rejoinder in 1551: this "Answer," as also the " Defence," undoubtedly exhibits Cranmer's views at the very time he was preparing the Prayer Book of 1552; for in a Letter to the Secretary of State, dated Sep. 29, 1551, he asks the King's Licence " for the printing and selling " of the Book which contained both. From the " Answer " I cite the following passages :—

"It is not I that wrestle with St. Ambrose, but you, who take great pain to wrest his words clean contrary to his intent and meaning. But where you ask this question, What can be more plain than these words of St. Ambrose, 'It is bread before consecration, and after, it is Christ's body?' these words of St. Ambrose be not fully so plain as you pretend, but clean contrary. For what can be spoken either more unplain or untrue, than to say of bread after consecration, that it is the body of Christ, unless the same be understood in,

thereby unto eternal life.' (Instit. book iv. ch. 17.) Again: ' We must therefore confess that the inward substance of the Sacrament is joined with the visible sign ; so that, as the bread is put into our hand, the Body of Christ is also given to us. This certainly, if there were nothing else, should abundantly satisfy us that we understand that Christ in His Holy Supper gives us the true and proper substance of His Body and Blood ; that, it being wholly ours, we may be made partakers of all His benefits and graces.' (Treat. of the Lord's Supper.) Again : ' The Son of God offers daily to us in the Holy Sacrament the same Body which He once offered in sacrifice to His Father, that it may be our spiritual food.' In these he asserts, as clearly as any one can, the true, real, and substantial presence and communication of the Body of Christ ; but how, he undertakes not to determine. 'If any one,' saith he, (Instit., book iv. ch. 17, num. 32,) ' ask me concerning the manner, I will not be ashamed to confess that it is a secret too high for my reason to comprehend ; or, to speak more to express ; or, to speak more properly, I rather feel than understand it : therefore, without disputing, I embrace the truth of God, and confidently repose on it. He declares that His flesh is the food, and His Blood the drink of my soul ; and my soul I offer to Him to be fed by such nourishment. He bids me take, eat, and drink, His Body and Blood, which in His Holy Supper He offers me under the symbols of bread and wine : I make no scruple, but He doth reach them to me, and I receive them.' All these are Calvin's own words."—*Cosin's History of Transubstantiation.* Ang. Cath. Lib. p. 167.

a figurative speech ? For although Christ's body, ·as you say, **be there after consecration,** yet the **bread** is not His body, nor His body is not **made** of it, by your confession. And therefore the saying of St. Ambrose, that it is Christ's body, cannot be true in plain speech. And therefore St. Ambrose in the same place, where he calleth it the body and blood of Christ, he saith, it is a figure of His body and blood. For these be his words : *Quod est figura corporis et sanguinis Domini nostri Jesu Christi.*—p. 179.

"And as for the word ' consecration ' I have declared the signification thereof according to the mind of the old authors, as I will justify.

"And for the writing of Melancthon to Œcolampadius, you remain still in your old error, taking Myconius for Œcolampadius. And yet the **change** of bread and wine in this Sacrament, which Melancthon speaketh of, is a **sacramental** change, as the nature of a sacrament requireth, signifying how wonderfully Almighty God by his omnipotency worketh in us his lively members, and not in the dead creatures of bread and wine.

" And the change is in the use, and not in the elements kept and reserved, wherein is not the perfection of a sacrament. Therefore, as water in the font or vessel hath not the reason and nature of a sacrament, but when it is put to the use of christening, and then it is changed into the proper nature and kind of a sacrament, to signify the wonderful change which Almighty God by his omnipotency worketh really in them that be baptized therewith ; such is the change of the bread and wine in the Lord's supper. And therefore, the bread is called Christ's Body after consecration, as St. Ambrose saith, and yet it is not so **really** but **sacramentally.** For it is neither Christ's **mystical** body, (for that is the congregation of the faithful dispersed abroad in the world,) nor His **natural** body, (for that is in Heaven,) but it is the sacrament both of His true natural body, and also of His mystical body, and for that consideration hath the name of His body, as a sacrament or sign may bear the name of the very thing that is signified and represented thereby.— p. 180.

. . . .

" And I express St. Cyprian's mind truly, and not a whit discrepant from my doctrine here, when I say, that **the Divinity may be said to be poured, or put sacramentally into the bread;** as the Spirit of God is said to be in the water of Baptism, when it is truly minis- tered, or in His word when it is sincerely preached, with the Holy Spirit working mightily in the hearts of the hearers. And yet the water in itself is but a visible element, nor the preacher's word of itself is but a sound in the air, which as soon as it is heard, vanisheth away, and hath in itself no holiness at all, although for the use and ministry thereof it may be called holy. And so likewise may be said of the sacraments, which, as St. Augustine saith, ' be as it were God's visible word.'—p. 181.

" . . . the bread after consecration is not called Christ's body, because it is so **in deed;** for then it were no figurative speech, as all the old authors say it is."—p. 182.

Such, then, were Cranmer's views of Consecration at the date of the publication of Edward's 2nd Book ; for, though published apparently some months before that Book, it is certain that he did not subsequently part with them for any lower standard: yet, whether the Archbishop's statements fully realized the mind of Catholic Antiquity or not, it will hardly be contended that the man who could write thus made light of that part of the Eucharistic Ritual, much less disbelieved or disavowed the Church's Doctrine concerning it.*

* Hence, as also for reasons mentioned at p. 35, I cannot accept the interpretation, there referred to, of the Rubric in the Prayer Book of 1552 "if any of the bread and wine remain, the Curate shall have it to his own use." It is to be regretted that Mr. Cheyne (*Six Sermons* p. 46, Note), in common indeed with others, should have (as I think) so mistaken, what I have no doubt is its true meaning, as to censure " Cranmer and his associates " in strong language for having thus "left" it. Even *Bucer*, in his Censures on the Book of 1549, while objecting to the oblation of the Elements "as implying a superstitious notion of the effect of Consecration: . . . allows . . . that at a very early period care was taken to avoid profanation of the remains of the consecrated Elements." (*Procter* p. 41.) And when we remember that neither he nor P. Martyr seem to have expected that their opinions would determine the changes (see their Letters quoted in *Procter* pp. 43 and 44), it is very unlikely that the Rubric in question could have been meant in the least to alter what no doubt was the then practice. It cannot be reasonably doubted, I think, that, as no Rubric existed in the 1st Book determining what was to be done with the unconsumed Sacrament when not reserved for the sick, so the Revisers of that Book thought it unnecessary to add a Rubric in the 2nd Book to determine a point which usual practice must have settled for a body of Clergy who, if not forbidden, would naturally do as they had done under the old Ritual. They were not likely, for the most part, to be irreverent on this matter.

I have already (Letter p. 35) expressed an opinion that reservation for the sick probably continued to be practised under the Book of 1552: in support of that view it may be as well to add here that (apart from the likelihood of the custom being continued by the Clergy of that day) the Office for the Communion of the Sick does not *forbid* it, though the Rubric of the 1st Book, *directing* it, was omitted. But in Elizabeth's Book the Office was precisely that of Edward's 2nd Book, and yet in her authorized Latin version the Rubric is retained, directing reservation at the public Celebration when notice had been given that a sick person desired Communion.

It would be no answer, I think, to this argument to say—that the Latin Book seems to have been designed for the use of the Universities : for the question at once arises—on what principle could reservation be accounted right in a College and wrong in a Parish? Besides, it would have to be shown that the *sacerdos* who, in the 3rd Rubric, is directed to reserve is not the *parochus* to whom in the 2nd Rubric the notice is ordered to be sent.

It is worth noticing, too, that P. Martyr in his Strictures on the Book of 1549 expresses his surprise that Bucer had not objected to Reservation for the sick.

In dealing with points of this kind we cannot too carefully bear in mind what were likely to have been the *habits* of Clergy accustomed to the Old Offices : by

Though, however, the Archbishop intended to maintain (as I believe) the Catholic Doctrine on Consecration; and, as his Letter to the Council proves, upheld the practice of kneeling at the Sacrament; we may well conclude that, under the circumstances of that particular time, he would readily consent to (perhaps suggested) an explanation of the latter act such as that contained in the Declaration. For, considering his anxiety as to what the Roman party had recently been doing at Trent, it was but natural that he should desire not to have the Church of England charged with upholding the Roman doctrine while insisting upon this act of external reverence.

It was barely seven months before, viz. March 20th, 1552, that he had written to Bullinger, Calvin, and Melancthon expressing his concern at the proceedings of the Council of Trent: addressing Calvin he thus writes:

" . . . . Our adversaries are now holding their councils at Trent for the establishment of their errors; and shall we neglect to call together a godly synod, for the refutation of error, and for restoring and propagating the truth? They are, as I am informed, making decrees respecting the worship of the host [περὶ τῆς ἀρτολατρείας]: wherefore we ought to leave no stone unturned, not only that we may guard others against this idolatry, but also that we may ourselves come to an agreement upon the doctrine of this sacrament. It cannot escape your prudence, how exceedingly the Church of God has been injured by dissensions and varieties of opinion respecting this sacrament of unity; and though they are now in some measure removed, yet I could wish for an agreement in this doctrine, not only as regards the subject itself, but also with respect to the words and forms of expression . . . ."—*Original Letters*, Parker Society Vol. 1. No. xiv. p. 24, and Lat. Orig. in *Cranmer's Remains*. Pt. 1, p. 431.

To this Letter Calvin replied from *Geneva* about a month afterwards, viz. in April 1552; he observes:—

" . . . I wish it could be effected, that grave and learned men from the principal churches might meet together at a place appointed, and, after diligent consideration of each article of faith, hand down to posterity a definite form of doctrine according to their united opinion. But this also is to be reckoned among the greatest

doing this we shall probably save ourselves from the common but, I think, most doubtful and unhistorical conclusion – that whatever was not *ordered* in Edward's 2nd Book ceased to be practised. Rubrical *omissions* must not be confused with Rubrical *prohibitions*.

evils of our time, that the churches are so estranged from each other, that scarcely the common intercourse of society has place among them ; much less that holy communion of the members of Christ, which all persons profess with their life, though few sincerely honour it in their practice . . . ."—*Orig. Letters.* Vol. 2, No. cccxxxvii. p. 713.

With so little hope, then, of attaining an agreement with other Churches on the Eucharistic question, Cranmer no doubt was the more desirous of securing concord in England ; it is likely, therefore, that we see one fruit of this wish in the xxixth Article of the Synod of this very year (1552) already noticed in the Letter p. 32 ; and nothing can be more probable than that the Archbishop had induced the Convocation to pass the 2nd paragraph (denying Transubstantiation) and the 3rd paragraph (rejecting "the reall and bodelie presence") —that very paragraph upon which, as I argued (Letter p. 36) the Declaration was obviously framed—on account of what he understood the Council of Trent to have been enacting ; though it is probable he did not know the precise language of the Decree and Canon which had been passed in its 13th Session, October 11th, 1551.

The Decree, which immediately follows that " On Transubstantiation " and is made to *depend* upon it, runs thus :—

" Wherefore, there is no room left for doubt, that all the faithful of Christ may, according to the custom ever received in the Catholic Church, render in veneration the worship of latria, which is due to the true God, to this most holy sacrament. For not therefore is it the less to be adored on this account, that it was instituted by Christ, the Lord, in order to be received : for we believe that same God to be present therein, of whom the eternal Father, when introducing Him into the world, says ; *And let all the angels of God adore Him ;* whom the Magi *falling down, adored ;* who, in fine, as the Scripture testifies, was adored by the Apostles in Galilee."—*Canons and Decrees of the Council of Trent* p. 79, Waterworth's Translation.

It is not improbable that the Archbishop may have been informed of the substance of this Decree: if so, he would no doubt consider that the earlier part of it (especially as based upon the Decree on Transubstantiation) tended to uphold the popular view of a *carnal* Presence ; and thus he would be the more eager to guard the Eucharistic Doctrine in those Articles which· were then passing. The Canon, indeed, which was founded upon this Decree is not, in its first clause, open to this objection : for it only declares :— ·

> " If any one saith, that, **in** the holy sacrament of the Eucharist, **Christ,** the only-begotten Son of God, is not to be adored with the worship, even external of latria ; . . . . let him be anathema."

But then, even if Cranmer had known of this Canon, he might naturally fear that the way in which it immediately proceeds to defend the *popular practices* of adoration would be likely to obscure this statement and foster the prevalent grosser belief : for it runs on, after the word "latria," thus :—

> " and is, consequently, neither to be venerated with a special festive solemnity, nor to be solemnly borne about in processions, according to the laudable and universal rite and custom of holy church ; or, is not to be proposed publicly to the people to be adored, and that the adorers thereof are idolators ; let him be anathema."—*Canon* vi. Ibid. p. 83.

In the Archbishop's judgment the practices thus maintained under the Council's anathema, and by it tied to the Doctrine of Transubstantiation, had been so connected in the minds of the people with the physical Presence, as to be neither safe nor profitable ; yet, in marked contrast with the vehemence of the Council, all that he and his Synod, speaking in the name of the Church of England, say, is—

> " The Sacramente of the Lordes Supper was not commaunded by Christes ordinàunce to be kepte, carried about, lifted up, nor worshipped."—*Art.* xxix of 1552.

He might well, therefore, think it all the more important to explain by way of Declaration that *kneeling* as ordered by the Church of England did not imply any belief in Transubstantiation ; especially as he knew that they who opposed the required practice would, probably, be only too ready to accuse her of maintaining, by a Ceremonial act prescribed to the people, what they would be compelled to admit she had disavowed in a Formulary to be subscribed by the Clergy.

Thus far I have argued Cranmer's probable meaning, upon the supposition that the objections to the Rubric enforcing Kneeling came from the Zwinglian party, and were based upon purely Doctrinal grounds : but, though we have no positive information on the subject, we are not left wholly to conjecture the source whence they proceeded: there is much reason for thinking that JOHN KNOX was really the objector whom the Archbishop had especially to withstand; yet doubtless he was the mouthpiece of a party and, too, we may be sure he would be no unwelcome advocate for those whom I have already noticed, notwithstanding their Doctrinal differences.

Knox (who had been ordained Priest about 1530) was appointed one of the Six Royal Chaplains in December 1551 : in this character he had, in October 1552, to revise the Articles then in preparation, as we learn from *Strype*, who, quoting the Council Book, says :—

" .... I find that ' October 2, a letter was directed to Mr. Harley, Bill, Horn, Grindal, Perne, and Knox, to consider certain Articles (which must be these Articles of Religion), exhibited to the King's majesty, to be subscribed by all such as shall be admitted to be preachers or ministers in any part of the realm ; and to make report of their opinions touching the same.' "—*Life of Cranmer*, Bk. ii. c. 28.

And in a Letter from JOHN UTENHOVIUS to HENRY BULLINGER, dated " London, Oct. 12, 1552," there occurs the following passage :—

" Some disputes have arisen within these few days among the bishops, in consequence of a sermon of a pious preacher, chaplain to the duke of Northumberland, preached by him before the King and Council, in which he inveighed with great freedom against kneeling at the Lord's supper, which is still retained here in England. This good man, however, a Scotsman by nation, has so wrought upon the minds of many persons, that we may hope some good to the Church will at length arise from it ; which I earnestly implore the Lord to grant."—*Orig. Letters*, Parker Society, p. 591.

Now, though Knox is not here mentioned by name, there can be little doubt that the passage refers to him ; for (1) First, his office of Royal Chaplain would account for his preaching before this congregation : (2) Next, the writer (who does not seem to have known much of the preacher) may, likely enough, have been ignorant of his recent promotion : (3) Thirdly, though there seems no more reliable record of his having been Chaplain * to the Duke, it may be inferred that he had been, both from his appointment in 1549 "to a preachership at Berwick-on-Tweed" by "the English Privy Council," (of which his Grace was then a most active member,) and also from the circumstance of his preaching "at Newcastle, April 4, 1550, before the Council of the North for public affairs":† (4) Fourthly, Northumberland's interest in Knox, probably because he had been his Chaplain, is shewn by his Letter to Cecil about the same time, (Oct. 28, 1552,) in which he writes :—

"I would to God it might please the King's Majesty to appoint Mr. Knocks to the office of Rochester bishopric ; which, for three purposes, would do very well. The first, he would not only be a whetstone, to quicken and sharp the Archbishop of Canterbury, whereof he hath need ; but also he would be a great confounder of the Anabaptists lately sprung up in Kent......"—*Orig.* St. P. Off. *Domestic*, in Tytler's Reigns of Edw. vi. &c. ii. p. 142.

That Knox did preach before Edward the Sixth is certain from the fact that he himself mentions it in his "Admonition to the professors of God's truth in England", published in 1554: he there relates, too, what he had said in his Sermon, as to the character of some of the King's councillors, which, supported as it is by other historical testimony, may fairly lead us to infer—that the sympathies of leading members of the Council were not so entirely with the Reforming movement as is commonly supposed, though other motives apparently induced them to forward it, for Northumberland himself died professing to be a Romanist. Knox repeats his conviction of the truth of his allegations in these words:—

"I affirme, that under that innocent Kinge pestilent Papistes had greatest authoritie. Oh! who was judged to be the soule and lyfe to the counsel in every matter of weiaghty importance ? Who but Sobna. Who could best dispatche busynesses, that the

* That he was not Chaplain to Northumberland on the 11th Dec. 1552 may be gathered from the fact, that on that day the Duke recommended his Chaplain "for the King's presentation to the Vicarage of Kidderminster, which Mr. Harley, now Bishop of Hereford, had." (Letter to Cecil. *Orig.* St. P. Office. Domestic Edw. vi. Vol. xv. No. 70.) At this time the serious dispute (mentioned below, p. 95,) had occurred between Northumberland and Knox.
† Hardwicke's Reformation, p. 148.

rest of the Counsel might hauke & hunt, and take their pleasure? None lyke unto Sobna. Who was most frantic and ready to destroy Somerset and set up Northumberland? Was it not Sobna?...... the Treasurer.' "

By Sobna, *i e.* Shebna, he " refers to Sir William Paulet, created in 1551 Marquess of Winchester, who was successively Comptroller, Secretary, and Lord Treasurer to Edward the Sixth, and was continued in that office by Queen Mary."—*Laing's* Knox, vol. 3, p. 283.

It may be thought, perhaps, that the way in which Knox here speaks of Northumberland is adverse to the supposition of the latter being his patron; but the fact is, that their regard for each other (whether ever very sincere or not) had undergone a material change. Elsewhere in the " Admonition" Knox calls the Duke " that wretched (alas) and miserable Northumberlande "; and, again, he asks " who, I pray you, ruled the roste in the courte all this time, by stoute corage and proudness of stomak, but Northumberland?" (*Laing,* pp. 277 & 280.) It was barely seven weeks after the Duke had recommended Knox for the Bishopric of Rochester that he wrote thus to the Secretary Cecil:

" Master Knox's being here to speak with me, saying that he was so willed by you, I do return him again, because I love not to have to do with men which be neither grateful nor pleasable. I assure you I mind to have no more to do with him but to wish him well, neither also with the Dean of Durham, because, under the colour of a false conscience, he can prettily malign and judge of others against good charity upon a froward judgment. And this manner you might see in his letter, that he cannot tell whether I be a dissembler in religion or not: but I have for twenty years stand [stood] to one kind of religion, in the same which I do now profess ; and have, I thank the Lord, past no small dangers for it."—*Orig.* St. P. Off. 7th Dec. 1552, in *Tytler's* Edw. vi. vol. ii. p. 148.

The breach thus opened was made wider by Knox's political preaching at Newcastle in the following year, in which he lamented the fall of Somerset, and thus led Northumberland to complain of him, in February, to the Council ; nor was it ever healed.

Another indication that Knox it was who had mainly provoked the Archbishop's Letter, occurs in one line of a "*Memoranda of matters to be brought before the Council,*" dated

Oct. 20, 1552, (St. P. Office. *Domestic*, Edw. vi. Vol. xv.
No. 20,) which runs thus:—

" Mr. Knocks—b. of Cat^{rb.} | ye book in y^t [*or* y^e] B. of Durh"

This note is just 13 days after the Primate's Letter
(p. 77), and 7 days before the Letter to the Lord Chancellor
(p. 35) to add the Declaration: the juxta-position of Knox
and Cranmer and the mention of *the book*, though separated
from their names, I cannot but conjecture to be notes touching
this dispute on Kneeling which was settled at the Council of
Oct. 27th by ordering the Declaration. The remaining part
of the Memorandum probably refers to the subject of
appointing a Bishop of Durham, which Northumberland was
then urging upon the Council: but whether " ye book " relates to some Document connected with the See of Durham,
or refers, as I think, to the Prayer Book then under discussion, the *former part* of the Note looks very much indeed
like an allusion to Knox's alleged complaint of the Rubric
on Kneeling and the Archbishop's defence of it.

Further, early in the next year, under date Feb. 2, 1552-3,
the Council Book contains the following entry:—

" At Westminster, the seconde of Fibruary 1552 A lettre to the
Archbusshop of Caunterbury in favour of Mr. Knokes, to be presented to the Vicaredge or Personage of Allhallows, in Bredestrete,
in his Lordship's disposition, by the preferment of Thomas Sampson
to the Deanry of Chichester."

This occurrence, and certain consequent proceedings of the
Council against Knox, related in the following passage, serve
still more to identify the Northern Reformer with the dispute
as to this Rubric on Kneeling. Mr. Laing remarks:—

" Knox's refusal of this living was one of the grounds upon which
he was summoned to appear before the Privy Council, as we learn
from a letter written by him in April 1553. The letter itself has
not been discovered; but Calderwood has preserved what seems to
be a full abstract of it, in his larger Manuscript History, in connection with some extracts from his ' Admonition,' which was written
and published the following year......
" ' In a letter, dated the 14th of April 1553, and written with his
own hand, I find (says Calderwood) that he was called before the
Council of England for kneeling, who demanded of him these

questions. First, Why he refused the benefice provided for him. Secondly, Whether he thought that no Christian might serve in the Ecclesiastical ministration according to the rites and lawes of the realme of England? Thirdly, If kneeling at the Lord's table was not indifferent?

"'....To the third he answered, That Christ's action in itself was most perfect, and Christ's action was done without kneeling; that kneeling was man's addition or imagination; that it was most sure to follow the example of Christ, whose action was done sitting and not kneeling.'

"'In this last question there was great contention betwixt the whole table of the Lords and him. There were present there the Bishops of Canterbury and Ely, my Lord Treasurer, the Marquis of Northampton, the Earl of Bedford, the Earl of Shrewsbury, Master Comptroller, my Lord Chamberlain, both the Secretaries, and other inferior Lords. After long reasoning, it was said to him, that he was not called of any evil mind *; they were sorry to know him of a contrary mind to the common Order. He answered, that he was more sorry that a common Order should be contrary to Christ's institution. With some gentle speeches he was dismissed, and willed to advise with himself if he would communicate after that Order."—*Knox's Works.* Vol. iii. p. 83. Edinburgh, 1854.

A careful examination of the Council Book,† though it enabled me to verify the extracts from Burnet and Strype at p. 35, has failed to furnish any additional particulars illustrative of the course pursued by the Council subsequently to the Archbishop's Letter. The Book contains, in fact, only short minutes of the Council's Meetings, any transcripts of Documents connected with the business transacted were kept elsewhere, and what remain are now preserved in the State Paper Office and other repositories of the Public Records. Perhaps the Council's Letter to the Lord Chancellor, Thos. Goodrick Bishop of Ely, (referred to at p. 35,) may have contained some *reason* for the insertion of the Declaration on Kneeling, but this Document does not seem to exist.

From the little we know of Goodrick himself, there is every reason to conclude that he was not likely to have been a party

---

* Certainly this is confirmed by the fact recorded (barely two months later) in the Council Book, under date June 2nd, 1553, that the Council, including the Abp. of Canterbury, wrote a Letter in favour of Knox to several gentlemen in Buckinghamshire. He quotes in his " Admonition" what he had preached at " Hammershame," *i.e.* Amersham, in that county.

† For the facility afforded me in doing this, I have to acknowledge the polite attention of Henry Reeve, Esq., of the Privy Council Office.

to any statement committing the Church of England to hete-
rodox teaching on the subject of the Real Presence; there
seems nothing to shew that he was at all a time-serving Prelate in the way of, what I may call, Continental Protestantism:
rather his tendencies, as alleged in the following Biographical
notice of him, appear to have been in the opposite direction :—

"he had a hand in compiling ...... the Institution of a Christian
man ...... in 1551, he was made Lord Chancellor of England, in
the room of Lord Rich, which office he discharged with singular re-
putation of integrity, though in matters of Religion he was suspected
by some, of too much disposition to temporize in favour of popery,
upon the accession of Queen Mary; and Dodd, though somewhat
faintly, claims him as a popish bishop.   It is certain he was suffered
to retain his bishopric to 'his death, although the seals were taken
from him."—*Chalmers' Biog. Dict.* Vol. xvi. p. 100.

Burnet's opinion coincides with this, though (as is too
often the case with that Prelate who yet was not quite the
person to be thus uncharitable) he indulges in somewhat
severe remarks upon the Chancellor: he says, with regard to
his promotion, that

" .... as *Goodrick* was raised by the Popish interest in opposition
to the Duke of *Somerset*, and to *Cranmer*, that was his firm friend;
so it appeared in the beginning of Queen *Maries* Reign, that he was
ready to turn with every tide: and that whether he joyned in the
Reformation only in compliance to the time, or was perswaded in his ,
mind concerning it; yet he had not that sense of it that became a
Bishop, and was one of those who resolved to make as much advantage by it as he could, but would suffer nothing for it."—*Hist. Ref.*
bk. ii. pt. 1, p. 173, fol. 1715.

Another link, however, in the chain of evidence is supplied
in *Foxe's* account of *Latimer's Disputation at Oxford,* April
18, 1554, already quoted from at p. 39.   *Weston,* one of his
opponents, thus addressed him :—

" Well, master Latimer, this is our intent, to will you well, and
to exhort you to come to yourself, and remember, that without Noah's
ark there is no health.   Remember what they have been, that were
the beginners of your doctrine :· none but a few flying apostates,
running out of Germany for fear of the faggot.   Remember what
they have been which have set forth the same in this realm : a sort
of fling-brains and light-heads, which were never constant in any one
thing ; as it was to be seen in the turning of the table, where like a

sort of apes, they could not tell which way to turn their tails, looking one day west, and another day east; one that way, and another this way. They will be like (they say) to the apostles, they will have no churches. A hovel is good enough for them. They come to the communion with no reverence. They get them a tankard, and one saith, I drink, and I am thankful: the more joy of thee, saith another. And in them was it true that Hilary saith, ' Annuas et menstruas de Deo fides facimus ;' that is, ' We make every year and every month a faith.' *A runagate Scot did take away the adoration or worshipping of Christ in the Sacrament, by whose procurement that heresy was put into the last Communion-book: so much prevailed that one man's authority at that time* . . . .—*Acts and Monuments,* vol. vi. p. 510.

These last words (which I have *italicised*) would naturally be thought to refer to Knox by any one aware of the prominent position which he at that time occupied; taken with the statements just before quoted they, apparently, are conclusive on the point. Moreover, the former part of *Weston's* accusation looks in the same direction; and (making due allowance for their author and for what we should call, the not very refined language of the period,) describes just such a character as that depicted by Cranmer in his Letter, where he deprecates the " gloriouse and unquiet spirites wᶜʰ can like nothing but that is after their own fansye," and who choose to assert that "whatsoever is not commaunded in the scripture is against the scripture, and utterly unlawfull and ungodlie."

But Dr. Townsend, the Editor of Foxe, throws a doubt upon *Weston's* meaning by appending to the expression, " a runagate Scot," the following note:—

" Alexander Ales, or Alesius, who translated the first Liturgy of Edward vi. into Latin. See Dr. Watkins' note in his life of Latimer, prefixed to his Sermons (Lond. 1824). p. ciii."

I have not succeeded in finding the book here referred to, and therefore are unable to examine the evidence which Dr. Watkins furnishes. The Parker Society's Editor of *Latimer's Remain's* affixes to Weston's expression a note similar to that of Dr. Townsend: he says—

" The person here alluded to is with reason supposed to have been Alexander Aless, a native of Edinburgh, and who was for some time an exile in Germany on account of his adherence to the doctrines of the reformation. He was employed to translate the first liturgy of King Edward vi. into Latin. See Wordsworth, Eccles. Biogr. Vol. v. pp. 247, note 2 ; 604, note 3, 3rd. Edit."—*Latimer's Remains*, Parker Society, Vol. 2. 1845.

Pursuing then the enquiry by this direction what does Dr. Wordsworth state ? His note upon Weston's expression runs thus; I quote from the 4th Ed. 1853, being the only one to which I have access :—

" ' Strype referring to these words of Weston, says, "But there was no Scot that ever I could read or hear of, that assisted at the review of ' that Communion Book.' " *Eccles. Memor.* vol. iii. p. 117. The person alluded to by Weston, I doubt not, was Alexander Aless, a Scottish exile, of whose good services we met with some account in the life of Cromwell (see p. 250), and who translated the first liturgy of King Edward into Latin, preparatory to the review in question, for the use of Martin Bucer, and Peter Martyr, who did not possess a sufficient knowledge of the English language, to qualify them to make their remarks upon the original. See Buceri *Scripta Anglicana*."—*Eccles. Biog.* Vol. v. p. 606. 4th Ed. 1853.

Yet though it is somewhat bold to question the conclusions of these three modern authorities, supported as they are by Strype, I venture to believe that a little examination of Strype's words and a comparison of dates will satisfactorily shew that *Alesius* could not have been the person intended by Weston.

For, as to Strype, (i.) First,(though he was probably accurate in concluding that "no Scot .... assisted at the review of ' that Communion Book,'" historically supporting this position, as he does, by adding to Dr. Wordsworth's quotation the sentence "And indeed Cranmer, Ridley, and Cox, were the chief that managed that affair, though they consulted with Bucer and Peter Martyr") he had either mistaken Weston's allusion and thought he was referring to the *revision* of Edward's 1st Book, or else he did not know or had forgotten at the time that the Declaration on Kneeling (to which Weston evidently refers) was not added until after the Book as revised had received the sanction of Parliament and the Crown.

(ii.) Secondly, Strype was apparently only imperfectly acquainted with Knox's movements at this time; for he thus continues the passage just cited:—

" And as for Knox, the Scotchman, he was hardly come into England (at least any further than Newcastle) at this time, much less had anything to do with that work."

But as we have seen (p. 93) Knox was appointed a Royal Chaplain in December 1551 ; the Act of Uniformity was not passed till April 6, 1552; and Knox, as Strype himself states (see p. 93), was appointed on Oct 2, 1552, to revise the Articles of Religion in his capacity of King's Chaplain. So that here is presumptive evidence of his presence not being wholly new in London or at the Court when called upon by the Council to assist in this latter responsible task.

(iii.) Thirdly, Strype was seemingly disinclined to believe Weston (as is often his wont with regard to Romanist writers); though had he known or remembered John Utenhovius's Letter (see p. 93) and Cranmer's Letter to the Council (on which I am now commenting,) it is very unlikely that he would have written as he did with regard to the allegation that " a runagate Scot " caused the " heresy," as Weston chose to call it, of the Declaration on Kneeling to be " put into the last Communion-book." It is much more likely that he would have coincided with the judgment of the Editor of Utenhovius's Letter, who says—

" The preacher referred to was probably Knox, though it does not appear that he was ' chaplain to the Duke of Northumberland': but possibly this may have been a mistake on the part of the writer." —*Orig. Letters*, Parker Society, 1847. Vol. ii. p. 592.

Thus much, then, with regard to Strype's statement. As to *Aless*, who is supposed by the writers I have quoted to be aimed at by Weston, *dates* seem to put it almost out of the question that he could have been meant. Indeed it is somewhat surprising that they all, apparently, omitted to enquire where Alesius was at the revision of 1552: this is the more remarkable in Dr. Wordsworth's case, for in his notice of *Alesius*, in the very volume from which I have been quoting, he thus speaks of him :—

" After the fall of Cromwell he returned to Germany, and was made professor of divinity at Frankfort on the Oder, which place he soon left in consequence of giving offence to the Elector of Brandenburg. He returned to Leipsig, and was there also chosen professor of divinity, which post he retained till his death in 1565."—*Eccles. Biog.* vol. v. p. 250.

I quote also another account of him: Chalmers says—

" The change of religion, which happened in England after the marriage of Henry viii with Anna Boleyn, induced Ales to go to London, in 1535, where he was highly esteemed by Cranmer, archbishop of Canterbury, Latimer, and Thomas Cromwel, who was at that time in favour with the King. Upon the fall of these favorites [*i. e.* in 1540], he was obliged to return to Germany [whither he had retired from his canonry of St. Andrew's some few years before], when the Elector of Brandenburg appointed him professor of divinity at Frankfort upon the Oder, in 1540."—*Biog. Dict.* Vol. i. p. 401.

It appears, therefore, that for 25 years, viz. from 1540 to 1565, that is to say during the latter part of Henry's, the whole of Edward's, and the former part of Elizabeth's reigns, *Aless* was residing on the Continent: nor am I aware that, beyond his translation of Edward's 1st Book already mentioned, there is anything to indicate that he took any part in or materially influenced the English Reformation movement, after he left England in 1540. Moreover everything tends to shew that the influence brought to bear upon the Privy Council, in reference to the question of Kneeling at the Sacrament was then a *local* one: and, too, that it was mainly a sudden movement, *subsequent* to the *completion* of the Book of 1552, and therefore one from which lack of time alone must probably have excluded the operation of any such distant action as that of Alesius.

All these considerations seem, consequently, to make it almost, if not wholly, a moral certainty that *John Knox* was, as I have argued, the person to whom Weston referred, whom Cranmer answered in his Letter to the Council, and whose objections led to the Declaration on Kneeling.

There is another noticeable point in Weston's words to Latimer. To the expression " They will be like (they say) to the apostles," Foxe appends a note which is specially to be observed; the more so as he was a *contemporary* historian, and certainly no favourer of Roman doctrine. He asks:—

" Who be these, or who be they, master'oblocutor, that will be like the Apostles, that will have no churches?—that be runagates out of Germany?—that get them tankards?—that make monthly faiths?—that worship not Christ in all his Sacraments?—Speak truth man and shame the devil."

Here we have a very just rebuke to Weston, the Prolocutor, whose object plainly was to damage the *English Reforms*, by identifying them with certain extreme offshoots of the Foreign Reformation; for, while it cannot be denied that the relations of these latter to the English Bishops were much too intimate not to be prejudicial to the Church of England, Weston was too well versed in the occurrences of Edward's reign not to know that he was libelling the Eucharistic Offices, which had been prepared under the King's authority, and was maligning their compilers. He could not but be aware that the Doctrinal, Ritual, and Ceremonial changes sprang mainly from the English Episcopate, and had been carried on by the Church of England's own organization. It was quite within the compass of his information—that, although certain leading Foreigners had been taken into counsel, yet, the English Ecclesiastical authorities were guided by principles definite enough to exclude heretical innovations in Faith and Practice; nor could he be ignorant of the fact that, eager as Cranmer and others were to provide comprehensive forms of Divine Service, they were fully alive to the danger of seeming to countenance the extravagancies of certain Continental residents in England who were anxious to shelter themselves under an apparent shadow of the English Reformation. Let it be assumed that even Weston's strong language is not an overdrawn description of some few of these (though Foxe's comment seems to bespeak a more charitable view) the acrimonious Prolocutor could not but have been fully cognizant of their antagonism to the leading Anglican Reformers. That they were a source of great disquiet to the Archbishop, notwithstanding all he was disposed to yield, must have been sufficiently evident at the time: his Letter to the Privy Council, now produced, furnishes *us* with important additional testimony to the same effect.

Though, however, we may fairly claim Foxe's responsive

question—" Who be these.... that worship not Christ in all his Sacraments ? "—as a proof that Weston's charge was both false and malicious when he asserted that the Declaration on Kneeling (for to that he must have referred) " did take away adoration or worshipping of Christ in the Sacrament"; it becomes all the more important to consider whether Knox *aimed* at such a result, now that we may say, I think, that *he* was the proximate cause of this explanatory addition to the Eucharistic Offices of Edward's 2nd Prayer Book.

To determine this point, two enquiries must be made; *First*, What was Knox's alleged objection to kneeling? *Next*, Was there anything in his opinions on the Real Presence which would lead him to deny that worship was due to Christ in the Eucharist?

With respect to the first of these questions some information has been already furnished in Cranmer's Letter (p. 77) and Knox's answer to the Privy Council (p. 97): his language on three other occasions is of precisely the same character. Thus, in "A Vindication of the Doctrine that the Sacrifice of the Mass is Idolatry. 1550", he says:—

" ....All wirschipping, honouring, or service inventid by the braine of man in the religioun of God, without his own express commandment, is Idolatrie...."—*Laing's Knox*, Vol. iii. p. 34.

So, again, in his " Faythful admonition unto the Professours of God's truthe in England," written probably at Dieppe (where he seems to have remained from the end of May to the 20th July 1554 in order, as he says, to " learn the estait of Ingland and Scotland".) and " Imprinted at Kalykow [apparently, as Mr. Laing thinks (Vol. 3, p. 253) a fictitious name for Dieppe], the 20. daye of Julii 1554"; he writes thus, evidently referring to Edward's 2nd Book:—

" And also God gave boldnesse and knowledge to the court of Parliament to take awaye the round clipped God, wherein standeth al the holines of the Papistes, and also to commaunde common breade to be used at the Lorde's table ; and also to take awaye the moste parte of superstitions (kneling at the Lorde's table excepted) which before prophaned Christes true religion."—*Laing's Knox*, Vol. 3, p. 279.

Six years afterwards he states his view even more expli-

citly in the " Buke of Discipline May 20. 1560 "; his words
are :—

" The Tabill of the Lord is then most rychtlie ministred, quhen
it approacheth most ney to Christis awin actioun. But plane it is,
that at that Supper, Christ Jesus sat with his discipillis, and thairfoir do we juge, that sitting at a table is most convenient to that holie
actioun :.. ..
" That the Minister breik the breid, and distribute the same to
those that be nyxt unto him, commaunding the rest, every one with
reverence and sobrietie, to breake with other, we think it nyest to
Christis actioun, and to the perfite practice [of the Apostles,] as we
read it in Sanct Paull.—*Laing's Knox*, Vol. 2, p. 114.

Such was Knox's studied and uniform language on five
occasions, at intervals from 1550 to 1560, that is to say *before
contemporaneous with*, and *subsequent to* the Book of 1552 :
and it is abundantly plain that he objected to kneeling at the
Sacrament from an alleged (need we doubt it a real, however
mistaken,) reverence for Christ's institution : he accounted it
a mere *human* (not even an *apostolic*) polity, and, as such, not
convenient, but *superstitious* and *idolatrous*.

Unless, then, it can be certainly affirmed that Knox held
that Christ was neither adorable nor adored when giving
Himself to His disciples at the institution of the Eucharist,
we are not, I conceive, entitled to argue that he refused to
kneel, when the Church commemorated that act, because it
betokened a worship of Christ: rather we ought, I think, to
argue that he designed to render the same honour to Christ
which was due and rendered by His Apostles when receiving
from Himself His Body and Blood; and that had he been
convinced of *kneeling* being the " most nigh to Christ's own
action" he would not have accounted it either *superstitious* or
idolatrous, but just that posture which "is most convenient
to that holy action," because he considered " that it was most
sure to follow the example of Christ" and " the perfect practice of the Apostles ".

But I proposed also to enquire whether kneeling, as implying worship of Christ, was obnoxious to the Scotch Reformer
on account of his views of Christ's Eucharistic Presence.

One statement of his opinions, two years before his remon-

strance against the Rubric of Edward's 2nd Book, occurs in
" A summary, according to the Holy Scriptures, of the Scra-
ment of the Lord's Supper.   1550"; it is as follows:—

"First, we confess that it is ane holie actioun, ordaynit of
God....
By it " he confirmeth and sealleth up to us his promeis and communion....
"And also that heirwith the Lord Jesus gathereth us unto ane
visibill bodie....and....calleth us to rememberance of his Death
and Passioun......
"And as concerning theis wordis, *Hoc est corpus meum*,....we
acknowledge that it [transubstantiation] is no artikill of our faith
which can saif us......And again, yf we do not believe his bodilie
presence in the bread and wine, that sall not dampn us, but the
absence out of our hart throw unbelief.
"Now, yf thai wold heir object, that....yit ar we bound to believe
it because of God's word....we answer, That we believe God's
Word, and confess that it is trew, but not so to be understand as the
Papistis grosslie affirme.   For in the Sacrament we receive
Jesus Christ spirituallie, as did the Fatheris of the Old Testament,
according to St. Paulis saying.   And yf men wold weill way, how
that Chryst, ordeyning this Halie Sacrament of his bodie and blude,
spake theis wordis Sacramentallie, doubtless thai wold never so
grosslie and foolischlie understand thame, contrary to all the Scriptures, and to the exposition of St. Augustine, St. Hierome, Fulgentius, Vigilius, Origines, and many other godlie writers."—*Laing's
Knox*, Vol. 3, p. 74.

Another evidence of what was uppermost in his mind, at
the time now under consideration, is found in a passage of
his " Admonition," of which I have already (at p. 104) quoted
the conclusion; he exclaims in his own, and indeed the
period's, strong and coarse style:—

" Transubstantiation, the byrde that the Devel hatched by Pope
Nicholas, and sythe that tyme fostered and nurryshed by al his
children, prestes, freres, monks, and other his conjured and sworne
souldiers, and in this laste dayes, chiefly by Stephen Gardiner and
his blacke broode in England,—Transubstantiation (I saye) was not
then clearly confuted and myghtely overthrowen, and therefore God
put wysedome in the tounges of his ministers and messengers to utter
[*i.e.* to disclose or expose] that vayne vanitie : and specially gave
such strength to the penne* of that reverend father in God, Thomas
Cranmer, Archebysshop of Canterbury, to cut the knottes of develyshe
sophistrie, lyncked and knyt by the Devil's Gardener, and his blynd
bussardes, to holde the veritie of God under bondage, that rather I

* Referring to "Cranmer's Defence," &c. 1550.

thinke they shal condemne his workes, (whiche, notwithstanding, shal continue and remaine to their confusion), then they shal enterprise to answer the same."—*Laing's Knox*, vol. 3, p. 279.

Further; two years after this; in "The maner of the Lorde's Supper" as "used in the Englishe Congregation at Geneva" 1556, "approued, by the famous and godly learned man, John Caluyn" and which Knox assisted to prepare, the "exhortation" says :—

" . . . . let us not suffer our mindes to wander aboute the consideration of these earthlie thynges (which we see present to our eis, and fele with our handes,) to seek Christ bodely presente in them, as if he were inclosed in the breade or wyne, or as yf these elementes were tourned and chaunged into the substaunce of his fleyshe and blood."—*Laing's* Knox, vol. 4, p. 194.

Once more; let me call attention to "The Confessione of the Faythe," 17 Aug. 1560, where in Chap. xxi, "Off the Sacramentis" we read thus :—

" . . . . in the Supper, rychtlie used, Christ Jesus is so joyned with us, that he becumis the verray nurishment and foode of our saullis. Not that we ymagine any transsubstantiatioun of bread into Christis naturall body, and of wyne in his naturall bloode, (as the Papistes have perniciouslie taught and dampnablie beleved;) but this union and communioun whiche we have with the bodye and bloode of Christ Jesus in the rycht use of the sacraments, is wròcht by operatioun of the Holy Ghost, who by trew faith caryes us above all thingis that ar visibile, carnall, and earthlie, and maikis us to feid upoun the body and bloode of Christe Jesus, whiche was ones brokin and schedd for us, whiche now is in the heavin, and appeareth in the presence of his Father for us. And yit, notwithstanding the far distance of place, whiche is betwix his bodye now glorified in the heavin, and us now mortall in this earth, yit we most assuredlie beleve, that the bread which we break is the communion of Christis body, and the cupp which we bless is the communion of his bloode. . . . . But all this, we say, cumis by trew fayth, whiche apprehendeth Christ Jesus, who onlie maikis his Sacramentis effectuall unto us ; and thairfoir, whosoever sclandereth us, as that we affirmed or beleved Sacramentis to be onlie nakid and bair signes, do injurie unto us, and speak against a manifest treuth. But this liberallie and francklie we most confess, that we maik ane distinctioun betwix Christ Jesus, in his naturall substance,* and betwix the elementis in the Sacramentall signes ; so that we will neather wirschip the signes in place of that which is signified by thame ; neather yit do we dispyse and interpret thame as unprofitable and vane ; . . . ."—*Laing's Knox*, vol. 2, pp. 114 and 115.

* " In the old printed copies, ' in his eternall substance.' "

Now it is unnecessary, for my purpose, to enquire whether these quotations imply a full appreciation, by their author, of the Catholic Doctrine of the Real Objective Presence ; though, in truth, some of the language exceeds what probably would be used by many who disclaim all sympathy with Knox, and would be sorry to lie under the least suspicion of not being greatly in advance of his Sacramental views. The question here is—are they inconsistent with such a belief in Christ's Eucharistic Presence as could accord worship to Him in the Sacrament of the Altar ("the Supper" as Knox calls it); or must they have excluded all idea of both from the mind of him who used them ? I humbly think not.

It is abundantly evident, indeed, that a vehement antipathy to the doctrine of TRANSUBSTANTIATION was uppermost in Knox's thoughts; and that he dreaded, as its necessary consequence, the belief of a "*carnall*," "*bodely*," "*naturall*," "*grosslie*" affirmed, presence of Christ "*inclosed*" in the elements : though, on the other hand, he advocates the use of the term "*sacramentallie*" as being consonant to Holy Scripture and the "exposition" of the Fathers, whose teaching he does not shrink from avowing, howsoever he may have construed it; and he, apparently, accepts Cranmer's published "Defence" as a true exponent of Eucharistic Doctrine.

But in his Formulary of 1560, which may not with any fairness be assumed to record higher and more Catholic sentiments than he held in 1552, he uses an expression which I cannot but consider as warranting the negative answer just given to the question suggested by the before-cited passages. For Knox's "Confession," after pointing out "ane distinctioun betwix Christ Jesus, in his naturall substance, and betwix the elementes in the Sacramentall signes," declares this conclusion—"so that we will neather *wirschip* the *signes* in *place* of *that which is signified* by thame; neather yet do we dispyse and interprete thame as unprofitable and vane." As, however, Sacraments are just before declared not "to be *onlie nakid* and *bair* signes"; but "the bread which we break is the *communion* of Christ's body, and the cupp which we bless is the *communion* of his bloode," "notwithstanding the

far distance of place, whiche is betwix his bodye now glorified in the heavin, and us now mortall in this earth," need we
infer that Knox meant to refuse adoration in the Sacrament
to Him Whose Body and Blood he declares (here and in the
"Summary") to be "spirituallie" communicated "in the
rycht use" of the Lord's Supper? Rather, should we not
endeavour to construe, in the most Catholic sense of which
they are fairly capable, the (necessarily well weighed) terms
of this public Formulary of Faith ; and therefore charitably
assume that he did mean to uphold the worship "of that
which is signified," while rightly condemning the worship of
"the signes." Let it be granted here, for argument's sake,
that *the utmost* he meant to teach was—that in the act of reception only Christ was sacramentally present to communicate
Himself—and there seems sufficient in such a doctrine to have
led him to kneel at that time in token of adoration of Christ,
if only he could have regarded *that posture* as consistent with
his theory of legitimate worship and, more especially, of the
pattern to be followed in the Celebration of the Eucharist.

Moreover it is important to recollect that at the very period
when Knox raised his objection to "kneeling at the tyme of
the receavinge of the Sacrament," he must have concurred in
the theological decisions of the English Convocation; unless
indeed he received the Forty-two Articles of 1552 in a non-
natural sense: for his signature (and the signatures of the
other five Royal Chaplains*) is attached to a copy of them

* As it is of some importance to know whether Knox was or was not one of
King Edward's six Chaplains, it seems worth while to advert to a statement made
by Mr. Barnes the Editor of a new Edition of Strype's Memorials of Cranmer,
2 vols., Routledge and Co., 1853.

At p. 423, Vol. 1, Strype, after mentioning the application to the Archbishop
(see p. 96) to present Knox to All-hallows Bread-street, makes this remark:—
"This Knox was the man whose name was so dashed in the King's Journal,
where the names of the King's six Chaplains were inserted, that Bishop Burnet
could not read it. (Collect. Vol. ii. p. 42.)"

To this passage Mr. Barnes the Editor, appends the following note "[vol. ii.
part 2, p. 43. Notwithstanding that Knox has been hitherto supposed to have
been one of Enward VI.'s chaplains, upon the authority of Burnet, of which
Strype availed himself, it is now positively proved that his was not the name,
'dashed in the King's Journal,' the Editor of this work for the Ecclesiastical
History Society, with the assistance of Sir Frederic Madden, having discovered
that the name erased was ' Eastwick,' and not ' Knox.']"

It is not clear whether the Editor intends in this note to deny absolutely that
Knox was one of the Royal Chaplains, or whether he only means to say that this

submitted for their consideration by the Privy Council on the 21st October; and in this Latin copy, which is in the State Paper Office, the Articles (with no very material and chiefly verbal differences) are found as finally published by Royal Authority in May, 1553.

Now of these Articles two only, the XXIXth and XXXth treat specifically of the Holy Eucharist ; the latter being intitled (in Latin) *"De unica Christi oblatione iu cruce perfecta,"* (in English) *" Of the perfeicte oblacion of Christe made upon the crosse"*; the former being headed (in Latin) *"De Cœna Domini"*, (in English) *" Of the Lord's Supper."* The English version of the XXIXth Article has been already given at p. 32, and consists of four Clauses : in the State Paper Office Latin version the last three parts are treated as separate Articles and denominated thus* (2) Art. XXX. *de Transubstantiatione ;* (3) Art. XXXI. *de Corporali Christi præsentia in Eucharistia ;* (4) Art. XXXII. *Sacramentum Eucharistiæ non asservandum.*

But it seems plain from an inspection of this Article that its whole aim and drift was against the *Roman* doctrine: with this it apparently contents itself: paragraphs 2 and 3 give no

passage in King Edward's journal must not be relied upon in proof of his appointment. So far indeed as anything I can find in Burnet applies he does not seem to have had any doubt who the Chaplains were ; for he says (Part ii. bk. 1, p. 162, fol. 1715) "These were *Bill, Harley, Pern, Grindal, Bradford,* and *Knox ?*' and this list corresponds with that which he furnishes in his copy of the King's journal. And though Strype says "Burnet could not read" Knox's name because it was "so dashed," he does not imply that Burnet was in error. It is not unlikely that Burnet's rendering may have been founded upon some contemporaneous evidence. Indeed if the erased name, in the journal of Dec. 18, 1551, *was* "Eastwick" this need only prove that another was selected in his stead : why may not *Knox* have been that other ? That one alteration was made in the List seems plain, for Strype, in quoting from the Council Book of Oct. 2, 1552, the names of the Chaplains to whom the Book of Articles was sent for revision, gives *Horn* instead of *Bradford* as one of the six—a reference " verified" as the Editor states (p. 394).

But whatever may be the history of the erasure in Edward's journal, it does not in the least detract from the evidence that Knox was a Royal Chaplain at the time of Edward's second Book receiving the sanction of Parliament: this is all that is necessary to identify him with the objection to the new Rubric on Kneeling. Not indeed that I think Mr. Barnes's remark at all discredits Burnet's original List which, it is well to observe, is (except in the case of Horn) *identical* with the Council's List of Oct 2, 1552, and with the names signed to the State Paper Office Copy of the Articles of 1552—a fair presumption, at all events, that Knox was one of the six Chaplains appointed in December 1551.

* See also *Hardwicke* on the Articles p. 300.

indication of being intentionally directed against two several views of the Real Presence; "the reall and bodelie [*realem et corporalem*] presence (as thei terme it) of Christ's flesh and bloude" deprecated in the 3rd Paragraph, seems neither more nor less than the "Transubstantiation" condemned in the 2nd Paragraph. It may, indeed, have been that the language of the 3rd Paragraph of the Article, asserting that "the bodie of Christe cannot bee presente at one time in many and diverse places", was meant to condemn a supposed ubiquitarian doctrine involved in Transubstantiation; if so, it of course tacitly pronounced likewise against Lutheran ubiquitarianism: though, whether or not its authors *contemplated* any allusion to Lutheran doctrine (while an immaterial question here) will be best determined by asking—to whom do the words "as thei terme it" allude? There can hardly be a doubt, I think, that they referred exclusively to the *Roman* party, considering with whom the Eucharistic controversy in England had been carried on and recollecting that the language which has been already quoted shows "**real** and **corporal**" to have been the current phrase which was therein maintained and opposed.

One other view of Eucharistic Doctrine besides the Roman seems indeed to have been *designedly* referred to in the *First* paragraph of the Article: of this probably it may be said (as Mr. Hardwick, p. 104, remarked of Art. xxvi.) that it was "directed....against the prevailing Zwinglian notion, that sacraments were no more than empty rites and external badges": but, as we have seen, the language of Knox alike condemns this. The object of the Article, then, seems limited to a denial of the doctrine of Christ's *absence* from this His Sacrament; and to a refutation of *such* a *Presence* as Transubstantiation was accounted to imply: in Mr. Hardwick's words—

"The twenty-ninth, 'Of the Lord's Supper', while avoiding the errors of the Zwinglian School, condemns the opposite dogma of a physical transubstantiation in the elements, as repugnant to the Word of God, and as inconsistent with the true humanity of our Saviour and his local residence in heaven."—p. 104.

Having regard, therefore, to all these considerations it may with some certainty be assumed, I think, that Knox's objection to kneeling at the Sacrament was not at all founded upon *doctrinal* grounds and that consequently any question of the worship due to Christ therein, or of kneeling being the expression of it, was *foreign* to his purpose in opposing the requirement of the Rubric; and this will further account for the entire absence of theological argument in Cranmer's Letter to the Council: he, as I think has been proved, had at that time mainly to resist an innovation ostensibly based upon a theory of purely Ecclesiastical Order which, in common with his co-advisers and most of (if not all) the Council, the Archbishop refused to recognize.

But, reasonably or not, the objection had been raised; raised, too, by one who was not likely to abandon his opposition but would probably use his opportunities to repeat it in public with the vehemence which had already attracted attention in high quarters and would be certain to secure him a favourable hearing from others also. Further, his indiscriminate charges of superstition, inapplicable though they were to the First Prayer Book, and most inappropriate to the revised English Office, were sure to draw towards the Second Book, that disaffection which had been already exhibited to the earlier Ritual by those who had but little sympathy with Knox save in his denunciation of the Mass.

To yield to Knox's objection was impossible without sacrificing that principle of deference to Antiquity which was a main feature in the English Reformation movement: Cranmer's Letter to the Council shews how hopeless he regarded the attempt; "If such men should bee hearde," he says, "although the boke were made everye yere anewe, yet should it not lacke faultes in their opinion": he declares that upon their theory it were best and necessary to "take awaie the hole boke of service. For what should men travell to sett an ordre in the forme of service, if no ordre can bee sett, but that is alreadye prescribed by the Scripture." This was his answer to Knox's theory of Church Polity; and consistently therewith the Archbishop and his coadjutors dismissed Knox's objection and decided, as the fact of the retention of the

" prescription of kneelinge," shews, that it was " fitt to remayne as a commandement" and ought not " to bee left out
of the boke." That the Scotch Chaplain was *not satisfied* with
their resolution of the Privy Council's question is clear from
the complaint two years afterwards, in his " Admonition"
(see p. 104), that this "parte of superstitions" had not been
taken away.

Yet with the prospect before them of a renewed strife when
the revised Prayer Book should make its appearance; and
looking to the probability that the new Rubric commanding
" kneeling at the tyme of receavinge of the Sacrament" would
be perversely identified with the " decrees respecting the
worship of the host" which the Archbishop lamented to learn
were being passed by the " adversaries....at Trent;" the
natural inference is—that, though Knox's complaint was un-
heeded, it was deemed prudent that the " some" who were
" offended", and all others who might join their ranks, should
be deprived of any such pretence as this for attacking the new
Eucharistic Office. Accordingly it was resolved that neither
by " ignorance and infirmitie" nor by " malice and obstinacie" should the order to kneel be " mysconstrued, depraued,
and interpreted in a wrong parte," as though the Church of
England's rule coincided with the Tridentine Canon then
lately enacted (see page 90) " περὶ τῆς ἀρτολατρίας"—*concerning
the worshipping of the bread with* LATRIA, i.e., *divine honour*—
for such Cranmer evidently feared would be a sort of popular
" idolatry" resulting from the Decree. " And yet because
brotherly charitie willeth, that so muche as conveniently
may be offences should be taken away;" therefore it was
determined to issue with the Rubric an explanatory Declaration of its object.

To whom, then, was the explanation to be addressed?
Not, certainly, to the general mass of the worshippers : for,
first, they were not the complainants : and, next, it would
practically be useless to them, placed as it was to be in a
Book of Public Offices, the price of which alone (though
fixed at a low rate by Royal Authority) limited its purchase,
for the most part, to just the number of copies required by the

Parish Priest and his Clerk or Clerks. Plainly, therefore, the intended exposition of the Rubric on Kneeling was meant to disarm the theological critics of the day, of whatever class, and to furnish the Clergy with an authoritative reply to any cavillers in their parishes who might *invent* objections, or be incited to urge them by some of those disaffected spirits whose position or attainments gained them more or less notoriety.

Such a manifesto, however, needed to be clothed in authorized language if it was to have weight with clergy and people : this in Cranmer's view would, no doubt, be the more necessary as it had to be issued with the Prayer Book which had already. received the sanction of Parliament. The obvious resource, if it furnished the requisite materials, was that Book of " Articles ......for the avoiding of controversie in opinion, and the establishement of a godlie concorde, in certeine matters of Religion" which was then about to be imposed upon the Clergy : it had already undergone the criticism of the *Prelates*, if indeed it had not been formally submitted to the Convocation (though this is not clear) ; and at that very time it was in the hands of Knox and the other Royal Chaplains for revision. If the Articles were not returned to the Privy Council by the 27th October, the day on which the Lord Chancellor was directed to add the Declaration, Cranmer had probably learned, during the five-and-twenty days that had elapsed since they were sent to the Chaplains, what was their judgment of them ; though, indeed, it is extremely likely that the views of the six revisers on the points discussed in the Articles were previously well known. Any *explanation*, therefore, of the Rubric on Kneeling, based upon the language of the Articles, was a course to which Knox could not object, however dissatisfied he might be at the retention of the Rubric itself ; and if the theological criticism of the principal objector was thus disarmed, no plan would be so likely to prove an effective defence against all other probable assailants from kindred quarters.

Now, in the XXIXth of these Articles (see p. 32) language would be found fully adequate to exclude every misinterpretation of the act of kneeling at reception which, so far I think as we can gather from their expressions, the Archbishop and his associates thought it of any moment to shut out. Was it feared that that token of adoration (for such in itself it really was) might be held to countenance Transubstantiation? Then, as the second paragraph of the Article condemned that dogma, it was only needful to import its teaching into the Declaration; this was done in the words "as concernynge the Sacramentall bread and wine, they remayne styll in their verye naturall substaunces, and therefore may not be adored."

Again: would it be thought that this posture of worship (for no one could doubt it to be such) implied a belief in that notion of a natural, organical, local presence of Christ's humanity which the reforming theologians of that day had been so vigorously opposing? The third paragraph of the Article taught the contrary, and, too, in an epitome of scholastic language,* which could hardly be unfamiliar to

---

* S. Thomas Aquinas, Summa, Pars 3, quæst. 75, art. 1, " *Utrum in hoc Sacramento sit Corpus Christi secundum veritatem.*"

It is objected, he says . . . . .

" 3. Præterea. Nullum corpus potest esse simul in pluribus locis, cum nec Angelo hoc conveniat: eadem enim ratione posset esse ubique. Sed corpus Christi est verum corpus, et est in cœlo. Ergo videtur quod non sit secundum veritatem in sacramento altaris, set solum sicut in signo."

To which he answers:—

" Ad tertium dicendum, quod corpus Christi non est eo modo in hoc sacramento, sicut corpus in loco. quod suis dimensionibus loco commensuratur; sed quodam speciali modo, qui est proprius huic sacramento. Unde dicimus, quod corpus Christi est in diversis altaribus, non sicut in diversis locis, sed sicut in sacramento: per quod non intelligimus quod Christus sit ibi solum sicut in signo; licet sacramentum sit in genere signi; sed intelligimus, corpus Christi hic esse, sicut dictum est (in corp. art.) secundum modum proprium huic sacramento."

Quæst. 75, art. 4. " *Utrum panis possit converto in Corpus Christi.*"

" . . . . . hæc conversio non est formalis, sed substantialis ; nec continetur inter species motus naturalis, sed proprio nomine potest dici transubstantiatio."

Quæst. 76, art. 5. " *Utrum Corpus Christi sit in hoc sacramento, sicut in loco.*"

" Respondeo dicendum, quod sicut jam dictum est (art. 3, hu. quæst.)† Corpus Christi non est in sacramento secundum proprium modum quantitatis dimensivæ, sed magis secundum modum substantiæ. Omne autem corpus locatum est in loco secundum modum quantitatis dimensivæ, inquantum scilicet commensuratur loco secundum suam quantitatem dimensivam. Unde relinquitur quod Corpus Christi non est in hoc sacramento sicut in loco sed per modum substantiæ eo scilicet modo quo substantia continetur a dimensionibus: succedit enim sub-

† " Præterea. Sicut dictum est (art. præc. and Art. 3. hu. quæst.) in sacramento est Corpus Christi cum sua quantitate dimensiva, et cum omnibus suis accidentibus. Sed esse in loco est accidens corporis : unde et ibi connumeratur inter novem genera accidentium. Ergo Corpus Christi est in hoc sacramento localiter."

most Priests then—which must have been well known to Knox, trained, as he was, in the disputations of the School-men : therefore (when the Declaration embodied this state-ment, and said, " it is against the trueth of Christes true naturall bodye, to be in more places then in one at one tyme ") the Catholic and the Protestant party would probably alike rejoice that they were bidden to defend the Church of England's view, as against the Papal party, by an appeal to such a witness as St. Thomas Aquinas, who had said that "in no manner is the Body of Christ in this Sacrament locally."

Once more : did any dread lest this new command to '·deliver" the Sacrament "to the people in their hands, *kneeling,*" (an order needless when the 1st Book was pre-pared, as then neither Clergy nor Laity presumed to do otherwise) should contribute to that very danger which Cranmer apprehended from the Trent "decrees respecting the worship of the host," how was their alarm subdued ? The Archbishop made no attempt to disguise a posture which, when employed in Public Worship, all knew to imply no less honour than that due to the Unseen though Present God : indeed he had himself pointed out in his Letter to the Council that "the people praying and geavinge thanckes, do kneele" in the "two praiers wch go before," and the " two" which "ymmediatlie followe" the "receavinge of the Sacrament"; and, moreover, he had expressly defended kneeling, in the act of reception, on the ground, that to abstain from it *then* "should rather import a contemptuouse then a reverent receavinge of the Sacrament"—words which surely can have but one natural meaning, viz., that such a *change* of posture would, at the least, be equivalent to a verbal denial of that Divine Presence *at that time* which

stantia Corporis Christi in hoc sacramento substantiæ panis: unde sicut sub-stantia panis non erat sub suis dimensionibus localiter ; sed per modum substantiæ, ita nec substantia Corporis Christi. Non tamen substantia Corporis Christi est subjectum illarum dimensionum, sicut erat substantia panis : et ideo substantia panis ratione suarum dimensionum localiter erat ibi, quia comparabatur ad locum illum mediantibus propriis dimensionibus ; substantia autem Corporis Christi comparatur ad locum illum mediantibus dimensionibus alienis ; ita quod e con-verso dimensiones propriæ Corporis Christi comparantur ad locum illum medi-ante substantia ; quod est contra rationem corporis loculi. Unde nullo modo Corpus Christi est in hoc sacramento localiter."

was attested to be there, immediately before and directly after, by the customary (and uncomplained of) act of kneeling.* But while maintaining this (and therefore necessarily holding that *in whatever way* Christ was present in the Sacrament, external worship was due to Him therein) the Primate had concurred in the 4th paragraph of the XXIXth Article which taught that " The Sacrament [Sacramentum) of the Lordes Supper was not commaunded by Christes ordinaunce to be . . . . worshipped [adorabatur]"—language this which most charitably and carefully avoids passing judgment upon those who, upon their view of the *Sacramentum* being only the *accidents* and not the *substance* of bread and wine, adopted a different conclusion. Here, too, then, was a warrant for anticipating the objection by saying in the Declaration (at no real risk of offending other Churches) that "the Sacra-

---

* While I am engaged upon this sheet the Bishop of St. Andrew's publishes his " Opinion on the Appeal of the Rev. P. Cheyne, delivered at the Episcopal Synod holden at Edinburgh, Nov. 4, 1858." As this is the " opinion" of the majority of that Synod (for the Bishops of Glasgow and Moray expressed their entire concurrence in it) it becomes the more important to notice a remark therein touching this act of Kneeling which the Declaration defends, especially as among the three "passages more particularly objected to", and which the Bp. of St. Andrew's expressed his *earnest hope* that Mr. Cheyne would "not refuse to recall . . . and express his regret for," was this : " 2. When he [the appellant] further declares that in the Lord's Supper 'we kneel to the Lord Himself, invisibly present under the form,' or 'under the veils of bread and wine.' " (p. 36.)

One argument advanced for this judicial request occurs at p. 29 where the Bishop says—" To order us to kneel in grateful acknowledgment of benefits received—those benefits being the Sacramental Body and Blood of our Lord and Saviour, Jesus Christ—this is natural, this we can understand. But in the actual, substantial Presence of Christ Himself, both God and man, we should expect to be directed to fall down and worship, not solely nor chiefly out of gratitude, but from those simpler motives of reverence and awe, which lie at the foundation of all the Divine honour which we pay to Almighty God."

Here the Bishop denies that the " REVERENCE" due to God was a motive for ordering the communicant to kneel when he received the Holy Sacrament : but Cranmer's Letter appears plainly to teach the very reverse of this ; he uses the precise word " REVERENT" as the *equivalent* of that " KNEELINGE" posture used by "the people praying and geavinge thanckes" immediately before and directly after the act of receiving ; therefore when he argues that not to kneel at that time "should rather importe a contemptuouse then a reverent receavinge of the Sacrament," he could surely mean nothing less than that to omit at such a moment *the recognized posture of* WORSHIP would be to withhold then that " Divine honour," proceeding from "motives of reverence and awe," which, the instant before and the instant after, they did not refuse as due to the Presence of God : in fact, while not touching upon the question of the Real Presence in the Sacrament, he points out the more than inconsistency of doing homage to God as present in devotions at the Sacrament, and refusing the like homage when *partaking of* " the Sacrament" itself.

mentall *bread and wyne* . . . may not bee adored, for *that* were *Idolatry* to be abhorred of *all* faithful Christians."

This comparison of the Article and the Declaration seems to leave no reasonable doubt whence the language was derived of this explanation of the Rubric on Kneeling which the Archbishop and his co-advisers deemed it desirable to publish. And the consideration that it was, evidently, drawn from a Doctrinal Formulary which was about to be imposed upon the Clergy, suggests that such a source would be, at once, a warrant for the acceptance of the Declaration itself and a guarantee that it contained nothing *contrary* to Catholic belief. For, when we recollect that the Articles of 1552 had undergone the criticism of the *Prelates*, and, as there are good grounds for believing, of the *Convocation* also; it is extremely unlikely, considering how many of these revisers (though not insensible of prevalent corruptions) were jealous of changes in the accustomed Theological language, that they would have assented to Definitions which were *opposed* to really ancient doctrine; and their watchfulness must naturally have resulted in part from the known views and tendency of some Bishops and leading Divines and from the operating influences of the foreign Reformers.

Mr. Hardwick, speaking of the preparation of these Articles, has observed :—

" . . . that the original draft of this document was made by Archbishop Cranmer, and by him submitted to a number of revisions during an interval of eighteen months. In what particulars it was modified or augmented by this long and varied criticism we are unable to ascertain precisely ; and yet the letter of the King to Ridley, bearing date June 9, 1553, as well as that of the Archbishop to Cecil in the previous September, would lead us to suppose that the amount of alteration had been very considerable ; for it describes the Articles, which were then publishing in their final form, as ' *devised and gathered with great study, and by counsel and good advice of the greatest learned part of our Bishops of this realm and sundry others of our Clergy.*' (Strype, Eccl. Mem. ii. 421.) We cannot, therefore, resist the conclusion, that they had been exposed to a searching review, and freely discussed and amended by a number of auxiliary hands, before the date of their general circulation."
—*Hist. of the Articles*, p. 83.

The " Visitation Book" of Bishop Hooper, 1551-2 furnishes a body of Articles which he endeavoured to enforce
in his own Diocese prior to the promulgation of the 42
Articles by Royal Authority in 1553: Hooper seems to have
drawn them mainly from those which the Archbishop sent
out for review, though they were apparently adapted to the
Bishop's own doctrinal notions: perhaps some of the other
Prelates took a similar course: a comparison of the two sets
of .Articles serves to illustrate the jealous caution, just
referred to, which determined the ultimate choice of phraseology. The XXIXth Article is that with which I am alone
concerned here: it so far corresponds with Hooper's Xth
Article as to deny plainly the doctrine of *Transubstantiation,*
but it is much more guarded in treating of the Presence ; it
contents itself with saying that " a faithful man ought not
either to believe or openlie to confesse the reall, and bodilie
presence (as thei terme it) of Christe's fleshe, and bloude,
in the Sacramente of the Lorde's Supper," whereas Hooper's
Article denies " any manner of corporal or local presence of
Christ, in, under, or with the bread and wine." These words
need not perhaps (as I have supposed at p. 30) mean more
than the rejection of a *carnal* and *natural* presence, but
(apart from the fact that Hooper also speaks of what we
receive as being " the confirmation and augmentation of all
the merits and deservings of Christ) obviously they are
sufficiently open to misconstruction, to have presented a formidable obstacle to the general acceptance of the XXIXth
Article, had it been couched in the same language.

Upon a careful consideration, then, of Cranmer's Letter,
combined with the illustrations it derives from the contemporary circumstances here related, the conviction is strengthened in my own mind—that the original Declaration was not
designed to be more than a denial of *such* Presence in the
Sacrament as was held, by the maintainers of Transubstantiation, to be the legitimate. conclusion from that Doctrine ;
though the words "reall and essenciall," if taken in their
usual acceptation and irrespective of their controversial
meaning in 1552, seem to condemn a *supernatural* no less

than a *natural* Presence " under the form of Bread and Wine."

Before quitting this Letter of Cranmer's there are two other points upon which it suggests observations. *First*, it corrects a statement made by Dr. Cardwell (and commonly adopted) as to the insertion of the Declaration on Kneeling in Edward's 2nd Book; he says that this " Rubric "

" had been added to the Communion Service by that King on his own authority after the publication of his second liturgy . . ."— *Hist. of Conferences*, p. 34.

But, if by is meant, as would seem—that the Bishops were not consulted—then the Archbishop's Letter, by reciting that the King desired him with others to reconsider the *Rubric* on Kneeling, leads to the inference that whatever was done had their concurrence. The, then recognized, authority of the King in Council would, in Cranmer's judgment, warrant an act which did not contravene anything that the Parliament had done in authorizing the Book: and as to the Doctrinal statement in the Royal Proclamation (for such it virtually was) the Archbishop had already the authority of his Synod for that, and in fact had more than a fortnight before (on Sept. 19th) written to Mr. Secretary Cecil saying :—

" I have sent the book of articles for religion unto Mr. Cheke, set in a better order than it was, and the titles upon every matter, adding thereto that which lacked. I pray you consider well the Articles with Mr. Checke ; and whether you think best to move the King's majesty therein before my coming, I refer that unto your two widoms."— *Cranmer's Remains.* Parker Society. Letter cccv. p. 439.

Most likely it is this identical " book of articles," in Latin, or a corrected copy of it, signed by Knox and the five other Royal Chaplains, which is still extant in the State Paper Office, (Domestic Edw. vi. Vol. xv. No. 28) dated October 20th, 1552 : at all events that copy contains the 29th Article as cited in English, at p. 32; and the order to insert the Declaration was not issued until October 27th. This fact therefore confirms the conjectures made in pp. 31 and 36.

Further, in a Note (*Hist. of Conf.* p. 34), Dr. Cardwell says :—

" This rubric does not appear in either of the Editions printed by Whitchurch in 1552, copies of which are now in the Bodleian; but it does appear in each of two editions by Grafton, printed in August 1552, copies of which may also be seen in the same library. The act of Parliament, which ratified the second Service-book, was passed in April 1552; and the order of Council requiring the insertion of the rubric bears date on the 27th of October, only four days before the book was to be generally used throughout the kingdom. It is found accordingly to have been inserted by cancelling the leaf, or some similar contrivance ; and the issuing of this order is a strong evidence of the alarm in which Cranmer and the Council were held on the subject of the real presence, even after the great alteration they had made respecting it in the service of the Communion."

Upon this I would remark (1.) that the copies of the *Whitchurch* editions which Dr. Cardwell mentions, may likely enough have got into circulation before the order of Sept. 27th " came to Grafton the printer in any wise to stay from uttering any of the books of the new service." Mr. Pickering's reprint is, however, from one by Whitchurch of 1552 and contains the Declaration : and there is in the British Museum (468. a. 7.) an old copy of the Whytchurche Book, with the Declaration : it is printed on a separate leaf, and follows the Rubrics at the end of the Communion Office. But indeed, as the Editor of the Parker Society's edition of the Two Liturgies observes, " Several copies are without it" of Grafton's edition : though there are two copies containing it in the British Museum, both evidently the same Ed. 1552 ; one imperfect, viz. (468. a. 6.) where it occurs at fol. 97 (clearly a misprint for 102 as it occurs between 101 and 103); the other perfect (468. b. 6.) has it on p. 102; in both copies it is found between the Rubric, beginning, " And if there be not above XX persons in the Parish," &c., and that commencing " And to take awaye the superstition which any person hath, or might have, in the bread and wine," &c.

2. With regard to Dr. Cardwell's remark that the Order in Council is evidence of the " alarm in which Cranmer and the Council were held on the subject of the Real Presence," I must, with all respect to so great an authority, profess my total inability to discover any grounds for his opinion. At pp. 35 and 36 I had sketched what I conjectured to be the

R

real history of this Declaration : Cranmer's Letter to the Council, now produced, entirely supports that view : and certainly the tone of that Letter indicates anything but " alarm :" it implies a settled conviction in the Archbishop's mind of the Doctrine to be maintained and indicates a resolution to maintain it—nay, it affirms that, so far as a prescribed act sustained the Doctrine, it had been " with just ballance waied " by himself and " a greate menny bushops and other of the best learned " men " at the makinge of the boke." The Declaration to which he now assented—probably prepared— was the deliberate judgment of the Church of England by representation, and no suddenly extemporized statement to meet a supposed new phase of a state of terror.

(3.) For the reasons already assigned at pp. 33 to 35 and elsewhere, I must venture to deny that there was *any*, much less " any great alteration," on the " subject of the real presence," in the Prayer Book of 1552.

The *Second* remaining point which the Archbishop's Letter leads me to notice is this,—That the way in which he regards " *kneelinge*" as the synonym for *reverence* may fairly suggest the true interpretation to be put upon the Rubric, in the present Communion Office, which directs that * "if any

---

* At p. 89, I have ventured to reject the opinion held by some—that the earlier part of this Rubric, as it stood in the Book of 1552 (" if any of the bread and wine remain, the Curate shall have it to his own use") referred to the *consecrated* Bread and Wine. It was not until long after those remarks were printed off that I noticed the following passages in Bp. Cosin's Notes on the Common Prayer, which, it will be seen, entirely support the opinion I had formed :—

1st Series, p. 130 Cosin's Works, Ang. Cath. Lib.—"*And if any of the bread and wine remain, &c.*] Which is not to be understood of the bread and wine already consecrated, but of that which remains without consecration ; for else it were but a profanation of the Holy Sacrament to let the Curate have it home to his own use. *Quam indigne faciunt, qui hac rubrica ad tantum facinus excusandum abutuntur, ipsi viderint.* It was Nestorianism once to think, that the consecrated bread, if it were kept *in crastinum*, became common bread again, if St. Thom. p. 3, q. 72, a. 11, ad 2, (a) quoteth St. Cyril of Alexandria right, *Ep. ad Calen.* Vide Maldon, de Sacram. p. 120. 'There was order taken for it of

(a) " [This reference is incorrect. The passage intended is in S. Thom. Aquinas, Summa Totius Theologiæ, pars. iii. quæst. 76, art. 6, ad secundum, where he speaks of ' quidam ponentes quod Corpus Christi non remaneat sub hoc sacramento, si in crastinum reservetur. Contra quos Cyrillius dicit,' etc. The same passage of S. Cyril is cited by him in the Aurea Catena on S. Luc. c. xxii. with the reference Ep. ad Calosyr. 'Insaniunt quidam dicentes mysticam benedictionem cessare a sanctificatione, si quæ ejus reliquiæ remanserint in diem subsequentim : non enim mutatur sacratum Corpus Christi, sed virtus benedictionis et vivificativa gratia jugis in eo est.' The Greek was found by Cardinal Mai in the Vatican MS. which contains S. Cyril's Commentary on S. Luke, and it is printed by him in the Classici Auctores, tom. x. p. 375, note . . . .]"—Editor's Note.

remain of that [Bread and Wine] which was consecrated, it shall not be carried out of the Church, but the Priest and such other of the Communicants as he shall then call unto him, shall, immediately after the Blessing, *reverently* eat and drink the same."

In Edward's 2nd Prayer Book (as indeed in the 1st) no direction whatever was given for the disposal of the remaining *Consecrated* Bread and Wine; the reasons are obvious, viz. (1) That, owing to the notice then *practically* as well as Rubrically required from those who proposed to communicate, not more probably remained of what was consecrated than could conveniently be consumed by the Celebrant: (2) That it must have been wholly unnecessary to prescribe a rule on this point for a body of Clergy who had been accustomed to follow those careful directions of the old Office Books which made even the cleansing of the Paten and Chalice a part of the Public Service; and so (though they should be considered as needlessly minute) guarded against a negligence and carelessness which (it must be confessed) is too commonly to be found in our own day among Clergy and Parish Clerks.

The similar absence of any Rubric in Elizabeth's Book (1559) may be accounted for on the like ground; for, could it even be shown that any general lax practice had grown up in the last year of Edward's reign, the restoration of the Missal by Mary must have corrected it; while the fact that James's Book (1604) made no alteration in this respect, may

old in the Church, which were well to be observed still, that No more should be brought, at least consecrated upon the altar, than would suffice to communicate the people, and if any remained, that the priests should reverently receive it. *Tanta in altari holocausta offerantur, quanta populo sufficere debeant. Quod remanserit (nimirum ex holocaustis et elementis consecratis) non servetur in crastinum, sed cum timore et tremore clericorum diligentia consumetur.* Clem. P. P. Ep. 2. de Consecrat. distinct. 2. *e. tribus gradibus.*" (b)

P. 131.—" *To his own use.*] We read in Clemens, (c) that after the Communion was done, the deacons took up that which was left, and carried it *in Pastophorium,* the room where the priests were lodged. In Origen, (d) that it was not

(b) [" Ap. Decretum, pars iii. de consecratione, dist. ii. c. 23, apud Corp. Jur. Canon., tom. i. The passage is taken out of a spurious Epistle of S. Clement, Epist ii. ad Jacobum fratrem Domini de sacratis vestibus et vasis, printed in the Concilia, tom. l. p. 99, A. B.]"—Ed. Note.

(c) "[.... Const. Apost. lib. viii. c. 13. Concilia, tom. i. col. 485. A]"—Ed. Note.

(d) " [... Origen in Levit. cap. v. 7. 15.) Hom. v. s. 8. Op. tom. ii. col. 211. B.]"—Ed. Note.

well lead to the belief that, though the objectors to kneeling at the reception of the Sacrament were increasing, no novel practice as to consuming the *remains* had crept in among those who adhered to and defended the Rubric.

But when the Scotch Prayer Book was prepared in 1636-7 the following Rubric was appended to the Communion Office :—" *And if any of the Bread and Wine remain, which is consecrated, it shall be reverently eaten and drunken by such of the Communicants only as the Presbyter which celebrates shall take unto him, but it shall not be carried out of the Church."* What is the legitimate inference from this? Surely, that in the preceding 30 years a growing Puritan irreverence in all that concerned the ministration of the Eucharist had shown the necessity of such a provision in a Book intended for use among a people who were deeply imbued with Knox's prejudices against Kneeling, and who were using his " Book of Common Order." If it be asked —why did not Abp. Laud then add a similar Rubric to the *English* Book? the answer is plain—that Ecclesiastical affairs were far too perilous at that time in England to adventure what would certainly have been denounced as a Popish innovation.

kept till the next day. In St. Jerome, (*e*) that after the Communion, they that had eaten it in the Church spent all that remained of the oblations. In Hesychius, (*f*) that after the example of the old law, all that was left was cast into the fire. In Evagrius, (*g*) that it was an ancient custom at Constantinople, that if any of the Sacrament remained, young children were called from the school to eat it up; which was retained in France, (*h*) as in *Concil. Masticon et Turon.*, held under Charlemagne." (*i*) See also Cosin's other Notes quoted *infra*.

So, too, Sparrow (whose language I had not before noticed) says—" *If any of the Bread and Wine remain, the Curate shall have it to his own use.* [*Rub.* 5. *after the Communion Service*] that is, if it were not consecrated: for if it be consecrated, it is all to be spent with fear and reverence by the Communicants, in the Church. *Gratian de Consecr. dist.* 2. *c.* 23. *Tribus Concil. Constant. Resp. ad. Qu.* 5. *Monachon. apud Balsam. Theophil. Alexand. Cap.* 7."—*Rationale* p. 241. Ed. 1672.

(*e*) "[In ecclesia convenientes oblationes suas separatim offerebant, et post communionem quæcunque eis de sacrificiis super fuissent, illi in ecclesia communem cœnam comedentes pariter consumebant.—Pseudo-Hieron. in 1 Cor. xi. 20. S. Hieron. Op. tom. xi. col. 9, 31, D. E.] "—Ed. Note.

(*f*) "[Hesychius in Levit., lib. ii. (in c. viii. 32.) ap. Bibl. Patr. Max., tom. xii. p. 86. C. Lugd. 1677.]"—Ed. Note.

(*g*) " [. . Evagrius, Hist. Eccl., lib. iv. c. 36, p. 416.]"—Ed. Note.

(*h*) " [. . . Conc. Masticonense II. A. D. 585. can. 5, Concilia, tom. vi. col. 675, C.D." —Ed. Note.

(*i*) " [. . . Con. Turonense III. sub Carolo Magno A. D. 813, can. 19; Ibid, tom. ix., col. 351, D.]"—Ed. Note.

To this Rubric of the Scotch Office may, no doubt, be traced the Rubric inserted in the English Book of 1662: nor need we wonder that Bishop Cosin and his co-revisers added this, when it is recollected that, in addition to the wide-spreading Puritanism of the quarter of a century which had elapsed since the Scotch Office was framed, the last 15 years of the period had witnessed the total banishment of the Prayer Book from the Public Services, and with it had abolished Ritual and Ceremonial practices which were very unlikely to be resumed in the absence of positive directions to both Clergy and People.

Now it may be safely assumed, I think, that had Archbishop Cranmer thought it needful to give any order for the consumption of the remaining Consecrated Elements, he would have used either the word "reverently" or the word "kneeling;" for, whether we regard his views on the Real Presence (see *e. g.*, p. 22) or his views on Consecration (see p. 85), it seems to me impossible to believe that (even taking his language in the lowest and loosest interpretation which has been, wrongly as I think, put upon it) he would have allowed that NOT to be *The Sacrament* which was consumed *after* the post-communion prayers, though it WAS *The Sacrament* when partaken of immediately after Consecration.

It seems clear, indeed, that the Archbishop held—that the Presence is *in the Ministration;* for, as he says, (see p. 88) "the [sacramental] change is *in the use,* and not in the elements kept and reserved, wherein is not the perfection of a Sacrament;" and again (answer to Gardiner, p. 271) "he is not present in the forms of bread and wine *out* of the ministration:*" but then it is essential to recollect that it was wholly unlikely for Cranmer (or indeed any Cleric or Laic of that day) to regard the consumption of the remains of the Consecrated Elements as anything else than *a part* of the Ministration:" it is difficult to understand that any one who tries to throw himself into that period will suppose it presumptuous to assume that no such thought entered the minds of the Churchmen of that time; rather the wonder would surely be

---

* Which, surely, implies that he considered Christ *was* present "in the forms" IN "the ministration."

how they could depart, except where distinctly ordered, from the traditional and rubrical theory and practice with which they had been bound up so long.

Assuming then, as I do without any doubt, that Cranmer so regarded it; the conclusion seems inevitable—that in whatever posture the Celebrant or his Ministers or the people made their *Communion*, in *that same* posture the Archbishop would have required them to consume the remaining Consecrated Elements when called upon to do so : *standing*,* was

* Bishop Cosin indeed seems, at one time at least, to have thought otherwise ; for in his 1st Series of Notes, A. C. L. p. 105, he thus writes—" *Then the Priest standing up, shall say the Prayer of Consecration.*] The transposing of this after that which goes before, otherwise than it was in King Edward's Book, hath left the Priest to receive the Sacrament standing, there being no Rubric or appointment to alter his gesture after this ; and upon this have the Puritans taken occasion to plead, and say that they may as well be left to their liberty and stand as the minister, when they receive. But see the answer infra."

The " answer" to which Cosin seems to refer, is the following Note p. 112, 1st Series—" Kneeling.] Kneeling here, for all the Puritans' objection, (a) hath reference as well to the minister himself, as to the people and other ministers."

But in this instance, as indeed in many other cases, the Puritans by taking the *literal* appear to have caught the true interpretation of the Rubric, though they argued very inaccurately from it. The Rubric, here referred to, stood thus in the Books of 1552, 1559, and 1604 :—" *Then shall the Minister first receive the Communion in both kinds himself, and next deliver it to other Ministers if any be there present (that they may help the chief Minister) and after to the people in their hands kneeling.*" · Bishop Cosin seems to have thought that the variation from the *order* of the 1st Book (in placing the prayer of Access *before* the act of Consecration) *apparently* changed the position of the Celebrant when communicating himself : but his error probably arose from his mistaking the meaning of the Rubric in the 1st Book ; that Rubric, except that it did not contain the words, " in their hands kneeling," was *identical* with the Rubric just quoted, and it is surprising that Cosin appears not to have considered the moral certainty of the Clergy of 1549 interpreting this Rubric by the practice which they must have pursued under " the Order of the Communion " of 1548. That supplementary Office directed " *The time of the Communion*" of the people to " *be immediately after that the Priest hath received the Sacrament, without the varying of any other rite or ceremony in the Mass (until other order shall be provided)* . . . ." then followed a longer and a shorter exhortation similar to those now used, the Confession, the Absolution, the Comfortable Words, and the Prayer of Access ; the very next Rubric orders " *Then shall the Priest rise, the people still reverently kneeling, and the Priest shall deliver the Communion, first to the Ministers, if any be there present, that they may be ready to help the Priest, and after to the other.*"

Now even if no such directions had been given, we may be sure that the Celebrant would have continued to communicate himself and the people, after the accustomed manner : but when told that, with certain variations, the Mass Office was to be strictly followed in other respects, it is clear that the Celebrant must have received the Sacrament himself STANDING " *cum inclinatione*," for that was the posture ordered in the Sarum and other Uses : no " other order " had been " provided," in this respect, down to the time at which Cosin penned this Note ; it follows, therefore, that the old *Rule* continued, even though the traditional *practice* may have been much invaded by Bishop Cosin's day, and so may have likely enough influenced the opinion recorded in his Note.

(a) Editor's Note.—" [' The Priest is expressly directed in the next rub. before, to stand, and not directly to kneel now.'—Survey, Ex. 22. quære 57. p. 70.]" A. D. 1606.

the posture of the *Celebrant; kneeling*, the posture of all others in making their Communion. The Post-communion consumption was just as much a part of "the use" and "the ministration" of the Sacrament as what had preceded: whatever reverence therefore ·Cranmer held to be due to Christ's Presence in the earlier part of "the use," he must necessarily, it would seem, have thought needful to be rendered so long as "the Ministration" lasted.

What that *reverence* was, we now know distinctly from his

Though, however, even Laud's Book of 1638 gave no direction as to the posture of the Celebrant when communicating, Bishop Cosin seems still to have retained his view when he wrote his Suggestions for alterations in the Prayer-Book; for at p. 517 A. C. L. this passage occurs—"58. In the Priest's taking of the Sacrament to himself, there is no direction either for his Kneeling when he takes it, or for the words which he is then to say; which is therefore needful here to be added, lest otherwise some contentious minister might say, that he is not enjoined to Kneel in this holy action himself, nor to say any words at all when he takes the Sacrament."

Accordingly, as the Editor of Cosin's Notes states "[The rubrics were thus prepared by Cosin: 'Then shall the priest that celebrateth receive the Holy Communion in both kinds *upon his knees*, and when he taketh the Sacrament of the Body of Christ he shall say, 'The body of our Lord Jesus Christ, which was given for me, preserve my body and soul unto everlasting life. Amen. I take and eat this for the remembrance of Christ who died for me, and I feed on Him in my heart by faith with thanksgiving.' And when he taketh the Sacrament of Christ's blood he shall say, 'The blood of our Lord, &c.' (then in Sancroft's hand, 'which was shed for me, preserve my body and soul unto everlasting life. Amen. I drink this for the remembrance of Christ who shed his blood for me, and am thankful.') 'Then shall he stand up and proceed to deliver the Holy Communion first to the ·bishops, priests, and deacons, if·any be present, in both kinds, and after that to the people in due order, into their hands, all humbly kneeling, and so continuing (as is most meet) at their devotions and prayers unto the end of the whole Communion.']"

But this proposed Rubric was not adopted in the Revision of 1662, though it is probable (see *infra*) that Cosin's Notes, &c. (especially his "Suggestions") were before the Reviewers at that time; Dr. Nichol's marginal note upon Cosin's Suggestion is "This seems to be altered, but still the rubric is not clear in this point:" looking however at the Rubric as it now stands, the probability seems to be that the question having been discussed and the old Office books weighed, either Bishop Cosin changed his opinion or was overruled by his co-revisers: perhaps there was sufficient difference of view among them to lead them to adopt here the recommendation of the Royal Commission by making no change. Anyhow they neither incorporated the old *Rubric* directing the Priest to stand; nor the *Words* ("The Body of our Lord Jesus Christ," &c.) which the Old Offices directed the Priest to use when communicating himself, though no form was prescribed for communicating the people. Clearly, then, we are free to interpret the Priest's *posture* by the analogy of the Old English Offices: while as to the *words*, probably the natural inclination of the Celebrant when receiving himself, is to use either secretly or openly (with the requisite change) the language he is bidden to employ in administering the Sacrament to the people.

Nevertheless the argument I have used in the text is in no way affected whichever view may be taken of the Rubric: that argument being—that the *same* posture, *whatever it is*, which is used by the Celebrant or others in making their Communion, must be also used in consuming the remains of the Sacrament.

own Letter; " Kneelinge," he considered the true external expression of it in the Church of England, in common with the rest of Western Christendom : to refuse this could only, in his mind, "importe a *contemptuouse* than a *reverent* receaving of the Sacrament." Can it be reasonably supposed that he would have thought otherwise of any (to whom the Rubric on Kneeling applied) who should then have offered to receive the *remains* of the Sacrament in any other than a *kneeling* posture ? I believe it cannot.

Now if this was true of Cranmer, how much more must it have been true of the last Revisers of the Prayer Book! Certain it is that the Reviewers of 1662, to whom we are indebted for the Offices as they now stand, could not have meant *less* by REVERENCE than the Archbishop did : their views (especially those *e. g.* of Sheldon, Cosin, Morley, Sanderson, Gauden, Heylin, Gunning, Pearson, Sparrow, and Thorndike) undoubtedly were not *lower* than Cranmer's : their experience of *irreverence* must have been *greater* among priests † as well as people. In, what we may be sure therefore was, their desire to promote due reverence among both, they added the following Rubrics or parts of Rubrics as being likely, in their judgment, to secure it :—

I. BEFORE THE FIRST LORD's PRAYER.—". . . . *the people kneeling.*"

II. BEFORE THE NICENE CREED.—". . . . *the people all standing up* [at the Gospel] . . . . *the people still standing* [at the Creed] *as before.*"

III. BEFORE THE OFFERTORY SENTENCES.—" *Then shall the Priest return to the Lord's Table, and begin the Offertory.* . . . ."

IV. BEFORE THE PRAYER FOR CHRIST's CHURCH MILITANT.—" *Whilst these sentences are in reading, the Deacons, Churchwardens, or other fit person appointed for that purpose,*

---

† A circumstance not surprising, when we find that so early as 1603 it was stated in the Hampton Court Conference that "the vicar of Ratesdale, ... by his unseemly and irreverent usage of the Eucharist, dealing the bread out of a basket, every man putting in his hand and taking out a prace, to have made many loath the Communion, and wholly refuse to come to Church."—*Barlow's Account* in Card. Hist. Corp. p. 210.

*shall receive the Alms for the poor, and other devotions of the
people, in a decent bason, to be provided by the Parish for that
purpose; and reverently bring it to the Priest, who shall
humbly present and place it upon the holy Table.*

"*And when there is a Communion, the Priest shall then
place upon the Table so much Bread and Wine, as he shall
think sufficient.*"

V. BEFORE THE FIRST EXHORTATION.—"*At the time of the
Celebration of the Communion, the Communicants being conveniently placed for the receiving of the holy Sacrament, ...*"

VI. BEFORE "IT IS VERY MEET," etc.—"*Then shall the
Priest turn to the Lord's Table, and say,*"

VII. BEFORE THE PRAYER OF CONSECRATION.—"*When
the Priest, standing before the Table, hath so ordered the Bread
and Wine, that he may with the more readiness and decency
break the Bread before the people, and take the Cup into his
hands, he shall say the Prayer of Consecration, ...*"

VIII. IN THE PRAYER OF CONSECRATION.—The manual
acts prescribed, "*Here the Priest is to take the Paten,*" etc.

IX. AFTER THE COMMUNION OF THE PEOPLE.—"*If the
consecrated bread or wine be all spent before all have communicated; the Priest is to consecrate more according to the form
before prescribed,*" etc.

"*When all have communicated, the Minister shall return to
the Lord's Table, and reverently place upon it what remaineth
of the consecrated Elements, covering the same with a fair linen
cloth.*"

X. AT THE END OF THE OFFICE.—"*. . . . but if any remain of that which was consecrated, it shall not be carried out
of the Church, but the Priest and such other of the Communicants as he shall then call unto him, shall, immediately after
the Blessing, reverently eat and drink the same.*"

Each of these Rubrics, as will be seen, was directed to a
separate point, some (*i. e.*, Nos. III., IV., and VII.) brought
out more distinctly the *Sacrificial aspect*; others (*i. e.*, Nos.
VIII., IX., and X.,) impressed more clearly the doctrine of
Consecration: but all combined in promoting one object,
viz., a more careful and orderly celebration of the Holy

Eucharist than had been accustomed; all tended to invest that Sacrament with a greater dignity than it *seemed* to possess when *Rubrically* shorn of some of its Ritual directions in the Offices subsequent to Edward's 1st Book : indeed, in some respects, the Rubrics of 1662 were fuller and more explicit than those of 1549 ; for the obvious reason—that the Clergy of Edward's days, familiar as they were with the Rules of the Old Offices, had no need of directions upon points which subsequent negligence or prejudice had obscured or would be likely to hide from the view of the Clergy of Charles the 2nd's reign, and their successors.

Moreover, the instructions given to the Commissioners were themselves calculated to favour this end; for, in "*the King's warrant for the Conference at the Savoy,*" they were directed " to advise upon and review the said Book of Common Prayer, comparing the same with the most ancient Liturgies which have been used in the Church, in the primitive and purest times." (Card. Hist. Conf. p. 300); and if those who exercised the most influence in the Conference desired (as there can be no doubt they did) to conform the Liturgy to the Ancient Offices as much as they could consistently with the King's direction to be careful in "avoiding, as much as may be, all unnecessary alterations of the forms and Liturgy wherewith the people are already acquainted, and have so long received in the Church of England" (*ibid*), there can be no question in what direction they must have been led: it would require no very extensive search among those ancient monuments of Eucharistic Doctrine and Ritual before they saw that whatever changes or additions they made in the Book under review must be of a nature to surround and pene- trate the Communion Office with protections and defences against Puritanical assaults and betrayals.

It follows, therefore, that any uncertainty which may now arise as to the construction of expressions, whether in the Rubrics or in the Substance of the Communion Office, can only be fairly and safely removed by a reference to those same Ancient Liturgies which were so distinctly and authoritatively com- mended to and employed by the Savoy Commissioners : the analogy of those Liturgies (including the old English Uses which the Reviewers could not but have regarded as the Church of England's traditional exposition of the Ancient Liturgies) must be followed in interpreting the language of the present English Liturgy if we at all wish to comprehend its letter and its spirit.

The word "reverently," now under discussion, occurs in three of the Rubrics just quoted, *viz:* Nos. IV, IX, and X; an examination and comparison of these will probably materially help to define the meaning of the term as used in No. X.—the Rubric now under consideration.

Rubric No. IV prescribes the mode of collecting and presenting the various Offerings of the people: the corresponding Rubric in the Books of 1549 to 1604 made a distinction in the method of receiving them. "*The devotion of the people*" was put "into the poor men's box" either by the people themselves (as in the Book of 1549), or by "the Churchwardens, or some other" who had gathered it: "*the due and accustomed Offerings*" were to be paid "to the Curate" by "every man and woman" on "the offering days appointed." But the Rubric of 1662 made no such difference; by that "*the Alms for the poor, and other devotions of the people'* were alike to be collected by "the Deacons, Churchwardens, or other fit person appointed for that purpose," who were to "reverently bring it to the priest:" considerations of convenience no doubt led to this change: the point however here to be observed is the act intended by the word "reverently:" I understand it to mean "Kneeling;" this belief is confirmed by the fact—that Bishop Cosin so explained the Rubric of 1604 in his 1st Series of Notes where (p. 97 A. C. L.) he says, quoting Bishop Andrewes—

"*And upon the offering days appointed, every man and woman shall pay to the Curate the due and accustomed offerings.*] . ? . W. ? 'They should not pay it to the curate alone, but to God upon the altar; from whence the curate hath his warrant to take it, as deputed by Him, and as the Apostle plainly alludes, 1 Cor. ix. 13, 14; Heb. xiii. 10. And this is not to be forgotten, though it be foregone, that whosoever gave any lands or endowments to the service of God, he gave it in formal writing, (as now-a-days between man and man) sealed and witnessed. And the tender of the gift was *super-altare,* and by the donor upon his knees."

Again, in his 2nd Series, p. 323, Bishop Cosin says :—

" *And upon the Offering-days appointed.*] It was one of the instructions set forth by the authority of King Henry VIII. in the Convocation of his clergy, *anno* 1536, to be generally observed in the Church of England, ' That the feasts of the Nativity of our Lord, of Easter Day, of the Nativity of St. John Baptist, and of St. Michael the Archangel, shall be accounted, accepted, and taken for the four general Offering-days.' Which order is in some places among us still observed. And the King or Queen in their Chapel-royal (or wherever they be at Church in those days) never omit it, but arise from their seat, and go in solemn manner to present their Offerings upon their Knees at God's altar. And then is read by the Priest or Bishop attending, this sentence here prescribed, 1 Cor. ix.: ' They which minister about holy things,' etc. . . . . "

Now if, as is implied in these two passages, *Kneeling* is the proper posture in which individuals should present their offerings ; it seems to follow that, when those Offerings are presented for them by another, their representative should also Kneel : * in the absence therefore of any direct evidence to show the precise intention of the Reviewers of 1662, it is a very reasonable supposition that the introduction of the word " reverently " into the Rubric, as then altered, had some reference to these opinions of Bishops Andrewes and Cosin ; especially as Bishop Kennett (Register p. 566) has this Note :

" Several Books and Papers, supposed to be laid before the Convocation while they were on this work of revising the Common Prayer.

" The Collections of Bishop Overall.

" The Notes of Bishop Cosins,

" And his additional notes in Latin.

" Notes of Bishop Andrewes."

* I have since met with the following passage in Jebb's Choral Service, p. 497 : — " According to regular Collegiate usage, the Clergy present their Alms severally themselves, kneeling in front of the Altar while making their offering. This custom is, I believe, unknown in Ireland, but it is one so reverential, and one which so distinctly exhibits the holy nature of almsgiving, and the purposes of God's Altar, that its revival were much to be wished. In some Colleges, all the lay members advance to the Altar rails, and then offer, one by one.

" A reverential mode of presenting the Alms ' offered to ' God's ' Divine Majesty,' is distinctly prescribed by the Rubric. Many interpret this to mean Kneeling ; and certainly the traditional practice of the Church, in the custom noticed in the last paragraph, would seem to justify the same posture in presenting the devotions of the people at large which was observed with respect to those of individuals."

And that such a meaning *was* designed, appears to be further indicated by the other word "*humbly*," which is employed to describe the posture of "the Priest," when he has to " present " the Offerings thus "reverently " brought to him. That a *different* posture was intended, is, I think, clear from the use of an expression which, though kindred in character, is not synonymous with "reverently "—the latter word implying (even according to the Dictionaries) more *respect, veneration,* and *awe.* Besides (recollecting the principles which guided the Reviewers) we cannot reasonably suppose that this choice of terms was made without reference to the directions of the old Offices; and in them there is nothing to indicate that *kneeling* was the Celebrant's posture when presenting Alms and Oblations, but quite the reverse : no direction indeed is given except as regards the Oblations of Bread and Wine ; these, according to the Sarum and Bangor rubric, he is to place " *diligenter* " (i. e., carefully, attentively) "*super medium altare,*" and then "*inclinato parumper elevet calicem utraque manu offerens sacrificium Domino,....* :" but, plainly, no other offerings would be made with *more* devotion than those which were presented for the express purpose of being consecrated for the Sacrament, and that this principle is meant to be retained now, may be clearly understood from the Rubric in our present Prayer Book, which merely bids the Priest to "*place upon the Table so much Bread and Wine as he shall think sufficient.*"

Moreover, it is important to remember that the act of presenting and placing upon the Altar, either the Offertory or the Elements is not the Priest's *formal oblation* of them, in our present Office, though the act of *bringing* the Offerings of the people to the Priest is their *formal oblation :* it is easy, therefore, to see why only the word "humbly " (equivalent to the " diligenter " of the Sarum and Bangor Rites) is used to prescribe the Priest's act, though the stronger term "reverently" prescribes the act of the people's representative. Indeed, some evidence of the intention in this choice of terms is apparently furnished by a comparison of this Rubric as it stood in Laud's book of 1637, where it reads "shall humbly present *it before the Lord* and set it upon the holy Table. And the Presbyter shall then *offer up* and place the bread and wine prepared for the Sacrament upon the Lord's Table : " the words which I have italicized not being incorporated with the Rubric of 1662. The Priest's *formal oblation* of the Offerings is made in the Church Militant prayer by the use of the words, " We humbly beseech Thee most mercifully [*to accept our alms and oblations,* . .] . . . which we offer unto thy Divine Majesty ; " and at that Prayer *standing* is plainly the posture of the Celebrant—with an *inclination* of his body, according to the above Rubric of the old Offices.

These considerations go very far, I think, towards proving that whoever presents the Offerings of the people to the Celebrant is to do so KNEELING; but that the Celebrant when presenting them on the Altar is to do so STANDING.

Rubric No. IX prescribes the mode in which the Celebrant is to return to the Altar " what remaineth of the Consecrated elements " after " all have communicated : " the term used to describe his action is " *reverently.*" It is to be noticed that this is the word which, in Rubric No. IV just considered, I have interpreted to mean " Kneeling ;" it might seem therefore that the same construction must be put upon the same word in this Rubric : but this by no means follows, as will be seen by a reference to the old Uses which, it must always be remembered, were not likely to be overlooked by the Reviewers of 1662 : the truth being that in Public Offices of Religion the *same degree of reverence* is not always expressed by the *same action* of the Minister and People, *e. g.*, the Versicles and Responses beginning "O Lord shew Thy mercy upon us," etc., in our present Morning and Evening Prayer, where " *the Priest* " is ordered to be " *standing up,*" though it is plain that he is engaged in exactly the same devotional act as the people; and again, in the ante-communion Service, the Lord's Prayer and two Collects are ordered to be said by " *the Priest standing :* " throughout this office indeed, except where expressly ordered otherwise, *standing* is the Celebrant's posture owing to the peculiar nature of that Ministration as a

" sacrifice," though in fact it is " our" *i. e.*, the people's as well as the Priest's " sacrifice of praise and thanksgiving."

There is no Rubric in the old Uses strictly corresponding to this Rubric No. IX, owing to some difference in their arrangement at this part from the present English Use: the analagous one in the Sarum and Bangor Offices is as follows:—

SARUM. • "*Hic sumat sanguinem: quo sumpto inclinet se sacerdos, et dicat cum devotione orationem sequentem:* Gratias tibi ago, Domine," etc.

BANGOR. "*Hic sumat totam sanguinem: quo sumpto et calice altari superposito, inclinans se sacerdos cum magna veneratione in medio altaris et crucem respiciens dicat hanc orationem sequentem.* Gratias tibi," etc.

To understand this (as applying to the Rubric No. IX) it must be remembered that the Celebrant had just communicated himself with the Sacrament of the Body which was still resting on the Altar: then having received in the other kind, taking the "*whole* of the Blood" according to the above Rubrics, he proceeded to communicate (in one kind) any of the people who desired to receive; this being done the ablution of the Chalice immediately followed and then the postcommunion prayers. But as the Chalice when replaced on the Altar necessarily contained some remains of the consecrated wine (which remains, as the Rubrics shew, were treated with as much care as the contents of the Chalice immediately upon Consecration) it cannot be reasonably doubted that any acts connected with returning the Chalice to the Altar were meant to be most reverential: yet, as has been seen, *Kneeling* was not the expression of it; nay, even in so solemn a part of the Office as the oblation of the *Sacrament*, no more demonstrative act is ordered than (Sarum, Bangor, Ebor) " *corpore inclinato* "=" *inclinet se devoto* " (Hereford)= "*profunde inclinatus* " in the present Roman Ritual: indeed in this latter Office the strongest expression throughout the whole action is " *genuflexus adorat*," *i. e.*, upon *one* knee: though even that does not occur in either of the four old English Liturgies.

This examination of Rubrics No. IV and IX will probably facilitate the investigation of No. X where "reverently" designates the posture alike of Celebrant, Clergy, and People in consuming the remains of the Sacrament. What, then, is the import of the word in this place, seeing that (as I have argued) it has two distinctly opposite meanings in the Rubrics just considered? Does it here mean *kneeling*, or *standing*, or some third posture? Clearly, I think, it means *both* kneeling and standing; and was designed as a *general* term to cover the *special* posture whether of Celebrant or others, for standing is just as much the Priest's *reverential* attitude as kneeling is the people's; if the *same posture* had been intended for *both* it is most natural to believe that the Rubric would have clearly *expressed* it, just as *e. g.*, the Priest is told to say the Prayer of Access "*kneeling down*"—a departure from his *ordinary* posture being designed, and one which the Office assumes he would not make unless so directed: but a *common* term being employed to state the Rule for both Priest and People, that term must, I contend, be interpreted in each case in conformity with the usage of the Office throughout and according to the analogy furnished by Rubrics IV and IX.

This view is confirmed, I think, by a similar *general* use of the word in the Office for "The Communion of the Sick," where the Rubric directs "*a convenient place in the sick man's house, with all things necessary*, to be "*so prepared that the Curate may* REVERENTLY *minister* . . . . ;" for as he is to "celebrate the Holy Communion" according to the *public* rite, except where otherwise ordered, and as that public rite prescribes *various postures* for the Celebrant, so it was needful to use a term which should include them all : such a term is the word "*reverently*."

So far, then, as the intention can be gathered from this comparison of the *relative* meaning of the word—and that meaning is surely a most important one—the interpretation proposed at p. 126 seems to be proved, *viz.*, that the posture in which any one makes his act of Communion must be also used when the same person consumes the remains of the Sacrament.

But it will materially help to *fix* this as the intended meaning, if-any support for it can be found in the opinions of those who are known to have been chiefly consulted or engaged in the revision of 1662.

One such opinion has already been incidentally noticed in the passage from Bishop Cosin (Note p. 123) where reciting the language of S. Thomas Aquinas on the consumption of the remains of the Sacrament, he translates (or rather paraphrases the words "*cum timore et tremore*" (quoted by that author) by the very expression in question—"*reverently :*" saying " There was order taken for it of old in the Church, ... if any remained, that the priests should reverently receive it." The passage, too, is the more noticeable as it may very likely have led to the insertion of the order in 1662 (though indeed it appeared in the Scotch Book of 1638) that "if any remain of that which was consecrated, *it shall not be carried out of the Church :*" for it will be seen that in the passage which St. Thomas quotes, the remainder of the Sacrament is expressly ordered *not to be kept for the morrow* ("non servetur in crastinum ")—words which we can readily believe to have been in Cosin's mind at the time of the Revision, though in the Note referred to he does not include them in his paraphrase of the original.

Another passage, showing plainly what was Cosin's view (when he wrote his 1st Series of Notes) of the Effect of Consecration (and consequently of the reverence due to the remains of the Sacrament) occurs in another Note upon the Rubric " *if any of the bread and wine remain* ; " for, at p. 131, he says :—

" *Bread and wine,* etc."] It is confessed by all divines, that upon the words of consecration the Body and Blood of Christ is really and substantially present, and so exhibited and given to all that receive it ; and all this not after a physical and sensual, but after a heavenly and invisible, and incomprehensible manner : but yet there remains this controversy among some of them, whether the Body of Christ be present only in the use of the Sacrament, and in the act of eating, and not otherwise. They that hold the affirmative, as the Luther-ans, *in Conf. Sax,*[*] and all Calvinists do, seem to me to depart

* *Editor's Note.* " [Docentur etiam homines, sacramenta esse actiones divi-

T

from all antiquity, which place the presence of Christ in the virtue of the words of consecration and benediction used by the Priest, and not in the use of eating of the Sacrament, for they tell us that the virtue of that consecration is not lost, though the Sacrament be reserved either for sick persons or other. Whereupon Cassander, Consul. Art. 10, saith, They are mad, *qui dicunt mysticam benedictionem Sacramenti cessare, aut virtutem suam amittere, siquæ reliquæ remanserint in dies futuros: non enim mutabitur SS. Corpus Christi, sed virtus benedictionis, et vivificativa gratia jugis in ipso est.* And this most of the Protestants grant and profess at first, though now the Calvinists make popish magic of it in their licentious blasphemy.*

Now if these were the only statements of Cosin upon this point there could be no room to doubt that the post-communion Rubric now under discussion should be interpreted in accordance with them, and consequently that the definition already given of "reverently" must be the true one. But it would be most unfair to pass over passages which, whatever ultimate conclusion may be made regarding them, certainly do seem at first sight to indicate some subsequent change of the Bishop's opinion. The first of these occurs in his 2nd Series of Notes, p. 345, and was apparently written about 1656 (see Note) within six years of the last revision of the Prayer Book, and is as follows:—

"Kneeling.] .... True it is, that the Body and Blood of Christ are sacramentally and really (not feignedly) present, when the blessed Bread and Wine are taken by the faithful communicants; and as true it is also, that they are not present, but only when the hallowed elements are so taken, as in another work (the History of Papal Transubstantiation)† I have more at large declared. Therefore whosoever so receiveth them, at that time when he receiveth them, rightly doth he adore and reverence his Saviour there, together with the sacramental Bread and Cup, exhibiting His own

nitus institutas, et extra usum institutum res ipsas non habere rationem sacramenti, sed in usu instituto in hac communione vere et substantialiter adesse Christum et vere exhiberi sumentibus corpus et sanguinem Christi.—Confessio doctrinæ Saxonicarum Ecclesiarum synodo Tridentinæ oblata. A.D. 1551. cap. 15. (p. 282. ap. Syllogen Confessionum, Oxon. 1827.)]

* *Nichol's Note.* "A line is worn out here, on the edge at the bottom of the page."

† *Editor's Note.* "[Historia papalis Transubstantionis, etc., cap. IV. s. 5. Cosin's Works, vol. IV., p. 49. That work was written in 1656, not printed till 1675. This indicates the date of this note. See the preface to volume IV. Cosin had first written 'Qui tantum sumentibus adest, et vera fide non destitutis;' this he altered into 'Quam communicantibus tantum adsit.' See the treatise itself.] "

Body and Blood unto them. Yet because that Body and Blood is neither sensibly present (nor otherwise at all present but only to them that are duly prepared to receive them, and in the very act of receiving them and the consecrated Elements together, to which they are sacramentally in that act united) the adoration is then and there given to Christ Himself, neither is nor ought to be directed to any external sensible object, such as are the blessed Elements. But our kneeling and the outward gesture of humility and reverence in our bodies, is ordained only to testify and express the inward reverence and devotion of our souls towards our blessed Saviour, who vouchsafed to sacrifice Himself for us upon the Cross, and now presenteth Himself to be united sacramentally to us, that we may enjoy all the benefits of His mystical Passion, and be nourished with the spiritual food of His blessed Body and Blood unto life eternal."

The real difficulty of this passage, so far as it concerns my present argument, is the writer's seeming denial of his former apparent belief—that the Body and Blood of Christ are present in the Sacrament *out* of its use: indeed his language, in the passage of his History of Transubstantiation to which he refers, looks like an unauthorized development of the cautious expression of the 28th Article, "The Sacrament of the Lord's Supper was not by Christ's ordinance reserved, carried about, lifted up, or worshipped;" whereas the Bishop says (p. 174 Oxford Trans.)" . . . . we deny that the elements still retain the nature of Sacraments, when not used according to Divine Institution, that is, given by Christ's ministers, and received by His people; so that Christ in the consecrated bread ought not—*cannot be kept and preserved* to be carried about, because he is present only to the communicants." I hope it is not too presumptuous to think that the words I have italicized are hardly warranted by the language of the Article, and it seems a legitimate question whether Cosin by the use of them does not create as great a difficulty as that which he wished to avoid; for, assume that in any given case * the Sacrament is reserved for a sick person, then,

* This is not a mere supposition, as the writer knows that a member of the present English Episcopate (and one who would certainly not be said to hold very high views on the Eucharist) not unfrequently, in his ministrations as a parochial Incumbent, reserved the Sacrament, at the public Celebration, for the use of the Sick. And too, it is no secret that during the cholera in Leeds some years ago, the Bishop of Ripon, while saying that he could not *authorize* reservation, did not feel himself justified in forbidding it in that emergency. A *real need* for thus acting doubtless has often arisen in the experience of many; it

according to the Bishop's argument, one of three views must be held (*a*) that being reserved *for the purpose of Communion,* "Christ in the consecrated bread ought" to and can "be kept and preserved;" and then this seems to make the Presence depend upon the intended object of the Priest: (*b*) or that the Presence *departs* from the *Sacramentum* when the Ministration is ended, but *returns* to it when used to communicate the sick person: (*c*) or that there could be no presence at all with the Elements, though consecrated at a public or private Celebration, if reserved for the use of the Sick, any more than if "preserved to be carried about."

But while, on the one hand, it is due to Bishop Cosin to suppose that he could have reconciled the apparent discrepancy; so, on the other hand, admitting its existence, it does not really militate against the point I am arguing; for, whatever may have been his exact opinion touching the consecrated Elements when *reserved*, he only denies to them "the nature of Sacraments, *when not used according to Divine institution:*" the question then is—are they used according to Divine institution ("that is," as he says, "given by Christ's ministers, and received by His people") when they are consumed, as expressly directed, by those very COMMUNICANTS who have just before been partaking of them? There seems to me nothing either in the passage from the History of Transubstantiation or in the Note on "*Kneeling,*" to imply that Cosin would have returned an answer in the negative; and if not, what he says of formal sacramental reception may surely be applied also to the participation in the remains of the Sacrament—"at that time when he receiveth them, rightly doth he adore and reverence his Saviour there together with the Sacramental Bread and Cup, exhibiting His own Body and Blood unto them;" and then it follows that the same "outward gesture of humility and reverence in our bodies" is to be used in both cases alike.

occurred once to the writer in a case where the sick person died just as the act of consecrating the Eucharist was finished; it is morally certain often to present itself again: but how is any one to resort to the obvious remedy—reservation—if view (*c*) suggested by Bishop Cosin's theory, is thought to be the most consistent one? Nay, what is to be thought of the authorized practice of reservation in the Scotch Episcopal Communion?

There is, however, another Note of this 2nd Series which must not be overlooked; it runs thus, p. 356 :—

" *And if any of the bread and wine remain, etc.*] which is to be understood of that bread and wine, that the churchwardens provided, and carried into the vestry, not of that which the Priest consecrated for the Sacrament; for of this if he be careful, as he ought to be, to consecrate no more than will suffice to be distributed unto the Communicants, none will remain.

" (Yet if for lack of care * they consecrate more than they distribute, why may not the Curates have it to their own use, as well as be given to children, (*Concil Mastic.* c. 2.) or be burnt in the fire (*Isych in Levit.*) for though the bread and wine remain, yet the consecration, the Sacrament of the Body and Blood of Christ do not remain longer than the holy action itself remains for which the bread and wine were hallowed; and which being ended, return to their former use again ?) "

If indeed this last paragraph is a record of Cosin's *opinion*, it undoubtedly would destroy the support I have been endeavouring to claim from him; unless (as seems probable from the passage just noticed, see also p. 127) he considered the consumption of the remains of the Sacrament *at the Altar* as part of " the holy action itself:" but from its bracketed form and the Editor's suggestion, it may be most reasonably supposed that it is nothing more than the real or imaginary language of an objector for whom the Bishop thought an answer should be provided.   No such answer, however, seems to be recorded by the Bishop: but, unless we are to resort to the very improbable surmise that he was not a consentient party, it may well be considered that his answer is furnished in the amended Rubric of 1662.

Yet by way of clearing up the difficulty, it will be well to consider what answer Cosin would probably have drawn from his knowledge of Ecclesiastical Antiquity ; and perhaps that answer can be given in no more concise and satisfactory way than in the words of Bingham ; for, treating of this very question, " *How the remains of the Eucharist were disposed of,*" he says, Bk. xv., c. 7., s. 4—

---

* *Editor's Note.*—"[This part of the note was written after the former, and because that occupied the page, this is carried down the margin ; it appears to be a sort of quero or ἀπορία in the way of discussion.]"

"Sometimes what remained of the Eucharist, was distributed among the innocent children of the Church. For, as I have briefly hinted before, whilst the communion of infants continued in the Church, nothing was more usual in many places than both to given children the communion at the time of consecration, and also to re-serve what remained unconsumed, for them to partake of some day in the week following. Thus it was appointed by the second Coun-cil of Mascon in France, Anno 588, 'That if any remains of the Sacrifice, after the Service was ended, were laid up in the vestry, he who had the care of them should, on Wednesday or Friday, bring the innocents to Church fasting, and then sprinkling the remains with wine, make them all partake of them. And Evagrius (lib. iv. c. 36) says, it was the custom of old at Constantinople to do the same: for when they had much remains of the Body of Christ left, they were used to call in the children that went to School, and distribute among them. And he tells this remarkable story upon it, that the son of a certain Jew happening one day to be among them, and ac-quainting his father what he had done, his father was so enraged at the thing, that he cast him into his burning furnace, where he was used to make glass. But the boy was preserved untouched for some days, till his mother found him: and the matter being related to Justinian the Emperor, he ordered the mother and the child to be baptized; and the father, because he refused to become a Christian, to be crucified as a murderer of his son. The same thing is related by Gregory of Tours (de. Glor. Martyr. lib. i. c. 10.) and Nicephorus Callistus (lib. xvii. c. 25), who also adds, that the custom continued at Constantinople to his own time, that is, the middle of the fourteenth century; for he says, when he was a child, he was often called to partake of the remains of the Sacrament after this manner among other children."

To what conclusion, then, is it most likely that Bishop Cosin must have been led by a consideration of the practice of the Church and the rule of the Council referred to in his question? Surely this—that the effect of the Consecration *was held* to "remain longer than the holy action itself re-mains for which the bread and wine were hallowed," for the children were to consume the remains *fasting*, this being the rule laid upon *Communicants;* and therefore that being *the Sacrament* still, according to Bishop Overall's definition in the Catechism, and not merely the *Sacramentum*, "the Curates" might not "have it to their own use," but it must be disposed of to the Communicants and with the same reverence as had accompanied the previous Sacramental action.

Again, with regard to the other practice, that of *burning* the remains, referred to in Bishop Cosin's note, the testimony of Bingham is equally explicit; he says, *Ibid* s. 5—

" In some places they observed the rule given by God for disposing of the remainders of the sacrifices of peace-offerings and vows under the old law, which was to burn them with fire. Lev. vii. 17. This was the custom of the Church of Jerusalem in the fifth century, when Hesychius, a presbyter of that Church, wrote his Comment upon Leviticus, where he speaks of it (lib. ii.) in these words: ' God commanded the remainder of the flesh to be burned with fire. And we now see with our own eyes the same thing done in the Church : whatever happens to remain of the Eucharist unconsumed, we immediately burn with fire, and that not after one, two, or many days.' From hence our learned writers generally observe two things : 1, that it was not the custom of the Church of Jerusalem to reserve the Eucharist so much as from one day to another, though they did it in some other Churches. 2. That they certainly did not believe it to be the natural body and substance of Christ, but only his typical or symbolical body : for what an horrible and sacrilegious thing must the very Jews and Heathens have thought it, for Christians to burn the living and glorified body of their God ? And how must it have scandalized simple and plain Christians themselves, to have seen the God they worshipped burnt in fire ? And with what face could they have objected this to the Heathen, that they worshipped such things as might be burnt, which is the common argument used by Arnobius, Lactantius, Athanasius, and most others, if they themselves had done the same thing ? If there were no other argument against transubstantiation and host-worship, this one thing were enough to persuade any rational man that such doctrines and practices were never countenanced by the ancient Church."

So far, however, from Bishop Cosin thinking this practice of the early Church any warrant for putting the remains of the Sacrament to the common uses permitted to the unconsecrated oblations of Bread and Wine, he must undoubtedly, I think, have regarded it as a most distinct precedent for a very reverent dealing with them; for the object was to prevent any risk of profanation—a precaution wholly needless if the Church had then held any such notion as that propounded in Cosin's supposed objection, *viz.*, that the Eucharistic action being ended " the bread and wine" which " were hallowed .... return to their former use again." There is no need, however, it seems to me, to perplex this subject, as some have even lately done, by raising questions of a gross and material character touching the oral manducation of the Sacrament: thus Mr. Goode (*on the Eucharist*, vol. i. p. 191,) speaking of the doctrine of the Real Presence as held by Dr. Pusey, the late Archdeacon Wilberforce, and Archdeacon Denison, says—

" If the Body and Blood of Christ are so joined to the bread and wine that the mouth of every communicant in receiving one necessarily receives the other, then brute animals eating and drinking the bread and wine receive the Body and Blood of Christ."

And he complains that Archdeacon Denison, having by anticipation noticed the objection, can only reply—

" . . . . that we are not told what the consecrated Elements may be to the brute creation, and therefore *cannot affirm anything on the subject*,"

whereas Mr. Goode says (p. 49)—

" . . . . the consistent Romanists maintain, that brute animals eating and drinking consecrated Bread and Wine, eat and drink the Body and Blood of Christ."

Yet, while it is no fair argument to assume—that a consequence connected with the doctrine of *Transubstantiation* by *some* of its maintainers, is also tied to a doctrine which its advocates assert to be the *reverse* of Transubstantiation—it may not be improper to consider how the objection can be met. Let it be granted that the Roman doctrine of the *change of substance* necessarily involves the result named (though Mr. Goode allows, p. 192, that "this is a view from which even many Romanists shrink," professing to hold, as S. Thomas Aquinas says, that " ' as soon as the Sacrament is touched of a mouse or a dog, the body of Christ ceases to be there ' ") why should a like result follow from that Sacramental *union* which the writers in question hold to be involved by the Real Presence of Christ's " Blessed Body and Blood under the form of Bread and Wine?" I say "from *that* Sacramental union which *the writers in question* hold; " for perchance Mr. Goode's expression—" that *the mouth* of every communicant in receiving one necessarily receives the other " might be rejected by those writers as implying a *sensible oral contact* opposed to the nature of the *res sacramenti* as by them understood. Passing over this, however, let me suggest, by way of answer, an analogical argument which I trust is not irreverent. The union, then, of the *sacramentum* and the *res sacramenti* is often explained as being *in kind* like that of man's soul and body; and, again, this latter is frequently used to illustrate the hypostatical union of the Word made flesh, as being also like it *in kind*.

Now, if a man is bitten maliciously by another human being or accidentally by an animal, we do not speak of it as though only a *corpse* had been so treated; yet, though we say "*he* was bitten," we do not mean that the man's *soul* was subjected to that same *physical* action which inflicted a visible injury upon his body : indeed, this is but an application of that truth conveyed by our Lord's words (S. Matt. x. 28.) " Fear not them which kill the body, but are not able to kill the soul."

But we estimate very differently the act of the human being and the act of the animal : the former we regard as a crime and a dishonour, because unnatural, and done by a being who is conscious that it is so; the latter we treat as neither an offence nor a degradation, because natural (in its present state) and done by a creature lacking that reasonable soul which is the source of moral responsibility.

Applying this to the Holy Eucharist, we may, perhaps, the better understand how, as St. Paul says, (1 Cor. xi. 27 and 29), " whosoever shall eat this bread, and drink this cup of the Lord, unworthily, shall be guilty of the Body and Blood of the Lord; " for such an one, though like the worthy receiver he cannot "carnally and visibly press with " his " teeth " more than " the Sacrament [*Sacramentum*] of the Body and Blood of Christ," (Art. XXIX) yet, "not discerning the Lord's Body " does dishonour to that *Res Sacramenti* by the very act of partaking with an evil mind, and therefore to " condemnation," the sign, or Sacrament [Sacramentum seu Symbolum] of so great a thing [tantæ rei.]"

Yet though no such dishonour as this can be done to the

Sacrament *(i. e.,* Sacramentum and Res Sacramenti) save where this faculty of discrimination exists, but is neglected; it is not the less a duty to guard it carefully from risks of seeming irreverence and, much more, of profanation. If, as is the case, we take precautions to preserve ourselves from harm, though from no feeling that our spiritual part can suffer physical injury; it would seem only the legitimate development of a natural instinct so to treat "the outward part or sign of the Lord's Supper" that "the inward part or thing signified" should not be subjected to *apparent* indignity even under circumstances where no design of disrespect could possibly exist. Hence, therefore, the precautions taken in the old English Canons against the Reserved Sacrament being kept so long as to become corrupt: thus Elfric's Canons, A.D. 957, prescribe that " The holy housel ought to be kept with great diligence, and not be permitted to be stale, but another be always hallowed anew for sick men, in about a seven-night or fortnight, so as that it may not be musty at least;" and the Legatine Canons at Westminster, A.D. 1138, Hubert Walter's Legatine Canons at York, A.D. 1195, and at Westminster, A.D. 1200, Archbishop Peckham's Constitutions at Reading, A.D. 1279, Archbishop Reynold's Latin Constitutions, A.D. 1322, alike forbid it to "be reserved above seven days after consecration:" hence, too, that reverent "custom of the Church of Jerusalem" to "burn with fire" such remains "of the Eucharist" as were "unconsumed," which, as furnishing the ground for Bishop Cosin's enquiry—"Why may not the curates have it to their own use?"—has led to these observations. I proceed now to notice another comment of his upon the same Rubric; it occurs in his 3rd Series of Notes, p. 481, and is as follows:—

"*And if any of the bread and wine remain, the curate,* etc.] which needeth not to be understood of that bread and wine which was blessed and consecrated, but of that which was brought to the Church, and not used for the Sacrament. And yet we read of some such things in the Constitutions of the Apostles, lib. viii. cap. 31, τὰς περισσευουσας ἐν τοῖς μυστικοῖς, etc. ' Let the deacons distribute the remains of the blessings at the mysteries to the clergy, according to the mind of the bishop or presbyters. To the bishop, four parts; to a presbyter, three; to a deacon, two; to the rest, subdeacons, readers, singers, or deaconesses, one part.'"

Upon this Note it may be remarked—that, if it was written (as there seems reason for thinking) subsequently to the one last considered, it may fairly be regarded as indicating the Bishop's later judgment, even though it were clear that the *bracketed* part of that Note conveyed his *opinion* at that time. It must be admitted that the passage presents a difficulty at first sight, and appears to imply some uncertainty in the Bishop's mind if, when he says, " And yet we read of some such things in the Constitutions of the Apostles," we understand the "such things" to refer to "that bread and wine which was blessed and consecrated : " but if we read " yet " in the not improbable sense of " beside " or " indeed," the passage is quite plain and entirely consistent with what I have supposed to have been Cosin's real view. Unless, however, there is any evidence to show that the Bishop believed the Constitution to refer to the Consecrated Elements, I see no reason for supposing that he took what, if Bingham be (as would seem) correct, is an entirely wrong view of the authority he quoted. Bingham's statement (Book XV., cap. vii., s. 3,) is as follows :—

" Some learned persons confound this division or consumption of the consecrated Elements with that other division of the oblations among the clergy, and allege the Author of the Constitutions for it, as if he intended this when he says, ' Let the deacons divide what remains of the mystical *Eulogiæ*, by the orders of the bishop or presbyters, among the clergy; to the bishops four parts; to the presbyter three parts ; to the deacon two parts ; to the rest of the clergy, subdeacons, readers, singers, deaconesses, one part. For this is acceptable to God, that every one should be honoured according to his dignity.' It is plain he speaks not here of the Consecrated Elements, but of the division of the people's oblations among the clergy, as Cotelerius rightly expounds it. For this was one way of maintaining the clergy in those days, as has been more fully shown in another place (Book V., chap. iv., s. 1.) And though he calls these by the name of the mystical *Eulogiæ*, yet that does not determine it to the Consecrated Elements: for, as has been noted before, *eulogiæ* is a common name that signifies both. And Socrates takes it for the oblations in this very case, when, speaking of Chrysanthus, the Novatian bishop, he says, he never received anything of the Church save two loaves of the *Eulogiæ* on the Lord's day. Where he certainly means, not two loaves of the Eucharist, but of the other oblations of the people, which it was customary for the clergy to have their proportional shares in."

There remains to be considered one other statement of Bishop Cosin on this subject: it occurs in these words, in his *Suggestions for alterations in the Prayer Book, p. 519*—

" 65, It is likewise here ordered, ' That if any of the bread and wine remain, the curate shall have it to his own use.' Which words some curates have abused and extended so far, that they suppose they may take all that remains of the consecrated bread and wine itself, home to their houses, and then eat and drink the same with their other common meats ; at least the Roman Catholics take occasion hereby to lay this negligence and calumny upon the Church of England; whereas the Rubric only intends it of such bread and wine as remains unconsecrate of that which was provided for the parish, (as appeareth by the articles of enquiry hereabouts in the visitations of divers bishops.) And therefore, for the better clearing of this particular, some words are needful here to be added, whereby the priest may be enjoined to consider the number of them which are to receive the Sacrament, and to consecrate the bread and wine in such a near proportion as shall be sufficient for them ; but if any of the Consecrated Elements be left, that he and some others with him shall decently eat and drink them in the Church before all the people depart from it."

How this *Suggestion* was carried out at the Revision of 1662 we know from that very Rubric which I am now discussing: Nichol's note upon Cosin's proposal is "The word ' unconsecrated ' is now put in ; " not of course that he means this only was added : perhaps Cosin had in mind the Rubric of the Scotch Office of 1638, which is in these words:—

" *And if any of the Bread and Wine remain, which is consecrated, it shall be reverently eaten and drunk by such of the Communicants only as the Presbyter which celebrates shall take unto him, but it shall not be carried out of the Church. And to the end there may be little left, he that officiates is required to consecrate with the least, and then if there be want, the words of consecration may be repeated again, over more, either bread or wine: the Presbyter beginning at these words in the prayer of consecration* (our Saviour in the night that he was betrayed, took, etc.)

The form, however, which the Rubric ultimately took in the hands of the Reviewers is more explicit than this or even than Cosin's suggestion; for, whatever it was meant to imply, the Scotch Rubric certainly did not expressly order the consumption to take place *before the rest of the people;* and Cosin only suggested that it should be made " before all the people depart," which word " all " *may* mean that only SOME *need* remain, though I think we can quite fairly regard it as *not emphatic* and only intending that the Congregation *in general* should stay until the consumption was ended : but the Rubric, as settled by Cosin and his co-revisers, directs the consumption to be " *immediately* after the Blessing," and therefore gives no opportunity for the people to leave the Church, not to say that *all* are clearly supposed to be waiting to see which of them the Priest " shall then call unto him." Taking, however, either view of Cosin's language it conveys the same idea as the Rubric—*viz:* that the consumption of the remains of the Sacrament is a *public religious act* and *a part of the Service;* such it clearly was under the old English Uses (as was remarked, p. 123); such we find it to have been in the early Church; recollecting, therefore, the terms of their Commission (see p. 130) it is most unlikely that the Reviewers of 1662 should have intended to suggest a different practice: of the rule of the Early Church Bingham thus speaks, (Book XV., cap. vii., s. 2):—

" If anything remained over and above what was necessary for these uses [*i. e.,* to communicate the sick, and to testify the communion of distant Churches one with another], then by other rules it was to be divided among the Communicants. As appears from the canons of Theophilus, bishop of Alexandria, one of which is to this purpose : ' Let the clergy and the faithful, (that is, the communicants) divide among themselves the oblations of the Eucharist, after all have participated, and let not a catechumen eat or drink of them.''

Yet it may be objected—that, as the Benediction is given before the consumption of the remains of the Sacrament, so, the Service must from its structure be considered to be over, and therefore that the argument maintained here and at p. 125 fails, inasmuch as the Ministration must be looked upon as

ended. But the like might be said of the Liturgy of the
Early Church, for the Bishop's Benediction preceded the
post-communion consumption; and yet there can be no doubt,
I suppose, that then that consumption was never regarded as
a mere supplementary act which had no connexion with the
Office itself: moreover it seems inconceivable that the
Christians, and especially the Clergy, of that day, should
have drawn a distinction between what was *reserved* and what
(not being needed for reservation) was *consumed;* therefore,
treating with the like reverence, as they did, what they
received in their public Communion and what was reserved
for the Communion of the Sick, it follows that they must have
paid the same regard to what *the Communicants alone* were
allowed to partake of in the post-benediction manducation.
And if this be so, is there the slightest ground for supposing
that the Reviewers of 1662 contemplated a procedure different
from that ancient practice which they took for their principal
guide, when there was nothing in the nature of the case to
call for such divergence, but, on the contrary, a Doctrinal
agreement which summoned them to take pattern by primitive
antiquity, and by the custom of the unreformed English
Church, so far as it coincided therewith? To me it seems
not, especially when we find Cosin, whose Eucharistic views
were certainly not higher than some of his most influential
co-revisers, writing thus in the 1st Series of those Notes
which we have been considering; unless, indeed, it can
be proved that this language is at variance with his latest exposition of Doctrine in his History of Transubstantiation: his
words are p. 155):—

" *The Body and Blood of Christ which are verily and indeed
taken,* etc.] Neither need there any fault be found with our Church
for thus distinguishing the outward sign from the thing signified,
the bread from the Body of Christ; for Maldonate affirms that the
Church of Rome never said otherwise, *de Sacram.*, p. 125 : *Respon-
dendum est, nos nunquam dicere, idem esse Sacramentum et rem
significatam; nam Sacramentum vocamus signum quod videtur, rem
significatam, Corpus Christi quod non videtur;* which approves of
our doctrine, and condemns that gross conceit of the ignorant
papists, that think they see, and taste, and chew the very Body of

Christ, corporally, which every man abhors to conceive, even the best learned among the papists as well as we. I cannot see where any real difference is betwixt us about this real presence, if we would give over the study of contradiction, and understand one another aright. Maldonate, *de Sacr.*, p. 143, after a long examination of the matter, concludes thus at last with us all, so the words be not taken *exclusivè*, as the Puritans will take them, *Corpus Christi sumitur a nobis sacramentaliter spiritualiter, et realitur, sed non corporaliter;* and as I have heard my Lord Overall preach it an hundred times.

There is one other objection which some might perhaps advance against this view for which I am contending—*viz :* that, if what is consumed "immediately after the blessing" by "the Priest and such other of the Communicants as he shall then call unto him" be as much the Sacrament as what they received before the Benediction, then they make a second Communion in one day, and this is forbidden by the Canons of the Church, at least to the Laity.

But *one* (and a sufficient) answer to this plainly is—that, as the old English Liturgies distinctly provided for the consumption of the remains of the Sacrament by the Celebrant in *just as reverent* a way as they ordered his communion to be made, and that too at a period when the authority of the then (and still existing) Canons * was recognized and acted upon, which forbade a Priest to *Celebrate* (and therefore to *Communicate*† twice in one day without necessity; so, to receive at any given Celebration of the Lord's Supper, *a second portion* of the Heavenly Food there set forth is not to make a second Communion. Moreover, since whatever the Consecrated Elements were to the Celebrant under either action, that also they must have been to those who united with him in those actions, it follows that if he did not then make a second Communion, neither did they ; and because the *nature* of the

---

* *viz :* The Canons made in King Edgar's reign, A.D. 960; Hubert Walter's Canons at Westminster, A.D. 1200; Archbishop Langton's Constitutions, A.D. 1222; Archbishop Langham's Constitutions, A.D. 1367.

† The old Law of the Church of England, "that it never be that a priest celebrate mass, and do not eat the housel himself," (*Edgar's Canons*, A.D. 960) is expressly re-enacted in Canon 21, A.D. 1603, which orders "that every Minister, as oft as he administereth the Communion, shall first receive that Sacrament himself;" and also by the Rubric in the present Communion Office, "Then shall the Minister first receive the Communion in both kinds himself."

Eucharist remains unchanged, whatever changes are made in the mode of its Celebration, therefore the like argument holds good now; and thus, (to make the comparison with all reverence) as he who partakes a second time of the same food at any repast (though he has returned thanks) is not thereby accounted to make more than one meal, so, he who (subsequent to thanksgiving) eats and drinks again of " that [Bread and Wine] which was consecrated," does not *repeat* his formal act of Sacramental Communion, but only *continues* to partake of that one " Supper " in which he is receiving the Body and Blood of the Lord.

Having regard, therefore, to these various considerations which have now been urged, especially, *viz :* the language of Cranmer's Letter; the Order of Communion 1548; the probable traditional practice through Edward 6th's reign, and in considerable part, at least, of Elizabeth's reign; the increasingly reverential character of later Rubrics; the known opinions, on the Real Presence, of the leading Reviewers of 1661; Bishop Cosin's Notes and Suggestions; the comparison of terms in the present Book; the directions of the Old Offices to which the Reviewers were referred, and the practice of the Early Church; the terms of the Rubric touching those whom the Celebrant is to call to him ; the time at which they are to be called: it seems to me that a sufficiently conclusive argument is furnished to sustain the theory here advanced—That, in ordering the remains of the Sacrament to be " reverently " consumed, the Church of England means them to be partaken of in that posture which belongs to the act of formal Sacramental manducation.

II. Having thus considered at some length Cranmer's Letter, and examined all the points of it which appear to touch the Declaration on Kneeling, as well as some other incidental questions which spring from the Eucharistic Office ; I proceed now to search for any other evidence calculated to sustain the position I have ventured to take up in my own Letter: this is the more necessary, since Archbishop Cranmer's Letter to the Privy Council (though of much value, as throwing a needful light upon the History of the Declaration) is so far disappointing—that it does not furnish any *Theological* arguments in favour of that rule of Kneeling at Communion for which he was contending. Knowing, however, as we now do, the basis on which he urged the opposed practice, we must be satisfied to look for the grounds of its support in Cranmer's known views at that time on the Eucharistic Presence. We have already seen that Prelate's opinions in the extracts given from his controversial language used contemporaneously with the publication of the Declaration. It is indeed, as I remarked when quoting it, a difficulty to reconcile some of his language with the rest, so as to make him speak consistently. It cannot be denied that he did frequently employ expressions which seem to contradict the Doctrine of what has been aptly termed The Real Objective Presence: but then it must always be borne in mind (1) that he did not scruple to adopt all the high language of Antiquity: (2) that he was most jealous of all attempts to use Patristic statements as a covering for the prevalent Roman Doctrine: (3) and that, owing to his *desire* of comprehending the Foreign Reformers, he may have been under the continual temptation of resorting to a phraseology which should not be obnoxious to the leading men in the several Reforming Schools. These considerations seem to suggest that it is due to the Archbishop to interpret his *lower* by his *higher* language, rather than to resort to the opposite course.

Now it must be allowed, I think, that (whatever expressions he suffered himself to use in controversy) Cranmer would well weigh the language he used or sanctioned as the medium of Catechetical Instruction for the Youth of the Kingdom in the Doctrines of the Church : we cannot fairly suppose that in such a Formulary he would permit statements or definitions at variance with what he believed to be the truth.

It was, then, in 1548 (the very year, be it remembered, in which the preparation of Edward's first Prayer Book was *completed*) that a Catechism, designated by Burnet "an easy, but most useful work,"* (*Hist. Ref.*, vol. 2, book i., p. 67.)

---

* Strype calls it "a very useful Catechism ;" and says that "The substance of this book is grave, serious, and sound doctrine."—*Ann.* book ii., c. 5.

appeared under Cranmer's immediate authority, indeed apparently revised if not translated by him, which must be held to express the Archbishop's belief at that time. It is a small volume, and is entitled :—

" CATECHISMUS, THAT IS TO SAY, A SHORTE INSTRUCTION INTO CHRISTIAN RELIGION FOR THE SYNGULAR COMMODITIE AND PROFYTE OF CHILDREN AND YONG PEOPLE. SET FORTH BY THE MOOSTE REUERENDE FATHER IN GOD THOMAS ARCHBISHOP OF CANTERBURY, PRIMATE OF ALL ENGLAND AND METROPOLITANE. *Gualterus Lynne* excudebat. 1548.

The following are all the passages which bear materially upon the subject of the Real Presence :—

[a] "Secondarily Christ saieth of the breade, this is my bodye, and of y⁰ cuppe he sayeth this is my bloud. Wherefore we ought to beleue y' in the Sacrament we receyue **trewly** the bodye and bloud of Christ. For God is almyghtye (as ye hearde in the Crede): He is able therefore, to do all thynges what he wil. And as saint Paul writeth he calleth those thinges whiche be not, as yf they were. Wherefore when Christe taketh breade, and saieth, Take eate, this is my body, we ought not to doute but we eat his **veray** body. And when he taketh the cuppe, and sayeth, Take drynke, this is my blod, we ought to thynke assuredly, y' we drynke his **veray** blode. And this we must beleue, yf we will be counted Christen men. And wher as in this perellous tyme, certayne deceitful persons be founde in manye places, who of very frowardnes, wil not graunt, that there is the body and bloude of Christ, but denye the same, for no other cause, but that they compasse by mans blynde reason, howe this thinge shoulde be broughte to passe, ye good children, shall with all dilygence beware of suche persons, that ye suffer not yourselues to be deceaued by them........ Wherefore eschewe such erroneous opinions, and beleue the words of our Lord Jesus, that you eate and drynke his **veray** body and blode although mans reason cannot comprehend how and after what manner y⁰ same is ther present."—Fol. ccxxxv.

[b] " Wherefore (good children) doubt not, but ther is the bodye and bloud of our Lorde, which we receaue in the lorde's supper. For he hath sayed so, and by the power of his worde hath caused it so to be. Wherefore seying Christ saieth do this as often as ye do it, in remembrance of me, it is euident hereby, that Christe causeth even at thys tyme, his bodye and bloude to be in the sacrament, after that maner and fashion, as it was at tyme, when he made his maundye with his disciples.......... And let not the foulyshe talke of unbeleuers moue you, who are wont to aske this question, How can the pryest or minister make the bodie and bloud of Christ? To the whiche I answer that the minister doth not this of himself, But Christ himselfe doth gyve unto us his fleshe and blode, as his wordes dothe euidently declare."— Fol. ccxxxvi.

[c] " For when ye do thus [i.e. examine themselves aright], then ye worthely receaue the body and bloud of Christ. And he that so receaueth it, receaueth euerlasting lyfe. For he doth not only, with his bodyly mouthe receaue the bodye and bloude of Christ, but he doth also beleue the wordes of Christ, whereby he is assured, that Christes bodye was gyuen to death for us, and that his bloude was shed for us. And he y^t this beleueth, eateth and drynketh the bodye and bloude of Christ spiritually."—Fol. ccxxxix.

[d] " Wherefore learne them [i.e. the words he had rehearsed] dilygently I pray you, y^t when ye be asked, what is ye Communion or the lordes supper? ye may answer, It is the trew body and true bloude of our lorde Jesus Christe, which was ordeyned by Christ him selfe, to be eaten and drunken of us Christen people, under the forme of breade and wine."—Fol. ccxl.

Looking at the language of these extracts, and especially of *b* and *c*, it would be bold to *deny* that their author or approver held the Doctrine of a Real Objective Presence in the Holy Eucharist.

Yet it has been, somewhat obscurely, implied, either that he did not *then* maintain *"the real* [meaning *bodily*] *presence,"* * or that he abandoned it soon after : the proofs furnished are two-fold ; (1) First, passages in the Letters of certain contemporaries; † (2) Next, a remark of Cranmer's own. ‡

---

* *Goode.*—" Nature of Christ's Presence," vol. 1, p. 46. The Explanation in brackets is Mr. Goode's.

† *Traheron to Bullinger,* Sept. 28, 1548. " ' That you may add yet more to the praises of God, you must know that Latimer has come over to our opinion respecting the true doctrine of the Eucharist, together with the Archbishop of Canterbury and the other Bishops, who heretofore seemed to be Lutherans.' "

John ab Ulmis to Bullinger, Nov. 27, 1548, " speaks of Cranmer as then ' in a great measure recovered from his dangerous lethargy' on the subject of the presence in the Supper, though he had spoken in different language of him so recently as the previous August."

Traheron to Bullinger, Dec. 31, 1548. " ' On the 14th of December, if I mistake not, a disputation was held at London concerning the Eucharist...... The Archbishop of Canterbury, *contrary to general expectation,* most openly, firmly, and learnedly, maintained your opinion upon this subject...... I perceive that it is all over with Lutheranism, now that those who were considered its principal and only supporters, have altogether come over to our side.' "

John ab Ulmis to Bullinger, March 2, 1549. " speaking of the Conference on the Eucharist above alluded to, he, like Traheron, remarks, that the Archbishop of Canterbury had, ' *contrary to general expectation,*' spoken on the subject correctly and clearly."

‡ *Cranmer's answer to Smith,* 1551. " ' But this I confess of myself that *not long before I wrote the said Catechism, I was in that error of the real* [meaning *bodily*] *presence,* as I was many years past in divers other errors, as of transubstantiation, of the sacrifice propitiatory of the priests in the mass,' &c."

But, as to the former, (1) considering the bias of the writers and their wish to claim Cranmer for themselves, nothing satisfactory seems capable of being drawn from them, even if the passages cited represented their sentiments accurately; I think, however, that all do not. With regard to the Letter of Sept. 28th, if *Traheron* meant to describe *Latimer* as one of the "Lutherans," then we have his own denial of it.* Mr. Goode's account of the Letter of John ab Ulmis, of Nov. 27th, has a somewhat different appearance when compared with the original: its words are:—

"That abominable and silly opinion of *a carnal eating* has been long since banished and entirely done away with. Even that Thomas [Cranmer] himself, about whom I wrote to you when I was in London, by the goodness of God and the instrumentality of that most upright and judicious man, master John a Lasco,† is in a great measure recovered from his dangerous lethargy."—*Orig. Letters.* Parker Society, p. 383.

That this passage could prove nothing as to Cranmer's view at that time on "the real [meaning *bodily*] presence" as distinct from Transubstantiation, is plain from the assertion that then, in 1548, it had been "*long since* banished," even if the expression "*carnal eating*" had not been used by the writer. That he was competent to vouch for the Archbishop's opinions may well be doubted when we find him (in that Letter of which Mr. Goode only says "he had spoken in different language of him [Cranmer] so recently as the pre-

* "*Latimer.*—I have long sought for the truth in this matter of the Sacrament, and have not been of this mind past seven years: and my lord of Canterbury's book hath especially confirmed my judgment herein. If I could remember all therein contained, I would not fear to answer any man in this matter.

"*Tresham.*—There are in that book six hundred errors.

"*Weston.*—You were once a Lutheran.

"*Latimer.*—No, I was a papist: for I never could perceive how Luther could defend his opinion without transubstantiation."—*Disp. at Oxford*, 1554. Foxe, vol. vi. p. 505.

Strype referring to this Disputation says, "It was but seven years before his burning that he [*i. e.* Latimer] relinquished that old error," *i.e.* of the "corporeal presence," or "transubstantiation," as he there shews.—*Life of Cranmer*, bk. i., c. 18.

† "'John ab Ulmis,' observes Dr. Jenkyns (in his Preface to Cranmer, p. lxxx.) 'is a competent witness respecting the time when the change in Cranmer's opinions became known, though he was mistaken with regard to the person by whom it was effected.' This was Dr. Ridley, afterwards Bishop of Rochester, and his fellow-martyr. See Strype, Cranmer, 97, and above, p. 13, *n.* 1."—*Editor's Note.*

vious August ") thus wholly misrepresenting the character of the Archbishop's Catechism :—

" . . . . I would have you know this for certain, that this Thomas has fallen into so heavy a slumber, that we entertain but a very cold hope that he will be aroused even by your most learned letter. For he has lately published a Catechism, in which he has not only approved that foul and sacrilegious transubstantiation of the papists in the holy supper of our Saviour, but all the dreams of Luther seem to him sufficiently well-grounded, perspicuous, and lucid."—*Orig. Letters.* P.S. p. 381.

Now let any one look at the extracts just given from this Catechism, and say whether they teach Transubstantiation, as John ab Ulmis so unscrupulously affirms : but, apart from its actual language, it must have been notorious enough that —whether its source was regarded, or the design of the Archbishop, or the alterations he made in the Translation, or his known opinion at that time—Cranmer's Catechism was not intended to teach the Roman Doctrine on the Eucharist.*
Certainly, then, this writer is no trustworthy witness of the Archbishop's views.

Of the two Letters dated Dec. 31, 1548, and March 2, 1549,† it seems enough to say that—as all we appear to know

---

* Else we may be quite certain that Dr. Rowland Taylor (in his Examination, January 22nd, 1554-5, when "Master Secretary Bourn said, ' Which of the religions mean ye of, in King Edward's days. For ye know there were divers books of religion set forth in his days. There was a religion set forth in a Catechism by my Lord of Canterbury : do you mean that you will stick to that ? ") would not have answered, 'My Lord of Canterbury made a Catechism to be translated into English, which book was not of his own making; yet he set it forth in his own name : and truly that book for the time did much good."— *Foxe*, vi. 685.

† But as Mr. Goode's extract affords but a very imperfect representation of these letters, it seems desirable to give them more at length here : they are as follows :—
Traheron to Bullinger, Lond. Dec. 31, 1548.—" . . . . . On the 14th of December, if I mistake not, a disputation was held at London, concerning the Eucharist, in the presence of almost all the nobility of England. The argument was sharply contested by the Bishops. The Archbishop of Canterbury, contrary to general expectation, firmly, and learnedly maintained your opinion upon this subject. His arguments were as follows :—The Body of Christ was taken up from us into heaven. Christ has left the world. ' Ye have the poor always with you, but me ye have not always,' &c. Next followed the Bishop of Rochester [Ridley], who handled the subject with so much eloquence, perspicuity, and power, as to stop the mouth of that most zealous Papist, the Bishop of Worcester [Heath]. The truth never obtained a more brilliant victory among us. I perceive that it is all over with Lutheranism, now that those who were considered its principal and almost only supporters, have altogether come over to our side. . . . . "—" [Postscript, added by John ab Ulmis.] Lo ! just as Master Traheron was about to send his

of the *Disputation at London*, on Dec. 14, 1548, is summed up in those words of King Edward's Journal: " There was a notable Disputation of the Sacrament in the Parliament House "—it would be a most unsafe course to determine Cranmer's views at that time from such notices of such writers upon a Controversy of which no records apparently remain.

(2.) With regard to Cranmer's own language about himself, it seems to furnish the best possible evidence that, though when (in 1548) he published his Catechism, he had abandoned those particular views on the subject of the Presence, which (in 1551) he declared to be unsound—yet that, at this latter date, he maintained the same doctrine which he had delibe-

letter, I happened to come into his room, and can do no otherwise than send you this brief salutation; for, owing to the great impatience of the messenger, I am unable to write more. I will tell you everything in a few days. In haste. London. The foolish Bishops have made a marvellous recantation."

It is not very clear whether this last sentence is meant to confirm Traheron's statement, or to imply some retractation of the opinion which Traheron thought the Bishops had pronounced : but the doubt does not affect my argument. The promised letter, however, seems not to exist; though in the following letter of John ab Ulmis to Bullinger, "dated March 2nd, 1548-9," and "written apparently from Oxford," he says "'. . . . I had most fully written to you respecting almost everything that I thought it would interest you to know, three days before I received your letter ; partly, too, because I was aware that Master Traheron . . . . had informed you of the discussion of the Council respecting the Eucharist." Afterwards he continues thus :—"'. . . . As to what they have reported respecting religion, namely, that there are great differences of opinion, I admit that such has been the case to a considerable extent ; but I can now assert that by the goodness of God, the minds of all good men are disposed to harmony and peace. For the cause of these dissensions is removed in this present parliament ; namely, the babbling and dogmas of Antichrist, which are now positively and effectually banished. I would here write you word what has been done and determined respecting the Lord's Supper, only that your most excellent and loving friend, Master Traheron, has already acquainted you with every particular. From him, therefore, you will learn the whole matter more completely, and from me these few things very briefly. The Archbishop of Canterbury, a man of singular worth and learning, has, contrary to the general expectation, delivered his opinion upon this subject learnedly, correctly, orderly, and clearly; and by the weight of his character, and the dignity of his language and sentiments, easily drew over all his hearers to our way of thinking. His opponent was that lying and subtle Cerberus, the Bishop of Winchester, together with a number of other babblers who were brought in, men who knew nothing else beyond a few quiddities, and those silly and false. Peter Martyr has openly declared to us all, on this very day on which I write this letter, what was his opinion upon this subject; and he seemed to all of us not to depart even a nail's-breadth from that entertained by yourself. Nay, more, he has defended that most worthy man, Zwingle, by the testimony of your opinion, and takes part with him against his adversaries, who falsely object to him that he makes the Sacrament a mere sign : he moreover declares that those persons are out of their senses, who make the body of Christ to be without any local habitation, uncircumscribed, in many places at once, void of shape, and other matters of the like kind. . . . ' "—*Original Letters*, p. 388.

rately put forth three years before. For (a) when he says, "I was in that error of the real presence" (whatever that error was) "*not long before* I wrote the said Catechism," he plainly means that he was *not* in that error *when* he wrote it; and (b) in another place he distinctly adheres to (in 1551) the language of the Catechism, only stipulating that no *carnal* sense is to be put upon it such as Gardiner, in his Articles of January 21, 1550—1 (see p. 27) had imposed for his own justification. His words are:—

"And in that Catechism I teach not, as you do, that the body and blood of Christ is contained in the Sacrament, being reserved, but that in the ministration thereof we receive the body and blood of Christ; whereunto if it may please you to add or understand this word 'spiritually,' then is the doctrine of my Catechism sound and good in all men's ears, which know the true doctrine of the Sacrament."—*Ans. to Gardiner.*

Moreover, Cranmer refers to and repeats in this part of his answer to Gardiner's criticisms upon his "Defence of the true and catholic Doctrine of the Sacrament," what he had written in that Treatise of 1550: the passage is as follows:—

"So doth St. John Chrysostem [in Joann. Hom. xlvi.] say, that we see Christ with our eyes, touch him, feel him, and grope him with our hands, fix our teeth in his flesh, taste it, break it, eat it, and digest it, make red our tongues and die them with his blood, and swallow it, and drink it.

"And in a Catechism by me translated and set forth, I used like manner of speech, saying, that with our bodily mouths we receive the body and blood of Christ. Which my saying divers ignorant persons, not used to read old ancient authors, nor acquainted with their phrase and manner of speech, did carp and reprehend for lack of good understanding.

"For this speech, and other before rehearsed of Chrysostum, and all other like, be not understood of the very flesh and blood of our Saviour Christ, (which in very deed we neither feel nor see,) but that which we do to the bread and wine, by a figurative speech is spoken to be done to the flesh and blood, because they be the very signs, figures, and tokens instituted of Christ, to represent unto us his very flesh and blood.

"And yet as with our corporal eyes, corporal hands, and mouths, we do corporally see, feel, taste, and eat the bread, and drink the wine, (being the sign and sacraments of Christ's body,) even so with our spiritual eyes, hands, and mouths, we do spiritually see, feel, taste, and eat his very flesh, and drink his very blood."—*Ibid.* p. 226.

Mr. Goode (vol. 1, p. 46) claims the Archbishop's statement, as to his change of opinion, in proof that when he put out the first Book of Homilies (in 1547) "he had not then embraced the true doctrine on the subject of the Eucharist," and that, consequently, we are bound to consider him as having subsequently abandoned the language of his Advertisement at the end of that Book, where a Homily is promised " of the due receiving of his blessed Body and Blood, under the form of Bread and Wine." Mr. Goode contends that the expression, "under the form of bread and wine," necessarily "expresses the doctrine of Transubstantiation;" though Cranmer (in 1551) distinctly states that he had, in 1548, "*many years past,*" abandoned that *error:* but Mr. Goode presses the same phrase into covering what he calls "the doctrine of the Bodily Presence," which doctrine he argues, from Cranmer's language, the Archbishop "held . . . . till after" the publication of the Homilies in 1547. Dates, however, prove, I think, that the words, "not long before," do not carry down Cranmer's belief of a " Bodily," *i. e.,* a *carnal* presence to the time of their publication, unless, indeed, it can be shewn that the Archbishop's opinions underwent a most material change within three or four months of that time. For the Homilies were prepared on purpose to be lodged in the several Dioceses, with the Royal Injunctions of 1547 by the King's Visitors as they proceeded through the kingdom that year: that Visitation was to have commenced in May or June, but was delayed until August; a delay which, it may be, was partly caused by the difficulties which Cranmer had to encounter from Gardiner, Bishop of Winchester, whose countenance and assistance he was anxious to obtain in the preparation of the Homilies, which, however, was ultimately refused, though he complained much of some parts of them when they were finished, pretty much because, as Cranmer thought, "he liked nothing unless he did it himself," (*Strype's Cranmer*, bk. ii., c. 3.) Now there was barely time for the Homilies to be distributed by the Visitors, before the Statute 1 Edw. VI., c. i., was passed on Nov. 4th.—" An Act against such as shall unreverently speak against the Sacrament of the Altar, and of the receiving thereof in both kinds :" to that Statute the Archbishop was clearly a consentient party, for in the contemporaneous Convocation, " Session V. November ult. . . . . Mr. Prolocutor exhibited . . . . a form of a certain ordinance, delivered by the most reverend the Archbishop of Canterbury, for the receiving of the Body of our Lord under both kinds, *viz.*, of bread and wine." (*Ib.* c. 4.) This Act was followed up by the Royal Proclamation of Dec. 27th, already quoted (see p. 6), the language of which, while expressly affirming "*that the body and blood of Jesus Christ is there,*" leaves no room for doubt that one object which Cranmer aimed at, in procuring the passing of the Statute, was to suppress the " unreverent " belief then popular, of a gross carnal presence, whether held in connexion with Transubstantiation or not; though it was also directed generally against those who " go about in their sermons or talks arrogantly to define the manner, nature, fashion, ways, possibility or impossibility of those matters." Mr. Goode may probably have mistaken Cranmer's views at this time from having, apparently, lost sight of the fact of this popular belief; for he says (p. 19), " That neither Romanists nor Lutherans have ever held a gross, visible, material presence, or a presence of the natural body after a natural manner." That this is an error, as regards the Romanists, an examination of the passages at pp. 6 and 28 will, I think, sufficiently demonstrate. Supposing it, however, to be even true that this sudden change of opinion did occur, (though, as I have argued, the evidence seems wholly against it,) it would be no proof that Cranmer repudiated the phrase, " Under the form of bread and wine;" on the contráry, in the Catechism of 1548, which was published shortly after the occurrences just referred to, *he actually employs the same language,* (see § *d,* p. 155) so that one of two conclusions must follow—(1) Either he maintained the *same* doctrine at the publication of the First Book of Homilies, as well as when the Catechism appeared; or (2) that he accounted the phrase, " Under the form of bread and wine," alike suited to express the doctrine which he held when he abandoned any notion of a *carnal*

Y

Presence. To my own mind, the evidence proves—that the Archbishop did not hold the doctrine of what Mr. Goode calls, "the Bodily presence," when he published the First Book of Homilies; that as he used the phrase in question then, so he employed it in his Catechism; and that, he neither had occasion, nor intended to disuse or to disown it afterwards;—for as to Cranmer's language to Gardiner, upon which Mr. Goode mainly relies for proof that the Archbishop *did* repudiate the phrase, it seems to me foreign to such an intention, as I have already suggested at p. 21; and moreover, such statements of Cranmer's doctrine as those furnished at p. 22 and elsewhere, are anything but inconsistent with a retention of the phrase.

It has, indeed, been suggested by a Prelate (who, like Mr. Goode, apparently desires to free Cranmer from the responsibility of the phrase) that it may have been "surreptitiously introduced:" but it seems inconceivable that this should have occurred, considering Cranmer's *personal superintendence* of the publication of the Homilies. Yet if it were so, it is no less difficult to imagine that the Archbishop should have been silent on the matter, when Gardiner wrongly quoted the language as being in the *Communion Office* of 1549, if a phrase which he is now said to have repudiated had found its way into an Advertisement of forthcoming Homilies, both without his knowledge and against his distinct convictions. But the same Prelate has further suggested—that "if we are to refer to the notice at the end of the one book, let us take with it the title page at the beginning of the second, and the titles of the two parts of the Homily itself. Neither here, nor in the words of the Homily, does the expression 'under the form of bread and wine' occur." If, however, there exists an apparent inconsistency, such as is here meant to be indicated, it may arise from insufficient attention to the *earlier* words of the Advertisement, which perhaps have hardly received due notice, on either side, in the controversy touching the disputed formula.

The terms, then, of the Advertisement imply that the object of the promised Homily was to treat "*of the due re-*

ceiving," rather than of the *Presence in the Sacrament ;* consequently, while the *Title* of the Second Book recognizes the *Notice* of the First Book, there need be no surprise (rather it was to be expected) that the *Title* of the promised Homily should convey the *specific purpose* of it; and so in " The Table of Homilies ensuing," the 15th is called " *Of the worthy Receiving of the Sacrament,*" while the "Homily" itself is intituled not merely " of the worthy receiving," but of the "reverent esteeming of the Sacrament of the Body and Blood of Christ : " as if in part to fulfil the promise of the PROCLA-MATION just noticed to " declare and set forth an open doctrine thereof, [*i. e.,* of the Sacrament], and what terms and words may justly be spoken thereby, other than be expressly in the Scripture contained in the act before rehearsed,"—a promise which Cranmer may have found it the more needful to redeem, considering the then growing irreverence on the subject. If, moreover, the Title be Cranmer's then it would seem that we may fairly read the word, " Reverent," by the light of the same language in his letter to the Privy Council already commented upon ; and, too, may consider these and the following statements of the Homily as being mutually expletive :—

Part I. (*a.*) " . . . . We must address ourselves to frequent the same [Table] in reverent and comely manner, lest as physic provided for the body, being misused, more hurteth than profiteth ; so this comfortable medicine of the soul, undecently received, tend to our greater harm and sorrow. And St. Paul saith, *He that eateth and drinketh unworthily, eateth and drinketh his own damnation.*"

(*b.*) " We must then take heed . . . . lest of two parts we have but one."

(*c.*) " For this table is not, saith Chrysostom, for chattering jays, but for eagles, who flee thither where the dead body lieth."

(*d.*) " . . . . Thus much we must be sure to hold, that in the Supper of the Lord there is . . . . no bare sign, no untrue figure of a thing absent."

(*e.*) " And truly, as the bodily meat cannot feed the outward man, unless it be let into a stomach to be digested, which is healthsome and sound ; no more can the inward man be fed, except his meat be received into his soul and heart, sound and whole in faith."

(*f.*) " It is well known that the meat we seek for in this supper is spiritual food, the nourishment of our soul, a heavenly refection,

and not earthly; an invisible meat, and not bodily; a ghostly substance, and not carnal; so that to think that without faith we may
enjoy the eating and drinking thereof, or that that is the fruition of
it, is but to dream a gross carnal feeding, basely objecting and binding
ourselves to the elements and creatures."

(*g.*) ". . . . The unbelievers and faithless cannot feed upon that
precious body."

(*h.*) "Wherefore let us prove and try ourselves unfeignedly, ...
so that at this His table we receive not only the outward Sacrament,
but the spiritual thing also; not the figure, but the truth; not the
shadow only, but the body; not to death, but to life; not to destruction, but to salvation. . . . ."

Part II. (*i.*) "You have heard with what constant faith we should
clothe and deck ourselves, that we might be fit and decent partakers
of that celestial food."

(*k.*) "St. Basil saith, it behoveth him that cometh to the body and
blood of Christ, in commemoration of Him that died and rose
again, to be pure from all filthiness of the flesh and spirit, lest he eat
and drink his own condemnation. . . . ."

(*l.*) "Dost thou neither fear God, the maker of this feast; nor
reverence his Christ, the refection of meat; . . . . ? "

(*m.*) "For surely, if we do not with earnest repentance cleanse
the filthy stomach of our soul, it must needs come to pass, that as*
wholesome meat received into a raw stomach, corrupteth and marreth
all, and is the cause of further sickness; so shall we eat this wholesome bread, and drink this cup to our eternal destruction."

(*n.*) "If they be worthy blame which kiss the prince's hand with
a filthy and unclean mouth, shalt thou be blameless which, with a
stinking soul, full of covetousness, fornication, drunkenness, pride,
full of wretched cogitations and thoughts, dost breathe out iniquity
and uncleanness on the bread and cup of the Lord? "

Now it is quite true, that neither in these passages, nor in
the rest of the Homily, is the expression used, "under the
form of bread and wine;" but the point to˙ be considered is,
whether *the same thing* is not taught *in other words*—whether
a Real Objective Presence in the Sacrament is not distinctly
set forth in the language of these extracts. It may well

---

* Is not this precisely the same idea as that conveyed in the Prayer of Access,
contained in all the Prayer Books, from 1549 to 1662, "Grant us therefore,
gracious Lord, SO to eat the flesh of Thy dear Son Jesus Christ, and to drink
His blood [1549, in these holy Mysteries, that we may continually dwell in Him
and He in us] that our sinful bodies may be made clean by His Body, and our
souls washed through His most precious blood. [1552-1662, and that we may
evermore dwell in Him and He in us]. Amen." Of what use is the word, SO,
unless it means that there is a right and a wrong way of partaking of the *same*
thing—that Thing being the Body and Blood of Christ?

enough have been that, in a Homily meant to be put out for popular instruction, Cranmer may have thought it desirable to drop that particular formula which to the popular mind conveyed then a false notion, and which was again and again employed by Gardiner and others, at that very time, to sustain their own views. But the *absence* of the particular expression can be no reliable proof that it was *rejected*, especially when Cranmer's Catechism was still in circulation; and there is nothing to show (so far as I am aware) that he wished to cancel that same expression which he had then used.

Of course if it can be shewn that this Homily was not written by Cranmer* or with his sanction, but was prepared or altered by Parker, or under his authority, my argument so far fails, that nothing can be drawn *one way or other* from this later Homily as regards Abp. Cranmer's views : but then it simply leaves his previous opinions untouched and becomes a standard by which to test only the mind of the Ecclesiastical Authorities of the beginning of Elizabeth's reign, instead of the intentions of the Episcopal Rulers of the latter years of the reign of Edward 6th.

I have urged Cranmer's employment of the phrase " under the form of bread and wine," in his Catechism, as disproving the theory that he abandoned that formula subsequently to his use of it in the Advertisement of the 1st Book of Homilies. Yet it may be contended, perhaps, that Cranmer was still in his " error of the real presence " when he published the Catechism ; for that, as Strype mentions (bk. ii., c. 5,)

" Bishop Gardiner, in his book against the Archbishop, takes advantage of two things in this Catechism against him, as though he himself, when he put it forth, was of the opinion of the corporal presence."

The " two things," Strype adds *(Ib.)* were these :—

---

* Though some proof of its being his may perhaps be found in the fact of its containing the same passage from *Eusebius Emissenus* (" When thou goest up to the reverend communion," &c.) which Cranmer quoted in his " Defence of the True and Catholic Doctrine of the Sacrament," and upon which he lays much stress in his " Answer to Gardiner," p. 228.

" The one was a picture that stood before the book, where was an altar with candles lighted, and the priest apparelled after the old sort, putting the wafer into the communicant's mouth. The other is an expression or two used somewhere in the book, ' that with our bodily mouths we receive the body and blood of Christ :' and, ' that in the Sacrament we receive truly the body and blood of Christ :' and ' this we must believe, if we will be counted Christian men.' "

That Strype did not believe the accusation to be well founded, is plain from his thus continuing his account :—

" But to both Cranmer in his next book against Gardiner, made answer, ' That as for the picture, it was that was set before the Dutch Edition of the book, and so none of his doing ; but that he afterwards caused the Popish picture* to be altered into a picture representing Christ eating His last supper with His disciples. ' As for the expressions,' he said, ' he taught, that we in the Sacrament do receive the body and blood of Christ spiritually ; and, that the words *really* and *substantially* were not used, but *truly?* And in his answer to Dr. Richard Smith's preface, wrote against the said Archbishop, who it seems had twitted him also with this Catechism, he spake largely of these his expressions in his own vindication." †

* Lest it should be inferred from this that Cranmer was *opposed* to the Lights and Vestments (and not merely to the picture as upholding the then popular view of the Mass as distinct from the Communion) it may be well to add here the following extract from a letter of " *Martin Bucer* and *Paul Fagius* to the Ministers at Strasburgh, dated at Lambeth April 26, 1549 :" after saying " We yesterday waited upon the Archbishop of Canterbury, that most benevolent and kind father of the Churches and of godly men ; who received and entertains us as brethren," they continue thus—" The cause of religion, as far as appertains to the establishment of doctrines, and the definition of rites, is pretty near what could be wished [here they mention the need of a suitable ministry] as soon as the description of the ceremonies now in use shall have been translated into Latin, we will send it to you. We hear that some concessions have been made both to a respect for antiquity, and to the infirmity of the present age ; such, for instance, as the vestments commonly used in the Sacrament of the Eucharist, and the use of Candles : so also in regard to the commemoration of the dead, and the use of chrism ; for we know not to what extent or in what sort it prevails. They affirm that there is no superstition in these things, and that they are only to be retained for a time, lest the people, not having yet learned Christ, should be deterred by too extensive innovations from embracing His religion, and that rather they may be won over. This circumstance however greatly refreshed us, that all the services in the Churches are read and sung in the vernacular tongue, that the doctrine of justification is purely and soundly taught, and the Eucharist administered according to Christ's ordinance, private masses having been abolished. . . . .
" At Lambeth, from the house of the Archbishop of Canterbury, near London."
—*Orig. Letters*, p. 535.
† The precise words of Cranmer to Gardiner are these—" And as concerning the Catechism, I have sufficiently answered in my former book [see p. 159.] But in this place may appear to them that have any judgment, what pithy arguments you make, and what dexterity you have in gathering of author's minds, that would gather my mind and make an argument here of a picture, neither put in my book, nor by me devised, but invented by some fond painter

167

Strype appears to have made some mistake in quoting Cranmer as to the *expressions* in his Catechism; at least I have not succeeded in finding, either in his *Answer to Gardiner* or in his *Reply to Smith* the language here attributed to him: there are five places in the former where reference is made to the Catechism viz. pp. 20, 188, 190, 226 and 227, (*Parker Soc. Ed.*) but in neither of them does Cranmer make the answer here imputed to him: *Gardiner*, indeed, (p. 20) says,

"Justus Jonas hath translated a Catechism out of Dutch into Latin, taught in the city of Nuremburg in Germany, where Hosiander is chief preacher, in which catechism they be accounted for no true Christian men, that deny the presence of Christ's body in the Sacrament. The words 'really' and 'substantially' be not expressed as they be in Bucer, but the word 'truly' is there, and, as Bucer saith, that is substantially. Which catechism was translated into English in this author's name [i.e. Cranmer] about two years past."

But Cranmer gives no reply whatever to this, whereas Strype apparently makes him *repudiate* the words "really" and "substantially." It is easy, indeed, to understand that the Archbishop may have been all the better pleased to trans-

---

or carver, which paint and grave whatsoever their idle heads can fancy. You should rather have gathered your argument upon the other side, that I mislike the matter, because I left out of my book the picture that was in the original before. And I marvel you be not ashamed to allege so vain a matter against me, which indeed is not in my book, and if it were, yet were it nothing to the purpose." Then follows the passage quoted at p. 159, "And in that Catechism," &c.—*Ans. to Gardiner*, p. 227.

The Archbishop's answer to Smith (who had said that "Peter Martyr at his first coming to Oxford, when he was but a Lutheran in this matter, taught as D. Smith now doth. But when he came once to the court, and saw that doctrine misliked them that might do him hurt in his living, he anon after turned his tippet, and sang another song") is in these words:—

"Of M. Peter Martyr's opinion and judgment in this matter, no man can better testify than I; forasmuch as he lodged within my house long before he came to Oxford, and I had with him many conferences in that matter, and know that he was then of the same mind that he is now, and as he defended after openly in Oxford, and hath written in his book. And if D. Smith understood him otherwise in his lectures at the beginning, it was for lack of knowledge, for that then D. Smith understood not the matter, nor yet doth not, as it appeareth by this foolish and unlearned book, which he hath now set out: no more than he understood my book of the Catechism, and therefore reporteth untruly of me, that I in that book did set forth the real presence of Christ's body in the Sacrament. Unto which false report I have answered in my fourth book, the eighth chapter," (*i.e.* the reply to Gardiner just quoted.) Then follows the passage "But this I confess of myself," &c., (see p. 155).—*Works.* Parker Society. ii. p. 374.

late a catechism in which these words were not used, considering the way in which many of the Roman party were continually employing them to express that notion of a *physical* presence which he was ever combating ;* and if he did in fact *prefer* the word " truly," this is no sort of proof that he *objected* to the other terms when not used in a *carnal* sense; especially when, as I have shewn at p. 62, those and other equivalent words were admitted to be legitimate by Cranmer, Ridley, and others, in the course of the Eucharistic controversy,

It may, moreover, be satisfactory to point out how the charge respecting the Catechism has been dealt with by Dr. Burton, who, in his Preface to the Oxford Edition of this Catechism 1829 (pp. xxi. to xxv.,) after quoting the passage from Cranmer relative to the picture (a fac-simile of which he gives at p. 174 of the Latin Edition) and remarking that "the Protestant reader will scarcely observe any thing which could justly have called for these remarks," says :—

" The Plate, which Cranmer introduced [viz. a Picture of our Lord and the Twelve sitting at a table; from a design by Hans Holbein who was then in England] instead of the one objected to by Gardiner, will be found in p. 204 of the English Catechism, and is totally different from that in the Latin. But though his answer is so far completely satisfactory, it must still be acknowledged, and Cranmer himself confessed, that he did not all at once shake off his former errors. The language, which is held concerning the real presence, in p. 208 of the English Catechism [*i.e.* the passage commencing " For God is Almighty," &c.] is extremly strong. The author of the Latin Catechism was undoubtedly a Lutheran and held consubstantiation, Cranmer is supposed at this time to have held the same doctrine; though the difference is remarkable, as has been already stated,† between the English and Latin Catechisms, the

---

* *e.g.* in this part (as in many other places) of his answer to Gardiner (who had claimed Luther, Bucer, Jonas, Melancthon Œpinus in favour of his own view) Cranmer says :—" And yet not one of these new men (whom you allege) do thoroughly agree with your doctrine . . . . For they affirm not such a gross presence of Christ's body, as expelleth the substance of bread, and is made by conversion thereof into the substance of Christ's body, and is eaten with the mouth."

† Page xviii. where, referring to p. 208 of his Edition of the English Catechism, he remarks " We may observe however that here it is, ' we *receyve* trewly the bodye and blood of Christ :' but in the Latin, p. 177, it is, ' quod vere corpus et sanguis ejus *sit*.' "

latter speaking of the Body and Blood of Christ being present in the Sacrament, the latter [sic query *former*] only of our receiving them. Cranmer was charged in his own day with having been first a Papist, then a Lutheran, and lastly a Zwinglian, in his opinion concerning the Sacrament : and Gardiner made much of the contradictions which appeared between the Catechism of 1548, and the Defence of the Sacrament, which was published in 1550. The same inconsistency appears to have been pointed out by Dr. Richard Smith in the Preface to a work, which he wrote against Cranmer's Defence, and which was entitled, *Confutation of a certain Book called, A Defence*, &c. The Archbishop answered this Preface, and after saying that the writer of it misunderstood Peter Martyr's sentiments, he adds, ' No more than he understood my book of the Catechism,' &c.—(See Note, p. 167.)

" But the heaviest charge was brought against Cranmer by Dr. Martin, in his examination at Oxford ; in which he accused him not only of versatility, but of actual dishonesty. Part of this dialogue has already been alluded to at p. vi. [viz. in a quotation from Fox, Acts and Monuments, vol. ii., p. 1877. ed. 1583.] ; but the whole of it is as follows,

" ' Martin. When King Henrye dyed, did you not translate Justus Jonas book ?

" ' Cranmer. I did so.

" ' Martin. Then there you defended an other doctrine touching the Sacraments, by the same token that you sent to Lynne your printer, that where as in the first printe there was an affirmative, that is to say, Christes body reallye in the Sacramente, you sent then to your prynter to put in a *not*, whereby it came miraculously to passe that Chrysts bodye was cleane conveyed out of the Sacrament.

" ' Cranmer. I remember there was two Prynters of my sayde booke, but where the same *not* was put in, I cannot tell.'

" It is impossible to say, to which sentence in the Sermon on the Lord's Supper Dr. Martin alluded ; for though we find the words, ' we receyve trewly the bodye and bloud,' and ' we eat his veray bodye,' yet the word 'reallye' does not occur throughout the whole of it : and if the reader will look to all the places, which appear to favour the real presence, he will find it almost impossible for the word *not* to have been inserted. Cranmer, it is true, does not actually deny the insertion, but his words may mean, that if it was made, it was without his knowledge ; and certainly no copy of the Catechism has as yet been produced, which contains the negative. It has been stated, that one of the Bodleian copies appears evidently to be a different edition from the others ; but the negative does not occur in it ; and the passage, to which Gardiner alluded, as quoted at p. xix.,* is

---

* viz. " ' We receave in the Sacrament the body of Christ with our mouthe, and such spenche other use, as a booke set forth in the archbishoppe of Canterburies name called a Catechisme, willeth children to be taught that they receave

z

not altered. This copy contains no list of Errata : but in the other copies, the word *not* is ordered to be inserted in the place which corresponds to page 139, line 1,* of this Edition, where it is evidently wanted ; but we can hardly suppose Dr. Martin to have confounded the two places. Strype (Memorials of Cranmer, p. 396) has certainly gone too far, when he said, ' In a second edition the word *not* was inserted in a certain place of the book, to alter the doctrine of the real presence, which was asserted in the first edition.' He appears to have taken this from the dialogue with Dr. Martin, in which nothing is said of a second edition; and upon the whole there is great reason to conclude, that the charge was altogether unfounded." †

In a Note Dr. Burton further says :—

" It is not impossible, that Dr. Martin may have remembered a passage in Gardiner's Answer to Cranmer's book upon the Sacrament, in which, after criticising Cranmer's version of a passage in Theodoret, he says, ' I wene the Printer left out a (not) and should have sayd, not changed into the godly substance,' p. 125. Cranmer denies that he or his Printer had made this omission, p. 322 ; and since the doctrine of transubstantiation formed the subject of dispute Dr. Martin may have confounded Cranmer's Defence of the Sacrament with his Catechism."

In further confirmation of these statements of Strype and Dr. Burton (which I have quoted to show that Cranmer adhered to the doctrine of his Catechism.) I cannot do better than cite the language of a recent author‡ whose doctrinal views are entirely on, what is called " The Evangelical side," but whose candour obliges him to deny that they can find support from the Prayer Book on the disputed questions touching the Sacraments: speaking of Cranmer's views on Baptism, Mr. Fisher says:—

" We have in the '*Answer to Gardiner,*'as well as in the aforesaid '*Answer to Smythe's Preface* ' a complete authentication of the Cate-

with their bodily mouth the body and bloud of Christ, which I allege because it shall appear it is a teaching set forth among us of late as hath been also and is by the booke of comen prayer beyng the most true Catholique doctrine of the substance of the Sacrament, in that it is then so Catholiquely spoken of, whicho booke this auctor doth after specially allow, howsoever all the summe of his teachyng doth improve it in that point.' "

* viz., in the Instruction on "The First Petition " of the Lord's Prayer— "' The name of God is halowed also, but lytle regarded and contemned, when the gospel and worde of God, is not boldely professed before the worlde.' "

† Strype does, indeed, defend Cranmer by adding—" But the Archbishop professed his ignorance concerning the foisting in of that word. The addition of which word, indeed, he thought was needless; still holding the body and blood *truly* present in the holy supper, though after a spiritual manner."—*Cranmer* p. 396.

‡ *Liturgical Purity our Rightful Inheritance,* by J. C. Fisher, Esq., Lond. 1857.

chism,' as being in the main a faithful exponent of the Archbishop's sentiments, not only in 1548, but even *so late as the close of the year* 1551—the very time, be it remembered, when under the especial superintendence of Cranmer, the Second Service Book of Edward VI. was actually in the course of preparation."—p. 169.

Again, referring to the Archbishop's opinion on the Real Presence, his words are :—

" . . . he does not seem to have finally renounced the figment of the 'corporal presence' until about the year 1548. And it is further evident, both from the Communion Office of 1552 and the disputations subsequently held at Oxford, that both he and Ridley maintained, to the very last, the *real* presence of Christ in the Eucharist ; understanding the term 'real,' not of course in its natural, but in its true and more appropriate *sacramental* import."[*] —*Fisher* p. 168.

It may help to bring out more clearly Cranmer's view at this time, if we compare it with Hooper's account of his own opinion on the subject at the same period ; writing to *Martin Bucer* from Zurich, June 19, 1548, after telling him that some "depart from your opinion in the matter of Eucharist, as I do myself," he thus continues, later in the Letter :—

" You write word, reverend sir, that you cannot believe the sacraments to be bare signs. Far be such a belief from the most unlearned Christian! The Holy Supper is not a bare sign, neither in it is **the true and natural body of Christ** exhibited to me in any **supernatural** or **heavenly** manner : nevertheless, I religiously and with all honour venerate and reverence the institution of Christ upon other grounds, because it is a sign of the good-will of God towards me, and an outward testimony added to the promise of grace. Not that this promise is applied to me by means of any sacrament, but because the promise previously applied to me by faith is thereby confirmed. In like manner the Church of God publickly receives him in baptism, who had been previously received by grace . . . . . . Thus the holy supper is a testimony of grace, and a mystery of our redemption, in which God bears witness to the benefits bestowed upon us by Christ : not that the remission of sins, which in believers ought to precede all use of sacraments, is there applied ; nor that the **true body** of Christ, which is in heaven and not on earth, is **exhibited together with the bread** ; but that it may confirm that faith which I have in the death and passion of that

---

[*] " This was the doctrine of Ratramn, by whose writings it is well known that the views of Cranmer and Ridley were considerably influenced."—See Foxe, vol. ii., p. 1610.

body which was alive, died, and rose again. And the minister gives what is in his power, namely, the bread and wine, and **not the body of Christ**; nor is it **exhibited** by the minister, and **eaten** by the communicant, otherwise than in the word preached, read, or meditated upon. And to eat the body of Christ is nothing else than to believe, as he himself teaches in the sixth of John. It is necessary therefore to bring Christ to the sacrament by faith, and not to look for him there. And thus the promise of grace is received by faith, as are also the Sacraments, of which faith they are the testimonies and the seals.' There are many other ends, but this is the chief; and those who thus use the sacraments do not make them bare signs. Thus John the Baptist said, that he baptized with water, but that there was one to come after him who should baptize with the Holy Ghost. He had water in his hand, by which remission of sins was confirmed in those who believed; but he had not in his hand the Holy Ghost, that he might give remission of sins to all that were baptized; for he baptized many hypocrites. From these sensible objects therefore faith teaches us to recognize things insensible and invisible. Regard these things, I pray you, in a godly spirit. I do not write for sake of dispute, but that I may testify to you, that the sacraments with us are not bare signs. For if faith shine forth in the mind of the recipient, the bridegroom is thereby joined* to the bride, so that none may put asunder what God hath joined together . . . . . ."—*Original Letters.* pp. 47-48.

Next to (perhaps even as much as) the *Roman* doctrine, what Hooper seems to have dreaded was the Lutheran belief: for in a Letter to " *Henry Bullinger*," dated at Antwerp, April 26, 1549, he thus expresses his fears :—

". . . . I hear that East Friesland has received the Interim. If this be the case, master à Lasco will soon return into England. I greatly regret his absence, especially as Peter Martyr and Bernardine so stoutly defend Lutheranism, and there is now arrived a third, (I mean Bucer,) who will leave no stone unturned to obtain a footing. The people of England, as I hear, all of them entertain right notions upon that subject . . . ."—*Original Letters*, p. 61.

In estimating Cranmer's Eucharistic views at this time, it would be a great omission not to take into account the Prayer Book of 1549 (for which he was mainly responsible) and the opinions entertained of it by those opposed to him on the *Roman* side. I have already (p. 9) referred generally to *Gardiner's* statements, in proof that he considered its language an adequate expression of ancient doctrine: the fol-

---

* [" The word is illegible in the MS."]

lowing passage, which is Gardiner's reply to a question on the subject, is to the purpose, as illustrating this point: he said, (and they are the words of a most unwilling witness), that—

" . . . . That book he could not have made after that form, but, as it was, he could with his conscience keep it, and cause others in his diocese to keep it, and diligently see that it should be kept, and the offenders punished. . . . . "—*Foxe*, vi., p. 114.

On the other hand, it would be unfair to pass over such a letter as the following, which claims the Archbishop as a convert, at that very time, to opinions of a much more advanced character in the direction of the Swiss school: it is from

"John Hooper to Henry Bullinger, *London, December* 27, 1549.

" . . . . The Archbishop of Canterbury entertains right views as to the nature of Christ's presence in the supper, and is now very friendly towards myself. He has some articles of religion, to which all preachers and lecturers in divinity are required to subscribe, or else a license for teaching is not granted them; and in these his sentiments respecting the Eucharist are pure, and religious, and similar to yours in Switzerland. We desire nothing more from him than a firm and manly spirit. Like all the other Bishops in this country, he is too fearful about what may happen to him. There are here six* or seven Bishops, who comprehend the doctrine of Christ, as far as relates to the Lord's Supper, with as much clearness and piety as one could desire, and it is only the fear for their property that prevents them from reforming their Churches according to the rule of God's word. The altars are here in many Churches changed into tables. The public celebration of the Lord's Supper is very far from the order and institution of our Lord. Although it is administered in both kinds, yet in some places the Supper is celebrated three times a day. Where they used heretofore to celebrate in the morning the *Mass* of the Apostles, they now have the *Communion* of the Apostles; where they had the *Mass* of the Blessed Virgin, they now have the Communion, which they call the *Communion* of the Virgin; where they had the principal, or high Mass, they now have, as they call it, the high Communion. They still retain their vestments, and the candles before the altars; in the Churches they always chant the *hours* and other hymns relating to the Lord's Supper, but in our own language. And that Popery may not be lost, the Mass-priests, although they are compelled to discontinue the use of the Latin language, yet most carefully observe

* "[It appears by the following letter, that the Bishops here referred to were Cranmer, of Canterbury; Ridley, of Rochester; Goodrich, of Ely; Farrar, of St. David's; Holbeach, of Lincoln; and Barlow, of Bath.]"

the same tone and manner of chanting to which they were heretofore accustomed in the papacy. God knows to what perils and anxieties we are exposed, by reason of men of this kind. . . . . "—*Original Letters*, p. 71.

A month later, *Hooper*, writing again to *Bullinger*, (Feb. 5, 1549-50) repeats his opinion of Cranmer's Eucharistic doctrine, in the following letter :—

" . . . . At Court I have been lecturing upon the Psalms, and God knows at what risk I interpreted the Sixth Chapter of St. John. . . . . Now as to what is doing in England. The Bishops of Canterbury, Rochester, Ely, St. David's, Lincoln, and Bath, are all favourable to the cause of Christ ; and, as far as I know, entertain right opinions in the matter of the Eucharist. I have freely conversed with all of them upon this subject, and have discovered nothing but what is pure and holy. The Archbishop of Canterbury, who is at the head of the King's Council, gives to all lecturers and preachers, their license to read and preach ; every one of them, however, must previously subscribe to certain Articles, which, if possible, I will send you, one of which, respecting the Eucharist, is plainly the true one, and that which you maintain in Switzerland."—*Original Letters*, pp. 75 and 76.

Now, fortunately, both these letters (though apparently unfavourable to the opinion which I am advocating—that Cranmer at this time held the doctrine of a Real Objective Presence in, or at least *in the ministration of* the Eucharist) furnish a definite test of the Archbishop's views, and one which is much more satisfactory than the personal opinions of those of his contemporaries who *wished* to prove his views to be consistent with their own. It will be seen that Hooper speaks in both letters, of "certain," or "some articles of religion," to be subscribed by preachers and teachers : these Articles (mainly based, probably, on the 13 Articles of 1538) were in fact, as seems now pretty well established, an earlier draft of the 42 Articles of 1552: the Article "respecting the Eucharist," to which Hooper refers, would therefore be the original casting of the 29th Article of 1552 (see p. 32): whether the language was the same at both dates, there seems no mode of ascertaining, but while such is probably the case (considering the attention which Cranmer and Ridley

had paid to the Eucharistic question before 1549,) it may
safely be concluded that the Eucharistic Article of which
Hooper speaks, was not framed in *less* Catholic language than
that of 1552; and as we know (see p.119,) that Hooper, in
his Visitation Articles, modified an important expression of
that Article to suit his own doctrinal view, so it is a most fair
conjecture (to say the least) that the Archbishop's Article of
of 1549 was not necessarily designed to bear the interpretation which Hooper put upon it, when he asserted it to
teach " that which you, " Bullinger, "maintain in Switzerland." What its language was apparently meant to teach,
and did convey, has already been considered at pp. 114-18;
and if such was Cranmer's belief in 1552, it may most safely
be asserted to have been his belief in 1549-50.

It is very commonly assumed that Cranmer's opinions at
this time were much influenced by those of Bucer, and that
the changes made in the Prayer Book of 1552 were mainly
due to his interference; how little ground there is for the latter
supposition has been already pointed out at p. 100; moreover,
it should be remembered that Bucer died at Cambridge,
February 27, 1550-1. (*Original Letters*, pt. 1; pp. 490 and
495.) Supposing, however, the assumption to be true, it is
worth while to see in what direction Bucer would have led
the Archbishop, on the subject of the Eucharistic Presence,
in 1550: commenting upon P. Martyr's Disputation at Oxford (quoted at pp. 9 to 13) he thus speaks in a letter "to
Brentius, dated at Cambridge, May 15, 1550":—

" . . . . I am as sorry for Master Martyr's book as any one can
be; but that disputation took place, and the propositions * were
agreed upon, before I arrived in England. At my advice he has
inserted many things in the preface, whereby to express more fully
his belief in the presence of Christ. Among the nobility of the
kingdom, those are very powerful, who would reduce the whole of
the sacred ministry into a narrow compass, and who are altogether
unconcerned about the restoration of Church discipline. [. . . .]†

* "*viz.*1. In the Eucharist there is no transubstantiation. 2. Nor are the
body and blood of Christ present under the species of bread and wine. 3. This
body and blood are united to the elements sacramentally."—p. 478.

† ["A sentence is here defective in the original MS."]

While they seek to provide against our bringing down Christ the Lord from heaven, and confining Him in the bread, and offering Him to the communicants to be fed upon without faith, a thing that none of our party ever thought of; they themselves go so far as, without any warrant of Holy Scripture, to confine Him to a certain limited place in heaven; and talk so vapidly about His exhibition and presence in the supper, (nay, some of them cannot even endure these words,) that they appear to believe that nothing else but the bread and wine is there distributed. No one has as yet found fault with me for my simple view of the subject; nor have I ever heard of any one who has been able to confute it from any solid passage of Scripture, nor indeed has any yet ventured to make the attempt. Their principal argument is, that the mysteries of Christ can be well and intelligibly explained, (which would be true, if they would add, ' to faith, but not to reason.') They now assume, that it cannot with reason be supposed of Christ, that He is in heaven without being circumscribed by physical space ; and since he is thus in heaven, as they take for granted, they insist, not only upon what no one will allow them, but also without any solid reason, that it cannot be understood that the same body of Christ is in heaven and in the supper: and when we reply, that no one supposes a local presence of Christ in the Supper, they again say that the body of Christ cannot be understood to be present anywhere without being locally circumscribed. The sum therefore of their argument is to this effect: Reason does not comprehend what you teach respecting the exhibition and presence of Christ in the supper ; therefore they are not true, and the Scriptures which seem to prove them must be otherwise interpreted. Let us pray for these persons. I have as yet met with no real Christians who were not entirely satisfied with our simple view of the subject, as soon as it had been properly explained to them. . . ."— *Original Letters*, pp. 544-5.

So, too, addressing Calvin, on Whitsunday, in the same year, he says :—

" . . . . We must observe, in addition to these evils, that not a few persons, laying aside all desire after true repentance, faith, good works, the communion and discipline of the Church, do nothing but dispute and contend, and often very profanely, how they may seclude Christ our Saviour from our sacraments and holy assemblies, and confine him to his place in heaven. . . . . "—*Ibid*, p. 547.

On the other hand, if it is to be inferred from P. Martyr's language to the Archbishop, (see p. 12,) that Cranmer preferred the terms used in the Oxford disputation to those which Bucer employed, then we are but thrown back upon the position which I have urged that P. Martyr defended on that occasion, *viz.*, that there is no "*substantial* and *real* presence" in the Sacrament, *i. e.,* (in the other words by which he also expresses his meaning) the Body and Blood of Christ are not there "*corporally*" in the sense of "*substantially* and *carnally;*" for thus in fact he interchanges his expressions, showing that in his mind *real* stood for *carnal.*

Two years later than Bucer's Letters just quoted, we have Cranmer's own definition of the word, "Corporal," from which it will be seen still further *in what sense* he accounted it obnoxious to a true description of the Presence; thus, in his Answer to Gardiner, he says:—

"And as for these words, 'carnally," and 'corporally,' I defame them not; for I mean by carnally and corporally, none otherwise than after the form and fashion of a man's body, as we shall be after our resurrection, that is to say, visible, palpable, and circumscribed, having a very quantity with due proportion and distinction of members, in place and order, one from another. And if you will deny Christ so to be in heaven, I have so plain and manifest Scriptures against you, that I will take you for no Christian man, except that you revoke that error. For sure I am that Christ's natural body hath such a grossness, or stature, and quantity, if you will so call it, because the word grossness, grossly taken, as you understand it, soundeth not well in an incorruptible and immortal body."—Bk iii., p. 140.

So, again, he replies to the same Prelate:—

"And as for this word, 'corporal,' you openly confessed your own ignorance in the open audience of all the people at Lambeth; when I asked you, what corporal body Christ hath in the Sacrament, and whether he had distinction of members or no, your answer was in effect, that you could not tell. And yet was that a wiser saying than you spake before in Cyril, where you said, that Christ hath only a spiritual body and a spiritual presence, and now you say, he hath a corporal presence. And so you confound corporal and spiritual, as if you knew not what either of them meant, or wist not, or cared not what you said. But now I will return to my book, and rehearse mine answer unto St. John Chrysostom, which is this."— *Answer to Gardiner,* p. 182.

Cranmer then goes on to quote from his *Defence of the true Doctrine,* etc., where he cites St. Chrysostom as saying *(In Sermone de Eucharistia in Encœniis.)*

"'When you come to these mysteries,' speaking of the Lord's board and holy communion, 'do not think that you receive by a man the body of God,' meaning of Christ. These be St. John Chrysostom's own words in that place.

" Then if we receive not the body of Christ at the hands of a man, *ergo*, the body of Christ is not really, corporally, and naturally in the Sacrament, and so given to us by the priest. . . . . "—p. 182.

And once more he writes:—

"And what this word, 'corporal,' meaneth, I am not ignorant. Marry, what you mean by 'corporal' I know not, and the opening thereof shall discuss the whole matter. Tell therefore plainly without dissimulation or coloured words, what manner of body it is that Christ hath in the Sacrament? Whether it be a very and perfect man's body, with all the members thereof, distinct one from another, or no? for that understand I to be a man's corporal body, that hath all such parts, without which may be a body, but no perfect man's body: so that the lack of a finger maketh a lack in the perfection of a man's body. Marry, if you will make Christ such a body as bread and cheese is, (wherein every part is bread and cheese, without form and distinction of one part from another,) I confess mine ignorance, that I know no such body to be a man's body. Now have I showed mine ignorance: declare now your wit and learning. For sure I am that Christ hath all those parts in heaven, and if he lack them in the Sacrament, then lacketh he not a little of his perfection. And then it cannot be one body that hath parts and no parts."—p. 228.

Before passing on to such statements of other writers as serve to illustrate that meaning of the Declaration for which, throughout, I have been contending, it may be well to produce two or three other passages from Cranmer's " Answer to Gardiner," touching the nature of the Presence, especially as they exhibit that prelate's latest belief at the time (1552,) when he had gone the farthest in the direction of low views of Eucharistic doctrine; it will, I think, be seen that, amid much loose language, he did not deny such *an objective Presence in the Ministration as justified Kneeling in token of adoration :* more than this is not necessary for my purpose, even if it can be produced from the Archbishop's later writings; for any question of the Presence as regards the Sacrament reserved, does not come into consideration here; nor is it needful to discuss the point—whether as great difficulties * would not have attended his view (in any case

* Though he quotes, apparently in defence of his opinion, the statements of

where necessity might have required, *e. g.*, the reservation of the Sacrament for a sick person) as wait upon the belief that whatever relation Consecration produces between the *Sacramentum* and the *Res Sacramenti*, such relation does not cease with the *Ministration* itself, but continues under the circumstances supposed.

The first passage I would quote, is one in which Gardiner cites against Cranmer the words of Eusebius Emissenus, who seems to have been a favourite writer with the Archbishop; his words are :—

"And where Emissene saith, that Christ hath taken his body from our sight into heaven, and yet in the sacrament of his holy supper he is present with his grace through faith, he doth us to understand, **that he is not present in the forms of bread and wine out†** of **the ministration,** (except you will say, that faith and grace be in the bread when it is kept and hanged up,) but when the bread and wine be eaten and drunken according to Christ's institution, then, to them that so eat and drink, the bread and wine is the body and blood of Christ, according to Christ's words: *Edite, hoc est corpus meum. Bibite, hic est calix sanguinis mei.* And therefore in the book of the holy communion, we do not pray that the creatures of bread and wine may be the body and blood of Christ, but that they may be to us the body and blood of Christ; that is to say, that we may so eat them, and drink them, that we may be partakers of his body crucified, and of his blood shed for our redemption."—p. 271.

With this reference to "the book of the Holy Communion," it is desirable to compare the following argument between Cranmer and Gardiner; the latter had said :—

"The body of Christ is by God's omnipotency, who so worketh in his word, made present unto us at such time, as the Church pray [prayeth] it may please him so to do, which prayer is ordered to be made in the Book of Common Prayer now set forth‡, wherein we

Roman writers, observing that "some say, that the body of Christ remaineth so long as the form and fashion of bread remaineth, . . . Some say, it remaineth no longer than the Sacrament is in the eating, and may be felt, seen, and tasted in the mouth." (p. 56.) Again, "And where you say that Christ undoubtedly remaineth in the man that worthily receiveth the Sacrament, so long as that man remaineth a member of Christ: how agreeth this with the common saying of all the papists, that Christ is contained under the forms of bread and wine, and remaineth there no longer than the forms of bread and wine remain?" (p. 59.)

† Does not this imply clearly, that Cranmer held that "*He is present in the forms of bread and wine* IN *the ministration*"?

‡ "Winchester here refers to these words in the first Service Book of Edward VI., in the prayer of Consecration, 'With thy Holy Spirit and word

require of God, the creatures of bread and wine to be sanctified, and to be to us the body and blood of Christ, which they cannot be, unless God worketh it, and make them so to be : in which mystery it was never taught, as this author willingly misreporteth, that Christ's most precious body is made of the matter of bread, but in that order exhibited and made present unto us, by conversion of the substance of bread into his precious body ; not a new body made of a new matter of bread and wine, but a new presence of the body, that is never old, made present there, where the substance of bread and wine was before. . . . ."—p. 79.

To this Cranmer answers :—

" Christ is present whensoever the Church prayeth unto him, and is gathered together in his name. And the bread and wine be made unto us the body and blood of Christ, (as it is in the book of common prayer,) but not by changing the substance of bread and wine into the substance of Christ's natural body and blood, but that in the godly using of them they be unto the receivers Christ's body and blood : as of some the Scripture saith, that their riches* is their redemption, and to some it is their damnation ; and as God's word to some is life, to some it is death and a snare, as the prophet saith. And Christ himself to some is a stone to stumble at, to some is a raising from death, not by conversion of substances, but by good or evil use : that thing which to the godly is salvation, to the ungodly is damnation. So is the water in Baptism, and the bread and wine in the Lord's Supper, to the worthy receivers Christ himself and eternal life ; and to the unworthy receivers, everlasting death and damnation, not by conversion of one substance into another, but by godly or ungodly use thereof. And therefore, in the book of the holy Communion, we do not pray absolutely that the bread and wine may be made the body and blood of Christ, but that unto us in that holy mystery they may be so ; that is to say, that we may so worthily receive the same, that we may be partakers of Christ's body and blood, and that therewith in spirit and in truth we may be spiritually nourished. And a like prayer † of old time were all the people wont to make at the communion of all such offerings as at that time all the people used to offer, praying that their offerings might be unto them the body and blood of Christ.

" And where you say, ' it was never taught as I say, that Christ's

vouchsafe to bless and sanctify these thy gifts and creatures of bread and wine, that they may be unto us the body and blood of thy most dearly beloved Son, Jesus Christ.' In the second Service Book of Edward VI., this prayer was changed as it now stands."—*Editor's Note.*

* It is important to notice here that Cranmer's whole argument is based upon the fact of the SAME THING, differently used, producing different effects.

† " Domin. 3. Post. Trin. Secret.—Munera tibi, Domine, quibus oblata sanctifica, ut tui nobis unigeniti corpus et sanguis fiant ad medelum."

body is made of the matter of bread,' you knowingly and willingly misreport me. For I say not of the matter of bread, but of bread ; which when you deny that the papists so say, it seemeth you be now ashamed of the doctrine which the papists have taught this four or five hundred years. For is it not plainly written of all the papists, both lawyers and school-authors, that the body of Christ in the Sacrament is made of bread, and his blood of wine? And they say not that his body is made present of bread and wine, but is made of bread and wine. Be not their books in print ready to be showed ? Do they not say that the substance of the bread neither remaineth still, nor is turned into nothing, but into the body of Christ ? And do not yourself also say here in this place, that the substance of bread is converted into Christ's precious body ? And what is that else but the body of Christ to be made of bread, and to be made of a new matter ? * For if the bread do not vanish away into nothing, but be turned into Christ's body, then is Christ's body made of it ; and then it must needs follow that Christ's body is made of new,† and of another substance than it was made of in his mother's womb ; for there it was made of her flesh and blood, and here it is made of bread and wine. And the papists say not, (as you now would shift off the matter) that Christ's body is made present of bread, but they say plainly without addition, that it is made of bread. Can you deny that this is the plain doctrine of the papists? *Ex pane fit Corpus Christi.* 'Of bread is made the body of Christ,' and that the substance of bread is turned into the substance thereof? And what reason, sentence, or english, could be in this saying, ' Christ's body is made present of bread ? ' Marry,‡ **to be present in bread** might be some sentence, but this speech will you in no wise admit."—pp. 79 and 80.

Again, with reference to Gardiner's charge, that he had unfairly used St. Chrysostom's language, Cranmer says :—

" But always you be like yourself, proceeding in amplification of an argument against me, which you have forged yourself, and charge me therewith untruly. For I use not this speech, that we receive not the body of God at all, that we receive it but in a figure. § For it is my constant faith and belief, that we receive Christ in the Sacrament verily and truly ; and this is plainly taught and set forth in my book. But that ' verily ' as I with Chrysostom, and all the old authors take it, is not of such a sort as you would have it. For your understanding of ' verily ' is **so Capernaical, so gross,** and so dull in the perceiving of this mystery, that you think a

* " [' And to be made anew of a new matter.' 1551.] "
† " [Is made new, 1551.] "
‡ What is this but the language of the contested Advertisement—" under the form of bread and wine ? "
§ Cranmer's marginal note is—" Christ is verily and truly present and received."

man cannot receive the body of Christ verily, unless he take him **corporally, in his corporal mouth, flesh, blood, and bones, as he was born of the virgin Mary.** But it is certain that Chrysostom meant not, that we receive Christ's body verily after such a sort, when he saith, 'Do not think that you receive by a man the body of God.' And yet, because I deny * **only this gross misunderstanding,** you misreport my doctrine, that I should say, we 'receive not Christ at all, but in a figure, and no body at all;' wherein you untruly and slanderously report me, as my whole book and doctrine can witness against you." [Then immediately follows the passage at p. 33: "For my doctrine is . . . . nor meant." And afterwards it continues,] "Turn, I pray thee, gentle reader, to the thirty-sixth leaf of my book, and note these words there, which I allege out of Chrysostom. 'Do not think,' saith he, 'that you receive by a man the body of God.' Then turn over the leaf, and in the twentieth line, note again my saying that, 'in the holy Communion Christ himself is spiritually eaten and drunken, and nourisheth the right believers.' Then compare those sayings with this place of this ignorant lawyer, and thou shalt evidently perceive, that either he will not, or cannot, or at the least, he doth not understand what is meant in the book of common prayer, and in my book also, by the receiving and feeding upon Christ spiritually."—p. 185.

The passage to which Cranmer here refers, is found in his "Second Book against Transubstantiation," and runs thus:

" . . . . 'Lo,' say they, 'Doth not Chrysostomus, the great clerk, say most plainly, that we see neither bread nor wine; but that, as wax in the fire, they be consumed to nothing, so that no substance remaineth?' But if they had rehearsed no more, but the very next sentence that followeth in Chrysostom, which craftily and maliciously they leave out, the meaning of St. John Chrysostom would easily have appeared, and yet will make them blush, if they be not utterly past shame. For after the foresaid words of Chrysostom, immediately follow the words:

"'Wherefore,' saith he, 'when ye come to these mysteries, do not think that you receive by a man the body of God, but that with tongues you receive fire by the angels seraphin.' And straight after it followeth thus:

"'Think that the blood of salvation floweth out of the pure and godly side of Christ, and so coming to it, receive it with pure lips. Wherefore, brethren, I pray and beseech you, let us not be from the Church, nor let us not be occupied there with vain communication; but let us stand fearful and trembling, casting down our eyes, lifting up our minds, mourning privily without speech, and rejoicing in our hearts.'

---

* Language which seems to include all that can be required in favour of the Real Objective Presence.

"These words of Chrysostom do follow immediately after the other words, which the papists before rehearsed. Therefore if the papists will gather of the words by them recited, that there is neither bread nor wine in the Sacrament, I may as well gather of the words that follow, that there is neither priest nor Christ's body.

"For as in the former sentence Chrysostom saith, 'that we may not think that we see bread and wine;' so in the second sentence he saith, that 'we may not think that we receive the body of Christ of the priest's hands.' Wherefore, if upon the second sentence, as the papists themselves will say, it cannot be truly gathered, that in the holy communion there is not the body of Christ ministered by the priest ; then must they confess also, that it cannot be well and truly gathered upon the first sentence, that there is no bread nor wine.

"But there be all these things together in the holy communion, * [a] Christ himself spiritually eaten and drunken, and [b] nourishing the right believers; [c] the bread and wine as a sacrament declaring the same ; and the priest as a minister thereof. Wherefore St. John Chrysostom meant not absolutely to deny that there is bread and wine, or to deny utterly the priest and the body of Christ to be there; but he useth a speech, which is no pure negative, but a negative by comparison."—p. 312.

Then, having cited 1 Sam. viii. 7 ; Ps. xxii. 6 ; St. Matt. x. 34 ; xxiii. 9 ; Rom. vii. 17 ; 1 Cor. i. 17 ; Gal. ii. 20; Eph. vi. 12, and other texts as some, of many, examples of " a negative by comparison," he thus continues :—

"Now forasmuch as I have declared at length the nature and kind of these negative speeches, which be no pure negatives but by comparison, it is easy hereby to make answer to St. John Chrysostom, who used this phrase of speech most of any author. For his meaning in his foresaid homily was not, that in the celebration of the Lord's Supper is neither bread nor wine, neither priest nor the body of Christ, which the papists themselves must needs confess ; but his intent was to draw our minds upward to heaven, that we should not consider so much the bread, wine, and priest, as we should consider his divinity and Holy Spirit given unto us to our eternal salvation.

" And therefore in the same place he useth so many times these words, 'Think and think not,' willing us by these words that we should not fix our thoughts and minds upon the bread, wine, priest,

---

* Does not Cranmer here give precisely the definition of the present Catechism [c] "the outward part or sign " = Sacramentum : [a] "the inward part or thing signified" = Res Sacramenti : (b) "the benefits" = Virtus. The original is "Atqui hæc omnia in sacrosancta cœna pariter existunt. Christus ipse spiritualiter perceptus et fideles pascens, panis et viuun id nobis demonstrantia sacramento, et sacerdos horum minister."

nor Christ's body: but to lift up our hearts higher unto his spirit and divinity, without the which his body availeth nothing, as saith himself: 'It is the Spirit that giveth life, the flesh availeth nothing.'

"And as the same Chrysostom in many places moveth us not to consider the water in baptism, but rather to have respect to the Holy Ghost, received in baptism, and represented by the water: even so doth he in this homily of the holy communion move us to lift up our minds from all visible and corporal things to things invisible and spiritual.

"Insomuch that although Christ was but once crucified, yet would Chrysostom have us to think that we see him daily whipped and scourged before our eyes, and his body hanging upon the cross, and the spear thrust into his side, and the most holy blood to flow out of his side 'into our mouths. After which manner St. Paul wrote to the Galations, that Christ was painted and crucified before their eyes.

"Therefore saith Chrysostom in the same homily a little before the place rehearsed: 'What dost thou O man? didst not thou promise to the priest which said, Lift up your minds and hearts; and thou didst answer, We lift them up unto the Lord? Art not thou ashamed and afraid being at that same hour found a liar? A wonderful thing! The table is set forth, furnished with God's mysteries, the Lamb of God is offered for thee, the priest is careful for thee, spiritual fire cometh out of that heavenly table, the angels seraphin be there present, covering their faces with six wings. All the angelical power with the priest be means and intercessors for thee, a spiritual fire cometh down from heaven, blood in the cup is drunk out of the most pure side unto thy purification. And art not thou ashamed, afraid, and abashed, not endeavouring thyself to purchase God's mercy? O man, doth not thine own conscience condemn thee? There be in the week one hundred and sixty eight hours, and God asketh but one of them to be given wholly unto him, and thou consumest that in worldly business, in trifling and talking: with what boldness then shalt thou come to these holy mysteries? O corrupt conscience!'

"Hitherto I have rehearsed St. John Chrysostom's words, which do show how our minds should be occupied at this holy table of our Lord, that is to say, withdrawn from the consideration of sensible things unto the contemplation of most heavenly and godly things. And thus is answered this place of Chrysostom, which the papists took for an insoluble, and a place that no man was able to answer. But for further declaration of Chrysostom's mind in this matter read the place of him before rehearsed, fol. 26 and 28."*—pp. 314-16.

* *i.e.* p. 273. "About the same time, or shortly after, about the year of our Lord 400, St. John Chrysostom writeth thus against them that used only water in the sacrament. 'Christ,' saith he, 'minding to pluck up that heresy by the roots, used wine as well before his resurrection, when he gave the mysteries, as

185

The especial design of Cranmer in these passages, as indeed throughout his whole *Answer*, may perhaps be best described in his own words at the commencement of his argument, where he says :—

" This therefore shall be mine issue : that as no scripture, so no ancient author known and approved, hath in plain terms your transubtantiation ; nor that the body and blood of Christ be **really, corporally, naturally, and carnally** under the forms of bread and wine ; nor that evil men do eat the very body and drink the very blood of Christ ; nor that **Christ** is offered every day by the priest a sacrifice propitiatory for sin. Wherefore by your own description and rule of a catholic faith, your doctrine and teaching in these your articles cannot be good and catholic, except you can find it in plain terms in the scripture and old catholic doctors ; which when you do, I will hold up my hand at the bar, and say, ' guilty,' and if you cannot, then it is reason that you do the like, *per legem talionis.*"— *Ans. to Gardiner.* Book i. p. 13.

And again, at p. 152, his language is :—

And as for pleading of those words, 'really,' 'corporally,' 'sensibly,' and 'naturally,' they be your own terms, and the terms wherein resteth the whole contention between you and me ; and should you be offended because I speak of those terms ? It appeareth now that you be loth to hear of those words, and would very gladly have them put in silence, and so should the variance between you and me be clearly ended. For it you will confess, that the body of Christ is not in the Sacrament **really, corporally,**

---

after at his table without mysteries. For he said, 'of the fruit of the vine ;'' which surely bringeth forth no water, but wine.'
These words of Chrysostom declare plainly, that Christ in his holy table both drank wine and gave wine to drink, which had not been true if no wine had remained after the consecration, as the papists feign. And yet more plainly St. Chrysostom declareth this matter in another place, saying : 'the bread before it be sanctified is called bread, but when it is sanctified by the means of the priest, it is delivered from the name of bread, and is exalted to the name of the Lord's body, although the nature of bread doth still remain.
" 'The nature of bread,' said he, ' doth still remain,' to the utter and manifest confutation of the papists, which say, 'that the accidents of bread do remain, but not the nature and subtance.'"
And p. 286 where, having quoted two passages from St. Chrysostom *ad Cæsarium Monachum.* " When thou speakest of God," &c. and " Wherefore Christ is both God and man" &c., he remarks " These words of Chrysostom declare, and that not in obscure terms, but in plain words, that after the consecration the nature of bread remaineth still, although it have an higher name, and be called the body of Christ, to signify unto the godly eaters of that bread, that they spiritually eat the supernatural bread of the body of Christ, WHO SPIRITUALLY IS THERE PRESENT, and dwelleth in them, and they in him, although COPORALLY he sitteth in heaven at the right hand of his Father.''

sensibly, and naturally, then you and I shall shake hands, and be both earnest friends of the truth.

" And yet one thing you do here confess, (which is worthy to be noted and had in memory,) that you read not in any old author, that the body of Christ is really and sensibly in the Sacrament. And hereunto I add, that none of them say, that he is in the bread and wine corporally nor naturally. No, never no papist said, that Christ's body is in the Sacrament naturally nor carnally, but you alone, (who be the first author of this gross error, which Smith himself condemneth, and denieth that ever Christian man so taught,) although some say that it is there 'really,' some 'substantially,' and some 'sensibly.'"

Having now produced these statements of Cranmer (perhaps at needless length except for the desire of giving the context fairly) I proceed to add a few passages from some of his contemporaries which may serve to illustrate further that (as I argued in the Letter) the physical Presence held to be bound up with Transubstantiation, together with its popular result, was the great point of opposition by the English reforming party. Thus *Ridley*, in his "Godly talk with Latimer in the Tower," A.D., 1555, mentions among the "things" which he says "do offend me in the Mass" that "the sign is servilely worshipped for the thing signified," (*Foxe*, Act and Mon. vii. 411) thus admitting here as elsewhere (see pp. 58 and 60) that adoration is due to "the thing signified."

So, too, in his Examination at Oxford, Sep. 30, 1555, in part quoted at p. 61, he thus writes touching the Sacramental change due to Consecration.

" Always my protestation reserved, I answer thus; that in the Sacrament is a certain change, in that, that bread, which was before common bread, is now made a lively presentation of Christ's body, and not only a figure, but effectuously representeth his body, that even as the mortal body was nourished by that visible bread, so is the internal soul fed with the heavenly food of Christ's body, which the eyes of faith see, as the bodily eyes see only bread. Such a sacramental mutation I grant to be in the bread and wine, which truly is no small change, but such a change as no mortal man can make, but only the omnipotency of Christ's word."—*Foxe*, vii. 528.

The next example is from a very different class of persons,

viz., two "husbandmen" called "John Simson and John Ardely, of the parish of Wigborough the Great in Essex," who where articled by Bishop Bonner, May 22, 1555; two of his accusations were these :—

"IV. Item, that albeit it be true, that in the Sacrament of the Altar there is in substance the very body and blood of Christ under the forms of bread and wine, and albeit that it be so believed, taught, and preached undoubtedly in the said Church of Rome, and all the other Churches aforesaid, yet thou hast not so believed, nor dost so believe ; but, contrariwise, thou hast and dost believe firmly and stedfastly that there is not in the said Sacrament of the altar, under the said form of bread and wine, the very substance of Christ's body and blood, but that there is only the substance of material and common bread and wine, with the form thereof; and that the said material and common bread and wine are only the signs and tokens of Christ's body and blood, and by faith to be received, only for a remembrance of Christ's passion and death, without any such substance of Christ's body and blood at all.

"V. Item, that thou hast believed and taught, and thou hast openly spoken, and to thy power maintained and defended, and so dost believe, think, maintain and defend, that the very true receiving and eating of Christ's body and blood, is only to take material and common bread, and to break it, and to distribute it amongst the people; remembering thereby the passion and death of Christ only."

To these charges they replied thus :—

"To the fourth they answer, that in the Sacrament, commonly called the Sacrament of the altar, there is very bread and very wine, not altered or changed in substance in any wise ; and that he that receiveth the said bread and wine, doth spiritually and by faith only receive the body and blood of Christ; but not the very natural body and blood of Christ in substance under the forms of bread and wine.

"To the fifth they say, they have answered, answering to the said fourth article, and yet nevertheless they say, that they have believed, and do believe, that in the Sacrament of the altar there is not the very substance of Christ's body and blood, but only the substance of the natural bread and wine."—*Foxe*, vii. 87 and 88.

The last illustration is from "Another Letter written to the Christian Congregation by Robert Samuel" who was "Minister at Barholt [i.e. Bargholt] in Suffolk;" he was burned Aug. 31st, 1555; in this Letter "he declareth the confession of his faith" thus :—

"The other Sacrament, which is the Supper and Holy Maunday of our Saviour Christ, whereby the Church of Christ is known, I believe to be a remembrance of Christ's death and passion, a seal and confirmation of his most precious body given unto death, even to the vile death of the cross, wherewith we are redeemed and delivered from sin, death, hell, and damnation. It is a visible word, because it worketh the same thing in the eyes, which the word worketh in the ears. For like as the word is a mean to the ears, whereby the Holy Ghost moveth the heart to believe; so this Sacrament is a mean to the eyes, whereby the Holy Ghost moveth the heart to believe; it preacheth peace between God and man; it exhorteth to mutual love and all godly life, and teacheth to contemn the world for the life to come, when Christ shall appear, which now is in heaven, and nowhere else **as concerning his human body.**

"Yet do I believe assuredly, that his **very body is present in his most holy Supper** at the contemplation of our spiritual eyes, and so **verily eaten with the mouth of our faith.** For as soon as I hear these most comfortable and heavenly words spoken and pronounced by the mouth of the minister, "This is my body which is given for you:" when I hear (I say) this heavenly harmony of God's infallible promises and truth, I look not upon, neither do I behold bread and wine; for I take and believe the words simply and plainly, even as Christ spake them. For hearing these words, my senses be rapt and utterly excluded; for faith wholly taketh place, and **not flesh,** nor the **carnal imaginations of our gross, fleshy, and unreverent eating after the manner of our bodily food,** which profiteth nothing at all, as Christ witnesseth; but with a sorrowful and wounded conscience, a hungry and thirsty soul, a pure and faithful mind, do fully embrace, behold, and feed, and look upon, that most glorious body of Christ in heaven, at the right hand of God the Father, very God and very man, which was crucified and slain, and his blood shed for our sins, there now making intercession, offering and giving his holy body for me, for my body, for my ransom, for my full price and satisfaction, who is my Christ, and all that he ever hath; and by this spiritual and faithful eating of this lively and heavenly bread, I feel the most sweet sap and taste of the fruits, benefits, and unspeakable joys of Christ's death and passion, fully digested into the bowels of my soul. For my mind is quieted from all worldly adversities, turmoilings, and troubles; my conscience is pacified from sin, death, hell, and damnation; my soul is full, and hath even enough, and will no more; for all things are but loss, vile dung, and dross, vain vanity, for the excellent knowledge-sake of Christ Jesus my Lord and Saviour.

"Thus now is Christ's flesh my very meat indeed, and his blood my very drink indeed, and I am become flesh of his flesh, and bone of his bones. Now I live yet not I, but Christ liveth in me: yea, I dwell in him, and he in me; for, through faith in Christ and for Christ's sake we are one, that is, of one consent, mind, and fellowship with the Father, the Son, and the Holy Ghost. Thus am I assured and fully persuaded, and on this rock have I builded, by God's grace, my dwelling and resting place for body and soul, life and death. And thus I commit my cause unto Christ the righteous and just Judge, who will another day judge these debates and controversies ; whom I humbly beseech to cast his tender and merciful eyes upon the afflicted and ruinous Churches, and shortly to reduce them into a godly and perpetual concord. Amen.

" Thus do I believe, and this is my faith and my understanding in Christ my Saviour, and his true and holy religion. And this whosoever is ashamed to do, among this adulterous and sinful generation, of him shall the son of Man be ashamed, when he cometh in the glory of his Father with the holy angels.

ROBERT SAMUEL."

I pass on now to consider somewhat more fully, than in the Letter, such occurrences in the reign of Elizabeth as touch the subject on which the Letter proposed to treat.

It was noticed at p. 63 that the Declaration on Kneeling did not appear in Elizabeth's Prayer Book, and the reason assigned by Burnet for the omission is there quoted : the same Prelate, in writing of the review of the 42 articles in 1559, gives the following account of the way in which the question of the Real Presence was then dealt with, and so furnishes a further illustration of the grounds on which he alleges the suppression of the Declaration itself :—

" In the Article about the Lord's Supper, there is a great deal left out, for instead of that large refutation of the Corporal Presence, from the impossibility of a body's being in more places at once ; from whence it follows, that since Christ's body is in Heaven, the faithful ought not to believe or profess a Real or Corporal Presence of it in the Sacrament. In the new Articles, it is said, *That the body of Christ is given and received after a spiritual manner ; and the means by which it is received, is faith.* But in the Original Copy of these Articles (M. S. S. Cor. Christ, *Camb.*), which I have seen subscribed by the hands of all that sat in either House of Convocation, there is a further addition made. The Articles were subscribed with that precaution, which was requisite in a matter of such consequence ; for before the Subscriptions, there is set down the number of the pages, and of the lines in every page of the Book, to which they set their hands.

In that Article of the Eucharist, these words are added, *Christus in Cœlum ascendens, corpori suo immortalitatem dedit, naturam non abstulit : Humanæ enim naturæ veritatem, juxta scripturas perpetuo retinet, quam in uno & definito loca esse, & non in multa vel omnia simul loca diffundi, oportet : Quum igitur Christus in Coelum sublatus, ibi usque ad finem Seculi sit premansurus, atque inde, non aliunde, (ut loquitur Augustinus) venturus sit ad judicandum vivos & mortuos, non debet quisquam fidelium, Carnis ejus & Sanguinis realem & corporalem (ut loquuntur) præsentiam in Eucharistia, vel credere vel profiteri.* In English thus : ' Christ, when he ascended into Heaven, made his Body immortal, but took not from it the Nature of a Body : For still it retains, according to the Scriptures, the Verity of a human Body ; which must be always in one definite place, and cannot spread into many, or all places at once. Since then Christ being carried up to Heaven, is to remain there to the end of the world, and is to come from thence, and from no place else, (as says St. *Austin*) to judge the quick and the dead ; none of the faithful ought to believe or profess the real, or (as they call it) the corporal Presence of his Flesh and Blood in the Eucharist.'

" But this in the original is dasht over with *minium :* yet so, that it is still legible. The secret of it was this ; the Queen and her Council studied, (as hath been already shewn) to unite all into the Communion of the Church : and it was alledged, that such an express definition against a Real Presence, might drive from the Church many who were still of that persuasion ; and therefore it was thought to be enough to condemn Transubstantiation, and to say, that Christ was present after a Spiritual manner, and received by Faith ; to say more, as it was judged superfluous, so it might occasion division. Upon this, these words were, by common consent, left out : and in the next Convocation, the Articles were subscribed without them, of which I have also seen the original.

" This shews that the Doctrine of the Church subscribed by the whole Convocation, was at that time contrary to the belief of a Real or Corporal Presence in the Sacrament; only it was not thought necessary or expedient to publish it. Though from this silence, which flowed not from their opinion, but the wisdom of that time, in leaving a liberty for different speculations, as to the manner of the Presence ; some have since inferred, that the chief pastors of this Church, did then disapprove of the definition made in King *Edward's* time, and that they were for a Real Presence."—*Hist. Ref.*, Pt. ii., Bk. iii., p. 375. See also *Hardwick on the Articles*, p. 375.

Mr. Harold Browne thinks that " the clause in the Article" of 1552 was " omitted in Elizabeth's reign ; lest persons inclined to the Lutheran belief might be too much offended by it ; and many such " he adds " were in the Church, whom it was wished to conciliate."—*Exposition of the 39 Articles*, p. 708.

Bishop Burnet was quoted as stating that the DECLARATION was left out of Elizabeth's Prayer Book for the sake of those "inclinable to the Communion of the Church, who yet retained the belief of the Corporal Presence :" Mr. Browne (p. 100) assumes that, as with the Clause in the Article, " it was omitted . . . . . from a wish not to offend the many persons of Lutheran sentiments then in communion with the Church." If, moreover, Mr. Hallam's statement be correct (and there is much reason for thinking it true) that " Pius IVth. . .despatched a Nuncio to England, with an invitation to send ambassadors to the Council of Trent, and with powers, as is said, to confirm the English Liturgy, and to permit, double Communion . . . . (*Const. Hist.* i. p. 155. See also *Strype Ann.* i. p. 221) it is likely enough that this* circumstance may have had its weight in determining the course to be followed with regard to both Clause and Declaration.

But though the Clause disappeared from the Article and the Declaration from the Prayer Book, it would seem that the object of them was not disregarded and that the Declaration was in some other way kept before the Members of the Church of England : for in a joint Letter from Grindal, Bishop of London, and Horn,Bishop of Winchester, addressed to Henry Bullinger and Rodolp Gualter, " dated at London, Feb. 6, 1566-7," they write thus :

"We allow of Kneeling at the receiving of the Lord's Supper, because it is so appointed by law ; the same explanation however, or rather caution, that the very authors of the Kneeling, most holy men and constant martyrs of Jesus Christ, adopted, being most diligently declared, published and impressed upon the people. It is in these terms : ' Whereas it is ordained in the book of prayers, that the Communicants should receive the holy Communion Kneeling ; yet we declare, that this ought not so to be understood, as if any adoration is or ought to be done, either unto the sacramental bread and wine, or to any real and essential presence of Christ's natural flesh and blood there existing. For the sacramental

---

* Mr. Fisher indeed goes so far as to say that "the new alterations [in the Prayer Book of 1559] were all, without exception in a *Romeward* direction . . . . . . How then was this effected ? Not of course by sanctioning directly, and in terms, the doctrine of *Transubstantiation ;* but by removing every previous protest against the doctrine of a real or *corporeal* presence, so as to leave the Service *open* in this respect, to a Papistical interpretation.

" We say – real *or* corporeal presence; for it must be plain to every unsophisticated mind, that these two terms, as employed in the Eucharistic controversy, mean virtually the same thing ; [?] . . . . Obviously there cannot be a ' real ' *presence* of Christ's human nature in the elements, without a *local* presence of the same being necessarily implied."—*Liturgical Purity,* pp. 281-2.

bread and wine remain still in their very natural substances, and therefore may not be adored, for that were horrible idolatry, to be abborred of all Christians; and as to the natural body and blood of our Saviour Christ, they are in heaven, and not here; it being against the truth of the true natural body of Christ, to be at one and the same time in more places than one.' "—*Zurich Letters*, 1st Series, p. 180.

It will be found, by a comparison of this statement with the form of the Declaration in Edward's 2nd Book (see p. 3) that there is some little difference in the language: whether this arises from mere accident on the part of the writers of the Letter, or from their quoting some other then recognized version of the Declaration, seems only matter for conjecture. But, however that may be, the fact of the Declaration being *then* recognized mainly in the form which it originally had, notwithstanding its exclusion and the exclusion of the Clause of the Article containing the words "reall and bodillie" from the public Formularies out of regard for those who held (what Burnet calls) " the Corporal Presence," is strong evidence that (as I have all along contended) "real and essential" simply meant what was then commonly understood by " corporal," and were not the equivalents of the " verily and indeed " of our present Catechism.

The order of dates brings me now to a Document of considerable importance on the question of the Real Presence, and therefore on the meaning to be attached to the Declaration on Kneeling as it appears to have been used in Elizabeth's days—I mean the, now well known, Letter of Bishop Geste to Secretary Cecil on the 28th Article which it will be convenient here to reprint.

The Letter of Edmond Geste [or Gheast], Bishop of Rochester,* to Cecil, Secretary to Queen Elizabeth, 22nd December, 1566.

" Greeting in ye Lord.

"Right Honourable—I am verye sorye yt you are so sicke, GOD make you whole, as it is my desyer and prayer. I wold have seen you er this, accordinge to my duetye and good will,

---

* State Paper Office, Orig. Domestic Elizabeth, Vol. xli. No. 51.

but when I sent to knowe whether I might see you it was often answered yt you were not to be spoken with.

"I suppose you have hard how ye Bisshop of Glocestre [*i.e.* Cheney] found him selue greeved with ye plasynge of this adverbe *onely* in this article, 'The body of CHRIST is gyven taken and eaten in ye Supper after an heavenly and spirituall maner onely,' bycause it did take awaye ye presence of CHRISTIS Bodye in ye Sacrament, and prively noted me to take his part therein, and yeasterdaye in myn absence more playnely vouched me for ye same. Whereas betwene him and me, I told him plainelye that this word *onely* in ye fore-saied Article did not exclude ye presence of CHRISTIS Body fro the Sacrament, but onely ye *grossenes* and *sensiblenes* in ye receavinge thereof: For I saied vnto him *though he tooke Christis Bodye in his hand, received it with his mouthe, and that corporally naturally reallye substantially and carnally* as ye doctors doo write, *yet did he not for all that see it, feale it, smelle it, nor taste it.* And therefore I told him I wold speake against him herein, and ye rather bycause YE ARTICLE WAS OF MYN OWNE PENNYNGE. And yet I wold not for all that denye therebye any thing that I had spoken* for ye pre-sence. And this was ye some of our talke.

"And this that I saied is so true by all sortes of men that

---

* Compare the following passage from his "Treatise against the Prevee Masse," 1548. "The last argument that ys alledged for tornekynd is thys, If Christes bodye be in thee bred (as undoubtedly it is), then it is enbreaded and his bloude enwyned, which was alway taken for a great heresy, In respect whereof transubstantiation nedes must be graunted as ryght true and belevable. To thys I answer in sorte thus, Notwythstandinge CHRISTES Body be presented in thee bred (as questionles it is) not placely as ther placed spaced and measured, but ghostly ; as ther unplaced unspaced, and not mesured ; Howbeit, it is not enbreaded no more then the deytie is recompted enfleshed for that it is substan-cially in us. No more then the sayde Godhede is demed enbreaded, for yt is en-tirely in eche bred. No more then the HOLY GHOST is accompted enbreathed for that He was presented in CHRISTES breathe. No more then the sayd HOLY GHOSTE is adjudged embodied or enharted, for yt He is wholly in us and in oure hartes. CHRISTES Body is adjudged of no man to be accidented notwythstanding it is presented in the accidentes of the bread. Why then shuld it be adjudged enbreaded for Hys presence in ye bread. The one is as reasonable as gatherable as thother is. Some are fule deceyved in the meanynge of these wordes thim-panacion of CHRISTES Bodye, whyche is not in simple any presence indeferently of ye sayd Body in ye bred : No more than the incarnation or enfleshing of CHRISTES Godhede is indifferently any presence therof in mans fleshe and nature. But only soch a presence of CHRISTES Body in the bread wherewyth they both shuld be unseverably personed and have al theyr condicions and pro-perties common and mutuall betwixt them. Soch a presence is the personal pre-sence of CHRISTES Godhede in Hys Manhode. Soch is ye presence of ye soul in ye bodye. In respect whereof as CHRISTES Body is not enpersoned in us, not-withstanding it be enbodied to us : Semblable though the sayd body be presented in ye bred, howbeit it is not become one person therewith which is properly termed ye impaning or enbreding thereof."—p. 86, ed. 1840.

c c

even D. Hardinge writeth ye same as it appeareth most evidently by his wordes reported in ye Busshoppe of Salisburie's [*i.e.* Jewel's] booke pagina 325, wich be thees : ' Then ye maye saye, yt in ye Sacrament His verye Body is present yea really that is to say in deede, substantially that is in substance, and corporally carnally and naturally, by ye wich words is ment that His verye Bodye His verye flesh and His verye humane nature is there not after corporall carnall or naturall wise, but invisibly unspeakably supernaturally spiritually divinely and by waye unto Him onlye knowen.' " *

"This I thought good to write to your honour for myn own purgation. The Almightye GOD in CHRIST restore you to your old health, and longe kepe you in ye same with encrease of vertue and honour.

Yours whole to his poore pow^r

"EDM. ROFFEN."

" To ye right Honourable and his singler good friend
  Sir Willm Cecil Knight Principall Secretaire
  to ye Queens Matie. "

It would have been unnecessary for my purpose to do more than quote this Letter, but from the circumstance that Mr. Goode (*Supplement to Work on the Eucharist*, 1858) has endeavoured to deprive it of the value which it seemed to possess, by producing "another letter of the same Bishop, which " he has " found in the same repository," *viz.*, The State Paper Office. I agree so far with Mr. Goode as to think that a "comparison" of the two Letters and " the internal testimony " of the latter, leave no *reasonable ground* (I cannot say no "possibility") for "a doubt that both are by the same hand." Mr. Goode has only printed the first paragraph, and so much besides of the Document as deals directly with the 28th and 29th Articles; I now print the whole (distinguishing by brackets [[ ]] the portions given by Mr. Goode,) for two reasons. (1) First, because I think other parts of the Document will help to clear up the difficulty which Mr. Goode has raised : (2) Next, because the entire Document, not having been hitherto printed, may prove interesting on other grounds. The Document is No. 37, Vol. lxxviii. of the State Papers " Domestic-Elizabeth," it is supposed to be

---

* The extract is here taken from Jewel's controversy with M. Harding, Art. v., Divis. v., p. 455, ed. P.S.

of the date, " May 1571," and is intitled (in Mr. Lemon's Catalogue) " [Anonymous] to Burghley. A long discourse, urging a unity in sound and true doctrine, *indorsed* ' toching coming to ye Church, and receaving ye Sacrament.' "

The Paper is as follows :—

(In dorso) [[* " To ye right honourable & his verye goode Lorde L of Burleye etc.

" I am bold to trouble your good Lordshippe ones agayne for unitie in sound and true ~~relig~~† doctrine. Ffor never was there better occasion when to performe it then nowe. Bycause ye Bisshoppes have gyven uppe ye booke of articles to ye Quenes ma^{tie} to peruse them and judge them. I have writen my mynde to your L. of some of ye articles that ye saied unitie might be performed and set forthe, knowynge you as willinge theunto as my selfe.]]

" Notes.

[I.] " 1. It is writen in ye begynnynge of ye article of predestination as it is in Laten thus : Predestinatio ad vitam]]‡ est eternã dei propositũ, quo ante jacta mũdi fundameta, suo consilio nobis quidem occulto constanter decrevit, eos quos in Christo elegit, ex hominũ genere a maledicto et exitio liberare, atq͞ɜ ut vasa in honorẽ efficta, per Christũ ad eternã salutem adducere. Thees wordes (suo consilio nobis quidem occulto) are to be putt out of ye booke for three causes The first is bycause ye scripture sheweth playnely ye cause why God hath predestined them to eternall life whome he hathe chosen in Christ, wiche is that, ye glorie of his mercie and grace might be praised. For thus Poule writethe, § Qui predestinavit ut adoptaret in filios per Jesũ Chrũm in sese juxta beneplacitũ sue voluntatis ut laudetur gloria gratie sue. The scond cause why ~~Goddes~~ ‖ it is not true, that goddes cõsell in predestinatinge us is not knowen unto us is, bycause Powle doth saye the contrarie,¶ Patefacto nobis arcano volũtatis sue juxta beneplacitũ suñ quod proposuerat in se ipso usq͞ɜ ad ad dispensatiõe plenitudinis temporũ ut sumatim instauraret oĩa per Chrũm. Here Poule

---

* This paragraph, and Sections 8, 9, 10, and 11, are reprinted from Mr. Goode's pamphlet; the rest is from a copy obtained at the State Paper Office.

† Erased *sic* in MS.

‡ The purport of the rest of this Section, and of Sections 2 to 7 inclusive, is then stated by Mr. Goode in a short paragraph.

§ Ephe. ii. ‖ Sic in MS. ¶ Ephe. i.

plainely shewethe that what tyme Christ came, God by him declared and opened yᵉ mysterie of our predestination and salvation. Therefore thees wordes, suo consilio nobis quidem occulto, are to be putt out of yᵉ booke. The thirde cause wᶜʰ the saied wordes are to bee putt out of yᵉ booke is, by-cause by those wordes it is to be gathered that there is a conṡell, & cause in God in predestinatinge us wiche is yet hidden and not knowen by yᵉ scripture, and therefore they gyve occasion to curiouse persons to searche out causes of Goddes predestination besides and without yᵉ scripture wich is a dangerous thinge and not to be used and condemned by Poule,* in that he saithe that he taught yᵉ Ephesians all yᵉ counsell of God ~~meanynge~~† for he meanethe thereby that there is no other coñsell and cause in God to predestinate elect and save us then he preached to yᵉ Ephesians.

"2. Agayne in yᵉ article of predestination about the ende there be thees wordes. Furthermore we must receave Goddes promises in suche wise, as they be generally set forthe to us in holy scripture. Thees wordes be not playne ynoughe. For they are spoken for no comfort and remedye against yᵉ tentation of predestination whereof was spoken in yᵉ sentence next before. Therefore they be chefely to be understanded of yᵉ promissees of God made unto us for salvation and life everlastinge. By yᵉ wiche we ought to learne two necessaire and comfortable lessons. The first is that God in his generall promissees of eternall healthe promisethe and offerethe salvation and eternall life to every man wiche hearethe them. For that is for yᵉ promisees of God to be generally set forthe unto us in yᵉ scripture. The second that every man must beleve that God promiseth unto him salvation & eternall life when yᵉ promisees of salvation be preached unto him. For that is to receave the promisees of god as they be generally set forthe in yᵉ scripture but it is to harde for yᵉ meane learned or yᵉ simple people to gather out thees nedefull lessons out of thees wordes folowynge. We must receave Goddes promisees in suche wise as they be generally set forthe in yᵉ scripture. Wherefore for ye better understandinge of them. I wolde wishe some more wordes to be putt unto for yᵉ expressinge of suche a meanyng. As thus, We must receave and beleve the promissees of God in Christ for eternall health and life to belong to every man as they generally be set forthe to all men in the holy scripture so that every man wiche beleveth to yᵉ ende in Christ shall

---

* Act. xx.   † Sic in MS.

be saved. And they wiche beleve not in him shall be
damned,* Qui credit filio habet vitam eternall. † ‡But he that
beleveth not in yᵉ name of yᵉ onely begotten Sone of God.

"3. In yᵉ ende of yᵉ article of predestination there be thees
wordes In our doyenges that will of God is to be folowed
wiche we have expressely declared unto us in yᵉ worde of
God. In that it is here saied that in our doyenges that will
of God is to be folowed wiche is expressed in yᵉ scripture ; it
playnely gyveth us to understande that there be two willes of
God, one in the scripture an other without yᵉ scripture and
that those two willes be contrarye or els why should it be
forbiddẽ to folowe any will of God in our doyenges.   Therefore the foresaied wordes be dangerous bycause to teache two
willes to be in God and them to be contradictorie the one to
will one thinge and yᵉ other not to will the same but yᵉ contrarie is a doctrine wich must nedes cause yᵉ comptempt§ of
Goddes will that it foloweth hereby, that what a man dothe
he dothe it by yᵉ will of God either open or secrete   Wherefore I wold wishe yᵉ above rehersed wordes and sentence to
be quyt put out. And in there place this to be placed as
necessaire to yᵉ mattier.

" We ought not to judge nor speake of predestination and
election nore of the causes of them, but as they be playnely
taught us in yᵉ worde of God.

"4. In yᵉ article of sacramentes, whereas it is writen a
litle after yᵉ begynynge in this wise, By the wiche he dothe
work invisibly in us, if there were putt in this worde ('salvation ') then yᵉ vertue of yᵉ sacramẽtes of baptisme and of yᵉ
Lordes supper shuld be more fully expressed bycause they
doe not onely confirme our faithe but also be meanes whereby
God worketh in us eternall healthe.

"5. And whereas a litle after it is saied, There are two
sacramentes ordeyned of Christ our Lorde in yᵉ gospell that
is to saye baptisme and yᵉ supper of yᵉ Lorde. In my
judgemẽt it were better saied thus. In this sort there be but
two sacramẽtes baptisme and yᵉ Lordes supper and yᵉ reast to
be lefit out bycause thees wordes (in this sorte) have a respect
to that wiche was spoken of before, whereby thees two sacramentes are showed to have no felowes.

"6. It folowethe in yᵉ booke. Thees fyve comõnly
called sacramẽtes that is to saye confermation penance orders
matrimonie and extreme annoylinge are not to be accompted
for sacramentes of yᵉ gospell. This is not true in all poyntes :

* Joan iii.   † Joan iii.   ‡ Sic in MS.   § Sic in MS.

For it is certein that Christ did order his apostles by thees his wordes, Sicut misit me pater ita ego mitto vos, hæc cũ dixisset flavit in eos et dicit eis.* Accipite spiritũ sãctũ quorũcuq͗ remiseritis peccata remittũtur eis, quorũcuq͗ retinueritis retenta sũt. Here Christ did not onely order and admitte his apostles to be preachers of his worde and to be ministers of his sacramentes but also by his breathinge gave them yᵉ Holy Ghost whereby they had yᵉ more grace to execute there office. It is nothinge worthe that is here objected that he wiche dothe order can not gyve to him wiche is ordered yᵉ Holy Ghost. For by Calvine (who is yᵉ autour of this sayenge) granteth that by orderynge he that dothe order dothe gyve unto him wiche is ordered authoritie to forgyve syne wich is as great a worke as to gyve yᵉ Holy Ghost yea it can not be gyven with out yᵉ Holy Ghost. Poule in steade of breathinge used in orderynge yᵉ laynge on of handes. Stirre up saithe he to Timothie yᵉ gift of God wich is in yᵉ layenge on of handes.† He hath yᵉ same in an other place whereby we learne that we ought to be ordered by imposition of handes and that thereby grace is gyven to him wiche is ordered.‡ So that it can not be well denyed but that orderynge is a sacramẽt of yᵉ gospel; but yet not such one, as baptisme and yᵉ Lordes supper be bycause by orderynge to the person wiche is ordered no forgynes§ of synes is offered, nor his faith ~~here~~ || herein is confirmed.

"7. Nowe further in yᵉ booke Being suche as have growen partely of yᵉ corrupt folowynge of yᵉ apostles. It is ment by thees wordes that confirmation, penance, orders, matrimonie have growen of yᵉ corrupt folowyng of yᵉ apostles, but this I see not to be true bycause they be all godly thinges, and maye be used with great profitt and godlynes. therefore there is no corruption but a puritie in usinge of them as the apostles did. Yeat as good and as godly as they be they are no suche sacramentes as baptisme and yᵉ Lordes supper are. Bycause none of them have appoynted of God yᵉ visible signe of His healthfull grace, and all of them (save penance) want that grace and so they are not to be accompted for suche sacraments as baptisme and yᵉ Lordes supper are, wiche have bothe yᵉ signe and Goddes heathfull¶ grace. Therefore by my judgemẽt, whereas it is saied those fyve comonly called sacramentes, that is to saye, confirmation, penance, orders, matrimonye, extreme annoylinge are not to be accompted for sacramentes of yᵉ gospell beinge suche as

* Joan xx. † 2 Timo. i. ‡ 1 Timo. iv. § Sic in MS.
‖ Sic in MS. ¶ Sic in MS.

have growen partly of ye corrupt folowynge of ye apostles, and so forthe to ye ende of the sentence I wishe all out of ye booke and to be in there stead of thees wordes folow-yenge confirmation penance orders matrimonye and extreme annoylinge are not to be taken for suche sacramentes as baptisme and ye Lordes supper be bycause none of them hathe appoynted of God the visible signe of his healthfull grace and all of them save penañce want that grace And so they are not to be accompted for suche sacramentes as bap-tisme and ye Lordes supper are, wiche have bothe ye signe and Goddes healthefull grace ordeyned of God to be signified and gyven by it.

"8. [[In ye Article of ye Lordes Supper it is thus said. The bodye of Christ is gyven taken & eaten in ye Supper after a heavenlye & spũall mañer onely. Thoughe it be true, that ye bodye of Christ can not be gyven taken & eaten in his supper, but it must nedes be truely gyven taken and eaten in ye supper, yet bycause some men for a more playnes wold have added this worde truely or in-dede, in this wise, The body of Christ is in dede gyven, taken & eaten in ye supper, it were well to putt it in, and Calvine agreethe thereunto for thus he writethe in his comentaries upon these wordes of Poule, hoc est corpus meũ. Concludo realiter ut vulgo loquũtur hoc est vere nobis dari in cena corpus Christi. And my L. of Sarisburie hath thees wordes. That we verelye & undoubtedly receave Christis bodye in ye sacrament it is neither denyed, nor in question.]]

"9. [[In that, in ye booke it is further saied after a spirituall & heavenly maner onely some be offended withe this worde onely, as my L. of Glocester, as thoughe this worde onely did take awaye ye reall presence of Christis bodye, or ye receavinge of y same by ye mouthe, whereas it was putt in onely to this ende, to take away all grosse & sen-sible presence, for it is very true that when Christis bodye is taken & eaten, it is neither seen, felt, smelt nor tasted to be Christis body, and so it is receaved and eaten but after a heavẽly & spirituall & no sensible manner. And whereas it is saied bycause ye mouthe receavethe Christis bodye, therefore it is sensibly received, The consequent is not true bycause ye mouthe in receavinge Christis bodye, doeth not feele it nor taste it, nor we by any other sence do perceave it. Yet for all this to avoyde offence & contention ye worde onely maye be well left out, as not nedeful. My L. of Glocester is pronoũced excom̃unicate by my lorde of Canter-burie & shall be cited to answer before him, and other bishoppes to certein errours whiche he is accused to holde. I think if this worde onely were put out of ye booke for his sake it were ye best.]]

" 10. [[It foloweth in ye booke, But ye mene whereby ye bodye of Christ is receaved & eaten in ye supper is faithe. If this worde profitably were put hereunto in this sort, But ye mene whereby ye body of Christ is profitably receaved & eaten in ye supper is faith, then shuld the occasion of this question, whether ye evill do receave Christis body in ye sacrament, bycause they lacke faithe (wiche risethe of ye forsaied wordes & causethe miche strife) shuld be quyte taken awaye, for that hereby is not denyed the unfrutefull receavinge of Christis body without faithe but ye frutefull onely affirmed.]]

[["My L. grace of Canterburie is purposed to present to ye Quenes Matie ye first copie of ye booke of articles (to the wiche ye most part of bishops have subscribed) to have it authorised by Her Matie, and there is this article.]]

" 11. [[Evill men receave not ye bodye of Christ, which article is not in ye prynted bookes either in Laten or Englishe. If this article be confirmed and authorised by ye Quenes grace it will cause muche busynes, bycause it is quyte contrarie to ye scripture & to ye doctrine of ye fathers, for it is certein that Judas as evill as he was did receave Christis bodye,* bycause Christ saied unto him take eate this is my bodye. It is not saied, if thou be a good or a faithefull man, take eate this is my bodye, but simply without any suche condition, take eate this is my bodye. So that to all men wiche be of ye churche & of the profession of Christ, whether they be good or bad, faithfull or unfaythefull (for to them onely Christ spoke thees wordes take eate this is my body and not to ye jewe turke, miscreant beast or birde) Christis body is gyven & they do receave it.† That is ye cause that poule saith whosoever shall eate of this breade & dryncke of ye cuppe of ye Lorde, unworthely, shall be giltie of ye body & bloude of ye Lorde, for he that eatethe or drynkethe unworthely eatethe & drynketh his owne dañation, bycause he makethe no difference of ye Lordes body. Note well thees wordes ye Lordes body. It [sic] not here saied ye signe or sacrament of ye Lordes body nor ye grace or fruite of the Lordes bodye, nor ye memorie of the Lordes passion, but plainely ye Lordes bodye, to teache us that ye evill men of the churche doo receave Christes bodye. Therefore

* Matt. xx.   † 1 Cor. xi.

Theodoretus (that anciant father) in his cõmentarie upon
y⁰ saied wordes thus writethe, Illud autẽ, Erit reus corporis et sanguinis domini, hoc significat, quod quẽãdmodũ
tradidit ipsũ Judas, Ipsi autem insultaverũt et eum probris et
convitiis affecerũt Judei, Ita eum ignominia et dedecore
afficiũt, qui sanctissimum ejus corpus immundis manibus
accipiũt, et in pollutũ incestũque os imittũt. God grant us
unitie in true & sounde doctrine for Christis sake. Amen.]]

[II.] "1. [B] Touchinge y⁰ first part of y⁰ bill wich is to
dryve ~~men~~* papistes to y⁰ churche, I thinke it both lawfull
& necessarie, ~~for y⁰ papistes have noo just cause to~~ † but
withall to enforce them to receave I think it utterly to be
unlawfull. For if we knowe y⁰ the papistes doo thinke y⁰ y⁰
cõmunion wiche we doo minister is no cõmunion or no lawful
cõmunion (as certainly they doo) and we do knowe it, then we
ought not to gyve it them bycause they receavinge wich‡ such
an evill opinion of y⁰ cõmunion shuld take it to theire cõdeña-
tion and so to gyve them y⁰ comunion what were it els, but to
go aboute to destroye them. And we have no power saith Poule
to destroye but to edifie.

"2. [B] Poule willeth no man to receave before he dothe
first examyn him selve, whether he judgeth right of y⁰ sacramẽt
or no and hath a pure faith and a good and a cleane conscience
or no. Let a man saith he examyn him selve and then leitt him
eate of that bread and drynke of that cuppe whereby he
teachethe us that no man shuld receave so long as he judgeth
not well of y⁰ sacramẽt ~~Chri~~ §

"3. [B] Christ forbiddeth us to gyve an holy thing unto
dogges ~~wiche~~|| and is not y⁰ cõmunion an holy thinge and those
papistes wich judge ill of our cõmunion be they not in respect
of theire ill judgmẽt as evill as dogges withe reverence I speake
it. Therefore we ought not to gyve y⁰ cõmunion to those
papistes wiche judge evill of y⁰ cõmunion.

"4. [B] Poule willeth us to shone an heretique after ones
or twise warnynge. And doo we not take the stoute papist
be an heretique. Then we ought to shone him leaving his
companye and not to gyve him y⁰ cõmunion the chefest
token of fellowshippe. If he will not heare y⁰ churche saithe
Christ Lett him be unto thee as an ethnicke and a publicane.

"5. [B] Chrisostome saith, that he had rather dye then he
wold wittingly gyve y⁰ sacramẽt to any man whom he knewe
wold take it unworthely. And will we gyve y⁰ sacramẽt to y⁰

* Sic in MS.　　† Sic in MS.　　‡ Sic, query *with*.
§ Sic in MS.　　　　　　|| Sic in MS.

D D

stoute papist, whom we knowe doth thinke evill of y⁰ sacra-ment, and so when he taketh it must nedes receave it to his dañation. Suerly if we gyve him y⁰ sacrament we can not with out repentance escape the perill that Chrisostome feared thereby.

6. [B] " The com̄union booke willeth none to receave wiche is a blasphemer of God, or an hinderer, or a slanderer of * of His worde. And do we not take the obstinate papist to be suche. Therefore by the com̄union booke, we ought not to gyve y⁰ com̄union to y⁰ obstinate papist.

7. [B] " The papist knoweth that he doth syne yf he should receave that for y⁰ com̄union wiche he judgethe to be no one.

8. [B] " And so if we shuld euforce him to receave we shuld cause him to syne against his conscience wiche is deadly syne. Qui edificat contra conscientiam edificat ad gehennā he that buildeth against conscience buildeth to hell.

" But it is here said y͵ Austene wold that y⁰ Donatistes shuld be enforced to receave. Therefore why shuld not y⁰ papistes be dryven to receave also. To this I an̄swer Austene confesseth y⁰ y⁰ Donatistes had y⁰ same word and sacramentes that y⁰ Catholiques had. For y⁰ Donatistes did confesse y⁰ an evill man did preache y⁰ same worde y⁰ a good mā did and did minister y⁰ sacramētes that a good man did; but they denied y⁰ y⁰ word wiche was preached by an evill man, and y⁰ sacramentes wich were ministered by an evill man were profitable to y⁰ hearer and y⁰ receaver as y⁰ worde preached by a good man and y ⁰sacramētes ministered by a good man were. As y⁰ papistes grant y⁰ baptisme wich is gyven to him wich is out of y⁰ churche is not profita-ble untill he wich hathe it come to y⁰ churche And yet y⁰ papistes take it for a true and perfitt baptisme in substañce notwithstandinge. Therefore Austene might well enforce y⁰ Donatistes to receave as agreeinge with y⁰ catholiques in y⁰ substance thereof. [9. B] But ye papistes thinke y⁰ we have no consecration and so no com̄union or sacramēt as the catholiques have. Therefore y⁰ example ᵒᶠ † or coñsell of Austene in forcynge y⁰ Donatistes to receave maketh not to enforce y⁰ papistes to receive our com̄union as a true and a perfitt com̄union ~~wiche~~‡ bycause in there conscience they take it to be no one. [III.] That wiche for hast I wrote cunfusely and unperfitly before, I have sent ᵢₜ§ you amended. [1. Bb] The bill for bynding men to come to churche I

* Sic. in MS.   † Sic. in MS.   ‡ Sic. in MS.   § Sic. in MS.

thincke it both lawfull and also necessarie for the papistes
have no just cause to absent them fro~ it bycause they can
not denye but it is y⁰ word of God wiche is there redde and
the prayers wiche be there saied be accordinge to y⁰ same
worde. And bycause y⁰ saied worde is y⁰ meane appoynted
of God to bring us fro~ errour to trueth and prayer is
there made to desyre God to bringe them fro~ errour wiche
be deceaved   Therefore y⁰ papistes wiche be in an errour
ought to be dryven by y⁰ lawe to come to y⁰ churche to
heare y⁰ worde of God there redde and preached and with
all y⁰ comon prayers yᵗ they may be brought from it.
Whereas y⁰ bill enforceth them to y⁰ comunion ever that·
be not well persuaded therein that is unlawful and that
in two respects. The one touchethe the comunicantes The
other ~~that~~* concernethe them that shall minister unto them.
[8. Bb] As touchinge them wiche judge not well of y⁰
comunion (as it was ministred and consecrated) this I have
to saye It is decreed by y⁰ counsell of Trident (as it was
before by y⁰ counsell of Florence) that y⁰ sacramēte must
be consecrated and ministred with y⁰ entention as the
churche dothe holde them but ye papist knowethe yᵗ we
doo not consecrate nor minister y⁰ sacrament withe y⁰ entent
of y⁰ churche, bycause y⁰ churche saithe that the bread is
transubstantiated and yᵗ Christis body is there really. And
our ministers doo consecrate ~~and minister~~† but to this ende
and entent, to make ye sacramēt of Christis body as it is in
heaven and not as it is in y⁰ sacrament. Therefore if y⁰
papist be enforced to y⁰‡ receave y⁰ sacrament he takethe it to
his condeñation bycause he judgeth it not to be y⁰ Lordes
body and so receaveth it unworthely (as it is in Poule).

9. [Bb] " The papist thinketh that we have no consecration bycause we speake not the wordes of consecration over
y⁰ breade by takynge it in our handes or by appoyntynge
unto it when these wordes are in utterynge, as Austine re-
quyreth Accedat verbum ad elemētu~ et sit sacramentu~
And to prove this to be true it is saied in y⁰ comunion booke
Heare us O mercifull Father we beseech thee and grant yᵗ
receavynge thees creatures of bread and wyne accordynge to
thy sone our Saviour Jesus Christis holy institution in remembrance of his deathe and passion maye be partakers of
his most blessed body and bloude. He saith not that we
maye be partakers thereby partakers of his body and bloude.
Note this worde thereby or y⁰ like is here left out, wiche

* Sic. in MS.   † Sic. in MS.   ‡ Sic. in MS.

shuld applye y⁶ wordes to y⁶ breade and wyne to make them
to be meanes to receave by, ye body and bloude of Christ;
wiche giveth us to understande that it is ment there that
Christis body is not given us by ye sacrāmet but otherwise
spiritually onely by faith wich is deeu both when we receave and when we doo not. As for the wordes wiche doo
after folow in y⁶ booke they seme to to * be spoken in y⁶
waye of a storie and not for entention of consecration.

["8.] As concernynge the ministers if they know any men
to be suche papistes, wiche holde that the comunion wich they
gyve is either no comunion or an unlawfull comunion he
ought not to gyve it them bycause he knoweth that he
shold gyve it them to there condemnation And we have
no power saithe Poule to destroye but to edifie. [5. Bb]
And Chrisostome saithe he had rather dye then he wold
wittingly gyve y⁶ comunion to any man, that wold unworthely
receave it. [3. Bb] And Christ comandeth that we shuld not
dare sanctū canibus. [4. Bb] And Poule saith hereticū post
unā aut alteram admonitionem de vita. If we ought to
shone y⁶ cōpaynye of him that is an heretique or of a contrarie opinion then we ought not to gyve him y⁶ comunion
y⁶ chefe signe of felowshippe. Therefore it is saied of Christ
Si ecclesiam non audierit sit tibi ethnicus et publican. [6. Bb]
The comunion booke willethe that none wiche is a blasphemer
of God or an hinderer or a slanderer of his worde etce shuld
receave And doo we not take y⁶ obstinate papist to be suche
Therefore if we enforce y⁶ papistes to y⁶ comunion we doo it
against Goddes lawe and y⁰ lawe of y⁶ realme and against
there our owne† conscience and ours the papistes.‡ Et qui
edificat contra conscientiā edificat ad gehennā wherefore for
y⁶ honour of God for y⁶ reverence of y⁶ sacrament and saftie
of mens solles cause the enforcement to y⁶ comunion to be
quyte putt out of the bill.

[IV.] "To ye other mattier Poule saith y⁶ corpora nrā
sūt membra Christi. Of y⁶ wiche it is to be gathered that
our bodies also be partakers of Christ as it is well seen by y⁶
comunion. There y⁶ first consell of Nice I reade Cyrill and
Calvine also that§ saye that our bodyes shall rise againe to
life eter‖ everlastynge bycause they be partakers of Christis
imortall bodye."

---

* Sic. in MS.   † Sic. in MS.   ‡ Sic. in MS.
§ Sic. in MS.   ‖ Sic. in MS.

Now Mr. Goode, remarking upon Bishop Geste's Letter of Decr. 22, 1566, says, (p. 6) :—

" From this letter it seems, that the words, ' the body of Christ,' etc., inserted in the 28th Article in the revision of 1562, were proposed by Bishop Geste, and proposed by him (with a subtility to be regretted) under the notion that they admitted his doctrine of the presence of our Lord's body in the elements.

" This is the utmost that the advocates of Bishop Geste's doctrine of the presence can extract from this letter in their favour."

But need they *wish* to " extract " more ? It is enough surely for those who hold the doctrine of the Real Objective Presence, to be able to maintain—that they are entitled to hold and teach that doctrine because the terms of the Article do " not exclude" it, and that this is affirmed by the Bishop who drew up the Article. They demand, and *justly* demand, complete toleration, at least, for what they believe to be much more than an *opinion*, yet certainly (as they think) an opinion meant to be comprehended by the language of the Article. Nor will they object to be accused, with Bishop Guest, of " subtilty," if by that is meant *refinement;* convinced that *nicety* of definition is not inappropriate to the subject of the Eucharistic Presence : though they would repudiate any intention of *cunning* or *artifice*, and might think it unbecoming in Mr. Goode to impute it to Bishop Guest, *if* here, as elsewhere, he *is* indulging that license of judgment which unfortunately he is apt to betray towards the *motives* of his opponents.

Mr. Goode admits, indeed (p. 7), that,

" . . . under some circumstances, it might have been difficult to show, that those who agreed to the Articles in the Convocation of 1562, did not use these words in the same sense as that attached to them by Bishop Geste. But," he adds, " fortunately these Articles were passed in Convocation with the *addition of another*, namely the 29th, which I shall now show, *by Bishop Geste's own testimony*, to be entirely irreconcileable with his view of the presence, and which therefore excludes his interpretation of the 28th. And accordingly we find that he did not subscribe the Articles in the Convocation of 1562. (See Lamb's Historical Account of the xxxix. Articles.)

" Now what Bishop Geste himself held to be the doctrine maintained in Article 29, he himself shall inform us : as also how far he would have been glad subsequently to modify the phraseology of Article 28."

In proof of his statements he then proceeds to quote §§ 8, 9, 10 and 11 of the Document above printed.

But, first of all, Mr. Goode (unless I mistake his words) argues upon an assumption which, to say the least, is quite unwarranted by the commonly received theory of the principle which guided the framers of the Articles, *viz.*, *a desire of comprehension.* If that theory be true (and there seems no reason to dispute its accuracy) it surely was not requisite that all " those who agreed to the Articles in the Convocation of 1562 " should use these words ['after an heavenly and spiritual manner onely '] in the same sense as " Bishop Guest did. Considering the various opinions which were then held, as to the nature and mode of the Presence, all that the acceptors needed to secure was—that the *language* of the Articles did not condemn such diversities as, it was understood, were meant to be tolerated. To imagine that Guest's doctrine was unknown to the Convocation, or that (as Mr. Goode says, p. 11) he "penned the words . . . with the secret intention of understanding them as he has explained them in his letter to Cecil ;" and that, consequently, he and the Convocation passed the Article with entirely opposite objects, is a notion wholly devoid of foundation, and totally alien to the important position he occupied in the revision of both the Prayer Book and the Articles: the opinions of the man who was intimately associated with Cecil and Parker in that work, and who was substituted by Cecil, in the time of the Archbishop's illness, to aid in preparing the Prayer Book of 1559, were not likely to be hidden from the Convocation of that day. That those opinions ran in, what would be called, a Roman direction, is sufficiently disproved by the fact that, in his answers to the Secretary touching certain proposed emendations in the Prayer Book, (1) he thought it needless to use the proper Eucharistic Vestments ; (2) proposed such a division of the Eucharistic Office, that non-communicants should not remain throughout ; (3) considered it not convenient "to continue the use of praying for the dead in the Communion;" (4) advised the omission of the Prayer of Consecration as it stood in Edward's 1st Book; (5) said that the Sacrament should be received in the hand and not in the mouth; (6) and deemed it "indifferent" whether the communicants partook of it standing or kneeling.—*Strype's Ann.* Vol. i., p. 83.

Mr. Goode further contends that the 29th Article, as understood by Guest, was "entirely irreconcileable with his view of the Presence," (p. 7), and "consequently was fatal to his mode of interpreting the 28th," (p. 11).

But it is noticeable that the words objected to by Bishop Guest, in § 11, are not the words which ultimately appeared in the Article, or in its title: he complains that in the Book about to be presented for the Queen's authentication, "there is this Article. Evill men *receave* not ye bodye of Christ:" and he uses the same word three other times in the course of his objections in this Section, besides three times employing the expression, "*take* eat." Yet neither of these words "*receive*" and "*take*" occur at all, either in the heading or in the body of the 29th Article of 1571. Was this a mere oversight of the writer? It is difficult to believe in such an absence of accurate quotation on the part of one so intimately acquainted with the Articles as Guest necessarily was, and that, too, on an occasion when he was complaining of *words* and *phrases*—the more so as, in all the other instances in this Letter, he cites the Articles exactly. May it not, then, have been the case that some change was made in the English title* of this Article before the Articles were presented to the Queen for ratification? If so, it must have been before May 11th, as on that day they were signed by the Bishops, including Guest himself; and this fact of his subscription at that time to the English copy of the Articles (Lamb, p. 30), helps to determine the *date* of this Document now under consideration; for if it be Guest's (and there seems every reason to believe that he was the author of it) there can be no

---

* The title of Article xxix., as signed by Guest, on May 11, 1571, is, "The wicked do not eate the Body of Christe in the use of the Lord's Supper."—*See Lamb's Reprint.*

reasonable doubt that it was written prior to May 11th, and
that his objections having been then in some way satisfied, he
was able to concur with his Episcopal brethren in attesting,
by his signature, his *acceptance* of the Articles; though, probably, not his entire *approval* of some of their *language*. Mr.
Goode, indeed, (p. 13) chooses to make a most unfair and uncharitable insinuation against the Bishop for thus acting : he
says :—

"That Bishop Geste, almost immediately after penning the above
letter to Lord Burleigh, should subscribe the Articles, including the
29th, is, I suppose, to be accounted for from what some modern
writers would style, 'The necessities of his position ;' but it is a fact
which does not seem very creditable to his candour. It did not,
however, go without its reward, for by the end of the year he was
promoted to Salisbury."

Now, as Mr. Goode does not offer a particle of evidence to
sustain his inuendo, and as there is nothing, so far as I am
aware, in what is recorded of Bishop Guest's character, to
justify such a surmise ; this suggestion of unworthy motives
may be dismissed with the remark—that that Prelate's conduct in signing the Articles is apparently more consistent
with candour than is Mr. Goode's in censuring him for his
act.

That the Articles did undergo a variety of changes of more
or less importance during the Convocation, which began April
3, and ended May 30, 1571, is plain from such slight notices
of its proceedings as remain in the Abstract made by Dr.
Heylin before its records were destroyed in the Fire of
London.   Bennett (Hist. of Articles, pp. 261—3) has quoted
from this a description of what occurred on the very day when
the Articles were signed by the eleven Bishops, of whom
Guest was one, which seems to suggest that, probably, it was
on this occasion that that Prelate was satisfied : he says :—

"*Fryday, May* 11, *the Bishops being met in a low Parlour at*
Lambeth,* de et super rebus Ecclesiæ et libro articulorum de doctrina (ut apparuit) secrete semotis omnibus arbitris tractarunt ;
*which may perhaps have been the subject of that two hours Con-
ference, which they had afterwards on Wednesday, May* 23. *Sess.* 8."

* Whither, on "May the 4th, the Convocation" had "been adjourned . . .
because of the Archbishop's indisposition, as it seemeth, . . ."—*Strype's Parker*,
Bk. iv., p. 319.

It is, indeed, extremely likely that the question of the re-adoption of Article 29 occupied a material place on this occasion (see also *Hardwick*, p. 154, and *Swainson*, p. 32), and that the Meeting was held for the very purpose of discussing the points raised in Guest's supposed Letter to Burleigh : the opinions of such a man could hardly be disregarded, and as it is not probable that he suddenly abandoned what, plainly, he had been holding for at least the five years preceding (apparently very much longer),* yet did then subscribe, there is certainly fair ground for believing either that some alteration was made, or that he was convinced of the phraseology of the 29th Article being not at variance with his belief. That the Archbishop was ready to meet as far as he could the difficulties which beset this question, seems plain from the occurrence related in his Letter to Lord Burleigh on June 4th (*Parker Correspondence*, No. cclxxxix., p. 381), when, apparently, the Articles were waiting for the Queen's ratification. For, though he retained his opinion as to the applicability of the passage quoted from St. Augustin, it seems (see *Bennet*, chap. 24) that he afterwards "removed" the *reference* from the margin of the Article, when some copies had been struck off, and so left the appeal to St. Augustine *more general*. It is, moreover, worthy of notice, that this marginal reference to St. Augustine is not in the copy (as reprinted by Dr. Lambe) signed by Guest on May 11, 1571. If Guest (though I doubt it) was the author of this objection, the Archbishop's course further confirms the view here suggested.

Now Guest's objection to the 29th Article arose from his opinion that it was " quite contrarie to yᵉ Scripture and to yᵉ doctrine of the Fathers :" he thought moreover (and indeed with a kind of prophetic mind, considering what has since happened) that it would "cause much busynes ;" therefore he was anxious for its omission, or for some modification of it, so as to avoid these evils. But it is quite easy to con-

---

* For in 1548 he published "A Treatise againste the Prevee Masse," in which occurs the passage given at p. 193, as illustrating his Letter of December 22, 1566.

ceive of Archbishop Parker having satisfied him that there was nothing in the language of the Article which contradicted the authorities he had referred to, or the view which he had expressed in § 11 of his Letter. For it is clear from Guest's language in this very Section that he never could have regarded "all men which be of y⁺ churche, and of the profession of Christ, whether they be good or bad, faithfull or unfaythefull," as "partakers of Christ," in the Sacrament, in that sense wherein our Lord spake when He said to Simon Peter, "If I wash thee not thou hast no part with Me." If, then, the Archbishop could convince Guest (as surely was not difficult) that this expression of the Article was not inconsistent with his belief—that "Judas as evill as he was did receave Christis bodye, because Christ saied unto him take eate this is my bodye"—seeing that the very same Father (St. Augustine) who was cited in the Article held the same * belief respecting Judas—Guest might naturally and consistently withdraw his opposition, and unite in a statement which had obtained the concurrence of his brethren.

Mr. Goode asserts that "*Bishop Geste's own testimony*" proves the 29th Article "to be entirely irreconcileable with his view of the presence" and one "which therefore excludes his interpretation of the 28th" (p. 7) and is "fatal to his mode of" explaining it (p. 11). But, first of all, it must be observed that Guest distinctly repeats in § 9 of this Letter the precise explanation of the words "after a spirituall and heavenly maner only" which he had given in his former Letter; and he speaks of their introduction into the Article, in such a way as entirely to destroy Mr. Goode's, not exactly charitable, theory that "he himself penned" them "with the secret intention of understanding them as he has explained them in his Letter to Cecil of December 22, 1566." For it seems utterly beyond belief that his former assertion should have remained unnoticed, so far as anything appears to the

---

* "The Lord Himself endureth Judas, a devil, a thief, and His betrayer: Ho allows him to receive among the innocent disciples, what the faithful know to be our Ransom."—*Ep.* 43, *ad Glor. Eleus.*, § 23, p. 99. Dr. Pusey's Catena, p. 503.

contrary, and that he should have ventured to assert again (in a Document obviously not designed merely for the Secretary's own private perusal) that " it was putt in onely to this ende, to take awaye all grosse and sensible presence "—thereby, in fact, as it seems to me, claiming for that interpretation of it the assent of the Convocation—unless he well knew that such a statement did not admit of contradiction. If however, this later Letter was not written by Bishop Guest, then it much increases the very *difficulty* which Mr. Goode seeks to remove; for the writer, whoever he was, becomes a most important witness to the truth of that positive statement made by Bishop Guest, but which Mr. Goode ventures to deny.

This consideration alone seems to warrant us in drawing, from Guest's language about the 29th Article, a conclusion materially different from that which Mr. Goode has furnished: for if, as I venture to maintain, the *silence* of the Bishops admits the truth of Guest's allegation respecting the 28th Article ; then if it does not *disprove* Mr. Goode's assertion —"that the meaning attached to the words of the 28th Article by Bishop Guest was not that in which they were passed by Convocation" (p. 11)—it shows that it was *a* meaning not designed to be excluded ; and therefore I submit that, whereas Mr. Goode says (p. 7) "no sense can be placed on Article 28, which is not consistent with the doctrine delivered in Article 29," it would be truer and more pertinent to state—that to disallow an interpretation of Art. 29 which is consistent with Guest's explanation of Art. 28, is to ignore the mind of the Convocation of 1571 which passed them both.

In further defence, however, of his theory Mr. Goode contends (p. 11) that—

" Even irrespective of that addition [of Art. 29] it would seem that the words [of Art. 28] appeared to others to enunciate so clearly a different doctrine from that which Bishop Geste ascribed to them, that even Bishop Cheney, who would have been glad to have subscribed them in that sense could not conscientiously do so. And Bishop Geste himself, on second thoughts, would have liked to eliminate the word ' only,' *in order to save Cheney from con-*

demnation ; which shows that Parker and the Bishops before whom
he was convened did not interpret the word in the sense attached to
it by Geste."

Upon this passage I remark (1) First, that if it be meant that
Cheney concurred with "others" in construing the disputed
words differently from Guest, it by no means follows that he
and they spoke the mind of those who passed the Article :
from the little that seems known of Cheney's opinion it appears that he held a somewhat *physical* notion of the Real
Presence, though not maintaining Transubstantiation : for
Strype (*Cranmer* p. 461) says, that, in the Convocation of
1553, he " owned the Presence with the Papists, but denied
the Transubstantiation ;" and again (*Ann.* 1. 282), after remarking that Goodman accused him of being a Papist, says,
" But I do not find anywhere that he was indeed of that
faith, any further than that he was for the **real,** that is the
corporal, presence of Christ in the Sacrament." This seems
confirmed by Guest's words in his letter of December 22,
1566, where he states that he told Cheney he " wold speake
against him herein," *i.e.,* apparently, for advocating that the
Body of Christ in the Sacrament was in some kind of way
cognizable by the *senses* as distinct from *faith* ; and his remarks in § 9 of the letter of 1571 seem to imply the same
opinion as being still held by Cheney : for he observes,
" And whereas it is saied bycause yᵉ mouthe receavethe
Christis body, therefore it is *sensibly* receaved ; the consequent is not true bycause yᵉ mouthe in receaving Christis
bodye, doeth not feel it nor taste it, nor we by any other
sense do perceave it." Moreover Campian the Jesuit,
writing to Cheney in Nov., 1571, exhorted him to return to
the Church for " that he was more tolerable than the rest of
the heretics, because he held the presence of Christ in the
Sacrament" (*Strype Ann.* i. 282) *i.e.* his, Campian's, view of
the Presence.* If this were so it would sufficiently account

---

* A consideration this which surely suggests how Mr. Goode really answers
himself when he says (p. 16), "Another testimony that the Bishops of that day
did not hold the doctrine of the real presence of Christ's body and blood in the
elements, may be found in the fact that Campian, one of the Romish divines of

for Cheney's objection to the phrase and for his continuing still to oppose it, notwithstanding Guest's explanation of its design: he "could not conscientiously" subscribe it in Guest's "sense" if, as would seem, he held a notion of "grosseness and sensibleness in yᵉ receaving" of the Sacrament, which Guest told him the words were meant to "exclude."

That Cheney did (about the date of Guest's Letter of 1566) hold some opinion on the Eucharistic Presence materially different from the opinions of his Episcopal brethren,＊ seems clear from a Letter. written by Jewel to Bullinger on Feb. 24, 1567, in which he says—"One alone of our number, the bishop of Gloucester, hath openly and boldly declared in Parliament his approval of Luther's opinion respecting the Eucharist, but this crop will not, I hope, be of long continuance." (*Zurich Letters*, 1st Series, p. 185.) But as Guest, both in 1566 and 1571, quotes Jewel's language as being confirmatory of his own statements touching the Real Presence, we are necessarily led to conclude that there was a difference between the belief of Cheney and Guest on this subject.

(2.) Next, I would observe that Guest's willingness " to eliminate" the word " onely" or, as Mr. Goode also expresses it (p. 7) "to modify the phraseology of Art. 28," on Cheney's account, is no proof at all that " Parker and the Bishops" held a different interpretation of it from Guest; rather I conceive it shews their agreement. Because (a) though he thought (§ 9) " if this worde onely were put out of yᵉ booke for his [Cheney's] sake it were yᵉ best," he clearly held that

that period, speaks of Cheney as more tolerable than the rest of the heretics, and distinguished from them *as holding the true presence of Christ on the altar* . . . ." The Italics are Mr. Goode's. Compare *Ridley* (p. 60)—"That Heavenly Lamb is" etc. See also Bishop Guest's " Treatise against the Preevee Masse," 1548 ". . . . the worthy counsayle of Nice wryteth to the disalowance of transubstantiation in sorte thus, let us not grossely beholde the bread and wyne proposed and set before our eyes but in faythe consider the Lambe of God in that hys sacred table having our heartes elevated and uplifted. . . ."—P. 82. Ed. 1840.

＊ Mr. Goode himself allows this, for he says (p. 16). "And Camden speaks of Cheney as distinguished from his brethren by being *Luthero addictissimum,* a warm adherent of Luther."

it made no real difference to the meaning of the Article, for in this same section he repeats distinctly that interpretation which Mr. Goode denies to be the true one. Again (b) there is nothing to shew, so far as I know, that Cheney was in danger of "condemnation" by the Bishops' for holding Guest's interpretation of the Article, though he may have been cited for teaching the doctrine which I just now suggested that he maintained: he had been excommunicated in Synod, in April, "for absence and contumacy" (*Strype Ann.* i. 281); but I have failed to discover anything to shew what were the "certain errours whiche he is accused to holde" and which Guest says he was to "be cited to answer before the Archbishop and other bishoppes."

It may, further, be noticed that § 8 also manifests Guest's real object in proposing any alteration in the terms of the 28th Article, though he himself was fully content with its wording: his design clearly was to obviate the difficulties of others by using language which, while not obnoxious to them, should yet convey the sense in which he declared the Article to have been framed: thus "bycause some men for a more playnes wold have added this word truely or in-dede," he said "it were well to putt it in" thus—"The body of Christ is in dede gyven taken and eaten in y* supper;" and he quotes the language of Calvin and Jewel as a reason for admitting the proposed phrase. Probably, in this suggestion, he designed also to meet the objection of Bishop Cheney.

Mr. Goode still further endeavours to fortify his position by the following observation (p. 12):—

"It is worthy of remark, also, that the very word which Archdeacon Denison would wish us to suppose is to be *understood* in the interpretation of the words, that we receive the body of Christ by faith only, namely ' profitably,' was *proposed for insertion by Bishop Geste,* but was *not inserted.*"

But the *non-insertion* of this word is no proof that it was *rejected;* if, indeed, it could be shewn that this was done, and done on the plea—that to insert it would alter the sense of the Article—some ground would be furnished for the notion (which I suppose Mr. Goode means to impute to the Bishops) that a "lively faith" is the necessary condition for *reception* of the Body of Christ. Guest's design in proposing the word, was to hinder the "miche strife" which the words of the Article caused in reference to "this question, whether y⁰ evill do receave Christis Body in y⁰ sacrament, bycause they lacke faithe:" yet the very form of his proposal shews that he did not consider the word to be *necessary* to such a construction of the Article as included his own belief; and if this was his view, it is not difficult to understand that, even supposing his Episcopal brethren did not share his interpretation (though I am not admitting such to have been the case) they would prefer to retain language which covered their diverse opinions on what was not a matter of essential belief; whereas the addition of the word would be a very likely bar to the Subscription of those who did not hold the doctrine of reception by the wicked; and might even raise difficulties in the case of those who held that, Christ being present in the Sacrament, His Body was *given* to all, and all *received* It, but that It was not *eaten* of the wicked because from such He then withdrew Himself. Besides, they might well think that the language they had adopted was most consonant to the *general* character of the words both of our Lord and of St. Paul, and therefore the more advisable to be retained, considering the range of opinions which, it is well known, the Articles were designed to include.

Mr. Goode, however, (p. 13, discovers another proof "that Archbishop Parker disagreed with Bishop Geste in his view of the doctrine of the Eucharist," from the language of the Archbishop's Letter to Lord Burleigh, of June 4, 1571, in which he "expressly defends the 29th Article against those who had endeavoured to prejudice him [Burleigh] against it."

But this is assuming, what has to be proved,—that Guest was the objector on this occasion—a most improbable thing, seeing that he *had signed* the Articles, including the 29th, on May 11th, nearly a month before. So then, when Parker says that St. Augustine's language "doth plainly affirm our opinion in the Article to be most true, however some men vary from it," the very word " our" would most naturally seem to *include* Guest, and therefore to recognise his interpretation of the Article as *not* disagreeing with the Archbishop's " view of the doctrine of the Eucharist."

It must be remembered, too, that Guest had expressly cited Theodoret, in § 11 of his letter, as supporting his doctrine of reception by the wicked, in these words :—

> "But 'he shall be guilty of the Body and Blood,' showeth this, that like as Judas betrayed Him, and the Jews insulted Him, so they dishonour Him, who receive His all-holy Body with impure hands, and bear It to their defiled mouth."

Yet St. Augustine, whose authority Archbishop Parker appealed to in the Article, and defended when it was demurred to, had said the same thing ; his words are:—

> "Ye remember of what it is written, ' Whoso shall eat the Bread or drink the Cup of the Lord unworthily, shall be guilty of the Body and Blood of the Lord.' And when the Apostle said this, the discourse was upon the subject of those who, treating the Lord's Body like any other food, took it in an undiscriminating and negligent way. If then this man is rebuked who does not discriminate, that is, see the difference of, the Lord's Body from other meats, how must he be damned, who, feigning himself a friend, comes to His table as a foe."—*Hom.* lxii. *on St. John. Dr. Pusey's Catena,* p. 516.

Further, in one of the Homilies of 1562, circulated under the express sanction of Archbishop Parker, it is distinctly said :—

> "If they be worthy blame which kiss the prince's hand with a filthy and unclean mouth, shalt thou be blameless which, with a stinking soul . . . dost breathe out iniquity and uncleanness on the bread and cup of the Lord ?"—*Second Part of the Sermon concerning the Sacrament.*

Comparing these three statements, I would ask—is there any such contradiction or discrepancy between them as would argue a serious difference of doctrine among those who appealed to them ? rather, are they not of such substantial identity as to encourage, if not to compel, the belief that Parker and Guest could have had no difficulty whatever in interchanging them as consistent expressions of the opinions which they held on this subject?

It is possible, indeed, that the person, who suggested the objection to Burleigh, was Cheney or some one holding the opinion ascribed to him at p. 212: in that case, what I have just said touching the opinions of the Archbishop and of Bishop Guest would be strengthened, and Parker's language in adhering to the quotation from St. Augustine would be satisfactorily explained.*

Mr. Goode produces " a still further testimony" to prove what were Archbishop Parker's views on the Real Presence, and to shew that those views were opposed to Bishop Guest's: but certainly it is not a little surprising that that "testimony" should be the Anglo-Saxon Homily of Ælfric on the " Paschall Lamb" to which I have referred at p. 68—a Homily, the "agreement" of which "with the tract of Ratramn is [as the Editors of the Oxford Edition of Ratramn, 1838, observe] not only doctrinal, but very often verbal:" this consideration is one reason why, as I suppose, it has commonly been regarded as an important witness to the English Church's belief of the Real Objective Presence in contradistinction to that mode of Presence which Transubstantiation is held to involve.

First of all, Mr. Goode draws attention to the circumstance —that the Preface to the Homily is "signed by Archbishop Parker and the Archbishop of York, and thirteen other Bishops (but not by Guest or Cheney):" meaning, I suppose, thereby to imply that they disapproved the Homily. But to this three answers may be made: (1) That the Preface from which Mr. Goode quotes, states the names attached to have been joined "With divers other personages of honour and credit: subscribing their names, the record whereof remains in the

---

* It seems to me a point quite open to discussion whether the objection to St. Augustine's authority came from this side of the controversy at all. In another publication (" Lawful Church Ornaments," p. 251) I ventured, in 1857, to raise this question, in opposition to Strype's statement that " some Papist had been nibbling at this new Article." The information requisite for deciding the point is still undiscovered.

hands of the most reverend father Matthewe Archbishope of Canterburye :"* therefore *Guest* and *Cheney* may have been among those "personages." (2) That while *Guest* and *Cheney* are not found among the published subscriptions, neither does so important a name as that of *Jewel* appear, nor are the names of some other Bishops attached, *e.g.*, Chester, Bath and Wells,Exeter, Peterborough, St. Asaph, Oxford. (3) That the signatures were appended not, apparently, to recommend the *doctrine* of the Homily, but, as the Preface states, to shew that—

" these here under written upon diligent perusing and comparing the same [Homily and old auncient bookes] have found by conference, that they are truely put forth in print without any adding or withdrawing anything for the more faithfull reporting of the same, and therefore for the better credit hereof have subscribed their names."

Next, Mr. Goode inaccurately includes in what he terms the " condemnatory notice" in the Preface, " of some things in this Homily," the sentence 'where it speaketh . . . of the mixture of water with wyne :'" but the note at p. 40, upon the words, "Holy bookes commaund that water be mengled to the wine which shall be for housell," is in these word, " No Scripture inforceth the mixture of water with the wyne": plainly shewing that the intention was not to condemn the ancient practice, but to guard against what the Preface seems to consider as " greate ignoraunce and superstition," viz., that the " command" had a *Divine* as well as an *Ecclesiastical* authority, and therefore made the mixed Chalice *essential* to the Sacrament.

Further, Mr. Goode remarks (p. 14), that—

" The doctrine of the Homily in the part here [*i.e.* the Preface] referred to with comparative approbation, is undeniably not that of a real presence of Christ's body in or under the elements, but that the elements become in a mystical and spiritual sense Christ's body and blood, as having a spiritual power and influence imparted to them."

In proof he quotes pp. 15 to 23, italicizing, as shewing the

---

* The MS. does not appear to be among the MSS. in the Lambeth Library.

sort of Presence he speaks of, the words which I have so distinguished in the following sentences from his extract :—

(1) "Now saye we to suche men, that *some thynges be spoken of Christ by signification, some by thyng certain.*" (2.) " Truely the bread and the wine which by the masse of the priest be halowed, *shewe one thyng without to humayne understanding, and an other thing they call within to believing minds.* Without they bee sene bread and wine both in figure and in tast : but they be truely after the halowing Christes body and hys bloude *through ghostly mystery.*" (3.) " Much is betwixte the invisible myghte of the holye housel, and the visible shape of hys proper nature. It is naturally corruptible bread and corruptible wine : and is by myghte of God's worde truely Christes bodye and hys bloude : *not so notwithstanding bodeley, but ghostly.*" (4.) . . . . *nothing is to be understoode therein bodelye ; but all is ghostlye to be understood.*"

But surely these italicized words which Mr. Goode regards as adverse to, are rather confirmatory of, " a Real Presence of Christ's Body in or under the elements : " they plainly indeed declare against any "bodely," *i.e.,* physical Presence, but they no less clearly pronounce for a Presence which is "ghostly," *i.e.,* spiritual, though withal Real. In truth, the word "within," which occurs in the second sentence may not unfairly be claimed as a witness for that "in or under" which Mr. Goode rejects ; and the italicized words in sentences (3) and (4) may well be deemed the equivalents of Bishop Guest's "after a heavenly and spirituall and no sensible manner." (§ 9).

Mr. Goode has, however, omitted to call attention to the important word " truely," which occurs three times in these same sentences—the very word which Bishop Guest (§ 8) was willing to have inserted in Art. 28 to meet the case of some who desired "a more playnes" in its terms. Neither has he particularly noted the words " is in " which I put in italics in the following sentence which he quotes :—" Whatsoever *is in* that housel which giveth substance of life, that is of the ghostly might, and invisible doing "—words again which cannot well be summarily dismissed as condemning the "in or under" which is supposed to be so obnoxious to "the doctrine of the homily."

It would seem, however, that Mr. Goode is not satisfied with the doctrine even as he interprets it; for he says, "This is not precisely the doctrine of our best divines," quoting Hooker, *Eccl. Pol.* V., lxvii. 6, and then he adds "But it is very different from what is called the doctrine of the Real Presence, and the difference between it and the sounder doctrine delivered by Hooker, is *comparatively* of secondary importance." Yet if this Homily is, as Mr. Goode says, a "testimony of Archbishop Parker's views;" if its doctrine is spoken of "in the way of commendation" by him and the other fourteen Bishops who signed the Preface; if, moreover, the doctrine so approved is to be taken, as Mr. Goode implies, as explanatory of the meaning of that 28th Article which these Bishops agreed upon—what is this but saying that Hooker held "a sounder doctrine," touching the Eucharistic Presence, than the Elizabethan Bishops delivered in the Article which they Subscribed themselves and put forth to be Subscribed by all the Clergy of the Realm? Would Hooker have admitted this? Can the answer be doubtful?

Having thus considered at some length, and I hope satisfactorily answered, Mr. Goode's remarks upon those passages in this Letter, which relate to the 28th and 29th Articles, I now proceed to notice some other statements in the same Letter, which, I think, further tend to shew the fallacy of those conclusions which Mr. Goode has drawn from it.

It will be seen that Bishop Guest, (the supposed writer) does not confine his objections to these two Articles; for the xviith and xxvth are alike the objects of his censure: he commences his Letter (§ 1) by urging that "Thees wordes (suo consilio nobis quidem occulto)* are to be put out of yᵉ book for three causes" which he then mentions: again, (§ 2) he complains that the words "Furthermore we must receave Goddes promises in such wise, as they be generally set forthe to us in holy Scripture," which occur in the last clause of the Article, "be not playne ynoughe;" and, once more, (§ 3) he expresses his opinion that the words "In our doyenges that

---

* These words are not in the *English* version, in the Fac-simile of the "Little Booke," printed by Dr. Lambe.

will of God is to be folowed wiche we have expressly declared unto us in yᵉ worde of God," forming part of the same clause, "be dangerous." But all these three expressions (which are found in our present 17th Article) *were retained* in that English copy of the Articles which Bishop Guest signed on May 11th, 1571.

So, too, in regard to the 25th Article, the Bishop wished (§ 4) to insert the word "salvation" in the sentence "By the which he dothe work invisibly in us." Again, he proposed (§ 5) that the second clause—"There are two Sacraments ordeyned of Christ our Lorde in yᵉ gospel"—should read thus: "In this sort there be but two sacraments, baptisme and yᵉ Lordes supper." Further (§ 6) he considered it was "not true in all poyntes" to declare, as stated in the third clause, "that thees fyve commonly called sacramentes that is to saye confermation penance orders matrimonie and extreme annoyling are not to be accompted for sacramentes of the gospell; and (§ 7) he also saw it "not to be true" to speak of them as "Beinge suche as have growen partely of yᵉ corrupt folowynge of yᵉ apostles" if "thees wordes" were "ment" to refer to "confirmation* penance orders matrimonie." This clause of the Article he therefore wished to be altered in the form he gives at the end of § 7, "Confirmation," etc.

But, as in the case of the 17th Article so, in this, the phraseology was adhered to, and Guest signed the Articles notwithstanding the objections put forward in the Letter.

Now how are we to account for this? Mr. Goode's solution of the difficulty, in respect of Articles 28 and 29, has been already noticed (pp. 205, 208); I must presume he would

---

* It is worth observing that the same objection, so far as regards Confirmation, was made by the *Puritans* at the Hampton Court Conference, 30 years later. (*Cardwell Hist. Conf.*, p. 181.)—"In the third point (which was about Confirmation) was observed either curiosity or malice, because the Article which was then presently read, in those words: 'These five, commonly called sacraments, that is to say, confirmation, penance, orders, etc., are not to be accounted for sacraments of the gospel, being such as have grown partly of the corrupt following of the apostles,' etc., insinuateth that the making of confirmation to be a sacrament is a corrupt imitation; but the Communion Book, aiming at the right use and proper course thereof, makes it to be according to the Apostles' example; which his Majesty observing, and reading both the places, concluded the objection to be a meer cavil. And this was for the pretended contradiction."—*2nd Day's Conference, January 14th*, 1603.

resort to the same explanation in reference to Articles 17 and
25 : I prefer the more charitable and the more likely opinion
—that he became convinced of the language not being
unsound, though it was not what he considered *the most
appropriate* to obviate difficulties and to meet objections. It
would needlessly encumber these pages, and would be quite
foreign to their purpose, to discuss the points raised in this
Letter upon the 17th and 25th Articles, with a view to
reconcile their language with the objections of Bishop Guest :
but it will be convenient to cite the words of the Homily
" *Of Common Prayer and Sacraments,*" as bearing upon his
remarks on the 25th Article.—

" Now with like, or rather more brevity, you shall hear how many
sacraments there be, that were instituted by our Saviour Christ, and
are to be continued and received of every Christian in due time and
order, and for such purpose as our Saviour Christ willeth them to be
received. And as for the number of them, if they should be considered according to the exact signification of a sacrament, namely,
for the visible signs, expressly commanded in the New Testament,
whereunto is annexed the promise of free forgiveness of our sins,
and an holiness and joining in Christ, there be but two, namely,
Baptism and the Supper of the Lord. For although absolution hath
the promise of forgiveness of sin; yet by the express word of the
New Testament it hath not this promise annexed and tied to the
visible sign, which is imposition of hands. For this visible sign (I
mean laying on of hands) is not expressly commanded in the New
Testament to be used in Absolution, as the visible signs in Baptism
and the Lord's Supper are : and therefore Absolution is no such
sacrament as Baptism and the Communion are. And though the
ordering of ministers hath his visible sign and promise ; yet it lacks
the promise of remission of sins, as all other sacraments besides the two
above named do. Therefore neither it, nor any other sacrament else
be such sacraments as Baptism and the Communion are. But
in a general acception, the name of a sacrament may be attributed to
that thing, whereby an holy thing is signified. In which understanding of the word, the ancient writers have given this name, not
onely to the other five, commonly of late years taken and used for
supplying the number of the seven sacraments ; but also to divers
and sundry other ceremonies, as to oil, washing of feet, and such
like ; not meaning thereby to repute them as sacraments in the same
signification that the two forenamed sacraments are. . . . . And
although there are retained by the order of the Church of England,
. . . certain other rites and ceremonies about the institution of
ministers in the church, matrimony, confirmation of children . . . . .

and likewise for the visitation of the sick ; yet no man ought to take these for sacraments in such signification and meaning as the sacrament of Baptism and the Lord's Supper are : but either for godly states of life, necessary in Christ's Church, and therefore worthy to be set forth by public action and solemnity, by the ministry of the Church, or else judged to be such ordinances as may make for the instruction, comfort, and edification of Christ's Church."

Now, comparing this passage with § § 4, 5, 6 & 7 of the Letter to Burleigh, is there not such identity of language as to shew that the same hand might have written both ? But this 9th Homily had been set forth by Archbishop Parker and the other Bishops nine years before, and was now again authoritatively recognized as containing " a godly and wholesome doctrine," in the 35th of those very Articles then awaiting the Royal Sanction. Is it at all an improbable conjecture —that Guest was referred to the Homily for proof that the 25th Article did mean what he thought it might, in words, more clearly convey ? Would not this be quite sufficient to account for the relinquishment of his objection, and for his consenting to sign the Article ? If so, does not this consideration support the theory for which I am contending— that Guest was convinced that the language of the Articles, to which he had been demurring, was not repugnant to the doctrine which he held, and, therefore, that he could consistently attach his signature ?

No doubt, too, Guest felt that having made this last attempt to get, what he considered, a more accurate phraseology introduced into these Articles, it was simply the path of modest duty to concur by his signature in the decision of " y* most of [the] Bishops," and to set an example of Subscription (though it was not required from the *Bishops* by the 13th Eliz. c. 12), unless he was convinced that those Articles really embodied unsound doctrine. *Bennet*, indeed, thinks (p. 187) that Guest's Subscription at this time proves that he " came off from those notions afterwards " which he had held about the Real Presence " (as divers persons in those early daies entertained different opinions at different times about the Sacrament)" : but then *Bennet*, apparently, was entirely ignorant of the existence of these Letters of 1566 and 1571, else he must have sought for some other reason to account for Guest's signature to "that very [29th] Article in the Convocation of 1571."

With regard to the question of Cheney's subscription, *Bennet* says :—

"Nor do I believe, that Bishop *Cheney* did ever subscribe the Twenty-ninth Article. For tho' the 13 *Eliz.* c. 12 obliged the inferior Clergy to Subscription ; yet the Bishops are exempted from that necessity by the very Letter of the Act."

It may be quite true that, as Mr. Goode supposes, Cheney "would have been glad to have subscribed" the Articles, as as well Guest; though not, as I have argued at p.212, "in that sense " which Guest puts upon the 29th ; but, unless he was constrained to do so by any other authority than that of the Statute, it can hardly be doubted that he would be anxious to avoid Subscription himself (though obliged to enforce it upon his Clergy), if he continued to hold that opinion of the Real Presence, which there seems ground for believing that he did maintain in May, 1571.

Having regard, then, to the various considerations now offered, I must confess myself unable to think with Mr. Goode, that "the question thus raised" by Bishop Guest's Letter of Decr. 22, 1566, which "has been appealed to as determining the sense of the 28th Article in a direction very different from that which has been ordinarily attributed to it," can " be easily set at rest, and the interpretation thus given to the 28th Article be shewn to be inadmissible" (p. 1): on the contrary, it seems to me that, although some obscurity still overhangs the subject, the view I have now presented will, at least, bear a favourable comparison with that which Mr. Goode has drawn, and requires some strong shadow to be thrown upon it, before it can be dissolved into his picture.

Some additional light is, however, cast upon, what I have represented as, Guest's opinions at this time, in Parts II. and III. of his Letter to Burleigh (see pp. 201—4), wherein he argues "toching coming to y⁰ Church, and receaving y⁰ sacrament." The Bill to which these words relate is conveniently referred to in the following passage of Mr. Swainson's Essay on Article xxix. : I have verified the dates, and added the words enclosed in brackets: speaking of the Parliament which met on April 2, 1571, he says (p. 15): —

" The Queen intended to bring at least one Bill concerning Religion before the House. That Bill was against the introduction of Popish Bulls into the country. It is uncertain whether she sanctioned " The Bill concerning coming to Church, and receiving the Holy Communion," which was read a first time, April 4. The Bill may have been a Government measure, and it may be desirable to trace it through the Houses. It was read the second time, April 6, and committed (D'Ewes, p. 157). Mr. Fleetwood, a ' Church Reformer,' speaking against some of its provisions, it came in a new form from the Committee, April 9: [and again " was read the first time " (D'Ewes, p. 159), it seems also to have had another reading, and was discussed, April 11th (D'Ewes, p. 161),] was read a second time, April 20 (D'Ewes, p. 176): re-committed [with additions,] April 21 ; ingrossed, April 30 : read a third time and passed, May 4 : received in Upper House, May 5 : [probably] read first time, May 7 : second time and committed, May 9 : third time (with amendments) ["conclusa dissentientibus Comitibus Wigorn and Southampton, and Dominis Windsor, and Vaux] May 17: received in the Lower House and conference ordered, May 19 : ' ordered upon the question to be general as to the body thereof,' May 22 : [in the Lords, May 24,] another conference, May 24 : again in the Lords, May 25. In the Journals of the Lords it is here marked *conclus.* But, for some cause or other, the Bill did not become law. No Act answering to the description received the Royal Assent this Session."

I may add, that no similar Act was passed during the rest of Elizabeth's reign, though two Acts were made, so far like it, as to require *attendance at Church,* but not enjoining the reception of the Sacrament : *viz.,* 23 Elizabeth c. 1, A.D. 1581, *"An Act to retain the Queen's Majesty's Subjects in their Due Obedience;"* and 35 Elizabeth c. 1, A.D. 1593, bearing the same title.

Now an examination of this part of Guest's Letter, to which I have just referred, will probably shew the true " cause " why " the Bill did not become Law:" if, as I have argued, p. 207, it was written before May 11th, that date corresponds with the date, May 5th, at which the Bill was received in the Lords : there it was *amended,* on May 17th, upon the third reading; and when it got back to the Commons there was a Conference " as to the body thereof." All this looks very much as if the Amendments of the Upper House materially affected the value of the Bill in the eyes of the Lower; and, when we come to read the objections of Bishop Guest, the conclusion seems almost unavoidable — that the Bill did not pass in consequence of his remonstrances, which, probably enough, took form and substance in the " Amendments " noticed.

It will be seen that this portion of Guest's Letter consists of two Parts, the latter of which (marked [III.], p. 202) is mainly a repetition and enlargement of Part [II.]:* the writer himself supplies the reason for this; he says, " That which for hast I wrote confusely and unperfitly before, I have sent you amended." This circumstance confirms, moreover, the suggestion just made—that the Letter was called forth by the introduction of the Bill into the House of Lords—and, further, helps to fix the date of the Letter itself, which I think may now be fairly held to lie between May 5th, the day on which the Bill reached the Lords ; and May 11th, the day on which Guest signed the Articles.

Two things are clear from this remonstrance of Guest: *first*, that he was no favourer of the Roman party ; for so far as the Bill was meant "to dryve papistes to y* church I thinke it," he says, " both lawfull and necessaire :" *next*, that he was entirely opposed to compelling them to communicate ; for he says, " To enforce them to receave I thinke it utterly to be unlawfull."

Whence arose this important distinction which he drew in their case ? Plainly because, as he himself shews, the two acts involved such very different consequences : he said ([III.] [I.B b]) that " ye papistes wiche be in an errour ought to be dryven by y* lawe to come to y* churche to heare y* Worde of God there redde and preached and with all y* comon prayers y* they may be brought from it ;" whereas, he adds

* For facility of reference I have marked by similar numbers the corresponding arguments in the two Parts : the Numbers not bracketed are in the MS. It will be seen that all the arguments are repeated in Part [III.] (though in a somewhat different order) except No. 2. [B], shewing that self-examination is a condition of worthy receiving.

([II.] [8.Bb]), " If y⁰ papist be enforced to receave y⁰ Sacrament he taketh it to his condemnation bycause he judgeth it
not to be y⁰ Lordes body and so receaveth it unworthily (as
it is in Poule);" and, as he had said before ([II.] 1.[B]),
" what were it els but to go aboute to destroye them, And
we have no power saith Poule to destroye but to edifie."

But, upon what *doctrinal* ground did the writer thus urge
this danger to " the papistes " in being " enforced to receave
y⁰ Sacrament?" Clearly, it seems to me, because he believed the Real Objective Presence : whereas " the papistes "
believed the Sacrament, as then celebrated in the Church of
England, to be *no* Sacrament ([II.] 7. [B]): because, (1),
they alleged ([II.] [9. B] and [III.] 9. [B b]) there was "no
consecration," owing to the absence in " y⁰ Communion booke"
of certain manual acts ([III.] 9.[B b]): because (2) they further
held (*Ibid*) that the absence of the word " thereby," in the
Prayer of Consecration, shewed that " the wordes " of that
prayer were not meant to " applye . . to y⁰ breade and wyne
to make them to be meanes to receave by the body and
bloude of Christ; wiche giveth us to understand, that it is
ment there that Christ's body is not gyven us by y⁰ Sacrament but otherwise spiritually onely by faith wich is deeu
both when we receave and when we doo not:" because (3)
they also said (*Ibid*) that the rest of the Prayer was " spoken
in y⁰ waye of a storie and not for entention of consecration :"
because (4) they argued, and the writer admitted ([III.]
[8. B b]) that the Sacrament was not consecrated or ministered
with " y⁰ entent of y₀ [*i.e.*, that] churche " which "saithe that
the bread is **transubstantiated**, and that Christis body is there
really;" whereas, says the writer, " our ministers doo consecrate * but to this ende and entent, to make y⁰ Sacrament
of Christis body as it is in heaven and not as it is in y⁰ Sacrament." †

---

* He had written here " and ministor," but afterwards erased it; shewing
how accurate he wished to be in his language.

† Compare the following passage from Guest's " Treatise on the prevee
masse," 1548 :—" These wordes, take, eat, in these wordes of the institution of
the Lorde's Supper, take, eate, this is My bodye, be no wordes of makinge of

The writer of the Letter, however, disallowed (as his language plainly implies) these objections of " the papistes " to be any disproof of the validity of the Sacrament ; thereby, in fact, claiming that Presence which was wholly independent of the faith or misbelief of the receiver, and so rendered the unworthy partaker obnoxious to the judgment to which the writer deprecated exposing " the papistes " by a Legal enactment.

It was, then, in consequence of this entire belief of the writer in the *reality* of the Church of England's Eucharist, that he pleaded against the enforced communion of " the papistes" on these grounds—That ([II.] 3. [B] and [III.] [3. B b]) it was to disobey the command of Christ, who " forbiddeth us to give an holy thing unto dogges:" that ([II.] 2. [B]) it was to disregard St. Paul's warning of their danger, who, neglecting self-examination, received unworthily ; and ([II.] 4. [B] and [III.] [4. B b]) to neglect his admonition " to shone an heritique after ones or twise warnynge :" that ([II.] 5. [B] and [III.] [5. B b]) it was to despise the example of St. Chrysostom,* who " saith, that

the Lorde's body, but of presenting and exhibiting the same to the receauers of the ryghte supper of the Lord. So that it is full open that the prieste can neither consecrate Christis body, neither make it. Howbeit this is alwaye grauntable, ye minister both consecrateth and maketh, though not Christes body and bloud, yet thallotted bread and wyne ye Sacramentes exhibitive of the same. For where as ye bread and wyne used at the Lordes Supper were prophane and unholy, before the wordes of the institution of the sayd supper were duely reported upon them. Nowe after thee due reporte and utterance of thee sayd wordes by thee minister, upon thee before-named bread and wyne, they be consecrate and made of prophane the holy sacramentes exhibitues, of Christes body and bloud. Thus also meaned the fathers by these words, consecration and making in this Sacramente. Nowe to transubstantiatyon or tornekynde, thee next entreatable matter, which is no lesse disallowable, then disceaueable. How can thys stande with our fayth that Christes body (whose creatyon is unrenuable) shulde be again made of the nature of bread (a vyle creature) through the exchange of the nature thereof into hys," etc. P. 79. Ed. 1840.

* " Let no one communicate who is not of the disciples. Let no Judas receive, lest he suffer the fate of Judas. This multitude also is Christ's body. Take heed, therefore, thou that ministerest at the Mysteries, lest thou provoke the Lord, not purging this body. Give not a sword instead of meat.
" But if thou darest not do it thyself, bring him to me ; I will not allow any to dare to do these things. I would give up my life rather than impart of the

he had rather dye then he wold wittingly gyve ye Sacrament to any man, whom he knewe wold take it unworthely :" that ([II.] 6.[B] and [III.] [6.B b]) it was to give no heed to " The Communion booke " which " willeth none to receave wiche is a blasphemer of God or an hinderer or slanderer of his worde :" that ([II.] 8. [B]) therefore it was to make light of "syne against his conscience wiche is deadly syne."

Wherefore, because of these weighty considerations—that ([III.] [6.B b]) to "enforce ye papistes to ye Communion we do it against goddes lawe and ye lawe of ye realme, and against their conscience and ours," he entreats Lord Burleigh "for ye honour of God, for ye reverence of ye sacrament and saftie of men's solles, cause the enforcement to ye Communion to be quyte putt out of the Bill."

Nor did he, as it seems, plead in vain ; for, as I have already remarked (p. 226), the proposal to compel the adherents of the Pope to Sacramental Communion was entirely abandoned.

It cannot, surely, be reasonably doubted (considering especially the reference to St. Chrysostom's strong language) that the writer believed distinctly the doctrines of the Real Objective Presence and of Reception by the Wicked ; but these are precisely the doctrines advocated by Guest in the former portion of this very same Letter : what, then, is the legitimate inference ? Certainly, as I must think, that the man whose counsel, apparently, prevailed to arrest this Bill by the Doctrinal pleas which he advanced, could hardly have had his proposals, as to the 28th and 29th Articles, rejected because his belief on the Eucharistic Presence was opposed to that of the rest of the Episcopate, as Mr. Goode contends : on the contrary, if, as it seems extremely probable, his influence defeated this Parliamentary attempt to coerce the Romanists to Communion, by his assertion of the practical consequences of a doctrine which he obviously *assumes to be*

Lord's Blood to the unworthy ; and will shed my own blood rather than impart of such awful Blood contrary to what is meet."—(*Hom.* lxxxii., § 6, p. 1094) *Dr. Pusey's Catena*, p. 672.

the recognized one ; it may very fairly be thought that, as I have already argued, his advice upon those Articles was only not adopted, except, apparently, as to the important alteration in the *Title* of Art. xxix. (see p. 207), because the changes he proposed were not needed to bring them into harmony with the Theological belief of himself and of his brethren, who unitedly signed them on May 11th, 1571.

The concluding paragraph of this Letter ([IV.]) suggests that some " other mattier " was also under discussion at that time, and that Bishop Guest's opinion was asked or offered in reference to it : the passage does not afford the means of deciding what the precise point was ; but, from the apparent reference to those words of the prayer of access in "ye Communion" Office, " grant us, therefore (gracious Lord), so to eat the Flesh of Thy dear Son Jesus Christ, and to drink His Blood, that our sinful *bodies* may be made clean by His *Body* . . ." it would seem that some question had been raised touching the *corporal* relation between Christ and Christians in virtue of the Incarnation. But, whether this conjecture is right or not, the answer shews the writer's belief—that in the reception of the Eucharist there was a participation of Christ so *real* as to affect not the soul only, but the body also : a belief which he might well treat (for his words imply it) as being the *received* doctrine, considering the language of the Homily* then in circulation. Yet, does not this further involve the same writer's belief of a Real Objective Presence in that Sacrament ? And, if so, have we not here Bishop Guest again proclaiming, in fact, (in no hesitating manner, as if it were merely his own opinion) that belief, with all its consequences, just as he had done before in treating specifically of the 29th Article ?

If this supposition be true respecting this last portion of the Letter, it confirms what I have said concerning Guest's

---

* " . . . thus much we must be sure to hold, that in the Supper of the Lord there is . . . . the Communion of the body and blood of the Lord, in a marvellous incorporation . . . . wrought in the souls of the faithful, whereby not only their souls live to eternal life, but they surely trust to win to their bodies a resurrection to immortality."—*Hom. of Sct.*, part I·

opinions as developed in the previous portions : yet, if this be not its purport, there is nothing in the passage at variance with the rest of the Letter, or calculated to weaken what he had before advanced.

Before passing, however, from this Document, it seems desirable to notice Mr. Goode's thrice repeated assertion (pp. 7, 11, 26), that Bishop Guest* did not Subscribe the Articles of 1562; it makes no difference, indeed, whether he did or not, to the preceding remarks upon that Prelate's two Letters ; though, if it were *absolutely certain* that Guest did sign in 1562, those remarks would be so far strengthened as Mr. Goode's argument would be weakened, in the disproof of the allegation (that Guest did not then subscribe) by which he endeavours to sustain his opinion as to the rejection of Guest's opinions in the Convocation of 1571.

It must be admitted, indeed, that there are grounds for doubting whether Guest did subscribe before 1571 : *Bennet* certainly has shewn (Essay ch. 5) that there are reasons for thinking that *Strype* was mistaken in asserting that he "did," upon the authority of " extracts " taken " out of the Registers of Convocation " (*Ann.* i. 325—326) before their destruction in the Fire of London : but it does not seem to me that he has produced sufficient evidence to warrant his conviction that Guest (as well as Cheney) was " stedfastly resolved

---

* In considering this question of Guest's Subscription it should not be forgotten that no less a person than Dean Nowell did not sign the copy of the Articles subscribed by the Lower House of Convocation in 1562, of which he was then Prolocutor ; that copy, like the one Guest did not sign, contained the 29th Article. In 1571, he like Guest, did sign ; but the printed copy of the Articles attached to the Bodleian MS.,† where his name appears, does not contain the 29th Article : yet as there seems to have been a *second* subscription of the Lower House to the Articles, as finally settled, including the 29th, he may, likely enough, have subscribed that. But this places Nowell and Guest in exactly the same position : is there any thing to show that Archbishop Parker and Nowell disagreed in the Real Presence ? I think not : yet, if so, how would Mr. Goode account for Nowell's non-subscription in 1562? Perhaps, what would explain Nowell's course then, would explain Guest's also at that time.

† Dr. Lambe (p. 40) has a curious note about this Bodleian MS. he says, "There is one copy, of which I ought to make some mention, *viz.*, that of Wolfe's edition of 1563, with the names of the Convocation of 1571 on a sheet of parchment sewed on to its cover. It is not at all clear that these names were subscribed to any Articles If they were, they must have been attached to an English copy in 1571, from which they have been separated and sewed to this book." But there is nothing about the book to indicate this ; and what reason can be assigned for such a surmise? It would seem that Dr. Lambe had not taken into account the *second* subscription mentioned by *Bennet*, pp. 273 and 315.

against it." There is nothing to shew, so far at least as I can discover, that Guest changed his belief on the Real Presence between 1562 and 1571 ; on the contrary, the two Letters of 1566 and 1571, which have been here considered, strongly attest his persistence in it. It is likely enough, therefore, that he had the same objection to the wording of Art. xxix., in 1562, which he stated to Lord Burghly when it was proposed to publish it in 1571: probably enough, therefore, Guest did *hesitate* to sign, as, indeed, the absence of his sig· nature from the Parker Latin MS. of January 29, 1562-63 attests. It by no means follows, however, that he would have *refused* to sign, had it been then determined to promulgate that Article with the rest: but the fact that it was allowed to remain dormant among the Convocation Records; that it did not appear in the Latin MS. (*State Papers, Dom. Eliz.*, Vol. xxvii. 41a) apparently sent to the Secretary Cecil ; and that, as the *English* contemporary MS. states of it, "this in yᵉ orynal book not prynted " (*Ibid.* 40, January 31, 1563) would furnish adequate reasons for Guest continuing to decline Subscription, indeed for his having no occasion to further consider the subject until it was re-opened by the proposal to publish this Article with the rest in 1571.

Though, however, these considerations would obviate any *necessity* for his Subscription in 1563, they do not prove, nor does it by any means follow, that he *did not* subscribe: it is not improbable that, as has been suggested, he may have done so in some subsequent Session: but perhaps the Original Records themselves would not have determined the point any more than the Extracts which have been preserved; for it does not follow that any notice of additional Subscriptions would have been entered in the Convocation Register : if the Parker MS. had remained with the Convocation Records, instead of being taken, apparently, to Lambeth by the Archbishop, it would in all likelihood have shared their fate; in that case what evidence would there have been as to who subscribed or who did not ? Possibly, then, Guest (it might also be true of Cheney) subscribed some other copy of the Articles which was destroyed with the Records themselves.

For the reasons above stated, however, I need not pursue the inquiry further; indeed it would seem nearly profitless to do so in the absence of other Documents than those known to exist : in fact, it does almost appear that the point could only be finally settled by the discovery of another copy of the Parker MS., with the Signatures lacking in that original. I close these observations therefore with the following remarks, which shew Mr. Hardwick's latest (published) opinions on the subject :—

"But formidable doubts have been excited as to the supreme authority of the Parker Manuscript, by collating portions of it with an extract taken from the actual Register of Convocation in the time of Archbishop Laud, and formally attested by a public notary to satisfy or silence his accusers. Besides exhibiting a different version of one Article ' On the authority of the Church,' . . . . the extract from the Convocation-records has preserved a catalogue of the assentient prelates, varying in some noticeable points from that surviving in the Parker Manuscript :* and fresh perplexity is added to

* "This MS. contains the subscriptions of the Archbishop of Canterbury, and the Bishops of London, Winchester, Chichester, Ely, Worcester, Hereford, Bangor, Lincoln, Salisbury, St. David's, Bath and Wells, Coventry and Lich-field, Exeter, Norwich, Peterborough, and St. Asaph, — besides the three above-mentioned [Young of York, Pilkington of Durham, Downham of Chester] who belonged to the other province. The copy of the Record produced by Arch-bishop Laud omits the three northern prelates, as well as those of Chichester, Worcester, and Peterborough. It, however, includes the name of Guest, Bishop of Rochester, although some persons have doubted whether he *subscribed* or not (Bennet, p. 184),--a suspicion which is somewhat strengthened, so far as Parker's draft is concerned, by what is known of Guest's opinions on the Eucharist. But when the 3rd clause in the Art. ' De Cœna Domini' [' Forasmuche as the trueth of mannes nature requireth,' etc., see p. 32] appearing to favour Zwinglian views as to the nature of the Presence, was struck out by the Convocation, Guest might be entirely satisfied, and so might subscribe ;—which strongly favours the conclusion that the extract produced at Laud's trial was taken from a *later* and more authoritative document. On the other hand, Cheynie, Bishop of Gloucester, though occasionally present at meetings of the Synod, never acquiesced in some of the decisions, which explains the omission of his name in *all* the lists, (Strype, *Annals,* I. 563). The Bishopric of Oxford was not full ; and Kitchen of Llandaff (apparently from want of sympathy) took no part in the proceedings."
This fact of the withdrawal of the Clause of Art. 29 here referred to by Mr. Hardwick, tends to shew (if his argument about Guest is well-founded, as it would seem to be) that there was not that great discrepancy between the opinions of Archbishop Parker and Bishop Guest, which Mr. Goode maintains to have existed, and which I have ventured to doubt. It confirms, too, I think what I have all throughout this Letter contended for—that " *real* and *essential* " in the *Declaration* of 1552, " *reall* and *bodelie* " [*Realem et Corporalem*] in the *Article* of 1552, meant no more than *carnal* and *physical*—else how could Arch-bishop Parker have consented to abandon so important a clause as this, which he had inserted in his draft of the Article of 1562, as copied from that of 1552 ?

this question by the circumstance that *both* the series of episcopal signatures are said to have been appended to the Articles on the same day, and in the same place.

"If one may safely hazard a conjecture in the midst of these clashing statements, it is possible that after the House of Bishops had subscribed the Primate's copy on the 29th of January, it was transmitted to the northern Convocation, without waiting for the criticism of the lower house, who had continued their discussions for another week; and that on its return it was deposited, like other private papers, with the Parker Manuscripts, where it is now surviving; while *the* copy of the Articles as left when finally authorized by the whole Synod on the fifth of the following month had found its natural place among the other records of Convocation, *viz.*, in the registry belonging to the See of Canterbury, at St. Paul's Cathedral." —*Hist. of Art.*, p. 135. 2nd Ed.

For if the language was intentionally Zwinglian, and Parker knew it so to be, then he must have been a Zwinglian in re-producing it: but no one, that I am aware, has ever accused him of holding this view of the Eucharistic Presence: it follows, therefore, that in proposing to re-impose that part of Article 28 of 1552, which denied "the reall and bodilie presence (as thei terme it) of Christ's flesh and blood," he knew full well he was only excluding a *carnal* presence. It is, however, quite consistent with this to suppose that the Archbishop consented to abandon the paragraph because the language might be (and was by some) misunderstood to favour Zwinglian doctrine.

That some were dissatisfied with the change is plain from the Letter of Humphrey and Sampson to Bullinger, in July, 1566, where, speaking of "some blemishes which still attach to the Church of England" they say, "13. Lastly, the Article composed in the time of Edward the Sixth respecting the spiritual eating, which expressly oppugned and took away the real [realem] presence in the Eucharist, and contained a most clear explanation of the truth, is now set forth among us mutilated and imperfect."—*Zurich Letters*, I., p. 165.

After all, however, was this the reason for the alteration in the Article? Is it not much more likely that the paragraph was omitted because the Declaration, which corresponded with it, had already been omitted in Elizabeth's Prayer Book? This seems to me to be the true explanation of the change; for though, as I have noticed at p. 191, the Declaration seems to have been in some way used; yet the omission of its language from the Prayer Book and the Article implied an intention not to constrain opinions too much on this point, by any publicly imposed formulary. The following extract from a Letter of Archbishop Parker to Sir William Cecil, on Feb. 6, 1570-71, will serve to shew what opinions the Archbishop did not hold, and also that there was a considerable unanimity of belief upon the Eucharistic question only two months prior to the opening of the Convocation, on April 3rd.—"Sir, As you desired, I send you here the form of the bread used, and was so appointed by order of my late Lord of London * and myself, as we took it not disagreeable to the injunction. And how so many churches hath of late varied I cannot tell; except it be the practice of the common adversary the devil, to make variance and dissension in the Sacrament of unity. For where we be in one uniform doctrine of the same, and

* The allusion is to Grindal, who, acting with Parker upon the Queen's Injunction, and the 26th Section of Elizabeth's Act of Uniformity (which gave power to the Queen by advice of the Ecclesiastical Commissioners or Metropolitan "to publish such *further* ceremonies" as tended to "the due reverence of Christ's holy Mysteries and Sacraments") had advised the substitution of Wafer Bread for Common Bread. The instance is not favourable to those who now propose to revive this power to suppress or control Ceremonial or Ritual developments.

These Records it must be recollected, perished in the great fire of London; and therefore Mr. Goode is not quite warranted in saying so positively (p. 26), in contradiction of Dr. Pusey's statement gathered from Strype, that "Neither [Cheney nor Geste] signed those Articles [of 1562], and the Articles of 1571 were never signed by Cheney. This is an important fact in relation to our present subject."

At p. 66 I suggested that it might be useful to examine the language of Bishop Jewel, as being a leading Elizabethan Prelate, to ascertain whether his arguments touching the Real Presence were not, like those of the Edwardine Divines, directed chiefly against the prevalent popular belief of a *carnal*, *physical* presence: this I proceed now to do, especially as Guest's reference, in both Letters, to his contemporary, makes it all the more important to learn what he held on the Doctrine for which Guest quotes him; the controversy with *Harding* furnishes numerous passages to support this opinion: Jewel, in his "Sermon at Paul's Cross," 1560, had challenged the Roman party to "bring any one sufficient sentence out of any old Catholic doctor, or father, or out of any old general council, or out of the holy scriptures of God, or any one example of the primitive Church. . . . For the space of six hundred years after Christ," to prove the truth of twenty-five several Doctrines or Practices which they used or held. Harding took up the challenge in 1563; and Jewel replied in 1565: the following are a few out of many passages which might be cited as shewing the language which runs throughout the disputation.

One proposition which Jewel denied to be proveable from the first six centuries was:—

"that the people was then taught to believe that Christ's body is

so cut off much matter of variance which the Lutherans and Zwinglians do hatefully maintain, yet because we will have some matter of dissension, we will quarrel in a small circumstance of the same, neither regarding God in His Word, who earnestly driveth us to charity, neither regarding the love and subjection we should have to our prince, who zealously would wish the devout administration of the Sacrament, nor yet consider what comfort we might receive ourselves in the said Sacrament, if dissensions were not so great with us." —*Parker Correspondence*, No. 286.

really, substantially, corporally, carnally, or **naturally** in the Sacrament."

Harding began his proof by saying that :—

" Christian people hath ever been taught that the body and blood of Jesus Christ, ... is present in this most holy Sacrament, and that **verily and indeed.**"

And he adds :—

" . . . . that the words of institution of this Sacrament admit no other understanding, but that he giveth unto us in these holy mysteries his self-same body and his self-same blood **in truth of substance,** which was crucified and shed forth for us."—*Of Real Presence; Works, Parker Society,* Vol. 1, p. 44-5.

Jewel (though indeed he seems here somewhat to overlay Harding's language by his own interpretation of it) says in reply :—

" The question is here moved, ' whether Christ's body be **really** and **corporally** in the Sacrament.' His answer is, that Christ's body is joined and united **really** and **corporally** unto us."

Then he proceeds to argue thus :—

" And, albeit M. Harding lay such hold upon these words of Christ, as if they were so plain, yet others of his friends, by their diverse and sundry constructions touching the same, have made them somewhat dark and doubtful, and cannot yet throughly agree upon them. Some of them say, ' Christ's **natural** body is in the Sacrament, howbeit not **naturally** ;' some others say, ' It is there both **naturally,** and also **sensibly** :' some of them say precisely, ' Never man used either of these two terms, **naturally** or **sensibly,** in this case of Christ's presence in the Sacrament.' Yet others of them put the matter out of doubt, and say, ' Christ is there present **naturally.'** And in the council holden in Rome under Pope Nicolas the Second, it was determined, and Berengarius forced to subscribe, that Christ is in the Sacrament **sensibly ;** or as they then **grossly** uttered it in Latin, *sensualiter.* Some of them say, ' Christ's body is not divided or broken in the Sacrament, but only the accidents.' But Pope Nicolas with his whole council saith, ' Christ's body itself is touched with fingers, and divided, and broken, and rent with teeth, and not only the accidents.' . . .

" Now, if this article cannot be proved, neither by any words of the Scriptures, as Doctor Fisher saith, and as it further appeareth by the dissension of the teachers, nor by any one of all the old doctors and fathers, as M. Harding granteth by his silence, then may godly and catholic christian people well stay their judgments, and stand in doubt of this carnal and fleshly presence. Indeed the question between us this day is not of the letters or syllables of Christ's words, for they are known and confessed of either party; but only of the sense and meaning of his words, which, as St. Hierome saith, is the very pith and substance of the Scriptures. . . . If it be true that M. Harding saith, that this is the only sense and meaning of Christ's words, that his body is in such gross sort really and fleshly in the Sacrament, and that, unless Christ mean so, he meaneth nothing; it is great wonder that none of the ancient catholic doctors of the Church, no, not one, could ever see it; or, if they saw it, yet, being so eloquent, lacked words, and were never able to express it.—*Ibid.* pp. 446-7.

"And whereas M. Harding thus unjustly reporteth of us, that we maintain a naked figure and a bare sign or token only, and nothing else; . . . he knoweth well that we feed not the people of God with bare signs and figures, but teach them that the Sacraments of Christ be holy mysteries, and that in the ministration thereof Christ is set before us even as he was crucified upon the cross; and that therein we may behold the remission of our sins, and our reconciliation unto God; and as Chrysostom briefly saith, 'Christ's great benefit and our salvation.' Herein we teach the people, not that a naked sign or token, but Christ's body and blood indeed and verily is given unto us; that we verily eat it; that we verily drink it; that we verily be relieved and live by it; that we are bone of his bones, and flesh of his flesh; that Christ dwelleth in us and we in Him. Yet we say not either that the substance of the bread or wine is done away; or that Christ's body is let down from heaven, or made really or fleshly present in the Sacrament. . . . .

"To conclude, three things herein we must consider: first, that we put a difference between the sign and the thing itself that is signified.

"Secondly, that we seek Christ above in heaven, and imagine not him to be present bodily upon the earth.

"Thirdly, that the body of Christ is to be eaten by faith only, and none otherwise.

". . . . .

"Now consider then, good Christian reader, with thyself, whether it be better to use this word 'figure,' which word hath been often used of Tertullian, St. Augustine, and of all the rest of the ancient fathers, without controlment; or else these new-fangled words, 'really,' 'corporally,' 'carnally,' etc., which words Mr Harding is not able to shew that, in this case of being really in the Sacrament, any one of all the old fathers ever used."—*Ibid.* pp. 448-9.

Harding continued thus:—

"Again, we cannot find where our Lord performed the promise he had made in the sixth chapter of John, 'The bread which I will give is my flesh, which I will give for the life of the world,' but only in his last Supper: where if he gave his flesh to his Apostles, and that none other but the very same which he gave for the life of the world, it followeth that in the blessed Sacrament is not mere bread, but that same his very body in substance. For it was not mere bread, but his very body, that was given and offered up upon the cross.''

To which Jewel replies:—

'' This principle is not only false in itself, but also full of dangerous doctrine, and may soon lead to desperation. For if no man may eat the flesh of Christ, but only in the Sacrament, as here by M. Harding it is supposed, then all Christian children, and all others whosoever depart this life without receiving the Sacrament, must needs be damned, and die the children of God's anger. For Christ's words be plain and general: ' Unless ye eat the flesh of the Son of man, ye shall have no life in you.' . . . . But our doctrine, grounded upon God's holy word, is this, that as certainly as Christ gave His body upon the Cross, so certainly He giveth now the self-same body unto the faithful; and that, not only in the ministration of the Sacrament, ... And therefore St. Augustine saith, *(De. Civ. Dei.* Lib. xxi. c. xx.) ' They eat Christ's body, not only in the Sacrament, but also in very deed.' Here St. Augustine saith, contrary to M. Harding's doctrine, that we eat Christ's body, not only in the Sacrament, but also otherwise; yea, and so far he forceth this difference, THAT HE MAKETH THE EATING OF CHRIST'S BODY IN THE SACRAMENT TO BE ONE THING, AND THE VERY TRUE EATING THEREOF INDEED TO BE ANOTHER THING.* . . . . To be short, of Christian children, and other faithful that never received the Sacrament, he writeth thus (*in Serm. ad Inf.* Citat. a Beda 1 Cor. x.), ' No man may in any wise doubt, but that every faithful man is then made partaker of the body and blood of Christ, when in baptism he is made a member of Christ: and that he is not without the fellowship of that bread and cup, although before he eat of that bread, and drink of that cup, he depart this world, being in the unity of Christ's body. For he is not made frustrate of the Communion and benefit of that Sacrament, while he findeth that thing which is signified by the Sacrament.' ''—*Ibid.* pp. 449-50.

Again, Harding had said:—

'' If the words spoken by Christ in St. John of promise, that he performed in his holy Supper, ' The bread that I will give is My flesh,' had been to be taken, not as they seem to mean, plainly and truly, but metaphorically, tropically, symbolically, and figuratively, so as the truth of our Lord's flesh be excluded, as our adversaries

---

* The words which I have printed in Capitals are very observable as shewing Jewel's opinion of the language of St. Augustine, and may fairly be appealed to in support of Guest's language, touching reception by the wicked, in his Letter, § 11, p. 200.

do understand them, then the Capernaites had not any occasion at all of their great offence."—*Ibid.* p. 450.

To this Jewel, quoting St. Augustine, St. Basil, Origen, Tertullian, and St. Chrysostom, replies:—

" Hereby it is plain that Christ's meaning is spiritual, as Christ Himself and all the old fathers and doctors of the Church have expounded it; not real, **carnal, gross,** and **fleshly,** as M. Harding imagineth. M. Harding will say, that the eating with the mouth and the grinding with the teeth is a work spiritual. By this sense he is a good proctor for the Capernaites, and must needs say, that they had a spiritual understanding. . . . .

" Now let us see what sense the Capernaites gathered hereof. Origen saith, ... ' It happeneth sometime that simple men, being not able to put difference between those things in the Scriptures that pertain to the inner man, and those that pertain to the outer man, are deceived by the likeness of words, and so fall into foolish fables and vain fantasies.' So saith St. Hierome, ... Whereas they are taken for the elders in the Church, and the chief of the priests, by following the plain letter, they kill the Son of God.' Even thus it happened unto the Capernaites: that Christ spake spiritually of eating with faith, they understood **grossly** of eating with the teeth; as though they should swallow down His **flesh** into their bodies, as other meats; even in such **gross** sort as M. Harding would now teach the people to eat Christ's body."—*Ibid.* p. 452.

The better to sustain his position Harding said thus:—

" . . . . if Christ would have been so understanded, as though He had meant to give but a figure only of his body, it had been no need for him to have alleged his omnipotency and almighty power to his disciples, thereby the rather to bring them to belief of his true body to be given them to eat. . . . . ' Doth this offend you?' saith he. . . . ."

Upon which Jewel remarks:—

" And again, would M. Harding make all the world believe, if Christ's body be not **fleshly** and **grossly** in the Sacrament, according to his fantasy, that then God therefore is not omnipotent? Verily the old catholic fathers acknowledge God's omnipotency in the water of baptism; yet is not Christ therefore **really** present in the water."— *Ibid.* pp. 453-4.

Then instancing SS. Chrysostom, Augustine, and Leo, he concludes:—

" It appeareth by these authorities, that Christ in the water of baptism sheweth his invisible and omnipotent power. Yet will not M. Harding say that Christ is therefore **really** and **fleshly** present in the water of baptism.

" Therefore it was but vain labour to allege Christ's omnipotent power to prove this **fleshly** presence in the sacrament."—*Ibid.* p. 455.

Further, Harding stated :—

" These places of the scripture, and many other reporting plainly that Christ at his supper gave to his disciples his very body, even that same which the day following suffered death on the cross, have ministered just cause to the godly and learned fathers of the Church to say, that Christ's body is present in the sacrament **really, substantially, corporally, carnally,** and **naturally.** By use of which adverbs they have meant only a truth of being, and not a way or mean of being. And though this manner of speaking be not thus expressed in the scripture, yet it is deduced out of the scripture. For if Christ spake plainly, and used no trope, figure, nor metaphor, as the scripture itself sufficiently declareth to an humble believer, and would his disciples to understand him, so as he spake in manifest terms when he said, ' This is my body which is given for you ;' then may we say, that in the sacrament his **very** body is present, yea, **really,** that is to say, indeed, **substantially,** that is in substance, and **corporally, carnally,** and **naturally**; by which words is meant that his very body, his very flesh, and his very human nature, is there, not after corporal, carnal, or natural wise, but invisibly, unspeakably, miraculously, supernaturally, spiritually, divinely, and by way to him only known."—*Ibid.* p. 455.

Mr. Goode (p. 12) endeavours to depreciate the value of Guest's reference (in his Letter of 22nd Dec. 1566) to these words of Harding; he says :—

" How different were the views of Bishop Geste on this point from those of Bishop Jewel, may be seen by comparing the way in which the former notices the passage he has quoted from Harding, and the remark of the latter on the same passage. Bishop Geste, as we have seen, quotes it as conformable to his own doctrine. But this very same passage is treated by Bishop Jewel i n the following way."

Then Mr. Goode proceeds to quote Bishop Jewel's answer, which (except the part in brackets) I had also selected, as illustrative of the position for which these extracts were made :—

[" M. Harding saith these words, ' This is my body,' must needs be taken without metaphor, trope, or figure, even as the plain letter lieth, and none otherwise. So saith M. Harding only upon his own credit. But the old catholic doctors of the Church, of whom, he saith, he hath such store, say not so. St. Augustine, St. Ambrose, St. Hierome, St. Chrysostom, St. Basil, Tertullian, and others call the Sacrament a figure, a token, a sign, an example, an image, a similitude, a remembrance ;] . . . . Upon these grounds of his own M. Harding reareth up this conclusion : ' Thus,' saith he, ' may we say, that Christ is in the Sacrament really,' etc. Indeed, a man may say much, that hath no regard what he say. But if he will say, as the old godly Fathers said, then must he say: *Hoc est corpus meum, hoc est figura corporis mei :* This is my body, that is to say a figure of my body. For so the old learned Father Tertullian saith, Then must he say . . . . ' Christ delivered unto his disciples a figure of his body.' For so the old learned father St. Augustine saith. Then must he say : . . . . . ' The sacrament of Christ's body after a certain phrase or manner, or trope, or figure of speech, is the body of Christ.' For so again St. Augustine saith.

" Here M. Harding, seeing the inconveniences and absurdities of his doctrine, thought good to heal it up with some plaister. By these words, **really, carnally,** etc., ' the godly learned fathers,' saith he, ' meant that Christ's very body and flesh is there, but not in any natural or carnal wise.' And thus M. Harding's doctors wrote one thing and meant another. For M. Harding knoweth that all adverbs, taken of nouns, signify evermore a quality, and never the substance ; which thing children are taught to know in the grammar school ; and may be resolved thus : *Viriliter, virili modo : muliebriter, muliebri modo.* . . . .

" But what are these old learned fathers, that say Christ's body is **really** and **fleshly** in the Sacrament? Where be their words? What be their names? If they have neither names nor words, how can they be allowed for sufficient witnesses. M. Harding well knoweth that the old learned fathers never said so: yet must he needs imagine both causes that moved them so to say, and also expositions, what they meant by so saying. . . . . "—*Ibid* pp. 456-7.

But what is there in this language of Bishop Jewel which, as Mr. Goode says, makes his views " different" from "the views of Bishop Geste ? " Guest, stating his disagreement with Cheney, says that " yᵉ DOCTORS doo write " the expressions " corporally naturally reallye, substantially and carnally:" he does not say, as Harding asserted and Jewel denied, that " the godly and learned FATHERS of the Church " wrote thus: he neither quotes Harding's reference to these Fathers, nor gives the remotest hint that he considered such reference accurate ; in fact, he does not use, or even allude to, this portion of Harding's argument at all : what he does is merely to use, as against Cheney, an *explation* to which Harding himself was compelled to have recourse when claiming a Patristic authority for the terms in question. Guest argues that " though .... Christ's Bodye " were " receaved .... corporally naturally reallye substantially and carnally *as ye doctors do write*, yet he did not for all that see it, feale it, smell it, nor taste it " in any PHYSICAL manner : and he fortifies his position not only by claiming for it the sanction of " all sortes of men," but especially by citing an important admission of the leading Roman controversialist of that day, who, as Jewel says of his doctrine, "thought good to heal it up with some plaister," by saying that Christ's "verye humane nature is there [in the Sacrament] not after corporall carnall or naturall wise, but invisibly unspeakably supernaturally spiritually divinely and by way unto Him onlye knowen." Guest, quoting as he did from "Jewel's controversy with M. Harding, of real Presence," could not be ignorant of this reply of the Bishop of Salisbury to which Mr. Goode refers us: nor can it be reasonably supposed that he would carelessly, much less wilfully, misrepresent Jewel as coinciding with him on a point upon which both their opinions were sufficiently well known, and therefore easily capable of comparison by the important personage to whom he wrote. Moreover, Guest was surely in a somewhat better position than we can be to understand the published language of his living contemporary; and therefore he may well enough have been persuaded of what seems to me to be true—that when Jewel says "thus M. Harding's doctors wrote one thing, and meant another," his objection was not to the words " corporally, carnally," etc., but to that popular perversion of them which was still very current, and which was fostered in the use made of them by such a writer as Harding. I will only further express my conviction—that it requires no very careful comparison of Jewel's Eucharistic statements with Guest's Treatise on the "Prevee Masse," already quoted, to shew the coincidence of their judgment, and to prove the improbability of that difference of opinion on the Real Presence which Mr. Goode ascribes to them.

Harding, however, proceeds to specify authorities; and

having quoted from St. Chrysostom, St. Hilary, Gregory Nyssen, and St. Cyril, he sums up thus:—

" Now this being and remaining of Christ in us, and of us in Christ **naturally** and **carnally,** and this uniting of us and Christ together **corporally,** presupposeth a participation of his **very** body, which body we cannot truly participate but in this blessed sacrament. And therefore Christ is in the Sacrament **naturally, carnally, corporally,** that is to say, according to the truth of his nature, of his flesh, and of his body. For were he not so in the Sacrament, we could not be joined unto him, nor he and we could not be joined and united together **corporally,**

" Divers other ancient fathers have used the like manner of speech ; but none so much as Hilarius and Cyrillus ; whereby they understand that Christ is present in the sacrament, as we have said, according to the truth of his substance, of his nature, of his flesh, of his body and blood."—*Ibid.* p. 472.

To which Jewel rejoins:—

" Now at the last M. Harding draweth near the matter, and bringeth forth the old fathers with these very terms, **'really,' 'substantially,' 'corporally,' 'carnally,'** &c., and allegeth these few, as he saith, instead of many, having indeed no more to bring. And although these fathers speak not any one word that is either denied by us, or anywise serveth to this purpose, yet he cunningly leadeth away the eyes of the ignorant with the shew of old names, and, like a juggler, changeth the natural countenance of things, and maketh them appear what he listeth.

" For whereas he hath taken in hand to prove that Christ's body is **really** and **fleshly** in the Sacrament, he finding his weakness and want therein, altereth the whole case, and proveth that Christ's body is **really, fleshly,** and **naturally** within us. But this matter was not in question, and therefore needeth no proof at all."—*Ibid.* p. 472.

The Bishop, after examining Harding's authorities, goes on to discuss what is meant by this **corporal** union of Christ and us: one of his remarks is:—

" Further, that we be thus in Christ, and Christ in us, requireth not any **corporal** or **local** being, as in things natural. We are in Christ sitting in heaven, and Christ sitting in heaven is here in us, not by a **natural,** but by a spiritual means of being .... Yet notwithstanding, the same conjunction, because it is spiritual, true, full and perfect, therefore is expressed of these holy fathers by the term **corporal,** which removeth all manner, light and accidental joining ; and **natural,** whereby all manner, imagination, or fantasy, and conjunction only of will and consent, is excluded: not that Christ's body is **corporally** or **naturally** in our body, as is before said, no more than our bodies are **corporally** or **naturally** in Christ's body ; but that we have life in us, and are become immortal, because by faith and spirit we are partakers of the natural body of Christ.

"M. Harding saith : We are thus joined unto Christ, and have him **corporally** within us, only by receiving the Sacrament, and by none other means. This is utterly untrue, as it is already proved by the authorities of St. Augustine, St. Basil, Gregory Nazianzene, Leo, Ignatius, Bernard, and other holy fathers ; neither does either Cyrillus or Hilary so avouch it. Certainly, neither have they all Christ dwelling in them that receive the Sacrament, nor are they all void of Christ that never received the Sacrament. Besides, the untruth hereof, this doctrine were many ways very uncomfortable. For what may the godly father think of his child, that, being baptized, departeth this life without receiving the Sacrament of Christ's body ? By M. Harding's construction, he must needs think his child is damned, for that it had no natural participation of Christ's flesh, without which there is no salvation ; which participation, as M. Harding assureth us, is had by none other means, but only by receiving of the Sacrament. Yet St. Chrysostom saith : 'In the Sacrament of Baptism we are made flesh of Christ's flesh, and bone of his bones.'

"For better trial hereof, understand thou, gentle reader, that both Cyrillus and Hilarius in those places dispute against the Arians whose error was this, that God the Father and the Son are one, not, by nature, but only by will and consent. Against them Hilarius reasoned thus :—

"Christ is as really joined unto the Father as unto us :
"But Christ is joined unto us by nature :
"Therefore Christ is joined to God the Father by nature."

After some explanation of this syllogism, Jewel concludes thus :—

"Christ's body is not **naturally** or **corporally** present within us ;
"Therefore much less is it **corporally** present in the Sacrament."
—*Ibid.*, pp. 477-8.

The disputants then go on to discuss another point, viz. :—

"That Christ's body is or may be in a thousand places or more at one time."

Harding alleged that—

"...... the ancient fathers of the Church have confessed and taught both these beings, of Christ in heaven and in the Sacrament together ......"—*Ibid.*, p. 485.

Jewel, in his reply, says :—

" But first, for the clearer conceiving of the answer hereunto, understand, good Christian reader, that by the record of the old fathers
Christ is present among us sundry ways: by his Holy Spirit, as
Cyrillus saith ; by his grace, as Eusebius Emissenus saith ; by his
divinity and majesty, as St. Augustine saith ; by faith dwelling in
our hearts, as St. Paul says. Thus is Christ most comfortably
present in his holy word, in the mystery of Baptism, and in the Sacrament of his body. We deny only that gross and fleshly presence that M. Harding here defendeth ; wherein we have the authority and consent of the old learned fathers. For, to allege one instead
of many, St. Augustine saith : . . . . ' The body wherein Christ rose
again must be in one place.' "—*Ibid.*, p. 486.

Farther on in the argument, Harding quotes the passage
from Bucer (already given at p. 73, as cited by Gardiner
to Cranmer), comparing Christ's Presence in the Sacrament to the Presence of the sun in the earth: Jewel thus
comments upon it:—

" . . . . the very similitude or example that he useth of the sun
putteth the matter out of all question. For like as the body or
compass of the sun, being in one certain place of the heavens,
reacheth out his beams, and giveth influence into the world ; even
so Christ, the sun of justice, being in heaven in one place at the right
hand of God, likewise reacheth out his beams, and giveth his influence into the faithful, and so feedeth them, not by bare imagination or fantasy, but truly, substantially, and indeed. And as
the sun is more comfortable, and more refresheth the world, being
absent, by his beams, than if his very natural substance and compass
lay here upon the earth ; even so the body of Christ, being in the
glory of his father, in the very substance and nature of our flesh, and
there evermore entreating mercy for our sins, is much more comfortable
unto us, and more quickeneth both our bodies and souls by his heavenly and spiritual influence, than if it were here present fleshly before
our eyes. And as the sun, not coming down from heaven, nor
leaving his place, is nevertheless present with us in our houses, in
our faces, in our hands, and in our bosoms ; even so Christ, being
in heaven, not coming down, nor leaving his room there, yet nevertheless is present with us in our congregations, in our hearts, in our
prayers, in the mystery of baptism, and in the Sacrament of his body
and blood."—*Ibid.*, p. 499.

Moreover, Harding, rejecting a *physical* presence, says :—

" And that all absurdities and carnal grossness be severed from
our thoughts, where true Christian people believe Christ's body to
be in many places at once, they understand it so to be in a mystery
. . . ."—*Ibid.*, p. 504.

Jewel, in his answer, makes this remark :—

" Again he [St. Augustine] saith : .... 'Christ by his Godhead is ever with us; but unless he had departed away bodily from us, we should evermore **carnally** see his body.' These words are specially to be noted. If Christ were **bodily** here, he should **carnally** be seen : therefore, by St. Augustine's judgment, if Christ were **bodily** present in the Sacrament, we should see him **carnally** in the Sacrament."—*Ibid*, p. 505.

Another proposition which Jewel challenged the Roman party to prove was :—

" That the people did then fall down and worship the Sacrament with godly honour."

Harding, in taking up the challenge, cited St. Chrysostom ; Jewel, in examining the passage, says :—

" In this wise therefore, having removed the people's hearts into heaven, and placed them even in the sight of Christ, he saith further unto them : For this body's sake thou art no longer dust and ashes ; this body hath made thee free ; this body was broken for thee upon the cross ; this body must we adore, as the wise men did ; this body not now upon the earth, but at the right hand of God in heaven ; this body that thou seest with thy spirit, and touchest with thy faith, whereof the Sacrament that thou receivest is a mystery. So saith Emissenus : . . . . 'With thy faith behold the holy body of thy God, touch it with thy mind, receive it with the hand of thy heart.'

" But M. Harding will reply, Chrysostom saith : ' As Christ was in the stall, so he is now upon the altar; and as he was sometimes in the woman's arms, so he is now in the priest's hands.' True it is Christ was there, and Christ is here ; but not in one or like sort of being. For he was in the stall by **bodily** presence ; upon the holy table he is by way of a Sacrament. The woman in her arms held him **really**; the priest in his hands holdeth him only in a mystery. So saith St. Paul: ' Christ dwelleth in our hearts;' and no doubt the same Christ that lay in the stall. It is one and the same Christ ; but the difference standeth in the manner of his being there : for in the stall he lay by presence of his **body**; in our hearts he lieth by presence of faith."—*Ibid.*, p. 539.

Once more ; Harding quoted the comment of SS. Ambrose and Augustin upon Psalm xix. 5 : Jewel ends his answer in these words :—

" But they will reply, St. Ambrose saith : ' We do adore Christ's flesh in the mysteries.' Hereof groweth their whole error. For St. Ambrose saith not, We do adore the mysteries, or the flesh of Christ **really** present, or **materially** contained in the mysteries ; as it is supposed by Mr. Harding. Only he saith, ' We adore Christ's flesh in the mysteries,' that is to say, in the ministration of the mysteries. And doubtless it is our duty to adore the body of Christ in the Word of God, in the Sacrament of baptism, in the mysteries of Christ's body and blood, and wheresoever we see any step or token of it, but especially in the holy mysteries ; for that there is lively laid forth before us the whole story of Christ's conversation in the flesh. But this adoration, as it is said before, neither is directed to the Sacraments, nor requireth any **corporal** or **real** presence. . . . ."—*Ibid.*, p. 542.

Another point in the controversy was this :—

" that in the Sacrament, after the words of consecration, there remain only the accidents, and shews without the substance of bread and wine."

In answering one of Harding's arguments, Jewel says :—

" The question between us is not, whether the bread be the body of Christ, or no ; but whether in plain and simple manner of speech it be **fleshly** and **really** the body of Christ." — *Ibid.*, Vol. II., p. 570.

So, too, when discussing the 12th Article :—

" that whosoever had said the Sacrament is a figure, a pledge, a token, or a remembrance of Christ's body, had therefore been judged for an heretic."

The Bishop, in reference to a quotation which Harding made from S. Hilary, remarks:—

" Further, we may say that Christ's body is in the Sacrament itself, understanding it to be there as in a mystery. But to this manner of being there is required neither circumstance of place, nor any **corporal** or **real** presence."—*Ibid.*, p. 604.

Again, comparing a passage from St. Gregory with one which Harding had cited from St. Augustin, Jewel observes:—

" Now, as Christ dieth in the Sacrament, so is his body present in the Sacrament. But Christ dieth not there **really** and **indeed** ; therefore Christ's body is not there **really** and **indeed**."—*Ibid.*, p. 618.

" And thus St. Augustine's meaning may well stand upright without any new secrecy or **real** or **fleshly** presence."—*Ibid.*, p. 619.

Further, in arguing the 17th Article :—

" that the priest had then authority to offer up Christ unto his Father."

Jewel remarks thus upon a sentence of St. Chrysostom :—

" Thus the death of Christ is renewed before our eyes. Yet Christ **indeed** neither is crucified, nor dieth, nor sheddeth his blood, nor is **substantially** present, nor **really** offered by the priest."— *Ibid* , p. 710.

Later, in the same argument, he observes thus :—

" Therefore St. Gregory saith : . . . . ' Christ, living immortally in himself, dieth again in this mystery. His flesh suffereth (in the mystery) for the salvation of the people.' I reckon, M. Harding will not say that Christ dieth **indeed**, according to the force and sound of these words, or that his flesh **verily** and **indeed** is tormented and suffereth in the Sacrament."—*Ibid.*, p. 726.

And, once more, he says :—

" In like manner the ministration of the holy communion is sometimes of the ancient fathers called an ' unbloody sacrifice ;' not in respect of any **corporal** or **fleshly** presence that is imagined to be there without blood-shedding, but for that it representeth and reporteth unto our minds that one and everlasting sacrifice that Christ made in his body upon the cross."— *Ibid.*, p. 734.

Moreover, in their dispute touching the 21st Article :—

" that then any Christian man called the Sacrament his Lord and God."

The Bishop of Salisbury replies to his opponent thus :—

" In the end, M. Harding confirmeth this doctrine by the confutation of an error, which, for the novelty and strangeness of it, may easily seem to be his own ; and therefore ought of right to be called ' M. Harding's error :' for I believe it was never neither defended nor imagined by any other.

" He surmiseth there be some that either have said, or else may say, that Christ's flesh is present **really** in the Sacrament ; howbeit dead and bloodless, and utterly void both of soul and Godhead. This is a new error, never tamed or touched before this time.*

---

* I should be most sorry to misrepresent, in the least degree, Mr. Freeman, and therefore I do not venture to say that he *has* made the kind of statement which Jewel here condemns ; but, in common with others, one hopes to see some explanation in his expected volume of certain passages contained in Sect. xii. (pp. 143—145) of his published " Introduction to Part ii." (J. H. & J. Parker, 1857). I subjoin the following as indicating what I refer to :—

" . . . . The Presence of Christ is assumed, without entering into any argument, to be a necessary result of the Presence of His Body and Blood."—p. 149.

" . . . . His [Christ's] Death being as real as any man's, His broken Body and His Blood poured out in Death were no more the Man Christ Jesus, than the body and blood of any other man are that man. True it is that from neither His Body nor His soul was the Divinity ever separated, but was so present with Both that neither could the One be left in Hell, nor the Other see Corruption . . . . . ."—p. 149.

"As for us we do constantly believe and confess that Christ, the very natural Son of God, received our flesh of the blessed virgin, and that, wheresoever that flesh is, there is also both the Godhead and the soul.

"Of this undoubted truth M. Harding gathereth an impertinent conclusion. For thus he reasoneth : 'If Christ be verily under the form of bread in the Sacrament, then is he there entire and whole, God and man.' Indeed, the first being granted, the rest must needs follow. But how is M. Harding so well assured of the first? What old doctor or ancient father ever taught him that Christ's body is **really** and **fleshly** present under these forms or fantasies of bread and wine ?"—*Ibid.,* p. 770.

Other passages, of a like character with these now quoted,

With much deference I cannot but ask Mr. F.—did not this Presence of the Divinity make exactly *that* distinction of union between *Christ's* Body and Soul after death, and man's body and soul after death, which points towards one answer to his following question ?—

"And next, if the broken and poured-out Body and Blood of Christ, in Their natural condition and manner of existence, were not Christ, —as certainly they were not,—have we any reason for saying or conceiving that in Their supranatural and sacramental manner of existence they are Christ ?...."—p. 150.

To my mind Ridley seemed to think so when he said (see p. 60), "....that Heavenly Lamb, is (as I confess) on the table ; but by a spiritual presence," &c. And again—"I grant the Priest holdeth the same Thing [which the woman did hold in her womb], but after another manner."

Pursuing the idea, Mr. F. further says:—

".... .The unreceived Elements are the Body and Blood of Christ, and no more : but 'he that eateth and drinketh' of them aright hath in him CHRIST Himself, and no less, and is united to Him."—p. 154.

But, again, to quote Ridley (see p. 56), "....I grant....*Christ* is offered in many places at once, in a mystery and sacramentally, and that He is *full Christ* in all those places," etc.

Once more Mr. F. writes :—

".. The natural Body of Christ, once slain,....was, nevertheless, after being received into the receptacle of God's appointing, the heart of the Earth, reunited to That Soul by the operation of the interposed Divinity; and so CHRIST HIMSELF once more truly alive, and rose again. And even so, when His Body and Blood, existing in a new and specially provided manner, have been received into the duly qualified bodies and souls of men, does the same vital reunion, as it should seem, take place, and so CHRIST HIMSELF, in Body, Soul, and Divinity, is in them of truth, and raises them, together with Himself, to a glorious immortality."—p. 154.

But Jewel says (see above), "....we do constantly believe and confess.... that, wheresoever that flesh is, there is *also* both the Godhead and the soul :" Mr. F. admits the " Body and Blood " = Flesh, to be " existing in a new and specially provided manner," i.e., I suppose, in the Sacrament; and Jewel only denies the *fleshly* presence of " Christ's Body ....under these forms or fantasies of bread and wine." therefore it seems necessarily to follow that the Sacramental *Body and Blood* of Christ *is* CHRIST, and that, as the Declaration seems also to teach, " *Christ* " is " therein *given* to all worthy Receivers," not *formed* in them, as Mr. F.'s language appears to teach.

K K

will be found in pp. 167, 464, 467, 475,* 483, 490-3, 500-4, 520, 548, 551, 601, 620, 708, 711-18, 733, 760, 765, 781, 785, 797, 798. In common, however, with the extracts here given, it will be found that they alike mainly aim at destroying the notion of a *physical, carnal* Presence ; as if that were *the* point continually prominent in Jewel's mind and the one which he felt he must ever present to his adversary; though it must.be owned that he did not always avoid, at least seeming, inconsistencies which blunted its sharpness, or, at least apparent, exaggerations which weakened its force ; and though, like other anti-Roman writers of that period, he not only at times deals with his opponent as though he thought it impossible for him to employ a fair or sound argument ; but also often himself uses language which seems barely, if at all, capable of, what the advocates of the Real Presence, would consider a Catholic meaning. But, I repeat, it is essential to a fair judgment of his words (as also in the case of Cranmer and other writers of the same period already quoted) to bear constantly in mind—that he was ever aiming at the destruction of that belief in a *natural* Presence, which had become so popular, and which was extremely likely to be sustained by any concession, however small, to the current phraseology of its advocates. It is, therefore, both fair and necessary, whenever possible, so to interpret what may be called his *lower* and *laxer* Doctrinal statements as to make them harmonize with his *stricter* and *higher* ones; while it would be an error, and unfair to Jewel himself, to interpret his statements by the opposite method, unless we determined wholly to ignore his repeated professions of submission to the teaching of the Catholic Church during the first six centuries. Perhaps Mr. Goode, like other writers on his side of the controversy, is not wholly free from this erroneous mode of dealing with Jewel and his sixteenth century contemporaries.

---

* "That we verily and undoubtedly receive Christ's body in the Sacrament, it is neither denied, nor in question."—This is the sentence quoted by Bishop Guest [I.] 8. (See p. 199).

In noticing Mr. Goode's "Supplement" my purpose was not to make any general answer to it, but only to consider his observations upon Bishop Guest's Letters: it seems to me, however, not out of place here to advert to some other passages which bear upon the subject of this Letter; this relevancy must be my excuse for noticing Mr. Goode's criticisms upon the statements and arguments of those for whom it would, else, be a presumption in me to attempt any reply: though, indeed, Mr. Goode himself invites it; for in no less than *seven* places within the short compass of *twenty-four* pages (23 to 47) does he "leave" points, which (as in fact his own notice of them proves) are far from unimportant, to "the reader to choose" between, or "to be disposed of" by him, or "to pass judgment" upon, or "to make his own comments" on, and the like.

First of all I must notice a strange oversight on the part of Mr. Goode; he complains (p. 18) of Dr. Pusey having written thus :—

"Mr. Goode frequently excepts against the belief in the oral reception of the Holy Eucharist. Isidore, embodying in his own statement the words of St. Augustine, states it as explicitly as words could express it : 'that in honour of so great a Sacrament the Lord's Body should enter the mouth of a Christian before any other food.' ([Real Presence] p. xxv.)"

Mr. Goode says that :—

" in this passage there is a double attempt to mislead the reader ; [1] for according to the sense in which the terms 'Holy Eucharist' and 'the Lord's body' are used by Dr. Pusey's opponents, I have, of course, never excepted against the belief in the oral reception of the former ; [2] and Isidore states nothing of the kind imputed to him by Dr. Pusey."

But surely Mr. Goode need not fear that any reader of ordinary discernment could be *misled* by Dr. Pusey's words : the passage itself plainly shews that he there used the term "the Lord's Body" as *equivalent* to "the Holy Eucharist ;" and that it was in "the sense" of Its *being* "the Lord's Body" that he spoke of Mr. Goode's exception to "the belief in the oral reception" of It : the whole context of the passage makes this still clearer.

To prove the second [2] part of the "attempt to mislead" Mr. Goode says (p. 19) :—

" As to the extract from Isidore, if *the context* had been given, there could not have been quoted, as I have already shown,* a passage more clearly showing the error of Dr. Pusey in affixing the meaning he does to the words he has cited ; for Isidore immediately afterwards says :—'*Bread*, inasmuch as it strengthens the body, is therefore *called the Body of Christ* ; but *wine*, inasmuch as it produces blood in the flesh, is therefore referred (or, likened) to the blood of Christ."

The Italics are Mr. Goode's.

Now will it be believed that Dr. Pusey had actually given this very " context" and that it is only separated by *two lines* from the passage ("Mr. Goode frequently," etc.) of which Mr. Goode complains? The two lines are these, they follow the words " the blood of Christ," and Mr. Goode would have done well to quote them in order to assist *his* readers in understanding *his* " context" from S. Isidore :—

" These, then, as being visible, yet sanctified by the Holy Ghost, pass into the Sacrament of the Divine Body."—(*Real Presence*, p. xxv.)

It is, however, very unfortunate that while Mr. Goode calls the passage he has cited from Dr. Pusey " an apt specimen of the unfairness of the mode of argumentation usually adopted by Dr. Pusey and his party" and blames Dr. Pusey for *not quoting* a context *which he had quoted*—(or perhaps, to be accurate enough for Mr. Goode, I ought to say—for not *re*-quoting a context which could only have benefitted the Printer)—it is, I say, unfortunate that Mr. Goode himself should have been guilty of a more serious omission than the one he deprecates : he tells us that " Isidore immediately afterwards" he had used the words " the Lord's Body should enter the mouth of a Christian before any other food," says, " ' Bread inasmuch,' " etc.

Now, really, when Mr. Goode alleges that it is " the unfairness of.... Dr. Pusey and his party, which renders it impossible for any one, perusing their works alone, to have an

---

* " See my Work on the Eucharist, p. 242, where other testimonies will be found of the sense in which such terms were used by the Fathers."

idea of the nature of the points in dispute " (p. 19), he ought
not to have made it incumbent upon his own readers to refer
to Dr. Pusey's own extract from S. Isidore in order to ascertain whether he (Mr. Goode) has used the word "immediately" in an *exact*, or in a *loose* "sense." Yet what does
the reference reveal? Why that S. Isidore *interposes* the
following most important words between the two passages
which I put in brackets to shew the connexion of the whole
paragraph—passages which Mr. Goode says follow "immediately" upon each other :—

" [For this took place then, as a mystery. I mean, that the disciples at first did not receive the Body and Blood of the Lord fasting.
But now by the whole Church it is received fasting. For so it
pleased the Holy Ghost through the Apostles, 'that in honour of so
great a Sacrament, the Lord's Body should enter the mouth of a
Christian before any other food,] and therefore is that custom kept
throughout the whole world." For the Bread which we break, is
the Body of Christ, Who said, ' I am the Living Bread which came
down from Heaven.' But the wine is His Blood, and this it is, which
is written, ' I am the true vine ;' but [bread, because it strengthens
the body, is therefore called the Body of Christ: but the wine, because it produces blood in the flesh, is therefore referred to the
Blood of Christ]."—(*Real Presence*, p. xxv.)

I would, then, beg Mr. Goode carefully to consider whether
the passage beginning, "and therefore," etc., and ending
"'true vine;' but" (which, indeed, he has also omitted in his
"Work on the Eucharist, p. 242," to which he refers us—
See p. 252) does not tell much more against him than the,
alleged, omitted "*context*" makes for him, even though one
could allow that he has so printed that context as to furnish
the true index to its meaning ?

But has he thus truly indicated the purpose of S. Isidore?
I speak only with the diffidence which becomes me when I
say that Mr. Goode appears to me to have entirely missed the
intention of that writer in the latter part of the paragraph.

For, first of all, his way of quoting it is calculated to mislead ; he prints it (See p. 252) as though the word "*Bread*"
began the sentence, instead of occurring, as it does, nearly in
the middle of it: next, his *italicizing* of the sentence is quite
partial, for he omits thus to treat the words "referred to the

Blood of Christ :" thirdly, he appears not to perceive, what seems to me observable, that S. Isidore is only explaining why "bread," and not "wine," is "called the Body of Christ;" why " wine," and not " bread," is "referred to the Blood of Christ ;" it matters nothing whether his theory of the relative nutritious properties of bread and wine would be sanctioned or not by modern Chemists and Physiologists ; his purpose was simply to furnish, what seemed to him to be, the reason for the Sacramental *bread* being termed " the Body " " of Christ " which God graciously gives for " the *strengthening ;*" and the *wine* being termed " the Blood " " of Christ " which is mercifully afforded for "the *refreshing* of our souls."

There is yet a fourth way in which Mr. Goode seems to me to have misrepresented (however unintentionally) S. Isidore's meaning: whether he has merely quoted Dr. Pusey's translation or not I cannot say ; however, they coincide verbatim, except Mr. Goode's Italics : but then Mr. Goode has thought it right to insert the words " (or, likened)," See p. 252, by way of explaining S. Isidore's expression " referred :" * but surely to make " *likened* " the equivalent of " *referred,*" though it may seem to serve Mr. Goode's argument by making " referred " the synonym of " called," wholly perverts S. Isidore's purpose, which, as I think, was only to shew that the " bread" and the "wine" were each " REFERRED " respectively and only to the "Body" and "Blood" of Christ, on the grounds which S. Isidore mentions : I cannot doubt that we were meant to explain (if indeed explanation be needed) "called" by "referred," and are not to interpret "referred" by " likened ;" and this, as it appears to me, removes all pretence for saying that S. Isidore (among the other Fathers whom Mr. Goode names) in giving " us reasons why the bread in the Eucharist is called Christ's Body, and the wine His Blood," shews that he " did not consider them so really, but only representatively." (*The Nature of Christ's Presence in the Eucharist,* p. 241.) On the contrary, it seems well nigh impossible for him to have spoken of them in stronger terms,

* " Refertur ": Mr. Goode gives the original of this " context" in his " work on the Eucharist, p. 242."

as being " so really," than in saying "..the Bread which we break IS the Body of Christ,......But the wine IS His Blood ..."*

To pass on now to another of Mr. Goode's remarks: he says (p. 19) :—

" .... in order to get rid of objections, a terminology is adopted which may enable Dr. Pusey to hold his doctrine, and at the same time deliver him from the necessity of meeting the difficulties attaching to it. Thus he says, ' In the Holy Eucharist, the Body and Blood of Christ do not (as Mr. Goode often represents us as teaching) form one whole [i.e. with the bread and wine] *except sacramentally*. There is no physical union of the Body and Blood of Christ with the bread and wine.' (p. xvii.) But what is the meaning of the words *except sacramentally?* Dr. Pusey holds that the two are so united that they necessarily go together into the mouth of the communicant. Whether Dr. Pusey chooses to call this union sacramental, ...or anything else, is a matter of indifference. The fact of such a union is the question in dispute. And to give it an ambiguous or incomprehensible epithet, in order to make it unassailable, is useless, except to mislead the reader."

But Mr. Goode ought rather to complain of the Reformation writers, who, as he must know, used these very terms : I will just refer to those already quoted in these pages.

FOXE says—that the *third* " conclusion" of P. Martyr's discussion at Oxford was, " The Body and Blood of Christ be united to bread and wine sacramentally."—p. 10.

DR. MADEW replied to *Dr. Glyn*,—" Forsooth He has but one very Body...; but the same is sacramentally in the Sacrament . . ."—p. 14.

CRANMER, explaining his uses of the word " Sacrament," says, I use to speak sometimes (as the old authors do) . . . of His sacramental presence."—p. 20.

---

* Since the above was in type I have met with the following corroborative passage in *Harding* v. *Jewel*:—" Likewise in the Sacrament of the holy communion, as the bread outwardly feedeth our bodies, so doth Christ's body inwardly and spiritually feed our souls. Thus is feeding an effect common unto them both. And therein standeth the resemblance and likeness of the Sacrament. Therefore Rabanus Maurus (lib. i. cap. xxxi.) saith : Quia panis corporis cor confirmat, ideo ille congruenter corpus Christi nominatur ; et, quia vinum sanguinem operatur in carne. ideo illud refertur ad sanguinem : ' Because the bread confirmeth the heart of our body, therefore is the same conveniently called the body of Christ ; and, because wine worketh blood in our flesh : therefore the wine hath relation unto the blood of Christ." '—p. 793.

Again, answering *Gardiner*, his words are—" We say, that the Body of Christ . . . . is in the Sacrament **sacramentally**, and in the worthy receivers spiritually, without the proper form and quantity of His Body."—p. 23.

" . . . . the bread is called Christ's Body after consecration, as S. Ambrose saith, and yet it is not so really but **sacramentally**."—p. 88.

"And I express St. Cyprian's mind truly, ... when I say, that the Divinity may be said to be poured, or put **sacramentally** into the bread ; . . . ."—p. 88.

RIDLEY, replying to *Weston*, says—" . . . . Christ is offered in many places at once **sacramentally** . . . ."—p. 56.

To *Smith* he answers—" . . . . by the **sacramental** signification He is holden of all men."—p. 57.

To *Ward* he replies—" . . . . He bade them take His Body **sacramentally** in material bread . . . ."—*Ibid.*

" I grant the bread to be converted . . . . by **sacramental** converting . . . ."—*Ibid.*

To *Glyn* he says—" . . . . the Body of Christ is present in the sacrament ; but yet **sacramentally** . . . ."—p. 58.

To *Tresham* his words were—" Evil men do eat the very true and natural Body of Christ **sacramentally**, and no further, as St. Augustine saith. But good men do eat the very true Body, both **sacramentally**, and spiritually by grace."—p. 59.

Moreover both forms of the very Declaration on Kneeling, which I am considering in these pages, twice speak of the "**sacramental** bread and wine" not, as I think, without a designed reference to that change, and union with the Body and Blood of Christ, which Consecration effects; for, else, the word **sacramental** might well have been omitted without affecting the sense (seeing that no one ever advocated Adoration of the unconsecrated elements) and this, too, seems to be indicated in the expression "there bodily," i.e. *materially* "received," their "*substances*" still remaining: thus differing from the *res sacramenti* Which is incapable of being *materially* received.—(See p. 31 line 4.)

These authorities for the use of the words "*sacramental*"

and "*sacramentally*" ought to content Mr. Goode, and to convince him that " the fact of such a union" was admitted by the English Reformers however much it may be " the question in dispute" now.

And when he demands from Dr. Pusey " the meaning" of these words, he seems to overlook that Dr. Pusey has so far explained them (p. xvii.) as to point out that " the *character* of the union . . . . is different" from that of the " two perfect Natures" in the " One Person" of "our Blessed Lord," and from " the two parts of one and the same nature . . . . in the one person of each of us ;" though " the *principle*" of the union " is the same." Thus, in saying what it is not, he states what it is, viz. a union *peculiar* to the Sacrament, and therefore properly called Sacramental : *Cranmer* (See p. 256) in Scholastic language, defines it to mean " without the proper form or quantity of His body :" to insist upon more than these explanations seems to me to be persisting in a demand which can only be satisfied by denuding the Sacrament of that Mystery which its very name imports.

Mr. Goode proceeds to say (p. 20) that :—

" . . . . on the same ground, Dr. Pusey's work on the testimony of the Fathers, ... is noticed by the present Bishop of St. David's only as being one of those compilations which are bringing the name of a *Catena* into suspicion and disrepute, as equivalent to *an organ of polemical delusion*.' (Charge for 1857, p. 26.)"

Now it *may* be that the Bishop intended to include " Dr. Pusey's work on the testimony of the Fathers" in this condemnatory notice of the " compilations ; " but certainly his Lordship does not *say* it is "one of" them, as I think will appear upon reading the *whole* passage which runs thus :—

" I believe however that the so-called catholic teaching, understood as I have said, [*i. e.*, (see Charge p. 25) in the sense attached to it by its opponents] is no less repugnant both to Scripture and to the whole stream of genuine primitive tradition, though, by means of compilations which are bringing the name of a *catena* into suspicion and disrepute, as equivalent to an engine of polemical delusion, it may be made to appear to have a great mass of patristic evidence in its favour."

It can hardly fail, I think, to strike anyone who reads this passage—that Mr. Goode's quotation of it could never have suggested that the Bishop points to a, not unimportant, distinction—viz., "Catholic teaching" as "understood" respectively "by its opponents" and by its advocates. But I will not dwell on this, as I cited the passage for a different purpose, viz., to ascertain whether Mr. Goode rightly quotes it as a designed condemnation of Dr. Pusey's "Notes" to his Sermon on 'the Presence of Christ in the Holy Eucharist." Now the only ground for so regarding it, is a *Note*, appended by the Bishop to the word "favour," which however Mr. Goode does not give; it is as follows:

"A very large part of the passages collected by Dr. Pusey, in his Notes on his Sermon, 'The Presence of Christ in the Holy Eucharist' would be deprived of all, even seeming, relevancy and argumentative value, by the simple insertion of the word *sacramental* or *sacramentally*."

The position thus revealed is at least a curious one: Mr. Goode, in no very gentle terms, reproaches Dr. Pusey for the *use* of "an ambiguous or incomprehensible epithet," which he says must "mislead the reader," and which makes his work "in an argumentative point of view, ... wholly useless:" the Bishop would have this very same "epithet" *employed* in order to measure the true value of passages in a book which Mr. Goode could only safely allege the Bishop to have condemned (so far as the Charge is concerned) by referring to this Note which seems to me inconveniently opposed to Mr. Goode's own protest against "sacramental" and "sacramentally."

But it must not be overlooked here—that Dr. Pusey has by anticipation done more than even the Bishop proposes: for he has given a long Note, extending from p. 264 to p. 314, the running title of which is "*Illustrations used by the Fathers imply sacramental change only:*" while at p. 307 he writes thus explicitly of "the Fathers:"—

" . . . . . all their instances harmonize in this one point—a power above nature put forth in things of nature; and there is a real, sacramental change, whereby what was before a mere element of this world becomes sacramentally the Body and Blood of Christ."

In passing now from Mr. Goode's notice of the Bishop of

St. David's Charge I cannot forbear remarking—that, whatever his Lordship thinks of the views of the advocates of "Catholic teaching," his tolerant and charitable spirit contrasts strongly with the tone of Mr. Goode towards his opponents on this subject : his Lordship referring to the prosecution of Archdeacon Denison, says (p. 25) :—

"After the closest attention which I could give to the subject, I ... have been led to the conclusion that the dispute, though undoubtedly indicating a wide discrepancy of views and feelings, is in itself mainly a verbal one, which would either. never have arisen, or have been easily settled, if there had been an earnest desire for mutual understanding, instead of a disposition to widen the breach."

And again (p. 26) :—

"Every man has a right, especially when he is on his trial, to explain his own opinions, and to require that they be judged according to his own interpretation of them, and not by the construction which may be put upon them by his adversaries. It may be that his explanation is perplexed and obscure ; it may involve manifest absurdity and contradiction : it may resolve itself into mere nonsense. But these are things for which, as I conceive, the author is fairly amenable to the bar of literary criticism, not to a tribunal which inflicts penalties affecting civil rights. To sustain a charge of unsound doctrine, involving such penal consequences, nothing as it appears to me, ought to suffice, but the most direct unequivocal statements, asserting that which the Church denies, or denying that which she asserts."*

---

* I cannot but subjoin here an extract from Mr. Fisher (whom I have before quoted) as shewing also the thoughts of a candid mind upon this subject : remarking upon the "guarded circumspection in the use of terms" as employed by Dr. Pusey and, more particularly, by the late Archdeacon Wilberforce, he says :—
"Of the important bearing of this fact upon the case of the Archdeacon, had his case been actually brought before the Ecclesiastical Courts, those who are still familiar with the details of that of Mr. Gorham will not need to be reminded. It will be remembered, that one of the most effective arguments, employed by Mr. Gorham's Counsel, was an argument that addressed itself in an especial manner to those feelings of deference and respect, which mankind are ever disposed to entertain for the authority of time-honoured names. It was alleged, that opinions, which could not ' in any important particular be distinguished from those of Mr. Gorham,' had been propounded and maintained, without censure or reproach, by many eminent and illustrious prelates and divines who have adorned the Church, from the time when the Articles were first established. Now the question at once arises—might not this self-same argument have been used, and with equal effect, had the occasion required it, in behalf of Archdeacon Wilberforce ? We believe most assuredly that it might have been thus used ; and, if so, what must *in all fairness* have been the issue of the proceedings brought against him ? We are told of Jewel, Usher, Jeremy Taylor, Whitgift, Pearson, Carlton, and

The next point to which Mr. Goode calls attention
(pp. 21 to 24) is Dr. Pusey's " discussion of the meaning of
the *Advertisement* at the end of the first Book of Homilies,
to which " he, Mr. Goode, had "already directed the attention of the reader " in his " Work on the Eucharist, pp. 40—
47." I have examined the subject at some length in a former
part of this Appendix (See pp. 152—171) where will be
found, what seem to me, adequate reasons for dissenting
from Mr. Goode's conclusions—that the *Advertisement* was
" opposed to the Doctrine established by authoritative Formularies subsequently published," (p. 21) : that it cannot
have the slightest force or value " except " That it may be
some indication of the views entertained *at the time* by the
person who inserted it . . . . " (p. 23) : and that it " is a mat-

Prideaux, as having held views, upon the subject of Baptism, which are undis-
tinguishable from those of Mr. Gorham. Certainly it would not be difficult to
cite a similar array of names in support even of the more extreme opinions of the
late Archdeacon, provided those opinions are taken according to the letter of his
published works. What, for instance, shall we say of such divines as Overall,
Cosin, Thorndyke, Sheldon, Bramhall, Jackson, and Morley—all men of mark
and eminence in the Church, and some of them Bishops and Archbishops? Nay,
what shall we say of the notorious Dr. Gunning himself ; the very man at whose
instigation the rubrical alteration, we are now considering, is known to have
been made ?* These divines may not have written upon the subject of the Eucharist at the same length, or with the same systematic precision, as the author
of the book we are now considering ; but they have all, and especially the last—
the chief actor be it remembered, in the revision of 1662—given utterance to
sentiments of which it may without hesitation be affirmed, that they cannot, ' in
any important particular be distinguished' from those of Mr. Wilberforce. And
when, moreover, all the other circumstances of the case are duly considered :
when we call to mind the special reason—namely, a compromise with Rome—
for which the Rubric now under consideration was omitted from the Liturgy of
Elizabeth, together with the strong language which has all along been allowed to
exist in certain portions of our present Communion Service : when we consider
the Scholastic phraseology introduced, as we have already seen, into the Church
Catechism by Bishop Overall ; and the final removal, *even from the Articles*, of
the one only clause contained in them, which was condemnatory, in express
terms of the ' Real Presence :' we see not with what appearance of equity, or
even common fairness, the late Archdeacon of the East Riding could, had his
case been actually brought before any of our Ecclesiastical Courts, have been deprived of the honours of his Archdeaconry ; Mr. Gorham continuing all the
while unmolested in the vicarical emoluments of Brampford Speke."—
pp. 388—391.

* In a note Mr. Fisher gives the passage which I had quoted from Burnet at p. 70, remarking upon it, "And yet it was to men capable of such extravagancies as this, that the final revision of our National Service-book was entrusted ; and we, forsooth, are content to accept
their handy-work as the expression of our own religious belief."

ter of secondary importance" to consider "whether the phrase used in this Advertisement . . . . . was used to express the doctrine of the real presence in the bread and wine, their substance remaining, ..." (p. 23).

My only reason for now adverting to this part of the "Supplement" is Mr. Goode's complaint that "Dr. Pusey, according to his usual custom of ignoring the strongest points of his opponents' argument, ... takes no notice" (p. 22) of his citation of Cranmer's reply to Gardiner who had said (See p. 21) that the expression "under the form of bread and wine" occurred "in the distribution of the Holy Communion."

Why Dr. Pusey did not notice this I do not know; he may have thought it, as certainly it seems to me to be, one of the *weakest* of Mr. Goode's arguments; for how the fact—that the phrase did not occur in so *improbable* a place as the Communion Office of 1549 — proves its lack of *authority* where it stands in the First Book of Homilies, is a position which I should have thought it impossible to maintain without very different evidence from what Mr. Goode has produced or, indeed, from any which seems to exist. Mr. Goode, however, resorts to a singular plea in order to maintain what he regards as Cranmer's fatal answer to any Doctrinal claim of the Advertisement: he says:—

"If the form of words in question occurred in any formulary of authority in our Church, that was equivalent to their being in the 'Communion Book.'"

They did occur, however, as Mr. Goode says, (p. 22) "at the end of an authoritative Formulary ;" that "Formulary" (to use Mr. Goode's nomenclature): being the first Book of Homilies: but suppose, for argument's sake, they had "occurred" in either of the Homilies themselves ; would Mr. Goode really consent to place these "Sermons" on the same footing as the Communion Office ? If so, is he prepared to accept all the consequences of such a theory, and to acquiesce in all the statements of these Homilies as readily as he is bound to admit the teaching of the Communion Office itself? It may be so, but I much doubt it. Yet, if not, of what use is his argument at all? But even if he is willing to be bound by the legitimate force of his own proposition, it by no means follows that, in that proposition, he represents the mind of Archbishop Cranmer or the Convocation : surely it cannot be seriously maintained that they ever contemplated such an identification of the Homilies and the Communion Office. It was a most legitimate and useful thing to propose to instruct the people in the true meaning of a current Theological term, by issuing a Homily in which it should be explained: it would have been, to say the least, a most doubtful proceeding to employ in a public Liturgy (where explanation was impossible)—that Liturgy, too, being a *reformed* one—an expression which was well known to be used in support of different Doctrines by different classes of religionists ; one of these Doctrines being that very one of Transubstantiation which the Church of England had ceased to hold when the Prayer Book of 1549 was issued. It is easy therefore to understand why Cranmer repelled in somewhat strong terms Gardiner's assertion, that the phrase was used "in the distribution of the Holy Communion;" but it seems to me most illogical to infer from this circumstance, that " Cranmer evidently repudiates the phrase altogether as one used by the Church of England." I am content to set against Mr. Goode's inference the facts—that at this very time (1551) Cranmer's Catechism of 1548 was still in circulation : that, in that Catechism, Cranmer had employed this precise phrase (See p. 155): that, in his " Answer to Gardiner," (1551) he used the very phrase (See p. 179 and Note) : that in this same Book he adhered to the Catechism* (See p. 159): and that there is nothing whatever to show that he ever abandoned it ; whereas, on the contrary, all that we know goes to prove that he maintained it to the end of his life.

But Mr. Goode, anxious to deprive the *Advertisement* of any possible weight, yet seemingly embarrassed by the con-

---

* ...... this document is, as has already been shown, authenticated by Cranmer himself, no less decisively at the *close* of the year 1551—when, according to Burnett, the SECOND Book of Edw. had *already* been drawn up—than at the time of its first publication."—*Fisher Lit. Pur.* p. 235. The Italics and Capitals are Mr. Fisher's.

sideration, that Archbishop Cranmer's opinions will naturally be regarded as a fair test of its meaning, further says (p. 23):—

"And the question as to what Cranmer's precise views were in 1547 will not determine the meaning of this Advertisement, for the authorship of the Advertisement is not known ; and such a notice, having no legal authority, might be inserted by any one to whom the office of editing the first book of homilies was entrusted ; and certainly few among the authorities of our Church had then given up the doctrine of Transubstantiation. It is clear, as I have just shewn, that Cranmer altogether repudiated the phrase occurring in it as one to which our Church was committed, and shows by his language, in several places respecting it, what he understood by it. And therefore it cannot be supposed that he inserted it."

Now we have just seen that the Archbishop *did* make the phrase his own, and, in a sense, the Church of England's too, by using it in his Catechism of 1548 : yet he certainly never "repudiated" that Catechism, but distinctly upheld it (See p. 159), in the very "Answer to Gardiner," wherein, according to Mr. Goode, he "altogether repudiated" it for "our Church ;" we are driven then to this conclusion—that Cranmer *held* and *taught* a Doctrinal phrase which he *well knew* and *openly declared* to be opposed to the mind of that Church over which he was Archbishop ; but, as for my own part I cannot believe that the Primate would thus dishonestly instruct the "children and yong people" of England so, the merest charity obliges to the persuasion, that Cranmer did not consider the phrase to be *disallowed* in the Church of England, even though he might not think her formally "committed" to it : if so, it may *most fairly and reasonably* "be supposed that he inserted it."

But, says Mr. Goode, "few among the authorities of our Church had then given up the doctrine of Transubstantiation :" yet certainly *Cranmer* had ; and therefore he was not very likely to entrust the "editing" of the book to any one by whom, perchance, the phrase in question might be introduced with the design of supporting that Doctrine. It is, however, a mere assumption on Mr. Goode's part, that the Archbishop employed any one to *Edit* the Homilies : certainly there is no known proof that he did, though there is sufficient reason for thinking that he did not : yet, if he did, is it in the least likely that he neglected to look at the Book when it came out of the printer's hands ? In that case could the *Advertisement*, or so important an alteration of it, have escaped his notice? On the supposition, indeed, that the Book *was* Edited by another, it is not impossible that a sentence of seven words might have been overlooked by the Archbishop, if inserted in the *body* of the Homilies ; but assuredly it is most improbable that he could have overlooked it in so conspicuous a place as it occupies at the *end* of the Book. As to Mr. Goode's assertion, that " the authorship of the Advertisement is not known," it no more detracts from its value than does the like ignorance diminish the worth of some of the Homilies themselves ; and when (to account for, what he considers, its *unwarranted* insertion) he says that it had "no legal authority," it seems to me enough to say—that I believe he would fail to produce any "legal authority" for the Homilies themselves which does not equally apply to this Advertisement.

I suppose Mr. Goode would allow that the Doctrine of Transubstantiation was authoritatively abolished in the Church of England when the 2nd Book of Homilies was published in Elizabeth's reign : yet Bishop Jewel, while denying Harding's doctrine of a *carnal* Presence, uses the phrase in question (See p. 249) without any indication that he objected to it except in the sense which Harding put upon the word "forms" viz. *accidents* without *substance;* or " fantasies" as Jewel calls them :* if, then, as there is good

---

* Jewel's language to Harding in "The Defence of the Apology" shews more clearly his meaning in the passage referred to above ; thus he says :—

" But ye tell us further of yourself, that the body of Christ in the Sacrament .... being (as you say) a very natural body, yet hath neither likeness nor shape of a body." – p. 258 Ed. P. S.

Again, quoting St. Augustine, " Hereof we may conclude that the body of Christ, which you have imagined to be contained grossly and carnally in the sacrament, forasmuch as by your own confession it hath neither quality, nor quantity, nor form, nor place, nor proportion of body, therefore by St. Augustine's doctrine it is no body."—*Ibid.* p. 259.

So, too, referring to Harding's distinction of "form" and "substance," he asks—" But now, what if all this great imagined difference be no difference ? What if these two words 'form' and 'substance,' as they be used by Fulgentius, be all one ?"—*Ibid.* p. 261.

reason to believe, Jewel edited the *Second* Book of Homilies, the natural conclusion seems to be that he could not have regarded the terms of the Advertisement as being either *unauthorized* by, or *repugnant* to the mind of, the Church of England :* else, though he might not have felt at liberty to omit it, he would never have recognized it so distinctly in the Title of the 2nd Book which declares that the " Homilies" therein contained were "*of such matters as were promised*

Then, referring to SS. Athanasius, Chrysostom, Augustine, and Leo, he further enquires—" Wherefore say you of your own head, that ' form' and ' substance' be so contrary, seeing the Catholic fathers say they be both one ? " —*Ibid.* p. 262. See also his remarks on "*forma*" and "*natura*," pp. 512-13.

* Since writing the above I have read for the first time Mr. Griffiths' copious and careful Preface to the new Oxford Edition (1859) of the Homilies : his " collation of" the published editions with what he seems reasonably to regard as "the original form" of the Homily of the Resurrection leads him to the following remarks :—" . . . . the omission of the words ' in form of bread' in p. 433, l. 22, was doubtless intentional, and ought to be borne in mind, when attempts are made to found an argument for the presence of Christ in the consecrated elements upon the retention of the words ' under the form of bread and wine' in the promise of more Homilies which closes the First Book : for its import is shewn by another omission, ' now received in this holy Sacrament,' in p. 435, l. 18."—p. xxxiv.

Now here it is important first of all to observe that Mr. Griffiths (who has very carefully investigated the subjects of Authorship, Editorship, and Editions of both Books of Homilies) never attempts to question (as Mr. Goode does) the genuineness or authority of this Advertisement : speaking of the First Book of Homilies he does not hesitate to say (p. xiv.) that " Cranmer intended from the first that more should follow, and put a promise to that effect at the end of the Book together with a list of subjects on which they should treat." With regard, however to the omission of the phrase "in form of bread" (which Mr. Griffiths seems to consider as *now* lessening the argumentative value of the expression— " under the form of bread and wine) it may fairly be supposed that it was considered best to avoid the incidental use, in this Homily, of a controverted term relating to a subject promised to be dealt with in another Homily treating exclusively of the Sacrament of the Body and Blood of Christ. As to the second change in the same Homily, viz. the omission of the words which I bracket in the following sentence—" Yea, how dare we be so bold to renounce the presence of the Father, the Son, and the Holy Ghost [now received in this holy Sacrament], (for, where one is, there is God all whole in Majesty together with all his power, wisdom, and goodness,) " &c.—I cannot see how it sustains Mr. Griffiths' opinion as to the former by shewing, as he says, the " import" of the other omitted sentence : rather it seems to me to have been left out as having been already better expressed just before (p. 433, l. 28, &c.) in the sentence, " Thou hast received his body to have within thee, the Father, the Son, and the Holy Ghost for to dwell with thee, to endow thee with grace, to strength thee against thy enemies, and to comfort thee with their presence." Indeed Mr. Griffiths' conjecture, if correct, would seem to *sustain* the authority and fitness of the terms " under the form of bread and wine" as being the *equivalent* of the phrase "in this holy Sacrament;" for I suppose the objectors to the Advertisement will not deny that the Church of England might sanction such a formula as this— " Of the due receiving of His Body and Blood in the Holy Sacrament."

It is convenient, and may be useful (as bearing upon what has been said at

M M

and intituled in the former part of Homilies." It is most improbable, too, that the History and Authorship of the Advertisement had been forgotten in sixteen years; for no longer
time had elapsed between the 1st Edition of the First Book
in 1547, and the 1st Edition of the Second Book published in
1563 under the sanction of the Queen and Convocation; yet
in that period no less than *twenty* Editions of the First Book
are known to have been published; viz. *fifteen* in King
Edward's reign, (between 1547 and 1552,) and *five* under
Queen Elizabeth (between 1559 and 1563) prior to the issuing of the Second Book.* The Title of the 1st Elizabethan Edition informs us also that they were "by her
Grace's aduyse perused and ouersene;" and, whether *Parker*
or *Cox* or *Jewel* performed this office, the Advertisement
could not have been unnoticed by either of them: what
Bishop Cox thought of its authority we know from the
Preface which Strype tells us he prepared for the Second
Book; for he there says that "whereas in the said [First]
Book of Homilies mention was made of other Homilies concerning certain necessary points of religion that were intended to be annexed to these, her Highness hath caused the
same to be faithfully drawn" &c.—(*Annals* c. **xxx.**) Moreover it cannot reasonably be doubted that the sense in which
Cranmer used the word "form," in the Advertisement, was

p. 209, relative to Art. **xxix.**) to notice here an alteration which Mr. Griffiths
says (Pref., p. xxi. and Note ii., p. 445) was also made in "The first part of the
Sermon concerning the Sacrament." He states that in "the original form"
above mentioned (which he believes to be the copy presented to Elizabeth of the
2nd Book of Homilies, as settled in the Convocation of 1563) the following
bracketed passage from St. Augustine occurs, though it was omitted in the first
and in all the subsequent published Editions:—"For the unbelievers and faithless cannot feed upon that precious Body: whereas the faithful have their life,
their abiding in him; their union, and as it were their incorporation, with him.
[Whereof thus saith St. Augustine; 'He which is at discord with Christ doth
neither eat his flesh nor drink his blood, although he receive to the judgment of
his destruction, daily the outward sacrament of so great a thing.'] Wherefore
let us," etc. In the margin was the reference "Lib. 4. de Trinit.," which was
also omitted. It will be recollected that Article xxix. was suppressed, although
it had been passed in the same Convocation of 1563. The Article was restored
in 1571, but not so this omitted passage of the Homily. Perchance this may
have influenced Abp. Parker in removing, as is said, (see p. 209) the *reference*
to St. Augustine from the *margin* of the Article.

* See Mr. Griffiths' Catalogue. pp. l. to lx.

well known at the time the Second Book was prepared; and, too, that that sense was none other than the anti-roman one, already quoted from Jewel, viz. *substance* and not merely *accidents*.

I have already drawn attention (pp. 162-165) to a point which seems not to have been sufficiently regarded by any in considering the notice of the promised Homily and its supposed production in the Second Book under the title "Of the worthy receiving and reverent esteeming of the Sacrament of the Body and Blood of Christ." The argument there was founded upon a probable conclusion (drawn from Bp. Burnet)* that this Homily was due to Cranmer's own fulfilment of the promise; though it was also shewn what would be the effect of the discovery that the Homily was certainly not prepared by *Cranmer*. It is in place here to observe that (assuming the Homily to have been compiled or revised by *Jewel*) what was there suggested (p. 165) as a reason which might have induced the Archbishop not to use in the Homily the words "under the form of bread and wine" applies equally to the Bishop; for Jewel at that time may have entertained the like fear of its being popularly accepted in Harding's sense, which Cranmer in his day probably had of its being interpreted by Gardiner's definition. Yet such an act of prudent consideration no more proves of Jewel than of Cranmer—that he objected to it as being at variance with the teaching of the Church of England—on the contrary it seems to me that a further proof of his acceptance of it, in the sense in which he must have known that Cranmer employed it, is to be found in "The twenty-sixth Article" of his controversy with Harding, against whom Jewel maintains that no proof can be found in the first six centuries "that the Sacrament is a sign or token of the body of Christ, that lieth hidden underneath it."

Harding had said:—

"That the outward form of bread, which is properly the sacra-

* " . . . . there were two books of Homilies prepared; the first was published in King Edward's time; the second was not finished till about the time of his death; so it was not published before Queen Elizabeth's time."—*Expos. of Art.* xxxv.

ment, is the sign of the body of Christ, we confess, yea, of that body which is covertly in or under the same, which St. Augustine calleth *carnem Domini forma panis opertam,* ' the flesh of the Lord covered with the form of bread:' "

To this Jewel answers thus :—

" These words of St. Augustine are alleged and answered before.* That holy learned father never said, neither that the forms and accidents be the sacrament, nor that Christ's body is **really** hidden under the same ; nor in this place speaketh any one word at all of any accidents.

" But the words wherein M. Harding is deceived are these, *forma panis ;* which words signify not the outward forms and accidents, as he untruly expoundeth them, but the very kind and substance of the bread.   So St. Paul saith : . . . . Christ, being in the form (or nature) of God, took upon him the form (or nature) of a servant,' . . . . I think M. Harding will not say, Christ took a body of forms and accidents, that he might be conversant and live with men . . . .

"And as touching the other word *operta,* ' covered,' St. Augustine meaneth not thereby that Christ's body is **really** contained and covered under the said form or kind of bread, but only that it is there AS IN A SACRAMENT OR IN A MYSTERY.   In this sense St. Augustine saith : . . . ' The grace of God lay hidden covered in the old Testament.'   And again: . . . ' The new Testament was hidden in the old, that is to say, it was secretly signified in the old.' "—pp. 796-7.

---

* That is at pp. 618 and 619 of the same Volume : I have given two short extracts from the answer at p. 247: but it may be useful to make a further quotation here: thus Jewel says—" In the second word, *operta,* which signifieth ' covered,' M. Harding wittingly dissembleth his own learning, and would seem not to know the manner and nature of all sacraments ; which is to offer one thing outwardly unto our senses, and another inwardly to our mind.   Hereof there is sufficiently spoken before, in the second and eighth division of this article." †—p. 618.

"Thus the Sacrament of Christ's flesh, which, according to the doctrine of St. Augustine, beareth the name of the thing that it signifieth, is called Christ's flesh, invisible, spiritual, and only to be conceived by understanding.   For the whole work hereof pertaineth, not unto the mouth or teeth, as St. Augustine saith , but only to faith and spirit."—p. 619.

† Viz. at pp. 594, 595, 604—*s. g.* "These things considered, it may soon appear how faithfully and how well to his purpose M. Harding allegeth this place of St. Augustine: *Hoc est, quod dicimus,* etc: (De Consecr. Dist. 2.)   ' This is it that we say, which we go about by all means to prove, that the sacrifice of the Church is made of two things, and standeth of two things ; of the visible kind (or nature) of the elements, and of the invisible flesh and blood of our Lord Jesus Christ; of the Sacrament, the outward holy sign, and the thing of the sacrament, which is the body of Christ.'   Hereof M. Harding gathereth that the body of Christ lieth hidden under the accidents.   St. Augustine's words be true; but M Harding with his guesses is much deceived.   For of this word *specie* he concludeth that the substance of bread is gone, and nothing remaining but only accidents ; and of this word *invisibili* he gathereth that Christ's body is there really inclosed.   And so he maketh a commentary far beside his text."—p. 594.

"Neither does this word ' visible' import any such external form as is here imagined ; but only excludeth the body of Christ, which is in heaven, invisible to our bodily eyes, and visible only to the eyes of our faith."—p. 595.

For the passage at p. 604 see p. 247.

But then, lest this illustration should be thought to prove too much, it is well to notice another illustration which Jewel gives, *together with it*, at p. 618 :—

" But as St. Augustine saith here, Christ's body is hidden under the form or kind of bread ; even so he saith : . . . ' The grace of God lay hidden in the old testament.' Even so Gregory saith : . . . ' As the chaff hideth the corn, so the letter hideth the Spirit.' Even so again St. Augustine saith : . . . ' The new Testament was hidden in the old.' But he expoundeth himself : . . . ' It was hidden, that is to say, it was secretly signified.' And thus by St. Augustine's own words and exposition, we may likewise say : . . . ' Christ's flesh is privily hidden, that is to say,' as St. Augustine expoundeth it, ' it is privily signified.' "

Now Jewel's quotation from St. Gregory in this passage removes a difficulty which it and the former passage might else present, and so helps us to see that he might (as I have argued that he did) accept the phrase " under the form of bread and wine," allowing a *true* yet denying a *physical* Presence therein and therewith of the Body and Blood of Christ. For it is clear that the " corn " hidden under the " chaff " is a *material* thing; but, as he himself says,* the like was not true of " the new Testament" which " was hidden in the old ;" why then (besides another) did he use two illustrations which are thus *at variance ?* I can imagine no other reason than that he wished to guard himself from seeming to unsay what (as Compiler or Editor) he had said two years before on behalf of the Church of England, in the Homily of " The Worthy Receiving," &c., viz. that the Sacrament of the Altar was " no *untrue* figure of a thing absent;" and further that (while by one illustration, from the two Testaments, he sustained his resistance to a *Carnal* Presence and by a second, from the chaff and corn, pointed to his

---

* " Here, lest M. Harding should take these words strictly and grossly, as he doth the rest, and say, the new testament indeed and really was covered in the old, St. Augustine himself hath prevented him, and opened his own meaning in this wise, as it is said before : *Occultabatur,* . . . *id est, occulte significabatur,* [De Baptism. contr. Donatist. Lib. 1. c. xv. 24.] : ' it was covered, that is to say, it was secretly signified.' By which exposition, being St. Augustine's, M. Harding might have learned likewise to expound these words : caro operta forma panis, id est, occulte significata : ' The flesh covered in the form or substance of bread, that is to say, privily signified in the form or substance of bread.' "—p. 797.

belief in a *Substantial* Presence) in comparing this Sacrament with "the grace of God [which] lay hidden in the old testament" and with "the letter [which] hideth the Spirit," he used a third analogy, which, varying from yet combining the other two, supported a *Sacramental* but withal a *True* and *Real* Presence.

There is, however, another reason—and a very forcible one —for believing that neither Cranmer nor Jewel nor their contemporary Authorities in the Church of England repudiated the phrase in question; for it occurs in one of the "Prayers of the Passion" in the first *Elizabethan* Edition (1559) of Hen. 8th's *reformed* Primer of 1545: the Prayer is as follows :—

"Our [1545. O, Jesu Christ, which] Saviour and Redeemer, Jesu Christ, which in thy last supper with thine Apostles didst *deliver* [1545. *consecrate*] thy blessed body and blood *under the form of bread and wine;* Grant us, we beseech thee, ever stedfastly to believe, and kindly to acknowledge, thy infinite and almighty power, thy incomprehensible love towards us, and that we may alway worthily receive the same blessed Sacrament, according to thy holy ordinance, that thereby we may obtain increase of all goodness [1545. godlynes] in unity of spirit with thee our head, and, by thee and thy Spirit, with all the company of them that be truly thine, which be thy spiritual and mystical body, and our spiritual and Christian brethren. Hear us, our Saviour Christ, for thine [1545. thy name sake. Amen.] name's sake."—*Private Prayers. Q. Elizabeth.* Parker Society, 1851, p. 86.

Now this Prayer first appeared (so far as any known Edition shews) in Hen. 8th's *reformed* Primer of 1545: several Editions of that Book were subsequently published down to the year 1575; omitting, however, the reign of Mary: the Book is wholly different both from the Sarum Primer (of which many Editions were printed, before and after 1545, in England and on the Continent) and also from Edward 6th's Primer of 1553; these therefore, as not furnishing any evidence either way, need not here be considered: but it seemed to me important to compare the different existing Copies and Editions of the Primer of 1545 and to note any variations of the phrase now under consideration. The result of this collation is shewn in the following Table which will, I think, materially aid the enquiry as to the *authority* of the phrase itself. The Copies in the British Museum I have myself examined; for the rest I am partly indebted to the kindness of friends upon whose accuracy I can rely.

All the Copies which are noticed in this Table were printed in *London:* the Continental Editions (of which there are many), being of no value in this enquiry, are not included.

No.	Date.	Size and Printer.	Where kept.	Variations in the Prayer.
1	1545 June [xix.	4to. E. Whitchurche.	B. Mus. C. 35. C.	"Our Saviour and Redeemer Jesu Christe, whiche in thy last supper with thyne Apostles didst *consecrate* THY BLESSED BODY & BLOOD UNDER THE FOURME OF BRED AND WYNE: Graunt" &c.
2	1545 June xx.	8vo. Edw. Whitchurche.	B. Mus. C. 35. b. C. 25. h. 10.	Ib. —— Ib. ——
3	1545 Sept. vi.	4to. Richd. Grafton.	B. Mus.—— 1	"O Jesu Christ, . . . *consecrate.* . . ."
4	1545	4to.	Q, Coll. Oxford.	Ib. —— Ib. ——
5	1545	4to. Grafton.	Bodl. Gough 39.	" . . . . *consecrate* . . . ."
6	1545	4to. Grafton.	Bodl. Douce BB 123.	" . . . . *consecrate* . . . ."
7	1545	4to. Whitchurch.	Bodl. P. 14. Th. Seld.	" . . . . *consecrate* . . . ."
8	1546 Aug. xx.	8vo. Ed. Whitchurche.	B. Mus. C. 35. a.	"Oure Savioure & redemer Jesu Christ . . *consecrate* . . . . ."
9	1546	4to. R. Grafton.	Bodl. P. 16. Th. Seld. C. 25. h. 6.	" . . . . *consecrate* . . . ."
10	1547	4to. R. Grafton.	B. Mus.—— 1—2.	"Our saviour & redemer Jesu Christ, . . . *consecrate* . . . ."
11	1547	4to. R. Grafton.	Bodl. Donce BB 122	" . . . . *consecrate* . . . ."
12	1549	4to. R. Grafton.	Bodl. Gough 44. C. 35 b.	" . . . . *consecrate* . . . ."
13	1551	12mo. R. Grafton.	B. Mus.—— 1—2. C. 25. h. 9.	"Our sauiour & redemer Jesu Christ, . . . *deliver* thy blessed body" &c.
14	1551 prob.	4to. Will. Powell.	B. Mus.—— 1 - 2.	Ib. —— Ib. ——
15	1559	. . . . see	above p. 270 . . .	" . . . . *deliver* . . . ."
16	1566 in Colophon. 1575	12mo. W. Seres.	Ball. Coll. Oxford.	" . . . . *delyuer* the Sacrament of thy *Blessed Bodye and Bloude*: graunt that we" &c.

No. 1—Wants Title, supplied in M.S. to agree with No. 2: the Colophon gives the date.
No. 2—"The Primer set forth by ye Kinges majesty and his cleargy, and none other to be used throughout his dominions. 1545." The date " xix. day of June 1545" occurs in the Colophon.

Having thus tabulated the results of the examination of these Primers, let us see to what conclusion they lead us: but, first, I must own that, confident as one felt of the

No. 3—"The Primer in Englishe and Latyn, set foorth by the Kynges majestie and his Clergie to be taught, learned, and read: and none other to be used throughout all his dominions. Lond. Richd. Grafton, vi. Sept. 1545. Cum priv."

No. 10—"The Primer set forth by the Kinges majestie and his Clergie to be taught, learned, and red: and none other to be used thorowout all his dominions.

"Imprinted at London the last daye of Nouember, in the first yere of the reign of our souereigne Lorde the Kyng Edward the vi. by Richard Grafton printer to his moste royall majestie, cum priv." &c.

No. 13—No title: in Colophon "The ende of the Primer. Imprinted at London by Richard Grafton, Printer to the Kynges majestié, 1551. cum priv."

No. 14—"The Primer set furth by the Kynges hyghness and hys Clergie, to be taught, learned and read, of all his louying subjectes, all other set aparte, corrected accordyng to the Statute made in the third, and, liii. yere of our soueraigns Lord the Kynges Majesties reigne.

"Cum priuilegio ad imprimendum solum."—Colophon. "Imprynted at London in Fletestrete, by me Wyllyam Powell, dwellynge at the sygne of the George, next to saynt Dunstans Churche."

The book has no date: it is supposed to be 1551: it may be later, but it must be subsequent to the Stat. of 1549-50, in pursuance of which it was printed.

The "Statute" here referred to is the 3 & 4 Edw. vi. c. 10. A.D. 1549-50. "An Act for the abolishing and putting away divers Books and Images." Section v. of which Provides ". . . that any person or persons may use, keep, have, and retain any Primers in the English or the Latin tongue, set forth by the late king of famous memory, King Henry the Eighth, so that the sentences of invocation or prayer to saints in the same Primers be blotted or clearly put out of the same; . . ."

No. 16—"The Primer and Catechisme, set forth at large, wyth meny godly praiers necessarie for all faithful Christians to reade. By Q. Elizabeth [these italicized words are written in ink.] Imprinted at London by William Seres. Anno 1566."

The Colophon reads thus—"Imprinted at London, by William Seres, dwelling at the West ende of Paules Church, at the sygne of the hedgehogge. Cum priuilegio ad imprimendum solum. Anno 1575."

Besides this Copy (which is in the Library of Balliol College, Oxford) there are two other copies, in the Bodleian Library, of which Mr. Lathbury (Hist. Bk. of Com. Prayer, 1858,) thus speaks:—"In 1575 another Primer was published . . . . Of this edition, there are two copies in the Bodleian. They have indeed usually been regarded as different editions. One has no title, the other no colophon. The title to the one has the date of 1566; the colophon to the other that of 1575. After a careful examination, I ascertained that they are of the same edition. The real date of the books is that inthe colophon, 1575; and the date in the title of one copy is merely that of some other book, for which the woodcut border had been used in 1566. Such variations between the title and the colophon of books in these times are very common. The woodcut border bore the date of the year in which it was first used; and in taking the block for this Primer the date was either forgotten to be removed, or designedly retained, and the proper year given in the Colophon."—p. 67.

Mr. Lathbury informs me that his recollection of these particulars is quite distinct, and that he still adheres to the same opinion as to the real date of the Book.

The Editor of the Parker Society's reprint of the Primer of 1559 (No. 15) also thinks that 1575 "after all, may be the true date even of the former volume," i.e. the book of 1566.

But, having myself carefully examined these two Bodleian copies (since I communicated with Mr. Lathbury), and compared them with the Balliol copy, I am strongly of opinion that 1566 is the true date at which they were originally printed, and that either there was a further issue in 1575 with a Colophon of that date appended, or that (as is just possible) the type was kept standing and fresh copies were struck off in 1575 That there was no re-composition is clear from little defects of printing (e.g. a lead standing up) which appear in the copies.

With regard to Mr Lathbury's particulars of the Editions I must remark that either he has fallen into an error, or one of the two copies he mentions is missing from the Bodleian: for both the copies now there have the Title Page, whereas Mr. L—— states that only one, of the two he saw, possessed it.

The two copies (which are both imperfect) are marked "Tanner 63" and "8o. C. 85 Line." The Title-page of both agrees exactly with the Balliol copy, except in not having like it the words "Q. Elizabeth" written: the "Tanner 63" has no Colophon and ends with a "Prayer. For the desire of the life to come:" the other copy has an additional page containing "Another Prayer. Almighty God, give us grace that we may cast away the works of darkness," &c.; and then comes a notice—

"¶ Thus endeth the Primer at large now newly Printed with the Kinges Psalmes." On the back of this page is the Colophon which agrees exactly with the Balliol copy. The contents of the Bodleian copies and of the Balliol copy are exactly the same: the Balliol has also the additional Prayer contained on the last leaf of the Bodleian "8o. C. 85 Linc."

authority attaching to the dogmatic expression "under the form of bread and wine," I had no idea that so much additional support could be found for it in the successive Editions of this Book of Devotions; and, next, I cannot but

Thus, then, it is clear that all three copies were printed from the same "forms": whether they were composed in 1566 or 1575 is the point to be decided: it could only be absolutely settled that there was an Edition of 1566 by the discovery of a copy bearing that date both in the Title-page and the Colophon, or by ascertaining with certainty that the " Tanner 63 " (or some similar copy) never had a Colophon.

It appears to me, however, that the following Almanack, which is found in all three copies (but which does not seem to have been considered sufficiently, if at all, before) goes very far to remove any doubt that 1566 is the original date of the Books.

¶ An Almanack for ix yeares.			
The yeare of our Lorde.	Easter Daye.	The Golden number.	The Sun dayes letter.
1566.	14 Aprill.	9	F
1567.	30 March.	10	C
1568.	18 Aprill.	11	D C
1569.	10 Aprill.	12	B
1570.	26 March.	13	A
1571.	15 Aprill.	14	G
1572.	6 Aprill.	15	F C
1573.	22 March.	16	D
1574.	11 Aprill.	17	C

Cꞁ The yeare hath, 12 months, or 52, weekes and one daye. And it hath in all 3 hundred and, 66 dayes, and 7, houres.

Now, looking at this Almanack, the question at once suggests itself—if this Book was printed in 1575 how is it that the Almanack only comes down to 1574? For all practical purposes it was wholly useless in 1575 to give the " Easter daye" for the nine previous years: but it would have been important, in a popular book printed in 1566, to furnish the date of that Festival for some subsequent years; and, accordingly, this Almanack gives it for the next eight years after 1566: it seems hardly possible, therefore, to avoid the conclusion that the Primer must have been originally printed in 1566. Moreover the continuance of this same Almanack in the copies with the Colophon date of 1575, (viz. the Bodleian "8o. C. 85 Linc" and the Balliol copy,) makes me decidedly think that they were simply a further issue of stock copies to which the Additional Prayer and the Colophon were added in 1575; and that the Bodleian " Tanner 63" is a copy of the Book as it appeared in 1566. This opinion is strengthened by the fact that the Primer of 1559 (No. 15) also contains an Almanack in which " Easter day" is given for the 15 years next following.

The two Bodleian copies contain the Eucharistic Prayer precisely in the altered form which occurs in the Balliol copy (No. 16) · if, then, my conjecture as to the date of these three Books is correct (viz. 1566), it is likely that the change in the language of the Prayer was made then, and not in 1575; and this is exceedingly probable, considering the circumstance mentioned by Mr. Griffiths (see p. 265) that similar words, viz. "in form of bread" had been already omitted in the *published* Editions of the Homily of the Resurrection as it first appeared in 1563—just 3 years before this Edition of the Primer was put forth.

Still it is possible (though, I think, unlikely) that these copies are a *revised* Edition published in 1575 of one printed in 1566 with the same Title-page, and worked off from the old "forms"; and that, consequently, the Prayer remained unchanged until the *later* date: but to establish this it is necessary to find a copy containing the *unaltered* prayer with the undeniable date of 1566.

This Edition of 1575 appears to be the latest *authorized* Edition of that of 1545: there are indeed in the Bodleian four copies of a professed reprint of the Ed. of 1546 (see No. 9), they are marked 8vo. Rawl. 218, and Gough Missal 5, 88, 93: they have no date however; the Typography leads to the belief that they are of about 1701 ; but, as there is nothing to shew that this reprint was published by authority so, no conclusion can be drawn from the fact of its containing the Prayer as it stood in 1546.

surmise that Mr. Goode did not contemplate the existence of this kind of evidence, else he must have allowed its force, and so have modified his language about the Phrase, or he would surely have produced it in order to shew, if he could, its inapplicability to the case. Moreover, in weighing the evidence of these Primers, it is of much consequence to remember— that (like Authors) Printers, and especially Royal Printers, were not free in those days to publish what Devotional or Theological Books they pleased, nor to retain or omit in them what they chose: the *cum privilegio* of that day was not only an *inhibition* to others, but also a *stringent law* to those who received it, binding them to print only what was sanctioned by the proper authority: so long, indeed, as that authority was not withdrawn from any given Edition, they were free to print it as often, and in as great numbers, as the demand for it warranted; but self-interest alone was a sufficient check to any departure from this rule by those who wished to retain their privilege. It is, then, worse than useless to allege (as Mr. Goode does of the Advertisement*) or to imply, that the *Printers* were responsible for the continuance of this Phrase in successive Editions of the Homilies, or of the Primer; for, to say the least, it is highly improbable that a Royal Printer of that period would have taken so venturesome a step as to create a precedent of even such *comparative* harmlessness as, it seems, Crown and University Printers have hazarded within about the last seventy years: viz., to alter, without I believe any authoritative direction, the Rubrics touching the time of Publication of Banns, in order to make them accord with an Act of Parliament† which was not designed to *abolish* the Rubrical time of publication (*i. e.* after the Nicene Creed); but was only meant to *legalize* another time in cases where compliance with the Rubric might lead to fraud.

---

* " And this *Advertisement*, though of course *forming no part of the Homilies* was repeated by succeeding printers in their editions of the Book, even *after the Second Book had been added, in which a Homily had been given on the subject, maintaining a totally different doctrine from that implied in these words.*"—*Goode on the Eucharist.* Vol. i., p. 41. But, on this alleged difference, see above, pp. 162—5.

† Stat. 26 Geo. 2, c. 33. A.D. 1753 "An Act for the better preventing of clandestine Marriages."

Premising thus much, we are bound to regard the Editions of the Primers set out in the above Table as having that full Ecclesiastical Sanction which is conveyed, in the Title-Page of the First and of subsequent Editions, by the words "set forth by the King's Majesty and his Clergy."

Further, as Cranmer was Archbishop of Canterbury, and the leading Prelate during the six years which produced the Editions comprised in the first *fourteen* copies mentioned in the above List, it must in all fairness be assumed (in the absence of any proof to the contrary) that he concurred in their publication. It can hardly be doubted that he was a party to the *first* Edition in 1545, when it is remembered that—as Strype informs us in writing of that year—(*Cranmer* Bk.. I. c. 30.) Henry 8th "had of late appointed some other of his chaplains and learned men," "with the Archbishop, to peruse certain books of Service, delivered by the King to them, wherein there were many superstitions fit to be amended. Which the Archbishop, in the name of the rest, at this time acquainted the King with . . ." For, though it is true that the Primer could not strictly, perhaps, be included among these "*Books of Service*," the fact that it appeared in a *reformed* shape in June, 1545, is a very strong indication that the Archbishop had to examine this among the other Books.

We have already seen (p. 160 and 263) that the Archbishop had abandoned *Transubstantiation* long before this time; and therefore if, as I have argued, he authorized the Primer of 1545, he could not have used the phrase, "didst consecrate thy blessed body and blood under the fourme of bred and wyne," as being (in Mr. Goode's words) "peculiar to those who held the Doctrine of Transubstantiation, and maintained that the *forms* or appearances only of bread and wine remained in the consecrated elements."—*Goode on the Eucharist*, Vol. i., p. 43.

But it may fairly enough be replied—that as Cranmer confesses himself to have been, apparently about this time, "in that error of the real presence, as I was many years past in divers other errors, as of transubstantiation," etc. (See p. 155, Note, and compare Foxe's account on p. 84), therefore the Phrase which he sanctioned in Henry's Primer cannot be regarded as a suitable formula for the Church of England's present Doctrine ; for that, whatever may now be her real belief as to the Presence, she certainly does not hold that "Corporal Presence of Christ's natural Flesh and Blood," which Cranmer is supposed to refer to in the above confession. (*See also* Strype's Cranmer, Bk. I., c. xviii.) Granting, however, for argument's sake, that Bishop Ridley, by means of *Bertram's* Book, had not *then* brought off the Archbishop from a *carnal* view of the Presence, which yet was not *Transubstantiation* ; the objection only further proves that Cranmer could use the Phrase in some other than a *Roman* sense ; and, if so, then it *may* be that it will further serve to express a Doctrine which is neither *Transubstantiation* nor the " Corporal Presence " of the Declaration on Kneeling.

Facts prove, I think, that Cranmer himself thought thus : for it is certain, from his own words just quoted, that in 1548 he had abandoned that "error of the **real** presence," of which he speaks : yet in 1549 another Edition of the Primer appeared without the slighest change in this Prayer. Nay more, the perpetuation of the Prayer was, in fact, sanctioned by the 3 & 4 Edwd. VI.' c. 10, which passed quite at the beginning of that year, (See Note No. 14, p. 272)—a Statute which the Archbishop is commonly supposed to have had a considerable share in procuring : yet that Statute required no other change in the Primer than the omission of " the sentences of invocation or prayer to saints."

But if any one thinks that the Archbishop's language about himself in 1548 is not clear enough to be wholly relied upon in this case, there can be no sort of pretence for saying that he had the slightest leaning towards a " corporal," *i.e.* *carnal* Presence, when he published, in 1550, his " Defence of the True and Catholic Doctrine of the Sacrament," and also, in 1551, his "Answer to Gardiner," vindicating that Book. Yet, in 1551, a new Edition of the Primer was printed, though not until this Prayer and the Phrase in question had been re-considered, as is shewn by the substitution of "*deliver*" for "consecrate." This alteration however, so far from indicating any doubt on Cranmer's part of the propriety of the terms of the Advertisement to the Homilies, which had then been *four years* in circulation, did but serve to bring the *Primer* Phrase into a closer *verbal* agreement with the *Advertisement* Phrase : this will be, readily seen if they are read side by side, thus :—

Advertisement, 1547.	*Primer*, 1551.
" Of the due receiving of His Blessed Body and Blood under the form of bread and wine."	" . . . . didst deliver Thy Blessed Body and Blood under the form of bread and wine."

Could language better harmonize than this? The Advertisement speaks " of the due receiving," *by a particular medium*, of *that same Thing* which the Primer teaches that Christ did " deliver " to His Apostles *through the very same medium*. Is it possible, then, that the Primate of all England and Metropolitan could instruct the King's " loving subjects " to pray in a Phrase which, at that very time, as Mr. Goode says, he *repudiated for the Church of England?* Whatever people may choose to think of the Archbishop's want of consistency, in some respects, they will scarcely be ready to answer " Yes " to this question: yet if any could be found to take so miserable an estimate of Cranmer's character, it will not be supposed that Mr. Goode would unite with them.

So far then as Archbishop Cranmer is concerned it seems to me that, while it was before shewn to be *morally certain* that he was responsible for the original appearance of the Phrase in the Advertisement to the First Book of Homilies, it is now proved to be, at least something like, *historically true* that he must have sanctioned and approved its continuance there.

Having regard, therefore, to all the known evidence, I cannot but think it clearly established—that (as the Archbishop must be held to have acted officially and legally in the matter, so) down to the end of the reign of Edward 6th the Formula in question had the *complete authority* of the Church of England.

It could hardly be expected that this *reformed* Primer would be re-printed in Mary's reign : its omission of certain Invocations would be alone sufficient to prevent its re-issue then : but it is hardly probable that the Phrase in the Prayer would have been thought an adequate expression of the Doctrine of Transubstantiation (then again held) unless it were accompanied with an explanation to shew that " form " meant only *accidents:* yet such an explanation might encumber a *Prayer,* and therefore make it seem better to reject it altogether.

The members of Convocation at the Accession of Elizabeth were of course those who represented the Clergy on the death of Mary : now the earliest act of the Lower House in Elizabeth's reign (Feb. 18th or 28th, 1558-9, under their Prolocutor, Nicholas Harpsfield, Archdeacon of Canterbury) was to present an Address to the Bishops, to be tendered to the Parliament, containing "certain Articles in defence of the religion established under Mary :" the " First" of them ran in these words :—

" That in the Sacrament of the Altar, by virtue of the words of consecration duly pronounced by the priest, the **natural** body and blood of Christ, conceived of the blessed Virgin, are **really** present under the *species* [=form] of bread and wine."

But it is clear that they did not think this language would cover *Transubstantiation;* therefore they proceeded to add :—

" Secondly, That after the consecration the substance of bread and wine does not remain, nor any other substance, excepting that of God and man."—*Fuller,* Ch. Hist., Bk. ix., § 1 ; and *Collier,* Eccl. Hist., Pt. ii., Bk. 6.

In fact they repeated what was done by the advocates of *Transubstantiation* in Henry 8th's reign, when they succeeded, against Archbishop Cranmer and others, in introducing this very same language into the first of the Six Articles of 1539, although three years before (1536) the Convocation had excluded Transubstantiation, while allowing a *physical* Presence, by expressing itself in the following language which was sanctioned by the king :—

" FOURTHLY.—As touching the Sacrament of the Altar, we will, that all bishops and preachers shall instruct and teach our people

....that they ought and must constantly believe, that, under the form of bread and wine, which we there presently do see and perceive by outward senses, is **verily, substantially,** and **really** contained and comprehended the very self-same body and blood of our Saviour Jesus Christ, which was born of the Virgin Mary, and suffered upon the cross for our redemption ; and that, under the same form and figure of bread and wine, the very self-same body and blood of Christ is **corporally, really,** and in **the very substance** exhibited, distributed, and received unto and of all them which receive the said sacrament ; and that therefore the said sacrament is to be used with all due reverence and honour ; ......"— *Fuller,* Bk. v., § 4.

So then, in what has just been said, is to be found a further reason for the Primer of 1545 not being re-published under Queen Mary, though an *unreformed* Primer was reprinted.

But, so soon as the Archiepiscopal throne was filled by Queen Elizabeth's appointment of Parker, no time was lost in re-producing *reformed* Office Books, and the same year (1559) which witnessed Elizabeth's Prayer Book, saw also a new Edition of the Primer, with no other change in the Prayer than that substitution of " deliver" for " consecrate," which was made in 1551. Thus, then, at the commencement of another distinct period in the Reformation, the Phrase which is said (though how truly I have already considered) to have been repudiated for the Church of England by one Archbishop, re-appears under the sanction of another Primate whose Theological soundness also is not questioned by those who object to the Phrase; moreover, it re-appeared at the same time in a new Edition of the First Book of Homilies, which had not been merely left to the Royal Printers to set up from any old Edition, but which had been (as before noticed) " by her Grace's aduyse perused and ouersene, for the better understandying of the simple people." Mr. Griffiths states (p. lviii.) that " many verbal alterations were made in the text, partly by substitution, partly by addition :" so that the Editor must have carefully read the Book; yet, either he carelessly passed over the Advertisement at the End of it, or he knew that it was meant not to be altered; can any one reasonably doubt that the latter was his real condition ?

I am not unmindful of the facts that Jewel was only Elected Bishop on August 21st, 1559, and was not Consecrated until the 21st January following: it may therefore be urged that, as he could not have been a party to the re-publication of the Primer in 1559 so, he must not be held responsible for the continuance of the unaltered Prayer, and, consequently, it ought not to be cited in proof that he used, either approvingly or as being authorized, the language quoted from him at pp. 249 and 264 Note. Yet, surely, if ever "silence gives consent," and use implies approval, it was so in this case: for his *Reply to Harding* was not published until 1565, nor his *Defence of the Apology* until 1567, yet both the Primer and the First Book of Homilies had been circulating for *six* years before the earlier of these dates; nay, more, for *two* years the Second Book of Homilies had also been distributed, under the Sanction of the Crown and the Convocation, as expressed in the XXXVth Article; and he, as a Diocesan Bishop, had to see that all were duly used. If, however, the Phrase in question was obnoxious to the Church of England, or even to Jewel himself, could there have been a better and fairer opportunity for him to have said so than when discussing with *Harding* its Theological significance? How came it to pass that, instead of merely defining the word "form" which occurs in it, he neglected so fitting an occasion to *repudiate* the Phrase altogether, either for himself, or for the Church of England, or for both? I can only suppose that he had no wish *personally* to disown it, or that, if he had, he felt he was not free to do so for the Church of England, so long as it remained in any of her authorized Books.

These remarks are also a further answer to Mr. Griffiths' observation, already noticed in the Note to p. 265.

But, having insisted so much on the repeated re-publication in the Primer of the language which Mr. Goode declares to have had no authority in the Advertisement of the First Book of Homilies, it would be unpardonable in me not to draw particular attention to the latest known Edition of the Primer, which is noticed in the preceding Table; for a very considerable change was made in the Prayer as given in that Edition; no less, in fact, than the *entire omission* of the alleged unauthorized formula; so that the Prayer reads thus:—

" Our Saviour and Redeemer, Jesus Christ, which in Thy last supper with Thine Apostles didst deliver the Sacrament of Thy Blessed Body : grant that we," &c.

There is some doubt (as I have pointed out in the Note at p. 272) as to the true date of this Edition of the Primer: the Title page calls it 1566, but the Colophon marks it as 1575: it is not unlikely that *both* dates are correct; the former (1566) indicating (as I have said) the period when it was first printed, the latter (1575) the time of its re-print or re-issue; this may have arisen from the very common practice with printers at that period of continuing to use an old Title page, if it was a *Block*, and printing the *real* date of an Edition in the Colophon. It is quite probable that there may have been an Edition in 1566, though, as no copy is known with that date only, there is no means of ascertaining whether the Prayer was altered at that time, or not until 1575: the true date of the alteration is not, however, *material* for my present purpose; though if it be 1575 it strengthens my argument, as, in that case, the alteration was four years after Bishop Jewel's death, and in the last year of Archbishop Parker's life.

Yet, *assuming* that the change was made in 1566, the change itself implies that the old phraseology was allowed up to that time : why, then, was it changed at all? As nothing is known of the history of the change the cause can only be matter of conjecture, but that, I think, a natural conjecture. It is well known that nothing better impresses Doctrine on the mind than the language of prayers which are in frequent or constant use : but the expression "under the form of bread and wine" *had* marked Doctrines which were no longer held by the Church of England, and which clearly were intended to be excluded by that Homily on the Sacrament which was authorized in the Convocation of 1563. But the continued use, in a Prayer, of a Dogmatic Phrase,

o o

claimed respectively by the holders of three different Doctrines, viz., *Transubstantiation* (either with or without a *Carnal* Presence)—a *Corporal*, i.e., a *Physical* Presence,—and a *Real*, i.e., a *True*, but not a *Material* Presence,—might perplex or mislead those who were not Theologians; especially as at that time the Declaration on Kneeling (which, as I am throughout contending, was designed to exclude every possible theory of a *Carnal* Presence) was not appended to the Communion Office, and so that authoritative safeguard was wanting. It has been seen (See p. 213) that Bishop Cheney (though opposed to *Transubstantiation*) apparently held a *Material* Presence, at this very period, therefore it may have more or less prevailed in his Diocese of Gloucester —perhaps elsewhere. To omit from the Primer, then in use, the Phrase which might be thus misunderstood, may well have been thought a likely mode of correcting the error, and of preventing its extension.

Yet, if this were so, why was not the like process of excision resorted to in the Homilies? Obviously, I think, because there was no similar danger of misunderstanding; for, (1) the Homilies were not Prayers; (2) they were not much in the hands of, or read by, the people; (3) though they were read to the people by the Clergy, the Advertisement of course was not read; (4) the Phrase did not occur in any *Homily*, being probably omitted on prudential grounds, as I have already suggested at pp. 165 and 267. It was one thing for the Bishops to remove from a Prayer or a Homily* language which did not involve any point of essential Faith, but which might be designedly perverted, or popularly misapplied; quite another to withdraw a Dogmatic statement, of real Theological value, from a *Notice* never designed to be publicly read, or privately meditated upon. The Advertisement at the end of the First Book of Homilies was a kind of Historic link which bound it to the Second Book, and which

---

* I am willing to concede to Mr. Griffiths that this feeling *may* have had its influence in the omission, from the Homily of the Resurrection, of the words "in form of bread;" though, as I have said in the Note, p. 265, I do not think his *argument* accounts for it.

showed how, and how faithfully, the intentions of those who authorized the earlier Book had been carried out, either by themselves, or by their successors, in the later Volume; and this alone would be a sufficient reason for its being retained in every Edition down to the present day, and for faithfully retaining it hereafter. But it was, and is, still more a duty not to *abandon* a Theological Formula which had acquired a definite meaning in connection with the settled Eucharistic Doctrine of the Church of England; though it might not be thought then, and may not be considered now, needful or profitable to employ it in the ordinary religious instruction of the people.

Having thus carefully examined and, I hope, fairly estimated the evidence for and against the contested language of the Advertisement, it does seem to me, and will I trust appear to others, clearly established that the Phrase " *Of the due receiving of His Blessed Body and Blood under the form of bread and wine,*" is a Theological definition strictly authorized by the Church of England, and therefore one which may be most fairly and confidently used in controversies touching the Doctrine of the Real Presence in the Holy Eucharist.

Pursuing this Historical Enquiry in the order of time, it is necessary to notice the very important additions which were made to the Church Catechism in the reign of James 1st: it is pretty generally allowed that, considering the known views of Overall their reputed author, these additional explanations of Sacramental Belief were designed to be in the direction of what is called High Doctrine. That there was no intention of being deterred from this by any clamour about Popish teaching, is plain from what the King said on the second day of the Hampton-Court Conference, January 16, 1603-4; for, in answer to Dr. Reinolds, one of the Puritan representatives, who " complained that the Catechism in the Common Prayer Book was too brief; . . . and . . . requested therefore, that one uniform catechism might be made," it is reported that,—

" His Majesty thought the doctor's request very reasonable : but yet so, that he would have a Catechism in the fewest and plainest affirmative terms that may be :"

and stating as one rule to be observed "in reforming of a Church"—

"that there should not be any such departure from the Papists in all things, as that because we in some points agree with them, therefore we should be accounted to be in error."—*Card. Hist. Conf.*, p. 187.

With respect to the nature and tendency of these Catechetical additions, I cannot do better than cite the language of the same candid but adverse writer whom I have before quoted.

Mr. Fisher, speaking of them, remarks that—

"Since the revision of 1604—or, at all events, since the year 1662—Sacramentalism most decidedly predominates. . . . . In short, it is not too much to say, that in the Catechism as it *now* stands, the SACRED ORACLES, considered as an inspired Code of religious belief, are completely overshadowed by the prominence given to a Patristic scheme of sacramental theology."—*Liturgical Purity*, p. 293.

Again he says :—

". . . . it lets in the whole system of Romish Sacramentalism, by the insertion of a series of questions and answers, both upon Baptism and the Lord's Supper, which are at least *open* to a Papistical interpretation. . . . .

"For instance—the old and essentially "Romish dogma of 'the real presence' receives, it may safely be affirmed, a plausible sanction at least, if nothing more, from the terms of the following question and answer :—

"'Q. What is the inward part or thing signified ? '

"'A. The body and blood of Christ, which are *verily and indeed* taken and received by the faithful *in* the Lord's Supper.'"

The italics are Mr. Fisher's.

And he argues that it is "assuming the very question in dispute" to reply, as some do, that the 28th Article teaches a different and the true Doctrine and " that the Church cannot contradict herself;" Mr. F., on the contrary, insists "that the Church is, in several important particulars, inconsistent with herself,"—pp. 297-8. Further, he adds :—

" It is a significant fact that the expression ' *verily and indeed,* is the very expression used in those definitions of the Eucharistic presence, which have at different times been adopted, for the purpose of bringing the sacramental doctrine of the East into the closest possible approximation to that of Rome."—p. 299.

In proof he quotes from *Neale's Hist. of the Eastern Church*, and *Palmer's Dissertations*, the Decree of the Council of Bethlehem, 1671—2.

It will not be out of place to insert here an extract from one of the

" Articles of Religion, agreed upon by the Archbishops and Bishops, and the rest of the Clergie of Ireland, in the Convocation holden at Dublin in the year of our Lord God 1615, for the avoyding of Diuersities of Opinion : and the establishing of consent touching true Religion."

The passage is as follows :—

" Of the Lord's Supper.

" In the outward part of the Holy Communion the Body and Blood of Christ is in a most lively manner represented : being no otherwise present with the visible Elements, than things signified and sealed are present with the signes and seales, that is to say, symbolically and relatively. But in the inward and spirituall part, the same Bodie and Bloud is **really** and **substantially** presented unto all those, who have grace to receive the Sonne of God, even to all those that beleeve on His Name. And unto such as in this manner doe worthily and with Faith repaire unto the Lorde's Table, the Bodie and Bloud of Christ is not only signified and offered, but also truely exhibited and communicated."—*Eccl. Injunctions*, 1559-1732, in B. Museum.

The rest of the Article is composed of the English Articles 28, 29, 30, and 31, with some slight variations. I quote the passage as an instance of the authoritative use of the words, " really and substantially" in reference to the *inward* part of this Sacrament—the " Bodie and Bloud " of Christ—which the Article seems to teach is thus "presented" to the worthy communicant only, though They are " represented" by " the outward part " to all " in a most lively manner." The definition is curious, making, apparently a Symbolical and *Real* Objective Presence to one class of Communicants—the worthy : a *Symbolical* Objective Presence only to another class—the unworthy.

Here it will be convenient, as I am referring to the Church Catechism, to notice Mr. Goode's objection to the sense attached to the words "*the faithful*" by the writers he is opposing : he says (*Supplement*, p. 24) that :—

"....where the common sense of every impartial reader tells him, that the words were meant to indicate that the Body and Blood of Christ were taken and received by *the faithful only*,* ....Dr. Pusey would fain have us suppose, that the Catechism maintains with him, that *all* receive the inward part, the Body and Blood, in receiving the outward ; but the faithful alone receive *the grace* that flows from them.   But this is directly contrary to what the Catechism really says, for it clearly limits the reception of *the Body and Blood* to *the 'faithful.'*

" The only possible mode of explaining away this statement of the Catechism is, either to say with Archdeacon Denison, that the statement does not mean to deny that the Body and Blood of Christ may be received by the *unfaithful* just as much as by the faithful ; or with one of his defenders, that the phrase ' the faithful ' merely means here all the baptized, that is, in fact, everybody who comes to communicate ; both which explanations I willingly leave in the hands of the reader."

This last sentence of course means, that no "reader " is likely to give any credence to these "explanations."   But, as it would be worse than useless to pen a Catechism in language of a loose and unauthorized character so, we may be sure that the terms employed in 1604 were such as had a definite Theological import.   Whether either of these " explanations " indicates the true meaning of the words seems, at least, worth considering ; and it might have been more to the purpose if, instead of thus remitting them to his readers, Mr. Goode had suggested some mode of determining who *are* meant by " the faithful " in the Catechism.

Perhaps Mr. Goode might reply that he has examined this point in the "Work" to which the "Supplement" belongs ; but, except a short passage in p. 754, I cannot find anything that really touches the question : Mr. Goode says :—

" I observe that an attempt has been made to affix to the words ' the faithful,' in that portion of the Catechism commented upon in pp. 668 et seq., above, the meaning of *all baptized Christians* as distinguished from *the heathen*.   To this, indeed, Archdeacon Denison himself alludes in his Sermon ; but as he declined to

---

* I omit some rather uncourteous language.

'insist' upon it, I did not think it worth while to detain the reader to discuss it. In reply to such an argument, I think it sufficient to point out, that all the numerous Commentaries on the Catechism that have ever been written by Archbishops, Bishops, and Divines of all views and parties, have agreed in interpreting the words as referring to true believers ; . . . ."—p. 754.

Mr. Goode had previously given (pp. 697—726) a series of extracts from *twenty-one* such Commentaries, ranging from 1623 to 1790: they appear to me, however, to contribute barely anything towards the settlement of the points which he notices in the above passages: an examination of them seems to furnish the following results : —

EIGHT, *not to the purpose*, viz. :—

" Dr. Comber, 1683 ; Bp. Ken, 1685 ; Bp. John Williams, 1690 ; Revd. John Lewis, 1700 ; Dr. Edwd. Wells, 1707 ; Bp. Burnet, 1710 ; Revd. James Salter, 1753 ; and Bp. Mann, 1790.

FOUR, *inadequate, viz.* :—

Bp. Nicholson, 1655 ; Dr. Simon Ford, 1684, who only says that " none but believers thus [*i.e.*, spiritually and by faith] receive them [*i.e.*, the Body and Blood of Christ] " ; Bp. Beveridge, 1704 ; and Revd. John Olyffe, 1710.

THREE, only speak of *worthy* receivers, viz. :—

The Oxford Catechism, 1679 ; Rev. Joseph Harrison, 1718 ; and Archn. Waterland, 1730.

THREE support, in different degrees, Mr. Goode's view, *viz.* :—

Dr. Mayer, 1623, who speaks of 'faith making Him [Christ] present unto the worthy receiver ; Abp. Wake, 1697, who says, " that which is given by the Priest . . . . The very Body and Blood of Christ as yet it is not. But being with faith and piety received by the Communicant, it becomes to him . . . . the very Body and Blood of Christ ;" and Rev. Peter Newcombe, 1712, who, denying "Christ's Body and Blood " to be " carnally present in these ele-ments," asserts " that a real Presence is not to be sought in " them, " but in the worthy communicants."

The remaining *three* seem to me to be favourable to those whom Mr. Goode is opposing, *viz.* :—

Revd. James Stillingfleet, 1787 ; Abp. Secker, 1771, who says,

" ....in one sense, all communicants equally partake of what Christ calls His Body and Blood, that is, the outward signs of them; yet in a much more important sense, *the faithful* only, the pious and virtuous receiver, eats His flesh, and drinks His Blood; shares in the life and strength derived to men from His incarnation and death :
.... In appearance the Sacrament of Christ's death is given to all alike; but *verily and indeed*, in its beneficial effects, to none besides the faithful. Even to the unworthy communicant He is present, as He is wherever we meet together in His name; but in a better and most gracious sense to the worthy soul; becoming, by the inward virtue of His Spirit, its food and sustenance." *

Dr. Sherlock, 1660, is the remaining one of these three; Mr. Goode quotes him as stating that :—

" .... as the bread and wine are truly taken and received corporally, so verily and indeed is the Body and Blood of Christ taken and received spiritually of every true faithful soul in the Lord's Supper if rightly administered."

But, as such language does not necessarily *exclude* a belief that those who are not " true faithful" communicants receive in some way the Body and Blood of Christ so, Sherlock's own words, published thirteen years later in his " Practical Christian " (1673) shew that he saw no contradiction in the two views; especially as his *Catechism* was reprinted during his lifetime (1677): the following passages from the " Practical Christian (*Ed.* 1846) seem to me to leave no doubt as to what he held :—

" The Sacramental Body of Christ is the consecrated elements of bread and wine in the Sacrament. This is expressly affirmed by our Lord saying, ' This is My Body, This is My Blood.' Who then dare say, (as the Fathers frequently observe,) This is not His Body, but a figure of His Body only?
" He discerns not this Body of our Lord, 1. who sees not with the eye of faith, Christ really present, under the species of Bread and Wine, though he conceive not the manner thereof . . . ."
" Those old verses, expressing the faith of the wisest of our first

* It is desirable to record here Archbishop Secker's opinion of the meaning of *The Declaration* in what it says as to *kneeling* :—" It is true, we also kneel at the Sacrament, as they [the Romanists] do: but for a very different purpose : not to acknowledge *any corporeal presence of Christ's natural flesh and blood;* as our Church, to prevent all possibility of misconstruction expressly declares; adding that *His body is in Heaven, and not here:* but to worship Him, who is everywhere present, the invisible God....." Compare the *Note*, p. 117, on the " Opinion" of the Bishop of St. Andrews.

Reformers, may satisfy every modest, humble, and sober-minded good Christian in this great mystery of godliness :

> ' It was the Lord that spake it,
> He took the Bread and brake it ;
> And what the Word did make it,
> So I believe and take it.'

" 2.   .   .   .   .

" 3. He discerns not this Sacramental Body of the Lord, who prepares not himself to receive the same with all 'reverence and godly fear ;' with ' hands washed in innocency ;' and into a ' pure and clean heart ;' into a soul ' cleansed from all filthiness, both of flesh and spirit ;'* and perfumed (as was our Lord's crucified Body) with the sweet odours of humility and compunction, of love and devotion, of obedience and charity.

.   .   .   .

" And he that receives Christ's holy Body and Blood into his soul, not first emptied of all his sins by holy faith, and all the sacred offices of true repentance, doth, with Judas, betray his Master into the hands of His enemies which crucified Him : for those were our sins. And therefore it is said of such unworthy receivers, that ' they are guilty of the Body and Blood of Christ.' "—Vol. I., pp. 182-4.†

If, then, Bishop Sherlock could write thus when dealing *expressly* with this question (though Mr. Goode's citation of his Catechism might lead to an opposite inference) it may well be that, many at least of, the other writers just noticed would have coincided with Bishop Sherlock if they had felt themselves obliged to discuss the point which he considered. It was one thing for them to write explicitly on,

---

* The following Prayer (which I do not quote as of any *authority now*, but only as an old explanation of the being "guilty of the Body and Blood of the Lord) occurs in the Sarum Primer of 1541 * and in Thomas Petyt's Editions of 1543 B. M.—C. 35 c.   1544 B. M. $\frac{\text{C. 35 b.}}{1-2.}$

" *When thou hast receyved the sacrament.*

"The verye true receyuynge of thy gloryous body of flesshe and bloode : my soueraygne lorde omnypotent is, that I caste it not forthe agayne to my dampnacyon and judgement but that I may optayne thereby remyssyon of my synnes : and that I may lyue in charytable lyfe whyles I am here lyuynge, so that I maye hereafter comme to eternall lyfe, by the vertue and grace.   So be it."

† Mr. Goode (pp. 864-6) tries, ineffectually as I think, to reconcile this language with his own views.

* This Primer (with other Books and a super-altare) was found, August 5, 1857, in the North wall of the (now rebuilt) Chancel of St. Mary the Virgin, Addington, Bucks. The only other copy, I believe, of this Edition is preserved in the Library of Stonyhurst College. In the first Prayer of the Dirige are the words, "and forgive them all their sins," which Mr. Maskell says (Mon. Rit., Vol. II., p. 121, Note) do not occur in any of the Editions of Henry VIIIth's Latin and English Primers which he had seen.

what I may call, the *positive* side of the Catechism, seeing that all concurred in the belief—that *worthy* Communicants received (in whatever manner) "the Body and Blood of Christ" with all Its "benefits;" quite another thing for them to argue the *negative* side, especially as there had always been great divergency of opinion in the Church as to the way in which those who discerned not the Lord's Body in the Sacrament were to be accounted guilty of It.

But it never can be unfair to interpret the language of a writer by his known opinions, unless there is clear evidence that he meant to speak in a different sense; if, therefore, as is commonly supposed, the Catechetical Questions on the Sacraments are due to Bishop Overall, his own supposed * statements elsewhere ought to be a satisfactory proof of his meaning in the Catechism: one (and the most pertinent) of these has been already given in full at p. 137 : here, therefore, it may suffice to quote the words—". . . the Body and Blood of Christ is really and substantially present, and so exhibited and given to all that receive it ; . . ."

In the extracts given from Mr. Goode at p. 286, he objects to any attempt to "affix to the words 'the faithful'"

---

* I say "supposed" because Mr. Goode (pp. 827-8) contends that the Notes in which these passages are contained "were neither written by Overall, nor claim the authority of being derived from his papers." And he adds, "By whom they were written cannot now probably be ascertained, but certainly it was not Bishop Cosin, who was Overall's chaplain, because his Notes, as we shall see presently, are of a very different kind."

But the learned Editor of Bishop Cosin's Notes (*Ang. Cath. Lib.*) carefully re-investigated this question of Authorship, and came to the conclusion that the whole three Series of Notes are Bishop Cosin's ; and thus he more than supports Dr. Nicholl's original remark, which Mr. Goode deems insufficient, that they are "supposed to be made from the Collections of Bishop Overall, by a friend or chaplain of his." Until, then, the result of this later enquiry is set aside by fresh evidence, the Notes may still be used as possessing the authority hitherto claimed for them.

As to Bishop Cosin's "Notes" being "of a very different kind:" the example which Mr. Goode gives (p. 855) will be found above, p. 138, where I have commented upon it: this Note is from the 2nd Series, contained in a Prayer Book of 1638, and supposed to have been written between 1638 and 1656: the Note cited in the text is from the 1st Series, which is believed to have been written between 1619 and 1638, and is found in a Prayer Book of 1619: the 3rd Series occurs in a MS. Book, and is considered to be mostly before 1640. But the very fact of the *difference* which Mr. Goode notices goes to shew that the earlier Note was, all the more probably, Overall's ; especially if it be the case, as is thought, that Bishop Cosin did alter his opinions in some respects in the course of writing those Notes.

the signification of *the Baptized* or the *Communicants*: it becomes necessary, therefore, to inquire whether this is at all a *new* meaning or is not rather a return to the definite Theological and Ecclesiastical sense in which the term has always been employed. In order to trace this, it will be best to examine—I. *The places in which it occurs in the New Testament.* They are the following :—

(a) Eph. i. 1. ".... to the *saints* which are at Ephesus, and to the *faithful* in Christ Jesus."

(b) Col. i. 2. "To the *saints* and *faithful* brethren in Christ which are at Colosse."

(c) 1 Tim. iv. 10. " .... the Saviour of all men, specially of those that *believe.*"

(d) 1 Tim. iv. 12. " .. be thou an example of the *believers..* "

(e) 1 Tim. v. 16. " If any man or woman that *believeth* have widows, let them relieve them .. "

(f) 1 Tim. vi. 2. "And they that have *believing* masters let them .... rather do them service because they are *faithful....*"

(g) 2 Tim. ii. 2. " .... the same commit thou to *faithful* men...."

(h) Titus i. 6. " .... having *faithful* children .... "

It will hardly be pretended, I suppose, that the first two passages, (a) and (b) do not refer to the *entire* body of the Christians, *i.e,,* the Baptized, in Ephesus and Colosse : nor is there anything to shew that the next three (c), (d) and (e) are to be taken in a more exclusive sense ; or that the "masters" spoken of in the following passage (f) are the *good* "believing" ones as distinguished from *Christian* masters in general : the succeeding passage (g) would naturally be taken primarily in the more limited sense of *trustworthy*, no less than well-instructed, Christians ; though, if they afterwards proved to be unreliable in their conduct, the word "faithful" would still not be inapplicable in regard of their Church-membership: while, as to the last instance (h), it can scarcely be supposed that St. Paul meant to forbid Titus to "ordain " any as " elders " unless their children were all *true* and *sincere* Christians, as well as being professed members of the Church, *i.e.* "faithful."

II. *Passages where it is found in the Ancient Liturgies.*

1. Liturgy of S. Mark.

(*a.*) " .. bless Thy *faithful* and orthodox people ; increase them to myriads of myriads.. ."—*Neale's Translation,* p. 10.

(*b.*) " Bless Thy *faithful* and orthodox people, them that do Thy holy will, with a thousand thousand and ten thousand times ten thousand blessings."—p. 20.

2. LITURGY OF ST. JAMES.

(*c.*) " . . . Thou only art holy,'Who sanctifiest, and art distributed to, Thy *faithful* people ; . . ."—p. 32.

(*d.*) " . . . the King of kings and Lord of lords, Christ our God, cometh forward to be sacrificed and to be given for food to the *faithful* ; . . ."—p. 40.

(*e.*) " The Lord shall bless us, and make us to receive with the pure tongs of our fingers the burning coal, and to place it in the mouths of *the faithful,* for the purification and renewal of their souls, and bodies, now and ever.

" O taste and see that the Lord is good : He that is broken, and not divided, distributed to *the faithful,**** and not consumed, for the remission of their sins and eternal life, now and ever, and to all ages."—p. 60.

3. LITURGY OF ST. CLEMENT.

(*f.*) " *And let all* THE FAITHFUL, *as they will, pray for them* [the Catechumens], *saying,* Lord have mercy."—p. 66.

(*g.*) "*And let the Deacons say :* Pass forward, ye Energumens. *And after this let him exclaim :* Pray, ye that are illuminated. Let us, *the faithful,* all pray earnestly for them, that the Lord may count them worthy, having been initiated into the death of Christ ......
Thou that .... didst through Christ give them the law of spiritual regeneration,—do Thou Thyself now look upon the baptized, and bless them and hallow them, and prepare them so as to be worthy of Thy spiritual gift, and the true adoption of Thy spiritual mysteries, the gathering together with them that are saved, through Christ our Saviour."—p. 70.

(*h.*) "*And let the Deacon say :* Depart, ye that are in penitence. *And let him add :* Let none of those that are not able to pray with us, pass forward : let as many as are *faithful* kneel with us."—p. 76.

(*i.*) "*And let the Deacon stand at the doors of the men, and the Sub-Deacons at those of the women, that no one may go out, and that the door may not be opened, even though it be by one of* THE FAITHFUL, *during the time of the anaphora.*"—p. 76.

4. LITURGY OF ST. CHRYSOSTOM.

(*k.*) " *Deacon.* Let all the Catechumens depart ; .... let not any of the Catechumens— ; let all *the faithful ;* — ...."—p. 105.

---

* Compare this and 2 *c.* with the following: " The Lamb of God is broken and distributed ; He that is broken and not divided in sunder; ever eaten and

(*l.*) " *The first prayer of* THE FAITHFUL, *after the unfolding of the Corporal.*"—p. 105.

(*m.*) " *The second prayer of* THE FAITHFUL."—p. 106.

5. LITURGY OF MALABAR.

(*n.*) " .... Pray, bearing in memory .... all *the faithful* who have departed from the living and are dead in the true faith."— p. 141.

It can hardly be questioned, I think, that in all these places (except 5 (*n.*) which refers to those who died in Church *communion;* and, *perhaps,* I. (*a.*) and (*b.*), which *possibly* include THE BAPTIZED in general) the word "*faithful*" means strictly THE COMMUNICANTS ; *i.e.* not only those who at any given Celebration *actually* communicated, but also all who were not *prevented* from communicating by any rule of Discipline. The expression "*the Communicants,*" in the Liturgy of St. Chrysostom, which is plainly the synonym of " *Thy faithful people* " and " *the faithful* " in the Liturgy of St. James, seems to me to prove this: while that (unless in the instances I have excepted) the term "*the faithful*" has this limitation, appears, also, to be shewn by the exhortation to *them,* in the Liturgy of St. Clement, to "pray earnestly" for "*the illuminated,*" i.e. "*the baptized,*" as the context shews.

III. *The testimony of Ecclesiastical Writers or Historians.*

And here it will be quite sufficient to quote Bingham, as his words do but profess to sum up the testimony of authorities whom he names. Thus he says, "in all which accounts" it is " proper to be remarked :"—

" That the name believers, Πιστοὶ, and *Fideles,* is here taken, in a more strict sense, only for one order of Christians,—the believing or baptized laity, in contradistinction to the clergy and the Catechumens, the two other orders of men in the Church. And in this sense, the words Πιστοὶ and *Fideles* are commonly used in the ancient Liturgies, and Canons, to distinguish those THAT WERE BAPTIZED, AND ALLOWED TO PARTAKE OF THE HOLY MYSTERIES, never consumed, but sanctifying THE COMMUNICANTS."—*Lit. of S. Chrysostom,* p. 121.

It is worth while to notice also this sentence as illustrative of the following passage in a Rubric at the end of the Communion Office in the Prayer Book of 1549:—"... every one [*i.e.,* of the Wafer Breads] shall be divided in two pieces, at the least, or more, by the discretion of the minister, and so distributed. And men must not think less to be received in part than in the whole, but in each of them the whole body of our Saviour Jesu Christ."

from the Catechumens, whence came that ancient distinction of the service of the Church into the *Missa Catechumenorum,* and *Missa Fidelium*; . . ."—*Eccl. Antiq.*, Bk. I., c. 3, § 3.

" The Πιστοὶ, or *Fideles*, being such as were baptized, and thereby made complete and perfect Christians, were, upon that account, dignified with several titles of honour and marks of distinction above the Catechumens :" viz., φωτιζόμινοι, *The Illuminate;* Ὁι Μεμνημίνοι, *The Initiated;* Τίλειοι, *The Perfect ;*—*Ib.* c. 4, § § 1, 2, 3.

" All these names (and many others might be added, which are obvious to every reader, such as Saints, and Sons of God, &c.) were peculiar titles of honour and respect, given only to those who were Πιστοὶ, or *Believers*."—*Ib.* § 4.

"And hence it was that, correspondent to these names, the *Fideles* had their peculiar privileges in the Church above the Catechumens. For first, it was their sole prerogative to partake of the Lord's Table, and communicate with one another in the symbols of Christ's body and blood at the altar . . . . ."—*Ib.* § 5.

"Another of their prerogatives above Catechumens was, to stay and join with the minister in all the prayers of the Church, which the Catechumens were not allowed to do ; . . . ."—*Ib.* § 6.

" More particularly the use of the Lord's prayer was the sole prerogative of the Πιστοὶ, or *Believers ;* for then it was no crime, or argument of weakness, or want of the spirit, to use it ; but an honour and privilege of the most consummate and perfect Christians . . ."—*Ib.* § 7,

" Lastly, They were admitted to be auditors of all discourses made in the Church, even those that treated of the most abstruse points and profound mysteries of the Christian religion ; which the Catechumens were strictly prohibited from hearing . . . . . when the Catechumens were dismissed, then they discoursed more openly of their mysteries before the *Fideles* . . . . . and in these, and the like privileges, consisted their prerogative above the Catechumens."—*Ib.* § 8.

No one can deny that *the baptized* have as full privileges in the Modern, as they had in the Ancient Church.

It must be borne in mind, too, that this Greek word Πιστοὶ (of which *Fideles* is the Latin equivalent) is *the Original* in *all* the places cited from the New Testament and from the Ancient Liturgies.

IV. *The places in which the term has been or is employed in the English Prayer Book.*

These will be most readily seen and compared in the following Tabular collection of them from all the Editions, together with the Latin translation in Queen Elizabeth's Book of 1560.

Coll. 4th Sunday after Easter.	"Almighty God, Which dost make the minds of all *faithful* men to be of one will: grant unto *Thy people*," &c.	"O Almighty God, Who alone canst order the unruly wills and affections of sinful men: grant unto *Thy People*," &c.	"Deus, qui *fidelium* mentes unius efficis voluntatis," &c.
Whitsunday.	"God, Which as upon this day hast taught [Who as at this time didst teach—1604 & 1662] the hearts of Thy *faithful* people," &c.	"Deus, qui corda *fidelium* sancti Spiritus illustratione docuisti," &c.
13th Sunday after Trinity.	"Almighty and merciful God, of Whose only gift it cometh that Thy *faithful* people do unto Thee true and laudable service;" &c.	"Omnipotens & misericors Deus, a cujus beneficentia proficiscitur ut tibi a *fidelibus* tuis digne & laudabiliter serviatur," &c.
21st Sunday after Trinity.	"Grant, we beseech Thee, merciful Lord, to Thy *faithful* people pardon and peace," &c.	"Largire, quæsumus, Domine, *fidelibus* tuis veniam placatus & pacem," &c.
25th Sunday after Trinity.	"Stir up, we beseech Thee, O Lord, the wills of Thy *faithful* people," &c.	"Excita, quæsumus, Domine, tuorum *fidelium* voluntas [voluntates]," &c.
Post Communion.	"Thy Mystical body [the Mystical body of Thy Son—1604 & 1662] which is the blessed company of all *faithful* people," &c.	"in corpore tuo mystico [incorporata], quod est sancta communio omnium *fidelium*," &c.
Burial of the Dead.	"Almighty God [1549—O Lord] with Whom do live the spirits of them that [be dead—1549] depart hence in the Lord, and in Whom the souls of [them that *be elected*—1549 to 1604] *the faithful*, after they are [be—1549 to 1604] delivered from the burden of the flesh, are [be—1549 to 1604] in joy and felicity;" &c.	"Omnipotens Deus, apud quem vivunt spiritus illorum, qui hinc decesserunt, & quocunq; animæ *electorum*, postquam exuerunt onus hujus carnis, lætitia & felicitate fruuntur," &c.

Now it is observable that every one of these passages (except that out of the Burial Service) is from *The Communion Office*, i.e. *The Liturgy;* for the *Collects* are, of course, a part of that Office. In all reason therefore we ought to interpret the word "faithful" according to continuous Ecclesiastical usage, unless anything has been anywhere said to imply the contrary; so far, however, is this from being the case, that everything we know about the history of the English Liturgy, whether as first compiled in 1549 or as subsequently Revised, proves that the intention all along was to make it embody the mind of Primitive Antiquity, especially as set forth in the Primitive Liturgies so far as they were then known, or were embodied in the USES which had long been familiar in this Kingdom.

The language of the five Collects quoted shews that "the faith-faithful" there spoken of are they who, being baptized, are Ecclesiastically *capable* of receiving those *Gifts* of God which are designed to procure for them the various *Benefits* of His Grace supplicated in the Collects themselves; possessing this *capacity* they are admitted (according to the Discipline of the Church as received and exercised in this English portion of it) to that COMMUNION which is a Divinely appointed means of conveying the requisite Gifts: but a *capacity* to *receive* a Gift by no means necessarily implies a *disposition* to *profit* by that Gift: and as, in the case now under consideration, it is obviously impossible that any exercise of Discipline could absolutely declare the existence of such *disposition*, so the terms of a Liturgy must necessarily be limited to that *capacity* of which alone the Church can be cognizant. Hence, as it seems to me, the necessity for those words of the *"Exhortation"* given *"at the time of the celebration of the Communion"* which emphatically point out the distinction between *Sacramental* and *Spiritual* participation of " that holy Sacrament ;" asserting that " as the benefit is great" to those who "receive" It with "a true penitent heart and lively faith . . . . so is the danger great" to them who "receive the same unworthily"—because the former " spiritually eat the Flesh of Christ and drink His Blood," whereas the latter eat and drink . . . . damnation [*i.e.* judgment], not considering the Lord's Body"; inasmuch as they "presume to eat of that bread and drink of that cup" which is "the holy Communion [*i.e.* communication] of" It. Hence, again, the need for that most expressive "SO" in the *Prayer of Access* (found practically, too, in the Ancient Liturgies*) which it is impossible to gloss over as though it was not designed to mean that there is a way "to eat the Flesh of" God's "dear Son, and to drink His Blood" in which the Benefits sought for by that Prayer cannot be obtained.

Again, take the sentence above quoted from the 2nd Postcommunion prayer; it can only be, as I think, by entirely ignoring the old Ecclesiastical sense of the words that the "all faithful people," who are there said to be the "mystical Body" of Christ, can be limited to those *really pious* and *godly* ones of the Church of whom it could scarcely be doubted that they "be meet partakers of these Holy Mysteries."

The passage from the Burial Service may appear at first sight to present an exception to that meaning of the words "*the faithful*," which I am here alleging to be the true one.

---

* *Liturgy of S. Mark.*—". . . Enlighten our soul with the divine rays of Thy Holy Spirit, that we, being filled with the knowledge of Thee, may worthily participate in the good things that are set before us, the spotless Body and precious Blood of Thine only-begotten Son, our Lord and Saviour Jesus Christ; . . ."—*Neale's Transl.*, p. 26.

Liturgy of S. James.—"*Priest, (before communicating)* . . . do Thou, who art a compassionate God, make me worthy by Thy grace to communicate without condemnation in the holy Body and precious Blood, for the remission of sins, and eternal life."—p. 61.

Liturgy of S. Clement.—"*And let the Deacon say,* . . . Having received the precious Body and precious Blood of Christ, . . . let us beseech Him that they may not be to us to judgment, but to salvation; . . ."—p. 90.

Liturgy of S. Chrysostom.—"*The Priest meanwhile saith secretly,* . . . make us worthy to partake of Thy heavenly and terrible mysteries of this holy and spiritual Table, with a pure conscience, for the remission of sins, forgiveness of transgressions, participation of the Holy Ghost, inheritance of the kingdom of heaven, boldness of access to Thee: not to judgment nor to condemnation."—p. 119.

Liturgy of Malabar.—"*The Priest saith:* . . . make us also worthy, by Thy love, that in all pureness and holiness we may receive the gift: and that it may not be unto us for judgment or vengeance, but for love and piety and the remission of sins, and resurrection from the dead, and eternal life: . . ."—p. 154. Other passages will be found at pp. 24, 25, 29, 61, 89, 119, 122, 154.

Q Q

It will, perhaps, be said that—granting the term, as elsewhere employed in the Prayer Book, to have the comprehensive sense contended for; it must be taken in a more limited sense here, where "*the faithful*" are pronounced to be "in joy and felicity;" and therefore it may have the like contracted meaning in the Catechism.

But, it seems to me, that the expression as here employed, so far from having a meaning at variance with its use in the other places cited from the Prayer Book, is entirely in accordance with them; because it is no more limited than they are to those whom I suppose Mr. Goode includes in the term "true believers." The way in which it is used in the Liturgy of Malabar * (See 5 (*n.*) p. 293) supports this opinion.

A reference to the Table (p. 295) will shew that the term was first inserted in this Office at the last Review (1662); and was then substituted for the expression "*the Elected*" which had been used up to that time in all the Reformed Prayer Books, and which was taken from the Salisbury Manual.† Now, though no other key is furnished to the meaning of the words than the context of the Prayer, it can hardly be supposed that it was used in a *narrower* sense than the words "saints," "faithful," "believers," quoted at p. 291 from the Apostolical Epistles, or than the word "*elect*" as applied to these persons in any of those same Epistles (Coloss. iii. 12; 2 Tim. ii. 10; Tit. i. 1) or to those "strangers" whom St. Peter addresses (1 Pet. i. 1 & 2).

Yet, whether this be or be not accepted as the true explanation of "*the Elected*," we are not left without a guide to the meaning of "*the faithful*"; for, when the former term was exchanged for the latter, a new Rubric was prefixed to the Office, distinctly limiting its use by saying, "*Here it is*

---

* The same *idea* is preserved in the following passages.
LITURGY OF ST. MARK.—"Give rest to . . . . every spirit that has departed in the faith of Christ. . . ."—*Neale's Trans.* p. 17.
LITURGY OF ST. CHRYSOSTOM.—"And further we offer to Thee this reasonable service on behalf of those who have departed in the faith. . . ."—p. 117.

† "Deus, apud quem spiritus mortuorum vivunt, et in quo *electorum* animæ deposito carnis onere plena felicitate lætantur," &c.—*Palmer*, Orig. Lit. p. 237.

to be noted, that the Office ensuing is not be used for any that die unbaptized, or excommunicate, or have laid violent hands upon themselves." So, then, while by not using the Office in these three cases the Church of England would abstain from any judgment upon them, and would leave them to the justice and mercy of God, she intended to regard all others as *" the faithful,"* and so partakers of *"joy and felicity"*— varying, we may well believe, with the varied degrees of faith and holiness in which they departed this life.

It will be no answer to this view to say—that this Office is often used for those who *ought* to be among the " excommunicate ;" for the Office, as revised in 1662, contemplated the *continued use*—or rather, the *stricter application*—of that DISCIPLINE enjoined in the Laws of the Church—Laws of whose existence the Canons of 1603-4 alone bear abundant proof; however much, whether from necessity, or unfitness, or other causes, they have, to a great extent, fallen into abeyance. It follows, therefore, that the Church meant to regard as *" the faithful"* all *validly baptized* persons (except such as "laid violent* hands upon themselves ") who had not been severed from her Communion by a "sentence of excommunication pronounced against them " (Can. 65) by an Ec-

---

* I must confess myself unable to agree with those who think that "violent hands" must be limited to cases pronounced by a Coroner's Jury to be *felo de se:* it is no want of charity, I trust, which compels me to believe that the Church of England did not contemplate *in this Rubric* any distinction between such cases and those in which a verdict of " temporary insanity" is given, but meant to forbid the use of *the Office* in both, though not the interment of the *latter* in consecrated ground : Wheatley (*Com. Prayer,* p. 481) supports this view : Shakspeare, too, represents this as the rule of his day—a rule from which, as it seems to me, the Church of England has not in theory departed : *Ophelia,* though " crowner's quest law" gave her " *Christian* burial," for else " She should in ground unsanctified have lodg'd," was only buried with " maimed rites;" for when *Laertes* asked, "What ceremony more ?" the *Priest* answered, " Her obsequies have been as far enlarg'd as we have warranty : Her death was doubtful;" (*Hamlet,* Act V.)

No doubt there are cases in which the omission of the Office would be a great trial to the friends of the deceased; but then it should be remembered (and would so far be a consolation) that, while its omission can be no injury to souls so passing out of this life (for God is their Judge), it might have a most salutary effect in deterring from self-destruction others for whom no sound plea could be urged. It is to be feared that (so-called) *charitable* verdicts and *charitable* use of the Burial Office in cases of suicide may have lessened the dread of the act itself, and so have encouraged its more frequent commission.

clesiastical Judge : the 68th Canon, treating of this impediment to Burial, says that " No Minister shall refuse " to
bury, "except the party deceased were denounced excommunicated *majori excommunicatione,* for some grievous and
notorious crime, and no man able to testify of his repentance."
But it is clear, from an inspection of her Laws, that such a
punishment would not be lightly inflicted even for those
greater offences to which it was limited ; and as, what would
be called, "truly religious people"—those bringing forth
" some sixty, some an hundred-fold"—ever bear but a small
proportion to ordinary Christians—the yielders of " thirty-
fold, so " *the faithful* " must of necessity have a meaning sufficiently large to comprehend the least and the feeblest of
those who are in any degree *willing* to do Christ service, as
members of the Household of Faith, however much hindered
by causes which must be remitted to that "Master" to Whom
each " standeth or falleth."

Moreover, unless the Liturgy is to be construed by a
different rule from the Articles, the XIXth Article plainly
supports the sense here alleged to be the true meaning of the
term " the faithful " in the places cited from the Prayer Book
Offices, when it says that " The visible Church of Christ is a
congregation of *faithful* men ; " and if there could well be a
doubt of the *comprehensive* meaning of the word here, the last
clause disposes of it by saying that certain portions of this
"congregation of faithful men" "*have erred* . . . . not only
in their living and manner of Ceremonies, but also in matters
of Faith."   Not the less strongly, though even more clearly
for the present argument, the XXXIIIrd Article teaches that
every one who is in " the unity of the Church " must be
reckoned in " the whole multitude of *the faithful;*" and " that
person" is evidently accounted to be in such unity who has
not been " rightly cut off from" it " by open denunciation of
the Church:" so that here a distinct meaning is authoritatively
assigned to the term " *the faithful*" by making it the equivalent of those who are *not formally* " *excommunicate.*"

Besides, the analogy of other similar words which are used

in the Prayer Book, serves to sustain that meaning of the expression "the faithful" to which Mr. Goode demurs: thus— " make Thy *chosen* people joyful" (*Matins, &c.*); " all estates of men in Thy *Holy* Church" (*Coll. Good Friday*); "the prayers of Thy *humble* servants" (*Coll. 10th Sund. aft. Trin.*); "Thine *elect*" (*Coll. for All Saints Day*); "*Good* people, these are they whom we purpose," &c. (*Ord. of Priests*) —these, one and all, refer to Christians in their *corporate* character; yet they cannot but *imply* the same truth which the xxvith Article *expresses* when declaring that "in the visible Church the evil be ever mingled with the good."

It rests with those who deny that the sense here contended for is the *true* sense of the words " the faithful" in the Catechism, to shew that in that Formulary they were *designed* to have a meaning wholly different from what I have argued must, in all consistency, be regarded as the meaning of " the faithful" in the other instances cited from the Prayer Book—*fideles* (πιστοί) being in every case the Latin equivalent, just as in the examples previously quoted from Ecclesiastical Antiquity.

At p. 72 of the Letter (after quoting a passage from Bishop Burnet to shew that it was " chiefly by *Gawden's* means " the Declaration on Kneeling was restored to the Communion Office in the Book of 1662,) I said that I was unable then to state whether there was " any evidence to shew that *Gawden* did not hold high views of the Real Presence, though denying Transubstantiation: " since that time I have collected what evidence I could procure respecting his Eucharistic belief; and this I now proceed to furnish.

But, first, it will be well to produce another extract from Bishop Burnet, because it gives some additional information as to the support which Bishop Gawden received in proposing the restoration of the Declaration: the passage occurs in the MS. volume* of his " Own Time," now in the British Museum, and is as follows:—

* Lord Macaulay, referring to the MS., says, " These memoirs will be found in a manuscript volume, which is part of the Harleian Collection, and is num-

" There were some small Alterations made in y° Book of.Common Prayer, together with some additions), the most important was y' concerning y° kneeling in y° sacrament, wch had been putt in y° Second Book of Comon Prayer set out by Edward y° 6th, but was left out by Queen Elizabeth, and was now by Bishop Gawden's means put in at y° end of y° office of y° Communion. Sheldon opposed it, but Gawden was seconded by Southampton and Morley. The Duke complained of this much to me, as a puritannical thing, and spake severely of Gawden, as a popular man, for his procuring it to be added (tho' I have been told y^t it was used in King James's time)."—*Harleian MSS.*, 6584.

Bishop Gawden is called by Chalmers (Biog. Dict.) a Prelate " of more fame than character :" certainly he does seem in some degree to have been a time-server. The *Biog. Britannica* states, " We are assured that Gawden took the covenant, notwithstanding he seems to deny it,* and published, in 1643, certain doubts and scruples of conscience about taking the Solemn League and Covenant : he was chosen one of the

---

bered 6584. They are, in fact, the first outlines of a great part of Burnet's History of his Own Times. The dates at which the different portions of this most curious and interesting book were composed are marked. Almost the whole was written before the death of Mary. Burnet did not begin to prepare his History of William's reign for the press till ten years later. By that time his opinions, both of men and things, had undergone great changes. The value of the rough draft is therefore very great: for it contains some facts which he afterwards thought it advisable to suppress, and some judgments which he afterwards saw reason to alter. I must own that I generally like his first thoughts best. Whenever his History is reprinted, it ought to be carefully collated with this volume." —*Hist. of England*, Vol. iii., p. 19, Note. Hearne's opinion of Burnet's History of his Own Time (which, however, does not make the Bishop an incompetent witness to facts) is thus expressed :—" Mar. 19, 1733-4. Learning is sunk so very low, that I am most certainly informed, that nothing now is hardly read but Burnet's romance or libel, called by him, *The History of his Own Time*. 'Tis read by men, women, and children. Indeed it is the common table-book for ladies, as well as gentlemen, especially such as are friends to the Revolution scheme."—*Hearniana*, ii., 808. See also p. 812.

* The following passage from Baxter's Life seems to imply that Gawden did take the Covenant, though with certain expressed or understood qualifications which satisfied his own scruples :—

" § 362. I come now to the non-subscribers' particular scruples, which are such as these.

" I. They say, That all men confessing that *an oath or vow is obligatory*, they must see good proof that *this particular vow* is *not so* before they can exempt it from the common force of vows ; but such proof they have never seen from Mr. *Fullwood*, Mr. *Stileman*, Dr. *Gauden*, or any that hath attempted it, and on whom it is incumbent ; but rather admire that men of so great judgment and tenderness of conscience should ever be satisfied with such halting arguments ; which they had long ago more fully confuted, if the law had not forbidden them."—p. 410, fol. 1696.

Assembly of Divines who met at Westminster in 1643 ;" but appears not to have sat in it, as his name was " struck off the list, and Mr. Thomas Goodwin put into his room."

The earliest publication of his which I have met with is intitled—

" Ἱερὰ Δάχρυα.
" *Ecclesiæ Anglicanæ Suspiria.*

"The TEARS, SIGHS, COMPLAINTS and PRAYERS of the CHURCH OF ENGLAND : setting forth Her former *Constitution*, compared with Her present Condition ; also The visible *Causes*, and probable Cures, of Her *Distempers.* In iv. Books. By JOHN GAUDEN, D.D. of *Bocking* in *Essex.* Jer. 8. 28. ' *Is there* no Balm in Gilead ? is there no Physician there? Why then is not the health of the Daughter of my people recovered ?'

" LONDON, Printed by J. G. for R. Royston, at the Angel in Ivie-Lane, 1659."

The following passages shew what were his opinions at this time.

" Chap. xvi. Irreconcilable differences between Reformed Truths and Romish Errors, which are as manifest and obstinate.

"This is their so great, rude and sacrilegious *maiming* of the *Lord's Supper*, by their partial *communicating* of the *Bread* only to the people, without the Cup ; then their strange *racking of Christians Faith* against all sense and reason, nay beyond all *scripture-phrase* and proportion of Sacramental expressions, or mysterious predications, to believe they doe not receive so much as Bread, but another substance under the accidents and shews of Bread.

" What learned *Romanist* can deny, but that both *Clergy* and *Laity* did, for above a thousand years receive the *Lord's Supper* in both kinds, after the constant use of all Primitive Churches, the Apostles Practise, and Christ's Institution. Nor is there any more doubt, but that the ancient Churches received those *Holy Mysteries* with an high *veneration* indeed of that *Body and Blood of Christ*, which was thereby signified, conveyed and sealed to them in the *truth and merits of the Passion* ; but yet without any *Divine Adoration* of the *Bread and Wine*, or any imagination that they were *transubstantiated* from their own seeming Essence and Nature to the very *Body and Blood of Christ.* Which fancy of (*Metemsomasis*) changing the Body and Substance of *Sacramental signes* into the bodily substance of the Thing *signified* and *represented* by them (as the incomparable *Primate* of *Ireland* hath observed out of *Irenæus*) began from the juglings of one *Marcus* a *Greek Impostor*, or jugling *Presbyter*, who using long *Prayers* at the *Celebration* of the *Eucharist*, had some *device* to make the *Cup* and *Wine* appear of a *purple* or *red* and *bloody colour,* that the people might think at his *invocation* the Grace from above did distill *Blood* into the *Cup.* After this the *imagination* spred from *Greeks* to *Latins,* by popular and credulous fancies, promoted much by one *Paschasius Radbertus,* who in a legendary spirit tells us of *Flesh* and *Blood,* of a *Lamb* and a *little Child,* of appearing to those *Receivers* that were doubtfull of Christ's *corporall presence* ; so he tells of *limbs* and *little fingers* found in the *hands* and *mouths* of *Communicants.* From hence *Damascen* among the *Greeks,* and *P. Lumbard* among the *Latins,* carried on this *credulity,* or vain *curiosity,* using all their wits to make good this strange and impossible transmutation of *disparate subjects* and *sub-stances :* in which having nothing from Sense or Reason, Nature or Philosophy, from Scripture-Analogy, or Sacramentall and Typicall predications, frequent in Scripture (as the *Lamb* is called the *Passeover,* so *Christ* our *Passeover; Christ* the *Rock, Vine, Door ;* these *drie Bones* are the *house of Israel ;* the *seven ears of corne are seven years,* &c. the *Tree is thou, O King)* to prove the *Miracle,* they flie to absolute *omnipotency,* whether God will or no, and shut out all reasoning from *Sense, Philosophy, Scripture.* Nor do they regard ancient *Fathers* and Councils : all which, though highly and justly magnifying the great *Mystery,* yea, and the *Elements* conse-crated, as related to and united with the Body of Christ, as Signs and Seals of its Reality, Truth, use and merit to a sinner; yet generally tbey hold them to be *substantially* and *physically Bread* and *Wine,* but *sacramentally, relatively* or *representatively* (onely) the *Body* and *Blood of Christ :* as the *Council* of *Constantinople anno* 754 consisting of 338 Bishops, did affirm, the *Bread to be the Body of Christ,* not φὺσ'ιι, but θισιι, not in substance, but in resem-blance, use and appointment. Which *Doctrine,* as *Catholic* was maintained to the *Emperor Carolus Calvus,* by *Bertrannus* or *Ratrannus,* anno 880, which was also maintained in *England* by *Johannes Scotus* in King *Alfred's* time, ur.till *Lanfranks* days, *anno* 1060, who condemned that Book of *Scotus* about the Sacrament agreeable to the opinion of *Bertram ;* whose *Homily* expressing his judgement at large against *Transubstantiation,* was formerly read publicly in Churches on *Easter day,* in order to prepare men for the right understanding and due receiving the *Lord's Supper.*

" Nor did the Doctrine of *Transubstantiation* obtain in the Church, untill the year 1225 when Pope *Innocent* the third in the *Council* of *Lateran* published it for an *Oracle, That the Body and Blood of Jesus Christ are truly contained under the forms of Bread and Wine, the Bread being transubstatiated into the Body of Christ, and the Wine into the Blood of Christ, by the power of God.*

" Hence followed the invention of *Concomitancy,* which presuming that the *Communicant* received under the accidents and *shew of Bread,* the whole *Body of Christ,* and so his *Blood,* it was judged rather *superfluous* than *necessary* (yea and lesse safe in some respects) for the *Lay-people* to receive the *Cup* or *Wine*, and *Blood of Christ* apart, as he instituted, and the Church of old, even the *Roman*, constantly practised, as do the *Greeks* at this day, according to what Christ commanded, and in what sense he *gave* it, and *called* it *reall Bread and Wine*: for such he *took*, such he *brake*, such he *blessed*, such he *gave* to the Disciples, when he said, that is, this *Bread*, is my *Body*, this *cup* is my *Blood;* such S. *Paul* understood them to be, and so declares this the mind of Christ, as he had *received* it immediately from Christ, *The Bread which we break, is it not the Communion of the Body of Christ?* For we are all *partakers* of that one Bread. So, *whosoever shall eat this bread and drink this cup unworthily. Let a man examine himself before he eat of that bread.*

" Certainly either the Apostle's expressions must be affectedly very dark, and his meaning different from his words, or he was quite of another mind than the *Papists* are at this day, who durst, in the all-daring *Council of Trent*, damn all those who follow Christs example, use his words, and are of the *Apostle's judgment*, expressing their sense of the *blessed Sacrament* in his words ; which we think much safer to follow, both in the use of *Sacramentall Bread and Wine*, communicated to all Receivers, and in the persuasion we have of our *receiving* true *Bread* and *Wine*, yet duly consecrated, and so *sacramentally* united to the *Reall Body* and *Blood of Christ*, which we faithfully *behold*, thankfully *receive*, and reverently *adore* in that *blessed Mysterie*, according to the ancient Faith, Judgment, Reverence and Devotion of the Church of Christ, void of sacrilegious novelties, and incredible *superstitious vanities*."—pp. 309-11.

Nothing can be clearer than that he distinctly repudiated Transubstantiation : at the same time the language of the last paragraph seems very plainly to enunciate his belief in the Real Objective Presence.

We next meet with him as Bishop of Exeter and learn his opinion, about Kneeling at the Sacrament, as set forth in a Folio Tract, called

" The COUNSELL which the Bishop of EXCESTER delivered to XLIV. PRESBYTERS and DEACONS, after they had been ORDAINED by him (with the assistance of other grave *Ministers*) in the Cathedral Church of Excester, after the Primitive, Catholic, and lawful way of the Church of England. January 13, 1660 [1].

" Printed by *J. Flesher*, and are to be sold by *R. Royston*, Bookseller to his Sacred Majesty, MDCLXI."

The following passages, like those just cited, are printed to correspond with the original :—

" *In like sort as if we had contended for our* Religion and Posterity, *or for the main* points *of* State *and* hinges *of* Empire, *we have canvassed those questions very sadly and superciliously, Whether God looks with more kindness and welcome on those that receive the* Lord's Supper sitting, *or* standing, *or* kneeling. *In which I conceive the* Christians *of the* first Ages *(for the most part) used* standing, *in the* presence *and* service of God ; *and possibly in the* holy Eucharist *too; expressing by the* uprightness *and* readiness *of that* posture *the* Faith *they had as to Christ's* Resurrection, *that great* Article *in which, as in one center, the whole* orb *of* Christian Faith *doth move.* Sitting at Church Tertullian *counts* rude and reproachful to the Divine Majesty ; *not only as too* familiar, *but as impudently testifying a* weariness in His Service.

"In after-ages of the Church, when the Arrian *Pest had infected farre and neare, the* Orthodox Christians *enclined more to* kneeling *at the* Sacrament, *as thereby owning and vindicating the* adorable Majesty *and* Divinity *of* Christ, *one and equal, as* God, *with the* Father *and the* Holy Spirit. *A gesture no doubt* variable, *because not* necessary, *having not the* mark *of* precept *and* institution *upon it, so much as of* occasion *and* custome : *yet it is* lawful *and* commendable, *because according to the general* tenour *and* analogy *of* Divine *worship ; at least it is* free, *and not to be rigidly* exacted, *accordiny to the* first gesture *of Christ, who followed the civil fashion of the* Jewish *nation in their* discumbency *or* lying down *at their* meales, *in a* leaning *posture: which few, if any, of the great* sticklers *against* kneeling *do observe.*

"Besides this, there is without doubt a vast difference *between the* Divine Majesty *of* Christ, *at first* instituting *these Sacred* Mysteries *of the* Lord's Supper *by his* soveraign autority ; *and* us, *poor worthless wretches, celebrating them with that* reverence *and* humility *which becomes our* vileness *and* distance, *when we are to receive those* heavenly dainties *from the* table *and* hands *of Christ with that* duty *and* obedience, adoration *and* gratitude which *is meet. Not that the* efficacy, grace *and* comfort *of the* Holy Sacrament *depends upon the* gesture *of the* Body ; *but upon the faithful, penitent and devout* temper *of the gratious* heart.

" Only it is for certain no sin in a Christian, both to express and excite the inward motives *of an* humble *and* devout soul, *by the* outward gestures *and sutable* motions *of the* body ; *as in* lifting up *the* hands *and* eyes *to heaven, so in the* bowing *of the* head *and* knees *and* whole body *toward the earth : By the one we shew the sense of our own* vileness *and* misery ; *by the other our hopes in God's* mercy *and* benignity."*—pp. 19 and 20.

It was only four months after giving this " counsell" that the Savoy Conference was held, Gauden being one of the Episcopal Commissioners : the Answers of the Bishops to the Puritan demand, that Kneeling at the Sacrament "may be left free," distinctly embody the opinions put forth by Bishop Gauden in both these extracts; thus they say :—

"§ 15. The position of kneeling best suits at the Communion as the most convenient, and so most decent for us, when we are to receive as it were from God's hand the greatest of seals of the kingdom of heaven. He that thinks he may do this sitting, let him remember the prophet Mal. Offer this to the prince, to receive his seal from his own hand sitting, see if he will accept it. When the Chuch did stand at her prayers, the manner of receiving was 'more adorantium,' (S. Aug. Psalm xcviii. Cyril. Catch. Mystag. 5,) rather more than at prayers, since standing at prayer hath been generally left, and kneeling used instead of that (as the Church may vary in such indifferent things). Now to stand at Communion, when we kneel at prayers, were not decent, much less to sit, which was never the use of the best times."—*Card. Hist. Conf.*, p. 350.

The Bishops say that the ancient custom of receiving the Communion was "more adorantium," even " when the Church did stand at her prayers :" Bishop Gauden, one of them, had published two years before that " we faithfully *behold*, thankfully *receive*, and reverently *adore* in that *blessed Mysterie*," the "*Reall Body* and *Blood of Christ*," and, too, " according to the ancient Faith, Judgment, Reverence and Devotion of the Church of Christ, void of sacrilegious novelties, and incredible *superstitious vanities*." Also in his, '' counsell" just noticed, he advocates Kneeling at the Sacrament on this very ground that it is most " suitable" at that time " when we are to receive those heavenly dainties from the table and hands of Christ with that . . . *adoration* and gratitude which is meet." Moreover, his argument throughout this latter Document is quite in accordance with the second Answer of the Bishops upon "The Communion Service," touching Kneeling, in which they say :—

"§ 10. Kneel at Sacr. Concerning kneeling at the Sacrament we have given account already ; only thus much we add, that we conceive it an error to say that the Scripture affirms the Apostles to have received not kneeling. The posture of the paschal supper we know ; but the institution of the holy Sacrament was after supper : and what posture was then used the Scripture is silent. The Rub.

at the end of the 1. Ed. C. that leaves kneeling, crossing, &c., indifferent, is meant only at such times as they are not prescribed and required. But at the Eucharist kneeling is expressly required in the Rub. following."—*Card.* p. 354.

But it was at the very same time when these Answers were given that the *same* Bishops (for there is nothing to shew that Gauden did not concur) as distinctly refused to restore the Declaration on Kneeling, though pressed to do so by the Puritans, "for the vindicating of our Church in the matter of kneeling at the Sacrament (although the gesture be left indifferent):" the Bishops' answer, which it may be as well to repeat here, though given at p. 70, is:—

"§ 12. This Rub. is not in the Liturgy of Queen Elizabeth, nor confirmed by law; nor is there any great need of restoring it, the world being now in more danger of profanation than of idolatry. Besides the sense of it is declared sufficiently in the 28th Article of the Church of England."—*Card.* p. 354.

How came it to pass, then, that (as Burnet tells us) Gauden "pressed" (p. 71) the Declaration, and that by his "means" it was "put in" (p. 302)? It may be, as "the Duke" said "severely," that Gauden did it as "a popular" measure, though it had been "resolved to gratify [the Puritans] in nothing" (p. 71): but then it in no way follows that he regarded it as anything more than a Protest against Transubstantiation: nor is there anything to indicate that the other Bishops viewed it differently; on the contrary their statement that "the sense of it is declared sufficiently in the 28th Article," plainly implies a like belief. It is, indeed, very likely that Gauden thought it would help to neutralize the effect of Puritan opposition if this Declaration against Roman doctrine were again adopted; and it was only what he had himself stated when he wrote (p. 303) "that the ancient churches received those *holy mysteries* with an high *veneration* indeed of that *Body and Blood of Christ*, which was thereby signified, conveyed and sealed to them in the *truth and merits of the Passion;* but yet without any *Divine Adoration* of the *Bread and Wine*, or any imagination that they were *transubstantiated* from their own seeming essence and nature to the very Body and Blood of Christ:" but it is beyond belief, as it seems to me, that he (or indeed his colleagues) could have designed thereby to express any concurrence* in the Puritans' denial of the Real Presence, or in their objection to Adoration, unless we entirely ignore his other statements already quoted, or persuaded ourselves that he had abandoned them.

Yet if this was *Gauden's* wish and design, *Sheldon's* opposition may naturally enough have arisen either from the fear that it would be accounted a concession to the Puritans which might prove inconvenient after the refusal which had been given in the Conference, or from a disinclination to provoke the Roman party by putting forth a Declaration which the Conference had said there was no " great need" of on the score of " danger" from " idolatry." Gunning's proposal to change the words " reall and essentiall" may, most likely, have met the difficulty and may have led to that agreement between Gauden, Gunning, and the Bishops which I ventured to assume (p. 73) took place—an opinion which is certainly confirmed by this additional information which has been considered.

That Gauden's Eucharistic belief, though most clearly opposed to Transubstantiation, not only presented no obstacle to Gunning's proposed change but readily fell in with it, may be further concluded from another work of Gauden's which, after many searches and inquiries in all likely quarters during some eighteen months, I have fortunately met with in the possession of a private individual.† When the Book was written I have been unable to ascertain: the *Biographia*

---

* It is with this qualification that we must read the following passage in *Kennett's Register and Chronicle*, p. 585 : —

" *The Concessions and Alterations that were now made for reforming the Book of Common Prayer.*

" ix. They desired that a Rubrick in the Common Prayer Book in 5 & 6 Edw. vi. for the vindicating of our Church in the matter of kneeling at the Sacrament. without the Declaration, &c., might be restored, and it was so."

Kennett's language reads as if he saw no *distinction* between the old and new *form* of the Declaration, whatever he may have thought both to mean.

† John Nealds, Esq., of Guildford, who, in answer to my enquiry in that most useful publication *Notes and Queries*, obligingly allowed me the loan of it.

Britannica speaks of it as published " Lond. 1681 :" Gauden, however, died Sep. 20, 1662, so that it was either a posthumous publication or a reprint of an Edition published in his life time : but from the circumstance that it was dedicated to "The Lady Rich," who died Nov. 12, 1657, it may most reasonably be concluded to have been published under Gauden's own auspices. The copy from which I now quote is dated 1707, being the Tenth Edition, and bears the *Imprimatur* of Archbishop Sancroft, 1686; whether the Archiepiscopal sanction was then for the first time given, or was appended to the Edition of 1681 or to any earlier Edition* I have not been able to learn : nor is the point material : the sanction of Sancroft, whenever appended, is a sufficient testimony of the value of the book itself. The Title is as follows :—

" The whole duty of a communicant : being rules and directions for a worthy receiving The most Holy Sacrament of the Lord's Supper. With Meditations and Prayers for every Morning and Evening throughout the Week. Also, some Useful Directions and Considerations, in order to a Holy Life after we have received the Blessed Communion.

" By the Right Reverend Father in God,
John Gauden, late Lord
Bishop of Exeter.
The tenth Edition.

" London : Printed for N. Boddington, at the Golden-Ball in Duck Lane ; and H. Hoodes, at the Star, the Corner of Bride Lane, Fleet Street. 1707."

The Frontispiece represents an Altar vested for the Holy Communion, with Linen Cloth on the *top* of the Table—two Flagons, two Chalices with covers—return Rails, so close to the

---

* I have since met with another, and perfect, copy belonging to the Rev. G. F. Lee, who has kindly allowed me the use of it : this is an earlier edition; it has the same Frontispiece, Imprimatur, and Dedication; the title page runs thus :—
"The Whole Duty of a Communicant : being Rules and Directions for a Worthy Receiving the Most Holy Sacrament of the Lord's Supper. By the Right Reverend Father in God, John Gauden, late Lord Bishop of Exeter.
"He being Dead, yet speaketh.
" The Fourth Edition with Additions, out of the Reverend Prelate's Original Copies.
" London; Printed by D. M. for Langley Curtiss near Fleet-Bridge, and Hen. Rodes, next door to the Swan-Tavern, near Bride-Lane in Fleet-Street, 1688."
Any different readings which occur in this Edition are thrown into Notes.

ends of the Altar that, apparently, the Celebrant could not stand
at the north *end*. Over the Altar appears a company of Angels
amid clouds and radiating light : kneeling on the lower steps
of the Altar are two Angels, looking North and South :—at the
bottom of the Frontispiece are the words, " The Angells admire the Divine Goodnes." It bears the—

" Imprimatur, Hen. Maurice, Reverendissimo in Chr. Pat.
and Dom. Domino Gulielmo Archiep. Cant. e Sacris Domesticis.
" May the 31st, 1686."

The Dedication is " To The truly Honoured The Lady
Rich," and is signed, " J. Gauden." In it he says :—

" . . , in an Argument of so mysterious a depth, good affections
are rather to be raised and inflamed, than Subtilties searched and disputed. When I come short in depth of knowledge, I endeavour to
supply in belief of the truth, in love to the goodness, in thanks for
the benefit, in admiration of the mercy and designation ;* the less I
reach to its height, the more I retire to my own heart, which I can
sufficiently prepare by humility, for the receiving of that, whose
Divine Excellency, tho' I cannot comprehend, yet the benefit and hap-
piness by it I may obtain."

The following are all the passages touching in any way the
subject of the Real Presence: the italics are in the original:—

" That great Solemnity and Angelical feast."—p. 1.

" II. [a]

" A Sacrament is a visible Sign of an invisible Grace, a holy Seal
ordained of God to strengthen our Faith in His promises in Jesus
Christ, for the free Remission of our Sins : Which God, therefore,
annexed to His Word, to confirm us by representing the Sufferings
of Christ to our sight and tasting, as the Gospel preacheth in to our
ears ; and it is called the *Lord's Supper*, because Christ *ordained it
as* His last Supper, Matt. xxvi. 26. Wherein to fulfil the Law He
eat the *Paschal Lamb*, and to shew the determination and change of
the *Levitical* Law and Priesthood, He ordained for this New Covenant of Grace, a New Sacrament and Seal thereof, that it succeeding
the Passover, might declare Him to be *the Lamb of God which taketh
away the sins of the world*, John i. 19, to shew and represent His
Death, until His coming again ; to leave His Church a Badge of
distinction from Infidels, and a parting Token and Pledge of His
great Love, assuring the Faithful of His continual Care of them."—
p. 2.

* " Dignation."—ed. 1688.   † "at."—ed. 1688.

" III. [a]

" The visible Signs are *Bread and Wine*, the thing signified is the participation *of the Body and Blood of Christ*, the benefit of whose Death and Passion being apprehended by faith accrue to us as our Mystick* Union with Christ, our Incorporation into Him, our Reconciliation with God, and the nourishment of our most precious Souls to Eternal Life, *John* vi. 54. *Whoso eateth my Flesh, and drinketh my blood, hath Eternal Life, and I will raise him up at the last day . . . . . ."*—p. 3.

" Secondly, *The Author by whom it was instituted.*
" II. [b]

" So that in this great Mystery . . . . Reason is quite dazled and blind, ... devolving all the Work of this Holy Mystery to Faith, which relies upon the Truth, Power and Love of the Institutor, Jesus Christ, who while He was yet on earth, by a corporal and natural Presence conversing with men, but chiefly with His choice and domestick Company, the Twelve Apostles, a little before His Death, instituted this Sacred Mystery, after His last Supper which He made with them."—p. 8.

" III. [b]

" By the Evidence of this Sacrament, exhibiting himself to them, and all believing Souls, . . . as . . . after His Ascension might be a continual Memorial and Seal of the Covenant of Grace, ... a lively Token and Pledge of His Spiritual Presence with His Church, during His Bodily Absence, till His second coming, as also a Badge of . . . . that mutual Love and Charity of Believers, who are all united by Faith to one and the same Saviour, of whom they are all Partakers in this One Sacrament, as well of the Invisible Grace as the Outward and Visible Signs, *the Bread and Wine*."—p. 8.

" Thirdly, *The Outward Means suitable to this End.*
" I. [c]

" The Choice of which familiar Signs, made by our Saviour for the Outward Means, discovered a wonderful Wisdom, ... Things . . . such as for the Community may be had of all Nations, ... though where the proper species of *Bread and Wine* cannot be had, those means of nourishment, which are proportionable may be used, so that no Nation or Man may think himself excluded from the use and comfort of this Sacrament of the Lord's-Supper."—p. 9.

" III. [c]

" For their Plainness and Simplicity, it is such as may take off Christian Minds from placing Piety and the Mysteries of Grace and Religion in any External Pomp and Vanity, which doth but dazle

---

* " mystical."—ed. 1688.

the Eyes and amaze the Senses, and detain Vulgar and Common Minds, by the Outward Glóry of the Senses Objects, from that inward retiring of the Spirit and Soul to its proper and comfortable objects, which are Spiritual, Invisible, and Intellectual, and far remote from the Senses, and abstracted from them, so that Christians cannot easily be so grossly and stupidly sensual, as to imagine any Efficacy in these small and simple Elements of themselves, no more than in Wax or Parchment, which not of their proper Virtue, but only of the Will of the Conveyer, have Power to Convey an Estate to the Receiver of them."—p. 10.

Fourthly, *The Mystical Union, by which they effectually attain and convey to us that End and Benefit which is propounded.*

" I. [d]

" For the Sacramental Union of the Outward Signs, which are the proper objects of our Senses, to the *Body and Blood of Christ*, which are the proper Objects of our Faith, this I conceive to be not by any Physical or Natural Union as the Fruit to the Tree, ... nor yet by any . . . changing the Substance of these Elements into the substance of *Christ's Body and Blood* . . . ."—p. 14.

" II. [d]

" Nor may Omnipotency . . . be so far extended by Human Fancy and Imagination to . . . . . . tell us jointly that they are *Bread and Wine*, and yet his Will is at the same, and about the same Thing, that . . . they are not *Bread and Wine*, but substantially *Flesh and Blood; . . .*"—p. 14.

" VI. [d]

" So that as the *Bread and Wine*, by their natural Qualities and Virtues, are fit to represent the spiritual Efficacy of the *Body and Blood of Christ*, yet by a natural Power, are no whit able to impart to a Communicant the *Body and Blood of Christ*, with the Benefits of them to the Soul : So that our Blessed Saviour hath made choice of them for the first, and hath given to them a Sacramental Virtue, and a Supernatural Efficacy for the Second, which they truly do as Remembrances, as Signs and Seals ; really conveying to the believing and prepared Soul, by the concurrent Spirit and Power of the Institutor, Jesus Christ, that which in their Nature they do fitly represent."—p. 17.

" IX. [d]

" We deny not a true and real presence and perception of Christ's *Body and Blood* in the Sacrament, which in reality even they of the other gross opinion do not imagine is to Sense, but to Faith ; which perceives its Objects as really, according to Faith's perception, as the Senses do theirs after their manner. I believe therefore, That in the Sacrament of the *Lord's Supper*, there are both Objects presented to, and received by a worthy Receiver; First, the *Bread and Wine* in their own Nature and Substance distinct, do remain as well as their Accidents, which are the true Objects of our Sense, and fit Signs to represent by them the inward Grace."—p. 20.

"X. [d]

" Also there are spiritual, invisible, and credible, yet most true and really present, Objects of Faith; the *Body and Blood of Christ,* that is *Christ Jesus himself,* whom by Faith I consider as suffering for my Sins, and cast my soul by His mercy offered me by the Merits of His Death. These two Materials of the Sacrament are so united, that it may be truly said (not in a Gross and Physical, but Divine and Sacramental Sense) the *Bread and Wine* are the *Body and Blood of Christ,* and *Christ's Body and Blood are Bread and Wine :* John vi. *Meat indeed, and Drink indeed,* not by transmutation of Nature, but by a similitude of Virtues, and proportionable Effects, by a Sacramental Union and Relation, depending upon the Truth, Authority, and Divine Power of the Institutor, *Jesus Christ.*"— p. 20.

"XI. [d]

" Whose Appointment of these Elements to such a Use or End, and uniting them in this near Relation to His *Body and Blood,* by the solemn Consecration of them, make up the firm and true Being of a Sacrament, which requires a Truth and Reality, both of the Signs and Symbols, and that which is by them represented and sig-nified ;* a Truth and Certainty of Relation and Connexion one with another : So that I receive not only *Panem Domini, the Bread of the Lord ;* but also, *Panem Dominum, my Lord Jesus Christ, the true Bread of Life eternal to my Soul and Body ;* this latter, as truly and really as the former, together with all the benefits which flow from Christ."—p. 21.

"XII. [d]

" On the other side, whoso unpreparedly and irreverently, and so unworthily, receives the one, contracts a Guilt of Damnation for Neglect, Indignity, and Irreverence offered to the other ; that is, *the Body and Blood of Christ,* which Faith only discerns and receives in this great Mystery : And whoso violates and contemns the Seal and authentick Letters of the King, becomes guilty of Indignity and Offence to his Authority and Majesty, which is not only re-strained to his person ; but also inseparably annexed to any Sign or Token by which he is pleased to Manifest His Royal Will and Pleasure, thus rightly informed, as I hope, in the Nature of this Sa-crament, what it is in itself, what it may be to me, of how Divine a Mystery and Dignity it is in itself to my Soul, either of Comfort and Salvation in a Worthy Receiving, or of Guilt and Damnation in an Unworthy Receiving of it."—p. 21.

* "also a."—cd. 1688.

" Fifthly, *How we ought to prepare ourselves.*
" I. [e]

" . . . . by a Self Examining, see what fitness there is in me, answerable to these Holy Mysteries, and the Grace of God by these offered to me, and most Effectually Conveyed, except the Unpreparedness, and Indisposition of my Heart do Frustrate and put an Obstacle."—p. 22.

"XI. [e]

" . . . . the sight of the Promises, and the Seals of the Sacrament annexed to them, in which I behold Jesus Christ crucified, does again establish my Heart . . . ."—p. 30.

"XVII. [e]

" The same holy frame, and devout temper of Spirit, I labour to continue in my receiving, carrying my Faith, by the visible Representations before me, and giving* to me to behold its invisible, but most credible Object, Jesus Christ crucified and dying for sin . . . ."
—p. 34.

" *Rules and Directions to a Week's Preparation.*
" I. [f]

"When thou hearest the warning read in the Church by the Minister, consider and contemplate with thyself that God Almighty hath sent forth His Servant to bid thee to this great Supper, where not His fat Oxen are killed, but His only beloved Son and thy dear Saviour (who was crucified on the Cross, for thine, and for the Sins of the whole World) is offered to thee to feed upon in thine Heart with Faith and Thanksgiving ; . . . ."—p. 39.

" Monday *Morning, a Preparatory Prayer to the holy Sacrament.*
" I. [g]

" . . . . I do hear thy Word, and thy dear Son is offered unto my Ear ; I receive this Sacrament, and now He is offered unto my Eye, in the Testimony of these two Witnesses, this Truth is established in my Heart, that my Saviour suffered Death for my Sin."—p. 47.

This copy is defective here, pp. 51 to 58, *viz.,* Self examination on the Ten Commandments.

" *A Prayer for Pardon and Remission of Sins.*
IV. [h]

" . . . . . Cleanse my heart throughly . . . . . that I may receive Jesus Christ with all the Benefits of His death and Passion. . . . . "
" *Meditations for* Monday *Evening on the* Holy Sacrament, of the Lord's Supper, showing the necessity of receiving it."

---

* "given."—ed. 1688.

"II. [i]

"O most wonderful Sacrament, what shall I say of thee! Thou art the life of my soul, and a Medicine to heal all my wounds!..."
—p. 62.

III. [i]

"..... Shall I who am loaden with sins, dare to present myself to that holy banquet; where Angels wait as ministering Spirits, sent out for the good of those who are to receive the Earnest of Salvation? Shall I with lascivious eyes, full of wanton looks, behold that Lamb without spot or blemish? With my polluted looks and lying tongue, shall I touch the Bread of Angels? or shall I lodge the KING of kings in a heart filled with foul concupiscence?"—p. 63.

"A prayer for Monday *Evening on the Holy Sacrament."*

"IV. [k]

"Grant, O Lord, that I may receive Thee with pure lips and a penitent Heart, that Thou dwelling in my Heart by Faith, I may find myself strengthened, comforted, and my Heart inflamed with the love of Thee; then shall I prostrate myself before Thee, and acknowledge in the Assembly of Thy Saints, that it is Thou alone who hast comforted me, and that there is no salvation in any beside Thee."—p. 65.

"Meditations for Tuesday *Morning on the Holy Sacrament."*

"VI. [l]

"....Christ conveyed unto us in this Sacrament."—p. 69.

"Meditations for Tuesday *Evening, on the Holy Sacrament."*

"I. [m]

"By means of this Divine Food, the soul is united to Christ, and receives that strength and vigour which continually sets it forward in its Spiritual Ascension. Who can give worthy thanks for so great a Benefit? Who will not be altogether dissolved into tears, when he sees Almighty God united to him? The more we go about to consider the Excellency and Virtues of this sovereign Mystery, the more do we want words to express it, and the more doth our understanding fail us."—p. 73.

V. [m]

"He hath given us of His own Bread, and of His own Cup; nay, He hath given us His own Body as Bread, His own Blood as Wine, for the Nourishment of our Souls;...."—p. 73.

"Meditations for Wednesday *Morning, on the Most Holy Sacrament.*

VI. [n]

"O then receive me a poor sinner at Thy Holy Table: this

most Holy Medicine cures all the wounds of sin ; this quickening Flesh overcometh all mortal sin. This is the most Holy Seal of Divine Promises, which we may shew before God's Judgment Seat ; having this Pledge we may glory, and be secure of eternal life: If Christ's Body and Blood be exhibited unto us, assuredly all other Benefits by that most Holy Body, and most Blessed Blood, are prepared for us ; . . . . "—p. 82.

" *Meditations for* Wednesday, *a preparation on the Holy Sacrament.*"

" V. [o]

" In this blessed Sacrament here, we have an unmoveable Centre to rest on ; God our Portion, Christ our Fulness, an Object larger than the Heavens. . . . . "—p. 92.

" *A Prayer for Faith.*

" O Almighty God, whose Nature is above our reach ; and whose secret operations no humane reason can conceive ! Give me that Faith, without which no man can know Thee, and without which no soul can please Thee : Lord I believe, but to believe unto righteousness, O God, increase my Faith. Concerning the great Sacrament of Thy precious Body and Blood, I believe that in the same Night that Thou, O Lord Jesus, wast betrayed, Thou didst give to Thy disciples Bread and Wine, which thou didst call thy Body and Blood, with a charge to eat and drink, and to do the same in remembrance of thee ; for as thou wast upon thy Departure, thou wouldst leave them and me a Sign of thy Body, a Figure of thy Blood, and a Memorial of thy bitter Death and bloody Passion ; lest I should forget thee, who wast ready to lay down thy life for me, who am the worst and vilest of sinners."—p. 111.

" II. [p]

" Therefore I take these Elements of Bread and Wine, for holy Signs of thy Body and Blood, believing that though they remain after the Consecration in their Substance both Bread and Wine, yet they are more than common Bread and Wine, being made by prayer and thy holy Word the Figures of thy Flesh and Blood; which in the Action and Use of the Sacrament, are really and effectually taken by the Faithful. So tho' I feel and taste Bread and Wine, yet by the Eye of Faith, I eat thy Body, and drink thy Blood, in Remembrance that thou didst Die for me, and for all Mankind."—p. 112.

" *Meditation for* Friday *Evening, on the Holy Sacrament.*

" II. [q]

" And the best way to strengthen our Trust in God, is by renewing our Resignation, and when can we more seasonably do it, than at our Receiving the blessed Sacrament, in which we have exhibited the Fulness of Christ's Merits, as the Propitiatory Sacrament and Atonement for our Souls, by whom we have Access unto the Father, ... "—p. 113.

" Meditations for Saturday *Evening, on the Most Holy Sacrament.*

" II. [r]

" O that I were now with an humble Heart at the Holy Table of my Lord, ... there is the universal Medicine for all our Dise; ses, and an Ark of Safety against all Dangers; there, O my soul, thou mayest by the Eye of Faith behold thy crucified Lord and Saviour, shedding his most precious Blood upon the Cross for thy sins, and burning with an unspeakable desire of thy Salvation. There thou mayest look upon him whom thou dost still crucifie afresh by thy sins daily and hourly. . . . . "—p. 112.

This copy is imperfect from here, p. 123 to 131, *" When the Minister is saying the Offertory,"* etc.*

[s]

" At the time of the Consecration fix your Eye upon the Elements, and at the Actions of the Ministers in ordering the Bread and Wine, we ought joyfully and thankfully to meditate after this manner.

" O who can but admire and wonder, that the Son of God should become food to the souls of Men, and to humble himself so low to be represented by Bread, which is the Poor Man's Food, though necessary for the Rich ; it is the staff of our life, and signifies that Body of thine, which thou gavest for the life of the World ; thou hast by thy holy Mystery made this Bread and Wine spiritual Food, as well as temporal ; O Lord, I beseech thee, let the operation of it be such as to strengthen my soul, that I may withstand all temptations whatsoever, and evermore serve thee in Spirit and Truth. Amen.

[t]

" When the Minister breaks the Bread, and pours out the Wine, use these Meditations.

" O Holy Jesus, thy Blessed Body was torn with Nails upon the Cross, and thy Precious Blood was inhumanly spilt by thy Crucifiers ; but I, unworthy Wretch, by my manifold sins have occasioned more torments to thee ; they crucified thee but once, but I crucifie thee daily ; they Crucified thee because they knew thee not, but I have known thee ; what thou art in thyself, the Lord of Glory, and what thou art to me, a most tender and merciful Father, and yet I have still continued to Crucifie thee afresh : O do thou work in me, first a great sorrow for my sins past, and then a great hatred, and a firm resolution against them for the time to come."—p. 134.

---

* But in the Ed. of 1688 at p. 133 occurs the following :—
"A Prayer before the Sacrament.
" II. . . . . . O then, dear Lord, fit me I beseech thee for thyself, that I may receive with that joy and spiritual comfort, this thy Body that was broken, and thy precious Blood which was shed for me, whereby I may partake of all the Benefits of thy bitter Death and Passion. . . . . "

[u]

" When the Minister is drawing near thee with the Elements, say,

" I adore thee, O most righteous Redeemer, that thou art pleas'd to convey unto my soul thy precious Body and Blood, with all the benefits of thy Death and Passion; I am not worthy, O Lord, to receive thee, but let thy Holy and Blessed Spirit, with all his purities, prepare for thee a lodging in my soul, where thou mayest unite me to thyself for ever. Amen.

[v]

" Ejaculations before the Bread.

" This is that Bread which came down from Heaven, whosoever eateth shall never hunger. Thou dealest thy Bread to those which hunger after Righteousness : O feed my fainting soul with this Bread of Life.

" O strengthen my Heart and Hand by a lively Faith, and open my mouth with fervent desires that I may Eat, not for bodily sustenance, but spiritual relief, and the refreshment of my soul.

" O let my soul feel the spiritual Efficacy of thy grace, that I may not eat unworthily, or to my condemnation. O Lord, I beseech thee, enable and direct me by thy holy and blessed Spirit to receive it worthily. Amen."—p. 136.

" When the Minister gives the Holy Bread, say softly with him

" The Body of our Lord Jesus Christ, which was given for me, preserve my Body and Soul unto everlasting life.

" Here take the Bread with reverence, then proceed :

" I take and eat this in Remembrance that Christ died for me, and will feed on him in my Heart with Faith and Thanksgiving. *Then answer audibly,* Amen.

After the Bread, say :

" I give thee hearty Thanks, O Lord most Holy, that thou hast refreshed my soul at this time, by my feeding upon thy Body which was broken for me; If I had lived innocently and had kept all thy Commandments, yet could I have had no proportion of merit to so transcendant a Mercy ; but since I have so loved Sin, and added Transgression to Transgression, thy Mercy is so glorious and infinite, that I stand amazed at the consideration of its immensity : O let me not throw off this Wedding Garment, or stain it with Pollution of deadly Sin, but let me be wholly united to thee, being transformed according to thy Holy Will and Life, who livest and reignest for ever. *Amen.*"—p. 137.

Or this :

" O Blessed Jesus, sanctifie this Bread to me that it may be to my Soul the Staff of Strength, whereby I may vanquish and overcome all the Assaults of the Devil, the World and the Flesh, and continue thy faithful Soldier and Servant to my Life's end. *Amen.*

. . . .

" *When thou receivest the Cup, say after the Minister, softly :*
" The Blood of My Lord Jesus Christ which was shed for me. preserve my Body and Soul unto everlasting Life ; I drink this in remembrance that Christ's Blood was shed for me, and am thankful, *Amen.*—p. 138.

" *After the Cup, say,*
" O how delightful is this Cup to me, Blessed Jesus, which was so heavy to thee ! it was thy Agony and bloody Sweat, thy bitter Death and Passion, which afforded me this Cup of chearfulness ; thou didst find it bitter, when thou wast appeasing an angry Father, but thou hast sweetened it by a reconciliation, and hast wrought out my Redemption and Salvation.

Or this :
"I Praise Thee, I Bless Thee, I Glorifie Thee, O Lord most Holy, that thou hast at this time so refreshed my Soul, and filled me with holy Desires ; O let thy tender Mercy always keep me in this happy temper, that I may never err, nor stray from thy Command-ments, but keep firm that Covenant which thou hast sealed with thy most precious Blood for my Redemption ; and direct me, O Lord, and guide me so here, that I may be a fit Member for thy Heavenly Kingdom hereafter. *Amen.*"—p. 139.

I have extracted thus fully from this Book, even at the risk of being tedious, in order that Bishop Gauden's opinions on such points as touch the subject of the Real Presence may be fairly judged by the context of those passages in which they occur ; and that thus he may, in fact, speak for himself. An analysis of the passages furnishes the expression of the Bishop's belief on the following Eucharistic statements which he enumerates :—

1. That the Eucharist is a sacrificial representation of Christ's sufferings " to our sight and tasting."—

II. [a] p. 311.   XI. [e] p. 315.   XVII. [e] p. 315.

2. That it has three parts (as defined in the Church Cate-chism), viz : (1.) The Sign—sacramentum. (2.) The thing signified—res sacramenti. (3.) The benefits—virtus sacra-menti.—III. [a] p. 312.   VI. [d] p. 313.   XI. [d.] p. 314.

3. That it is a Mystery explicable only to Faith.—

II. [b] p. 312; and ineffable—I. [m] p. 316.

4. That it is a "lively token and pledge of" Christ's "Spiritual Presence with His Church, during His Bodily Absence."—III. [b] p. 312. VI. |n] p. 317.

5. That the "Sacramental Union of the Outward Signs .... to the Body and Blood of Christ" is not "any Physical or Natural Union," nor yet Transubstantiation.—I. and II. [d] p. 313. X. [d] p. 314. XI. [d] p. 314.

6. That the Bread and Wine by "a supernatural Efficacy" really convey what they are designed also to represent, viz., The Body and Blood of Christ.—VI. [d] p. 313. V. [m] p. 316. II. [p.] p. 317. [s] p. 318: *i.e.*, Christ Himself Who is therein offered to feed upon:—I. [f] p. 315. I. [g] p. 315. VI. [l] p. 316: even "that Bread which came down from Heaven."—[v] p. 319.

7. That there is " a true and real presence and perception of Christ's Body and Blood in the Sacrament."—to faith, not to sense.—IX., X. and XI. [d] pp. 313, 314.

8. That such Presence is Objective and irrespective of the character of the receiver.—III. [i] p. 316. V. [o] p. 317. Note p. 318.

9. That this Presence is due to Consecration.—XI. [d] p. 314. II. [p] p. 317.

10. That in some sense the Body and Blood of Christ are received by the wicked.—XII. [d] p. 314. III. [i] p. 316. [v] p. 319.

11. That Adoration is due to Christ in the Sacrament.— [u] p. 319.

It will be at once seen that these Eleven Propositions involve mainly the very questions which were raised in the Case which originally led to the preparation of this Letter, and which have been brought into discussion also in other cases ; it can hardly be denied, I think, that Bishop Gauden's language concerning them is sufficiently strong and decided to shield those who have been accused of employing an unwarranted phraseology; especially when it is recollected that the man who thus wrote was one of the principal Savoy Commissioners and Reviewers of 1661-62, and that to him is very mainly owing the re-introduction of that Declaration on

T T

Kneeling, which the language condemned has been declared to contravene, though no proof has yet been furnished that the Declaration was ever designed to do more than (as I have argued throughout this Letter) exclude the Doctrine of Transubstantiation, and any consequences to which it necessarily led.

Bishop Gauden was not, however, the only Prelate who urged the re-production of this Declaration : we have learned from Bishop Burnet (see p. 302) that he " was seconded by Southampton and Morley:" why Southampton interested himself on the subject, or what opinion he held on the Doctrinal question, I have been unable to learn, nor is it of the least moment in considering the actions and opinions of the *Divines* who were concerned in the Revision of 1662. But it is very desirable to ascertain any particulars as to Bishop Morley's opinions : little, however, seems to be known of him :"* Chalmer's (*Biog. Dict.* Vol. xxii. London, 1815) says that he :—

* Richard Baxter, in his Account of the Managers of the Conference between the Episcopal and Presbyterian Divines, says of him :—" Bishop Morley was oft there, but not constantly, and with free and fluent words, with much earnestness, was the chief speaker of all the Bishops, and the greatest interrupter of us ; vehemently going on with what he thought serviceable to his end, and bearing down Answers by the said fervour and interruptions."—*Life*, p. 363, fol. 1696.

It may be as well to hear his opinion of others, whose names have been mentioned in the course of these pages.

" Bishop Cosin was there constantly, and had a great deal of talk with so little Logick, Natural or Artificial, that I perceived no one much moved by anything he said. But two Virtues he shewed (though none took him for a Magician): One was, that he was excellently well versed in Canons, Councils, and Fathers, which he remembered, when by citing of any passages we tried him. The other was, that he was of a rustick wit and carriage, so he would endure more freedom of our discourse with him, and was more affable and familiar than the rest."—*Ibid.*

" Bishop Gauden was our most constant helper; he and Bishop Cosin were seldom absent. And how bitter soever his pen be, he was the only Moderator of all the Bishops (except our, Bishop Reynolds): he shewed no Logick ; nor meddled in any dispute, or point of learning ; but a calm, fluent, rhetorical tongue ; and if all had been of his mind, we had been reconciled : but when by many days' Conference in the beginning, we had got some moderating Concessions from him (and from Bishop Cosin by his means) the rest came in the end and brake them all."—*Ibid.*

" Dr. Pierson and Dr. Gunning did all their work (beside Bishop Morley's discourses), but with great difference in the manner. Dr. Pierson was their true Logician and Disputant, without whom, as far as I could discern, we should have had nothing from them, but Dr. Gunning's passionate invectives mixt with some Argumentations : he disputed accurately, soberly, and calmly (being but once in any passion) breeding in us a great respect for him, and a persuasion that if he

" .... was sent over by Chancellor Hyde," from the Hague, " to help to pave the way for " Charles II.'s Restoration : to " the heads of the Presbyterian party " he " avowed himself a Calvinist, because he knew that they entertained the most favourable opinion of such Churchmen as were of that persuasion. His chief business, however, in this kind of embassy, was to confute the report that Charles II. was a papist. In this he was probably more successful than correct." He was author of " An Argument, drawn from the evidence and certainty of sense against the Doctrine of Transubstantiation," and also of a " Vindication of the Argument drawn from sense against Transubstantiation." London, 1683.

From this latter work I extract the only four passages which afford any clue to Bishop Morley's opinions, so far as they relate to the Doctrinal grounds, on which he probably counselled the insertion of the Declaration on Kneeling : the *Italics*, etc., are his own : the first occurs when explaining the word " Mysteries," where he says :—

" .... and in this sense likewise both the *Sacraments* may be and are called *Mysteries*, but especially that of the Lord's Supper, which none were permitted to be present at, or to see administered, in the *Primitive Church* of old, nor are not in *Protestant Churches* at this day, but such as are receivers and partakers of it. And from hence the word *Missa* or *Masse* came to be taken for the *Sacrament* itself; because when that part of the *Divine Service* (which was before the *Sacrament*, and at which the *Catechumeni* and others (that were not to be partakers of the *Sacrament* might be present) was done, " the *Deacon* dismissed that part of the People by saying, *Missa est*, that is, Your part of the Service is done, and you are to depart ; and then none staid but such as were to communicate, whom they called *fideles*. But that which was not lawful and counted a profanation of this holy mystery in the *Primitive Church*, is now in the *Romish* not only counted lawfull but meritorious ; I mean the standing by, and looking on the celebration of the *Lord's*

had been independent, he would have been for peace, and that if all were in his power, it would have gone well : he was the strength and honour of that cause which we doubted whether he heartily maintained."—p. 364.

" Dr. Gunning was their forwardest and greatest speaker ; understanding well what belonged to a disputant ; a man of greater study and industry than any of them, well read in Fathers and Councils ; and of a ready tongue ; (and I hear and believe of a very temperate life, as to all carnal excesses whatsoever) : but so vehement for his high imposing principles, and so over-zealous for Arminianism, and Formality, and Church Pomp, and so very eager and fervent in his discourse, that I conceive his prejudice and passion much perverted his judgment, and I am sure they made him lamentably over-run himself in his discourse."—*Ibid.*

Supper, or the *Masse* (as they call it) without receiving of it."—
pp. 17 and 18.

The other passages are found in his refutation of the argument—that Transubstantiation is a Miracle : upon which he writes thus :—

" (3rd.) There is no such Miracle as Transubstantiation, because God never works any *miracle,* but for some great *end,* and such a one, as cannot be obtained without such a miracle, according to the old and true saying, both in Philosophy and Divinity, *Deus nihil agit frustra,* God doth nothing in vain.   But supposing a *Transubstantiation,* or a miraculous change of the *Bread* and *Wine,* into the body and blood of *Christ,* such a miracle would be to no purpose ; because, as *Christ* himself tells them (that though he would have given them his very flesh to eat) *the Flesh profiteth nothing :* his meaning is, that the eating of his *flesh,* or the very substance of his flesh in that gross and *carnal* manner, as they then, and the *Papists* now, think it is to be eaten, would doe no man any good at all. For it is not the taking of *Christ's body* into our mouths, in the very flesh or corporeal substance of it (if it could be so taken) that can nourish our souls into everlasting life ; for then all that received this *Sacrament,* should be saved ; which yet they doe not, nor dare not affirm : but it is the *Spirit,* saith *Christ,* that *quickeneth,* that is, it is the spiritual eating of his flesh and drinking of his blood, that nourisheth us in the life of *grace* here, and will bring us unto the life of *glory* hereafter ; and according to this manner of eating and drinking, it is, that *Christ* saith, *John* vi. 54, that ' *Whosoever eateth his flesh and drinketh his blood, hath eternal life ;*' and in order to the eating and drinking of *Christ's flesh* and *Christ's blood* in this spiritual manner, and to that spiritual end, there neither is nor can be any need or use of *Transubstantiation ;* and consequently being of no Necessity, nor of no Use, there can be no such *Miracle.*

" (4th.) And lastly, There can be no such miracle as *Transubstantiation,* because all *Miracles* are possible ; but *Transubstantiation* is impossible as implying many real and proved *contradictions* : as the being of *Accidents* without *Subjects,* the nourishing of *Substances* by *Accidents,* and the generation of other *Substances* out of the corruption of *Accidents;* as likewise that there should be a *Body* without *quantity,* a *quantity* without *extension,* or extension without extending itself in any space or place : Or lastly, that one and the same *Body* should be in *diverse places* at one time, and yet not fill any place, nor be in any of the spaces betwixt those places, and consequently to be united and not united, divided and not divided ; nay, that the same body which is in Heaven *circumscriptivè,* or *tanquam in loco proprie dicto,* should be at the same time out of that place, and consequently *in loco* and *extra locum,* that is circumscribed and not circumscribed, or circumscribed in one place and not circumscribed in another : Besides many others the like inconsistencies and contradictions, which you may see demonstrated at large in Dr. *Whitaker,* Bishop *Morton,* and Mr. *Chillingworth.* Now that whatsoever implyes a *Contradiction* cannot be done, no not by *miracle,* is *their* doctrine, as well as *ours ;* because, this would rather argue an impotency than an omnipotency in God.

" To conclude all, Whereas the *Author* of this *Pamphlet* saith that all *Catholics,* he means *Romanists,* hold that *Christ's body* and *blood* have a *spiritual presence* in the *Sacrament ;* and that (saith he) being once granted, there can be no difficulty in believing that our Saviour's body and blood may be in many places at the same time, because it is granted to all *Spirits.*

" I answer, supposing it were true (as it is not) that all *Romanists* hold *Christ's body* to have a *spiritual presence* in the *Sacrament,* and supposing it were true likewise, that a true humane body (as Christ's is) could have a *spiritual presence,* that is, (as I suppose his meaning to be) could be present as *Spirits* are present without filling the place, or space wherein they are ; which is most false. For a *Body* cannot be a body and no body, as it must be if it were a *Spirit;* and nothing can have the presence or propriety of a *Spirit* but a Spirit : and consequently nothing can be anywhere as a *Spirit* but a Spirit. But supposing (I say) it were true, that *Christ's body* were in the *Sacrament* in a *Spiritual* manner, or after the manner of *Spirits,* yet would it not follow that *Christ's body* could be in diverse places at the same time. For no *created Spirit* can be in many, or in more places than one at the same time, no more than a Body can. Indeed there is a difference between the presence of a *Spirit,* and the presence of a *Body,* the former being where it is, *definitivè,* and the other *circumscriptivè;* But that which is *definitivè,* where it is, cannot be anywhere else than where it is at one and the same time, no more than that which is *circumscriptivè ;* and consequently, to be in many places at once, is as inconsistent with the nature of a *Spirit,* I mean of a finite and created Spirit, as it is with the nature of a *Body.* For the Angel *Gabriel* was not with the Blessed *Virgin* at the same time that he was in Heaven, nor in heaven at the same time that he was with the Blessed *Virgin ;* and it was one of the Arguments whereby the Ancient *Fathers* prove the *Holy Ghost* to be God, because He may be, and is, in many places at the same time, which no *Spirit* can be but He only.

" There is therefore no such *Miracle* as *Transubstantiation,* it being not only a useless thing if it were so, but an impossible thing that it should be so."—pp. 23-27.

Neither of these passages contains, indeed, any *direct* statement of Bishop Morley's belief on the Real Presence ; *indirectly,* however, they furnish some clue to it, and to the sense in which he must have sanctioned the Declaration on

Kneeling : for, in the first place, the argument drawn (in the passage, p. 323) from the (erroneously alleged*) rule of the Primitive Church and the custom of the "Protestant Churches" in his own day, to prove that "both the *Sacraments* may be and are called *Mysteries,* but especially the *Lord's Supper,*" implies the belief of something more distinct and peculiar about the Eucharist than pertains to the other Sacrament; if not, how could Bishop Morley account for the fact that Baptism was not as secretly administered as he states the Eucharist to have been in the ancient Church ? What could account for the desire to secure the Eucharist from risk of profanation (for that it was which led to the *actual* practice of the Early Church) but the belief of Christ's true Objective Presence therein ? Else surely it mattered little then, and matters less now that our congregations are not divided into "Catechumeni and others," *who* was or is present at an Office which claimed to be no more than a *memorial* of an *absent* Christ.

But, again, his argument against Transubstantiation, while it supports the language of the Declaration on Kneeling, (especially in the 4th passage, which is a contemporaneous commentary on the final clause which condemns Ubiquitarianism), is in no way adverse to such language concerning the Presence, as I have all along contended the Declaration did not design to exclude; for the 2nd passage (p. 324) shews that what he objected to was any notion of a Real Presence after what he calls a "gross and *carnal* manner," such as the Capernaites misunderstood our Lord's words to mean ; and his remark that any oral reception "of Christ's body" "in the very flesh or corporeal substance of it was both impossible and unbeneficial," shews that he must have understood the words of the Declaration—"any Corporal Presence of Christ's natural Flesh and Blood,"—to be simply the *equivalent* of *gross* and *carnal, i.e., Capernaiacal.*

But in the absence of any more direct proof of Bishop Morley's belief, from his own language, it is most natural to

---

* On this point I venture to refer the reader to "The Anglican Authority for the Presence of non-communicants during Holy Communion."— Masters, 1858.

quote the words of Bishop Morton, the only one of his three authorities whose language, in the lack of any more distinct reference, I can satisfy myself he may have referred to in the 3rd passage (p. 325). The Book to which Bishop Morley seems to refer, is the Treatise of Bishop Morton, intitled, " *Of the Institution of the Sacrament of the Blessed Bodie and Blood of Christ (by some called) The Masse of Christ*," LONDON, 1631 ; where, at p. 148, he writes as follows :—

"That Protestants, albeit they deny the Corporall Presence of Christ in this Sacrament ; yet hold they a true Presence thereof in diverse respects, according to the judgment of Antiquitie.

"Sect. II.

" There may be observed four Kindes of Truthes of Christ his Presence in this Sacrament : one is *Veritas Signi*, that is Truth of *Representation* of Christ his Body ; the next is *Veritas Revelationis*, Truth of *Revelation ;* the third is *Veritas Obsignationis*, that is a Truth of *Seale*, for better Assurance ; the last is *Veritas Exhibitionis*, the Truth of *exhibiting* and deliverance of the Reall Body of Christ to the faithfull *Communicants.* The truth of the *Signe*, in respect of the thing signified, is to be acknowledged so farre, as in the *Signes of Bread* and *Wine* is represented the true and Reall Body and Blood of Christ, which Truth and Reality is celebrated by us, and taught by ancient Fathers, in contradiction to *Manichees, Marcionites*, and other other old Heretikes ; who held that Christ had in himself no true Body, but merely *Phantasticall*, as you yourselves well know. In confutation of which *Heretikes* the Father *Ignatius* (as your Cardinall witnesseth) called the *Eucharist* itself, *the flesh of Christ.* Which saying of *Ignatius*, in the sence of *Theodoret* (by whom he is cited against the Heresie of his time) doth call it the *Flesh and Blood* of Christ, because (as the same *Theodoret* expounded himselfe) *it is a true signe of the True and Reall Body of Christ :* and as *Tertullian* long before him had explained the words of Christ himself [*this is my Body*] that is (saith hee) *this Bread is a Sign or Figure of my Body.* Now because it is not a *Signe*, which is not of some *Truth* (for as much as there is not a figure of a figure) therefore *Bread* being a signe of Christ's *Bodie*, it must follow that Christ had a true Body. This, indeed, is Theologicall arguing, by a true *Signe* of the *Body* of Christ to confute the *Hereticks*, that denied the *Truth of Christ's Body.* Which controlleth the Wisdome of your *Councell of Trent*, in condemning Protestants, as denying Christ to be *Truly present in the Sacrament, because, they say, he is there present in a Signe*, or *Figure ;* which were to abolish all true *Sacraments*, which are true *Figures*, and *Signes* of the things which they represent."

Here, again, we have another illustration of the meaning of

the word *corporal* in the Declaration, *i.e.*, if, as it cannot be reasonably doubted, Bishop Morley (who was, it must be remembered, one of the Reviewers of 1662) accepted the language of Bishop Morton as written thirty years before; for the latter clearly advocates "a true" in distinction from a "Corporall Presence of Christ in this Sacrament," basing his judgment upon the teaching of primitive antiquity, and deprecating the Roman condemnation of those who, "because they say, that Christ is there [*i.e.*, in the Sacrament] present in a Signe," are alleged to deny that He is "truly present in the Sacrament."

This, however, is not the only statement of Bishop Morton on the Real Presence; and as Bishop Morley has only given a *general* reference to him, it is desirable to know what he elsewhere says : thus, in another work of his, the "*Catholic Appeal*," (p. 93, ed. 1610), he writes (the italics here, too, as before, are his) :—

" . . . . the question is not absolutely concerning a *Reall Presence*, which *Protestants* (as their own Jesuits witnesse) *do also professe;* Fortunatus (a Protestant) holding that Christ is *in the Sacrament most really; Calvin* teaching that *the presence of Christ's bodie in respect of the soules of the faithfull, is truly in this Sacrament, and substantially received : with whom* (they say) *Beza and Sadael* (two other Protestants) *do consent,* which acknowledgment of our adversaries may serve to stay the contrarie clamours and calumnious accusations, wherein they used to range Protestants with those *heretickes, who denied the true Bodie of Christ was in the Eucharist, and maintained only a figure and image of Christ's Bodie :* seeing that our difference is not about the truth or realitie of the Presence, but about the true manner of the being and receiving thereof."

Such is Bishop Morton's language towards the *Roman* side of the Eucharistic controversy : now let us see how he speaks to the *Puritan* opponents of the Church of England. In a book called, "A Defence of the innocencie of the three ceremonies of the Church of England, *viz.*, the *Surplice, Crosse* after *Baptisme*, and *Kneeling* at the receiving of the blessed Sacrament:" London, 1619 :—he thus says (p. 299) :—

"Sect. xl.
" *Our fourth Confutation of the non-conformists, and justification of ourselves, issueth from the non-conformists owne Practise.*

" First, by their Intentional Reverence.

" You would account it an extreme injury to bee censured as contemners or prophaners of these holy mysteries ; or not to celebrate and receive them reverently, with the truely religious affections of your hearts and mindes : which you professe will be the dutie of every worthy Communicant that shall rightly *discerne* in this Sacrament *the Lords body.* This being granted (which without impietie cannot be denied) it ministreth unto us an argument, whereby you may be comforted (as I suppose) without all contradiction.

" First, I may reason thus : that manner of Reverence, which it is lawfull for a Christian to conceive in his mind, the same is as lawful for him (the case of scandall excepted) to expresse in his outward gesture of bodie. But it is lawfull for a Christian to conceive such a *Relative Reverence ;* as from the sight of the Sacrament (being *Objectum à quo*) to raise his thoughts to a contemplation of the mysticall and spirituall object of faith, signified thereby : and upon the understanding of the mysticall, even the body and blood of *Christ* really (albeit not corporally) exhibited unto us in this Sacrament, to receive these visible pledges of our redemption, by the death of *Christ,* (as the *Objectum propter quod*) with all holy and reverent devotion of heart and mind. Therefore it is lawful to perform a sensible and bodily reverence at our outward receiving thereof."

There are two other Publications by Bishop Morton* which I have not had the opportunity to examine ; but those already quoted are, I think, sufficient for the purpose: *viz.,* to ascertain whether he held the Doctrine of the Real Objective Presence in the Eucharist : the language cited seems to shew that he did :† if so, then, I think, it must be allowed that Bishop Morley held it too ; for it is at least a fair presumption that he did not disapprove the language of Bishop Morton, considering the general way in which he refers to him as one of those who demonstrated the " inconsistencies and contradictions" of the Roman doctrine: consequently, Bishop Morley may well be claimed as one of those Reviewers who, therefore, could have had no further design in urging the republication of the Declaration on Kneeling, than to guard against a belief in Transubstantiation, which his own language shews him to have opposed.

* *Viz.* (1) " Apologia Catholica," etc., and (2), " Totius doctrinalis controversiæ de Eucharistiæ decisio," etc.

† Though Mr. Goode (*Nature of Christ's Presence,* &c. p. 831) says, " It would be difficult to name any one who has more expressly, fully and learnedly *refuted* the doctrine he is here [viz. *The Doctrine of the Real Presence as set forth in the works of Divines and others in the English Church since the Reformation.* Parker, Oxford, 1855.] cited in support of." To prove this he quotes from the " Catholic Appeal" pp. 113, 118, 121 — 131 ; but the extracts seem to me not to the purpose.

Among the Divines who were engaged in the Savoy Conference and the Revision of 1662, was Dr. Heylin ; he thus writes when noticing some of the changes in the English Reformed Communion Office :—

"In the first Liturgy of King Edward, the Sacrament of the Lord's Body was delivered with this benediction, that is to say, ' the Body of our Lord Jesus Christ, which was given for the preservation of thy body and soul to life everlasting ; The Blood of our Lord Jesus Christ,' etc., which, being thought by Calvin and his disciples to give more countenance to the **gross** and **carnal** presence of Christ in the sacrament, which passeth by the name of **transubstantiation** in the schools of Rome, was altered into this form in the second Liturgy, that is to say, ' Take and eat this in remembrance that Christ died for thee ; and feed on him in thy heart by faith with thanksgiving. Take and drink this, etc. But the revisers of the book [in 1559] joined both forms together, lest under colour of a **carnal**, they might be thought also to deny **such** a **real** presence as was defended in the writings of the ancient Fathers. Upon which ground they expunged a whole rubric at the end of the Communion service, by which it was declared that kneeling at the participation of the Sacrament was required for no other reason than for a signification of humble and grateful acknowledging of the benefits of Christ given therein unto the worthy receiver, and to avoid that profanation and disorder which otherwise might have ensued, and not for giving any adoration to the Sacramental bread and wine there bodily received, ' or in regard of any real and essential presence of Christ's body and blood.' " —*Heylin*. Hist. Ref. Vol. II. p. 285. Cambridge, 1849.

Now if Heylin was a consenting party to the changes of 1662 (and there is no reason to suppose that he was not) this passage seems to prove that he did not consider the Declaration, as then re-annexed, to militate against "*such* a *real* presence as was defended in the writings of the ancient Fathers :" though, apparently, he thought the words " real and essential," in the older form, might seem contrariant : and alleges (erroneously, as I think I have shewn) that the Elizabethan Services "expunged" the Edwardine Declaration as seemingly denying the Patristic Doctrine. No doubt the change of language proposed by Gunning, as Burnet tells us, and adopted by the reviewers, satisfied Heylin by removing any doubt which might attach to the meaning of the Declaration as it originally stood : he must, therefore, be regarded as another witness—that it is now only a protest against a "*gross* and *carnal*" presence of Christ in the Sacrament," whether implied by Transubstantiation or by any other theory of the mode of Presence; even if these pages fail to convince any that it was not designed* to be *more* than this in its earlier form.

It is beyond a doubt that Bishop Cosin's Opinions materially influenced the course taken by the Reviewers in 1662: I have already had to consider carefully such of his Notes upon the Common Prayer as bear upon the questions discussed in these pages: his latest opinions upon the Eucharistic question must be considered to be contained in his " History of Popish Transubstantiation ; " for that work was written in 1656, six years only before the last revision of the Prayer Book. and he consented to its publication only a few months before his death in Jan. 15, 1572: so that here we have the matured convictions of the last fifteen years of his life—convictions be it remembered which he maintained, and which therefore must have influenced his decisions, while engaged upon the Review of the Prayer Book in 1661-2: it is most natural then to turn to that publication for an explanation of the sense in which he accepted the Declaration when consenting to append it to the Communion Service ; and it seems to me that that sense cannot be better stated than by quoting at length the following chapter:—

"CHAPTER III.

" WHAT THE PAPISTS DO UNDERSTAND BY CHRIST BEING SPIRITUALLY PRESENT IN THE SACRAMENT. 2. WHAT S. BERNARD UNDERSTOOD BY IT. 3. WHAT THE PROTESTANTS. 4. FAITH DOTH NOT CAUSE, BUT SUPPOSE THE PRESENCE OF CHRIST. 5. THE UNION BETWIXT THE BODY OF CHRIST AND THE BREAD IS SACRAMENTAL.

* Mr. Fisher, like others, seems to have thought (Lit. Pur., p. 382), that it had a further design, for he says—it will be remembered, that, not only was the Romanizing dogma of the "*Real Presence*" virtually abandoned by our first Reformers, when they undertook to revise the Liturgy for the second time in the reign of Edward ; but that the very *word* ' Real' was then deliberately, and with evident design, repudiated by them, as a word of unsound and most perilous import. Notwithstanding their lingering attachment to the refinements of Ratramn upon the meaning of this term, and their occasional use of it in their own writings."

Mr. Fisher's error in this passage seems to lie in supposing (though I am not sure he means as much) that the word *Real* was eschewed as being equivalent to *true ;* whereas the object was to avoid a term which the Roman party continually employed to denote the Presence implied in Transubstantiation: I think the preceding pages show that this was the true ground for the avoidance of the term.

" Having now, by what I have said, put it out of doubt that the protestants * believe a spiritual and true presence of Christ in the

* I venture to request the reader's attention to §§ 7, 8, and 9 of the following document, as shewing how much was held on the subject of the Real Presence by certain French Protestants only thirteen years after Bishop Cosin's death. The whole Paper, (which I met with accidentally some five years ago) is so interesting that it seems worth while to re-print it entire: from its allusion to "the persecution" which its authors were "under," it appears to have been elicited by the prospect or the fact of the Revocation of the Edict of Nantes by Louis XIV., on Oct. 12, 1685.

"A True copy of a project for the re-union of both religions in France.

" We whose names are here underwritten, Ministers of the Reformed Religion ; being desirous to carry our obedience to his Majesties Commands as far as the great interest of our Consciences will give us leave; and hoping, from the great goodness of his Majesty, that in consideration of this our compliance, and the steps we make towards the Religion he professes, he will be pleas'd to command the persecution we are under to cease; do promise to contribute, what lies in our power, to the Religious design which he has of uniting all his Subjects under one Ministery, and do resolve to re-unite ourselves to the Gallican Church, which in its Pastoral letter does likewise say that they will yield some of their right in favour of the publick Peace, and will rectifie those things that want redress, provided the wound of Schism be once heal'd. We do likewise on our side engage ourselves, that if the following Articles are *bona fide* granted to us, we will with all our hearts give his Majesty that satisfaction which he desires.

" 1. That there shall be no Obligation upon any body to believe Purgatory, that all disputes on this Article shall cease; every one speaking with great moderation of the state of souls after this life.

" 2. That the pictures of the Holy Trinity shall be taken out of the Churches ; and those which shall be left shall be only as Ornaments, &c. That the Pastours shall carefully instruct the people to avoid upon this subject the abuses which are but too common among the ignorant.

" 3. That such Relicks of Saints as shall be undoubtedly own'd to be true, shall be preserv'd with respect, but shall not make any essential part of the cult of Religion, and that none shall be bound to Worship them.

" 4. That it shall be taught that God alone is the true Object of our Adoration, and that the people shall be warn'd not to attribute to any Creature though never so eminent, that which is peculiar and proper to God : But nevertheless since the Saints in Heaven do concern themselves in our miseries we may pray to God to grant that to the Prayers of the Church triumphant, which the indifference and coldness of Ours cannot obtain from Him.

" 5. That amongst the Sacraments of Christian Religion Baptism and the Eucharist shall be reputed the chiefest, and that the others shall have the Name of Sacraments in a more large Sense only.

" 6. That touching the necessity of Baptism the Canon of the Council of *Trent* shall be the Rule, and it shall not be intended to any other than the natural sense of these words. *Si quis dixerit Baptismum liberorum ad salutem non esse necessarium anathema sit.* And therefore there shall be no modification to the tenth Canon of the preceding Chapter; which declares, that it is not lawful for all persons to administer the Sacraments, that power belonging only to the Ministers of the Gospel who have received it from Jesus Christ.

" 7. That Jesus Christ is really present in the Sacrament of the Eucharist, though the manner of His presence be incomprehensible to the Wit of man, and therefore none shall be oblig'd to define the manner of His Presence, neither shall there be any dispute about it, since it passes our understanding, and that God has not reveal'd it.

" 8. That in receiving the Sacrament One shall be in a posture of adoration, the Communicants at that time paying to Christ those supreme honours which

Sacrament, which is the reason that, according to the example of the fathers, they use so frequently the term *spiritual* in this subject,—it may not be amiss to consider, in the next place, how the Roman Church understands that same word. Now they (Bell., de Euch., l. i. c. 2. § 3.) make it to signify, 'that Christ is not present in the

are only due to God; but no more shall be exacted from any body for the species of the Bread and Wine, than that respect we pay to Sacred things.

"9. That none shall be obliged to kneel before the Host, except at the Communion.

"10. That the people shall have the Liberty of reading the Scripture, which shall be read publikly in the Churches, and that the Service shall be perform'd in the Vulgar Tongue: That the Cup shall be given to the people, and that no other Sacrifice shall be own'd, but that upon the Cross, that it shall be taught that Christians have but one victim which was sacrificed once for all, and that the Eucharist is only a Sacrifice of commemoration or the representation, which the true Christian makes to God of the Sacrifice of the Cross.

"11. That before we be oblig'd to receive Auricular confession, all abuses proceeding from it be redressed, and those necessary modifications added, which may contribute to the quiet of our Consciences.

"12. That all Fastings and other Mortifications shall be looked upon only as helps to Piety, and to preserve us in a state of Grace: That all the Orders of Religious Men or Women shall be reform'd, particularly the Mendicants. And those only shall be preserv'd that are most Antient, such as the Benedictines, together with the Jesuits and Fathers of the Oratory, all which shall be subject to the inspection and authority of the Bishops alone.

"13. That the Ministers shall be preserved in the state Ecclesiastick, and shall have in the Church a particular Rank; except only those who have been twice married, who shall be consider'd some other way.

"14. That Jesus Christ having bestowed on his Ministers the power of administering the Sacraments *gratis*, that they shall likewise dispense them *gratis*, and without selling them as is now practic'd.

"15. That the people shall be dispens'd from that great number of Holy Days which now so burthen them, and shall be oblig'd to celebrate only the Mysteries of the Nativity and Resurrection; with those of the Apostles and Saints of the first century.

"16. That the limits which the last Assembly of the Clergy of *France* have set to the Pope's authority shall be inviolable, and that as to the Rank he is to have amongst the Bishops, he be look'd upon only, as *Primus inter pares*.

"17. That those Observations and Ceremonies, which are beneath the Majesty of the Christian Religion, and of which there is no foot-steps in Antiquity, shall be abolish'd; such as Torches at Burials, Canonizations, Processions, Pilgrimages, and the postures of the Priests at the Altar.

"18. That upon all questions of the merit of good Works, and the power of grace, the opinion of St. *Austin* shall be followed, and the exposition of the Bishop of *Meaux*.

"19. That the gaining of Pardons and Indulgences shall be reform'd, & that the people shall be instructed as much as possible, that they are to hope for the remission of their sins by the blood of Jesus Christ.

"May the Lord send down His Spirit upon men, that they be all one heart, and one soul, and that we may in our days see this blessed Reunion. It is the Vows and Prayers of all good people of both Communions, and to which all ought to contribute according to their talent both by word and writing. *Amen fiat.*
Signed by
Dubourdieu
La Coste.
And above sixty more.

London, Printed by *Randal Taylor,* 1685."

Sacrament, either after that manner which is natural to corporal things, or that wherein His own Body subsists in Heaven, but according to the manner of existence proper to spirits whole and entire, in each part of the host; and, though by Himself He be be neither seen, touched, nor moved, yet in respect of the species or accidents joined with them, He may be said to be seen, touched, and moved;" "and so (part I.), the accidents being moved, the Body of Christ is truly moved accidentally, as the soul truly changeth place with the body; so that we truly and properly say, that the Body of Christ is removed, lifted up, and set down, put on the paten, or on the altar, and carried from hand to mouth, and from the mouth to the stomach:" "as Berengarius (§ 5) was forced to acknowledge in the Roman council under Pope Nicholas, that the Body of Christ was sensually touched by the hands, and broken and chewed by the teeth of the priest." But all this, and much more to the same effect, was never delivered to us either by Holy Scripture or the Ancient Fathers.* And, if souls or spirits could be present, as here Bellarmine teacheth, yet it would be absurd to say, that bodies could be so likewise, it being inconsistent with their nature.

"2. Indeed, Bellarmine confesseth with S. Bernard, that 'Christ in the sacrament is not given to us carnally, but spiritually :' and would to God he had rested here, and not outgone the Holy Scriptures and the doctrine of the Fathers. For endeavouring, with Pope Innocent III. and the Council of Trent, to determine the manner of the presence and manducation of Christ's Body with more nicety than was fitting, he thereby foolishly overthrew all that he had wisely said before, denied what he had affirmed, and opposed his own opinion. ' His fear was, lest his adversaries should apply that word *spiritually*, not so much to express the manner of presence, as to exclude the very substance of the Body and Blood of Christ : therefore, saith he, 'upon that account it is not safe to use too much that of S. Bernard, ' the Body of Christ is not corporally in the Sacrament,' without adding presently the above mentioned explanation. How much do we comply with human pride and curiosity, which would

---

* This alleged consequence of the Presence to which Bishop Cosin here objects may perhaps help to explain his meaning in the passage referred to, p. 138. With his objection may be compared the language of the Bishop of Brechin,— " . . .Either Christ is present, or He is not. If He is, He ought to be adored; if He is not, *cadit questio.*

" And yet this does not involve those extreme results of the doctrine mentioned before. It is quite compatible to hold this, and yet not to be able to accept the ceremonies of the festival of Corpus Christi, or of the Forty hours' Adoration. One may distinctly believe all this, and yet accept the words of the Article that "the Sacrament of the Lord's Supper was not by Christ's ordinance..worshipped.' Our Lord ordained the Sacrament to be the perpetual application of His Sacrifice, and to be the means of our union with Him. He did not ordain it to be a Palladium to confine His Presence to certain local bounds. Historically, we find evidence of the reservation of the Sacrament in the very earliest times, for the purpose of communicating the sick. The reservation for the purpose of adoration was much later."— *Charge*, p. 29, 2nd Ed.

seem to understand all things! Where is the danger? and what doth he fear, as long as all they that believe the Gospel own the true nature and the real and substantial presence of the Body of Christ in the Sacrament, using that explication of S. Bernard concerning the manner, which he himself, for the too great evidence of truth, durst not but admit? And why doth he own that the manner is spiritual, not carnal, and then require a carnal presence as to the manner itself? As for us, we all openly profess with S. Bernard, that the presence of the Body of Christ in the Sacrament is spiritual, and therefore true and real ; and, with the same Bernard and all the ancients, we deny that the Body of Christ is carnally either present or given. The thing we willingly admit, but humbly and religiously forbear to inquire into the manner.

" 3. We believe a presence and union of Christ with our souls and body, which we know not how to call better than sacramental, that is, effected by eating ; that, while we eat and drink the consecrated bread and wine, we eat and drink therewithal the Body and Blood of Christ, not in a corporal manner, but some other way, incomprehensible, known only to God, which we call spiritual ; for if, with S. Bernard and the fathers, a man goes no further, we do not find fault with a general explication of the manner, but with the presumption and self-conceitedness of those who boldly and curiously inquire what is a spiritual presence, as presuming that they can understand the manner of acting of God's Holy Spirit. We contrariwise confess, with the Fathers, that this manner of presence is unaccountable and past finding out, not to be searched and pried into by reason, but believed by faith. And, if it seems impossible that the Flesh of Christ should descend and come to be our food through so great a distance, we must remember how much the power of the Holy Spirit exceeds our sense and our apprehensions, and how absurd it would be to undertake to measure His immensity by our weakness and narrow capacity, and so make our faith to conceive and believe what our reason cannot comprehend.

" 4. Yet our faith doth not cause or make that presence, but apprehend it as most truly and really effected by the words of Christ ; and the faith whereby we are said to eat the Flesh of Christ is not that only whereby we believe that He died for our sins (for this faith is required and supposed to precede the sacramental manducation), but more properly that whereby we believe those words of Christ, ' This is My Body ;'—which was S. Austin's meaning when he said, ' Why dost thou prepare thy stomach and thy teeth ? Believe and thou hast eaten (*super Joh. tract*, 25).' For in this mystical eating, by the wonderful power of the Holy Ghost, we do invisibly receive the substance of Christ's Body and Blood, as much as if we should eat and drink both visibly.

" 5. The result of all this is, that the Body and Blood of Christ are sacramentally united to the bread and wine, so that Christ is truly given to the faithful [credentibus], and yet is not to be here considered with sense or worldly reason, but by faith, resting on the words of the Gospel. Now it is said, that the Body and Blood of Christ are joined to the bread and wine, because that in the celebration of the Holy Eucharist the Flesh is given together with the bread, and the Blood together with the wine. All that remains is, that we should with faith and humility admire this high and sacred mystery, which our tongue cannot sufficiently explain, nor our hearts conceive."—*Oxford Trans.*, pp. 169—171.

Such being Cosin's own statement of his belief upon the Real Presence, it may be well to compare his language with that of the Declaration, and observe how far the latter expresses what Cosin held to be the judgment of antiquity. The Declaration, then, states:—

(I.) That Kneeling at the Sacrament is " a signification of our humble and grateful acknowledgment of the benefits of Christ therein given to all worthy receivers." Bishop Cosin says (§ 3), " We believe a presence and union of Christ with our soul and body . . . . . effected by eating ;" and (§ 5), "that Christ is truly given to the faithful [credentibus]."

(II.) The Declaration states that Kneeling is "for the avoiding of such profanation and disorder in the Holy Communion, as might otherwise ensue." Bishop Cosin indicates the ground of profanation when he says (§ 2), there is a "real and substantial presence of the Body of Christ in the Sacrament," and that such presence is *objective* because (§ 4) "our faith doth not cause or make" it, "but apprehends it as most truly and really effected by the word of Christ" in the act of Consecration (§ 3).

(III.) The Declaration denies any adoration* to be intended

---

* Bishop Burnet thus defends Kneeling as a posture of Adoration in the Eucharistic Office :—" For the Posture, it is most likely that the first Institution was in the Table-Gesture, which was, lying along on one side. But it was apparent, in our Saviour's practice, that the *Jewish* Church had changed the Posture of that Institution of the Passover, in whose room the Eucharist came. For though *Moses* had appointed the *Jews* to eat their Paschal Lamb, standing with their loins girt, with staves in the hands, and shoes on their feet; yet the Jews did afterwards change this into the common Table-Posture: of which change, though there is no mention in the Old Testament, yet we see it was so in our Saviour's time; and since He complied with the common custom, we are sure that change was not criminal. It seemed reasonable to allow the Christian Church the like power in such things with the *Jewish ;* and as the *Jews* thought their coming into the Promised Land, might be a warrant to lay aside the Posture appointed by *Moses*, which became travellers best ; so Christ being now exalted, it seemed fit to receive this Sacrament with higher marks of outward

ordue "either unto the Sacramental Bread or Wine there bodily received, or unto any Corporal Presence of Christ's natural Flesh and Blood." Bishop Cosin adopts (§ 2) the words of S. Bernard, as accepted by Bellarmine, that "the Body of Christ is not corporally [*i.e.* carnally] in the Sacrament, and declares "that, while we eat and drink the consecrated bread and wine, we eat and drink therewithal the Body and Blood of Christ, not in a corporal manner."

(IV.) The Declaration asserts that "the Sacramental Bread and Wine remain in their very natural substances," and that "the natural Body and Blood of our Saviour Christ are in Heaven, and not here; it being against the truth of Christ's natural Body to be at one time in more places than one." Bishop Cosin, while declaring "it would be absurd to say that bodies could be" "present" in the way "Bellarmine teacheth," "it being inconsistent with their nature;" bids us consider, "the power of the Holy Spirit" in case "it seems impossible that the Flesh of Christ should descend and come to be our food through so great a distance;" and states (§ 5) "the result of" his argument to be "that the Body and Blood of Christ are sacramentally united to the bread and wine."

I argued (at p. 73 of this Letter) that although the substitution of "corporal" for "real and essential" was due primarily, as it seemed, to Bishop Gunning,* the majority, at

respect, than had been proper in the first Institution, where He was in the state of humiliation, and His Divine Glory not yet fully revealed. Therefore in the Primitive Church they received standing and bending their body, in a Posture of Adoration. But how soon that Gesture of Kneeling came in is not so exactly observed, nor is it needful to know. But surely there is a great want of ingenuity in them that are pleased to apply these Orders of some latter Popes for Kneeling at the Elevation to our Kneeling; when ours is not at one such part, which might be more liable to exception, but during the whole Office; by which it is one continued Act of Worship, and the Communicants kneel all the while." —*Hist. Ref.* Part ii. Bk. 1, p. 163, fol. 1715.

* Mr. Fisher, having observed that the Declaration was omitted in Elizabeth's Book "for the purpose of propitiating the Romanists," thus speaks of its changed language when restored in 1662. "Up to the period of the Restoration, the balance was maintained with an even hand between the two opposing parties— between the Romanizer on the one hand, and the avowed Protestant on the other. But when in the eventful year, 1662, the Liturgy was once more subjected to an authoritative revision, this state of equilibrium was no longer maintained. The Reviewers of that year laid hold of the discarded Rubric of 1552: and had they only re-inserted it in its original form, they would then indeed have conferred an

least, of the Bishops must have consented to the change : the language of Bishop Cosin, just cited, is sufficient evidence that he was one who could have had no difficulty in accepting the alteration, though, in all probability, he was indisposed to Gunning's alleged theory of the *mode* of Presence notwithstanding that Cosin commonly called him, in 1657, his "most affectionate friend and servant:" whether Burnet's account of Gunning's theory (see p. 70) be accurate or not, there seems no means of ascertaining: perhaps some light would be thrown upon the subject if we could find "A view and connection of the Common Prayer, 1662" which Gunning is said to have written (see *Chalmer's Biog. Dict.*); but a careful search and inquiry in all likely quarters has failed to discover it.

Here, perhaps, might safely be left the oft-repeated question—Does not the Declaration deny a Real Objective Presence of the Body and Blood of Christ in the Sacrament of the Lord's Supper? For Bishop Cosin's language, unless deprived of the weight justly due to it in any Historical answer, seems to me to furnish the clear reply—That such a Presence is not only not denied, but is, in fact, admitted by the very terms which exclude a *material* Presence. Mr. Goode, however, in his "Nature of Christ's Presence in the Eucharist," has made some statements upon this point which need to be considered, though indeed he has only so far

inestimable boon upon the Church ; by re-establishing one of those wholesome barriers, which had been so prudently contrived against the mischievous inroads of Papal doctrine.

"Such, however, was not the design of Dr. Gunning and his Laudian coadjutors. They re-inserted the Rubric, it is true : but they re-inserted it in an altered form, omitting the words 'real and essential'—obviously the most important in the passage *—and substituting the word '*corporal*' in their place.

"Now mark the inevitable consequence of this proceeding. Such a substitution, deliberately and designedly made, must necessarily be considered as involving nothing less than a positive, though tacit, recognition of the '*real and essential*,' as distinguished from the '*corporal*' presence ; and consequently, as having established a most plausible, though subtle pretext, for the maintenance of one of the most dangerous and delusive errors ever invented by the great deceiver of mankind. . . . .

"Nor have the leaders of the present 'Tractarian' movement been at all backward to avail themselves of the support, which this Rubric, in its present altered form, so palpably affords them."—*Lit. Pur.*, p. 382.

* I need scarcely say that I do not concur in Mr. Fisher's view of the meaning of these words in the original Declaration ; my argument in these pages being—that they were only meant to be equivalent to *carnal*.

noticed the above very important Chapter from Bishop Cosin, as to quote part of §. 5 which, with deference to his contrary view, I cannot but think makes entirely for the case of the writers he is opposing. Thus, then, at p. 30, he says :—

". . . . . . by the Rubric at the End of the Communion Service repudiating the doctrine of the corporal presence in the Lord's Supper, *because it is against the truth of Christ's natural body that it should be in more than one place at the same time*, she has forbidden the doctrine that there is a presence of Christ's natural body in the Supper, either in a natural or supernatural or spiritual manner, and either adjoined to the elements, *or distinct from them.*

The *Italics*, etc., here and in the following quotations, are Mr. Goode's.

Yet, surely, whatever he may think to have been the *intention* of the Declaration (though, indeed, the citations in these pages appear to me to preclude that notion of intention conveyed in the above passage) Mr. Goode has no right thus to wrest its *language* from its literal, grammatical construction; what is denied is "*any Corporal* presence of Christ's natural Flesh and Blood;" by this, says Mr. Goode, "is forbidden the Doctrine of" Its "Presence . . . . . . either in a *natural,* or *supernatural,* or *spiritual* manner :" a *natural* Presence of Christ's natural Flesh and Blood " is of course a "Corporal" Presence, *i.e.*, the Presence of a Body after the manner of a Body, and therefore is denied to be in the Eucharist; but unless a "supernatural," or "spiritual" Presence is *necessarily* a "Corporal" Presence, then neither such "manner" of Presence is denied by the terms of this Declaration.

In a Note to this passage, p. 32, Mr. Goode adds:—

"And the supposition of the real presence of the body in a supernatural way is a mere subterfuge, resorted to for the purpose of escaping the condemnation of the Rubric, but in vain, because such a presence *is* a *corporal* presence."

But why should Mr. Goode impute this motive to the persons of whom he speaks? He may think their notion of a *supernatural* Presence of a *natural* Body very bad philosophy : still if they say that they do not mean a Corporal, *i.e.*, *material* Presence with form and quantity, he is not warranted in speaking thus; for, to say the least, the term *supernatural* may as fitly be used with an *intention* to exclude such Presence, as were any of the strong terms which I have given, at p. 62, in the List No. 2 of expressions *allowed* by those Authorities in the Church of England of whose *bonâ fide* acceptance of this Declaration Mr. Goode would not, I feel sure, raise the smallest doubt. And when we recollect those remarkable words of our Lord (St. John iii. 13), "No man hath ascended up to heaven, but he that came down from heaven, even the Son of Man which *is* in heaven,"— words which, I suppose, would *popularly* be held to mean that His Body, though *naturally* on earth, was in some sense also *supernaturally* in Heaven through its union with the Divine Word Which is inseparable from the Godhead—it may not be thought unfitting, now that the "Son of Man" by a *local* change "hath ascended up to heaven," to call His coming "down from heaven," to be in some manner in the Holy Eucharist a *supernatural* Presence ; provided only that they who thus speak no more intend what the Declaration calls a "Corporal" Presence than, as we may well believe, did our Lord when uttering the words related by the Evangelist.

"Supernatural" is not, however, the only term which Mr. Goode asserts to be thus condemned by the Declaration ; for he says that it equally forbids "a Presence of Christ's natural body in the Supper, ... in a . . . . *spiritual* manner:" yet, at p. 89, he appears to retract this expression ; for he says " . . . that glorified Saviour is present with us in the rite. His human nature is, in a spiritual sense, really present with us, though not bodily." I assume that he does not mean to draw a distinction between the words "sense" and "manner;" and the illustration which he annexes warrants me, I think, in so doing; for he says immediately :—

"As the sun, though bodily far away from us, is really present with us when we have the presence of his light and heat, so the human nature of Christ, though bodily far away from us, is enabled by that Spirit to which it is united, to be present in power and influence throughout the earth, and thus to communicate to those who by a living faith are united to it, as the members of a body to the head, those spiritual energies and graces that dwell in it abundantly for communication to the members of His mystical body, the true Church."

The illustration here used by Mr. Goode has already been noticed in these pages as having been employed by others : thus, at p. 73, *Bishop Gardiner* was mentioned as having cited it with approbation from *Bucer* ; and *Archbishop Cranmer* was quoted as saying in reply, "In this comparison, I am glad that, at the last we be come so near together; for you be almost right heartily welcome home, and I pray you let us shake hands together." But Cranmer alleged that "Martin Bucer saith not so much as you do." I said, too, p. 75, that " the illustration here used is *Ridley's* also." Again, at p. 245, the same simile is referred to as having been quoted by *Harding* from *Bucer;* and *Jewel* was there shewn to have readily accepted the comparison as one that " putteth the matter" of a " fleshly " Presence " out of all question," though proving that " Christ . . . . . is present with us . . . . . in the Sacrament of His body and blood,"

Now the supposed aptness and value of the illustration is shewn by the very fact of its being thus resorted to by these seven writers, *viz.*, two noted Roman controversialists, Gardiner and Harding ; three leading Reforming Bishops, Cranmer, Ridley, and Jewel ; one principal Foreign Reformer, Bucer; and lastly by Mr. Goode. The lack of agreement in their application of the illustration may have arisen, less from an unwillingness to arrive at a common understanding of terms, than from the difficulty of deciding a question which (though perhaps *more capable* of being solved now than three centuries ago) even yet does not admit of a satisfactory reply owing to our still limited knowledge—perhaps real ignorance—of the actual nature and properties of matter. That question is—Can the presence of the sun in the earth be truly regarded as anything more than what is called a virtual Presence ? For, if it can be so regarded, then, possibly, it offers the truest analogy of the Real Presence in the Eucharist, and admits of being pursued with reverence to the farthest limits which must bind every comparison of things Spiritual and Material: while the fact that our Lord is spoken of in Holy Scripture as "The Sun of Righteousness" (Mal. iv. 2) would of itself naturally prompt a resort to that "Sun" which "He maketh" "to rise on the evil and on the good" (S. Matt. v. 17), when a figure was needed which might serve the best to explain His own Sacramental Presence in His Church.

I am not so presumptuous as to think that I can now, any more than when formerly noticing the point, at p. 75 of the original Letter, contribute any suggestions which will materially tend towards answering the Enquiry; but it may not be out of place, or overbold, to state here some few thoughts which seem to bear upon the subject, and which appear to me not less worthy of a little consideration than I ventured to regard them as being, four years ago, though at that time the opportunity of mentioning them did not occur.

It would be strange if the great advance made in Physical Science since the 16th century, furnished no fuller or more accurate methods of elucidating Theological Questions by Natural Phenomena than were available to controversialists Three Hundred Years ago: it was no fault of theirs that they did not apply scientific facts or theories which had then to be invented or discovered: but the very circumstance, that they did use them so far as their knowledge enabled them, implies how they would have acted now; and fully justifies us in having recourse to them under their more developed aspects.

Archbishop Cranmer (*Ans. to Gardiner*, p. 89) had drawn this "comparison":—

"They say, that Christ is **corporally** in many places at one time, affirming that his body is **corporally** and **really** present in as many places as there be hosts consecrated. We say, that as the Sun **corporally** is ever in heaven, and no where else, and yet by his **operation** and **virtue** the Sun is here in earth, by whose **influence** and **virtue** all things in the world be corporally regenerated, increased, and grow to their perfect state ; so likewise our Saviour Christ bodily and corporally is in heaven, sitting at the right hand of his Father, although spiritually he hath promised to be present with us upon earth unto the world's end."

Bishop Gardiner, in replying to this, had said : —

" But to the purpose of this similitude of the Sun, which Sun, this author saith, 'is only corporally in heaven, and no where else,' and in the earth the operation and virtue of the sun : so as by this author's supposal, the substance of the Sun should not be in earth, but only by operation and virtue: wherein if this author erreth, he doth the reader to understand, that if he can in consideration of natural things, it is no marvel though he err in heavenly things. For, because I will not of myself begin the contention with this author of the natural work of the Sun, I will bring forth the saying of Martin Bucer, ... he useth the similitude of the Sun for his purpose, to prove Christ's body present really and substantially in the sacrament, where this author useth the same similitude to prove the body of Christ really absent."—p. 90.

Then Gardiner proceeds to quote the passage from Bucer as already given at p. 73, and adds :—

" Thus hath Bucer expressed his mind, whereunto, because the similitude of the Sun doth not answer in all parts, he noteth wisely in the end, how this is a matter of faith, and therefore upon the foundation of faith we must speak of it, thereby to supply where our senses fail. For the presence of Christ, and whole Christ, God and man, is true, although we cannot think of the manner 'how.' The chief cause why I bring in Bucer is this, to shew how, in his judgment, we have not only in earth the operation and virtue of the Sun, but also the substance of the Sun, by means of the Sun-beams, which be of the same substance with the Sun, and cannot be divided in substance from it ; and therefore we have in earth the substantial presence of the Sun, not only the operation and virtue. And howsoever the Sun above in the distance appeareth unto us of another sort, yet the beams that touch the earth be of the same substance with it, as clerks say, or at least as Bucer saith, whom I never heard accompted papist ; and yet for the real and substantial presence of Christ's very body in the sacrament, writeth pithily and plainly, and here encountereth this author with his similitude of the sun directly ; whereby may appear, how much soever Bucer is esteemed otherwise, he is not with this author regarded in the truth of the sacrament, which is one of the high mysteries of our religion."—p. 90.

It was by way of rejoinder to these arguments that Cranmer employed the language before cited at pp. 74 and 75, wherein he seems to rest his difference with Gardiner solely upon this one point, which the Roman controversialist called "the substantial presence of the sun;" for, though he says "if the substance of the sun be here corporally present with us upon earth, then I grant that Christ's body is so likewise," and observes that "Bucer saith not so much as" Gardiner, he asks, "and yet if you both said that the beams of the Sun be of the same substance with the Sun, who would believe either of you both?"

Gardiner had endeavoured, apparently, to guard himself against misunderstanding as to his use of the term corporally, by saying:—

> "The word 'corporally' may have an ambiguity and doubleness in respect and relation: one is to the truth of the body present, and so it may be said, Christ is corporally present in sacrament; if the word corporally be referred to the manner of the presence, then we should say, Christ's body were present after a corporal manner, which we say not, but in a spiritual manner; and therefore not locally nor by manner of quantity, but in such manner as God only knoweth, and yet doth us to understand by faith the truth of the very presence, exceeding our capacity to comprehend the manner 'how.'—p. 89.

In the argument between Jewel and Harding upon "the similitude of the Sun," the question did not actually arise—*whether the beams be of the same substance with the Sun?* Jewel seems to have thought it enough to confute a Corporal Presence in the Eucharist by the allegation (which of course Harding would allow) that "the Sun is more comfortable, and more refresheth the world, being absent, by his beams, than if his very natural substance and compass lay here upon the earth." In thus using the term "compass" Jewel may fairly be taken to have indicated the exact sense in which he employed the words "very natural substance;" namely, as necessarily implying, *in his argument,* form and quantity, and so that sort of local physical Presence in which it was essential to disavow any belief: though it does not, I think, follow that he would have denied the possibility of a substantial presence of the Sun in the Earth, which might more fitly be called a "very natural" presence than one of mere "operation and virtue."

The great controversial Theologians of the 16th Century, such as these whose statements have just been quoted, could hardly be ignorant altogether of the theories then in existence respecting the nature of Light and Heat, and so of their bearing upon this question of the character of the Solar Rays; even though, as is likely enough, they may not have thought it needful to take any definite view themselves of the subject: their acquaintance, *e.g.*, with the writings of S. Thomas Aquinas was sufficient to afford them some information on the matter: he had discussed the question (*Pars. prima.* quæst. 67. Art. 2 and 3)—Whether light was a *body* or a *quality*—and had concluded against the *corporal* theory for this reason, among other grounds of objection—" That two bodies cannot be together in the same place: but the light is with the air: therefore light is not a body."

Probably, however, it is not assuming too much to assert—that what is now known of the nature of the Sun's light would lead Philosophers to reject, as an *absolutely* true proposition, Aquinas's premiss, " That two bodies *cannot* be together in the same place ;" and with it, his conclusion that "light is not a body." For, whether we adopt the *Newtonian* (*i.e.*, the *Corpuscular*) theory, which regards Light as a peculiar matter projected in all directions from Luminous Bodies in a rapid succession of particles—a theory which appears very similar to that of Vision held by Pythagoras; or whether (having regard to the fact of the *polarization* of Light, which has revived the Doctrine of *Descartes* and others) we accept the *Undulatory* theory, which maintains that a highly attenuated fluid or ether is universally diffused throughout space, and, though inappreciable by our senses while at rest, is thrown into a succession of waves when acted upon by a luminous body: it seems that all the known phenomena of Light may be explained upon either hypothesis.

Moreover, whichever hypothesis is adopted, it is held that Light must be regarded as a MATERIAL SUBSTANCE, possessed of certain properties, from which this character of it is argued: such are—its capability of deflection; its being arrested by some bodies, though passing through others; its reflection by polished surfaces; its condensation and diffusion in passing through certain media; its producing chemical changes; its absorption and spontaneous emission from particular substances, *e.g.*, the Diamond which, having been exposed to the Sun's rays, continues to shine in the dark for a short time.

Further, these theories about *Light* are held to be mostly applicable to *Heat* also; and, as the Rays of the Sun furnish Heat as well as Light, so the belief in the *Materiality* of those Rays receives a further confirmation; indeed it is thought that Light and Heat may be only *modifications* of the same Matter, inasmuch as in the Sun's Rays they are so blended that hitherto Science has not been able entirely to separate them.

Without, then, resting too much upon present conclusions of Science which future discoveries* may vary, it can scarcely be considered *unphilosophical* now to hold as, at least, a probable opinion—" that the beams of the Sun be of the same substance with the Sun "—and it may be presumed that were Archbishop Cranmer living in the present day he would hardly feel warranted in saying, of Gardiner and Bucer (if they still asserted their belief in *corporeiety*, and he in *quality*) " Who would believe either of you both ?"

Yet this conviction of their *Materiality* and *Identity* with the Sun by no means implies a LOCAL *presence* of what Bishop Jewel called the "*very natural substance and compass*" of the Sun itself wherever the *Beams* of that Luminary are present. It may be permitted, surely, to hold without reproach—that they are the *same* THING, though not after the *same* MANNER.

Again: it will probably be generally admitted that the Sun's Rays, *i.e.*, his *Material* Light and Heat do combine with; interpenetrate; occupy the same space as; are, in

* See, *e.g.*, the recent discovery of Iron and Magnesium in the Solar Atmosphere.—" Researches on the Solar Spectrum," etc., *Edinburgh Review*, October, 1862.

fact, in, with, and under other Bodies, whose *Materiality* is appreciable to the senses in ways which cannot be predicated of the Sun's Beams. And this being so, it follows, upon the theory of their *identity* with the Sun, that the same admission may be fairly asked and readily conceded touching the SUN itself.

There are two ways in which THE SUN can be regarded as thus **substantially** present: for the sake of distinctness they may be called *General* and *Special*. By *General*, I mean its ordinary diffusion, by means of its Beams, through the *Material World:* by *Special*, I intend its particular localization when, those Beams being brought to a focus in a Lens or Mirror, a distinct *Image* is formed of the Heavenly Luminary. It is hardly necessary to point out that these two modes of Presence are not only diverse in their character, but also distinct in their effects: the former being, what may be called, an Atmosphere of Heat and Light, whose Influence is everywhere naturally exerted in some degree upon all Objects in Nature coming within it: the latter being a precise spot where that Heat and Light are scientifically centred and brought to act upon some given object selected for their peculiar and more powerful operation.

Now, it seems to me, that these considerations may reverently be used analogically to explain and illustrate those two kinds of the DIVINE PRESENCE which are commonly known as the *Universal* and the *Particular:* the First being expressed in that question concerning His Omnipresence which God asked through the Prophet Jeremiah, (xxiii. 23, 24), "Am I a God at hand, saith the Lord, and not a God afar off? Can any hide himself in secret places that I shall not see him? saith the Lord. Do not I fill heaven and earth? saith the Lord." The Second being described in that promise, "My Presence shall go with thee," which God made to Moses, who (when oppressed with the burden of care for the people) complained, "Thou hast not let me know whom Thou wilt send with me." (Exodus xxxiii. 12, 14.) Of both these manifestations of God's

Presence it is alike true that they were God in the Verity of His Eternal Substance, exhibiting Himself, and operating diffusedly or concentratedly (so to say); though He speaks of Himself, and is spoken of, as having a *local* habitation, as when Job asks, (xxii. 12), " Is not God in the height of heaven," or when Micaiah declared, (1 Kings xxii. 19), " I saw the LORD sitting on His throne, and all the host of heaven standing by Him on His right hand and on His left."

But it is more to my present purpose to apply this analogy to that remarkable distinction between the Old Dispensation and the New, which St. Paul so precisely points out in the Epistle to the Hebrews (x. 1) when he speaks of "the Law having a shadow (σκιὰν) of good things to come, and not the very image (αὐτὴν τὴν εἰκόνα) of the things." The Law was, and the Gospel is, as his words seem to mean, an exhibition upon Earth of the "good things [which are even yet] to come." (ix. 11.) What those "good things" are, may be gathered from the fact of " Christ being come an high Priest of" them ; for in the discharge of His Sacerdotal Functions of Oblation and Intercession—begun on Earth and continued, by reason of His "unchangeable Priesthood, (vii. 24), when "He entered in once" for all "into" Heaven "the Holy Place"—He "obtained eternal redemption for us," (ix. 12), "perfected for ever them that are sanctified," (x. 14), "is able to save them to the uttermost that come unto God by Him, seeing He ever liveth to make intercession for them." (vii. 25.) Thus by His Atonement He is working out that Reconciliation and Peace which are to result in such a Perfection of His Mystical Body, as will fully realize the Psalmist's words, (Psalm xvi. 11), " Thou wilt shew me the path of life : in Thy Presence is fulness of joy ; at Thy right hand there are pleasures for evermore ;" because, "all things " being then "subdued unto " Christ, God will "be all in all." (1 Cor. xv. 28.)

Yet the Exhibition of this Divine goodness under the Law was but an *Adumbration* of It; nevertheless it was *identical* with it (as are the Beams of the Sun with the Sun), being a Shadowing forth of Itself—a Cloud resplendent with the Divine glory, such, *e.g.*, as that in which God appeared "upon the mercy seat" of the Tabernacle, (Lev. xvi. 1), or, later, in the Temple, when "the cloud filled the House of the Lord, so that the priests could not stand to minister because of the cloud: for the glory of the Lord had filled the house of the Lord." (1 Kings viii. 10, 11.) It was not a Shadow projected from an Object by a Luminary shining upon it, but an Emanation of, though not a separation from, the Divine Presence Itself; and, therefore, though only a Shadowy outline of it yet still, the Presence of Him Who is Divine.

Under the Gospel, however, it became more than this: it developed into the *Delineation* of the "good things" themselves which then began to "shine" (2 Cor. iv. 4) in Christ, in Whom "dwelleth all the fulness of the Godhead bodily," (Col. ii. 9); for He was "the Image of the Invisible God." (Col. i. 15.) His Visible Presence among men answered Solomon's question in a way little, if at all, contemplated— "Will God indeed dwell on the earth?" For though he said, "Behold, the Heaven and Heaven of Heavens cannot contain Thee, how much less this House that I have builded?" (1 Kings viii. 27); human eyes nevertheless beheld "the Word" of God "made Flesh, and" dwelling "among" men, "full of grace and truth." (St. John i. 14.) And so it came to pass, that though "No man hath seen God at any time: the Only Begotten Son, which is in the bosom of the Father, He hath declared Him," (St. John i. 18); for "God was manifest in the Flesh." (1 Tim. iii. 16.) The Invisible and Incomprehensible God vouchsafed to assume Form, and to be enshrined in Matter, in order that His creature, Man, might behold Him and approach Him, and thus come sensibly within the sphere of His operation, (even as some object brought to the focus of a Lens in which the Sun's beams have been concentrated into his Image): though His Infinity was not thereby bounded, nor His

Invisibility consequently destroyed: He remained the Eternal Spirit though He was born in Time of Mary His creature.

But, then, although there was the most complete and perfect identity between God sitting on His throne and God walking among men; it was nevertheless true that the Presence of God in Christ reconciling the world unto Himself" (2 Cor. v. 19) was only a *local* Presence, by reason of Christ's Humanity. Men had, indeed, in the visible tabernacling of Christ in the midst of them, all the sympathy of "perfect Man" and all the power of "perfect God :" but the conditions of Manhood Physically limited His Incarnate Presence to one place at one time; though the conditions of Godhead enabled the God-Man to extend Himself after a Spiritual manner, and to exert both His Power and Sympathy where He was Corporally absent, as, *e.g.*, when He said, "Thy Son liveth." (St. John iv. 50.)

Yet this extension, from the nature of the case, could be but *partial* in its effects; for it necessarily involved applications to Christ of a local and personal character which were commonly difficult, and as regarded the great mass of mankind must be practically, if not absolutely impossible. The invitation of the Sun of Righteousness was " *Come* unto Me *all* that travail and are heavy laden, and I will refresh you," (St. Matt. xi. 28): but the answer must soon have been, "I sought Him, but I could not find Him," (Cant. v. 6), even by those at no great distance, and though He went hither and thither never so much in the plenitude of His zeal to enlighten the Nations.

The Ascension of the Incarnate Sun of Righteousness, though it was to a local habitation in "Heaven," whence, as "Light of Light," He "came down," removed this difficulty of Universal Presence, arising out of the limitations imposed by His Humanity. One especial object which Christ had in determining to "go away" from His Disciples was to "come again" to them, (St. John xiv. 28): this return, which was to be effected by the coming of the Holy Ghost, " the

Comforter," Who was to "abide with" them "for ever," (xiv. 16), had moreover a further purpose than their own personal consolation; it had reference to "the world," which that Divine Spirit was to "reprove (*or* convince)" of the very same things which Christ had already been convicting it of, *viz.*, "Sin," (*e.g.*, St. John xv. 22); "Righteousness," (*e.g.*, St. Matt. xxi. 28—32); "Judgment," (*e.g.*, St. Matt. vii. 2). And directly connected with this purpose was another, and that other a re-production, (so to say), when Christ should have gone away, of that same "image of the things" still "to come," which men had been beholding in Him, and which needed to be perpetuated, unless the Gospel were to exhibit less than the Law: "Howbeit," said our Lord, "when He the Spirit of Truth is come,......He will shew you THE THINGS TO COME," (St. John xvi. 13), words not a little remarkable when compared with those of St. Paul, (Heb. x. 1), already spoken of, especially if we bear in mind his "visions and revelations of [*i.e.*, given him by] the Lord" when he was "caught up to the third heaven....into paradise, and heard unspeakable words which it is not lawful [*or* possible] for a man to utter." (2 Cor. xii. 1—5.) Nor are we left wholly to guess in what the Holy Ghost's manifestation of these "things to come," primarily at least, consisted; "For," said our Lord, "He shall glorify Me : for He shall take of Mine, and shall shew it unto you. All things that the Father hath are Mine: therefore, said I, that He shall take of Mine, and shall shew it unto you." (St. John xvi. 14, 15.)

Now, whatever may be the details of this Manifestation by which the Spirit was to "glorify" the Incarnate Son, there can be no doubt that they all converge towards, and centre in, that perfect love of God which caused the entire Oblation of the Eternal Son, wrought it out through all its stages, and completed it in the final act of Christ's sacrifice upon the cross. That the Memorial of this final act was in fact subsequently made among Christians is plain from St. Paul's remonstrance with the "foolish Galatians....

before whose eyes," as he says, "Jesus Christ hath been evidently set forth crucified among you." (Gal. iii. 1.) How it was, and was to be perpetually "set forth," may be no less plainly gathered from his recital to the Corinthians of that account of the Institution of the Eucharist which he "received of the Lord," (probably in that Heavenly Vision already referred to), wherein he says, "For as often as ye eat this bread, and drink this cup, shew ye the Lord's death till He come." (1 Cor. xi. 28.) The evidence of this perpetual Commemoration, hitherto, is matter of the plainest History, as in the Acts of the Apostles, (e.g., ii. 42; xx. 7), and the witness of Liturgies; it exists, moreover, in the living experience of this crowning act of Worship in the Universal Church. The realization of the promise to the first Disciples (and in them to all others)—"I will come to you," (St. John xiv. 18)—is not less surely to be found in the Invocation of the Holy Ghost, whether expressed or implied, to make present in that "Divine Service" the Body and Blood of Christ, i.e., Christ Himself. The effect of that realization—"I will see you again, and your heart shall rejoice," (St. John xvi. 22)—finds its distinct confirmation in that description of "the ministration of the Spirit" which St. Paul gives—"We all, with open face beholding as in a glass the glory of the Lord, are changed into the same image from glory to glory, even as of the Lord the Spirit." (2 Cor. iii. 18.)

Unless, however, this Manifestation of Christ in His glory, as exhibited by the present Ministry of the Spirit in (what I may properly call) the Eucharistic Mirror, is an *equally* TRUE shewing forth of the God-Man with that which was beheld when He said, "I am come a Light into the world," (St. John xii. 46); then, His Presence now must be said to have lost in *Intensity*, while it has gained in *Universality*. But the Sun of Righteousness in declaring the purpose of His shining to be "that whosoever believeth IN ME should not abide in darkness," (*Ibid.*), described the precise *Object* on which the Faith of Christians was ever to be exercised, in order to effect their spiritual Illumination : that *Object* was none other than *the Incarnate Son* **really** present among them, gradually scattering the darkness of sin which obscured the Image of God, wherein Man was created, and, in so doing, bringing out afresh the golden outlines and features of the Divine character still existing in him. It is upon *this very same* OBJECT, only in its glorified condition, that "we all" are believingly to gaze, in order that by the "knowledge" of Christ so acquired we may be transformed into "the image of Him that created" us, (Col. iii. 10), *i. e.*, into the likeness of Christ Himself, the *imago* (εἰκών) of the Gospel, Who thus carries on the Sanctification of the Will of the regenerate ; advancing them "from glory to glory ;" "the inward man" being "renewed day by day," towards the perfection of its re-creation, "while we look not at the things which are seen" with bodily eyes in Sacraments, "but at the things which are not seen," except by spiritual discernment : "for the things which are seen are temporal ; but the things which are not seen are eternal." (2 Cor. iv. 16—18.)

That this **substantial** Eucharistic Image is capable of being multiplied as indefinitely throughout the Kingdom of Grace as is the Solar Image throughout the Visible World, might fairly be gathered from the Church's practical application, in regard to the Sacrament of the Altar, of such a promise as that of her Lord, "Where two or three are gathered together in My Name, there am I in the midst of them." (St. Matt. xviii. 20.) *HOW* this *Presence* is produced it is as hopeless as needless to attempt to *decide :* but this is no sufficient ground for refusing to admit the FACT of that *Presence.* If, by whatever law—known, or to be discovered —the mirrored image of the Sun produces Natural Effects like to what we *suppose* would be the local action of that Luminary, and therefore may be fitly called the Real Presence of the Sun ; it cannot surely be a condemnable proposition to hold—that, as the same Spiritual Effects are now caused by Eucharists which we *know* to have been caused by

z z

the actual Presence of Christ upon earth, therefore He is now as **Really** present in these Sacramental Mirrors as He is in His local Session at the Right Hand of His Eternal Father. Yet this is no more a *Material, i.e.,* a *Corporal* Presence, in the ordinary acceptation of the term, than is the Image of the Sun in a Mirror the *Corporal* Presence of that Luminary. Archbishop Cranmer (in 1551, when his doctrine of the Real Presence was at what may be called its lowest ebb), arguing with Bishop Gardiner against the Presence of Christ's **Natural** Body as the result of Consecration, professed to hold with St. Cyprian, " that the Divinity may be said to be poured, or put sacramentally into the bread." (See p. 88.) The question is—Considering that in the " one Christ " are " two whole and perfect Natures,....the Godhead and the Manhood,....never to be divided," (Art. ii.), can His Humanity be accounted present in Eucharistic Elements in such a manner as not necessarily to involve its Ubiquity? It seems to me that a statement made by Cranmer in the previous year, and certainly not abandoned when he penned the above words, may be claimed as supporting an affirmative answer: he complained of being misrepresented in being accused of holding "that the spiritual receiving" of the Eucharist " is to receive Christ ONLY by His Divine Nature," and emphatically replied, "which thing I never said nor meant." (See p. 23.) The context of the sentence can, I think, be cited to shew that the Archbishop would not have thought it inconsistent to apply to *the Spiritual* PRESENCE what he here says of *the Spiritual* RECEIVING : but I do not press it as *his* argument, since the passage may be thought hardly clear enough to warrant it. What has now been advanced by way of analogy, drawn from the Presence of the Natural Sun, may possibly point to a mode of illustrating and defending the Real and Substantial Presence " of the Body and Blood of Christ under the Forms of Bread and Wine." It may be that in time to come He, Whose honour is most especially concerned in a right apprehension of the Doctrine to be believed on this Mystery, will give wisdom to some man, combining the requisite Theological and Scientific knowledge, and enable him so to explain this long-contested, and too often uncharitably disputed subject, as shall tend to Peace and Unity among His Mystical members, and so to His own greater glory in His Church and in the World.

These remarks are partly connected with that portion of a long Note quoted at p. 340 from Mr. Goode's Work on the Eucharist: but it is necessary to notice also the other statements contained in that Note: adverting to the exclusion of the Declaration on Kneeling, from all the Editions of the Prayer Book between 1552 and 1662, he says:—

"The reason for this exclusion may have been that it was not felt desirable to be rigidly strict at that time against *all* notions of a bodily presence. The great point was to exclude the carnal notion of an *oral* eating of the Body of Christ present *in the Elements*, and all the evil consequences resulting from such a doctrine; and to establish the doctrine that '*the mean* by which the Body of Christ was eaten was *faith*.' The notion of a bodily presence in the Supper to the faith of the receiver was one of a more harmless speculative nature, and therefore was left open to those who chose to entertain it. But the revival in our present Prayer Book of the Rubric of the second Prayer Book of Edward VI. clearly put an end even to this doctrine."

One error in this statement seems to me to lie in Mr. Goode's assuming that "the notion of a bodily presence IN THE SUPPER to the faith of the receiver .... was left open" yet not that of "the Body of Christ present IN THE ELEMENTS:" but here, at all events, he stands opposed to Bishop Burnet and Mr. Harold Browne (see above, pp. 63, 189, 190-1; and further, *Browne on the Articles*, p. 708 *) the latter of whom

---

* "The meaning of it [the Rubric] clearly is, not to deny a spiritual, but only a 'corporal presence of Christ's natural * Flesh and Blood,' 'and a consequent adoration of the elements, as though they did not remain still in their very natural substances.'"

* "There may be a difficulty in reconciling this doctrine [viz., of Christ's natural having become a spiritual, His corruptible an incorruptible body'], which is the plain doctrine of Scripture and the Primitive Christians, with the language of the Rubric at the end of the Communion Service quoted above. If they be at variance, the language of a not very carefully-worded Rubric, adopted not without some hesitation by the Reformers, ought not to be pressed: but it is plain, that the writers of the Rubric did not mean by the words 'natural body' to convey the same idea as St. Paul attaches to the term in 1 Cor. xv. The doctrine, which they meant to teach, was only, that we must not consider the manhood of Christ changed into His Godhead." I must venture so far to differ from Mr. Browne as to express my belief that what has been advanced in these pages shews that the "Rubric" *was* "carefully-worded."

considers that the Declaration and its corresponding Clause in the 28th Article of 1553 were omitted out of regard to the Lutherans; the former perhaps referring the act to a like consideration for the Roman party as well: if, however, as certainly was the case, the suppression was designed to conciliate one or both of these; then, clearly, the belief of a Presence *in, with, or under the Elements* was not forbidden, for the Lutherans held it; nor can we suppose it was meant to be denied to the Romanists if they were content to allow the protest of the Article against Transubstantiation.

Again, Mr. Goode contends that "the great point" at that time was to determine against "the carnal notion of an *oral* eating of the Body of Christ present *in the Elements*" and in favour of *manducation by "faith:"* * but it is obvious from

---

* At p. 34 Mr. Goode says—"The Article maintains that the Body and Blood of Christ are received only by faith, and therefore not by the mouth of the communicant, and consequently they are not in or under or substituted for the consecrated elements; and the Rubric asserts, that there is no substantial presence of the natural Body of Christ at all in the Supper; and therefore the words 'verily and indeed taken and received' do not mean that the substantial Body and Blood of Christ, whether we suppose them present in a natural or a supernatural way, are received by the communicant."

But, unless Mr. Goode holds that Eucharistic reception and manducation of the Body and Blood of Christ are nothing more than a kind of mental contemplation, there seems no purpose to be answered by his argument, even if it were a sound one. For if, as surely is the case, there needs to be a real Union and Communion between man and his Incarnate God, there must be some means of effecting them; Christ has provided this in the two Sacraments of Baptism and the Lord's Supper; though we know they are not *absolutely* essential to this end: but Mr. Goode is here speaking of the *ordained* means of Communion, *viz.*, Eucharistic *feeding:* now seeing that He, Who could have fixed upon any other mode of Communion, *chose* to appoint this, it may well be thought to have a designed significance, and to have been meant to teach us—that so far as any *organ* or *sense* at all is the instrument by which faith effects its purposes, the *mouth* is that organ in the case of Sacramental Communion of the Body and Blood of Christ. The 28th Article does not say, as Mr. Goode represents, that "the Body and Blood of Christ are received only by faith;" its words are "the mean whereby the Body of Christ is received and eaten in the Supper is Faith." But the mention of an *agent* does not necessarily exclude an *instrument;* and so the mouth of a Christian may be the VISIBLE *instrument* by which an INVISIBLE *faith* effects Communion between his soul and Christ: just as, when in His risen Humanity He appeared to the disciples, Thomas in *touching* Him *touched* GOD (See p. 50); though it is as true to say that no man ever *touched* God, as to say that "No man hath *seen* God at any time" (St. John i. 18). I have already (at pp. 143—146) ventured a suggestion as to the compatibility of *oral* manducation with a *Real*, yet not carnal, Presence: here, therefore, it will be enough humbly to express my conviction that such a theory may suffice to correct that, perhaps not needless, dread of a gross and material conception of Eucharistic feeding which apparently runs through Mr. Goode's observations and arguments on this point.

the Article of 1563 and 1571 that an equal prominence was given to the condemnation of Transubstantiation and, what is more, the very Clause which declares that "*faith*" is "the mean whereby the Body of Christ is *received* and eaten," also declares that It "is *given*.... only after an *heavenly* and *spiritual* manner"—terms which Bishop Guest tells us as emphatically in his Second Letter (p. 199), as in the First, were designed "to take away all grosse and sensible presence"— a statement to which, it has been proved I think, we are bound to give the fullest credit.

But, further, Mr. Goode says that the restoration of the Declaration in 1662 "clearly puts an end even to this doc-

A reference to some extracts already given will shew that such a dread is not new, and will at the same time support, I think, what has been advanced in this note. Thus (See p. 12) though P. Martyr held "that we are incorporated into " Christ "by communication . . . . of the matter of the Sacrament, namely, the Body and Blood of Christ; but he meant it in *mind* and *faith*;" such language does not *necessarily* exclude *oral* "communication;" the ground, for this expression of the mode, being his anxiety "that they mixed not the Body and Blood of Christ *carnally* with the bread and wine by any *corporeal* Presence"—a then not unpopular corruption which it was deemed needful to guard against.

Again: Dr. Redman (see p. 28) when distinctly asked "his opinion, whether we received the very body of Christ with our mouths and into our bodies, or no?" did not deny such reception, but said "It is a hard question," adding "but surely we receive Christ in our souls by faith," and expressing his fear lest "When you do speak of it otherways, it soundeth grossly, and savoureth of the Capernaites."

Once more: Cranmer though, in answer to Weston (see p. 49), *he denied* that we receive "the Body by the mouth;" taught in his Catechism (See p. 155) that a rightly prepared communicant "doth . . . with his bodyly mouthe receaue the bodye and bloude of Christ;" the seeming contradiction being reconciled by the language of his "Defence" (See p. 159), and especially by his comment upon Gardiner's use of the word "verily" (See p. 181), which he says "is so *Capernaical*, so *gross*, and so dull in the perceiving of this mystery, that you think a man cannot receive the body of Christ verily, unless-he take Him *corporally* in his corporal mouth, *flesh, blood, and bones*, as he was born of the Virgin Mary." Looking at these statements and considering the prevalence at that time of carnal notions on the Presence, it is not difficult, I think, to understand the admission "that Christ entereth into us both by our ears and by our eyes" (See p. 49)— language which was hardly capable of a carnal construction—yet to comprehend the evident reluctance to endorse *oral* reception: though no one surely will deny that Christ *can* enter the soul by the mouth as well as by any other organ.

I will only further remark upon the above extract from Mr. Goode—that it is of the utmost importance in this controversy (especially if it is to become profitable by promoting any agreement) to be *accurate* in the use of language: Mr. Goode says "the Rubric asserts, that there is no substantial presence of the natural Body of Christ at all in the Supper:" but what is denied is "any *Corporal* Presence of Christ's natural flesh and blood:" unless Mr. Goode can prove that a *substantial* Presence *must* be a *Corporal* Presence this interchange of terms is not permissible.

trine" of "a bodily presence in the Supper to the faith of the receiver," which he thinks may have been allowed to be held during the exclusion of the Declaration.* Now it is immaterial to consider whether the statement of Bullinger and Gualter in their Letter of Feb. 6, 1566-7 (see p. 191) strictly represents the general practice at that time, when they say that that "same explanation" was then "most diligently declared, published and impressed upon the people :" though, of course, if, as there seems no reason to doubt, such was the case, its absence from the Prayer Book was of no practical importance. It is a complete answer, I think, to Mr. Goode's assertion to refer to the reply of the Bishops in 1661 (see p. 70) when the restoration of the Declaration was demanded: they said that "the sense of it is declared sufficiently in the 28th Article of the Church of England;" for if, as the Bishops in effect say, the Declara- and the Article mean the same thing; then, if the Article *without* the Declaration did not condemn the Presence of which Mr. Goode speaks, it follows that the Article *with* the Declaration does not now condemn it. Nay, more, by the same reasoning, if the Article *minus* the Declaration did not " take awaye yᵉ presence of Christe's Bodye in yᵉ Sacrament," as Bishop Guest asserted (See p. 193) how can the Article *plus* the Declaration have a precisely opposite effect ? There is but one answer, let him accept it who will,—that two statements *substantially alike* when separate, produce one *essentially different* when they are united.

In support of these three statements upon which I have been commenting, Mr. Goode refers to "the able Roman

* Yet Mr. Goode had said just before (p. 29) "There may be a real presence of Christ, even in the sense attributed to the words by the Archdeacon [who, Mr. G. says, "has confounded two things entirely distinct, the real presence of Christ in the Sacrament or rite to the worthy receiver, and His real presence in the consecrated elements; as also a *real spiritual* with a *real bodily* presence], *in the Supper*, though it be not in the elements. And, in the true sense of the words, our Church no doubt holds a real spiritual presence of Christ in the sacrament or rite to every faithful communicant, but not in the sacramental bread and wine."
So again (p. 12) "The Body might be present even materially, and yet not in the Bread."

Catholic writer, Abraham Woodhead,"* quoting passages from his "Two Discourses concerning the Adoration of our Blessed Saviour in the Holy Eucharist. Oxf. 1687, 4to., pp. 18, 24:" where the writer argues that the "reason" of the Declaration—viz., that the same body cannot be at the same time in different places—" seems necessarily to exclude . . . . the *real* and *essential* presence, as well as *corporal* and *natural*;" and contends that "the same objections, absurdities, etc.," are thus presented to those who "say that Christ's Body is really or essentially present in the Eucharist, ... not to the Elements, but to the receiver; and that not to his body, but to his soul," as they "afflict others" with, "for making it present with the signs." Upon Woodhead's reasoning, which he quotes at length, Mr. Goode says (Note p. 31):—

"These remarks are perfectly true. The denial that our Saviour's body can be in two places at the same time, is a denial that there can be any real bodily presence of our Saviour at all in the Eucharist, either in the Elements, or apart from them . . . . . The restoration, therefore, of this Rubric to our Prayer Book at the last revision precludes those who have subscribed it from holding *any* bodily presence at all in the Eucharist, even apart from the consecrated elements. While it was excluded, such a view might no doubt be held by our Divines, and some of them, perhaps, who lived at that time did maintain it. *But even these give no countenance to the doctrine opposed in this work*, because that doctrine is, that *the presence is by priestly consecration* IN THE ELEMENTS, *and to be adored as in the elements*; a notion which was decidedly opposed, as I shall show hereafter, by those who held the highest doctrine of the Real Presence ever maintained in our Reformed Church. And this is distinctly admitted by the Roman Catholic author just cited, even when endeavouring to show how near these authors come to the Roman Catholic doctrine of the Real Presence. He is obliged to admit that this notion of the Real Bodily Presence was that it was a Presence *to the receiver*, but *not to the elements*. (See work already cited in various places; and his Compendious Disc. on Euch., Oxford, 1688, p. 30, et seq., and App. 2, p. 212.)"

* He was born in 1608; educated at University College, Oxford; fellow in 1633; soon after took Holy Orders; was Proctor in 1641; subsequently went to Rome with pupils, where he is thought to have joined the Church of Rome; was deprived of his Fellowship in 1648, by the Parliamentary Visitors, on the ground of absence; died at Hoxton, May 4, 1678.

Now when Mr. Goode assigns his reasons for saying, " These remarks are perfectly true," he makes a statement which is certainly not the counterpart of Woodhead's argument; that writer considers " the reason" of the Declaration to be fatal to the " *real* and *essential* " no less than to the " corporal and natural" Presence ; and that, too, whether the Presence is held to be to the Receiver, or in the Elements: Mr. Goode seems to ignore the distinction between these two sorts of Presence, *viz.*, the *real* and the *corporal,* by saying what, in fact, the Declaration more accurately expresses—*viz.*, that there is not " any *real bodily* Presence of our Saviour at all in the Eucharist;" consistently enough, therefore, he contends that the restored Declaration " precludes . . . . . . from holding *any* bodily Presence." But he is here fighting with a phantom; for the writers whom he is opposing have nowhere set up the notion of such a Presence ; on the contrary, they distinctly put forward the teaching of the Declaration : so that, unless Mr. Goode means by " any bodily Presence " something really different from "any corporal Presence of Christ's natural Flesh and Blood," his argument is useless, and may only mislead.

It is clear, however, from his other language, that Mr. Goode's objection travels beyond some real or supposed doctrine of " any bodily Presence," and runs up into, what he calls, the doctrine " that *the presence is by priestly consecration* IN THE ELEMENTS, *and to be adored as in the elements:*" by the expression " the Presence " I presume Mr. Goode does not mean that " bodily Presence " of which he had just been speaking, but such other Presence as the Church of England believes: here, however, I am not concerned to discuss the abstract questions of Consecration, or of the nature and mode of the Presence ; though, indeed, they have been noticed already in different parts of these pages, so far as was necessary for the elucidation of points in the historical survey which they take; it is only needful, therefore, to enquire—whether *the terms of the Declaration* exclude "the doctrine" here stated by Mr. Goode to " be decidedly opposed, ... by those who held the highest doctrine of the Real Presence ever maintained in our Reformed Church?" And I think it may be somewhat confidently answered that, having regard to the evidence which I have already offered, the statements of those who were responsible for the introduction and re-introduction of the Declaration, prove that no such exclusion was contemplated.* In saying this I do not mean to imply that their contemporaries, of whom Mr. Goode speaks, are to be wholly disregarded; but that any statements of theirs which are, or seem to be, opposed to those authorities I have cited, must not be allowed to outweigh them. But as Mr. Goode invokes Woodhead's admissions in support of his own opinion as to the teaching of the writers he mentions, it is desirable to consider what that author states in proof of their holding that " the Real bodily Presence was," as Mr. Goode says, " a Presence *to the receiver,* but *not to the elements."*

In referring to the first of his two Publications † which Mr. Goode cites (See p. 359), it is important to notice at the outset that Woodhead seems to have been ignorant or unmindful of one important circumstance as to the Declaration; and this may therefore have coloured his views of its meaning, and of the language of its authors and maintainers: speaking of the change in the form of delivering the Sacrament, he says (p. 2) that it was made by "the Composers of the

---

* Even Woodhead (p. 4), to whom Mr. Goode here refers, says that the authors of the present Declaration "either leave this undetermined, whether there be not another Presence of Christ's Flesh and Blood as real and true as is the Corporeal, to which an adoration is at this time due: or else do determine, as seems concludable from their present Proposition [viz., that the natural Body of Christ is not there] that there is not any such real Presence of the Body at all, and so no adoration due in any such respect."

† The following extract seems to explain a Typographical peculiarity in these two Publications, *viz.,* the frequent insertion of passages in square brackets, apparently by some one else than Woodhead himself; and also removes the doubt, which has been sometimes entertained, whether the author was Abraham Woodhead or Obadiah Walker:—" In October following [*i.e.*, 1686] Mr. Walker obtained a License from his Majesty [James II.] to print certain books lying by him, because he knew they would not pass through the Licenser's hands, and in Jan. following that, he published, ' *Two Discourses concerning the Adoration of our Blessed Saviour in the Eucharist,*' etc., penned by his quondam tutor, Abraham Woodhead."—*Wood, Ath. Oxon,* vol. iv., p. 440, London, 1820.

Second [Prayer Book of Edward VIth.] ..... suitable to their *Declaration*, which denies any real or essential presence of this Body [of Christ] in the Eucharist:" Whereas the fact is that the Declaration was subsequent to the completion, and even printing of many copies, of the Book : the proof of this has already been given, so that there is no need to relate it here : I need scarcely add that a perusal of Woodhead's book plainly shews him to have been uninformed of those other important matters in the history of the Declaration which are now for the first time, I believe, published. It is well to notice, too, that Woodhead does not here accurately represent the teaching of the Original Declaration; it condemned the notion of "any reall and essenciall presence .... of Chryste's natural Fleshe and Bloude :" this does not necessarily mean the same thing as "real or essential Presence of [Christ's] Body," though Woodhead may have designed to interchange the language.

I pass over some other difficulties which Woodhead (p. 2) raises as to the omission of the Invocation and the Manual Acts, in the Second Book of Edward VIth.; merely drawing attention to what has been already stated (See pp. 34 and 35) in proof that those who were responsible for the Revision of 1552 did not intend it to teach a different Eucharistic Doctrine from that which the First Book set forth; and of which Bishop Gardiner could say (See p. 26) that "touching the truth of the very Presence of Christ's most precious Body and Blood in the Sacrament, there was as much spoken in that book as might be desired."

Now Woodhead discusses Three Subjects:—

" 1. That here [*i.e.*, in the Declaration] the present Clergy do profess expressly, that *the natural Body and Blood of our Saviour Christ are not in the Blessed Sacrament.*"—p. 4.

With reference to this he says :—

" ....the learned Protestant writers seem to me, at least in their most usual expressions, to have heretofore delivered the contrary; *viz.*, ' That the very substance of Christ's Body, that His natural Body, that that very Body that was born of the Blessed Virgin, and crucified on the cross, etc., is present, as in heaven, so here in this

Holy Sacrament, either to the worthy Receiver; or to the Symbols."—p. 5.

But this is certainly not the same thing as saying (in Mr. Goode's words)—that they only held "a Presence to the Receiver, but not to the Elements."

In proof, Woodhead cites Calvin on 1 Cor. xi. 24; *Instit.* 4, l. 17, c. 11 §; *ib.* §§. 16 and 19: "Beza, and others of the same sect, related by *Hospinian, hist. Sacram. parte altera*, p. 251": Hooker, *Eccl. Pol.*, 5, l. 67, §: Bp. Andrews, *Resp. ad. Apol. Bell.*, 1 c., p. 11; *ib.*, 8 c., p. 194: "Is. Causabon's Letter written by the King's command to Card. Perron," §. 11, n. 2: Bp. Hall, *De pace Ecclesiastica*, §. 12: Bp. Montague, *Appeal*, pp. 289 and 779: Abp. Laud, *Conf. with Fisher*, §. 35, n. 3 and 6: "Bp. Taylor, one of the last who hath written a just Treatise on this subject, 1. §., 11 n., p. 18,* and §. 12: Bp. Forbes, *de Eucharistia*, 2. l., 2 c., 9 §., and 3. l., 1 c., 10 §.: the Archbishop of Spalato, *de*

---

* Though I am unwilling to multiply quotations, it seems desirable here to give the passage cited from Bp. Taylor:—"It is enquired whether, when we say we believe Christ's body to be really in the Sacrament, we mean that body, that flesh, that was born of the Virgin Mary, that was crucified, dead and buried? I answer I know of none else that He had, or hath; there is but one body of Christ natural and glorified: but he* that saith that body is glorified, which was crucified, says it is the same body, but not after the same manner; and so it is in the Sacrament, we eat and drink the body and blood of Christ that was broken and poured forth; for there is no other body, no other blood of Christ: but though it is the same we eat and drink, yet it is in another manner. And therefore when any of the Protestant Divines, or any of the Fathers deny, that body which was born of the Virgin Mary, that was crucified, to be eaten in the Sacrament, as Bertram, as St. Hierom, as Clemens Alexandrinus expressly affirm; the meaning is easy, they intend that it is not eaten in a natural sense: and then calling [it] Corpus *spirituale*, the word *spirituale* is not a substantial predication, but is an affirmation of the manner; tho in disputation it be made the Predicate of a Proposition, and the opposite member of a Distinction. That Body which was crucified is not the Body that is eaten in the Sacrament, if the intention of the Proposition be to speak of the eating it in the same manner of being: but that Body which was crucified, the same Body do we eat, if the intention be to speak of the same thing in several manners of being and operating; and this I noted, that we may not be prejudiced by words, when the notion is certain and easy. And thus far is the sense of our doctrine in this Article."—p. 9.

"Again, §. 12, p. 288:—'They that do not confess the Eucharist to be the flesh of our Saviour, which flesh suffered for us, let them be Anathema. But *quo modo* is the question,' etc."—*Conf., Bp. Heber's Ed.*, 1839, vol. x., p. 73.

* The reference here is to "Bp. Ridley's Answer to Curtop's first argument in his Disputation at Oxford, Fox, Martyrol, p. 1451, vet. Edit."—See Bp. Heber's Edit., 1839, vol. ix., p. 431. (See p. 59.)

Rep. Eccl., 7. l., 11 c., 7 §.: and Mr. Thorndyke, *Epilogue to the Tragedy*, 3. l., 3 c.; *Ib.*, 2. c.; 3. l. 23 c.; 3. l., 5. c.; and 3. l., 30 c.

Of these *twelve* writers *ten* speak as distinctly as possible, in the passages quoted,* of the Real Presence being in or under the Elements, or in the Sacrament: *Hooker*, the eleventh referred to, in the place cited, represents the controversy as being "whether, when the Sacrament is administered, Christ be whole within man only, or else His Body and Blood be also externally seated in the very consecrated Elements themselves:" while Bishop Hall, the twelfth writer quoted, observes that the difference between the Calvinists and Lutherans is not as to the *Thing* present, but as to the *manner* of Its Presence.

While, however, this disposes, I think, of Mr. Goode's conclusions from Woodhead's reference to these writers so far; it is of equal importance to notice that they none of them maintain a *Corporal* Presence of Christ's Natural Body; and therefore I cannot see that Woodhead has proved his allegation—that they have "delivered the contrary" of the protest in the Declaration against "any Corporal Presence of Christ's Natural Flesh and Blood" in the Eucharist: for even granting to the full, for argument's sake, that they all allowed (as he says) "the very substance of Christ's Body" to be "present," it cannot be maintained, I think, that they accounted It present "*as* in heaven, *so* here in this Holy Sacrament;" if by *so* is meant in *such manner :* indeed, it appears to me, that Woodhead really reconciles his own alleged difference between the Writers and the Declaration, when he says, in commenting upon Bishop Taylor's language, "now by exclusion of the natural manner is not meant (surely) the exclusion of *nature*, or of the thing itself, (for, then, to say a thing is there, after a natural manner, were as much as to say, the thing is not there :) but the exclusion of

* I am not here concerned to enquire whether the passages are *accurately* quoted (though the accuracy of the citation from Bp. Taylor favours the supposition of their fidelity) because, like Mr. Goode, I have only to deal with them *as* quoted.

those *properties* which usually accompany nature, or the thing."—p. 10.

The next subject of which Woodhead treats is :—

" 2. That they [*i.e.*, the present Clergy] urge for this Non-presence there [*viz.*, in the Eucharist] this reason or ground out of Natural Philosophy, That *it is against the truth of a natural body, to be in more places than one at one time ;* here seeming to found their Faith in this matter on the truth of this position in Nature."—p. 4.

Upon this point he says :—

" Here also, first, I find Protestants, and especially our English Divines generally, to confess the Presence of our Saviour in the Eucharist to be an ineffable mystery, (which I conceive is said to be so in respect of something in it *opposite* and contradictory to, and therefore incomprehensible and ineffable by, human reason.) "—p. 13.

The authorities he quotes are, Calvin, *Inst.*, 4. 1., 17 c., 24 §. ; §. 32 ; §. 25 ; §. 7 : King James' Answer to Card. Perron, §. 20, n. 2 : and Bishop Taylor, *Real Presence*, §. 11, n. 28 ; *Liberty of Prophecy*, 20, §. 16—n. He then proceeds to comment upon their language, and urges these objections :—

1. That by *ineffable mystery* they appear to admit that "some seeming *contradiction* to reason may yet be verified in this Sacrament."—p. 14.

But their words appear to me, at most, only to speak of the mode of Presence being not *fully comprehensible* to reason.

2. That " these Writers must hold this particular seeming contradiction, or some other equivalent to it, to be true ; so long as they affirm a *real* and *substantial Presence* . . . . . . contra-distinct to . . . . . a Presence of Christ's Body in its *virtue, efficacy, benefits, spirit,* etc., which is the *Zuinglian's real Presence :* for " if the *substance,* the *essence,* the *reality,*" of Christ's Body, " *naturally* or *locally* in Heaven," be " present to the *symbols,* or to the *receiver,* . . . . we must affirm that this *essence* or *substance* of the same Body at least is at the same time in diverse *places.*"—p. 14.

He contends, further, that there is no escaping this conclusion

" unless we defend one of these two things ; either (1) *That this Body is both here and there by an incomprehensible continuation, as it were, thereof,* (which sounds somewhat like the *ubiquity* of some Lutherans)....Or (2) Unless we will explain ourselves, that, by the *essential, real, substantial presence of Christ's Body in the Eucharist, we mean only the presence of the true and real effect, blessing, virtues* of this Body, (as Dr. Taylor sometimes seems to do) but this is, after professing with the highest in our *words*, a relapsing into Zuinglianism in our *sense*."—pp. 15 and 16.

After quoting passages* from Bp. Taylor, in proof of his statement, he goes on to point out,

" that the Schoolmen do not all agree on one and the same" *mode* of Presence; some, with *S. Thomas,* denying "the Body of Christ to be either *circumscriptivè,* or *definitivè* in this Sacrament," and affirming " *that Idem Corpus non potest, per miraculam,* or *potentiam divinam, esse in pluribus locis simul,* i.e. *localiter,* or, in the forementioned wayes, circumscriptively or definitively."—(p. 17.)

But he explains :—

" 1. That they take *circumscriptivè,* and *definitivè,* in such a sense, as that these two do exclude, not only such a bodie's being *ubique,* every where, but absolutely its being *alibi,* any where else ; and that these modes of Presence would infer, that the same individual is divided from itself, (contrary to the nature of *individuum,* or *unum,*) if such body should at that time be any where else."—*Ib.*

And then he mentions :—

" 2. That they put a third way of Presence of Christ's Body in the Eucharist, real and true, and tho not *per modum quantitatis dimensivæ,* yet *per modum substantiæ,* which they say is a mode proper to this Sacrament, and such as hinders not the same body at the same time to be *alibi,* elsewhere, and yet to remain, tho it be elsewhere,

---

* "[I will set you down the Doctor's words. (*Real presence* § 11. n. 17.) where, after he hath said, ' that there is not in all School-Divinity, nor in the old Philosophy, nor in nature, any more than three natural proper ways of being in a place, *circumscriptivè, definitivè, repletivè,* and that the Body of *Christ* is not in the Sacrament any of these three ways,' (quoting *Turrecremata** for it) he replies thus to those Schoolmen, that rejecting these three ways, do say, that *Christ's* Body is in a fourth way, viz. *Sacramentally* in more places than one.— ' This, saith he, is very true; that is, that the Sacrament of Christ's Body is [*in more places than one*]; and so is this Body [*in more places than one*] figuratively, tropically, representatively in being [or *essence*] and really in *effect* and *blessing.* But this is not a natural real being in a place, but a relation to a person.' Thus he. But if thus Christ's Body be held by us, as to its essence, only *figuratively, tropically,* and *representatively* in more places than one; and *really* in those places only in its *effect* and *blessing,* what will become of our *præsentiam non minus quam illi veram,* (See before § 11.) if others hold the presence of Christ's very *essence* and *substance* in the Eucharist, we only the presence there of its *effect* and *blessing?"*—p. 16.

* This is an error; Bp. Taylor only quotes Turrecremata as denying the first two modes of Presence.

indivisum in se; which the other Presences, in their acception of them, do hinder."—*Ib.*

In stating this, however, he also takes care to mention that :—

"Meanwhile other Schoolmen and Controvertists take liberty to dissent from these. See *Scotus* in 4 sent. dist. 10. q. 2. and *Bellarm.* de Euchar. 3. l. 3. c. and it seems not without reason. For, why should this their *Substantial* or *Sacramental* way (as real and true as any of the other) of Christ's Body being at the same time in Heaven and in the Eucharist, consist with this Bodie's remaining *indivisum in se;* more than the *circumscriptive* or *definitive* way, rightly understood, and freed of their limitations ; or, why impose they such a notion on these two ways, that they must imply an exact adequation of the place and the placed, or exclude it from being at all anywhere else ; any more than the other Substantial or Sacramental way (which they maintain) doth ? "—p. 18.

Now, no doubt, Woodhead in these observations starts real difficulties and raises perplexing questions : but, perchance, they *can* be answered and overcome, so far as the present limits of knowledge and the nature of the subject admit. It may be that some such theory as the one already suggested (See pp. 341—54) touching the *substantial* presence of the Natural Sun in this world of the First Creation, indicates a not impossible mode of the Real Presence of the Incarnate Sun of Righteousness in the Eucharists of the New Creation of God : and so, perhaps, defenders of that Presence need not stumble at the language of the Declaration ; or be reduced, in maintaining it, to the *alternative* which Woodhead propounds : for if, as I venture to think, the presence of the *inorganic* Sun here and in the Heavens might not be unphilosophically regarded as *identical,* rather than as " an incomprehensible continuation," or as " the presence of the true and real effect" ; then (to speak with all reverence) it is surely as possible that the like may be predicated of the *organic* Body of Christ; especially if, as is necessary, we remember that that Body is now a SPIRITUAL (though a REAL) Body, and consider also what may be effected by the active Power of His Will as compared with the passive force of that " Greater Light" which He made. So, then, it seems to me that a " presence of Christ's very *essence* and *substance* in the Eucharist" is conceivable, which is not, what is usually understood by, a *material* presence; and which, after all, may be free from the objections which Woodhead enumerates.

But even should it be otherwise, and these apparent contradictions remain unreconciled, such a result would not, I think, here any more than in the former part of Woodhead's argument, support **Mr. Goode's** inference from, what he calls, that writer's admissions: for the difficulties apply quite as much to what he terms " the Real bodily presence ... *to the receiver*" as they do to that Presence if alleged to be "to the Elements."

Woodhead proceeds, however, to urge his difficulties as an argument against the *original* language of the Declaration; contending that—

" ....these words [*Real and essential presence*] seem as truly denied to be in the Eucharist, by the first composers of the foresaid Declaration in the latter end of King Edward's dayes, as the words [*Corporal* and *Natural presence*] are in this 2nd Edition thereof in A.D. 1661...."

But if I have correctly alleged throughout that the " *reall* and *essenciall* presence" of the first Declaration was designed to mean exactly the same as the " *corporal* presence" of the second Declaration, then Woodhead's argument falls to the ground; because " real and essential" did not import what he assumes them to have meant; and that this was so, is plain, I think, from the language of Bp. Ridley, who, it cannot be reasonably doubted (See Cranmer's Letter, p. 77) had an important share in framing the first Declaration ; for in his " Disputation at Oxford," full two years afterwards, he distinctly opposes *Transubstantiation* (from which, he says, " they gather that Christ's Body is really contained in the Sacrament of the Altar") on this very ground that " it maintaineth a **real, corporal,** and **carnal** presence of Christ's Flesh, ... and that not by *virtue* and *grace* only, but also by the whole **essence** and **substance**" thereof. (See p. 53.) Here, then, are the very words of the Declaration "real"= *corporal*:

" essential "$=$ *substantial:* each term and its synonym being, (as it seems to me) in Ridley's mind, the equivalent of "carnal." Moreover, in that very argument, he drew a distinction between "really"$=$"*transcendenter,*" in "which sort" he says "we also grant Christ's Body to be **really** in the Sacrament;" and "really"$=$"the *true manner* of His Body," "in which sense . . . . it may not be said to be here in the Earth."

I am not here overlooking Ridley's statement that the Presence is "by *virtue* and *grace* only:" yet I cannot but think that by those terms he meant *more* than, what is now called, a *virtual* Presence, *i. e.*, a mere *potential* Presence by an *agent* or *substitute;* though it is true (See p. 14) that in the Cambridge Disputation, 1549, he resorts to an illustration which seems scarcely to exceed it: but then his later language, in 1555, where he takes his example from the Sun (See p. 44) must be held, surely, to surpass this; unless, indeed, any will contend that there is no difference between the Presence of a King by his "mighty power and authority [which] is everywhere in his realms and dominions" and the Presence of the Sun " by its beams, light, and natural influence, when it shineth upon the Earth." In truth, this is just one of those instances of want of consistency in the use of terms which I have already had occasion to notice as rendering the arguments of the Reformation Writers so perplexing at times to us. However, in this very argument (also of the later date, 1555) where Ridley uses the words " *virtue* and *grace* " he allows (See p. 55) that if by " real presence " is not meant " real and corporal substance," but " something that appertaineth to Christ's Body," then " the ascension and abiding in Heaven are no let at all to that presence :" and he adds, " Wherefore Christ's Body, after that sort, is here present to us in the Lord's Supper ; by *grace*, I say, as Epiphanius speaketh of it." Perhaps, too, this last expression may be advantageously noticed in connection with another remark, made by Woodhead, as to the " *contradiction* " of saying " that the natural Body of Christ is not here in the

B B B

Eucharist, but only in *heaven;* yet;....that the natural Body of Christ is here in the Eucharist received. *It,* the *body* that was born of the B. Virgin, not a *grace* only, not a *Spirit* only, but *it* itself,...." Ridley, it will be observed, does not speak of the Presence *of the grace* of Christ's Body, but of Its Presence *by grace.*

The third subject of which Woodhead treats is the statement of the Declaration, that by Kneeling,

" no adoration is intended, or ought to be done unto any corporal presence of Christ's natural flesh and blood."—p. 4.

With reference to this he quotes Bishop Andrews, Bishop Taylor, Bishop Forbes, the Archbishop of Spalato, and Mr. Thorndyke, " to shew that the Church of England hath heretofore believed and affirmed such a Presence to *which* they thought Adoration due " (p. 28): yet he, somewhat strangely, argues that the Declaration, owing to the *reasons* assigned in it,

" seems clearly to deny Adoration due to Christ's Body as any way present in the Eucharist; contrary to the fore-cited doctrine, and contrary to the religion of King James and Bishop Andrews published to the world abroad. Or at least, in thus denying adoration due to a corporal presence, and then not declaring any other presence of Christ's body in the Sacrament that is adorable, when as such a Presence they believe ; it seems to betray the communicants to a greater miscarriage in their behaviour, as to such our Saviour's presence at the receiving of these dreadful Mysteries ; and to abridge this duty of that extent in which it had formerly been recommended by this Church."—p. 29.

But such reasoning seems to me most illogical, and not a little surprising, as coming from a writer like Woodhead; surely the very fact that the Declaration condemns one particular mode of Presence implies that its framers did not design to exclude the belief of any other than that mode: everything connected with the history of the Declaration, and the opinions of its framers and revisers, goes to prove, I think, that, as they had neither the desire nor the intention of needlessly paring down opinions on so difficult a subject so, they contented themselves with asserting what alone they thought it essential to maintain in the way of negation. If this be so, there could be no contemplated discouragement of any Adoration short of what necessarily involved the maintenance of that manner of Presence which was explicitly denied : while, so far from the Declaration tending " to betray the communicants to a greater miscarriage in their behaviour " we may fairly believe that it was thought a not improbable security against that irreverence which past experience had found to result from the popular notion of just such a *Carnal* Presence as it was the object of the Declaration to condemn and to discourage.

In passing now from this notice of Woodhead's Book, which has been necessitated by Mr. Goode's reference to it, I will only further observe—that if Woodhead's citations from English Divines, under the two former portions of his argument, do not sustain the inference which Mr. Goode draws from them, still less can such an inference be made from the language of those Authors quoted in the argument last noticed.

But Mr. Goode refers also to Woodhead's " Compendious Discourse on the Eucharist: Oxford, 1688, p. 33 et seq. and App. p. 212," for further proof that that writer, when commenting upon the language of " those who held the highest doctrine of the Real Presence ever maintained in our Reformed Church," was " obliged to admit that their notion of the Real bodily presence was that it was a presence *to the receiver*, but *not to the elements*."

Before, however, examining Woodhead's statements, it is of consequence to notice that Mr. Goode's expression " Real bodily presence " is inaccurate and tends to mislead ; for by " bodily " is almost certain to be understood " corporal "— the very idea condemned by the Declaration and by the writers in question. Nor, indeed, does Woodhead use this word in reference to these writers : he speaks of their holding " the *real* or *substantial* presence of Christ's body ;" but this is a very different thing ; and, in fact, involves the precise point upon which the Declaration turns—viz., the distinction between a *bodily=organical* Presence of Christ's Body ; and a *substantial=spiritual* Presence of Christ's Body —a distinction not (as many might be inclined to think) without a difference, and that the really important one which, it must have been observed, continually appears in the controversies which have been referred to in these pages.

Woodhead's statement, in the passage (p. 30, &c.) to which Mr. Goode refers, is as follows ; he says :—

" Now to come to the *second* thing, its affirming, or denying, the *real* or *substantial* presence of Christ's body with the *signs*, and that, *ante usum*. And this I think to be generally denied by the 2nd opinion,* (tho' I see not with what reason they can deny a possibility thereof, since they grant such a *presence* with the worthy receiver.) See Mr. Hooker 5. *l.*, 67. *s.*, p. 359. ' The *real presence* of Christ's most blessed *body* and *blood* is not to be sought for in the Sacrament, but in the worthy receiver of the Sacrament.' "

This is the well known passage so often quoted to prove that Hooker was *not* one of those Post-reformation Divines " who held the highest doctrine of the Real Presence ;" and therefore he cannot be fairly cited *by Mr. Goode* as a witness in this case : whether his language necessarily implies a *denial* of such Presence " in the Sacrament" may, I think, be fairly questioned. His object seems mainly to have been to discourage controversy on this point, and to promote unity by drawing attention to the fact that "no side denieth but that *the soul of man* is the receptacle of Christ's presence :" though, plainly, he was also moved by the consideration—that those who held that "Christ's body and blood be also externally seated in the very consecrated elements themselves ; . . . . are driven either to *consubstantiate* and incorporate Christ with elements sacramental, or to *transubstantiate* and change their

---

* The *Second* Opinion goes beyond this [*i. e.* a "Virtual Presence"], or at least seems so (for I must confess I do not well understand it, and we shall look more into it anon) and affirms a *real Presence* of Christ's Body, not in its *virtue*, but in its very *substance* ; but in this, not after a *natural* or *carnal*, but *spiritual*, manner ; not to *all* : but only to the *worthy* Receivers. *To them*, (*i.e.*) to their *Souls* and *Spirits*, by the susception of *Faith*, and not to their *Mouth* or their *Body*. Again, to *them*, but not to the *symbols* at all ; or if in some sense to these (as Mr. Hooker, *l.* 5., *s.* 67, saith, they really *exhibit*, but not *contain* in them, that which *with*, or *by*, them God bestoweth), yet not *ante usum*, or before the act of Receiving." ". . . . . ."—p. 1.

substance into His; and so the one to hold Him really but invisibly moulded up with the substance of those elements, the other to hide Him under the only visible show of bread and wine, the substance whereof as they imagine is abolished and His succeeded in the same room." If, then, there be a mode of Presence in, with, or, under the elements, which yet is neither of these two, Hooker's language does not exclude a " Real presence in the Sacrament." *

But Woodhead goes on to say :—

" See Dr. Tailor, p. 14. ' By spiritual we mean, present to our spirits only : that is, *saith he*, so as Christ is not present to any other sense but that of faith, or Spiritual susception.' Where (to digress a little,) I wonder why he and some others (so Dr. Hammond saith, [*for our souls to be strengthened*, etc.,] quoted before †) do not say,

* " . . . Hooker considered the very life and substance of saving truth to be in jeopardy, as on the side of the Romanists, so on that of the Lutherans also, by reasonings likely to be grounded, whether logically or no, on the tenet which they taught in common of the proper ubiquity of our Saviour's glorified Body in the Eucharist. Evidently it was a feeling of this kind, rather than any fear of exaggerating the honour due to that blessed Sacrament, which reigns in those portions of the fifth Book, where he lays down certain limitations, under which the Doctrine of the Real Presence must be received. The one drift and purpose of all those limitations is, to prevent any heretical surmise, of our Lord's manhood now being, or having been at any time since His incarnation, other than most true and substantial. Whatever notion of the Real Presence does not in effect interfere with this foundation of the faith, that, the genuine philosophy of Hooker, no less than his sound theology, taught him to embrace with all his heart. No writer, since the primitive times, has shown himself in this and in all parts of his writings more thoroughly afraid of those tendencies, which in our age are called Utilitarian and Rationalist. If at any time he seem over scrupulous in the use of ideas or phrases, from which the early fathers saw no reason to shrink, it is always the apprehension of irreverence, not of the contrary, which is present to his mind. For example, let the three following passages only be well considered and compared: *i. e.*, as they stand with their context; for in these critical parts more especially, no separate citation can ever do Hooker justice.

" 1. 'Christ's body being a part of that nature, which whole nature is presently joined unto Deity wheresoever Deity is, it followeth that His bodily substance hath everywhere a presence of true conjunction with Deity. And forasmuch as it is by virtue of that conjunction made the body of the Son of God, by whom also it was made a sacrifice for the sins of the whole world, this giveth it *a presence of force and efficacy* throughout all generations of men.'— Eccl., Pol. v. lv. 9."—The other two pages referred to are Ibid. v. lvi. 9 and 13. —Keble's Preface, pp. lxxx—lxxxii.

† " I will add to these of Dr. Taylor's, an expression of Dr. Hammond's. *Pract. Cat.* where he speaks of the Eucharist,—" God bestows the body and blood of Christ upon us not by sending it down locally for our bodies to feed on, but *really* for our souls to be strengthened by it. As when the Sun is com-

that Christ's *body* is substantially present to the bodies of worthy receivers, as well as to the souls, (yet, perhaps, they deny it not); for tho' the body of Christ be only *spiritually* there, yet may a *spirit* be present to a *body*, for our souls (spirits) are so....."

Yet, surely, such lanugage is no *denial* of a Real Presence "to the Elements." Taylor's words are but another way of expressing what Bishop Guest said, (See p. 193,)—"*though he tooke Christ's body in his hand, received it with his mouthe, and that corporally, naturally, reallye, substantially, and carnally,* as ye doctors doo write, *yet did he not for all that* see *it,* feale *it,* smelle *it,* nor taste *it."* Seeing, therefore, that Guest held,—that the belief of Christ's Body being *not cognizable by the senses* was entirely consistent with the belief of "ye presence of Christe's Bodye in ye Sacrament"—the same may fairly be asserted of this passage which Woodhead quotes.

Again, his language is :—

" See what Bishop Forbes saith, *Euchar*) 1. l. 1. c. 27. s. 'Verum Christi corpus non tantum animæ, sed etiam corpori nostro, spiritualiter tamen, hoc est, non corporaliter, exhibetur, et sane alio ac diverso nobis et propinquiori modo, licet occulto, quam per solam fidem. . . . . Fides, qua proprie Christi caro in Eucharistia spiritualiter, hoc est, incorporaliter manducatur, non est ea sola, qua Christus creditur mortuus pro peccatis nostris, etc., ea enim fides præ-supponitur, etc. Sed ea fides est, qua creditur verbo Christi dicentis. Hoc est corpus meum. Credere enim Christum ibi esse præsentem etiam carne vivificatrice, et desiderare eam sumere ; nimirum hoc est spiritualiter et recte eam manducare in Eucharistia. *Sect.* 25. Proinde male docetur a multis Protestantibus, hanc præsentiam et communicationem per fidem effici. . . . . Fides magis proprie dicitur accipere, etc., apprehendere, quam præstare. Verbum Dei et promissio, cui fides nostra nititur, præsentia reddit quæ promittit, non nostra fides.' Tis not *faith* that confers Christ's body, though by the faithful it is only worthily, or, (as they say,)

municated to us, the whole bulk and body of the Sun is not removed out of its sphere, but the Rays and Beams of it, and with them the Light and Influences are *really* and *verily* bestowed and darted out upon us." Thus he. As, therefore, not the Body of the Sun, but only the Beams thereof, can be said to be *really* and *locally* here below; so, I conceive the Doctor means, that not the *very body* of Christ but the *vertue* and *efficacy* thereof only, are *really* here *present* to the worthy receiver."—p. 27. But, the question arises,—Are not the Beams of the Sun something more than "the *vertue* and *efficacy*" of the Sun ? And if (as I think and have already argued) they are, then the Eucharistic Presence of Christ is also something more than "the *vertue* and *efficacy*" of His body.

only received, but received equally, and immediately both by the soul and body : whether this *body* of Christ be disjoined from, as they think, or conjoined with the Elements."

But does the passage quoted from Bishop Forbes bear out the inference which Woodhead would apparently draw from it ? I cannot think it does: and, indeed, Woodhead himself here, as elsewhere, speaks doubtfully of this writer, and of the class to which he considers him to belong. To my mind it needs some *positive statement* to that effect, before any absolute negation of a Real Presence *in* or *with* the Elements can be safely concluded from such a passage as this.

Woodhead ends this Section by quoting the four following passages from Bishop Taylor :—

"See Dr. Tailor, p. 7. 'After the Minister hath consecrated the bread and wine, the symbols become changed into the body and blood of Christ in a Spiritual, real manner.'

"So, p. 21. 'The question is not, whether the Symbols be changed into Christ's body and blood or no, for it is granted ; but whether this conversion be Sacramental and figurative, or natural and bodily, etc.'

"So, p. 265, 266. 'Before consecration it is mere bread, but after consecration it is, verily, the body of Christ, truly his flesh, and truly his blood.'

"But especially see such full expressions in his *Great Exemplar*, *3d. part. disc.* 18, p. 109, in the former Edition, *Sect.* 3, where amongst other things he saith : 'It is hard to do so much violence to our sense, as not to think it *bread ;* but it is more unsafe, to do so much violence to our faith, as not to believe it to be Christ's *body.*' (Again.) 'He that believes it to be *bread,* and, yet verily to be Christ's *body,* is only tied also by implication to believe God's *omnipotence,* that he who affirmed it, can also verify it. And if we profess we understand not the *manner* of this Mystery, we say no more, but that it is *a mystery,* etc.' "

It is plain, however, that Woodhead himself was perplexed by these passages when citing Bishop Taylor as one of those who held what he terms "The Second Opinion," (*See* p. 372) ; for he prefaces the First quotation with these words—

" . . . whilst this *second* opinion seems to hold no *presence* at all, *to* or *with,* the signs, but to the receiver, they only making the signs to be (as well as I can understand them) after Consecration *sanctified* instruments, upon receit of which by those who believe, God gives the other, the *body* and *blood* of his Son: as also in Baptism upon receiving the *water*, God gives the *Spirit;*"

And then, remarkably enough he adds—

" Yet I say, some other expressions of their's seem not so suitable to such a meaning, and may easily cause a mistake in the unwary reader; and why they use them I cannot tell, unless it be to imitate the phrase of the words of Institution, and also of the Fathers."—p. 32.

So again, most significantly, I think, he thus comments on the last quotation from Bishop Taylor:—

" Strange expressions! when the thing required to be believed is this: That Christ's *body* is in no way present to the *bread*, neither by the bread being changed into it, nor joyned with it; but only it given and present to the faithful, upon the receipt of this sanctified bread.

" Now would any discourse of the waters of Baptism, by which the Spirit is received, on this manner; *It is hard to do so much violence to the sense, as not to think it water, but it is more unsafe to do so much violence to our faith, as not to believe it to be the Spirit.* Would not he rather explain himself, that the one is not the other; but the one received, by God's free gift, upon the receiving of the other?"—p. 33.

Seeing, then, that Woodhead confesses this difficulty in Bishop Taylor's language, we may fairly refuse to accept the unqualified conclusion which Mr. Goode has drawn from the way in which Woodhead has appealed to the Bishop's arguments: moreover, the very difficulty is itself a presumption that the passages do not condemn the opinion which Mr. Goode would cite them to disprove: and it is worth observing, in confirmation of this remark, that Woodhead says "perhaps some of them [*i.e.*, the holders of this 'Second Opinion'] do not," in the passages he quotes, "peremptorily condemn the conjectures of others."—(p. 24). In proof of this he goes on to say thus:—

" See for what I have now said (besides the quotations before, p. 2, in the relation of this *second* opinion) many places in Dr. *Tailor*, the very Title of his book, wherein *Spiritual* must be took in such a sense, as not to deny *real;* and of *Christ*, must be understood of the *Body and Blood of Christ:* For this he saith often in the Book, namely, p. 7, see p. 20, where, in answering some hard sayings of the Fathers, &c., as if the same Body that was *crucified*, was not *eaten* in the Sacrament, he saith, ' That Proposition is true, if we speak of the eating of Christ's Body in the same manner of being [' for it had one manner of being on the Cross, and another in the Sacrament ']. But that Body which was crucified, the same Body we do eat, if we speak of the same thing in a several manner of being, &c. Christ's Body therefore is in the Sacrament, not only in its operation, but being ; though after another manner of being than it was on the Cross. And what Dr. *Taylor* saith, methinks, answers several arguments brought afterward by himself out of the Fathers against *real presence under*, or *with* the *symbols*, see p. 311. *Non hoc quod videtis*, &c. See p. 288. *They that do not confess the Eucharist to be the Flesh of our Saviour*, &c. See p. 5, where he will have *spiritual presence* to be particular in nothing, but that it excludes the *corporal* and *natural* manner, &c. See ArchB. *Laud*, p. 286, where he saith, *The worthy Receiver is by his Faith made Spiritually partaker of the true and real Body and Blood of Christ*, &c. And ArchB. *Cranmer* (as the ArchB. quotes out of Fox, p. 1703) confesseth, that though he was indeed of another opinion, and in-clining to that of *Zwinglius*, yet B. *Ridley* convinc'd his *judgment*, and settled him in the *point*."—pp. 24-25.

Woodhead's remark, that Bishop Taylor "will have *spiritual presence* to be particular in nothing, but that it excludes the *corporal* and *natural* manner," seems to me per-tinent to, what I think is, Mr. Goode's aggravation of the confessed difficulty of this question, in assuming, as he does, that "the supposed presence in the Eucharist is only a pre-sence of his [Christ's] body after a spiritual and super-natural manner, that is, a state of existence after the manner of a spirit." (*On the Eucharist*, p. 49). He insists upon this in several places* in his "Work on the Eucharist." But

---

* p. 50. "And as to its [Christ's Body] being present only after the manner of a spirit, I ask, with Bishop Jeremy Taylor, ' Can a body remaining a body be at the same time a spirit?' "
p. 183. " This doctrine supposes the body and blood of Christ partaken of in the Eucharist to be immaterial and like a spirit, while the words of our Lord shew us, that the body to be eaten there is the material body that was crucified on the cross, and the blood to be drunk there is the blood shed on the cross."
p. 184. "This doctrine supposes an *oral* manducation of an *immaterial* thing, a thing present only after the mode of existence belonging to a spirit; which is a manifest absurdity."
p. 211. "But those who are not so easily influenced by words and names are inclined to carry their researches a little further. They naturally ask them-selves the question, whether our old divines really thought that a body re-maining a body could be at the same time a spirit, and that our Lord's body,

"the manner of a spirit" may be, in one sense, said to be *the manner of a body;* for though a Spirit is an *immaterial* Body (using the word *immaterial* in a *popular,* and not a *strictly philosophical* sense), it is nevertheless a *body,* by reason of its non-ubiquity, while yet capable of motion in a manner which does not pertain to *material* bodies. Therefore, to make *spiritual presence=the manner of a spirit,* seems equivalent to the holding of the "Corporal Presence," which the Declaration condemns on the ground of "it being against the truth of Christ's natural Body to be at one time in more places than one." Bishop Taylor (in the passage quoted by Mr. Goode, p. 843), complaining of Bellarmine, says that

" *Spiritually with him signifies after the manner of Spirits,*" and adds that "They say that Christ's body is truly present there [in the Sacrament] as it was upon the Cross, but not after the manner of all or anybody, but after that manner of being as an angel is in a place. That's their *spiritually.* But we by the real spiritual presence of Christ do understand Christ to be present as the Spirit of God is present in the hearts of the faithful by blessing and grace; and this is all which we mean besides the tropical and figurative presence."

The Bishop's objection to regarding the Eucharistic Presence as "after that manner of being as an angel is in a place" is forcible enough; for such a Presence is really the "Corporal Presence of" a "natural Body" (here limiting the word *Natural* to a *Created Being,* and not referring it to, *e.g.,* the atmosphere): the point to be considered is—how he understood that "the Spirit of God is present in the hearts of the faithful by blessing and grace?"—could he do otherwise than consider it as a REAL presence when he remembered, as he must have done, that aspiration of St. Paul for the Ephesian Church "to be strengthened with might by His [Christ's] Spirit in the inner man; That Christ may dwell in your

remaining in heaven in a material form, could at the same time be present on hundreds of thousands of communion tables all over the world in the form of a spirit; so united, as a whole and perfect body, to every minute fragment of the Eucharistic bread, or form of bread, as to be eaten with it by every communicant; ...."

hearts by faith " (Eph. iii. 16 and 17)? It seems to me that he could not. And I venture to think that, in rejecting the Analogy which he condemned, Bishop Taylor might willingly and consistently enough have accepted what appears to be the only practicable analogy in this case, namely, that of the Natural Sun which has been already considered: to my mind, it meets the difficulty in a way which no other comparison does, and has the advantage of being both Scriptural and not new, though it is legitimate enough (as I have already argued) to view it in any new aspect which the Light of modern Science affords.

Mr. Goode refers also to, "App. p. 212," of Woodhead's Discourse : he does not give the words, but I presume he must refer to the following passage :—

" . . . . Afterward Archbishop Laud restor'd it, [*i. e.*, the sentence '*that these Thy Gifts and Creatures of Bread and Wine may be to us the Body and Blood of Thy Dear Son,*'] in the *Scottish Liturgy.* For which he was severely censur'd by *Baily's Laudensium Autocatacrisis.* This being, as he saith, a notable Argument for *Transubstantiation ;* at least, for the *real presence* to the *Receiver* it was. Though it is most certain, the Archbishop did not incline to defend *Transubstantiation,* but only the *real presence* to the *Receiver,* according to the Doctrine of the Church of *England,* misunderstood by that *Puritan.*"

It is just worth observing that this *Appendix* seems not to be Woodhead's at all, and perhaps Mr. Goode does not quote it as such: but this is not material to the question which hinges upon the quotation, viz., whether Archbishop Laud, as one of "those who held the highest doctrine of the Real Presence ever maintained in our Reformed Church," held only "a Presence *to the receiver,* but not *to the elements.*" The Appendix writer asserts that the Archbishop defended "only the *Real presence* to the *Receiver :*" but a careful consideration of his language, as subsequently given at pp. 390-3, can scarcely fail to raise a grave doubt as to the accuracy of the allegation.

As touching, however, this point upon which Mr. Goode so much insists, of the Presence being " *to the Receiver but not to the Elements,*" it will be as well to notice here the following passages in his " Supplement" p. 29 : he says :—

" His [Dr. Pusey's] argument that the rubrical direction as to the reverent reception of the remainder of the Elements by some of the communicants 'shows that the Church of England believes an abiding objective presence of the Body and Blood of Christ in the Elements, apart from the act of reception,' (p. 231), and that the direction as to the covering of the remainder of the consecrated elements with a fine linen cloth 'contains the same doctrine,' I leave to be disposed of by the reader. I confess to a feeling of impatience under the infliction of such apologies for arguments."

But it often happens that no " feeling of impatience," however strong, will get rid of awkward facts; and such is the case here : the Rubric as to the reverent reception of the remains of the Sacrament exists, and needs to be accounted for : its meaning has already been discussed at length in these pages (See 122—152) : it will be enough, therefore, now to supplement what was there said, by referring to a most unsuspicious witness, from whom I have already had occasion to quote.

Mr. Fisher, wrongly assuming that the Rubric in the Service Books of Edward and Elizabeth "—" and if any of the Bread and Wine remain, the Curate shall have it to his own use"—refers to the *consecrated* Elements, thus remarks upon the change in 1662 :

" This was, of course, much too concise and simple to suit the refined Scholastic taste of theologians like Dr. Gunning or Bishop Cosin. Consequently, as might have been anticipated, it was in 1662 very considerably enlarged, and most materially modified in its dogmatic import. It now stands as follows :—

" ' And if any of the Bread and Wine remain unconsecrated the Curate shall have it to his own use : but if any remain of that which was consecrated, it shall not be carried out of the Church, but the Priest and such other of the Communicants as he shall then call unto him, shall, immediately after the Blessing, reverently eat and drink the same.'

" This change, it will be observed, is in perfect keeping with those already noticed. Some indeed may be disposed—and not altogether without reason—to consider it as one of the most important alterations which the Communion Office has ever undergone ; involving as it does so palpable a recognition of that mysterious virtue, which is supposed, according to the theory of Rome, to be infused into the elements by the priestly act of Consecration. It is indeed, in this respect, all that the most zealous adherent of the Tridentine doctrine could desire. Such is the mystical sanctity of the newly ' *conse-crated* ' bread and wine, that they are not, we are told, to be used, even by the Priest himself,·anywhere except within the hallowed precincts of the altar." *—p. 400.

But though Mr. Fisher is in error in supposing that the change in, or rather the addition to, the Rubric arose from any unfitness in it to "the refined Scholastic taste" of which he speaks; his opinion is none the less valuable as to the meaning of the Rubric in its present form. The old Rubric was sufficient for its purpose in 1552, when, the minds of the Clergy being still thoroughly imbued with the Missal Rubrics, no Priest would have been at a loss how to dispose of the remains of the *Consecrated* Bread and Wine : but the

---

* This passage, and the other quotations from Mr. Fisher, were taken from the 1st Ed. of his Book : but a 2nd Ed. having been published in 1860 it is due to him to notice any variation he may have made in his statements. The passages cited at pp. 170, 284, 331, and above, are unaltered: that at p. 337 is substantially the same, though fuller, and even more explicit (in 2nd Ed., p. 296, &c.) : the one given at p. 262 seems to be omitted, but its purport is found elsewhere (2nd Ed., pp. 129, 151, &c.) : the passage at pp. 259-60 looks as if re-cast, and now ends thus (2nd Ed., p. 300) :—" Of course it is not for us to say, what might have been the decision of our Ecclesiastical Judges in the case of Mr. Wilberforce, had legal proceedings been actually instituted against him : but it is certainly difficult to see how, with this Rubric before them, [*i.e.*, the Declaration on Kneeling], they could have come practically to any conclusion condemnatory, in a penal sense, of his doctrine." The other remaining quota-tion, that at p. 171, ". . . he does not seem," &c., appears to be withdrawn, and the following substituted—" It has been ascertained, as we believe beyond a doubt, that, between the year 1548 and the period of the Second revision of the Prayer-Book, Cranmer's opinion respecting the corporeal presence of CHRIST in the Eucharist underwent a very marked and decisive change. During that short interval, indeed, he appears to have abandoned the Lutheran doctrine altogether. Now observe the change which the Communion Office underwent, at the time of this second revision. It was not enough, as some might have supposed, that the Rubric *alone* should be altered. There were, it seems, ex-pressions even in the *Service* which might seem to sanction the discarded doc-trine. The Service accordingly was made to undergo a precisely corresponding process of alteration." (2nd Ed., p. 145). Now I do not pretend to know what has caused this entire change, as it seems, in Mr. Fisher's opinion on this point : but, having paid due attention to what he has urged here and elsewhere in his 2nd Ed., I feel very confident in maintaining that his second thoughts are not the accurate ones; and I cannot but think that in this instance, as in others, it will be found that the supposed old and true maxim must be altered, and that it may yet appear that his *first* and *third* thoughts will be best. In support of this belief I must refer to what has been already said at pp. 6, 20-26, 46, 48, 49, 84, 154-59, 166-70, 174-78, 179-86, and 276.

gross irreverence with which the Sacrament had come to be treated before the end of the following Century, must have furnished a most cogent reason, quite apart from any " Scholastic taste," not only for removing any uncertainty (if such existed, though it may well be doubted); but also for furnishing a direction, with regard to the remains of the *Consecrated* Elements, of so explicit a character that no one could possibly plead the old Rubric in excuse for treating them as *common* Bread and Wine, and so seek to cover negligence or irreverence in disposing of them.   Indeed, I venture to think that this consideration is the true key to the meaning of the words, "it shall not be carried out of the Church :" it seems to me fairly open to discussion, whether these words were designed absolutely to prohibit *reservation for the sick* in cases where anything like a real difficulty (such as mentioned at p. 139) might arise about *Consecrating* at a Communion of the Sick : the Revisers of 1661 were not likely to have been unmindful of the Rubric in Elizabeth's Latin Prayer Book, which permitted it (See p. 89); and they may not have intended wholly to exclude its operation, though probably deeming it best not to encourage a habit of Reservation for ordinary cases which presented no difficulty in using the Office provided for " The Communion of the Sick."

With regard to the other fact—the direction to cover *" what remaineth of the consecrated elements . . . with a fair linen cloth "*—it may suffice, I think, to quote the following passage from the late Professor Blunt's " Duties of a Parish Priest " 3rd Ed. p. 339 :—

"This, you will observe, is the first mention that is made of covering the elements with a cloth, or 'corporal,' as it was called. So that the practice of thus veiling them, when *originally* placed upon the Table, though, as it should seem, obtaining in the early Greek Ritual (See *Lit. of S. Chrysostom*, Neale's Tetralogia Litùrgica pp. 63, 64), is unauthorized by our own, which would appear to consider them as common bread and common wine (however oblations to God) till after consecration, and therefore as not to be treated with any mysterious reverence ; but, *after consecration*, to be no longer common bread, οὐ Κοινὸς ἄρτος ; and no longer a common cup, οὐ Κοινὸν ποτήριον (Justin Martyr 1 Apol. §. 66); and now therefore to be screened frem the gaze of the congregation. So much doctrine is there contained in these Rubrics when duly studied and applied."

There is another statement made by Mr. Goode (Supp. p. 34) which needs to be noticed : he says that "the whole object of the Declaration is to point out, that the act of kneeling is not an act of adoration to Christ as so present," *i.e.* "as whole Christ, God and Man" (p. 33) by " an *immaterial* presence" (such as he alleges Dr. Pusey to hold); and he quotes in support of his position *First*, the parenthetical language of the Declaration as to our acknowledgment by kneeling " of the benefits of Christ therein given to all worthy Receivers ;" *Next*, the words of the 7th Canon of 1640. But, with respect to the former, surely it may, at least, be fairly said that Christ "being *therein* given " He *is there* WHEN given, and so ought to be adored : and that "whole Christ, God and Man" *is given*, though not after a natural manner, seems to me to be necessarily allowed by Mr. Goode himself; for he says :—

". . . I maintain, that the Body and Blood of Christ that we are to eat and drink in the Lords' Supper, are the true material body and blood of our Blessed Lord, of which He spake when he said of himself to his disciples after his resurrection,—'a spirit hath not flesh and bones, as ye see me have.' But I contend that this eating and drinking are of a spiritual kind, the act of the soul only ; but, in the case of the faithful, accompanying the eating and drinking of the sacred symbols by the mouth."—*Nature of Christ's Presence,* etc. p. 82.

Here, as I understand him, Mr. Goode contends for the *spiritual* partaking of a *material* Thing : it is difficult, then, to see why he should object, as he seems to do, to the *spiritual* PRESENCE and *spiritual* GIVING of that same *material* Thing *i.e.* of the risen (and ascended, for it was the same) Christ— God and Man. Surely the whole analogy to be drawn from the Elements sustains what he appears to disallow : for if the Bread and Wine must *be there*, in the Sacrament, before they can *be given* to the Communicants to be by them *consumed;* it follows that the *Body and Blood of Christ (i.e.* Christ Himself "whole Christ, God and Man ") must also *be there*, " in the Lord's Supper," before *they* can be *given* to the faithful to be by them " verily and indeed taken and received" in order to be "eaten" and drunk " after an heavenly and spiritual manner." (Art. xxviii.) Indeed Mr. Goode says (p. 82) "I must add, that as to any spiritual presence, our Lord may be present *in the Supper*,* and quite as effectually present, though he does not enter into or become annexed to the earthly elements of bread and wine." Yet I cannot but think that, having regard to the terms of the Declaration, Mr. Goode thus raises a difficulty (if it be a difficulty) quite as great as the one he opposes ; for precisely the same reason, *viz.* "it being against the truth of Christ's natural Body to be at one time in more places than one," applies to a "*spiritual* presence" of "the true material body and blood of our Blessed Lord " "*in the Supper*," as to a "spiritual presence" of it *in, with, or under the Elements :* in fact the Declaration says nothing whatever as to the *where* of "any spiritual Presence" of "Christ's natural Flesh and Blood;" though it does most distinctly pronounce *how* Christ is not present, when it rejects "any *corporal* presence of Christ's natural Flesh and Blood : FOR [*i.e.* because] . . . . the natural Body and Blood of our Saviour Christ are in Heaven, and not here."

But, as I am most anxious not to misunderstand (and so to misrepresent unconsciously) Mr. Goode's language, let me here take the precaution of saying that it is possible he may have intended to *emphasize* the word " benefits " and not the word " Christ " in his quotation from the Declaration upon which I am now commenting : in that case it would be necessary to enquire what he understands by the word " benefits " as there used—whether it is to be taken in the same sense as in the Catechism or in some other meaning.

I have not been able to find any passage in Mr. Goode's Work on the Eucharist or in his Supplement which will clearly guide to his opinion on this point : the only remarks, so far as I know, which bear upon it are the following which

---

* I have already noticed (See p. 358) a still stronger expression used by Mr. Goode as to a possible kind of Presence " in the Supper."

he makes in commenting upon a statement of the late Arch-deacon Wilberforce :—

" . . . . His main argument [*i.e.* in " his ' Charge,' pp. 285—8."] is this, that we are told that 'the Body and Blood of Christ are verily and indeed taken and received by the faithful in the Lord's Supper,' and then afterwards it is stated, what *the benefits* are of which we become partakers by *this reception ;* showing he contends that beyond the reception of certain benefits, there is, besides, the reception of *a thing* from which these benefits flow ; and he reasons as if this proved, that the Body and Blood of Christ must be in the elements.

" But the conclusion does not follow from the premises. No doubt there is a reception *by the soul* of the Body of Christ. And the consequence of that reception is, the enjoyment of certain benefits by the soul, namely, (as described in the Catechism) its being strengthened and refreshed by the Body and Blood of Christ, as our bodies are by the bread and wine. But this does not prove a reception of the Body and Blood of Christ by the mouth in con-junction with the elements. . . . . .

" And the Catechism, so far from drawing this distinction between receiving the body of Christ and receiving the benefits derivable from it, remarkably connects (I had almost said, identifies) the two. For in two previous answers it makes the second part of a sacrament, and the inward thing signified by the outward element, to be, an ' inward and spiritual grace ; ' not the *res sacramenti*, but the *virtus* or gratia sacramenti."—*The Nature* &c., p. 695.

Now, though not immaterial in itself, it is immaterial to me to discuss here the remarkable distinction drawn in the Catechism (and not in this place pointed out by Mr. Goode,) between the two Sacraments, by the additional third question as to the "benefits" of the "Sacrament of the Lord's supper." It is enough to observe that he regards the " benefits " of the Eucharist as "*the consequence* of" the soul's *reception* "of the Body of Christ : " it seems to me therefore, most probable that he *similarly* regards "the benefits" named in the Declaration ; for, coupling the words just cited with his remarks as to the nature of the Presence quoted before. (See p. 384) I cannot fairly suppose him to maintain so improbable an intention on the part of the Framers of the Declaration as either, a precise identification of "those benefits" as "being" (in the language of Bishop

Wordsworth, see Note, p. 117) "the Sacramental Body and Blood of our Lord and Saviour, Jesus Christ;" or an "acknowledgment" of an *effect* instead and to the exclusion of a *cause :* for, while the Bishop's explanation introduces a new Body such as Mr. Goode appears to disavow, it seems too unreasonable to suppose that they (the Framers) could have been so inexact in the wording of such an important public Theological statement as to lead us to contemplate *primarily* in the act of Kneeling at Reception the *subsequent* " benefits" of the Gift of " Christ" then and there bestowed upon " all worthy receivers"—Benefits which, however closely or remotely following upon the Gift, must be (analogically) considered as *later than* not *coincident with* that Gift.

Mr. Goode's second reference in support of his opinion as to "the whole object of the Declaration" is thus stated (the *Italics* are Mr. Goode's) :—

"And a similar reason for such a posture [*i.e.* Kneeling] is asigned in the seventh of the Canons of 1640, drawn up under the presidency of Archbishop Laud, where such a gesture 'in the celebration of the Holy Eucharist' is said to be not 'upon any opinion of a corporal presence of the body of Jesus Christ on the holy table, or in mystical elements, *but only* for the advancement of God's Majesty, and to give him alone that honour and glory that is due unto him, and *no otherwise.'*"—Sup. p. 34.

But, first of all, it must be said that the Canon is not treating at all of that " Kneeling" at receiving the Sacrament of the Lord's Supper with which the Declaration deals: it refers entirely to another custom which had much fallen into disuse and was then sought to be revived : this will be best seen by an inspection of the entire final Clause of the Canon which runs thus (the *Italics* are mine) :—

"And lastly, Whereas the Church is the house of God, dedicated to his holy worship, and therefore ought to mind us, both of the greatness and goodness of his Divine Majesty, certain it is that the acknowledgment thereof, not only inwardly in our hearts, but also outwardly with our bodies, must needs be pious in itself, profitable unto us, and edifying unto others. We therefore think it very meet and behoveful, and heartily commend it to all good and well-affected people, members of this Church, that they be ready to tender unto the Lord the said acknowledgment, *by doing reverence* *and obeysance, both at their coming in, and going out of the said Churches, Chancels or Chapels,* according to the most ancient custom of the primitive Church * in the purest times, and of this Church also for many years of the reign of Queen Elizabeth. The reviving therefore of this ancient and laudable custom, we heartily commend to the serious consideration of all good people, not with any intention to exhibit any religious worship to the Communion-Table, the East, or Church, or anything therein contained in so doing, or to perform *the said gesture,* in the celebration of the holy Eucharist, upon any opinion of a corporal presence of the body of Jesus Christ on the holy Table, or in mystical Elements, but only for the advancement of God's Majesty, and to give him alone that honour and glory that is due unto him, and no otherwise ; and in the practise or omission of this Rite, we desire that the Rule of Charity prescribed by the Apostle, may be observed, which is, that they which use this Rite, despise not them who use it not ; and that they who use it not, condemn not those that use it."

Now it is clear, from the language of the Canon, that " *the said gesture* " recommended to be used " in the celebration of the Holy Eucharist" was precisely that " doing reverence and obeysance" which was counselled to be performed at "coming in and going out" of Church : what that *gesture* was may be pretty certainly inferred† from the direction of the 52nd of Elizabeth's Injunctions of 1559 as to bowing at the Name of Jesus in Church ; it is there ordered—

" that due reverence be made of all persons young and old, with lowness of courtesie, and uncovering of heads of the menkind, as thereunto doth necessarily belong, and heretofore hath been accustomed."

I have no doubt that the traditional practice observed in some Cathedrals and Parish Churches, especially *Country* Churches, points to an identity of gesture between the Canon and the Injunction. But, as I have before intimated, this has no connexion with *kneeling at receiving :* that was *expressly required* by the Rubric of the Prayer Book in use

---

* " Nothing more frequent in the writings of the ancient fathers than *adoration towards the East,* which drew the primitive Christians into some suspicion of being worshippers of the sun."—*Heylyn's Cyprianus Anglicus,* Introduction, p. 17. Quoted in " Hierurgia Anglicana." p. 50.

† For proofs that this " gesture " was *bowing* and that it still prevailed in many places before the passing of the Canon in 1640, see " Hierurgia Anglicana" pp. 50—58.

both in Elizabeth's days and in Archbishop Laud's time; it was enforced by the, still unrepealed, 27th Canon of 1603 which ordered that "No Minister, when he celebrateth the Communion, shall wittingly administer the same to any but to such as kneel, under pain of suspension:" and, moreover, the circumstance—that the Canon of 1640 makes no pretension of *dispensing* with these then and now existing Laws yet allows a *liberty of action* with respect to the *gesture* it recommends—seems to me an unanswerable argument that the gesture of the Canon and the gesture of the Declaration are not identical.

Yet if they were, all that can be argued from the Canon is, I think, that it is more *explicit* than the Declaration; inasmuch as it denies "a corporal presence of the body of Jesus Christ on the Holy Table, or in mystical Elements"; but it is equally *implicit* in not excluding a *spiritual* Presence Can anything be cited from Archbishop Laud, "under" whose "presidency" (as Mr. Goode says,) the Canon was made, to indicate the reverse of this? I think not. On the contrary, how he would have defended the direction of the Canon, may be pretty certainly inferred from what he said only three years before, and which I suppose no one will think him likely to have unsaid in 1640; his words (which I only met with some time after writing the above) are as follows:—

"One thing sticks much in their stomachs, and they call it an *innovation* too; and that is, *bowing, or doing reverence at our first coming into the Church, or at our nearer approaches to the Holy Table, or the Altar,* (call it whether you will), in which they will needs have it *that we worship the Holy Table,* or GOD knows what.

"To this I answer, first, that God forbid we should worship any thing but God Himself. Secondly, that if to worship God when we enter into His house, or approach His altar, be an innovation, 'tis a very old one. For Moses did reverence at the very door of the Tabernacle. (Numb. xx. 6.) Hezekiah, and all that were present with him, when they had made an end of offering, bowed and worshipped. (2 Chron. xxix. 29.) David calls the people to it with a *Venite, O come let us worship and fall down, and kneel before the Lord our maker,* (Ps. xcv. 6): and in *all* these places (I pray mark it) 'tis *bodily worship.* Nor can they say this was Judaical worship, and now not to be imitated. For long before Judaism began, Bethel, the House of God, was a place of reverence, (Gen. xxviii. 17): therefore, certainly of and to God. And after Judaical worship ended, *Venite adoremus,* as far upwards as there is any track of a Liturgy, was the Introitus of the priest all the Latin Church over. And in the daily Prayer of the Church of England this was retained at the Reformation : and that psalm in which is *Venite adoremus,* is commanded to begin the morning service of every day. And for ought I know, the priest may as well leave out the *venite* as the *adoremus,* the *calling* the people to their duty, as the *duty* itself, when they are come. Therefore, even according to the Service-book of the Church of England, the priest and the people both are called upon for *external* and *bodily* reverence and worship of God. Therefore they which do it do not *innovate* . . . . For my own part I take myself bound to worship with *body,* as well as in soul, whenever I come where God is worshipped. . . . .

"And you, my honourable Lords of the Garter, in your great solemnities you do your reverence, and to Almighty God I doubt not; but yet it is *versus Altare,* towards His altar, as the greatest place of God's residence upon Earth—I say the greatest, yea, greater than the pulpit ; for *there* it is *Hoc est Corpus Meum,* this is my Body ; but in the pulpit 'tis at most but *Hoc est verbum Meum,* this is My word. And a greater reverence, no doubt, is due to the *Body* than to the *word* of our Lord ; and so, in relation, answerably to the *Throne,* where His Body is usually present, than to the *seat* where His word useth to be proclaimed. And God hold it there at His word ; for, as too many men use the matter, 'tis *Hoc est verbum Diaboli,* this is the word of the devil, in too many places : witness sedition and the like to it ;—and this reverence ye do when ye enter the Chapel, and when you approach nearer to offer. And this is no *innovation,* for you are bound to it by your order, and that's not new. And idolatry it is not, to worship God towards His Holy Table : for if it had been idolatry, I presume Queen Elizabeth and King James would not have practised it, no, not in those solemnities. And being not idolatry, but true Divine worship, you will, I hope, give a poor priest leave to worship God as yourselves do : for if it be God's worship, I ought to do it as well as you ; and if it be idolatry, you ought not to do it more than I. I say again, I hope a poor priest may worship God with as lowly a reverence as you do, since you are bound by your order and by your oath, according to a Constitution of Hen. V. (as appears *In Libro Nigro Windasoriensi,* p. 65), to give due honour and reverence *Domino Deo et altari Ejus, in modum virorum Ecclesiasticorum ;* that is to the Lord your God, and to His Altar, (for there is a reverence due to that too, though such as comes far short of Divine worship) ; and this is the manner, as ecclesiastical persons both worship and do reverence . . . . . Now if you will turn this off, and say it was the superstition of that age so to do,

Bishop Jewel will come in to help me there: for where Harding names divers ceremonies and particularly *bowing themselves and adoring at the Sacrament*—I say adoring *at* the Sacrament, not adoring *the* Sacrament; there Bishop Jewel (that learned, painful, and reverend prelate) approves all, both the kneeling and *the bowing*, and the standing up at the Gospel (which, as ancient as it is in the Church, and a common custom, is yet fondly made another of their innovations).* And further, the Bishop adds, ' That they are all commendable gestures and tokens of devotion, so long as the people understand what they mean and apply them unto God.' Now with us the people did ever understand them fully and apply them to God, and to none but God, till these factious spirits and their like, to the great disservice of God and His Church, went about to persuade them that they are superstitious if not idolatrous gestures ; as they value everything else to be where God is not served slovenly."— *Speech in the Star Chamber June* 14, 1637—*pp.* 43, 52. Cited in Hierugia Anglicana, pp. 55—6.

This, then, may be regarded with *moral* (I can scarcely doubt with *absolute*) certainty as Abp. Laud's explanation of that " *bowing* " " gesture " of the Canon which Mr. Goode inaccurately cites in proof—that " *Kneeling* is not an act of adoration to Christ [" whole Christ, God and man "] as so present" *i.e.* in, what he calls, "an *immaterial*" manner. What the Abp. thought of *kneeling* " at the Sacrament " is abundantly clear from this same passage : *why* he thought *adoration*=kneeling due then, is plain from what he says of the " Altar " where It is celebrated and of the " Body " which " is usually present" there. It will tend to complete his view of the point if his opinion of Christ's Presence in that Sacrament is here added ; and this may be satisfactorily gathered from the following passages in his celebrated controversy with *Fisher* the Jesuit. The *Italics* &c. are mine. Thus he says :—

" Thirdly, A.C. [*i.e.* Fisher] doth extremely ill to join those cases of the Donatists for baptism and the protestants for the Eucharist together, as he doth. For this proposition in the first, concerning the Donatists, leads a man (as is confessed by himself) into known and damnable schism and heresy ; but, by A. C's. good leave, the latter, concerning the protestants and the Eucharist, nothing so.

" * Bishop Jewell's Reply to Harding's Answer, Art. 3, Div. 29."

For I hope A. C. dare not say, that to believe the **true**, ***sub-stantial** *presence of Christ* is either known or damnable schism or heresy. Now as many and as learned† protestants believe and maintain this, or do believe the possibility of salvation (as before is limited) in the Roman Church: therefore they, in that, not guilty of either known or damnable schism or heresy, though the Donatists were of both.

" Fourthly, whereas he imposes upon the protestants ' the denial or doubting of the **true** and **real** *presence of Christ in the Eucharist*,' he is a great deal more bold than true in that also ; for understand them aright, and they certainly neither deny nor doubt it. For as for the Lutherans, as they are commonly called, their very opinion of consubstantiation makes it known to the world, that they neither deny nor doubt of His **true** and **real** *presence there ;* and they are protestants. And for the Calvinists, if they might be rightly understood, they also maintain a **most true** and **real** *presence*, though they cannot permit their judgment to be transubstantiated ; and they are protestants too. And this is so known a truth that ‡ Bellarmine confesses it ; for he saith, ' Protestants do often grant that the **true** and **real** *body of Christ is in the Eucharist*." But he adds, ' That they never say (so far as he hath read) that it is there **truly** and **really**, unless they speak of the supper which shall be in heaven.' Well ; first, if they grant that the **true** and **real** *body of Christ is in that* blessed sacrament, (as Bellarmine confesses they do, and it is most true,) then A. C. is false, who charges all the protestants with denial or doubtfulness in this point. And secondly, Bellarmine himself also shews his ignorance or his malice ; ignorance, if he knew it not, malice, if he would not know it. For the Calvinists, at least they which follow Calvin himself, do not only believe that the **true** and **real** *body of Christ* is *received* in the Eucharist, but that **it is there**, and that we *partake* of it **vere et realiter**, which are § Calvin's own words ; and yet Bellarmine boldly affirms that to his reading ' no one protestant did ever affirm it.' .... Nor can that place by any art be shifted, or by any violence wrested from Calvin's true meaning *of the presence of Christ in and at the blessed*

---

* " Cœterum his absurditatibus sublatis, quicquid ad exprimendam veram substantialemque corporis a sunguinis Domini communicationem, quœ sub sacris cœnœ symbolis, fidelibus exhibetur, facere potest, libenter recipio. Calv. Inst. lib. iv. c. 17. §. 19.—In cœnœ mysterio per symbola panis et vini Christus vere nobis exhibetur, &c. Et nos participes substantiae ejus facti sumus. Ibid. §. 11."

† " Sect. 35. numb. III."

‡ " Bellarm de Euchar. lib. i. c. 2. §. Quinto dicit. Sacramentarii sœpe dicunt reale corpus Christi in cœna adesse, sed realiter adesse nunquam dicunt, quod legerim, nisi forte loquuntur de cœna quœ fit in cœlo, &c.

" And that he means to brand protestants under the name of *sacramentarii* is plain. For he says the council of Trent opposed this word *realiter, figmento Calvinistico*, to the Calvinistical figment. Ibid."

§ " Calv. in 1 Cor. x. 3. vere, &c. Et in 1 Cor. xi. 24. realiter. Vide supra num. III."

Sacrament of the Eucharist, to any supper in heaven whatsoever..
...... And for the Church of England, nothing is more plain
than that it believes and teaches the **true** and **real** *presence of Christ
in the *Eucharist*, unless A. C. can make a body no body, and blood
no blood, (as perhaps he can do by transubstantiation) as well as
bread no bread, and wine no wine : and the Church of England is
protestant too. So protestants of all sorts maintain a **true** and **real**
presence of Christ in the Eucharist ; and then, where is any known
or damnable heresy here ? As for the learned of those zealous men
that died in this cause in queen's Mary's days, *they denied not the*
real *presence simply taken*, but as their opposites forced *transubstantiation* upon them, as if that and the *real presence* had been all
one.   Whereas all the ancient Christians ever believed the one, and
none but modern and superstitious Christians believe the other ....
Now that the learned protestants in queen Mary's days *did not deny,*
nay, *did maintain* the **real** *presence*, will manifestly appear.   For
when the commissioners obtruded to Jo. Frith the *presence* of Christ's
natural *body in the Sacrament*, and that *without all figure or similitude*, Jo. Frith acknowledges,† ' That the inward man doth as verily
receive Christ's body as the outward man receives the sacrament
with his mouth.'   And he adds,‡ ' That neither side ought to make
it a necessary article of faith, but leave it indifferent.'   Nay, Abp.
Cranmer comes more plainly and more home to it than Frith.   ' For
if you understand,' saith he,§ ' by this word **really, reipsa** ; that is
in very deed and effectually ; so Christ, by the grace and efficacy
of His passion, is **indeed** and **truly** *present*, &c.   But if by this
word **really** you understand ‖ **corporaliter**, ¶ **corporally** *in His*

* " ' The Body of Christ is given, taken, and eaten in the supper (of the Lord)
only after an heavenly and spiritual manner.   And the means whereby the body
of Christ is received and eaten is faith.'   Eccl. Ang, Art. xxviii.   So here is
the manner of transubstantiation denied, but the body of Christ twice affirmed.
And in the prayer before consecration thus : ' Grant us, gracious Lord, so to eat
the Flesh of Thy dear Son Jesus Christ, and to drink His blood ' &c.—And
again in the Second Prayer or Thanksgiving after Consecration, thus : ' We give
Thee thanks, for that Thou dost vouchsafe to feed us, which have duly received
these holy mysteries, with the spiritual food of the most precious Body and
Blood, of Thy Son our Saviour Jesus Christ ' &c."

† " Jo. Fox.   Martyrolog. tom. ii. London, 1597, p. 943."
‡ " Fox, ibid."   § " Cranmer apud Fox, ibid. p. 1301."
‖ " I say *corporaliter*, corporally ; for so Bellarmine hath it expressly : Quod
autem corporaliter et proprie sumatur sanguis et caro, &c., probari potest omnibus
argumentis, &c.   Bellarm. de Eucharist. lib. i. c. 12. §. Sed. tota.   And I must
be bold to tell you more than that this is the doctrine of the Church of Rome ;
for I must tell you too, that Bellarmine here contradicts himself : for he that
tells us here, that it can be proved by many arguments that we receive the flesh
and the blood of Christ in the Eucharist *corporaliter*, said as expressly before,
(had he remembered it,) that though Christ be in this blessed sacrament *vere et
realiter*, yet (saith he) non dicemus corporaliter, i.e. eo modo quo sua natura
existunt corpora, &c.   Bellarm. de Eucharist lib. i. c. 2. §. Tertia regula.   So
Bellarmine here is a notorious contradiction : or else it will follow plainly out of
him, that Christ in the sacrament is existent one way and received another,
which is a gross absurdity. ......"

¶ This expression, " corporally," should be especially noticed by those who

natural and **organical** *body, under the forms of bread and wine,* it is contrary to the holy word of God." * And so likewise bishop Ridley. Nay, bishop Ridley adds yet further, and speaks so fully to this point, as I think no man can add to his expression : and it is well if some protestants except not against it. 'Both you and I,' saith he,† 'agree in this ; that *in the Sacrament is the* very true and **natural** *body and blood of Christ,* even that which ascended into heaven, which sits on the right hand of God the Father, which shall come from thence to judge the quick and the dead : only we differ *in modo,* in the way and manner of being. We *confess* all one **thing** *to be in the Sacrament,* and *dissent* in the manner of being *there.* I confess Christ's **natural** *body to be in the Sacrament by* **spirit** and **grace,** &c. You make a **grosser** *kind of being,* inclosing a **natural** body under the shape and form of bread and wine.' So far and more, bishop Ridley. And‡ Archbishop Cranmer confesses that he was indeed of another opinion, and inclining to that of Zuinglius, till bishop Ridley convinced his judgment and *settled him in this point* . . . ."—*Laud.* v. *Fisher.* Cardwell's Ed., Oxford, 1839, pp. 245-49.

III. I have now produced fully, though not, I hope, at greater length than was needed, such additional Authorities and Arguments as seem to me fairly to support the Opinions maintained in the Letter ; it will be well, however, to complete or explain, so far as I can, any other statements which were unavoidably left imperfect.

Thus, at p. 65, I alluded to a statement of Strype's, which I was then unable to find, touching a Puritan proposal, in Elizabeth's reign, of *prostration* at the Holy Communion : I have now recovered the passage, which is as follows :—

"Another whose name was Snagg, entered into discourse of some of the Articles, which Strickland had laid down before. Whereof

find a great difficulty in those words of the Declaration "the *natural* Body and Blood of our Saviour Christ are in Heaven, and not here" : it is often argued by such—that these words (1) either *deny* any *real presence* of Christ's Body in the Eucharist (2) or *affirm* Him to have *two bodies :* but, as there can be no reasonable doubt that Cranmer is responsible for the terms of the original Declaration so, the Archbishop's language in the above quotation must, in all fairness, be taken as their true exponent : consequently when Christ's "*natural Body and Blood*" are said to be "not here," it must be understood that they are not here "*corporally*" i.e. *naturally=organically.*

* See also the passage as given above p. 46.
† " Apud Fox, ibid. p. 1598."—See also the passage as given above, p. 61.
‡ " Apud Fox, ibid. p. 1703."

E E E

one was, not to kneel at the receiving of the holy sacrament ; but to lie prostrate (to shew the old superstition) or to sit, every man at his own liberty. And the directions were thought fit to be left out of the book [of the Office of Communion] for that posture. Which should be a law ; and every man left to do according to his conscience."—*Strype Ann.* II., p. 93.

It is quite in place here to commend that proposal to the attention of devout persons amongst ourselves, whose vivid belief of Christ's Presence in the Sacrament of the Altar has drawn them into acts of prostration and other supposed reverential postures, which are a departure, not only from the established practice (which with us might have become very lax), but from the recognized rule of Western Christendom : that rule, which is even *more accurately defined* in the Latin Communion than in the Church of England, makes KNEELING the *external expression* of the honour due to Christ in the Sacrament : and it is plain from the Puritan proposition, which described it as " the old superstition," that those religionists accounted it a distinct mark of Adoration. Variations in the mode of Kneeling were, of course, meant to be allowed ; if for no other reason, at least, because it would be no less impossible than unnatural to prescribe any uniform angle which the worshipper's body must present when in that position ; but, in appointing a *definite* posture whereby to manifest a thankful allegiance to the Heavenly King, clearly all *self-chosen* ways of doing Him homage were as much designed to be excluded, as are marked departures from that manner of approaching an earthly Monarch which the forms of his Court provide. Such gestures, while regarded as pardonable extravagancies resulting either from ignorance or from good intentions, are not accepted by a temporal Sovereign as tokens of any deeper loyalty than is felt by those who conform to the rules of his Presence Chamber : still less may it be presumed that He, who fully knows and entirely accepts the hidden homage of the devoutest heart, regards more favourably any self-appointed tokens of it, however lowly and reverend they are designed to be, than

He does that conformity to the Prescriptions or Usages of His Church, which is so real an evidence of the humble and obedient will.

This device of the Puritans' to adopt any other posture than that of Kneeling, in order to shew "the old superstition" which they considered Kneeling to involve, implies a then continued adherence to that " superstition," *i.e.*, to that Adoration of Christ in the Eucharist, which Mr. Goode denies the Church of England to have allowed at that time, or to permit now. This bears upon a statement of his (Supp. p. 32) when commenting upon Dr. Pusey's remark that those words of Art. 28—"'the *Sacrament* was not by Christ's ordinance reserved, carried about, lifted up, or worshipped'.... By no honest interpretation can .. be extended to a worship, *not* of the *Sacrament*, but of Christ present there;" for Mr. Goode says:—

" Now, if Christ is present in an adorable form inside the bread, so that the two form (call the union sacramental, or what you will) *one whole*, that one whole is a legitimate object of worship, just as Jesus Christ was a proper object of worship. We ought to bow down to that which lies upon the Communion table as the sacrament, because, according to Dr. Pusey, Christ forms a part of it....."

It is certain, however, that two at least of the Reformers, who ought to have weight with Mr. Goode, would disagree with him here, for they make just the distinction which he ignores. First, Dr. Redman in 1551 (See p. 29) says— " That nothing which is *seen* in the Sacrament, or perceived with any *outward sense*, is to be worshipped," *i.e.*, with the honour due to God—words which surely imply that What is not thus cognizable by the Senses is to be so worshipped : next, Bishop Ridley in 1555 (See p. 58), when arguing against *Glyn* the Romanist, used these memorable words— " *We adore and worship Christ in the Eucharist.* And if you mean the external Sacrament ; I say, *that also is to be worshipped as a Sacrament.*" Perhaps Mr. Goode might say that this was a distinction well enough to be made by a Theologian like Ridley, but that it is incapable of being appreciated by the popular mind. This, however, was just one of those very questions involving popular acts on which the Bishop would be especially careful not to propound an *unpractical* theory. Are the mass of people, however, so inclined to a practical *Eutychianism* as Mr. Goode's argument seems to imply? I think not: though, no doubt, the Apostle's words are not inapplicable in this case too— " There must be also heresies among you, that they which are approved may be made perfect." (1 Cor. xi. 19.) For, if we come to consider it, people do I suppose almost universally, by a sort of natural or religious instinct which recognizes *co-existence*, separate in their own minds what, to the moral or physical sense, appears to be a *commingling*. It is so, surely, when men look upon, honour, or dishonour their fellow men; they do mentally separate soul and body, no matter whether it be done consciously or unconsciously. The like *was* the case with those who, having learned the truth of Christ's Nature, worshipped the God-Man when He was upon Earth—*is* their condition who, being similarly informed, worship Him now that He sits upon His Heavenly Throne: they did and we do—even the young or the uneducated, no less than the old or the wise—with no great difficulty distinguish between His "unity of Person " and any "confusion of substance." A kindred habit clings to us in viewing a solid body heated to incandesence, or in touching one whose temperature is not visible. Precisely so, it seems to me, is the separation we mentally make between the *Res Sacramenti* which Faith alone perceives, and the *Sacramentum* which Sight beholds; though at the same time we no less vividly recognize their Sacramental Union.

It may be that Mr. Goode's proposition, which has led to these remarks, was not unconnected in his mind with an assertion he, elsewhere, makes in the following passage :—

" Of the two, I must confess that I had rather have to defend the Romish doctrine than that of Dr. Pusey and Archdeacon Denison ; for when we read the words, ' This is my Body,' it seems a necessary conclusion that they must mean one of these two things,—either, ' This is a figure of—represents—my Body,' or, ' This is really and substantially my Body.' But if the doctrine of Dr. Pusey and Archdeacon Denison is the true one, they must be equivalent to saying, '.This is bread and my Body together.' Now certainly a *compound* of two essentially different things cannot be truly or properly described by a name that belongs only to one of them."— *Work on the Eucharist*, p.58.

To this last sentence it is that I refer as apparently raising a difficulty about *Sacramental Union*, which seems to me to be met at the outset by two of perhaps the best remembered and most commonly quoted texts of Holy Scripture : thus (Gen. ii. 7) we read " man became a living soul ;" and again (Ezekiel xviii. 4) " Behold, all souls are mine." It needs no argument surely to prove that in both these places " a compound "— man — consisting " of two essentially different things "—soul and body—is both " truly " and " properly described by a name "—soul—" that belongs only to one of them." So then, if He who " formed man of the dust of the ground," when He had " breathed into his nostrils the breath of life " called him by a name which no one supposes to have implied any *change* of his *earthly substance* into the *Divine Afflatus*, though the two formed " one whole " (to use Mr. Goode's term): why may not Bread, the product of a like Divinely formed earthy matter, when the Life-giving Breath of the Heavenly Spirit has been invoked upon it, be also called by a name which, though none (not even the Latin Communion) apply it to that material substance, does belong to Him who decreed the Consecrating Benediction " till He come " personally and visibly again ? Certain it is that "*when*" the Minister *delivereth* THE BREAD to anyone, he shall say, THE BODY of our Lord Jesus Christ, which was given for thee, preserve thy body and soul unto everlasting life ;" and certain also it is that " The Body of Christ is given . . . . in the Supper [though] only after an heavenly and spiritual manner " (Art. xxviii.)—language, which in its plain grammatical sense will, I think, *seem* to most (as in truth the very objections to it indicate) to imply an intention of recognizing a union which involves the Presence both of *the Bread* and of *the Body of Christ;* as Archbishop Cranmer said (See p. 20), "When I use to speak sometimes (as the old authors do) that Christ is in the Sacraments, I mean the same as they did understand the matter; that is to say, not of Christ's *carnal* presence in the outward Sacrament, but sometimes of His Sacramental Presence."

It will have been observed, probably, that in the paragraph embodying the sentence just discussed, Mr. Goode thinks one necessarily alternative meaning of "This is my Body" must be "This is a figure of—represents—my Body." But, as the object of all controversies on this subject should be to promote "a godly union and concord," it will be well to enquire whether such a meaning, if rightly understood, is not *uniform* rather than *alternative.* What, then, does Mr. Goode understand by his *alternative?* His meaning appears to be very plainly set forth only eight pages after the above sentence; for he says (p. 66, the Italics are his):—

"Now there is but one way in which bread can *be* the body of Christ, and that is by representation. It *is* the body of Christ as a picture *is* the person whom it represents. There is absolutely no other way of interpreting the words without doing violence to them. There is nothing in the whole account which involves more than a change of *character* and *use.*"

One obvious answer to this statement is—that it contradicts the Homily which says "that in the Supper of the Lord there is . . . . no untrue figure* of a thing absent;" for *this* "a picture *is* [of] the person whom it represents:"

---

* In reference to this point it may be useful to give the following passages from a Letter written by *Bucer* to *P. Martyr*, dated Cambridge, June 20, 1549.— Bucer is replying to a Letter from *P. Martyr* at Oxford, June 15, 1549, in which the latter endeavours to reconcile with Bucer's opinions the arguments he had used in his Disputation at Oxford (See pp. 9—13); he thus answers P. Martyr: —"I confess that, if you had thought good to consult with me on the framing of your Propositions [See p. 10], I should have entreated you to have expressed the second in these, or in similar words:—2. *The Body of Christ is not contained locally in the Bread and Wine, neither is it affixed or adjoined to those things by any manner of this world.* And to have added at the end of your third:—3. . . . *so that, to them, that believe, Christ is here truly exhibited; to be seen, however, received, enjoyed, by faith, not by any sense or manner of this world.* . . . . The reason why I should have preferred your second Proposition expressed in the words which I have judged [more appropriate.—*Ed.*], or, in similar terms, rather than in words which deny the **real** and **substantial presence** of Christ in the Sacrament (or rather in the Eucharist, so that the celebration [actio.—*Ed.*] and the Sacred assembly, rather than the symbols only, would have been

it may be never so speaking a likeness, but no one dreams
that it does more than quicken the recollection or the imagination of the *absent* person.   Is this, however, *all* that the
Sacrament of the Altar does?   Did our Lord design it to do

expressed), and also that something should have been added to your third, concerning the Exhibition of Christ, are these:—

" We ought always to endeavour with the greatest diligence, to edify in the
faith and love of Christ whomsoever we can, and to offend no one, since the
necessary obedience of Christ does not require that; and for this reason, in order
that we should not only think but also speak the same things, especially concerning Mysteries of Christ so great and so generally prized; we should, moreover, take care not to give any occasion to the evil-disposed for criminating,
much less of persecuting, the Church of God. Now, among those who can be
edified in Christ by the present Disputation, I think there are positively none of
those with whom I have ever had any communication on this point (—and I
have investigated the Sentiments of very many persons, both in their writings
and by personal converse, during that entire septennary in which, rolling as it
were the stone of Sisyphus, I have striven for the concord of the Churches as
regards this matter—) who imagine an impanation of Christ, or his local connexion with the symbols of this world.—But some, like your Antagonists, contended, that Christ is here exhibited, not in Bread and Wine, but in their
accidents, and that, as long as those accidents remain; yet they denied that He
is here contained locally.—Or they held, that undoubtedly nothing more is here
exhibited than Bread and Wine, as signs of Christ altogether absent, by which
we ought to make only a remembrance of Him, and to advance in the faith of
Him : however, some hold, that, by this remembrance, their minds are lifted up
into heaven, so that there they enjoy Christ.—Or they were of opinion that, in
this Sacrament, Christ exhibits himself whole, God and Man ; and hence, for
the purpose of preserving this their faith, and also of declaring that they do not
agree with those who here introduce naked and empty symbols, they like to
make use of these forms of speech, and to say, that the Body of Christ is here
exhibited Corporally, because His Body is exhibited ; Substantially, because
His Substance ; Carnally, because His flesh.—And there were a very few who
chose to use these words after that first fervour of the contention which arose in
the early struggle of this Disputation.   And those who chose to use these words
contended, that at least the right of using those forms of speech ought to be left
to them : nevertheless those persons always plainly affirmed that here they
thought nothing about a descent from heaven, nothing about a local inclusion :
and as to that which they maintained about the eating by the wicked, that also
subsisted in collation.*—A good number were of opinion, that the presence of
Christ was exhibited to them, in the Sacrament, simply, for their salvation, if
they received that [presence.—*Ed.*] with faith; and altogether withdrew their
mind from [any speculation as to.—*Ed.*] the manner in which He is present.

" I have found these and no other opinions, about the presence of the Lord in
the Sacred Supper, among those with whom I have ever conferred on this matter—
(I have conferred, however, certainly with very many) among whom, some
introduced more, some less, of a carnal contention; nevertheless I have decidedly
found not one person who insisted either on a local presence of Christ, or on a
connexion with the symbols after any fashion of this world.   It is for us, however, if we wish to edify and in nothing to offend, to labour with the utmost
diligence, that we may lead them into consent, as to the truth of Christ, both

* " It not being clear to the Editor what was the precise meaning which Bucer intended to
convey by this word—'*collatione*'—it has been left in its Latin idiom. Probably it was
intended to signify a mere '*bringing together*' of the elements and of the receiver, *without
any beneficial effect.*"

no more? Did St. Paul think it did no more, when he addressed the Galatians (iii. 1) in words already referred to (See p. 352)? Is not the Sacramental Picture rather the RE-presentation, *i.e.*, the *presentation* of the RES=the THING

between themselves and us, and with the universal Church of Christ. I cannot discover any more speedy and certain method of persuading all, who are not contentious, and who can be edified in this matter, to [adopt this.—*Ed.*] consent,—than this,—since we agree in sentiment with the Word of the Lord, and with the whole of the ancient Church, that we should freely use the words of Scripture and of the ancient Church ; and so, that we should both express and proclaim, in very full and certain words, that which is the principal thing in this sacred [matter.—*Ed.*]; as we see in the holy Fathers was the custom of the early Church. Now in the words of Christ, of the Apostle, and of the holy Fathers, we observe that the very [ipsam.—*Ed.*] exhibition of Christ is everywhere most fully expressed ; and the presence, not the signification [That is, the representation of Christ by a Sign.—*Ed.*] and absence, of the Lord. When, indeed, we are treating of the Bread and Wine,—they are properly called signs—to them this term is properly attributed, yes, even to the whole celebration. But neither the signs themselves, nor the signification of Christ, is the principal thing which is here in discussion ; but the very exhibition and spiritual eating of Him. On this account the holy Fathers used the word, Represent (which is the same as the word Exhibit), rather than Signify.

" Moreover, since here we all acknowledge that by faith we verily take Christ and have Him present; and that this taking and presence, not feigned, and verbal only, but real, and of the very substance of Christ; I see no reason why [the proposition—*Ed.*] that Christ is not taken **really** and **substantially,** should be defended as if it were a dogma of the Christian religion. It is far better, I think, that these terms [Signification and Absence.—*Ed.*] should be discontinued, which method of concord was lately adopted with great advantage in the German Churches; since they are not [the words.—*Ed.*] of Scripture ; nor do they even, as I believe, conduce very much to express the truth of Scripture ; nor are they taken in the same sense. For,—when those points are so much contended, that Christ is so in heaven, that He is **really** and **substantially** absent from the Sacred Supper, and is only present by signification,—I have found one result,—that there has been a wonderful confirmation of the impious profanation of the Sacraments by those who acknowledge only naked signs in the Eucharist. [I have found, also,—*Ed.*] that those who are truly on our side, but who are oppressed by a certain superstition with respect to words, and by the obscurity of the matter itself, are much disturbed by this disputation, and are too much led away [from us. — *Ed.*] by those who deny a real presence of Christ in the Supper, and admit nothing more than its significatory character. [I have found.—*Ed.*] that those, moreover, who have a more full understanding of this Mystery, and are not held [in bondage.—*Ed.*] by a superstition with respect to words, are not a little offended; because they see how many,—through this negation of a real presence of Christ in the Eucharist, and through the establishment of a signified presence,—are either precipitated by Satan into an absolute contempt of Sacraments, or are armed by him [to a battle.—*Ed.*] against the Church of God, by the pernicious crime of Christ excluded from the Sacrament.

" Well weighing these considerations, I am truly unwilling that Christ should not be [allowed to be.—*Ed.*] **really** in the Sacred Supper ; I am unwilling, also, that against those [your opponents.—*Ed.*] the matter should be urged by the arguments—Christ is in heaven, circumscribed by place ; therefore He is not in fact [Re ipsa vel realiter.—*Ed.*] or **really,** (which two expressions are, I think, equivalent,) in the Sacred Supper :—but rather, therefore He is not **locally** in the Supper. For thus this argument ought to be concluded, unless it become an empty sophism. But, if it be so concluded, against whom is the contest?

of the Sacrament (*Sacramentum*), *i. e.*, Christ Himself? Bishops Latimer and Ridley shall answer the question; the former declares (See p. 40) "this same [*spiritual*] presence may be called most fitly a *real* presence; that is, a presence

For even the Schoolmen did not affirm, that Christ was in the Supper or in the signs locally ; and who would tolerate antagonists who should affirm such a proposition ? Indeed, I know that this argument has given grave offence to an innumerable multitude of the holiest brethren ; who think that they are defamed by that false accusation ; as if, in truth, they included Christ locally in the Bread, or even in the celebration of the Supper. You [now.—*Ld.*] have the reason why I could have wished that you had not placed in your second Proposition, nor defended as a necessary dogma of our religion,—That Christ is not in the Supper, nor given and taken really ; and I should have preferred that all those words,—Really, Substantially, Carnally, Corporally,—had been omitted.

" The reason why I could have wished that, in your third Proposition, you had more distinctly expressed the exhibition of Christ in the Supper,—is this ; that I cannot desire that either yourself (who have a very great name among the Churches of Christ in every land, and who are among the dearest of my acquaintance) or that the Church of England should anywhere fall under suspicion, as if you acknowledged nothing in the Lord's Supper besides empty signs of Christ through which the remembrance of Christ now absent ought to be excited. For, although you say, in your subsequent responses, that you maintain an *efficacious* signification and exhibition of Christ; yet nearly the whole Disputation runs on in such a manner, that I fear too many who may read the Acts of this Disputation will come to the conclusion that you maintain that Christ is absent altogether from the Supper, and that whatsoever is done in it has no further result than that faith, excited concerning Christ truly absent, is increased through the Spirit of Christ, by His benefits brought to mind and by meditation ; and that you do not acknowledge that the very Christ, (beginning [to do this.—*Ed.*] in Baptism, and continuing [to do it.—*Ed.*] more and more in the Eucharist,) exhibits and communicates Himself present to His own by that communication, by which they verily are and remain in Him, and have Him being and remaining in themselves. To sum up : they will think you maintain the presence, not of Christ, but only of the Spirit of Christ, and of His influence ; although I know that you acknowledge that Christ exhibits Himself present to faith."

Then, having given P. Martyr his advice as to the publication of his Disputation, he goes on to say : — " Moreover, I could desire (you will certainly find a suitable place, possibly in your Peroration,) that you would very clearly define those words, ' *Esse in Sacramento Christi Corpus realiter*,' [That the body of Christ is **really** * in the Sacrament,—*Ed.*] and in such terms as shall point out the altogether absurd and impious sense of those words ; and that you would then add, that some persons go astray into that absurd and impious sense ; in order that it might more distinctly appear that you here by no means wish to traduce any Churches or brethren who are most averse from that sense which you oppose. Lastly. [I wish that.—*Ed.*] you would confess (if you can do so with a safe conscience,) ' that Christ undoubtedly is (since we must speak with simplicity) in His Sacraments, and present † in them, not absent from them ' ;

* *That* is *carnally, organically* : this was contended for by some on the Roman side, as P. Martyr's Disputation proves, and as I have shewn throughout.

† Bucer's anxiety on this point is further shewn in the following passage from his Letter a year later to *Theobald Niger*, dated Cambridge, April 15, 1550 : in it he says " Dr. Peter Martyr's Disputation was planned, and his Propositions communicated, before I came into England. I could have wished a modified Proposition, composed in words altogether different, and those [the words—*Ed.*] of Scripture. I am well assured, however, that he by no means wished that the Supper of the Lord should be [viewed as—*Ed.*] a mere administration of Bread and Wine ; he acknowledges the presence and exhibition of Christ ; but, since the

not *figured*, but a *true* and a *faithful* presence :" the latter says, distinctly enough as it seems to me (See p. 186) :—" in the Sacrament is a certain change, in that, the bread, which was before common bread, is now made *a lively presentation**

but that you would always add, 'that we may enjoy † Him by Faith,' as Paul says, that 'He dwells in our hearts by Faith.' For though we should grant you, that He is circumscribed even in heaven by a physical place, how is that inconsistent with His being now truly present to us by faith; even as the Sun, in whatever part of the world we behold him, is truly present to us by sight. Certainly all errors which can possibly arise from the name 'Presence,' may be altogether excluded by such words, which can neither disturb any of the brethren, nor arm our enemies against us by false criminations : I mean,—if we deny, together with transubstantiation, both a local presence, and any [presence—*Ed.*] of this world's character."—*Gorham's Reformation Gleanings*, pp. 83-90.

These last words are especially noteworthy as shewing how large a liberty of belief Bucer was willing to accord, and so they may with the utmost probability be accounted a valuable indirect confirmation of what was said, at p. 4 and elsewhere, as to the like freedom which the Authorities in the Church of England designed to allow : Bucer's statement ought, moreover, to have especial weight with those who hold that he influenced the changes in the 2nd Prayer Book of Edw. VIth to a much greater extent than (as I have already pointed out) Historical statements seem to warrant us in believing. In further proof of this last remark may be quoted the following passage of a Letter from *P. Martyr* to Bucer, written at Oxford early in February 1551 :—" On the 1st of February I received your letter dated January 22nd. Concerning the Reformation of the Rituals [Rituum—*Ed.*] I cannot write anything else as to what will be [done—*Ed.*] except that the Bishops have agreed among themselves on many emendations and corrections in the published Book. Indeed, I have seen the alterations on which they have decided, noted in their places; but as I am ignorant of English, and could not understand them, so I am unable to give you any certain information about them. However, I do not think they have gone so far as to determine on adopting the whole of your and my suggestions. To our [Archbishop — *Ed.*] indeed, I said, more than once, that, having undertaken this correction of the Rituals, they ought to

---

* Even P. Martyr, in his "Confession of the Lord's Supper, exhibited to the Senate of Strasburgh, about the middle of May, 1556, when he was called to Zurich," could thus speak : — " I would grant, moreover, that the bread itself is, in its own peculiar manner, the Body of Christ, and is so called because, namely, it is its Sacrament. For both Scripture and the Fathers often so speak of the Sacraments. But they who hold the opposite opinion will themselves, too, perhaps, concede a trope in the words cited; or rather, being compelled of necessity, they thus explain that phrase :—' This is my Body,'—*i.e.*, 'With this—namely, bread—is my Body given.' And I, too, should not object to admit this interpretation, if they would understand that the Body of Christ is given without a **substantial** or **corporal** presence. But, since they will not allow this, I, for the avoiding of ambiguity, abstain from that kind of trope, and am contented with the common and received one of *signification*, which the Fathers, too, of old employed."—*Gorham's Reformation Gleanings*, p. 362.

Zurich people have here many and great followers, this excellent man was drawn, I hardly know how, to consent to use the word, 'Signification,' although he added, 'efficacious,' by which he understands the exhibition of Christ, as he himself explains it in the Preface to his Disputations ; in which [Preface—*Ed.*], by my advice, he added many observations to his own, and withdrew some (—the Disputations were already published—); for he is most desirous of a pious concord."—*Gorham's Reformation Gleanings*, p. 142.

† I notice this word as being something like an answer to the following complaint which Mr. Goode makes against Dr. Pusey.—". . . he then seeks to *strain* in a similar way a very

of Christ's body, and not only a figure, but *effectuously* representeth his body . . . . which the eyes of faith see, as the bodily eyes see only bread." What is this, too, but in part the language of Art. xxv., " Sacraments ordained of Christ . . .

look well to it; that the restoration they make should be so simple, chaste, and pure, that there may be no further need for emendations : for, if frequent changes should take place in these matters, it might at length easily come to pass that they would fall into general contempt.* And I am persuaded that, if the business had been committed to his individual hand, purity of ceremonies †would without difficulty have been attained by him : but he has colleagues who offer resolute opposition. Cheke is the only person there, who openly and earnestly favours simplicity . . . ."—*Gorham's Reformation Gleanings*, p. 231.

The following passage from Mr. Fisher is also in place here : —". . . although foreigners, and belonging to a school of theology different in many respects from his own—they [*i.e.*, Bucer and P. Martyr] are, nevertheless, supposed to have swayed materially the mind of our great Reformer [Cranmer] in his treatment of the Service-book. This, however, it should be observed, is mere surmise; and a surmise, too, based upon the purest assumption. Probably both Bucer and P. Martyr—at least the former—might be *consulted* by the Archbishop; but we have no proof that he was really *influenced* by either of them in his preparation of the Liturgy. (See Lawrence's Bampton Lectures, p. 247). Indeed, there are letters extant which seem to shew very clearly, that P. Martyr himself was by no means deeply in the confidence of Cranmer . . . ."—*Lit. Purity*, 2nd Ed., 1860, p. 136.

With regard to the *doctrinal* questions, of "transubstantiation," and "a local presence," mentioned at the end of Bucer's Letter, and also as supporting the allegation made throughout these pages—that Transubstantiation was the main point of attack by the English Reformers—it is desirable to cite the following passage from Bucer's letter to Niger, April 15th, 1550, already quoted from at p. 401 : "Up to this time nothing further is established in this kingdom concerning that controversy, than that Transubstantiation is not to be affirmed. In the Public Prayers, however, at the Lord's Supper, a true exhibition of the Body and Blood of Christ is expressed in words exceedingly clear and weighty."—*Gorham's Reformation Gleanings*, p. 143. The Editor remarks in a Note "The words in Edward VIth's first Liturgy, 1549, which Bucer so highly approved were :— 'With Thy Holy Spirit and word, vouchsafe to ble+ss and sanc+tify these thy gifts, and creatures of Bread and Wine, that they may be unto us the Body and Blood of Thy most dearly beloved Son Jesus Christ.' In the Second Liturgy, 1552, they were expunged, and the following substituted : 'Grant that we, receiving these thy creatures of Bread and Wine, according to thy Son our

plain passage of one of the Homilies. The words of the Homily being,—' so that to think that without faith we may enjoy the eating and drinking thereof, or that that is the fruition of it, is but to dream a gross carnal feeding.' Dr. Pusey actually fixes upon the words 'enjoy' and 'fruition' as shewing that the writer meant that we *may* '*eat* and *drink*' thereof,' but not 'enjoy' that eating and drinking! He says that the writer of the Homily 'lays down, that faith is essential, not to *any* reception of our Lord's Body, but to '*the* fruition' of it, or the benefits resulting from it. In that he denies, that 'eating without faith' is '*the* fruition of it,' he even implies, that it may be a *reception* of it, although not the *fruition* of it. He lays the emphasis upon the words 'enjoy,' 'fruition.' (p. 219.) Faith is 'the mean,' according to him, by which a man healthily receives 'the spiritual food' of the Body and Blood of Christ.' (*ib.*); where the word 'healthily' is put in by Dr. Pusey, so as to change entirely the character of the doctrine delivered. Such is the way in which the plain statement of the Homily is explained away!"—*Supplement*, p. 28.

* Cranmer's Letter (See p. 77) plainly shews that he thought so too, and that he considered there was "no further need for emendation" after the changes which had been made in the revisions embodied in the 2nd Book.

† This seems plainly to imply that neither Martyr nor Bucer were dissatisfied with the *doctrine* of the First Book.

be .... *effectual* signs of grace ...." Can any one truly say of a PICTURE what Latimer, Ridley, and the Article here say of the Sacraments? Surely not.

But having thus noticed the one, what can be said of the

Saviour Jesus Christ's holy institution, in remembrance of his death and passion, may be partakers of his most blessed Body and Blood.'"

Now if Mr. Gorham is correct, though I think he is not, in supposing that Bucer referred to the words of Invocation, then the commonly received notion—that they were altered at his instance—is unfounded. Judging from Bucer's language as to P. Martyr's Eucharistic Statements, the probability is that *if either of them* induced the alteration it was P. Martyr; especially as Bucer died seven months before the completion of the Book, and P. Martyr was one of those whom the Privy Council wished Cranmer to consult touching the proposal to omit the Rubric on kneeling at receiving the Sacrament. Mr. Goode, however, (Work on the Eucharist, p. 618) takes the opposite view to Mr. Gorham; speaking of the Invocation he says :—" Now, no doubt, these words may be so explained as not to countenance the doctrine of a real presence *in the Consecrated Elements*, but they are very open to an interpretation of that kind. And accordingly we find Bucer, in his remarks on the Prayer Book, written at the request of Archbishop Cranmer for his use in the revision of the Book, taking particular exception to them, as open to an interpretation involving the Romish doctrine of Transubstantiation, and he proceeds to use words which exclude Archdeacon Denison's doctrine as much as that of the Romanists. He says,—

"'The holy Fathers understood no other change of those elements from these words, than that by which the bread and wine, remaining in every respect in the properties of their own nature, were then so changed from their vulgar and common use, and as it were translemented, as to be *symbols* [*] (symbola) of the same Body and Blood, and so of Christ himself, God and man, the bread which came down from heaven to give life to the world: so that whoever should take them according to our Lord's institution, and with true faith in Him, should be partakers of a fuller communion with the Lord, and enjoy [†] Him for the meat and drink of eternal life, by which they might more and more live in Him, and have Him living in themselves.'—*Buceri Censura in Ordinat Ecclesiast.* Op. ed. Basil, 1557, p. 471.

" Accordingly these words were altered, and *remain altered*, to the very words which we have seen Dr. Brett [‡] quoting as proof that the Church of England

[*] But not, as he says (See p. 401), "Empty signs of Christ, through which the remembrance of Christ now absent ought to be excited."

[†] The same expression as I have noticed at p. 402.

[‡] The passage which Mr. Goode cites from Dr. Brett is the following :—"I was and am very desirous to believe that the Church of England holds the doctrine so plainly taught by our Saviour. But I know not how to reconcile the Consecration prayer in the present established Liturgy to this doctrine, for that makes a plain distinction betwixt the Bread and Wine and our Saviour's Body and Blood, when, as Mr. Spinckes shows, and the words will bear no other construction than that, it was the Bread which Christ said was His Body; whereas the Consecration Prayer evidently supposes them to be two distinct things. 'Grant that we, receiving these thy creatures of Bread and Wine, may be partakers of Christ's Body and Blood.' Which manifestly implies the *Bread and Wine* to be distinct or different things from *the Body and Blood*. For if the Bread be Christ's Body, as Mr. Spinckes proves the words of Institution teach, then he that receives or partakes of the Bread must be a partaker of the Body. And except they are supposed to be two things, then the Prayer is, that we, *receiving or partaking of the Body and Blood of Christ, may be partakers of His Body and Blood*. This nonsensical interpretation must be given of this Petition, if the Prayer is understood in the sense which Mr. Spinckes declares and proves to be the necessary inevitable consequence of our Saviour's words, and which I verily believe to be so. But the ancient Church, as appears from all the Liturgies, never prayed in this manner. They never prayed, that, *receiving Bread and Wine, they might be partakers of Christ's Body and Blood*, but that they might be *worthy partakers*, that they might partake of it to their benefit, and not to their condemnation."—" *Brett's Discourse concerning the necessity of discerning the Lord's Body in the Holy Communion.* London, 1720. Preface, pp. xix.—xxi."

other "alternative" which Mr. Goode presents? He states it to be that—" This is my Body" must necessarily seem to mean " This is really and substantially my Body." The admission or rejection of this must, however, turn upon the

holds, that the consecrated Bread and Wine may be received where the Body and Blood of Christ are *not* received. and therefore do not include in themselves a real presence of the Body and Blood of Christ; namely, the words, 'Grant that we, receiving,'" &c.

With respect to Dr. Brett's difficulty it is enough to say here—that it seems to me fully met by the fact of the different language employed in the Prayer of Access and in the Consecration Prayer: the former, simply contemplating the approach of Communicants after the act of Consecration, says, " Grant us therefore, gracious Lord, *so* to eat the *Flesh* of thy dear Son Jesus Christ, and to drink his *Blood*, that our sinful bodies may be made clean," &c.: the latter necessarily contemplates the Elements in a two-fold aspect, (1) what they alone are before the recital of the words of Institution—"creatures of bread and wine"—(2) what they also become after such recital—Christ's " most blessed Body and Blood."

An examination of the "Censura" shews, I think, that Mr. Gorham was wrong and that Mr. Goode is right in supposing that Bucer's commendatory words referred to the Invocation: the following passage seems to prove that it must have been the *Prayer of Access* to which he referred:—

" Postremò sunt verba in hac præcedenti precatione, quæ incipiunt, Vue doe not presume to come to this, &c., verba de vera perceptione & manducatione bibitionemque; corporis & sanguinis Domini, quæ oro Dominum, ut det ita ut posita sunt, retineri, illa scil. in hac quidem oratione, Humblye beseechinge thee, &c. Valde namque; pura hæc verba sunt, & verbis spiritus S. consentientia. Omnino enim instituit Dominus hanc sui communionem κοινωνίαν corporis & sanguinis sui, ut eam vocat spiritus S. 1 Corint. 10. ut ea recipiamus, non panem tantum & vinum, dicenda alio qui fuisset uno corporis & sanguinis Domini, sed panis ac vini communio. Tum, nec causa fuisset, ut Dominus, cum distribuendo panem & vinum discipulis dixisset, Accipite & manducate & bibite, subjiceret, Hoc est corpus meum, Hic est sanguis meus. Recepimus ergo hîc non panem tantum & vinum, sed simul corpus & sanguinum ejus: & non quidem hæc sola, verum una totum Christum, Deum & hominem. At quia verum hominem, & simul verum Deum, ideo & carnem & sanguinem recepimus. Est emim hæc caro, quia est filiii Dei, sic & sanguis ζωοποιος, ut D. Cyrillus, contra Nestorium pulchrè explicat, & probat, & ex eo, quòd Dominus contra Capernaitas affirmauit de carne & sanguine suo, cum ipsi indignum putarent, quòd dixisset, se panem esse qui descendisset de cœlo, vitamque : daret mundo : quando quidem ipsi eum, ut filium que Josephi, ita nihil amplius existimabant, quàm alium quemque ; hominem constantem carne & sanguine."—*Scripta Anglicana*. Basileæ, p. 473.

But when Mr. Goode says " Accordingly these words [*i.e.*, the Invocation] were altered and *remain altered* to " the words " Grant that we receiving these thy creatures of bread and wine, according to thy Son our Saviour Jesus Christ's holy institution, in remembrance of his death and passion, may be partakers of his most blessed Body and Blood: who, in the same night," &c., he seems to me to represent inaccurately that they were adopted from Bucer, though his suggestion may have led to them: his proposition was to " change" the Invocation " into these or similar words," viz.—" Hear us, O merciful God our Father, and bless us, and sanctify us by Thy word and Holy Spirit, that we may receive the Body and Blood of Thy Son from His own hand in these mysteries by a true faith for the meat and drink of eternal life, which Thy Son, in the same night in which He was betrayed," &c.

sense in which he uses, or others receive, these terms; for that they have been used in opposite senses for Three Centuries these pages have, I think, abundantly shewn.   If, therefore, by *Really* is not mean—*carnally*, *sensibly*, *na*-

Now it will be seen, I think, that between Bucer's language and the language of the Prayer Book might be found the whole doctrine of the *objective* presence *in the Elements* or *in the Mysteries* irrespective of the Faith of the Receiver; even though it may have been, judging from the Letter just quoted and other statements, that Bucer intended no more than the exclusion of a *local organical* Presence.*   The Consecration Prayer as altered in 1552 makes the *participation*, and therefore the *presence*, depend upon *receiving according to the Institution:* Bucer's language apparently makes it to depend upon *the* receiver's *sanctification* and his *true faith*—conditions which need not in the least imply an *objective*, but only a *subjective* presence.   The change, then, as made by Cranmer and his co-revisers, while avoiding the doubtful terminology of Bucer, met his objection (which, whether forcible or not, was, in part, as we have seen, common enough then)—"that we are not taught by any precept of Christ our Saviour, by any word or example of His Apostles, to ask for such a benediction and sanctification of the bread and wine as that they may be to us the Body and Blood of the Lord; and we know that this prayer is still, at this day, wrested by Antichrist to the retaining and confirming of that dogma of infinite impiety and contumely against God, the **transubstantiation** of the bread and wine into the Body and Blood of Christ. For by that chiefly subsists the αρτολατρεια, bread being adored as Christ; resorted to as a present deity in all emergencies."

These considerations also answer, I think, Mr. Goode's remark that Bucer's words (which he quotes) "exclude Archdeacon Denison's doctrine as much as that of the Romanists."

* Compare remarks on P. Martyrs's Letter, Note, p. 402: also the following passage from Bucer's Letter to P. Martyr, June 20, 1549,—"One thing, however, has very much astonished me; that you seem to fear I shall be offended at your denying, That Christ is at the same moment in many places; and that it has escaped you that I, with Master Philip [Melancthon—*Ed.*], abominate from my whole heart that Ubiquity (as Philip calls it,) of Christ as man which some have laid down [as a dogma—*Ed.*]. I have never felt disposed, nor am I up to this moment disposed, to come forward in that controversy, Whether Christ is circumscribed by any Physical place in the heavens, He sits at the right hand of God; He has left the world; He is conversant with these good things which have not entered into the [heart of man here [below—*Ed.*]. I refrain, therefore, from transferring our modes of existence and Physical conditions to this subject, further than this;—that I always acknowledge and confess both the true nature of a human body and also soul to be actually in my Head and Saviour, and glory that I am flesh of His Flesh and bone of His Bones . . . And certainly if you have told anyone that I maintain that Christ is at the same time in many places, I mean locally,—I, who in these Mysteries exclude all idea of place,—I intreat you to have the kindness to explain to such an one my sentiment more correctly: which is this: that Christ exhibits Himself at the same moment and truly, by the Word and by His Sacraments, present to us, although we are existing in many places; but that we see and apprehend Him, present, by faith only, without any idea of place."—*Gorham's Reformation Gleanings*, p. 91. See, too, his Letter to Calvin, August, 1549, *Ibid.*, pp. 99—108; and the testimony of A. Lasco to Bullinger, April 10, 1551:—"D. Bucer began a Treatise on the Sacraments, a little before his death, but did not finish it. He was preparing, as I hear, answers to my [observations—*Ed.*]; but I saw nothing of them, though I could have wished to see them. However, as far as I can understand, he remained firm in his sentiment concerning the presence, and the real exhibition of the Body and Blood of Christ, in the signs, or through the signs."—*Ibid.*, p. 248.

The following short extract of a Letter from *P. Martyr* to *Calvin*, Strasburgh, March 8, 1555, is worth inserting here:—"He [*i. e.*, Marback] got so far as not to include the Body of Christ in the bread, but he insists that an actual and most real presence must be asserted, so far as the communicants are concerned, of the Body and Blood of Christ, and such a presence that even the wicked and they that eat unworthily do partake it; which clearly shows that he does not attribute the reception to faith, unless we speak of a living and salutary reception; as though there were a certain other true and (as they say) real eating of Christ's Body: which even the wicked may share."—*Ibid.*, p. 341.

turally; and if by *Substantially* is not meant—*materially, corporeally, organically:* then, but not otherwise, there need be no hesitation in accepting this interpretation, and supporting it by Bishop Ridley's authority (See p. 18), " These words, ' This is My Body,' are meant thus : by grace it is My *true* Body, but not My *fleshly* Body, as some of you suppose : " or, again, by Abp. Cranmer's words " Marry, *to be present in bread* might be some sentence, but this speech you [Gardiner] will in no wise admit," (See p. 181.) It seems to me, then, that we may accept both the one and the other "alternative" of Mr. Goode, if only we receive them in the sense wherein I have tried to shew they can be rightly understood. Indeed, in one place Mr. Goode seems unwilling to commit himself to a doctrine of mere "representation" or "picture;" for he says (*Work*, p. 215, the Italics are mine.) " We maintain a real spiritual presence of Christ's body and blood to the faithful communicant as much as they [Archdeacons Denison and Wilberforce and Dr. Pusey] do. But as the body and blood of Christ are food for the soul only, so their presence is vouchsafed, *primarily at least*, only to the soul, and for this there is no need of local proximity." I cannot but ask—how do we know that "there is no" such "need"? and I must add—that what has just been said in reference to the sense of Mr. Goode's *alternative* is, I think, also an answer to the following (somewhat harshly-worded) passage in his Supplement (p. 46):—

" . . . . men who have not given themselves over to a spirit of delusion on such matters, will, I suspect, agree with me, that if there is a real substantial presence of the body of Christ in the bread, there is a bodily presence, and that the presence of Christ's human body involves the presence of a material substance ; and that we are not to be deterred from saying so, because these authors [Archdeacon Denison and Dr. Pusey] finding inconvenient articles and rubrics in their way, deny in one *form* of words, what they assert in another."

In connexion, too, with those same remarks above made upon the Nature of the Presence, it may be useful to notice this observation in Mr. Goode's Supplement (p. 41); where, referring to his Work, he says :—

" I have stated that all those expressions in the Prayer-Book of 1549, which might seem to indicate that the presence of the Body and Blood of Christ was to be looked for in the consecrated elements, are carefully expunged or altered in the subsequent Prayer-Books to the present time,......"

The "expressions" themselves, as altered in the Book of 1552, are thus given by Mr. Goode in pp. 617 to 619 of his Work; they will be most conveniently compared when placed in parallel columns; the Italics are his :—

1549.	1552.
1. "... he hath left in those holy mysteries, as a pledge of his love, and a continual remembrance of the same, his own blessed Body and precious Blood, for us to feed upon spiritually, to our endless comfort and consolation."	1. " he hath instituted and ordained holy mysteries, as pledges of his love and [and for a, *in Ed.* of 1662] continual remembrance of his death to our great and endless comfort; "
2. "With thy Holy Spirit and word vouchsafe to bless and sanctify these thy gifts and creatures of bread and wine, *that they may be unto us the Body and Blood of thy most dearly beloved Son Jesus Christ.*"	2. " Grant that we, receiving these thy creatures of bread and wine, according to thy Son our Saviour Jesus Christ's holy institution, in remembrance of his death and passion, may be partakers of his most blessed Body and Blood."
3. "... beseeching thee that whosoever shall be partakers of this Holy Communion, may *worthily receive* the most precious Body and Blood of thy Son Jesus Christ."	3. "... beseeching thee, that all we who are partakers of this Holy Communion, may be fulfilled with thy grace and heavenly benediction."
4. "... so to eat the flesh of thy dear Son Jesus Christ, and to drink his blood, *in these holy mysteries.*"	4. "... so to eat the flesh of thy dear Son Jesus Christ and to drink his Blood."
5. "... hast vouchsafed to feed us in these holy mysteries with the spiritual food of the most precious Body and Blood of thy Son our Saviour Jesus Christ, and hast assured us (duly receiving the same) of thy favour and goodness towards us."	5. "... dost vouchsafe to feed *us which have duly received these holy mysteries* with the spiritual food of the most precious Body and Blood of thy Son our Saviour Jesus Christ, and dost assure us thereby of thy favour and goodness towards us."

The following portion of a Rubric of 1549 was *omitted* in 1552 :—

6. "And men must not think less to be received in part, than in the whole, but in each of them the whole body of our Saviour Jesu Christ."

Now to say—that the changes made in the first *Five* passages do not appear to me to exclude the doctrine which Mr. Goode says they "might seem to indicate" would be merely to set my own * opinion (uselessly to say the least) in opposition to his. It is much preferable therefore to refer to the citations already tendered at pp. 33-35 in proof that, at the time of the publication of the 2nd Book of Edw. VIth, these changes were not designed or regarded in the sense which Mr. Goode attaches to them. And this is, I think, materially supported by the evidence that, whatever Doctrine was taught by it, the omitted portion of the Rubric of 1549 (No. 6) was distinctly maintained by Abp. Cranmer when he prepared the revised Book of 1552. For in his Answer to Bp. Gardiner, published at that particular time, he quotes this very Rubric (See p. 22) remarking that "although it say, that in each part of the bread broken is received the whole body of Christ,

* But it may be useful to quote the following opinion of Mr. Fisher—"*Reformatio in Anglia ob rem Sacramentariam obtineri nequit :*—We have quoted these memorable words, in order to shew, what was the opinion of a foreign divine [Peter Martyr], highly distinguished for learning as well as piety . . . . respecting the progress which the Protestant movement had already made in England at the time when Edward the Sixth's *second* Prayer Book was enacted . . . . . The '*res Sacramentaria*' of the Anglican Establishment is not to be considered now, as it was in the sixteenth century, a mere impediment to the *progressive* advance of Protestant Principles. On the contrary, it is confessedly the very life and soul of a vigorous *retrogressive* movement within the Church . . . ."—*Liturgical Purity.*, p. 151.

In his 2nd Ed., 1860, the passage stands thus :—" He [P. Martyr] says emphatically—'*Reformatio in Angliâ ob rem sacramentariam obtineri nequit.*' (Hess. Cat. p. 60.) True, he admits in another letter—'*quod Liber seu ratio rituum ecclesiasticorum atque administrationis sacramentorum est emendatus, nam inde omnia sublata sunt quæ superstitionem fovere poterant.*' (Letter, ed. by Goode, p. 15.) But then it appears from the context, that he is here alluding to certain errors of the *Communion* Office which the Primate himself had but recently repudiated, and which had been, on that account, very carefully removed from the Prayer Book upon its second revision in 1552."—*Lit. Pur.* p. 137. I have already ventured to express (Note, p. 381) my entire dissent from Mr. Fisher's (apparently altered) view as to Cranmer having "but recently repudiated" the "certain errors of the Communion Office" to which he

yet it saith not so of the parts unbroken, nor yet of the parts or whole reserved, as the Papists teach......we be as truly fed, refreshed, and comforted by Christ, receiving a piece of bread at the Lord's holy table, as if we did eat an whole loaf. For .... whole Christ and the Holy Spirit, sacramentally, ..be..in every part of the bread broken, but not *corporally* and *naturally*, as the Papists teach."

The noticeable thing in these words is the marked connexion which the Abp. makes between the *breaking* of the bread and the presence of "whole Christ....in every" such "part of" it: and this, to say the least, involves an *objective* presence in what "is received," not merely a *subjective* presence in the receiver: but as the fraction of the bread is a formal part of the act of Consecration, it seems to me to follow from Cranmer's own reasoning—that the Presence exists in the *Sacramentum* before the Communion of the Priest; therefore irrespective of the Communion of the People: and this, I must think, admits the whole Doctrine of a Real Objective Presence, due to Consecration, in with or under the Elements. In the words of Bp. Cosin:—

" So, then, (to sum up this controversy by applying to it all that hath been said,) it is not questioned whether the Body of Christ be

alludes: and it seems to me that "the context", which Mr. Fisher refers to, sustains my objection; for P. Martyr (after saying, as above quoted, "that the Book or Order of Ecclesiastical Rites and the Administration of the Sacraments is reformed, for all things are removed from it which could nourish superstition ") adds—" But the chief reason why other things which were purposed were not effected, was that the subject of the Sacraments stood in the way; not truly as far as regards **transubstantiation** or the **real presence** (so to speak), either in the bread or in the wine, since, thanks be to God, concerning these things there seems to be now no controversy as it regards those who profess the Gospel; but whether grace is conferred by virtue of the Sacraments, is a point about which many are in doubt."—*Gorham's Ref. Gleanings*, p. 281. It can scarcely be doubted (especially recollecting the terminology of that period already so fully examined in these pages) that P. Martyr means here by **real, a carnal** presence, whether or not in this place he only employs the word as the *equivalent* of Transubstantiation. And, as I have already proved, I think, (in the passages referred to, Note, p. 381) that Cranmer had distinctly abandoned this doctrine of a **carnal presence** *before* the publication of the 1st Book in 1549; so, therefore, the change of language in the Communion Office of 1552 could not have been "on that account," as Mr. Fisher says: the alteration only goes to prove the *identity* of *doctrine* in the two Books on this point; though verbal changes were admitted to content, apparently, those who feared that certain expressions in the 1st Book might still be quoted as favouring (what I may call) *popular Roman* belief.

absent from the Sacrament duly administered according to His institution, which we protestants neither affirm nor believe; for, it being given and received in the communion, it must needs be that it is present, though in some manner veiled under the sacrament, so that of itself it cannot be seen. Neither is it doubted or disputed whether the bread and wine, by the power of God and a supernatural virtue, be set apart and fitted for a much nobler use, and raised to a higher dignity, than their nature bears; for we confess the necessity of a supernatural and heavenly change, and that the signs cannot become sacraments but by the infinite power of God, whose proper right it is to institute sacraments in His Church, being able alone to endue them with virtue and efficacy. Finally, we do not say that our blessed Saviour gave only the figure and sign of His Body, neither do we deny a sacramental union of the Body and Blood of Christ with the sacred bread and wine, so that both are **really** and **substantially** received together; but (that we may avoid all ambiguity) we deny that, after the words and prayer of consecration, the bread should remain bread no longer, but should be changed into the substance of the Body of Christ, nothing of the bread but only the accidents continuing to be what they were before. And so the whole question is concerning the transubstantiation of the outward elements, whether the substance of the bread be turned into the substance of Christ's Body, and the substance of the wine into the substance of His Blood; or, as the Romish doctors describe their transubstantiation, whether the substance of bread and wine doth utterly perish, and the substance of Christ's Body and Blood succeed in their place, which are both denied by protestants."—*Hist. of Transubstantiation.* Ch. iv. § 6. Oxford Trans. p. 175.

There remains to be further noticed one other point which was mentioned in the Letter at p. 70, *viz.* the statement of the Bishops in 1661—that there was not "any great need of restoring" the Declaration on Kneeling, "the world being now in more danger of profanation than of idolatry;" and the opinion which, evidently, they were also careful to express at the same time—that "the sense of it is declared sufficiently in the 28th Article of the Church of England." It will be well to consider *how* that "sense," then, "is declared" there. An analysis of the Declaration shews that it mainly contains *Four Propositions* which correspond with the *Four Clauses* of the Article; this will be best seen by placing them in parallel columns thus:—

412

DECLARATION.

1. " . . . it is ordained in this office . . . that the communicants should receive . . . . kneeling; (which order is well meant, for a signification of our humble and grateful acknowledgement of the benefits of Christ therein given to all worthy Receivers . . .)"

2. " It is hereby declared, That thereby no adoration is intended, or ought to be done, unto the Sacramental Bread or Wine there bodily received."

3. "For the Sacramental Bread and Wine remain still in their very natural substances, and therefore may not be adored; (for that were Idolatry, to be abhorred of all faithful Christians;)"

4. "[...no adoration is intended, or ought to be done,] . . . unto any Corporal Presence of Christ's natural Flesh and Blood. For . . . the natural Body and Blood of our Saviour Christ are in Heaven and not here;"

ARTICLE XXVIII.

Clause 1. " . . . to such as rightly, worthily, and with faith, receive the same [*signum* or *sacramentum*], the Bread which we break is a partaking [*communicatio*] of the Body of Christ; and likewise the Cup of Blessing is a partaking [*communicatio*] of the Blood of Christ."

Clause 4. " The Sacrament [*Sacramentum*] of the Lord's Supper was not by Christ's ordinance . . . . worshipped."

Clause 2. " Transubstantiation (or the change of the substance of Bread and Wine) in the Supper of the Lord, cannot be proved by Holy Writ; but it is repugnant to the plain words of Scripture, overthroweth the nature of a Sacrament, and hath given occasion to many superstitions."

Clause 3. " The Body of Christ is given, taken, and eaten, in the Supper, only after an heavenly and spiritual manner. And the mean whereby the Body of Christ is received and eaten in the Supper is Faith."

Now of these Four Clauses the 2nd and 4th give " the sense " in which the Bishops thought the Declaration no longer needed as a Protest and Safeguard touching Practice : for they " declared " against " the change of the substance of Bread and Wine " and therefore " sufficiently " against that " adoration " of the *Sacramentum* which the Declaration said " were Idolatry to be abhorred of all faithful Christians." The 1st and 3rd Clauses describe the " sign," the " manner," and the " mean " of the *communication* of the Body and Blood of Christ; all three necessarily excluding " any Corporal Presence of Christ's natural Flesh and Blood," as the Declaration said, " unto " which " adoration is intended or ought to be done ; " not because, like " the Sacramental Bread and Wine," It is not adorable, but because It is not there to be adored.

But this question now arises—Whether these *exclusive* terms of the Article are not necessarily *inclusive*, or do not *admit*, of a " sense" which does not contradict them : whether in fact they do not *imply* and *assume* an Objective Presence quite as *Substantial* and *Real*, though *Spiritual* and *Invisible?*

The Article, using the language of St. Paul (1 Cor. x. 16,) distinctly connects Κοινωνία = the *imparting* of the *Res Sacramenti* (" the inward part or thing signified ") with the Bread *broken* and the Cup *blessed*—it declares that each " *is* a partaking" or " a communion " (as in the English Article of 1552) of What it signifies : that they have become, by that Consecrating action, the Vehicle *carrying* the Gift of the Body and Blood of Christ ; and not merely, in Legal language, the Deed *conveying* It—a term utterly inadequate to express and wholly foreign from the idea of receiving " the Supper of the Lord " of which the Article treats. It follows, therefore, that (to say the very least) the Gift *is present* with the Sign at the time that Sign is given * to "such

---

* Compare the following passage of a Letter from *Calvin* to *Bullinger*, dated Geneva, June 26, 1548." . . . we say that that which is figured by them [Sacraments] is *exhibited* to the Elect ; lest God should be believed to mock our eyes with a fallacious sight . . . . When, in the Supper, the signs of the flesh and blood of Christ are held out [porrigi—*Ed.*] to us, we say, that they are not held out in vain so that the Thing itself also is not actually before us [Res nobis ipsa constet.—*Ed.*] Whence it follows that we eat the flesh and drink the blood of Christ."

But it might be thought one-sided not to add what follows : he goes on to say —" Thus expressing ourselves, we neither make the thing out of the Sign ; nor do we confound each of them in one ; nor again do we imagine that it is * infinite [? without limits—*Editor*] ; nor do we dream of a **carnal** transfusion of Christ into us ; nor do we lay down any other such fancy.

" You say, that Christ is in Heaven as regards His human nature : we acknowledge the same.—The word, heaven, conveys to your ears the impression of distance of place : we, also, willingly embrace that [opinion—*Ed.*] ; that Christ is at a distance from us by the interval of places.—You deny that the body of Christ is without limits ; but [affirm—*Ed.*] that it is contained within

---

* Editor's Note.—"Infinitum esse fingimus " the sentence seems a little obscure, but probably alludes to the *Ubiquitarian* doctrine of Brentius, the *unlimited* diffusion of the Body of Christ."

as " under the conditions named " receive the same ; " and being so present *to* these, how can It be otherwise than present *before* all others who are where they are? What is this but an Objective Presence whether men have Faith to discern it or not? If, then, such a Presence be recognized in, what I may call, the *donative* act of " The Administration; " need there be or is there any real difficulty in recognizing a like Presence in, with, or under " the Communion " before " the Minister first receive " It " himself " or " proceed to deliver the same to " others ? It cannot be said there *is* not, for the very fact of the controversy proves the contrary ; but it is hard to see why the difficulty should exist.

If what has been now said does not inaccurately represent the meaning of the 28th Article (as I hope and believe it does not) then, on the dictum of the Bishops at the Savoy Conference, this is " the sense " of the Declaration on Kneeling ; and therefore that Declaration does not *forbid* but *allows* the belief of a Real Objective Presence of the Body and Blood of Christ in the Eucharist, and consequently the Adoration of Christ as so Present. I do not say it *defines* whether that Presence is " in the Supper," as some express it ; or, as Abp. Cranmer (its Author) appears to have held, " in the forms of bread and wine [*in* but not] out of the ministration " (See p.

its own circumference : we assent; aye, and we, undisguisedly and openly, declare this.—You deny that the Sign is to be mingled with the Thing : we diligently inculcate that the one is to be distinguished from the other.—You sharply condemn [the notion of—*Ed.*] impanation : we subscribe [to your decision—*Ed.*].—To what, then, does our opinion amount ? [To this.—*Ed.*] Since here upon earth we see Bread and Wine, [we hold.—*Ed.*] that our minds are to be lifted up into heaven, that we may enjoy Christ; and that *then* Christ is present to us, when we seek Him above the elements of this world. For it is not permitted us to suspect that Christ is deceiving us; which would be the case, unless we hold that truth is exhibited to us together with the Sign : and even you yourselves allow that the Sign is by no means an empty one. It remains only for us to define what it contains. To this we briefly answer :— We are made partakers of the flesh and blood of Christ, so that He dwells in us and we in Him, and in this way enjoy all His good things. I ask, what is there either absurd or obscure in these expressions ? especially since we exclude, in express words, whatever wild imaginations might enter the mind. And yet we are severely criticised, as though we had departed from the simple and pure doctrine of the Gospel. But I should like to know, What is that simplicity to which we are challenged to return ? . . . ."—*Gorham's Reformation Gleanings*. London. 1857. p. 49.

125) : nor do I assert that it *compels* a belief in either of these modes. But I do humbly and respectfully maintain, and I venture to think that the foregoing pages have proved— That, as the language of the Declaration does not *exclude* the belief which I have endeavoured to shew is also consonant with the 28th Article, so every member of the Church of England is entirely free to hold it and every Minister free to teach it, "provided" only (as I said at the outset of this Letter, p. 4) they do not thereby intentionally " involve that Doctrine which, I allege, was *disavowed* in the Declaration."

If it be feared, as Mr. Goode and others seem to fear, that such a belief tends to make us so localize the Presence of Christ on earth as to hinder us from raising our thoughts to Him in Heaven : if, as he tells us, (Work, p. 451) " the Fathers constantly" are " admonishing us that ' he who approaches to this body must have his mind aloft ; ' that ' we have our victim above, our priest above, our sacrifice above,'* and that Christ is ' absent ' in heaven, and only to be laid hold of by faith :"—it seems to me enough to say, That the permissive belief for which I am contending no more involves the dreaded consequence than does any belief of the Substantial Presence of the Sun in this earth of ours hinder us from that lifting of our thoughts to the Glorious Luminary as he shines above, which I suppose is an instinctive feeling of every man who sees his Light or feels his Heat. It may assist also in calming such fears, to recollect that Bp. Latimer once said (See p. 41) " We do worship Christ in the Heavens, and we do worship Him in the Sacrament."

This (I fear too-lengthened) Postscript being now completed, it is necessary to sum up the result of both it and the Letter ; and this will, I think, be most conveniently done in the following Nine Propositions :—

* A lay friend noticing, after they were printed off, the following words of Robert Samuel (See p. 188) "there now making intercession, offering and giving his holy body for me, for my body, for my ransom, for my full price and satisfaction," says "might not this be italicized as expressing an important doctrine—the *juge sacrificium ?*"

1. That a (1) Carnal (*or* Capernaical) belief on the Real Presence, which it was (2) considered necessary to disperse, prevailed extensively among (3) Clergy and (4) Laity in the middle of the 16th Century.

Bp. Shaxton's Recantation Articles 1546, p. 5. (1)—Stat. Edw. vi., c. i., p. 6. (1. 2. 3. 4.)—Conversation between Cranmer and Bonner, Sep. 10, 1549, p. 6 : Argument pp. 7, 9 : The Lord Paget's opinion of Bp. Gardiner's Doctrine, p. 28. (1)—Articles ministered by Bp. Hooper to Will. Phelps, 1551, p. 30. (1. 2. 3.)—Conference in the Tower between Bp. Ridley and Sec. Bourn, 1553, p. 39 : Disputation at Oxford, Ap. 18, 1554, p. 39 : Exam. of J. Rogers, 1554-5, p. 42. (1)—Cranmer's Ans. to Gardiner, p. 181. (1. 2. 3.) —Argument from Jewel v. Harding, p. 250. (1. 2. 3.)—Jewel's "Defence of the Apology." Note 264. (1. 3.)

2. That, as this belief (1) mainly though (2) not entirely resulted from the popular Doctrine of Transubstantiation so, (3) a continuous effort was made to suppress that Doctrine.

Bp. Shaxton's Recantation Articles, No. 1, p. 5 (1)—P. Martyr's Disput. at Oxford, June 11, 1549, pp. 10 to 13. (1. 3.)—1st Disputation at Cambridge, June 20, 1549 : 2nd Disputation, June 24, 1549 : 3rd Disputation : Bp. Ridley's Determination of them p. 18. (1. 3.)—Cranmer's Ans. to Gardiner, p. 25. (1. 3)—Bp. Hooper's Visitation Articles 1551-2, p. 30. (1. 3.)—Assertion of the Sacrament by J. Winter, Nov. 8. 1551. p. 31. (1. 3.)—Article xxix. 1552, and Argument, p. 32. (1.3.)—Argument, p. 38 : Archdn. Philpot, Disp. at Lond. Oct. 18, 1553, p. 38 : Examn. of J. Bradford, Jan. 29, 1554-5, p. 41 : Conference between Ridley and Latimer, 1555, p. 42 : Ridley's "Brief declaration of the Lord's Supper," 1555, p. 43 : Cranmer's Disput. at Oxford, Ap. 16. 1555 : Ridley's Disput. at Oxford, 1555, p. 52. (1)—Cranmer's Letter to Calvin on Council of Trent, March 20, 1552, p. 90 : Arguments thereon, pp. 91 to 92. (1. 3.)—Knox's Objections to Kneeling, pp. 104-8. (1. 2. 3.)—Art. xxix. of 1553, and Mr. Hardwick's remarks thereon, pp. 110 and 111 (1. 3.).—Cranmer's account of opinion of Luther &c. Note p. 168. (1).—Opinion held by Cranmer and others between 1545 and 1548, pp. 275 to 278. (1. 2. 3.)—Bucer's Letter to Niger, Ap. 15, 1550. Note p. 403. (1.)

3. That, in doing this, there was no intention to deny or discourage a belief in the Real Objective Presence of the Body and Blood of Christ, in the Ministration of the Sacrament *or* under the Form of Bread and Wine, if such Presence was not held to be *Natural* or *Organical.*

Foxe's opinion of P. Martyr's Disputation at Oxford, June 11. 1549, p. 9.—Argument, p. 10.—Cranmer's opinion of Bertram's Doctrine, p. 20—Cranmer's Answer to Gardiner, pp. 20 to 26.—Dr. Redman's communication to R. Wilkes and Master Nowel, Nov. 1551, pp. 28, 29.—Young's Letter to Cheke concerning Dr. Redman, p. 29.—Articles against Bp. Ferrar, 1553-4, p. 37.—Comparison of terms, p. 62.—Argument between Cranmer and Gardiner on the presence of the Sun, pp. 73 to 75.—Cranmer's Letter to P. Council, Oct. 7. 1552. pp. 77 to 79.—Argument thereon, pp. 79 to 84.—Foxe's Estimate of Cranmer's opinion, p. 84.—Cranmer's language as to Consecration, pp. 85 to 89.—Cranmer's Belief compared with Calvin's, Note pp. 86 to 87.—Argument from Bp. Hooper's Articles of 1551-2, p. 119.—Cranmer's language as to Presence in the Ministration, p. 125.—Cranmer's Catechism, 1548, p. 154.—Argument therefrom, pp. 155-9, and from Hom. of 1547, pp. 160 to 168.—Gardiner's opinion of P. Book of 1549, p. 173. —Cranmer's definition of Corporal p. 177; his language to Gardiner, pp. 180 to 186.—Ridley's Exam. at Oxford, Sep. 30, 1555, p. 186. —Ans. of two "husbandmen" to Bp. Bonner, May 22. 1555, p. 187.—Letter of Rob. Samuel Aug. 31, 1555, p. 188.—Jewel's controversy with Harding, pp. 267 to 269.—Reformed Primers 1545 to 1559.—Bucer's Letter to P. Martyr, June 20, 1549, Note pp. 398 to 402.—Bucer's Letter to Niger, Ap. 15. 1550. Note p. 401.—P. Martyr's "Confession of the Lord's Supper," &c., May 1556. Note p. 402.

4. That the (1) Doctrine of the Real Objective Presence was Authoritatively taught in 1549; and that (2) the same Doctrine was also Authoritatively taught during the rest of the Reign of King Edward VIth.

Letter of Duke of Somerset to Cardinal Pole, June 4, 1549, p. 7.
(1)—Argument from Bp. Gardiner, p. 9. (1) – Bp. Gardiner's " Long
Matter Justificatory," 1550-1, p. 26. (1)—Articles exhibited by
Bp. Gardiner, Jan. 21, 1550-1, p. 27 (1. 2.)—Testimony of John
White, Feb. 20, 1550-1, p. 27 (1)—Argument, p. 32 : Act of Uni-
formity, 1552 : Statement of Bp. Latimer, 1554 : Argument and
Note p. 35. (2.)—Argument pp. 121 to 122 : examination of Mr.
Goode's comparison of the P. Books of 1549 and 1552, pp. 409 to
410. (1. 2.)

5. That, when (1) in 1552 objections were made
to that Rubric of the new Prayer Book
which enjoined Kneeling at reception of
the Sacrament, (2) the Declaration explaining it was framed in conformity with the
considerations advanced in these four Propositions; and that, consequently, (3) the
words "real and essential" were not meant
to be a denial of that Real Presence mentioned in Proposition 3.

Argument pp. 36, 73 (1.2.3.)—Letter of Utenhovius to Bullinger,
Oct. 12, 1552, p. 93 : Note in Co. Book, Oct. 20, 1552, p. 96 :
Exam. of Knox by P. Council, 1553 p. 97 (1)—character of the
Ld. Chancellor, Bp. Goodrick p. 98 : Weston's language as to
(prob.) Knox, in 1554 :—Foxe's remark on Weston's words, p. 102
(1. 2.)—apparent ground of Knox's objection pp. 104 to 108. (1)—
Argument pp. 113 to 118 (1.2.)—Argument from Cranmer's Letter
p. 119 (3.)

6. That the (1) omission of the Declaration from
the Prayer Book of 1559 (though it seems
to have been still in (2) some way Authoritatively used) together with (3) other Proceedings, (4) especially the Revision of the
Articles, in the Reign of Queen Elizabeth,
is evidence of (5) a purpose then to avoid
any appearance of denying that doctrine.

Bp. Burnet's account of the omission, p. 63 : Collier's account, p. 64 (1. 5.)—Kneeling not left indifferent, as proposed by Guest, p. 64 : refusal to Puritans to prostrate themselves, pp. 65 and 393 : direction for Wafer Bread p. 65 : Grindal's Dialogue, p. 66 : Ælfric's Anglo-Saxon Homily, p. 68, (3. 5.)— Omission of Sec. 3, in Art. xxix. of 1552 (4. 5.)—Bp. Burnet's account of revision of Art. 28 : Mr. Harold Browne's opinion of it, pp. 189 to 191 (4. 5.)—Letter from Grindal &c. Feb. 6, 1566-7 : Mr. Fisher's opinion of P. Book 1559 (2. 3. 5.)—Bp. Guest's Letter to Cecil, Dec. 22, 1566 p. 192 ; 2nd Letter, May 1571, pp. 195 to 204 : Argument thereon, pp. 205 to 235 (3. 4. 5.)—Bp. Jewel's controversy with Harding ; and Arguments thereon, pp. 235 to 250 (3. 5.)—Argument from New Ed. of Homilies and from Reformed Primer, pp. 264 to 283 (3. 5.)

7. That this recognition of the Doctrine of the Real Presence was not withdrawn, but was supported by such Eucharistic (1) Documents and (2) Statements as were put forth by Ecclesiastical Authority, from the death of Elizabeth until the Restoration.

Bp. Overall's additions to the Catechism ; Mr. Fisher's opinion of them, p. 283 to 284 : Irish Articles, 1615, p. 285 (1).—Ans. of Bps at Savoy Conference, 1661, pp. 70, 307 (2).—Can. vii., 1640, p. 386 (1.)

8. That (1) the Revision of the Order of the Holy Communion in 1662, (2) the known Opinions of the Leading Reviewers, and (3) the circumstances connected with the re-insertion of the Declaration then—(4) all concur to prove a continued acceptance of that Doctrine.

Non-conformist objection to Kneeling and demand for re-insertion of Declaration, p. 70 : refusal and ultimate consent of the Bishops, p. 70 : change of words " real and essential " at Bp. Gunning's instigation, p. 70 : probable opinion of Gawden, p. 72, (3. 4.)—Argument on Rubrics in Communion Office of 1662, p. 122 to 152, (1. 4.) —Bp. Cosin, effect of Consecration, p. 137-9, 150. (2. 4.)—Bp. Gauden's " Tears, Sighs," &c. pp. 303-5 : his " Counsell . . . to xliv. Presbyters," &c. p. 305. (2. 4.)—Bp's. defence of Kneeling, at Savoy Conf., p. 307 (1.4.)—Argument, pp. 307 to 9 (1.2.3.4.) —Bp. Gauden's "Whole duty of a Communicant," &c.; and Argument therefrom, pp. 310 to 322. (2.4.)—Bp. Morley's Argument against Transubstantiation; and his references to Bp. Morton, pp. 323 to 329 (2.4.)—Heylin's account of changes in Com. Service, p. 330 (2.4.)—Bp. Cosin's Hist. of Transub. c. 3; and Argument therefrom, pp. 331 to 337 (2)—Mr. Fisher's opinion of the design in alteration of "real and essential," Note, p. 337. (3.)—Bp. Cosin's Hist of Transub. c. 4, p. 410 (2.4.)—Comparison of Declaration and Árt. xxviii, suggested by the Bps. at the Savoy Conference, and Argument thereon, pp. 411 to 415 (3.4.)

9. That therefore, as the previous Propositions combine to shew, (1) both forms of the Declaration had the same meaning; and that meaning is entirely consistent with the (2) Belief in, and the (3) Practice of Adoration to, Christ *Really* though *Spiritually* present in the Eucharist under the Form of Bread and Wine.

Argument, pp. 3 and 4 (1. 2. 3)—Argument, pp. 338 to 355 (2) —Opinion of Mr. Harold Browne, Note p. 355 (2)—Argument from Mr. Goode's citations from Abraham Woodhead, pp. 361 to 379 (2. 3)—Examination of Mr. Goode's comment on Dr. Pusey's reference to Rubric on remains of Sacrament, pp. 380 to 383 : Argument, pp. 383 to 384 (2)—Speech of Abp. Laud, June 14, 1637, pp. 388 to 390 (2. 3)—Laud's controversy with Fisher, pp. 390 to 393 (2)—Argument from Puritan proposal for Prostration at the Sacrament p. 395 (2. 3)—Argument from the nature of Sacramental Union pp. 396 to 407 (2).

These Nine Propositions may themselves be advantageously summed up in the following Statement :—

That the leading English Reformers (even in in their latest days) together with those Successors down to the early part of the 17th Century who, like themselves, were mainly responsible for the Authorized Books which

declared the belief of the Church of England—
intended no denial of the Real Presence and of
Eucharistic Adoration—and, That the Caroline
Revisers were careful to alter or eliminate
those expressions which, however erroneously,
had been, or might be likely to be, held to
involve such a denial.

———

In a Note at p. 248 I drew attention to some of Mr.
Freeman's language on the nature of the Presence, and compared it with Bp. Jewel's notice of an apparently similar
theory broached (for the first time as he thought) by Harding; expressing also a hope that in the then expected
Volume some explanation would be given of the opinion
propounded by Mr. Freeman. That Volume has now
appeared, and in it Mr. F. re-affirms his former statements;
for in a Note, at p. 479, he says :—

" It has been abundantly demonstrated in the Introduction to
this volume, that in the view of antiquity, and of the English Church,
the consecrated Elements are, in a profoundly mysterious but most true
sense, the Body and Blood of Christ ; but nevertheless, as not being
identified with Christ Himself, nor containing Him personally, are
not objects of Divine worship. The latter part of this position has
been of late years, with some variety as to expression, but on the
whole to the same effect, disallowed by some among us. It may be
necessary, therefore, to say a few words in vindication of it."

Now my object in these pages has been to shew what is
" the view . . . of the *English Church* " in reference to the
Eucharistic Presence and its legitimate consequences, as
defined in the Declaration on Kneeling: I have *assumed*
throughout, as there is every ground for doing, that that
view was designed to be and is " the view of antiquity."
Yet, so far as any evidence is furnished by the Authorities
here cited, the testimony seems to me to prove the *novelty*

and not the *antiquity* of Mr. Freeman's theory which *severs* the *Presence* of CHRIST from the *Presence* of the BODY and BLOOD of Christ *"with"* " the consecrated Elements;" for I presume this to be the sense in which he uses the word "identified," and also to be the ground on which he alleges their *not* "containing Him personally." This *separation* he assigns as the reason for their being "not objects of Divine worship." But, assuming for argument's sake the truth of the proposition which Mr. Freeman denies, would " *the consecrated Elements*" be objects of *such* worship even then ? It seems to me that what has been already said at p. 395 furnishes an authoritative reply in the negative : while a consideration of Abp. Cranmer's great fears (mentioned at pp. 90 and 113)—that the Tridentine decree would result in Divine worship (*latria*) of the Elements, instead of that inferior honour (*dulia*) which Bp. Ridley said was to be accorded—shews that on no theory short of Transubstantiation could the claim of this worship be made and allowed; though it must not be forgotten that as defenders of even that doctrine repudiate any Divine Worship being given to the Accidents, we have no right to fasten it upon them as though it were an inevitable consequence of their belief.

But Mr. Freeman asserts that "the latter part of this position" of his "has been of late years, . . . disallowed by some among us ;" this, then, seems to me, *in effect*, accusing them of holding that very *Roman* doctrine which (unless I mistake the persons to whom he alludes) they are careful to deny. In support, however, of his allegation he offers " a simple statement of the fearful language—it is impossible " he says, " to characterize it otherwise—which the upholders of " the Doctrine he speaks of "have, by the necessity of their position, been driven to use. One of the most learned of them," he states, " yet no intentional fautor of Roman views, has declared that he considers that the same worship is due to the Elements as to the Blessed Trinity." Mr. Freeman should, however, have remembered the inconvenience of thus making a charge without clearly indicating the *person* and the *passage* to which he refers. As it is, one can only vaguely guess to whom and to what he alludes. Possibly, then, he may refer to Dr. Pusey: though, so far from his writings on the Eucharist containing any statement which warrants the above representation, no words could well contradict it more plainly than those he has again and again employed in his latest publication—" The Real Presence" &c., 1857 ; to shew this, it is amply sufficient to quote the two following running titles ; p. 316, " *To adore Christ present, is not to adore the Sacrament;*" and, p. 336, " *We adore, not the Sacrament, but our Redeemer.*" Strangely enough Mr. Goode (Supp. p. 33) makes a very similar indirect charge in the sentence already quoted at p. 395; and says of a passage which he cites from Dr. Pusey (p. 329, "People have profanely spoken of 'wafer-gods.' They might as well have spoken of ' fire-gods,' of the manifestation of God in the flaming fire in the bush " &c.)— " According to this doctrine, then, as the Second Person of the adorable Trinity was connected with the human nature in the person of Jesus Christ, so is Christ with the wafer in the Sacrament." Yet an obvious exception to the accuracy of this assertion is, That it ignores the words of the Second Article of the Church of England—"the Godhead and Manhood, were joined together in one Person, *never to be divided*"—and keeps out of sight the fact, That no one alleges a *permanent* Union of the *Sacramentum* and the *Res Sacramenti ;* and that even Roman Theologians admit the cessation of the Presence when the Accidents become corrupt.

If, however, the Author of " Eucharistical Adoration " be pointed at in Mr. Freeman's remark which I am here noticing; it is enough to reply—that Mr. Keble says (p. 58— 2nd Ed. 1859) "no plain and devout reader of Holy Scripture and disciple of the Church would, of his own accord, find a difficulty in adoring the thing signified, apart from the outward sign or form ;" again, the running title of p. 151 is

"*Adoration claimed for the Inward Part only;*" and further in noticing (p. 152) a comment made upon Art. xxviii., he says " Is not this expressly maintaining that the worship of the outward part is the only worship forbidden (if it be forbidden) in that Article?" : where the parenthetical expression "if it be forbidden" plainly means—that that point is probably beside the purpose of the Article.

But perhaps the reference is to Mr. Cheyne who, in his "Reasons of Appeal" 1858, gives an Appendix on the "Declaration concerning Kneeling" where he says (p. 64) "We are enjoined to receive the Blessed Sacrament of our Lord's Body and Blood, in that very manner, and with that very act, which denotes the highest degree of worship—the worship which we pay to the Blessed Trinity, Father, Son, and Holy Ghost." But then—going on to defend Eucharistic Adoration and remarking (p. 56) "If, then, as Bishop Andrews says, the Body and Blood of our Lord Jesus Christ be there, and Those not without His Soul, nor That without His Deity, and if we are then directed to use the same gesture which we use in the worship of Almighty God, what can the simple-minded suppose, but that which loving faith would dictate, that we worship *Christ*, Whom we are about to receive "—Mr. Cheyne proceeds to make this very explicit statement which, it seems to me, puts his meaning beyond all doubt : his words are " The Declaration tells us what our act of adoration is *not* directed to. It is not directed to the Bread and Wine. The Appellant never said that it was ; he said on the contrary that it is not—' we do not kneel to the outward signs '—we do not worship *them*. Neither do we worship (it says) any ' corporal presence of Christ's natural Flesh and Blood.' The Appellant never said that we do. His words do not imply anything of the sort. ' We kneel to the Lord Himself invisibly present, under the form of bread and wine,' or, as Sherlock says, ' under the species of bread and wine.' "

Mr. Freeman's second witness is thus exhibited:—"Another

writing to a newspaper, says, ' It is difficult, of course, for one to believe that *yonder piece of Bread is my God;* but I am bound to believe it.' " Here, again, not the slightest hint is given where the sentence may be found ; not, indeed, that it is of much importance to notice in a discussion of this subject the incautious language of a Newspaper Correspondent ; though it may be remarked that, supposing he had substituted for " my God " the words " the Body and Blood of Christ," many who hold *Them* to be *Christ* would complain of language which nevertheless could be technically justified by Mr. Freeman's own theory.

The third example is given thus :—" Another eminent person, and of high rank in the Church, affirms that Divine worship is indeed due to Christ, as contained, as God and man, under the Elements ; but recommends *moderation* in offering that Worship ; in which he considers that the Continental Churches run into excess. Excess in worshipping and adoring God Almighty ! " This, I presume, must refer to the Bp. of Brechin, and perhaps to that passage of his Lordship's Charge which I have quoted at p. 334 : whether Mr. Freeman's paraphrase quite represents it may easily be judged by a comparison.

But the writer goes on to say :—

" When grave divines of the English Church find themselves carried into positions such as these, it must be obvious, even to themselves, that there is a mistake somewhere. Nor is there in reality any escape from the admission of all mediæval and Roman eucharistic doctrine with respect to the Eucharist, otherwise than by falling back upon the truth, that the Elements while they are, as the Scripture assures us, the Body and Blood of Christ, still are *not*, as the Scripture nowhere affirms they are, Christ Himself."

The observation which naturally presents itself to the beginning of this passage is—That if Mr. Freeman has, as I believe he has, himself forcibly " carried " these divines " into positions " which they had not and have not any intention of willingly occupying, the only thing, one would

I I I

think, which "must be obvious, even to themselves" is, that the "mistake" lies with him who has thus thrust them out of the position which they claim to be their own. Moreover, it seems to me that, Mr. Freeman has himself used language which, at least, goes some way towards convicting him of having made a mistake in asserting that Doctrine, which he repeats at the close of the above passage, to be "*the truth.*" Thus, at p. 15, he says:—

". . . it may safely be laid down, that the one great and ruling purpose of all sacrifice was, *to restore to man by degrees, and ultimately to enhance immeasurably, his original capacity for enduring and enjoying the Divine Presence ; and to furnish a medium for acceptable presentation in It.* We shall find that an ever-increasing measure of that Presence, joined to proportionately enlarged methods of safe and beatifying access to it, characterize the whole history of Sacrifice and Priesthood."

When, then, Mr. Freeman, speaking of the "memorial offering" of the Church, says (p. 198) " One intervention of her High-Priest sends up her Eucharistic Gift to God in Christ, and brings down Christ, her Eucharistic Food, from God," he appears to me to point out that the Christian Sacrifice furnishes the *full* "measure" of and the *completely* "safe and beatifying access to" the "Divine Presence ;" and further that that Presence is the Presence of " *Christ Himself*" in that "Eucharistic Food" which is His "Body and Blood."

Moreover, Mr. Freeman seems to me to correct his own theory by "the reason" which (at p. 19) he mentions "as to the *cause* of God's withdrawing His indwelling, or rather the original measure of it, from man and creation at the fall ;" he says :—

". . . it is to be found in the condition of *Death* into which man, and all creation with him, had now fallen . . . This plainly appears from various sacrificial provisions of the old law, ... but above all, from that shrinking from, and loathing of Death, as such, which was doubtless a chief ingredient in the Agony of Christ. This detestation of Death, on the part of the Divine Nature, extends, as it should seem, to all the processes and phenomena of it ; and to the dissolution of any living or even inanimate organism. The exact disqualification, therefore, which had to be removed by sacrifice was this deathlike and deadly condition in all its degrees and effects, as well as in its ultimate and highest manifestation, namely, the permanent and eternal dissociation of the body and soul of man."

But then it would seem likely that this Divine abhorrence of "the condition of Death" is precisely a reason why *that* Sacrifice, which was *effectually* to *remove* the "disqualification" for God's renewed "indwelling" with His creatures, should not present this "deathlike" aspect: and it may have been from some such view of the case that Mr. Freeman says (p. 27) :—

" This Death alone, accordingly, had no offensiveness in the sight of God, as not being directly the work of the Devil or of sin, but springing solely from the acquiescence of a perfectly Holy Being. In accordance wherewith it alone was unaccompanied by any corruption. The dissolution of that Soul and Body was an operation as pure and holy as the joining together of Adam's soul and body, or of His Own at His Conception by the Holy Ghost. The Death was pure, because the Subject of it was innocent."

Yet this theory, however true in itself, looks inconsistent with a statement, in the passage last quoted,—that the Divine " detestation of Death . . . . extends . . . . to all the processes and phenomena of it"—one of which is there said to be the "dissociation of the body and soul of man." Perhaps, therefore, it may the rather be that the absence of " offensiveness in the sight of God," when beholding the Death of Christ, was due to the *materially different aspect* which was presented by the separation of His Soul and Body as compared with the like separation in the case of all other men : for, though the Soul of the Man Christ Jesus was in Hades and His Body in the Tomb, the conjunction of Deity with Both held Them in a state of union and a condition of reunion which is untrue of every other separated soul and body.

And if, as would seem likely to be the case, the perpetual presentation of that Sacrifice in the Heavenly Court manifests It in a character pleasing to the Divine Father; then the Apocalyptic vision of It certainly makes It instinct with

Life, though not hiding the feature which betokens Death: "I beheld, and lo, in the midst of the throne and of the four beasts, and in the midst of the elders, stood * a Lamb, as it had been slain " (Rev. v. 6.); and again (xiv. 1) " I looked, and, lo, a Lamb stood on the mount Sion, and with him an hundred forty and four thousand, having his Father's name written in their foreheads."

It follows therefore, I think, that the Memorial re-presentation on the Church's Earthly Altars of Christ's "one oblation of Himself once offered," must be no less free from any cause of " offensiveness " which would render it unacceptable "in the sight of God" than is the Eternal High Priest's continual Offering above with Which It is united: hence, then, an apparent necessity that What is thus presented in Eucharists to the Eternal Father should not be in that "deadly condition " of "dissociation " which seems more than implied in Mr. Freeman's statement "that the Elements, while they are, ... the Body and Blood of Christ, still are not, ... Christ Himself."

In saying this I am not unmindful of what he has written at pp. 207—9 " as to the sense in which Christ presents continually in Heaven His Sacrifice of Himself." He argues—

"That in some true sense He does so, were it only in the sense of pleading it, all must allow. But we are nowhere told in Holy Scripture that He actually and literally carried the Sacrifice of His broken Body and poured-out Blood, by a local translation, into the Heavenly Places. When He gave Himself at the last Supper, and when He was offered on the Cross : the Sacrifice abode still, locally, upon earth."

But this sounds like making " the Sacrifice " an *idea*, a *mere abstraction*, something *separate from* Him who gave Himself to be the Sacrifice; and so it is very much like speaking of "a local translation " of Christ's Will and Inten-

---

* STANDING (*i.e.* in its natural living position: . . . . it was not lying, but standing) AS IF SLAIN (*i.e.* retaining the appearance of death-wounds on its body: looking as if it had been slain . . . .)"—*Dean Alford*, in loc.

tion in offering Himself. Surely there was *no need* of our being " told" that " *the Sacrifice* of His broken Body and poured-out Blood " was " actually and literally carried . . . into the Heavenly Places," when we *are* told (Heb. ix. 24) that " Christ," Who showed His pierced Hands and wounded Side to the Apostles, " is " really " entered into heaven itself, now to appear in the presence of God for us " by " a local translation" of His Body Which was sacrificed. Indeed Mr. Freeman seems to anticipate some such objection as this, for he goes on to say :—

" When He ascended to Heaven, it was as Risen, and with a re-united Body, Soul, and Spirit. And though it is said, in the Revelation, that there appeared in the midst of the Throne a ' Lamb as it had been slain,' the language is qualified, meaning apparently ' as if it had once been pierced or slain :' and the context refers to the Sacrifice as a past event ; ' Thou wast slain, and didst redeem us unto God by Thy Blood.' "

No doubt it does ; yet this seems only consistent with that display of *life in death,* already noticed, which made Christ's death not obnoxious to God as was the death of all others : it appears, moreover, to point to that aspect of the Incarnation which rendered a God-man the only possible Being Who could die to satisfy Divine justice, yet not fall under the dominion of that very Death (*i.e.* destruction), which His Own death was designed to destroy. Hence, perhaps, those words of our Lord touching His Own life (S. John x. 18)—" I have *power* to lay it down, and I have *power* to take it again ;" hence, too, the especial recommendation and acceptableness of that Voluntary Offering for sin (ver. 17)—" Therefore doth My Father love me, because I lay down my life, that I might take it again ;" hence, further, it may well be, that triumphant announcement of Himself to the beloved Apostle in the very opening of the Apocalyptic vision (Rev. i. 18)—" I am He that liveth, and was dead ; and, behold, I am alive for evermore, Amen ; and have the keys of hell and death."

To support, however, his opinion of the *non-local transla-*

tion of the Sacrifice, Mr. Freeman suggests "with caution" that—

> "[It] is in Heaven, in the sense in which the Mosaic burnt-offering entered into the Holy place by means of the incense at the time of its offering, and by the personal appearance there of the High Priest once a year . . . . . It is as borne upon the Incense of His Intercession, and as presented evermore in a mystery in His Holy Hands, not locally, that the once broken Body and poured-out Blood of the Sacrifice is pleaded. So the sprinkling of His Blood towards the True Mercy Seat, which, from the analogy of the Mosaic scheme, doubtless took place in some sense, would seem to have been accomplished, though really, in mystery only, not physically or locally. And accordingly St. Paul does not say it was *with* His own Blood, but '*by it*,' that He entered in once into the Holy Place."

But, perhaps, the consideration—that Christ is *at once* the Eternal High Priest and the Ever-living Sacrifice—meets this and any kindred difficulty arising out of the pursuit of an exact analogy between the Type and the Anti-type; and so, His corresponding local entrance as High Priest to plead the shedding of "His own Blood," when He "suffered without the gate" in order "that He might sanctify the people with" It (Heb. xiii. 12), need not interfere with the idea that, being " burned without the camp " by the consuming fire of God's anger which He resolved to appease, He could not *in that condition* come "into Heaven itself;" any more than could " *the bodies* of those beasts, whose *blood* is brought into the sanctuary by the high priest for sin," have " entered into the holy places made with hands :" thus, then, there was no "local translation" of What in Its aspect of destruction was a Sacrifice unpleasing to God ; though in that "lifting up of " Christ's Hands," which speaks of Life while yet They bear the impress of Death, there is the ceaseless Memorial that (to quote the words which Mr. Freeman cites from Bp. Andrews as favouring his own view) it is " The same Body as now, but not the Body *as* it is now." And the fact embodied in this sentence seems also to indicate the "sense" in which the Blood of Christ may be said to have been even "physically and locally" sprinkled before the Heavenly

Mercy-Seat : for, remembering carefully the Divine declaration (Gen. ix. 4) " the life . . . is the blood "—as when the "blood" of "the sin offering, . . . for the people" was brought "within the vail " by the High Priest to "sprinkle it upon the mercy seat, and before the mercy seat," it also made "an atonement for the holy place " (Lev. xvi. 15, 16) ; so when Christ Who is "the Life" came as High Priest "to appear in the presence of God for us" He did, surely, bear with Him thither His Own Blood by Which, too, "the Heavenly things themselves" were "purified ;" though indeed, it was *by virtue* of that Blood before shed, that He procured and claimed admission to the Celestial Sanctuary.

These considerations lead me, though with much deference, to conclude differently from Mr. Freeman when he says (p. 209) :—

" Hence no inference can be drawn, as has been attempted of late years, to the effect that the consecrated Elements, whether separately or conjointly, are the Living and Risen Body of Christ. What the Living and Risen Christ presents and pleads evermore in Heaven, is His mighty wonder-working DEATH, undergone ages ago ; . . . And so, too, what the Church evermore pleads and presents, is His Body and Blood, such as they were when the One was broken and the Other poured forth upon the Cross ; which condition of them is in a mystery perpetuated still :"—

For, if "the voice of many angels round about the throne and the beasts and the elders " (Rev. v. 11) may, as perhaps it may, indicate what Christ Himself pleads there, then, its sound distinctly mingles the two ideas of *Life* and *Death* and does not more prominently, much less solely, speak of *Death*—" Worthy is the Lamb [*i.e.* the ever-living Lamb] that was slain to receive power, and riches, and wisdom, and strength, and honour, and glory, and blessing " (ver. 12) : and if, too, the echoing voices of the " every creature which is in heaven, and on earth, and under the earth, and such as are in the sea, and all that are in them " may be accounted as the thankful expression of Redeemed Creation for the Sacrifice Which restored it, then, further, it corresponds with that same idea; for when they were heard saying " Blessing, and honour, and glory, and power, be unto Him that sitteth upon the throne, and unto the Lamb for ever and ever" (ver. 13), we seem to have described the Church's *Gloria in Excelsis* and therein the pleading and presentation of that Memorial Sacrifice with Which it is united—the *living* "Lamb of God, . . . that *takest* away the sins of the world, ... that sittest at the right hand of God the Father" though also Eucharistically re-presented and Eucharistically worshipped; while the responsive acknowledgment of and communion with It still resounds (we may well believe) in the Temple above (ver. 14)—"the four beasts said, Amen. And the four and twenty elders fell down and worshipped Him that liveth for ever and ever."

Mr. Freeman, however, in this Note upon which I am commenting, proceeds to defend himself thus (p. 480):—

" And while the doctrine contended for [he should rather have said, to be accurate, *which I allege to be contended for*] labours under these weighty objections, I am not aware that more than one objection has ever been brought against the opposite view upheld in the pages. It is said that if the Elements are the Body and Blood of Christ, the doctrine of the Hypostatic Union (or of the inseparable conjunction, once for all, of the Divine and Human Natures in the One Person of Christ) obliges us to believe that they are Christ Himself: that otherwise we divide Christ and are guilty of a kind of Nestorianism. This at first sight looks plausible: but it will not bear the slightest examination. To uphold it, is to press one mystery to the utter forgetfulness of another. The position is, that wherever the Body of Christ is present, it must, for the reason just stated, be *so present as to be an object of worship*. This is the exact point contended for. But the defenders of it themselves are not prepared to carry it out to its legitimate results. Is not, (I would ask,) is not the Church the Body of Christ? and that in a most true and real sense, though in a manner perfectly mysterious to us? They cannot deny it. Will they affirm, then, that the Church, as being Christ's Body, is to be worshipped? And if not, why the Elements of Bread in the Eucharist, as being that Body?"

Now, first of all, I would observe—that, however allowable as a piece of abstract reasoning, it is scarcely justifiable to raise so subtle a question upon the groundless assumption (as I think I have shewn it to be) that the School, here apparently referred to, advocate Divine worship to the " Elements of Bread in the Eucharist as being " the " Body " of Christ. Yet, if the pursuit of such a logical consequence as this, on so confessedly mysterious a matter, is to be insisted upon as a necessary result of applying " the Doctrine of the Hypostatic Union " to the subject of Christ's Sacramental Presence, it might be some answer to say—that quite as great difficulties could be raised touching that Divine Union and Communion with the Church, which we must believe and maintain because it was so fully and plainly set forth by our Lord in His last discourse with His disciples (S. John xiv.—xvii.) : or, again, which is so strikingly expressed in that answer of " the Lord," from Heaven, to Saul the first great enemy of His infant Church (Acts. ix. 5) " I am Jesus whom thou persecutest :" or, once more, which is declared in St. Peter's assurance (2 S. Pet. i. 4) that there "are given unto us exceeding great and precious promises : that by these ye might be partakers of the *Divine nature*."

Yet, as it is not impossible to furnish explanations on these Scriptural difficulties, relating to the Mystical Body of Christ, provided that Reason be not called upon to invade the Province of Faith and Mental Demonstration be not demanded where Moral Vision can alone be accorded, so, probably, such explanations would be an approach towards meeting the question which Mr. Freeman here starts : it would be beyond the compass and beside the purpose of these pages to enter upon the needful length of such an intricate enquiry ; here, therefore, it must suffice to say that the *Revealed* FACT of Christ dwelling in His Church is, surely, the reason for acknowledging His Presence therein ; and so is the very ground of these and such like questions or counsels in the Apostolical Epistles—(Rom. xvi. 5.) " Greet the Church," (1 Cor. x. 32.) " Give none offence . . . . to the Church of God," (xi. 22.) " Despise ye the Church of God ? ", (vi. 15, 19.) " Know ye not that your bodies are the

K K K

members of Christ? . . . Know ye not that your body is the temple of the Holy Ghost, which is in you?", (1 S. Peter ii. 17.) "Love the brotherhood."

Moreover it might be a perfectly legitimate enquiry— whether some of these expressions, in describing "a manner perfectly mysterious to us" whereby "the Body of Christ" is present on Earth, do not further indicate the *nature* of the worship due to It, as being either mental or moral or physical —modes these which, perhaps, are not wholly inapplicable to explain the kind of worship due as Bp. Ridley said (See p. 58) to, what he called, "the external Sacrament;" bearing in mind, of course, the difference between Christ's living Members and inorganic Eucharistic Elements. If it should be objected—that Eucharistic Adoration cannot be compared with such a worship of Christ's Body the Church as is here suggested, because the latter lacks that external token of worship, *viz.* the prescribed act of kneeling which the former presents—it may be replied—That, though both are founded upon the same principle, *viz.* a Presence of Christ, the Eucharistic Manifestation of it may well have a different form of recognition, seeing that it is diverse from His exhibition of Himself in His members. Though, at the same time, it must be remembered that the Mystical Body receives the greater distinction, the recognition being *avowedly* or *intentionally* given to it; whereas, in the case of the Sacramental Body, the Kneeling is designedly not to the Species but to Christ thereby displayed to the eye of faith.

But, further, the dilemma on which Mr. Freeman apparently seeks to place those whom he is opposing, appears to me to be mainly due to his seeming not to recognize here, argumentatively, the distinctive characteristics of Christ's Body in the three various aspects under which, perhaps, It may be, not inaccurately, regarded :—(1) Its local corporal Presence, above; unclothed and in Majestic Session at the Right Hand of God the Father; (2) Its sacramental Presence, below; clothed upon yet not incorporated or commingled with the substances of the Eucharistic Elements; (3) Its incorporation with our fallen frames, which are thus raised to their true dignity in becoming Christ's Mystical Body.—The comparison already drawn (at pp. 341-55), between the Presence of the Natural Sun and the Presence of the Sun of Righteousness, may, perhaps, suggest modes of illustrating the relative honour to be paid to Christ's Body under these Its several manifestations. Mr. F. does, indeed, advert to a distinction of Presence (and, so far, impliedly allows a difference of worship) ; for he speaks of "the Body of Christ in its Eucharistic condition," when reverting just afterwards "to fearful doctrinal positions," already noticed, as a reason for concluding that what he considers a "plausible" but "a mistaken inference" respecting It "should *ex animo* be abandoned:" yet the inference would seem to be his own, and to be deduced from the imaginary "position" in which he (of course unintentionally) places others by writing as though they claimed the *same kind* of worship for the Body of Christ *however* as well as "wherever" present. So, too, when Mr. F. adds that "The only escape there is, when this parallel is pressed upon the upholders of the worship of the Elements, or of the Body of Christ, in the Eucharist, is to represent that the Church is only *figuratively*, not really, the Body of Christ"—he must not be surprised if in this instance also one thinks he has (unconsciously) misrepresented those to whom he refers; especially as the only clue he gives, in saying " this position, ... has been avowed by the most eminent and most universally esteemed of the divines in question," affords no means of comparing his own language with that of which he complains. It is indeed strange, and difficult to reconcile with controversial fairness, that he should persist in fixing upon others results which he draws from their belief; yet so he does again in a passage immediately following; for (p. 482) assuming it to be held that "the unreceived Elements demand Divine Worship," he asks "must not this, *à fortiori*, be extended to the communicant, who receives these Elements, and who is further declared to be—which the Elements are not—' one with

Christ, and· Christ with him?'" This question has been partly answered, I think, in what has been already said; I can now only again remark in addition, and that by way of counter inquiry—First, Who is it that demands Divine worship for the Elements? Next, is not our Sacramental Union and Communion with Christ the very argument for that reverence, *i.e.* worship, which is so continually insisted upon as due from us to both our own bodies and to the bodies of our brethren in Christ?

Exactly the same misrepresentation (I do not mean wilful) pervades the remaining portion of his Note (p. 482) where he says "It is now avowed as one principal purpose of the celebration of the Holy Eucharist, to be present simply to offer divine worship to Christ as present under the Elements: that is, as has been shewn to the Elements themselves." To this last sentence I cannot but reply—that it seems to me Mr. Freeman has entirely failed to shew any such identity as he here alleges. With regard, however, to the former part of the passage—though incautious or exaggerated language on the part of some may furnish ground for warning lest *communion* should be neglected or superseded by the advocacy of *worship*—if Mr. F. intends to deny the *lawfulness* of non-communicating worship, then I must venture respectfully to differ entirely from him : that he appears to do so, seems to follow from his asking "What single prayer or invocation has the English Church, at any rate, provided for this purpose?" But the mere absence of any such provision would not prove the illegality of such worship ; to establish this it would be necessary to shew that the Service itself, either in terms or by clear implication, forbids it ; otherwise, that it is contrary to some Law of the Church elsewhere recorded : with some confidence I express my belief that not only no such prohibition can be gathered from either source, but that the Evidence proves the contrary : this is not the place to investigate the subject,* yet it may be desirable to point to

---

* But I may be permitted here again, as at p. 326, to refer to a Publication where it is discussed.

the following Rubrics as shewing that non-communicating attendance of "the faithful" was designed to be allowed:— "At the time of the celebration of the Communion, the *Communicants* being conveniently placed " &c., " Then shall the Priest say *to them that come to receive*" &c., "Then shall this general Confession be made, in the name of *all those that are minded to receive*" &c., " Then shall the Priest, ... say in the name of *all them that shall receive*" &c., " Then shall the Priest say the Lord's Prayer, *the people* [not merely *the Communicants*] repeating after him every petition." To these may be added the Rubric directing the consumption of the remains of the Sacrament by " the Priest and such other of *the Communicants* as he shall then call unto him "—an order which would be wholly superfluous if none but Communicants might be present during that portion of the Service from which, by a comparatively modern custom, non-communicants usually withdraw.

I presume, however, that Mr. Freeman objects, to non-communicating attendance for worship, on another ground than that of the non-provision of "prayer or invocation ;" for, at p. 278 he writes thus :—

" Another remark is, that among the results of `this investigation we cannot reckon the faintest trace or intimation of any worship to be paid *to a sacrifice*. This is indisputable. The worship is throughout presented *by means* of the sacrifice, not directed to it. There is no countenance then, from this quarter at least, for the mediæval opinion, lately re-introduced by some earnest minds among us, that the supreme purpose, or, however, a very principal one, of the Eucharist, is to provide in the ordained media of the rite,—the consecrated Elements,—an object of Divine Worship. However ingeniously it has been endeavoured to invoke the countenance of Fathers and liturgies to such a view, it would seem absolutely fatal to it, that the ancient sacrificial system, Divinely accredited to us as an exact type or copy of the Gospel scheme, gives not the remotest hint of such a feature as destined to have place in it."

Without, however, meaning to use the expedient of endeavouring to refute an Author's statements by other passages in his writings when he was in the same mental phase (a resort always of questionable value unless there can be no reasonable doubt of his whole mind having been fairly grasped) I can-

not but compare what Mr. Freeman here says, with a remark
which he has elsewhere made in the same Volume; because
it seems to me to furnish ground for modifying the conclusion
at which he has here arrived: thus, at p. 4, after observing
of "the Holy Eucharist" that "by the distinct intimation of
our Lord Himself, its nature was to be ascertained by
reference to a system in itself sacrificial," he says:—

"As to the *range* which that reference, or parallel, was to take, it
may be observed, that though our Lord might not unnaturally, at
first sight, have been understood to point exclusively, (as doubtless
He referred very especially) to the Mosaic system, under which the
Apostles were brought up, His words contain, in truth, no such
limitation. No one dispensation or covenant is specified as having
an exclusive commission to interpret the New Ordinance: much less
is any particular rite of the Mosaic Institution so distinguished;
such as, for example, the Passover . . . . . Doubtless the Church
. . . . was to apply to those words of her Lord [*i.e.* the words of
Institution], with the utmost universality, what St. Paul has said,
in a more restricted sense, of certain words of Jeremiah: ' In that
He saith, A New Covenant, He hath made the first,' even all former
sacrificial dispensations, ' old.' And He referred to them all in
their entire extent, as His interpreters. The Eye of the Saviour,
in pronouncing those memorable words, glanced, we cannot doubt,
over the whole religious experience through which He Himself had
conducted mankind."

Yet this very argument, of the parallel to the Eucharistic
Sacrifice having to be sought in the " entire extent " of " all
former sacrificial dispensations " and not in the Mosaic alone,
supports the further consideration which can hardly fail to
suggest itself—That the parallel cannot be carried throughout, because " the Lamb slain from the foundation of the
world " is an Object of Divine Worship, which the Victim in
all other Sacrifices could not be.—Hence, then, the Body
and Blood of Christ being (as Mr. F. holds) really present
in the Memorial Eucharistic Sacrifice, *i.e.* Christ Himself
being present (as is contended in opposition to Mr. F. and as
may, further, be reasonably inferred from the fact that—
though the command under the Old Covenant was (Deut. xii.
23) " Be sure that thou eat not *the Blood;* for *the blood* is
the life; and thou mayest not eat *the life* with *the flesh*,"—the
bidding of CHRIST is (S. Matt. xxvi. 27, 28.) " Drink ye

all of it ; for this is My Blood [*My Life*] of the New *Testament :*" as Bp. Ridley declared (See p. 54) " I say also with St. Augustine, that we eat *life* and we drink *life ;)* it would seem to follow that the worship may and must be " directed to " as well as " presented by " Him " our Passover " Who " is sacrificed for us " (not however to " the consecrated Elements " as Mr. F. again repeats) : and this though, or rather because, there be not (as Mr. F. says) " the faintest trace or intimation of any worship to be paid *to a sacrifice.*" In fact Mr. Freeman evidently expected some such reply as this and endeavours to anticipate it ; for he says (p. 279) :—

" But it will perhaps be contended that this is among the number of the things in which the Old system could not justly mirror forth the New ; arising as it does out of the Divine Nature of the Gospel Sacrifice and Priest. But to this there is the fatal objection, that St. Paul, when setting forth to the Hebrews the points in which the Gospel sacrificial system transcends that of the Law, makes no mention of this as one. Nor is there, confessedly, a single word in the New Testament, any more than in the Old, of direction or instruction to the effect contended for. It is purely a matter of inference ; an inference the unsoundness of which, as well as the fearful conclusions which (by the admission of the upholders of it themselves) follow from it, has been pointed out elsewhere," *viz.,* as his Footnote mentions, in the " Note at the End of the Volume " upon which I am here commenting ; and in his " Introd. to Part II., pp. 142—145 " already noticed at pp. 248-9.

Yet, on consideration, this alleged silence of St. Paul need not be " the fatal objection " which Mr. Freeman avers ; and therefore, as not dealing directly with the subject like the Epistle to the Hebrews, the silence of the rest of Holy Scripture is of less moment. For, besides that the argument of St. Paul seems in its nature limited to shewing how " the Gospel sacrificial system *transcends* that of the Law " *where* it *corresponds* with it, his reticence as to its other higher aspects may, perhaps, be accounted for by the hindrance which he there mentions (vv. 11, 12) before making his comparison :—" Of whom we have many things to say, and hard to be uttered, seeing ye are dull of hearing. For when for the time ye ought to be teachers, ye have need that one teach you again which be the first principles of the oracles of God ; and are become such as have need of milk, and not of strong meat." And though it might seem at first that Mr. Freeman's theory is upheld apparently in the Apostle's Eucharistic exhortation (xiii. 15) "*By him* therefore let us offer the sacrifice of praise to God continually, that is, the fruit of our lips, giving thanks to His name;" the theory of "worship to be paid *to a sacrifice*" may perhaps be a very legitimate "inference" from the opening language of the Epistle (i. 6) "When He bringeth in the first-begotten into the world, He saith, And let all the angels of God worship Him ;" for if the Incarnate One Sacramentally comes in again by His Own appointed Eucharist, it cannot but be that so great a condescension to those who are lower than the Angels demands from them at least as deep an Adoration; He the true Melchizedeck "of whom it is witnessed that he liveth" (vii. 8) receiving "there," where He ever intercedes for them, the "tithes" of His people's deep devotion. In such "an inference" there surely is not "the unsound ness" which Mr. Freeman may well indeed deprecate; though, happily, "the fearful conclusions" he refers to, so far from being an "admission" on the part of those whom he so indistinctly indicates, are really, as I think I have-shewn, the erroneous inference which he so unaccountably imputes to them.

There is one other statement which Mr. Freeman makes, in connexion with his observations just considered, which needs to be noticed : he says (p. 279) :—

" Neither, again, does the ancient system, rightly understood, and taken in conjunction with Christ's own ordinance, lend any support to another mediæval habit, closely allied to the former one, of taking part, as it is called, in the sacrifice, without receiving. In the old system, the kind of offering which, and which alone, was of power to retain the people in the covenanted estate, was the peace or eucharistic offering. This, offered and partaken of thrice a-year at least, was, as has been shewn, the condition and channel of Israelitish life."

But the latter portion of this passage appears to me to correct the former and to admit even more than is contended for by those against whom Mr. Freeman urges his objections: if, indeed, they advocated *habitual* non-communicating attendance, there would be a force in his objection and a fitness in his parallel: but, as their contention expresses or implies *frequent* or at least the *prescribed* Communions (the case excepted of those who may be preparing for Communion) so, it seems to me, the complaint is *irrelevant;* though, at the same time, it furnishes an argument wherewith to justify a practice which would be strictly *lawful* according to the rule of the English Liturgy. For, if a person, acting upon the Rubric, were to "communicate three times in the year, of which Easter to be one;" and were to be present throughout "the Divine Service," without Communicating, during the rest of the year, he could defend his habit on that very requirement of "the old system" which, Mr. Freeman says, was "the condition and channel of Israelitish life." I do not say that such a habit of minimum reception would be an *expedient* one; nor am I forgetting that more frequent Communions are by distinct implication counselled in this Rubric and should therefore be continually and carefully recommended as the means of attaining those increased spiritual "benefits whereof we are partakers thereby;" yet that the "taking part, as it is called, in the sacrifice, without receiving" has its own blessing, appears to me to be practically admitted in Mr. Freeman's argument, and seems even more plainly implied by his saying elsewhere (p. 243) ". . . . it could not be but that admission to the Presence would, apart from sacramental reception, involve a measure of such communion" as he points out was one "of the needs of man" provided for "under the older dispensation."

It is not without much consideration and great diffidence, remembering the learning and ability of Mr. Freeman, that I have hazarded these few remarks upon his Note: they have been made in the hope of removing the erroneous impressions, touching the alleged opinions of others, which it seems too calculated to produce; and also, with the object of shewing that, when accurately represented, they are not contrariant to the Doctrine and Discipline of the Church, and, moreover, may apparently be harmonized with that ancient Doctrine of Sacrifice and Communion so elaborately discussed in a Work which one regrets, in common with others, may perchance be deteriorated in value by the peculiar theory of Eucharistic Presence so entirely and exclusively asserted in that Note and throughout Mr. Freeman's Volume.

———

To conclude. The preceding pages have been written under a strong sense of the great importance of not only not widening in the least the breaches caused by recent Eucharistic controversy; but, on the contrary, of doing everything possible to heal dissensions, so far as can be done consistently with what is due to the full and dispassionate consideration of all the reliable Evidence which is producible, however conflicting it may, or may be thought to, be. Moreover the *moral*, and in the case of Clergy the *legal* obligation of not contradicting the Decisions of the Catholic Church—represented to us in this Kingdom by the Church of England— has been carefully borne in mind; they were meant not to be, and it is hoped and believed they are not, infringed by any opinions expressed or conclusions drawn in this Volume. The sole aim has been to promote *Peace* and *Concord* touching a subject which, from its special relation to Him Who is " the Author" of the one and "the Lover " of the other, pre-eminently demands their culture. If what has now been said shall lead any to a juster appreciation of the English Reformation period than that in which, there is reason to believe, it is too commonly held; and if, in doing this, it shall further tend in the very smallest degree to reconcile differences, to remove doubts, to attest continuity of ancient Doctrine, to promote reverence, to deepen Faith, to encourage Hope, and especially to enlarge and strengthen Charity—the not unpleasing task of investigating a question of some Historical and Theological interest will have found a more than sufficient recompence.

INDEX.

LONDON: W. J. PERRY, PRINTER.

By the same Author.

REVIEW OF LENT TEACHING.—A Sermon preached in the Parish Church of St. Peter the Great, or Subdeanry Chichester, on the Sunday next before Easter, 1849. 6d.

THREE PRESENT SPECIAL DANGERS TO CHRISTIAN SANCTIFICATION.—A Sermon preached in the Parish Church of St. Peter the Great, or Subdeanry, Chichester, on Sunday, February 24, 1850. 6d.

PRAISE, A DUTY IN THE CHURCH'S ADVERSITY.—A Sermon preached in the Temporary Church of All Saints, St. Marylebone, on the Feast of All Saints, 1851. 6d.

LAWFUL CHURCH ORNAMENTS :—being an Historical Examination of the Judgment of the Right Hon. Stephen Lushington, D.C.L., in the case of Westerton v Liddell, &c. And of "Aids for determining some disputed points in the Ceremonial of the Church of England," by the Rev. William Goode, M.A. With an Appendix on the Judgment of the Rt. Hon. Sir John Dodson, D.C.L., in the Appeal Liddell v Westerton, &c., 1857. £1 1s. 0d.

THE ANGLICAN AUTHORITY FOR THE PRESENCE OF NON-COMMUNICANTS DURING HOLY COMMUNION.—Reprinted from "The Ecclesiologist" of August and October, 1858. 6d.

SOME ANALOGIES BETWEEN THE HUMAN AND THE MYSTICAL BODY, APPLIED TO DIFFICULTIES AND DUTIES IN THE CHURCH.—Part I., Difficulties in the Church, 1863. 2s.
Part II., DUTIES IN THE CHURCH.—*In preparation.*

Edited by the Same.

DIRECTORIUM SCOTICANUM ET ANGLICANUM.—Directions for Celebrating the Holy Communion according to the Rite of the Church in Scotland and of the Church of England. By the late Rev. W. Wright, L.L.D., 1855. 3s. 0d.

A MANUAL OF DAILY PRAYERS—for persons who are much hindered by the duties of their calling. With a Preparation and Devotions for Holy Communion. *Sixth thousand, with additions.* 1859. 4d.

MEDITATIONS FOR A WEEK, ON THE LORD'S PRAYER. 6d. or 25 for 8s. 6d.